"An excellent guide to the thinking behind S&P's influential corporate governance ratings."

"*Governance and Risk* is a useful and timely contribution to the topic, helping the reader to understand the complexity and providing analytic and comparative frameworks to support a more systematic approach to assessing corporate governance standards."

"Comprehensive in scope and cross-disciplinary in analysis, *Governance and Risk* begins with the premise—correctly in my view—that corporate governance is, at its core, an important risk factor for any corporation. Through this conceptual prism, they employ economic, legal and social analyses to provide fresh insight into how we should best understand and govern the inherently conflicting interests that comprise the modern corporation. Anyone seeking a rigorous analysis of these issues—from directors, managers and lawyers to shareholders and corporate and community activists—should include this volume in their reading. It is an important addition to the corporate governance literature in this post-Enron age."

"This is a courageous and successful effort to classify what has never before been analyzed and presented in such a comprehensible manner."

"*Governance and Risk* is an excellent piece of work. It is a comprehensive and carefully written manual that will be an invaluable source of information for managers and investors. It deserves careful study by anyone with an interest in the management of firms. It should make a significant contribution to the improvement of corporate governance of corporations around the world."

"I have found *Governance and Risk* to be one of the most comprehensive surveys of the field. It is an excellent reference work."

J. Mark Mobius, Ph.D., President,
Templeton Emerging Markets Fund, Inc.

"This is an important, timely book which brings much needed rigour and discipline to the analysis of corporate governance practices. It is the great merit of this handbook that it provides a bridge between recent scholarly research and the day to day interests of market practitioners and policy-makers. This handbook sets out a comprehensive framework for examining the many interlocking components of corporate governance. This new book will be of immense value to everyone who takes a global perspective on corporate governance trends. If you are looking for a reliable guide through the confusing maze of corporate governance, this book is an excellent place to start."

Paul Coombes,Director,
Corporate Governance Practice,
McKinsey & Company, Inc.

"Standard and Poor's has taken on a truly Herculean task by synthesizing corporate governance standards and best practices into a unified analytical structure. I am particularly gratified at the extensive parameters the book offers for comparative analysis between U.S. and foreign practices. Although the book is primarily a handbook for analysts and investors, the questions would be very helpful for boards in developing their own metrics for self-evaluation, using the "strongest analytical profile" as a draft benchmark. Congratulations on this giant accomplishment."

Roger W. Raber, President and Chief Executive Officer,
National Association of Corporate Directors

GOVERNANCE AND RISK

An Analytical Handbook for Investors, Managers, Directors, and Stakeholders

Edited by
GEORGE S. DALLAS
Standard & Poor's
Governance Services

McGraw-Hill

New York Chicago San Francisco Lisbon London Madrid
Mexico City Milan New Delhi San Juan Seoul
Singapore Sydney Toronto

Copyright © 2004 by The McGraw-Hill Companies, Inc. All rights reserved. Printed in the United States of America. Except as permitted under the United States Copyright Act of 1976, no part of this publication may be reproduced or distributed in any form or by any means, or stored in a data base or retrieval system, without prior written permission of the publisher.

1 2 3 4 5 6 7 8 9 0   DOC/DOC   0 9 8 7 6 5 4

ISBN 0-07-142954-9

This publication is designed to provide accurate and authoritative information in regard to the subject matter covered. It is sold with the understanding that the publisher is not engaged in rendering legal, accounting or other professional service. If legal advice or other expert assistance is required, the services of a competent professional person should be sought.
> —From a Declaration of Principles Jointly Adopted by a Committee of the American Bar Association and a Committee of Publishers and Associations.

McGraw-Hill books are available at special discounts to use as premiums and sales promotions, or for use in corporate training programs. For more information, please write to the Director of Special Sales, McGraw-Hill Professional, Two Penn Plaza, New York, NY 10011-2298. Or contact your local bookstore.

 This book is printed on recycled, acid-free paper containing a minimum of 50% recycled de-inked paper.

Library of Congress Cataloging-in-Publication Data

Dallas, George S.
  Governance and risk / by George S. Dallas.
      p.   cm.
  ISBN 0-07-142954-9 (hardcover : alk. paper)
    1. Corporate governance.   2. Risk management.   I. Title:
  governance and risk.   II. Title.
  HD2741.D35 2004
  658.4—dc22

                                                                    2003016499

C O N T E N T S

FOREWORD

When George Dallas asked me to write a foreword to this comprehensive work on corporate governance, I was somewhat taken aback by his statement that I was a "champion" for corporate governance. I think it would be more appropriate to state that I am fortunate enough to lead an organization that has been a "champion" of corporate governance since its earliest days in the mid-nineteenth century. The work George and his colleagues at Standard & Poor's do today is an extension of not only our heritage but of our parentage—The McGraw-Hill Companies.

In 1854, Henry Varnum Poor, the founding father of Standard & Poor's, took to task the New York Central Railroad—then viewed to be the best managed railroad in the country. He criticized harshly the Road's practice of issuing "watered" stock without full disclosure of how the proceeds would be used. But the reasons for his criticism are noteworthy in their prescience and applicability to today's environment. First he said, "It set a pernicious precedent as the New York Central, the largest business combination yet created in the United States, was being carefully watched by the whole business community."[1]

In short, leaders should act as leaders especially in setting standards for financial behavior. But Poor considered this risk insignificant "… in comparison with the wrong done to private right, to the commerce, and to the general welfare of the country."[2] A harsh lesson relearned in a disastrous fashion in early twenty-first-century America.

Obviously, corporate governance is a *sine qua non* of efficient capital markets which ultimately depend on trust and integrity no matter how stringent the regulatory regime. Certainly markets require sound

---

1. Henry Varnum Poor; Alfred D. Chandler; Arno Press, 1981
2. Ibid.

supervisory practices and enforcement, but they also require leadership—leadership by major corporations in establishing best practices for their commercial peers. Markets need analysts—yes, even critics—of weak practices because all of us who participate in the vibrancy of these markets are damaged by abuses and benefit by compliance. Clearly, it is in the best interests of all market participants, corporations, investors, bankers, and analysts to advocate and reward sound corporate governance practices.

On that basis, this book, aptly named *Governance and Risk*, provides solid conceptual grounding on the key themes of governance in corporations and other organizations, and is a practical handbook for those market participants who wish to better understand the dynamics of governance practices of companies in a multinational context. To the extent this work advances the understanding and practical advocacy of corporate governance, Standard & Poor's is honored to "champion" its development.

Leo C. O'Neill
President
Standard & Poor's

PREFACE

$\mathbf{A}$ccording to an old folktale, a traveller from the city once toured the rural countryside during a driving rainstorm, and came upon a farmer sitting contentedly in his house with rainwater pouring through the roof. The city gentleman was bemused by this, and said to the farmer: "I see your roof is leaking. Why don't you fix it?" The farmer looked at the visitor from the city with surprise and annoyance, and said: "Well, right now it's raining too hard. And when the sun is shining, it doesn't leak."

If we replace the rain with corporate governance failures, and if we replace the complacency of the farmer with the historical attitude of many corporate managers, directors, and shareholders about corporate governance, we see one of the roots of the governance problem that has become increasingly visible in markets around the world.

But complacency is on the wane. Two years following the spectacular, and tragic, demise of Enron, the corporate governance debate continues to grow in prominence, as the combination of corrupt governance practices in certain cases, and merely substandard governance in less extreme situations, is taking its toll. For shareholders, the fallout has contributed to depressed share prices and lack of market confidence. Other stakeholders, including creditors, employees, suppliers, customers, and local communities also have felt, often with considerable pain, the negative effects of corrupt or ineffective corporate governance practices. Governance has emerged as an explicit risk factor for investors, nonfinancial stakeholders, and policymakers.

Much of the attention to corporate governance has been focused on the emerging markets, following the financial crises in Asia and Russia in the late 1990s. However, the list of corporate casualties continues to grow in all markets, including prominent companies domiciled in countries with developed legal systems, sophisticated accounting standards, and mature financial markets.

BOOK PURPOSE AND STRUCTURE

This book is an analytical handbook for investors, stakeholders, and other analysts wishing to achieve a better practical understanding of key corporate governance issues in individual companies. It also can be used by company managers and directors as a basis for self-assessment. It is global in perspective, and addresses the challenge of understanding and comparing diverse approaches to corporate governance in different regions and countries.

Part One begins by framing corporate governance as an explicit risk factor, reviewing the development of the governance debate and recent empirical research relating to corporate governance. This part also addresses methodological approaches to corporate governance analysis, focusing in particular on how to achieve an objective assessment of many qualitative governance-related issues.

Part Two presents an analytical framework for looking at corporate governance in individual companies. It follows the criteria that have been developed at the Standard & Poor's Governance Services unit to evaluate and score corporate governance, focusing on factors such as ownership structure, shareholder rights, stakeholder relations, transparency and disclosure, the audit process, and board effectiveness.

In Part Three, macro, or country-related, influences also are addressed, as is a way to view the interplay of firm-specific versus country-related factors. The influence of the legal and regulatory environment is given particular attention. Attention also is given to issues of reporting and disclosure practices. This part addresses the issue of "quality" of earnings through Standard & Poor's Core Earnings initiative. As the interests of non-financial stakeholders are beginning to receive greater attention, the importance of meaningful social and environmental reporting also is addressed.

Together, Parts Two and Three focus on governance from the perspectives of finance, economics, law, and accounting. Some references are made to academic literature to establish a basic conceptual framework for evaluating corporate governance. These two parts are intended to link this conceptual framework to more granular analyst questions and instructions. These questions, in turn, serve as a practical guide on how to assess and benchmark governance standards in individual companies in a meaningful way.

Part Four explores related themes that are contiguous to corporate governance. This includes an examination of sustainable development to address an approach to governance that extends beyond the shareholder or financial stakeholder. Directors' and officers' liability insurance also is discussed, particularly with regard to its links to corporate governance. The scope of governance is extended beyond the strict corporate realm to consider dimensions of governance relating to managed funds and the public sector. Finally, leaving law and economics aside, we need to remember that ultimately it is people who govern. A capstone chapter in this part focuses on the human side of corporate governance.

The final part of the book includes a number of individual country studies, comparing the diverse market, legal, regulatory, and informational infrastructures in a wide range of countries around the world. This framework draws from the criteria developed in Part Two, and should provide a consistent basis of comparison of key governance themes in countries with differing economic, cultural, and legal institutions.

We include in Appendix A two "case studies," in the form of corporate governance evaluations that Standard & Poor's has conducted for Fannie Mae in the United States and the Central Telecommunication Company in Russia. These cases show practical applications of corporate governance analysis in two very different contexts. Appendix B also contains an article published in 2002 by Clifford Griep and Solomon Samson in Standard & Poor's Credit Markets Services group about the evolving linkage of governance to credit risk analysis.

This book is a contributed edition, bringing together a wide variety of technical and geographic expertise relating to corporate governance. The core of the book is written by colleagues at Standard & Poor's, most of whom are in the Governance Services group. This book is very much a team effort—not only with the individual contributions, but also with the underlying team "groupthink" that has supported the development and application of the analytical criteria presented in this book. The members of the Governance Services team who provided key support to this project include Gurinder K. Badial, Amra Balic, Nick Bradley, Ian Byrne, Andrea Esposito, Laurence Hazell, Hiroko Kiguchi, Julia Kochetygova, Dan Konigsburg, Katrina Tai, and Calvin Wong. The book also benefits from the contributions from other Standard & Poor's colleagues in our Credit Market Services and Investment Services units: David Blitzer, Liliane Bwakira, Gerben de Noord, Daniela Mesquita, and Sandeep Patel.

Gurinder K. Badial, in addition to her own editorial contributions, warrants particular recognition for playing an important coordinating role in this project, working with authors both internal and external to Standard & Poor's, as well as working closely with our publisher, McGraw-Hill. Kelli Christiansen at McGraw-Hill has been generous with both practical guidance and general encouragement about the editing and shaping of this book. George Gulla at Standard & Poor's also has provided considerable feedback that has been important to this project. We also are grateful for the administrative support that Chloe Lacroix of our Governance Services group has provided to this effort.

The external contributions to this book provide distinctive insight and expertise.

These include the individual contributions from Melsa Ararat of Sabanci University on Turkey; John Elkington and Peter Zollinger of SustainAbility on social and environmental reporting; Matthew Kiernan of Innovest on sustainable development; N. S. Kim and H. S. Kim of the Korean rating agency NICE on Korea; G.V. Mani of the Indian rating agency CRISIL on India; Lynn McGregor of Convivium on the human side of governance; Meyrick Payne of Management Practice Inc. on managed fund governance; Merlin Underwood of Lintstock Ltd. on Germany; and Stephen Wallenstein of Duke University and Robert Milbourne of Chadbourne & Parke LLP on the legal environment for governance. Jonathan Bates and his associates at Institutional Design in London also have provided considerable helpful input into our analytical criteria and methodological approach.

It is important to acknowledge Standard & Poor's advocacy of improved corporate governance standards through independent research and analysis. In particular, Leo O'Neill, President of Standard & Poor's, warrants recognition as "champion" for the development of corporate governance services at Standard & Poor's. Vickie Tillman, Roy Taub, Ed Emmer, Cliff Griep, and Petrina Dawson of Standard & Poor's Credit Market Services also have provided critical internal support.

Standard & Poor's began its development work in corporate governance in early 1998, and the Governance Services unit became operational in 2000, focusing on corporate governance evaluations and scores in emerging markets. We are now conducting corporate governance analysis in both developed and developing countries on a global basis. Our project began using Russia as a laboratory for testing our analytical criteria for a wide range of governance abuses. Standard & Poor's Moscow office played a special role in this regard and recognition is due to Moscow office head Cynthia Stone and our local team leader Julia Kochetygova.

My friend and colleague Nick Bradley has been a key force in the development of the governance group at Standard & Poor's from early on. We have worked together very closely, at times interchangeably, through all aspects of developing analytical criteria, building a team, and promoting the development of governance analysis in global financial markets. Nick warrants particular recognition and acknowledgment for his contribution to the development of the corporate governance capability that makes possible the publication of this book.

The development and institutionalization of corporate governance analysis is a long-term journey. But it is one worth taking. Good governance should be rewarded, and bad governance should be punished. To do this in practical terms, the market needs strong analytical tools and reliable benchmarks to assess governance risk. In this context we hope that this book can serve to help market participants more effectively identify and manage governance-related risks. The ultimate goal of more robust corporate governance and higher standards of integrity, fairness, and accountability is one that offers wide-ranging benefits to financial markets, governments, investors, companies, directors, and all other stakeholders who are affected by corporate behavior.

George Dallas
Managing Director and Global Practice Leader
Governance Services
Standard & Poor's
London
December 2003

AUTHOR BIOGRAPHIES

Dr. Melsa Ararat

Dr. Melsa Ararat is the Executive Director of the Corporate Governance Forum of Turkey (CGFT) and practicing faculty member at the Graduate School of Management at Sabanci University. Dr. Ararat has held various senior management and board positions in multinational companies in Asia, Japan, and Europe and was an associate of International Business Leaders Forum before assuming her current role. Her business experience includes strategic partnerships, international joint ventures, and mergers and acquisitions. She holds a Ph.D. in Management in the area of organization and strategy and an MSc in Thermodynamics. Dr. Ararat teaches Corporate Strategy and Governance at the graduate level, advises Standard & Poor's on corporate governance evaluations, and is involved in research. She serves on the editorial advisory board of the journal *Corporate Governance, Business in Society*.

Gurinder K. Badial

Gurinder K. Badial is a Research Consultant in the Governance Services group of Standard & Poor's, based in London. Ms. Badial has a degree in Business Studies and a Masters in Management from the London School of Economics and Political Science and also has a Masters in Personnel and Development. Prior to joining Standard & Poor's, Ms. Badial worked for Shell International and IBM Corporation. In addition, Ms. Badial is a member of the Chartered Institute of Personnel and Development (CIPD) and the Chartered Institute of Marketing (CIM).

Amra Balic

Amra Balic is Director in Standard & Poor's Governance Services group, based in London. She is active in providing individual company corporate governance evaluations and customized governance research in western Europe, emerging Europe, and Asia. Ms. Balic has been involved with the development of Standard & Poor's corporate governance analytical criteria, and with the development of the Standard & Poor's Transparency and Disclosure study. Prior to joining Standard & Poor's Ms. Balic was with the European Bank for Reconstruction and Development in London, where she worked in different analytical and research roles. Ms. Balic holds a B.A.Hons. in Economics from London Guildhall University and an MSc in International Accounting and Finance from London School of Economics and Political Science.

David M. Blitzer

David M. Blitzer is Managing Director and Chairman of *the Index Committee at Standard & Poor's*. Dr. Blitzer is the Chairman of *the S&P 500 Index Committee*, Chairman or member of Standard & Poor's other index committees, and a member of Standard & Poor's Investment Policy Committee. He is also the Chairman of the Standard & Poor's Core Earnings Committee and the leader of the team that developed Standard & Poor's Core Earnings. Dr. Blitzer is the author of *Outpacing the Pros: Using Indices to Beat Wall Street's Savviest Money Managers* (McGraw-Hill, 2001) and *What's the Economy Trying to Tell You? Everyone's Guide to Understanding and Profiting from the Economy* (McGraw-Hill, 1997). A graduate of Cornell University with a B.S. in Engineering, Dr. Blitzer received his M.A. in Economics from the George Washington University and his Ph.D. in Economics from Columbia University.

Nick Bradley

Nick Bradley is Managing Director and European Practice Leader for Standard & Poor's Governance Services group, based in London. This unit was formed in 2000, and provides corporate governance evaluations and customized governance research to companies and institutions in developed and emerging markets. Prior to joining the Governance Services group, Mr. Bradley was European Regional Practice Leader for Standard & Poor's Product Development group where he had specific responsibility for developing the corporate governance analytical criteria and service offering. Prior to joining Standard & Poor's in 1993, Mr. Bradley held a number of positions in corporate banking with Bank of America, Bank of Boston, and Credit Agricole. He studied Business at Coventry University and holds an MBA from Aston University Business School.

Liliane K. Bwakira

Liliane K. Bwakira is Manager in Portfolio Services at Standard & Poor's in New York. Ms. Bwakira joined Standard & Poor's in 2000. She has been instrumental in designing, implementing, and providing analysis of transparency and disclosure rankings initiated on S&P index constituents. In addition to corporate governance research, Ms. Bwakira writes emerging market reviews and index analyses published by Standard & Poor's. Ms. Bwakira holds an MIA in International Finance and Business from Columbia University, an MS in Mineral Economics from Michigan Technological University, and a degree in Political Economy from L' Université du Burundi.

Ian Byrne

Ian Byrne is the Business Development Director of the global governance services group of Standard and Poor's. As such, he is responsible for the sales and marketing activity of the group worldwide. Prior to this role, Mr. Byrne was Business Development Director at Standard & Poor's DRI, an economic analysis and information company, with special responsibility for major global relationships. He joined the Standard & Poor's group in 1991. Mr. Byrne had previously held senior positions in economic consultancy across Europe, and as a quantitative analyst, focusing on economic forecasting and model building in two major U.K. companies: Midland Bank (now HSBC) and Courtaulds plc. Mr. Byrne holds a B.A. (Econ) from the University of York and an MSc (Econ) from the London School of Economics.

John B. Chambers

John B. Chambers has been Deputy Head of the Sovereign Ratings group of Standard & Poor's since 1997. He is also Chairman of the Sovereign Ratings committee, which assigns credit ratings to 93 national governments. Before joining the sovereign ratings group, Mr. Chambers was head of Standard & Poor's Latin American financial institutions department.

Before joining Standard & Poor's in 1993, he was with Banque Indosuez, Paris. He has an M.A. from Columbia University and is a chartered financial analyst.

George S. Dallas

George Dallas is Managing Director and Global Practice Leader for Standard & Poor's Governance Services group, based in London. This unit was formed in 2000, and is active in providing individual company corporate governance evaluations and customized governance research in both developed and emerging markets. Mr. Dallas has been involved actively with the development and application of Standard & Poor's corporate governance analytical criteria in diverse markets around the world. Prior to this assignment, Mr. Dallas held several managerial and analytical positions at Standard & Poor's, including Head of Global Emerging Markets, European Region Head, and practice leader for the company's European corporate ratings group. Mr. Dallas joined Standard & Poor's in New York as a corporate credit analyst in 1983, prior to which he was a corporate lending officer at Wells Fargo Bank. Mr. Dallas holds a B.A., with Distinction, from Stanford University and an M.B.A. from the University of California at Berkeley.

Gerben de Noord

Gerben de Noord is European Affairs Representative for Standards & Poor's, based in London. In this role he is responsible for monitoring and influencing regulatory developments at the EU level with respect to rating agencies. He also is involved with public affairs for Standard & Poor's. Prior to joining Standard & Poor's in January 2002, Mr. de Noord was educated at Strathclyde University, Glasgow, UK (Master of Science in Finance), and Groningen University, Netherlands [Master (Doctorandus) in Economics].

John Elkington

John Elkington is Chairman of SustainAbility, based in London, Washington, D.C., and Zurich. A co-founder of the company in 1987, he has been professionally involved in the environmental and sustainable development fields for over 30 years. Mr. Elkington has worked with many of the world's leading corporations, with government agencies and with such NGOs as Amnesty, Greenpeace, and WWF. He also chairs the Environment Foundation, founded by the U.K. insurance industry in 1983, and sits on the advisory boards of a number of organizations. He has written or co-written 16 books, including *The Green Consumer Guide* (a No. 1 bestseller), *Cannibals with Forks* (which explained the concept of the triple bottom line, a phrase he coined in 1994), and over 20 published reports. He was elected to the UN Global Roll of Honor in 1989 for his "outstanding environmental achievements."

Andrea M. Esposito

Andrea Esposito serves as the North American Regional Practice Leader for Standard & Poor's Governance Services. In this capacity she is responsible for the analytical oversight of Standard & Poor's corporate governance evaluations and research in North America and with their commercial development. During her 20 years at Standard & Poor's, Ms. Esposito has had extensive analytical, managerial, marketing, and sales experience across corporate and government sectors both in the United States and Latin America, including 5 years she spent living and working in Latin America as a senior manager. Prior to joining Standard & Poor's, Ms. Esposito worked for the consulting firm Braxton Associates in Boston, Massachusetts. She holds a B.A.(*cum laude*) in Economics from Harvard University.

Dr. Matthew Kiernan

Dr. Kiernan is founder and Chief Executive of Innovest Strategic Value Advisors, Inc. Dr. Kiernan had previously co-founded a strategy consulting company which he later sold to KPMG Peat Marwick, where he then served as a senior partner. From 1991 to 1992, he was Director of the Business Council for Sustainable Development, which served as the Principal Business and Industry Advisor to the Secretary General of the UN Earth Summit in Rio de Janeiro, and Dr. Kiernan directed the group's Capital Markets Task Force. He also has lectured on environmental finance in senior executive programs at the Wharton School, Columbia Business School, and Oxford University. He holds advanced degrees in political science and environmental studies, as well as a Ph.D. in strategic environmental management from the University of London. His articles have appeared in a variety of leading business journals.

Hiroko Kiguchi

Hiroko Kiguchi is a Director in Standard & Poor's Governance Services group, based in Tokyo. She is actively involved with Standard & Poor's corporate governance scoring evaluations and research in both Japan and Korea. Ms. Kiguchi also manages Standard & Poor's Risk Learning Institute in Risk Solution group for Japan/Korea, after serving as a corporate ratings analyst at Standard & Poor's. She holds a B.A. from the International Christian University.

Hyung Suk Kim

Hyung Suk Kim is a Senior Credit Analyst with the Structured Finance Rating Department of National Information & Credit Evaluation (NICE), a credit rating agency domiciled in South Korea. He is primarily responsible for developing credit rating criteria and assigning NICE's credit ratings to asset-backed securities. As part of the local analytical team working with Standard & Poor's, he also participated in the first corporate governance scoring project conducted by Standard & Poor's in South Korea. Mr. Kim holds a B.A. in Business Administration from Korea University.

Nam Soo Kim

Nam Soo Kim is a Senior Credit Analyst with the Research & Development Department of National Information & Credit Evaluation (NICE), a credit rating agency domiciled in South Korea. Mr. Kim has 8 years of experience as a credit analyst in the telecommunications, textile, and shipbuilding industries. He is currently responsible for formulating credit rating criteria, developing new products, and conducting analyst training programs. As part of the local analytical team working with Standard & Poor's, he also participated in the first corporate governance scoring project conducted by Standard & Poor's in South Korea. Mr. Kim holds a B.A. in Economics from Seoul National University.

Julia Kochetygova

Julia Kochetygova is a Director in the Governance Services group at Standard & Poor's in Moscow. She manages the Moscow team responsible for Standard & Poor's corporate governance scoring and evaluations in Russia. Ms. Kochetygova joined Standard & Poor's in 1999, and was a member of the newly launched Governance Services group in 2000. Prior to joining Standard & Poor's she spent 5 years at Skate Information and Consultancy (Moscow) in senior analytical and managerial roles. Initially she served as Head of Equity Analysis running a team of analysts who were responsible for all fundamental equity analyses, including earnings and valuation estimates. She also managed the company's product development, including the development of safety ratings of equities, fixed income instruments and funds, plus the management of investor relations programs for Russian companies. Subsequently, she became Chief Operating Officer, then Chief Executive Officer, of Skate. Ms. Kochetygova holds an M.A. (Econ) from the Moscow Institute of National Economy and a Ph.D. (Econ) from the Institute of Economics, Russian Academy of Sciences.

Dan Konigsburg

Dan Konigsburg is a Director in Standard and Poor's Governance Services group, based in London, and acts as the global methodology and criteria coordinator for the group. He is responsible for the development and application of services to evaluate and measure the corporate governance practices of companies in emerging and developed markets. Mr. Konigsburg has spoken widely on the topic of corporate governance as an investment risk. Prior to this role, Mr. Konigsburg was a senior analyst at Institutional Shareholder Services, a corporate governance consultancy, based in Washington, D.C. Mr. Konigsburg holds a B.A. from Yale University.

G. V. Mani

G.V. Mani is a corporate governance and credit risk specialist with experience in analysis of corporate governance and credit risk spanning across the manufacturing, services, and financial sectors. In his current capacity as Director of Corporate Governance Services for CRISIL, India's premier rating agency, Mr. Mani has been involved with development of CRISIL's Governance and Value creation rating tool and its application across companies in India. Mr. Mani is also Director of Financial Sector Ratings and is in charge of all ratings in the financial sector for CRISIL. Mr. Mani is a Chartered Accountant and also has a degree in Cost Accounting.

Lynn McGregor

Lynn McGregor is Managing Director of Convivium, a company that specializes in assessing board and executive human capital and providing techniques for upgrading board and executive performance. The work has been based on over 20 years of research and experience. Ms. McGregor is recognized as a leading figure in her field and is well known as a keynote speaker. She has written books and numerous articles on the subject. She has a B.A.Hons. and an M.Phil (Social Sciences) from London University.

Daniela F. Mesquita

Daniela Fonseca Mesquita is a consultant to the Standard & Poor's office in Brazil. Prior to working as a consultant Ms. Mesquita was a corporate governance analyst and product manager at Institutional Shareholders Services (ISS), based in Washington, D.C. Ms. Mesquita holds a BA from the Catholic University of Rio de Janeiro (PUC-RJ), an MSc from the University of Oxford, and an MA, with Distinction, from the University of Reading.

Robert Milbourne

Robert Milbourne is an attorney with the International Project Finance practice group of Chadbourne & Parke LLP, and is based in Washington, D.C. Mr. Milbourne has represented developers, international financial institutions, and political risk insurers on project finance and capital markets transactions throughout Latin America and the Asia-Pacific region. He holds an A.B. from Dartmouth College and a J.D. from Duke University School of Law.

Sandeep A. Patel

Sandeep A. Patel is a Managing Director of Investment Analysis at Standard & Poor's. Dr. Patel is responsible for constructing model portfolios and has been closely involved with the content, design, and analysis of the Standard & Poor's Transparency and Disclosure study. At Standard & Poor's, Dr. Patel's team has been responsible for equity indexes outside the United States, for the implementation of Global Industry Classification

Standard, and for constructing and maintaining indices for alternative asset classes. Dr. Patel joined Standard & Poor's in February 2000. Prior to joining Standard & Poor's, he worked with J. P. Morgan Investment Management and with Tudor Investment Management. He has over 15 years of experience in the research and management of equity and fixed income portfolios. His research has been published extensively in such titles as the *Journal of Finance, Financial Analysts Journal, Emerging Markets Quarterly,* and *Journal of Investing.* Dr. Patel is an Adjunct Professor at the Stern School of Business, New York University, and is a frequent speaker at investment conferences. Dr. Patel holds a Ph.D. in Finance from the Wharton School at the University of Pennsylvania, an MBA from the Indian Institute of Management in Ahmedabad, India, and a B.A. from the Maharaja Sayajirao University of Baroda in Vadodara, India.

C. Meyrick Payne

C. Meyrick Payne is senior partner of Management Practice Inc. (MPI), a consulting firm focused on the governance of American mutual funds based in Stamford, Connecticut. MPI conducts an annual survey of mutual fund director compensation and governance practices as well as a survey of the profitability of mutual funds to the sponsors. Mr. Payne has written extensively about mutual fund governance in both the United States and Canada. He is a qualified Chartered Accountant in England and a Certified Public Accountant in the United States. He received his early education in England and holds an MBA from the Tuck School of Business at Dartmouth College.

Monica C. Richter

Monica Richter is a Managing Director in the International Public Finance Department of Standard & Poor's Ratings group. She has managerial responsibility for a team of analysts working on European (Western, Central, and Eastern), Middle Eastern, and African local and regional government ratings. In addition, Ms. Richter's team is involved with the assignment of ratings to health care, housing, and higher education institutions as well as public/private partnership financings. Ms. Richter has been with Standard & Poor's for a combined 12 years working first in New York and Frankfurt and more recently, in London. Prior to rejoining Standard & Poor's in Europe, Ms. Richter worked as a management consultant. She holds an

M.B.A. in strategic management from the Wharton School at the University of Pennsylvania and a B.A. in mathematics from Wellesley College.

Katrina Tai

Katrina Tai is a Director in Standard & Poor's Governance Services group, based in Hong Kong, where she is active in analytical work and market development in the Greater China region. From 1998 to 2001, Ms. Tai served as Director of Business Development for Standard & Poor's Ratings Services, during which time she had gained extensive exposure to the Chinese business community. Prior to joining Standard & Poor's, she worked as an equity analyst for international investment banks, including Socgen-Crosby Securities and Yamaichi International, covering the red-chips, telecom, and hi-tech sectors of the Hong Kong, Shanghai, and Shenzhen stock markets. She also has worked in a financial planning role for a Mainland China–related company in Hong Kong. Ms. Tai holds two B.Sc. degrees from McMaster University, and an MBA from the University of Toronto.

Merlin Underwood

Merlin Underwood is a director of Lintstock Ltd., a London-based consultancy that provides independent corporate governance advice. He has provided advisory services to Standard & Poor's in the review of its governance scoring criteria. Mr. Underwood holds a B.A. in Law from the University of Cambridge and a European Masters in Law and Economics from the Erasmus University of Rotterdam.

Stephen M. Wallenstein

Stephen Wallenstein is the Executive Director of the Duke Global Capital Markets Center, a unique collaboration between the Fuqua School of Business and the Duke School of Law, and is Professor of the Practice of Law, Business & Finance. He is also program director and founder of the Duke Directors' Education Institute, an ongoing series to address the corporate governance failures of diligence, ethics, and controls in corporate America. Professor Wallenstein is a graduate of the

Yale Law School, holds a Masters in Government from Harvard University, and a B.A. from Cornell where he was elected to Phi Beta Kappa in his Junior year.

Calvin R. Wong

Calvin Wong is the Hong Kong–based Managing Director for Governance Services, a position he assumed in April 2002. In his position, Calvin manages Standard & Poor's activities in Asia relating to corporate governance scores, evaluations, and customized research. Calvin also serves concurrently as the Asia-Pacific Regional Practice Leader for Structured Finance Ratings. He assumed this position upon moving to the region in January 1998. He is responsible for Standard & Poor's Structured Finance business in Australia/New Zealand, Southeast Asia, Greater China, and Korea. He manages the analytical teams in Hong Kong and Melbourne, Australia that are involved with ratings, criteria development, and surveillance for all types of asset securitization and structured financings. Prior to joining Standard & Poor's in 1987, Mr. Wong spent four years as a corporate lending officer for Irving Trust Company in New York. He holds a B.A. in Economics from Cornell University and an MBA in Finance from the Wharton School, the University of Pennsylvania.

Peter Zollinger

Peter Zollinger joined SustainAbility as a Director in 1999. In January 2001 SustainAbility's board of directors appointed him Executive Director. Besides managing the company, his focus is on corporate governance, in particular the role of corporate boards in the context of sustainable development. After graduating with an MBA in Finance from the University of St. Gallen, Switzerland, Mr. Zollinger was Executive Assistant of Swiss industrialist Stephan Schmidheiny, founder of the Business Council for Sustainable Development (now WBCSD). His emphasis there was on strategic management and communication. His career included a secondment to World Resources Institute, WRI, Washington, D.C., to help it engage the business community, with an emphasis on sustainable forestry and energy/climate protection. For several years, Mr. Zollinger acted as Director Strategic Development of FUNDES International (part of Schmidheiny Group), where he co-managed this network for small business development in nine countries of Latin America.

Introduction

Part One contains two chapters that establish a foundation for the subsequent parts on company governance criteria and country analysis. Chapter 1 presents corporate governance as a risk factor, and reviews the development of codes and recent academic research on key governance issues. Chapter 2 focuses on methodological issues in analyzing corporate governance. It lays out the framework for the criteria that will be addressed in Chapters 3 through 7, and discusses several challenges to applying governance criteria for meaningful analytical conclusions.

CHAPTER 1

Corporate Governance as a Risk Factor

George Dallas and Sandeep A. Patel

DEVELOPMENTS IN THE CORPORATE GOVERNANCE DEBATE

Corporate governance issues have always been integral to business practices, beginning with the creation of corporate structures and the distinction between owners and managers. The "agency problem" between owners, managers, and the directors who represent the owners began to become formalized in economic literature in the 1930s. Since that time, what we now would label as governance issues can be seen to have been an important part of business history as they relate to family empires, financial-industrial groups, nationalizations, privatizations, monopolies, conglomerates, and the hostile takeover movement, to name but a few areas.

In more recent years corporate governance has established a greater standalone identity as a field of study—and as an area of risk. The wide wake of damage and disenfranchisement caused by recent corporate governance failures has made corporate governance not just a concern for financial markets, but also an issue of political economy on a global basis. Policymakers, market participants, and academics are studying comparative governance structures and practices, with a view to identifying areas of risk and to develop policy responses for reform and improvement. But in a global setting, which includes pluralistic market environments, legal systems, ownership structures, and cultures, a standardized approach to corporate governance has yet to emerge that is relevant in all countries or business contexts. As such, these policy responses are also far from uniform.

Many governance observers cite the release in the early 1990s of the Cadbury Code on corporate governance in the United Kingdom as a key development in the modern literature on corporate governance in practice. This code, and the development of the U.K. Combined Code which was to follow, was catalyzed by several visible U.K. corporate failures of the late 1980s/early 1990s. The Cadbury Code became a standard model, or at least a reference, for much of the subsequent thinking on corporate governance codes. At the same time in the United States, large pension funds such as California Public Employees' Retirement System (CalPERS), and Teachers Insurance and Annuity Association-College Retirement Equities Fund (TIAA-CREF), began to use their influence as institutional investors to advocate improvements in corporate governance and stimulate greater shareholder activism.

However, given the relatively strong economic and stock market performance in developed markets during most of the 1990s, the urgency of the corporate governance debate during the late 1990s shifted more toward the emerging markets, as weak corporate governance was often diagnosed as contributing to the financial crises such as those that emerged in Asia and Russia. These crises put the spotlight on governance problems in regimes with weak protection of investor rights, and helped to stimulate the development of the corporate governance guidelines by the Organization of Economic Cooperation and Development (OECD) in the late 1990s. This was an attempt to create a general framework for corporate governance to have relevance over a wide range of legal jurisdictions, market practices, ownership structures, and cultures. Complementing the OECD Guidelines, the International Corporate Governance Network (ICGN) has carried on the development of outlining governance practices and policies for global or multinational application.

Since that time, we have seen these efforts to build a general global framework complemented by the development of many country-specific codes of best governance practice. The years 2002 and 2003 have given rise to wide-ranging attempts to legislate and regulate governance standards in markets around the world, perhaps most visibly in North America and Europe. The Sarbanes-Oxley legislation in the United States and the new listing rule proposals by the New York Stock Exchange and NASDAQ are prominent among these legal and regulatory initiatives, and were introduced with both urgency and rapidity.

Across the Atlantic, corporate governance reforms on company law at the European Union (EU) level were proposed by the Winter Report. The United Kingdom witnessed the Myners report on governance, the consultation paper on proposed changes to U.K. company law, and the Higgs report on nonexecutive directors. In continental Europe, governance codes also took shape in several key countries. These include the review of the French governance code led by Daniel Bouton, the publishing of the German governance code chaired by Gerhard Cromme, the review of company boards in Italy led by Stefano Preda, and the development of Spanish code of corporate governance led by the Aldama Commission. Elsewhere around the world—in Asia, Latin America, developing Europe, and other emerging markets—individual governance codes and guidelines have been introduced in many countries. The OECD itself is in the process of reviewing and updating its own principles, reflecting in part the dynamic debate in corporate governance in recent years.

TOP-DOWN POLICY REFORMS AND BOTTOM-UP MARKET-DRIVEN SOLUTIONS

These initiatives at legal, regulatory, and exchange reform represent efforts to control or mitigate governance-related risks, or to provide an "enabling environment" for healthy governance practices. On balance, these "top down" reforms represent a positive framework for improving governance standards and practices. However, they have their limitations and incumbent risks. A limitation in a collective sense is that while the numerous country codes and guidelines articulate many similar—or at least similar sounding—themes, there will be significant differences in how these may be applied or interpreted in individual jurisdictions around the world. Notwithstanding the efforts of the OECD and ICGN, there are no equivalent international governance principles that have built general global acceptance in the way that has been the case in the accounting area, for example, with International Accounting Standards. Global differences in governance practice and interpretation still exist and are not likely to go away in the foreseeable future.

A second limitation of top-down reforms is that externally imposed rules do not necessarily ensure a true culture of governance and shareholder/stakeholder value in individual companies. In other words, you can take a horse to water but you can't make it drink—even though the horse might be pretending to do so. Nominal compliance on its own can be form without substance. It can give rise to false comfort for those regulators, investors, or external analysts who focus on a superficial "box ticking" approach to assessing corporate governance. Compliance to laws and regulations does not mean that investors can rest easily and assume that all companies will comply in the same manner—nor that all companies who are in compliance have the same level of governance quality. There remains scope for differentiation. Moreover, there is the risk of cynical manipulation by companies or individuals who may wish to "game" the system by creating a façade of high governance standards while hiding a rot that is concealed beneath the surface.

As such, while many of these new laws, regulations, and listing rules are positive steps forward, shareholders and stakeholders cannot rely solely on laws and guidelines for protection. They themselves must assume the responsibility and develop the tools to monitor and assess governance at the individual company level to ensure or incite compliance both in form and substance, and to avoid conclusions that could result in false positives or false negatives.

Evaluating governance in individual companies must start with an assessment of a company's given governance "architecture." However, good or bad governance ultimately is less a question of architecture and more a question of the people who are governing from within this architecture. This requires an assessment, not only of codes and guidelines, but also of how effectively—or ineffectively—a company's managers and directors interact to create value for shareholders while respecting the interests of the company's stakeholders. For many audiences the governance debate extends further to the interests of key stakeholders, either in a normative sense of social responsibility or in a more economic sense of minimizing potential operational risks that could come from poor employee, community, or environmental relations.

DEVELOPMENT OF GOVERNANCE ANALYSIS CRITERIA AND RATING SYSTEMS

On that basis, there is scope for more nuanced understanding and analysis of qualitative governance risks that can enable investors and stakeholders to draw clearer conclusions about governance as a risk factor in individual companies. This has given rise to the development of corporate governance rating systems, such as those developed by Standard & Poor's and several other firms. The premise of this new field of rating analysis is that governance ratings can isolate and provide a diagnostic of the "soft," but nonetheless real, factors that affect how a company is governed with regard to the interests of its financial stakeholders. In principle, corporate governance rating or scoring systems can provide a positive complement to traditional credit or equity analysis by placing emphasis on factors that might not be heavily weighted in financially driven analysis.

The framework that Standard & Poor's uses in its corporate governance scoring process is a prominent feature of this book. As this, or other, methodologies on governance assessment become institutionalized and gain broad acceptance, market participants will be able to use governance ratings and scores as an analytical tool—to screen investment opportunities to assess degrees of governance-related risk, and to develop relevant governance risk premia on a firm-specific basis. Moreover, a governance rating system can benefit companies and company directors by providing an independent, third-party diagnostic of its relative strengths and weaknesses. In behavioral science as in the physical sciences, the act of measurement can have an effect on that which is being measured. Applied to the area of corporate governance, this suggests the potential for an effective governance rating system to serve as a positive discipline and incentive for improvement.

This in turn can affect a company's valuation, as well as its access to and cost of capital. If it becomes clear that there are financial rewards or penalties that are explicitly linked to governance quality, this can become an important "invisible hand" motivating the protection of shareholder rights, higher standards of transparency and disclosure, and the robust engagement of independent directors in the governance process.

Regulators may benefit from more established governance rating systems, as enhanced public disclosure and understanding about governance risks can contribute to greater market confidence and resilience. Other beneficiaries of such a system can include nonfinancial stakeholders, directors and officer liability insurers, and financial intermediaries.

GOVERNANCE AS A RISK FACTOR

Empirical research can provide essential guidance in the development of governance rating systems by highlighting the desirable and empirically relevant characteristics of corporate governance structures and processes. Academic research on corporate governance is nascent but very active. Luigi Zingales (1997) writes in the New Palgrave Dictionary of Economics and Law, "While some of the questions have been around since Berle and Means (1932), the term 'corporate governance' did not exist in English language until twenty years ago. In the last two decades, however, corporate governance issues have become important not only in academic literature, but also in public policy debates."[1] Over the last 25 years, and especially in the 5 years since Zingales, many academic studies have examined various mechanisms of corporate governance and the benefits of good corporate governance. For example, a search on the Social Science Research Network (SSRN) produced more than 400 articles on corporate governance since 1997. Much of this research has been driven within the academic disciplines of economics, finance, and law, looking for links between governance structures and practices and more tangible (or at least quantitative) measures of performance and valuation.

A few academic surveys provide detailed overviews of the literature on corporate governance—Shleifer and Vishny (1997), Karpoff (1998), Patterson (2000, 2003), Bhagat and Romano (2001, 2002), Denis and McConnell (2002), and Mathiesen (2003). These studies demonstrate that the gamut of corporate governance research is broad—and growing. The empirical focus of the studies has evolved in response to the availability of data, activism of shareholders, and developments in creating measures to reflect sound corporate governance processes.

There are various ways of characterizing the various themes of governance research. A convenient way of categorizing research is to group studies by the focus of governance mechanisms—*internal/firm-specific* or *external/systemic*. Studies focusing on governance mechanisms internal to a firm address shareholder rights, takeover defenses, accounting and auditing policies, risk management, board characteristics, independence, and executive compensation. Research focusing on governance mechanisms external to a firm include studies of the legal environment, especially commercial law, ownership structures, and policies in labor and product markets. This list of subcategories is far from exhaustive, but indicative of some of the key research themes.

Internal Factors

A key impetus to empirical research on corporate governance was the intellectual and business climate in the 1980s in the United States. This period is characterized by an explosion in mergers and acquisitions, the development of theoretical arguments supporting takeovers as a managerial discipline mechanism, and attempts by managements to avert hostile takeovers by the adoption of mechanisms such as poison pills. Not surprisingly, initial empirical research in the United States on corporate governance focused on the effects of takeovers and anti-takeover provisions on shareholder wealth. This focus gradually expanded to other internal corporate governance mechanisms such as board characteristics and independence and executive compensation.

The business context of growing leveraged buyouts and hostile takeovers coincided with the development of modern finance theory, and the empirical refinements in event study methodology as a means to test efficiency in capital markets.[2] Event study methodology is particularly suited to examining immediate effects of specific changes in corporate governance, such as increasing the number of independent members in the board of directors, adopting anti-takeover provisions, or changing the parameters of the chief executive officer's compensation. Bhagat and Romano (2001a, 2001b) summarize the key role event studies played in advancing the corporate law scholarship in the 1980s and its effect on legal policy. Early empirical research on the effect of internal corporate governance mechanisms on shareholder wealth is largely inconclusive, except for the strongly established stylized fact that takeovers increase the wealth of the acquired firm's shareholders. There are a number of valid reasons for the lack of convincing evidence, ranging from poorly framed hypotheses to sample selection biases and other econometric problems.[3]

The principal drawback of early studies of the effects of internal corporate governance mechanisms, however, turns out to be the event study methodology. Researchers such as Metrick and Ishii (2002) note that the perceived advantages of event studies are possibly its real disadvantages—for example, a limitation of event studies is that they force researchers to focus on one narrow aspect of corporate governance. In addition, effective use of event study methodology needs a clear definition of event and event date, and assumes that the effects of changes in corporate governance are realized over a very short time. In practice, internal corporate governance mechanisms evolve over time and are better characterized by a balance between a number of policies, procedures, and practices.

To overcome the limitations of event studies, recent studies such as Botosan (1997); Millstein and MacAvoy (1998); and Gompers, Ishii, and Metrick (2001) construct indices based on several measures that capture broad aspects of corporate governance such as financial disclosure, effectiveness of board, and takeover defenses, respectively.

Gompers, Ishii, and Metrick (2001) construct a broad index of shareholder rights ("Governance Index"), and document a positive correspondence between the governance index and long-horizon returns, after controlling for riskiness or "style" differences. This revealed that companies ranking most highly in this governance index enjoyed superior returns (over 8 percent) during the timeframe of the study (the 1990s). Botosan (1997) develops a broad measure of financial disclosure and finds that for firms followed by few financial analysts, cost of equity capital decreases by as much as 9 percent as the annual report disclosure level increases. Millstein and MacAvoy (1998) develop a broad measure of board independence and provide arguments and evidence, based on holistic board surrogates generated by CalPERS, to show that an active board of directors aligned with shareholder interests enhances value to shareholders.

While this firm-specific research does present some positive evidence linking corporate governance–related themes to tangible performance measures, open questions remain about specific governance features such as board structure and composition, executive compensation, and anti-takeover devices. As such, it is difficult to prescribe generic structures or a "one size fits all" approach to many aspects of governance at the individual company. Companies must be assessed on a case-by-case basis, and in the context of their macro or country environment.

External Factors

Researchers have focused on several macro or external influences affecting corporate governance, such as the legal environment and especially commercial codes on takeover and bankruptcy, ownership structure, and competition in labor and product markets. While the above macro themes are interlinked, the role of law is one of the key issues in recent corporate governance research. In the United States, corporate law is largely decided by states, and one small state, Delaware, has come to dominate the incorporation process. As a result, initial empirical research on the effect of corporate law in the United States focused on the effect on stock prices of a change in state of incorporation. Minor variations in legal regimes within states in the United States and infrequent changes in state laws as well as in corporations, limited the range of issues to be examined.

LaPorta, Lopez-de-Silanes, Shleifer, and Vishny (LLSV) (1997) broadened the range of issues researchers can examine around the theme of "Rule of Law" by focusing on cross-country differences in protection of investor rights. LLSV hypothesize that the extent to which a country's laws protect investor rights—and the extent to which those laws are enforced—are fundamental determinants of the ways in which corporate finance and corporate governance evolve in that country. Their empirical evidence indicates that there are significant differences across countries in the degree of investor protection, and that countries with low investor protection are generally characterized by a high concentration of equity ownership within firms and a lack of significant public equity markets.

An interesting, and provocative, finding of LLSV stemming from this research is that differences in the level of investor protection among countries are explained by differences in origin of their legal systems. In particular, the LLSV research finds civil law regimes less protective of ownership rights than in many common law regimes. This in turn is offered as an explanatory factor on why ownership is less concentrated in common law regimes with strong protection of ownership rights.

There is considerable literature about ownership structures as they relate to corporate governance, and these are outlined in greater detail in Chapter 3. Studies on ownership show that there is a large diversity of ownership structures, including markets where shares are widely held and markets where there are concentrations of ownership.[4] However, it is important to note here that the themes of ownership research differ markedly depending on the economies or markets under review. In markets where ownership is concentrated (Asia, Europe, emerging markets), the focus is largely on the potentially negative influences of blockholders. However, in markets such as the United States, where shares are more widely held, research focuses more on the role of institutional investors, either as activists or in the proxy process. Linked to this is research related to the market for corporate control and the use of poison pills, staggered boards, and other anti-takeover devices.

For example, Black (2001), Gillan and Starks (1998), and Karpoff (1998) provide reviews of research on shareholder activism. General studies, such as an examination of proxy proposals, show an inconclusive relationship between shareholder activism and performance.[5] However, studies focusing on actions of specific large shareholders such as TIAA-CREF or CalPERS suggest a positive effect of shareholder activism [Prevost and Rao (1998) and Carleton, Nelson, and Weisbach (1997)]. With regard to the market for corporate control, poison pills and other anti-takeover devices are often viewed as limitations of ownership rights, notably the right to sell one's share to a legitimate bidder. However, counter to this conventional wisdom, Heron and Lie (2000) provide evidence in defense of introducing poison pills—showing that poison pills enhance the bargaining power of managers, and stimulate increases in bid premiums and higher shareholder gains without materially altering the likelihood of takeover success.

In addition to legal and ownership issues, governance research draws attention to other market forces in terms of shaping corporate governance in individual companies. In this context it is worth citing examples from product and labor markets to illustrate how external governance influences can differ.

Beginning with product markets, Allen's study of Japan (2001) points out, with the example of Toyota, that the product market plays an important role in the efficient operation of Japanese companies in Japan. Hanazaki and Horiuchi (2000) also have provided empirical support that it is competition rather than bank monitoring that is important for Japanese companies. In the area of labor markets, Khanna and Palepu (2001) provide a very interesting case study of the Indian software company Infosys, making the argument that both product and labor market factors were drivers behind the development of world-class governance standards at Infosys.

These diverse legal, ownership, and economic forces can be complex and country specific. They complicate, if not render impossible, the search for absolute governance structures and solutions that are consistently applicable in all companies in all jurisdictions. In this regard, the concept of path dependency explored by several governance researchers[6] speaks to the notion that many governance environments may be resistant to institutional changes that may come with overall governance reforms. Countries will retain their own identities, which in turn link to historical legal, market, and cultural frameworks. However, this does not exclude the potential for some convergence of governance norms in individual companies, at least among firms that seek capital in the same international financial markets. This is often referred to as "bonding," particularly with regard to firms from developing markets who "bond" with financial markets whose requirements are more exacting (see Coffee, 2002).

COMPOSITE MEASURES IN RESEARCH

Much of the research that has been defined thus far has approached corporate governance from the perspective of a single explanatory variable, e.g., law, shareholder rights, ownership structure, board characteristics, and the like. However, increasingly there is a focus on developing composite measures for governance research, reflecting the notion that a reliable governance index for research projects will rely on a broad range of explanatory factors.

For example, the Investor Opinion Surveys conducted by the consulting firm McKinsey & Company defined corporate governance in individual firms as an abstract combination of "effective boards of directors, broad disclosure, strong rights and equal treatment of shareholders."[7] In its first pan-regional survey on corporate governance conducted in 2000, McKinsey found that a significant majority of institutional investors were willing to pay a premium for well-governed companies, a premium that varied from 17.9 percent in the United Kingdom to 27.6 percent in Venezuela.[8] Three-quarters of investors emphasized that board practices are at least as important to them as financial performance. The survey in 2002 re-emphasized the use of these composite corporate governance criteria to drive investment decisions, and highlighted the importance of factors such as greater financial disclosure, strengthened shareholder rights, and more board independence.

Empirical research also is beginning to focus on governance measures which draw from a broad range of explanatory factors to serve as a governance proxy. For example, in Black's study of corporate governance in 21 major companies in Russia[9] he uses crude governance ratings compiled by the Russian brokerage Brunswick Warburg with strong statistical conclusions. These ratings were assessments by Brunswick Warburg analysts based on a range of governance-related characteristics. Moreover, in Black, Jang, and Kim's 2002 study of corporate governance in 540 companies in Korea[10] a corporate governance index for individual companies was created using a composite of 42 variables which were categorized into four groups: shareholder rights, boards of directors, outside directors, and transparency/disclosure.

Outside the realm of academia, the brokerage CLSA has established a rating system for emerging market corporations in Asia, Latin America, and emerging Europe, based on a template-driven questionnaire completed by its equity analysts. This rating system produces a composite scope comprised of aspects of shareholder rights, strategy, transparency, board structure, and other governance-related factors. CLSA and Klapper and Love (2002) tested aggregate metrics of corporate governance against various performance measures, and generally found that the strongest scoring companies outperform companies whose governance parameters scored the weakest.[11]

The development of new corporate governance rating systems as a commercial service also stands to provide a source for further research into benchmarking companies for governance quality—and for testing these benchmarks empirically. Governance ratings can embody a balanced and objective range of factors that help to determine governance quality—and governance risk—in individual firms. At this point in time governance ratings or scores are still new to financial markets and have yet to be institutionalized. As these ratings develop in terms of critical mass and a time series, they also can be tested empirically for their use as predictive tools. In the interim, these can still be used as guides for research both into benchmarking companies' overall governance standards and in trying to identify more clearly the driving factors behind good governance.

GENERAL CONCLUSIONS AND AGENDA FOR FURTHER RESEARCH

Broad conclusions emerging from the research based on broad measures of governance in global markets over the last 5 years are that:

◆ *Corporate governance does matter.* Investors say that this is an important concern and some empirical studies show positive linkages with governance-related variables and performance measures.

◆ Investor research suggests the concept of a *corporate governance risk premium.* Investors are willing to pay a higher price for companies with better corporate governance. Or they may wish to pay a lesser price to compensate for lower governance standards. This is difficult to test in practice, as established benchmarks to help investors readily identify governance quality in individual companies have yet to be institutionalized.

◆ *Governance is not a "one size fits all" concept.* There are few insights from empirical research about ownership structures, investor rights, stakeholder relations, transparency standards, or board structures that have universal applicability. Companies need to be assessed on a case-by-case basis.

◆ *A holistic approach involving multiple explanatory factors*—not a single factor—provides the most robust conclusions in corporate governance research.

Where is there scope for more research? While it is unlikely that research, at least in the near term, will resolve all the open issues currently being debated in the governance area, there are several themes where further research can guide and provide a more solid foundation to efforts to systematically assess or benchmark governance standards as a risk factor in individual firms. These themes include the following:

◆ *Country risk:* Is it possible to meaningfully benchmark or calibrate country risk as it relates to governance at the individual company level? What is the relationship between countrywide governance risks, such as an ineffective legal system? Should a company's governance quality be viewed as intrinsically flawed or limited if it is incorporated in a jurisdiction with weak protection of investor rights?

◆ *Governance risk premium:* To the extent that corporate governance is itself a standalone risk factor, how can this risk be assessed to allow investors to rationally reflect a governance risk premium (or discount) in investment decisions? How high should such premia be? What is the influence of country risk in determining these risk premia?

♦ _Comparative governance structures and principles:_ Even though a meaningful "recipe" or prescription for corporate governance has yet to find universal applicability, "best practices" still can be researched for relevance in individual markets. Particularly with the recent articulation of new governance codes and principles in many countries around the world, there is scope to review how compliance with tighter rules and standards may—or may not—improve individual company governance standards. Areas of focus in this context can include board structure and composition, executive compensation, the working of the audit committee, and ownership rights—including the role of takeover defenses.

♦ _The human side:_ To achieve an understanding of board effectiveness that goes beyond structural issues the personal, or human, side of the board must be considered. This raises issues of organizational behavior, including diversity, teamwork, engagement, creativity, constructive tension, and "true" independence of mind. How can a company truly change its governance culture? What can be done to ensure proper "tone at the top"? How can boards best create an atmosphere of constructive tension? At the top end of the governance scale, the human side is likely to be the greatest differentiator between good and great companies. Attention and vigilance always should be paid to companies that may look good on the structural side, but where the human side may be missing.

♦ _Sustainable development:_ In many parts of the world the corporate governance debate is beginning to blend the interests of financial stakeholders such as shareholders and creditors with a broader awareness and greater prioritization of nonfinancial stakeholders, including employees, customers, suppliers, communities, governments, and environmental interests. With the sustainable development agenda growing and with the development of more social and environmental reporting, there is scope to begin to integrate social and environmental performance into broader assessments of governance. From a financial perspective, this can be explored on the basis of firms with stronger social and environmental performance having either better or at least more stable economic performance—possibly less subject to operational disruptions or to losses in brand value. If this were possible, the case for sustainable development would be stronger if more tangible links could be made to the "business case" for improving social and environmental performance—framing these as intangible assets or contingent liabilities in some shape or form. From the perspective of strategic management, relations with nonfinancial stakeholders should be viewed with regard to the extent they help a company to establish sustainable competitive advantage.

SUMMARY

A mosaic of evidence from research is emerging that is giving shape to the connection of governance with performance measures. But at the same time, it is fair to say that a "holy grail" has yet to be written establishing an empirical linkage between governance practices and economic performance and valuations that has consistent global applicability.

With all the recent attention given to corporate governance, this remains a relatively young field for analysis and research. Research will benefit from more institutionalized corporate governance analysis at the individual company level. Governance ratings, however, remain at an early stage of development and will gain greater urgency to the extent that empirical validation continues to grow. Continued research and more empirical evidence are required to validate existing governance principles and to seek new alternatives to the laws, guidelines, and standards that are being used to direct corporate governance reform at the macro level and guide corporate governance analysis at the micro level.

NOTES

1. Zingales, 1998.

2. MacKinlay (1997) reviews the use of event study in economics and finance, and explains, "The event study is an important research tool in economics and finance. The goal of an event study is to measure the effects of an economic event on the value of firms. Event study methods exploit the fact that, given rationality in the marketplace, the effects of an event will be reflected immediately in security prices. Thus, the impact can be measured by examining security prices surrounding the event."

3. For example, Borsch-Supan and Koke (2000) identify four categories of econometric problems that limit the conclusiveness of causal effects of corporate governance: reverse causality, missing variables, sample selectivity, and measurement error in variables.

4. Barca and Becht, 2002; Claessens, Djankov, and Fan, December 2002; La Porta, Lopez-de-Silanes, and Shleifer, 1999.

5. This finding suffers from a sampling bias, as Chidambaran and Woidtke (2000) and Carleton, Nelson, and Weisbach (1997) show that large shareholders negotiate their proposals with the management before they are voted, and most empirical studies ignore the role of negotiated proposals that are withdrawn.

6. Bebchuck and Roe, 1999; Coffee, 2002.

7. McKinsey Global Investor Opinion Survey on Corporate Governance, 2002.

8. McKinsey Global Investor Opinion Survey on Corporate Governance, 2000.

9. Black, 2001.

10. Black, Jang, and Kim, 2002.

11. CLSA Emerging Markets, February 2002; Klapper and Love, 2002.

REFERENCES

Allen, F. "Do Financial Institutions Matter?," Presidential Address, American Finance Association, *Journal of Finance*, 2001.

Barca, F., and M. Becht. *The Control of Corporate Europe*, Oxford University Press, 2002.

Bebchuck, L. A., J. C. Coates IV, and G. Subramanian. "The Powerful Antitakeover Force of Staggered Boards: Theory, Evidence and Policy," *Stanford Law Review*, 54, 2002.

Bebchuck, L. A., and M. J. Roe. "A Theory of Path Dependence in Corporate Governance and Ownership," *Working Paper No. 131*, Columbia Law School Working Paper Series, 1999.

Berle, A., and G. Means. "The Modern Corporation and Private Property," Macmillan, New York, 1932.

Bhagat, S., and B. S. Black. "The Uncertain Relationship between Board Composition and Firm Performance," *Business Lawyer*, vol. 54, 1999, pp. 921–963.

Bhagat, S., and B. S. Black. "The Relationship between Board Composition and Firm Performance," *Comparative Corporate Governance: The State of the Art and Emerging Research*, K. Hopt, M. Roe, and E. Wymeersch, (eds.), Oxford University Press, 1998.

Bhagat, S., and R. Romano. "Event Studies and the Law: Part I: Technique and Corporate Litigation," *American Law and Economics Review*, vol. 4, no. 1, 2002.

Bhagat, S., and R. Romano. "Event Studies and the Law: Part II: Empirical Studies of Corporate Law," *Working Paper*, International Center for Finance at the Yale School of Management, April 2001.

Black, B. "The Corporate Governance Behavior and Market Value of Russian Firms," *Emerging Markets Review*, vol. 2, 2001, pp. 89–108.

Black, B. S., H. Jang, and W. Kim. "Does Corporate Governance Affect Firm Value? Evidence from Korea," *Working Paper*, Stanford University, Korea University Business School, and KDI School of Public Policy and Management, 2002.

Borsch-Supan, A., and J. Koke. "An Applied Econometricians' View of Empirical Corporate Governance Studies," *Working Paper*, University of Mannheim and Centre of European Economic Research (ZEW), 2000.

Botosan, C. A. "Disclosure Level and the Cost of Equity Capital," *The Accounting Review*, vol. 72, 1997, pp. 323–349.

Carleton, W. T., J. M. Nelson, and M. Weisbach. "The Influence of Institutions on Corporate Governance through Private Negotiations: Evidence from TIAA CREF," *Working Paper*, University of Arizona, 1997.

Chidambaran, N. K., and T. Woidtke. "The Role of Negotiations in Corporate Governance: Evidence from Withdrawn Shareholder-Initiated Proposals," *New York University Law and Business Research Paper*, no. 99-12, 2000.

Choi, F. D. S. ed. *International Finance and Accounting Handbook*, 3d ed, Wiley & Son, October 2003.

Claessens, S., J. P. H. Djankov, and L. Fan. "Disentangling the Incentive and Entrenchment Effects of Large Shareholdings," *Journal of Finance*, vol. LVII, no. 6, December 2002.

CLSA Emerging Markets, "Corporate Governance in Emerging Markets," February 2002.

Coffee, J. C. "Competition among Securities Markets: A Path Dependent Perspective," Columbia University School of Law, 2002.

Coombes, P., and M. Watson. "Three Surveys on Corporate Governance," *The McKinsey Quarterly*, 2000.

Coombes, P., and M. Watson. "Global Investor Opinion Survey: Key Findings," McKinsey & Co., 2002.

Core, J. E., R. W. Holthausen, and D. E. Larcker. "Corporate Governance, Chief Executive Compensation, and Firm Performance," *Journal of Financial Economics*, vol. 51, 1999, pp. 371–406.

Denis, D. K., and J. J. McConnell. "International Corporate Governance," *Working Paper*, Purdue University, 2002.

Durnev, A., and E. H. Kim. "To Steal or Not To Steal: Firm Attributes, Legal Environment, and Valuation," *Working Paper*, University of Michigan, 2002.

Franks, J., and C. Mayer. "German Capital Markets, Corporate Control and the Obstacles to Hostile Takeovers: Lessons from Three Case Studies," *Working Paper*, London Business School, 1993.

Frost, C. A., and K. P. Ramin. "Corporate Financial Disclosure: A Global Assessment," in

Gillan, S. L., and L. T. Starks. "A Survey of Shareholder Activism: Motivation and Empirical Evidence," *Contemporary Finance Digest*, vol. 2, no. 3, Autumn 1998, pp. 10–34.

Gompers, P., J. Ishii, and A. Metrick. "Corporate Governance and Equity Prices," *Quarterly Journal of Economics*, 2001.

Hanazaki, M., and A. Horiuchi. "Have Banks Contributed to Efficient Management in Japan's Manufacturing?," *Working Paper CIRJE-F-76*, Faculty of Economics, University of Tokyo, 2000.

Heron, R. A., and E. Lie. "On the Use of Poison Pills and Defensive Payouts by Targets of Hostile Takeovers," *Working Paper*, Indiana University and The College of William & Mary, 2000.

Jenson, M. C., and W. H. Meckling. "Theory of the Firm: Managerial Behavior, Agency Costs and Ownership Structure," *Journal of Financial Economics*, vol. 3, 1976, pp. 305–360.

Karpoff, J. M. "The Impact of Shareholder Activism on Target Companies: A Survey of Empirical Findings," *Working Paper*, University of Washington, 1998.

Khanna, T., and K. Palepu. "Product and Labor Market Globalization & Convergence of Corporate Governance: Evidence from Infosys and the Indian Software Industry," *Working Paper*, Harvard Business School, September 2001.

Khanna, T., K. Palepu, and S. Srinivasan. "Disclosure Practices of Foreign Companies Interacting with U.S. Markets," *Working Paper*, Harvard Business School, 2002.

Klapper, L. F., and I. Love. "Corporate Governance, Investor Protection and Performance in Emerging Markets," *World Bank Working Paper*, 2002.

La Porta, R., F. Lopez-de-Silanes, A. Shleifer. "Corporate Ownership around the World," *Journal of Finance*, vol. 54, 1999, pp. 471–518.

La Porta, R., F. Lopez-de-Silanes, A. Shleifer, and R. Vishny. "Legal Determinants of External Finance," *Journal of Finance*, vol. 52, 1997, pp. 1131–1150.

MacKinlay, A. C. "Event Studies in Economics and Finance," *Journal of Economic Literature*, vol. 35, no. 1, 1997, pp. 13–39.

Mathiesen, H. "Encyclopedia of Corporate Governance," http://www/encyco-gov.com (accessed August 2003).

Metrick, A., and J. Ishii. "Firm-Level Corporate Governance," *Working Paper*, Wharton School of Business and Harvard Business School, 2002.

Millstein, I., and P. MacAvoy. "Active Board of Directors and Performance of the Large Publicly Traded Corporation," *Columbia Law Review*, vol. 98, 1998.

Monks, R. A. G., and N. Minow. "Corporate Governance," Blackwell Publishers Ltd., Oxford, 2001.

North, D. C. "Institutions, Institutional Change, and Economic Performance," Cambridge University Press, New York, 1990.

Patterson, J. D. "The Link between Corporate Governance and Performance: Year 2000 Update," The Conference Board, August 2000.

Patterson, J. D. "Corporate Governance and Corporate Performance Research: Overview Updated for 2003," The Corporate Library, 2003.

Prevost, A., and R. Rao. "Of What Value Are Shareholder Proposals Sponsored by Public Pension Funds?," *Working Paper*, Texas Tech University, 1998.

Shleifer, A., and R. W. Vishny. "A Survey of Corporate Governance," *Journal of Finance*, 52, 1997, pp. 737–783.

Zingales, L. "Corporate Governance," *The New Palgrave Dictionary of Economics and the Law*, P. Newman, ed., Macmillan, New York, 1998.

CHAPTER 2

Methodological Overview: Perspective of an External Analyst

George Dallas

The analysis of corporate governance in an individual company is a complex process, combining an objective assessment of company governance structures with a more qualitative interpretation of the effectiveness and integrity of the company's governance processes and culture. Once viewed largely as a somewhat narrow area of corporate procedure, the study of corporate governance has widened considerably in recent years to include several disciplines, including law, management, finance, and economics. The scope of analysis can be extended to include dimensions of behavioral sciences, political science, and ethics. This complexity increases further when doing comparative analysis in a multinational context. Differing legal regimes, stages of economic development, cultural norms, and diverse approaches to the role of business in society impose additional complications to rigorous and objective analysis of corporate governance in individual firms on a global basis.

BASIC DEFINITIONS

Building a framework to assess corporate governance in a multinational context starts with the process of defining governance and the boundaries of the firm in a way that is at once rigorous, but also flexible enough to accommodate meaningfully the different approaches to corporate governance that exist in companies throughout the world. Given the broad interpretations of corporate governance, and differing views globally about the role of the firm and its relationship with stakeholders outside the firm (e.g., employees, community, environment), achieving a universally acceptable definition can be a problematic undertaking.

The approach to defining governance focused on in this book, and which is the focus of Standard & Poor's Governance Services analytical criteria, is driven by the *financial dimension* of corporate governance. This implies a concentration on the effects of governance from the perspective of its key financial stakeholders, both *shareholders and creditors*—with particular emphasis on a firm's shareholders. And given the potential influences of blockholders (holders of majority or substantial minority blocks of shares), which will be discussed in subsequent chapters, it is *minority shareholders* whose interests are at the core of this analysis.

This is not the only way to approach corporate governance. Indeed, in certain countries and cultures, corporate governance may be defined in ways that place relatively greater weight on the interests of nonfinancial stakeholders. For example, in Japan the interests of employees arguably take equal or greater precedence over the interests of a company's shareholders. In other contexts, governance may be defined more broadly, taking a "triple bottom line" perspective into account—to accommodate how a company's governance affects not only its financial stakeholders, but also employees, local communities, and environmental interests. The role of nonfinancial stakeholders will be explored in greater detail in Chapter 3 on ownership and external stakeholders, Chapter 10 on social and environmental reporting, and Chapter 11 on sustainable development.

These external stakeholder interests are both important and legitimate. However, for purposes of this chapter, and the subsequent chapters on analytical criteria relating to individual company governance, the starting point will be to define the boundaries of the firm and the corporate governance problem somewhat more narrowly, to facilitate the examination of corporate governance from a financial perspective. On that basis, a simple, but overarching, definition of corporate governance to guide this book is as follows:

> At its most basic level, *corporate governance* is the interaction of a company's management, its board directors, and its shareholders to direct and control the firm, and to ensure that all financial stakeholders (shareholders and creditors) receive their fair share of the company's earnings and assets.

This definition effectively frames corporate governance as a potential risk factor for investors. If governance standards are poor, this speaks to the possibility that financial stakeholders may not receive appropriate investment returns, either due to corrupt governance practices in extreme cases, or ineffective governance practices in less extreme situations.

This is an approach that is consistent, for example, with that taken by the Combined Code in its series of reports on corporate governance in the United Kingdom. The perspective is obviously of greatest relevance to a company's investors. But it also should be of interest to nonfinancial stakeholders as well. As will be evident throughout this book, even this somewhat narrower approach to the evaluation of corporate governance still involves considerable analytical challenges, as well as the need to objectify aspects of company governance, which are qualitative in nature and difficult to quantify or reduce to ratings or scores.

As such, this approach to corporate governance is geared primarily to the interests of investors or external analysts who are assessing companies from a financial perspective. For those with interests that extend beyond financial stakeholders, this approach can serve as a foundation or springboard for further examination of the corporate governance problem. It can help to set the stage for analysis in which the boundaries of the firm are defined to be wider than the interests of its shareholders and creditors.

CRITERIA FRAMEWORK

Having established a working definition of corporate governance, focusing primarily on the interests of financial stakeholders, the next step is to develop a framework of analysis that breaks down aspects of governance into key component parts to facilitate consistent analysis and comparison—from company to company and from country to country. Particularly in a multinational context this can be an ambitious undertaking. There is no one model of corporate governance that works in all countries. Indeed, there exist many different codes of "best practice" globally, which take into account differing legal traditions, business practices, cultural norms, stakeholder priorities, and governance structures.

This represents a potential minefield of confusion for analysts, particularly for those who wish to reconcile on a consistent framework the governance practices that exist in differing geographic jurisdictions. While there has been considerable debate on the question of "convergence" of global governance standards to a single global model, it is unrealistic to expect that one size will fit all in terms of specific governance structures and practices. Apart from legal and cultural norms, differing patterns of ownership structure can play a key role in how companies are managed and governed. This is particularly true with regard to the structure and functioning of a company's board of directors—one of the key aspects of the governance process.

Rules versus Principles

In this context, debate and analysis that begins with a prescriptive "cookie cutter" view of governance rules and compliance procedures is fraught with peril and runs the risk of either missing the point or confusing the forest for the trees. At the same time, however, objective standards are required—both to facilitate meaningful comparative analysis and to bring a fundamental discipline to addressing the definition of corporate governance presented above—e.g., to ensure that financial stakeholders receive their fair share of a company's earnings and assets. This raises the broad issue of *rules versus principles.*

The discussion with regard to rules versus principles is most frequently referenced in the debate over accounting standards, most notably in discussions on the merits of rules based on the United States' Generally Accepted Accounting Principles (U.S. GAAP) as opposed to International Accounting Standards (IAS). These latter accounting principles focus on a company's adherence to broad principles that speak to its solvency and its ability to operate as a going concern. But the issue of rules versus principles is just as relevant in the external assessment of corporate governance in a comparative context. Is it more important to have compliance with a detailed and complex set of governance rules and standards that are meant to address the interests of a company's financial stakeholders? Or is it better to assess specific governance structures and practices less prescriptively, and more on the basis of overarching principles?

Clearly, within the realm of governance analysis there is scope to address both specific rules as well as broader principles. Both are required. However, for purposes of this book and the criteria that follow, it is principles that hold the ultimate trump card. Principles need to guide the interpretation of rules. But what principles are these to be?

In this regard it is worth drawing from the Business Sector Advisory Group of the Organization for Economic Cooperation and Development (OECD) in the development, during the late 1990s, of what are now commonly referred to as the OECD corporate governance guidelines. This multinational group faced a similar task of building a set of core corporate governance guidelines that have relevance in a global context. In so doing, the OECD guidelines were developed based on a platform of guiding core principles, which are relevant for the development of criteria for corporate governance analysis. These guiding principles are as follows:

- *Fairness*: The equality of treatment of all financial stakeholders, and in particular avoiding fraud, insider dealing, or any form of

expropriation by a company's managers or controlling shareholders.

♦ _Transparency_: To provide clear and equal access of material company information on a regular basis to all investors to allow for
  informed investment decisions and the ongoing monitoring of
  the company's activities.

♦ _Accountability_: The existence of legitimate systems of control—
  particularly to provide shareholders and creditors with an
  effective structure to enable them to express and enforce their
  interests and concerns over the actions of a company's managers
  and controlling stakeholders.

♦ _Responsibility_: Adherence to the prevailing laws of the jurisdictions in which the company operates, and the management of
  relationships with key constituencies or stakeholders to promote
  long-term sustainability and avoid potential disruption.

Conscious acknowledgment of a "principles based" approach to
corporate governance is particularly important when conducting analysis
in differing countries and regions. Otherwise, the pluralistic approaches
toward governance structures across the world would hinder meaningful
comparative analysis. The principles outlined above are broad enough to
transcend individual jurisdictions and have relevance across a range of
differing governance environments. Effectively, for an analyst of corporate governance, these overarching principles can serve as a "lens" or a filter through which individual company practices or structures can be
interpreted.

Hence, when confronting potentially contentious governance issues
(e.g., one-tier versus two-tier boards, combined versus split chairman/
CEO roles, etc.), a principles-based approach provides for greater flexibility
of analysis. Rule-driven models (e.g., two-tiered boards are intrinsically
bad) can be superficial and culturally insensitive. This can lead to inaccurate, or at least misleading, analysis. A principles-based approach, however,
provides an opportunity for wider reflection; in some ways it serves as an
analytical "court of appeals." Rather than simply dismiss an anomalous
structure or practice on the basis that it violates a prescriptive rule, the principles-based approach suggests that the analyst should take a step back and
pose the following questions: Is this fair, is this transparent, is there an
appropriate level of accountability, and is the company acting responsibly?

On that basis, core principles form the foundation of the broad corporate governance analytical framework that is to follow. This is the

springboard. For those interested in extending the assessment of governance beyond these outlined principles to address more explicit financial or economic issues of profitability, competitive advantage, valuation, and the like, the implicit hypothesis then becomes that adherence to these principles helps to enhance a firm's performance and its perception by those who value it externally. Ultimately this becomes a topic of study for empirical researchers. For others, adherence to these broad principles can be viewed as an end in and of itself, in some ways as a *hygiene factor*— something that may be viewed as necessary, but not intrinsically sufficient, to ensure a company's successful long-term performance.

Key Analytical Components

Assessing corporate governance in an international context calls for a two-pronged analytical approach:

Individual company analysis: the effectiveness of the interaction among a company's management, board, shareholders, and other stakeholders. This focuses on the firm-specific *internal* governance structure and processes at an individual company.

Country assessment: the effectiveness of the legal, regulatory, informational, and market infrastructure. This focuses on how *external* forces at a macro level can influence the quality of an individual company's corporate governance practices.

Both these micro and macro components are important to a full appreciation of corporate governance in individual companies. Specific factors can be identified in order to analyze governance practices and facilitate objective and comparative analysis of corporate governance practices at individual companies. Inclusion of country analysis enables the individual company evaluations to be placed in a more international context, facilitating a comparison of country governance environments.

This book will focus on both these individual company and country dimensions in much greater detail. For purposes of this chapter, the basic framework is outlined in Table 2-1.

This framework provides a basis by which one can score or rate a company in terms of governance issues. The company scoring methodology is at the core of this book. It focuses on four main components, and their subcategories, to evaluate the corporate governance standards of individual companies. These four components, and the subcategories, are presented below.

T A B L E   2-1

Corporate Governance Analytical Framework

Country Analytical Structure	Company Analytical Structure
◆ Market Infrastructure ◆ Legal Infrastructure ◆ Regulatory Environment ◆ Informational Infrastructure	◆ Ownership Structure and External Influences ◆ Shareholder Rights and Stakeholder Relations ◆ Transparency, Disclosure, and Audit ◆ Board Structure and Effectiveness

This is the criteria framework used by Standard & Poor's Governance Services in its governance scoring and evaluation process for individual companies. This analytical approach has been under development since early 1998, and has been subject to ongoing revision and modification to reflect changes in thinking about governance issues and to accommodate corporate governance issues in a wide range of countries and economies around the world, including both developed and emerging markets.

Company Analytical Components and Subcomponents

Component 1: Ownership structure and external influences

Subcategories:

- ◆ Transparency of ownership structure
- ◆ Ownership concentration and influence
- ◆ Influence of external stakeholders

Component 2: Shareholder rights and stakeholder relations

Subcategories:

- ◆ Shareholder meeting and voting procedures
- ◆ Ownership rights and takeover defenses
- ◆ Relations with nonfinancial stakeholders

Component 3: Transparency, disclosure, and audit

Subcategories:

- ◆ Content of public disclosure

- Timing of, and access to, public disclosure
- Audit process

Component 4: Board structure and effectiveness

Subcategories:

- Board structure and independence
- Role and effectiveness of board
- Director and senior executive compensation

These four components and their subcomponents draw from a wide variety of codes and best practices that have been published in countries around the world. Sources include literature from multilateral organizations, institutional investors, academics, law firms, brokerages, regulators, and exchanges. In particular, many codes of best practice were reviewed, reflecting a variety of country and individual company perspectives from around the world. In the development stage, this methodology was shared for feedback with various specialists in corporate governance, including investors, lawyers, economists, bankers, and social scientists. Further refinement came through a pilot project in which this methodology was tested on a range of companies, from large listed companies to closely held, small and medium-sized enterprises. Combining the four components, their individual subcategories and individual analytical factors that comprise these subcomponents, the Standard & Poor's governance scoring methodology comprises roughly 80 individual factors. The spirit of the methodology is to synthesize the key elements of corporate governance on a global basis, and not to impose the standards of any particular country or jurisdiction. As mentioned earlier, the approach is to understand individual governance practices and structures through the lens of overarching principles, such as those emphasized in the OECD corporate governance guidelines. The key is to ensure sufficient flexibility to accommodate different governance structures in the scoring process without compromising the assessment of the ultimate substance of a company's governance standards.

Companies versus Countries

This framework for analysis of corporate governance requires sensitivity to the country context in which individual companies operate. Ultimately, it is important to assess companies on their own merits, since many companies have firm-specific governance features that may or may not be dictated by the prevailing norms in their country of domicile.

However, the macro country environment can be important in motivating good or bad internal governance practices by individual companies. It is important to determine:

+ How key investor rights are defined, and
+ How effectively the relevant infrastructure in a given country
  encourages and protects these rights in practical terms.

The first question attempts to clarify what investor rights exist as
defined by legislation and regulation. The second question addresses the
relevance of these rights in practice.

In addition to an assessment of pertinent laws and regulation, the
analytical process may involve discussions with investors, company
directors, lawyers, accountants, regulators, stock exchange officials, economists, and relevant trade associations.

The four main areas of focus in this analysis are:

+ *Market infrastructure:* Ownership structures, role of financial
  markets, role of state or banking sector, historical market practices
+ *Legal infrastructure:* Written law and its enforcement
+ *Regulatory infrastructure*: Regulatory purview and effectiveness
+ *Informational infrastructure*: Accounting standards, timing, fair or
  continuous disclosure, auditing profession

Chapter 7 of this book will address this analytical framework in
greater detail. It will explore how these country factors may affect or
influence governance at the individual company level, and will also
review the issue as to whether a "sovereign ceiling" is a relevant concept
in governance analysis. Part Six will elaborate on these factors in detail for
a wide range of countries in differing regions, economic environments,
and political regimes.

ANALYTICAL PROCESS: MODELING AND CLINICAL APPROACHES

With the broad parameters of criteria in place to assess corporate governance both at the individual firm, as well as in a country context, it is also
important to consider questions of methodology and the analytical
process. In other words, how will these criteria be applied in practice?

It is worth exploring two fundamental approaches to assessing corporate governance that external analysts can use to draw conclusions

about a company's governance standards. One might be labeled a *modeling* approach, driven by data inputs and predictive algorithms. The other approach is more *clinical* in nature, which involves in-depth, case-by-case assessments of companies, their managers, and directors often conducted on an interactive basis.

Both the modeling and clinical approaches are used in corporate governance evaluation services that currently exist in the public domain. The approach taken in this book will identify factors that can be used in both approaches, but will place particular focus on the methodology for clinical or interactive governance evaluations (and this is the approach taken by Standard & Poor's in its governance scoring services). However, it is important to understand the relative strengths and weaknesses of both the modeling and clinical approaches, which are summarized in Table 2-2.

Modeling

The modeling approach often is used by analysts who wish to develop coverage over a wide universe of companies with relative ease. This process involves the construction of a model for ideal governance practices and populating this model with data against which algorithms can be applied to draw overarching conclusions or scores. These data can consist of inputs from publicly disclosed company data, or also can be expanded to include the results of surveys and questionnaires.

Particularly when analysts are not in a position to have direct access to a company's managers and directors, the modeling approach offers the main option to assess individual company governance standards. Because company cooperation is not necessarily required (unless the survey format is used), this facilitates a wide scope of coverage, customizable to the analyst's particular specifications. Models often are used in this context as "screening tools," to pass a wide range of companies through a filter to identify cases in which company governance might appear as particularly strong or weak, either to set the stage for more in-depth case-by-case analysis or to exclude or include a group of companies for investment purposes based on governance-related criteria. In particular they can be applied to broader company or country indices (such as the S&P 500, for example) to create subindices that are wholly governance focused.

In addition to the wide basis of coverage that a modeling approach provides, its benefits also can include greater objectivity and comparability from one company to another along the defined criteria. In partic-

T A B L E   2-2

Strengths and Weaknesses of Analytical Approaches

	Advantages	Disadvantages
Modeling Approach	◆ Broad coverage easily obtainable ◆ Company buy-in not necessarily required ◆ Facilitates wide level of comparisons on a consistent basis ◆ Objectivity: clarity of variables and the algorithms used to weight them ◆ Greater scope for rigorous quantitative analysis	◆ Limited or no direct access to company managers and directors ◆ Focus on governance "architecture" often to the exclusion of interpersonal dynamics ◆ Reliance on quality and breadth of public disclosure or accuracy of survey results ◆ Models can be misleading or too rigid to meaningfully accommodate subjective governance factors ◆ More susceptible to "gaming"?
Clinical/ Interactive Approach	◆ Deeper and more holistic assessments ◆ Interactive access to managers and directors: accommodates both interpersonal and "architecture" issues ◆ Access to germane nonpublic information (e.g., board minutes) ◆ Greater scope for case-by-case interpretation of individual variables: less rigid ◆ Greater flexibility and analytical discretion: less subject to gaming	◆ Coverage slow to build ◆ Requires company buy-in (e.g., self-selecting) ◆ Field researchers subject to bias or influence of company managers or directors? ◆ Greater subjectivity means can result in "black box" concerns of how individual variables are assessed and weighted

ular, since models are driven by data that are typically expressed in numerical terms, it can be relatively easy to build matrices and data sets for rigorous quantitative analysis. This facilitates empirical research to identify and weight the driving analytical factors and to test for causality or relationships with economic or financial performance parameters. As discussed in Chapter 1, models developed by academics for single-country analysis have already been developed, including those by Black in Russia (2001); Black, Jang, and Kim in Korea (2002); and Gompers, Ischii, and Metrick in the United States (2001). Governance models and databases also have been applied for practical research applications by brokerages, proxy advisors, proxy solicitors, and specialized governance research and rating firms.

The main disadvantage to the modeling approach is that governance can be very difficult to model in a meaningful way. This is particularly true in an international context where many overarching or subjective factors may be important in certain jurisdictions and companies, or less important in others. Moreover, given that governance is both about the specific governance "architecture" of an individual firm, but also about the people who govern, the modeling approach has difficulty in capturing what behavioral scientists might call the "human side" of corporate governance. It is also the case that specific aspects of governance architecture may be good or bad in certain contexts and relatively immaterial in others.

To cite one example, cumulative voting often is seen as a very positive way to ensure that minority shareholders are in a position to gain board representation when a blockholder ownership structure exists. However, for companies that are widely held, this urgency is less apparent. Examples of this nature underscore the complexity of creating viable models for governance that are robust in a multicompany or multicountry context.

The key risk here is a "garbage in, garbage out" scenario, out of which misleading results—false positives or false negatives—stem from issues relating to data quality and availability, model relevancy (e.g., the right mix and weighting of variables), and model rigidity (the lack of flexibility to accommodate for many subjective factors). Even for models that can overcome these weaknesses, there also runs the risk that the model can be "gamed" or manipulated in a cynical way by companies that "window dress" public data to beat the system to achieve a higher score than might be justified in a more interactive assessment.

Clinical/Interactive Approach

The clinical, or interactive, approach involves a more intensive examination of individual companies than is possible with the modeling approach, often with the collection of a wider range of supporting information. In particular, for corporate governance research this typically involves interviews with company managers and directors, as well as other relevant sources, which can include the company auditor, major blockholders, or other stakeholders. In addition to interviews, the clinical approach also can provide access to additional information, including board minutes, remuneration structures, or other internal documentation that can enhance the understanding of a company's governance environment.

This amounts to conducting field research, both to generate additional information that may be available in the public domain. But it also allows analysts to "kick the tires" or have a general "smell test," to provide a broader context with which to assess specific data items or structural features, and possibly to raise analytical issues that might otherwise not have been raised. In particular, this approach allows for a better insight of the people who govern, and lessens reliance on the analysis of governance architecture in the abstract—ultimately to facilitate assessment of substance over form.

Given the subjective nature of many important aspects of corporate governance analysis—such as gauging board effectiveness, board independence or CEO/blockholder dominance—the clinical/interactive approach can provide a greater depth and quality to the overall governance assessment. It provides a greater flexibility to the analytical process, facilitating case-by-case interpretation of individual company governance practices. Moreover, in providing scope for greater analyst discretion, the potential for companies to manipulate or "game" the process can be significantly lessened—though not necessarily eliminated.

While one of the strengths of the clinical approach is its greater flexibility, this also can be one of its main weaknesses. Giving analysts greater discretion in the collection and interpretation of company governance information also introduces greater subjectivity into the process. Though this is not necessarily a bad thing, it can run the risk of making the analysis less transparent, creating a "black box" situation in which it is difficult to understand exactly which specific factors and factor weightings drive the overall analytical conclusion. In this regard, it is important that criteria and decision guidelines for clinical governance analysis are clearly articulated.

The analyst's interpretive role in the clinical process can run the risk of distorting the overall objectivity of the analysis and its conclusions. While the interview process with company managers and directors represents perhaps the greatest source of new information and analytical insight, the personal interactions between analysts and company representatives can run the risk of creating a nonobjective bias (either positive or negative) in the individual analyst that can consciously or subconsciously influence the analyst's assessment and conclusions. These potential conflicts, however, are manageable. In an analytical context, the influence of management bias can be mitigated by having clear public criteria, ensuring that more than one analyst meets with company officials, and ensuring that analytical conclusions are determined not by individual analysts, but by committees including committee members that did not meet with management.

A less analytical—and more practical—problem with the clinical/interactive approach is that it depends on company willingness to participate in the analytical process. Otherwise it would not be possible for the analyst to have access to company managers, directors, and other nonpublic information. For companies to submit themselves to an interactive analytical process for which they often pay and whose outcome they cannot control, the costs of this undertaking often can be perceived as outweighing the potential benefits. Consequently, coverage of this form of analysis, notwithstanding its potential strengths and incremental insights, can be slow to build and establish interactive governance scores and ratings as a practical market tool.

Even as coverage does begin to build, there is also the issue of "self selection." Until market forces institutionalize interactive governance assessments or ratings, there is likely to be a Darwinian-type bias for the strongest companies going through the process first. These are the companies with the best stories to tell, and they will have the highest scores. At least initially, this will mean that interactive governance scores that are in the public domain run the risk of being skewed toward the high end until market forces come to demand this form of analysis from all listed companies. It will not be until market forces (investors, stakeholders, regulators) demand governance scores as a matter of normal market practice that a comprehensive range of companies will submit to this interactive process.

Is One Approach Better Than the Other?

Given the strengths and weaknesses of the modeling versus clinical approaches outlined above, it is inappropriate to be categorical about whether one approach is intrinsically better than the other in corporate governance analysis. Both can be done well or poorly.

However, given the qualitative nature of many of the important factors that indicate corporate governance quality in individual firms, *the clinical or interactive approach—if well managed and conducted—is arguably the most effective.* This is particularly so given the importance that company manager and director interviews can play in adding insight to the analytical process.

But happily this is not an "either/or" situation. These two broad approaches to analysis need not be mutually exclusive. Elements of both can be legitimately combined in a governance rating or scoring process, bringing together an objective model with a qualitative overlay. Each can be employed in a complementary way that can provide the benefits of each approach and offset some of the disadvantages of the other. In particular, to the extent that architectural dimensions of governance can be meaningfully modeled, this can represent an objective basis from which to test or challenge the more qualitative conclusions that come from the clinical or interactive approach.

OTHER PROBLEMS OF GOVERNANCE ANALYSIS

Weighting of Analytical Factors

Both for the modeling and clinical approaches, the weighting of specific analytical factors can be problematic. In Standard & Poor's interactive governance scoring methodology, for example, roughly 80 analytical factors are considered in assessing individual firms. Inevitably some factors will be more important than others. This leads to the question of how specific factors should be weighted.

The problem is that these weightings are not necessarily fixed. An extreme example in this context is the issue of share registration. In most jurisdictions, an independent share registrar is a given, and therefore it would appear inappropriate to give this issue a high weighting in an overall governance analysis. However, there are cases in Russia in which companies serving as their own share registrar actually erased individual shareholders from the share register, particularly if that shareholder was proving to be contentious. In such cases, this issue should be extremely highly weighted (perhaps 100 percent weighted from the perspective of the stricken-off shareholder!) in the governance scoring process.

Fortunately, most of the weighting issues normally encountered are not as dramatic. But the issue still exists even in more mundane circumstances. Factor weightings are important, but can be difficult to fix. While an issue such as board effectiveness, for example, should normally be more important than transparency of ownership structure, there may be cases in which extreme distortions could create exceptions to this.

Two ways of resolving this issue present themselves. One is to incorporate a "nonlinear" weighting rule to help legislate for extreme situations. This effectively means that a very low assessment in one particular factor of the analysis can pull down or place a ceiling on an overall governance score or conclusion. In the case of the Russian company with the corrupt in-house shareholder registrar, for example, this means that the overall governance score would be capped at a low level, notwithstanding the fact that other factors in the analysis might be assessed much more positively. Particularly in the modeling approach to governance assessment, nonlinear weightings provide a good basis for addressing anomalous situations. However, even in these situations, there runs the risk that nonlinear weighting algorithms can be overly mechanistic and distort final scores or analytical outcomes.

In the clinical/interactive approach nonlinear weighting rules also can be applied. But since the analytical process is more subjective, analysts are in a position to assess each company on a case-by-case basis and determine which are the most appropriate weightings to apply for individual companies at particular points in time. In effect this amounts to customized weightings for each individual company. This approach runs the risk of analytical inconsistency when comparing governance scores from one firm to another. However, if done with rigor and full attention focused on the ultimate goal of the governance score—i.e., an assessment of the extent to which a company's governance practices fairly represent the interests of its financial stakeholders—the approach of case-by-case weightings offers the most meaningful way to address the potentially thorny problem of factor weighting.

Limitations/Scope of External Analysis

No external analysis of corporate governance is foolproof. There is no perfect crystal ball. Particularly given the many subjective factors that comprise this form of analysis, there is scope for both false positives (bad governance situations that look good on the surface) as well as false negatives (good governance situations that look bad on the surface).

As close as a governance analyst can get to a company director or senior executive, there are limits to the understanding that can be achieved by external analysts. A particular problem, for example, is one of "proving negatives." For example, company public reporting or interviews with company managers are often unlikely to produce voluntarily disclosed information relating to inequitable related party transactions, lack of director independence, or dysfunctional board dynamics. It is difficult, if not in some cases impossible, to address these issues first hand. Moreover, the governance analysis outlined here stops short of being an audit. Rather it simply forms the foundation for an intelligent and informed opinion on the governance dynamics in individual companies.

In many cases, the best that can be done is to isolate areas in which relevant governance issues can neither be proven nor disproven in the analytical process and then seek explicit management representations about these points. Whether or not management is telling the truth, this approach at least isolates particular areas of potential concern, and can establish a public record of management's representation.

This leads to consideration of a final limitation of governance analysis: It is not equipped to legislate for, or to surface, instances of *fraud*. In this regard, it warrants emphasizing that the governance analytical structure and process outlined in this book is not a forensic exercise. While proper analysis needs to be conducted with a spirit of constructive skepticism, it is neither realistic nor practical to begin every analysis under the assumption that all information provided by the company is corrupt. External analysts need to rely on information given to them by sources they deem to be credible, and need to exercise a degree of judgment, and potential skepticism, on the information they are given to work with. However, when a firm is publicly in compliance with exchange and regulatory oversight, and when it is audited by a reputable accounting firm using reliable accounting standards, it is normal practice to accept company public reporting and statements as base material for analysis in good faith. But the analyst should be alert to detect any signs that may challenge the acceptance of company representations. In extreme situations, the additional inputs of forensic accountants might be required by investors to complement the basics of the governance analysis presented here.

GOVERNANCE IN CREDIT ANALYSIS

Links between governance and credit quality can be real, but often indirect. Indeed, it can be difficult—and sometimes possibly misleading—to automatically associate a company's specific corporate governance practices and structures to its fundamental credit quality. While there is likely to be a positive correlation between credit ratings and corporate governance scores, this correlation will not be one to one. In cases where governance features are benign or positive, industry, competitive, or financial factors may negatively impact a credit rating. Equally, there can exist situations where governance structures disfavor shareholders, while having a neutral impact from a credit perspective. However, governance is a relevant subject for credit analysts to the extent that corporate governance can be identified as a cause, or as leading to a cause, of weaknesses in a company's financial strength. At Standard & Poor's, governance issues are examined by credit ratings analysts in the context of assessing a company's management quality, accounting, and financial controls. There are times when governance-related issues will be a driver in shaping a company's credit rating; there also will be times when governance is not a key issue in the credit rating. At Standard & Poor's the role of governance issues in credit analysis continues to evolve as more cases of governance and management-related failures illustrate the links of these issues with a company's credit profile. In Appendix B, The Evolving Role of Corporate Governance in Credit Rating, an article published by Clifford Griep, Standard & Poor's Chief Credit Officer and Soloman Samson, Chief Quality Officer of Standard & Poor's Corporate Ratings group, explores the evolving role of governance in credit analysis in greater detail.

REFERENCES

Global Governance Codes and Guidelines

Gregory, H. G. "International Comparisons of Corporate Governance: Guidelines and Codes of Best Practice in Developed Markets," Weill, Gotshal & Manges, LLP, 2001.

Gregory, H. G. "International Comparisons of Corporate Governance: Guidelines and Codes of Best Practice in Developing and Emerging Markets," Weill, Gotshal & Manges, LLP, 2000.

International Corporate Governance Network, "ICGN Statement on Global Corporate Governance Principles," 1999.

Organization of Economic Cooperation and Development, "OECD Principles of Corporate Governance," 1999.

Many other global codes exist that are relevant for individual countries and regions. The website of the European Corporate Governance Institute, www.ecgi.com, offers a comprehensive basis of links to the major corporate governance codes around the world. Another good source is the Corporate Governance website: www.corpgov.net/library/olarticles.html-codes.

Governance Modeling

Black, B. "Does Corporate Governance Matter? A Crude Test Using Russian Data," 149 U. Pa. L. Rev. 2131, 2001.

Black, B. S., H. Jang, and W. Kim, "Does Corporate Governance Matter? Evidence from the Korean Market," *Working Paper,* Stanford Law School, Korea University and KDI School of Public Policy and Management, 2002.

CLSA Emerging Markets and the Asian Corporate Governance Association. "CG Watch, Corporate Governance in Asia," Hong Kong, www.clsa.com (accessed August 2003).

Gompers, P. A., J. L. Ischii, and A. Metrick. "Corporate Governance and Equity Prices," *Working Paper,* Harvard Business School, Harvard University and the University of Pennsylvania, 2001.

Clinical Interactive Research

Bazerman, M. H., G. Loewenstein, and D. A. Moore. "Why Good Accountants Do Bad Audits," *Harvard Business Review,* 2002.

Tufano, P. "Harvard Business School-Journal of Financial Economics Conference Volume: Complementary Research Methods," *Journal of Financial Economics,* vol. 60, 2001, pp. 179–185.

Corporate Governance and Credit Risk

Griep, C. M., and S. Samson. "The Evolving Role of Corporate Governance in Credit Rating Analysis," *Standard & Poor's Ratings Direct,* October 10, 2002.

Corporate Governance: Micro Perspective

INTRODUCTION

This part builds from the analytical framework for the corporate governance methodology, presented in Chapter 2.

Component 1: Ownership structures and external influences

Subcomponents:

- Transparency of ownership structure
- Concentration and influence of ownership
- Influence of external stakeholders

Component 2: Shareholder rights and stakeholder relations

Subcomponents:

- Shareholder meeting and voting procedures
- Ownership rights and takeover defenses
- Stakeholder relations

Component 3: Transparency, disclosure, and audit

Subcomponents:

- Content of public disclosure
- Timing of, and access to, public disclosure
- Audit process

Component 4: Board structure and effectiveness

Subcomponents:

+ Board structure and independence
+ Role and effectiveness of board
+ Director and senior executive compensation

Chapters 3 through 6 present a framework for analysts to conduct an evaluation of these four components, isolating the key analytical factors and addressing how they can be evaluated. This includes a list of questions and analytical instructions that can guide the evaluations. Some guidance also is provided with regard to key source documentation and identifying other questions that can be addressed in interviews with managers, directors, or their professional advisors.

Each of the chapters in Part Two follows a similar template. There is an initial overview of the analytical component, discussing the main themes, and in many cases making reference to relevant codes, research, or other sources. After the introductory overview, the analytical framework is presented for assessing the individual component, again drawing from the methodological approach used by Standard & Poor's in its governance evaluations.

Each of the four analytical components is broken into three subcomponents. The analysis of these individual subcomponents, in turn, is determined from the assessment of individual factors. For example, audit committee independence is a factor that contributes to the audit process subcomponent of our analysis. The audit process itself is a subcomponent of the larger transparency, disclosure, and audit component.

The purpose of each of the chapters in this part is to link conceptual thinking about the key governance issues to practical and granular ways of evaluating individual companies from a governance perspective. To aid in this context, the discussion of each subcomponent concludes with a presentation of factors that make for a strong or weak analytical profile. By attempting to define the extreme ends, the foundation of scoring or rating guidelines can be established. Further rating or scoring calibrations can be made on the basis of evaluating and weighting the relevance of the analytical factors as they exist in individual companies.

CHAPTER 3

Ownership Structure and External Influences

George Dallas

OVERVIEW

The influences of a company's owners and other stakeholders on its governance processes can be profound. These influences can be benign or malevolent to the interests of a company's minority shareholders, and can be driven by the separate, and potentially conflicting, agendas of management, blockholders, employees, governments, or other external stakeholders. For purposes of this chapter, *stakeholders* are defined as nonshareholding constituencies who are affected by, or have a legitimate interest in, the activities of a given company.

An appreciation of these real—or potential—influences is a fundamental first step in assessing a company's overall governance framework. A particular starting point is an understanding of a company's *ownership structure*—particularly the extent to which the company is widely held or controlled by one or several blockholders. A company's ownership composition is a key determinant of its governance structures and influences. It helps to shape other key aspects of company governance, including how shareholder rights are defined and how transparent a company is, and it also influences the composition and effectiveness of the company's board of directors.

Ownership structures are firm specific, though, as will be noted below, there are patterns of ownership structure that exist from country to country. In the short term, ownership structures should be seen as a "given" in that this is not usually something that a company's managers can directly affect. Over time, however, ownership structures can evolve or vary, either tending toward dispersed shareholdings or becoming concentrated from a once widely held structure.

The separation of ownership and control is one of the defining problems of corporate governance. The classic 1932 paper by Berle and Means on this subject forms a foundation for much subsequent literature in the field of governance. It defines the fundamental agency problem between a company's shareholders and the management that the shareholders employ as their agent. The problem is one of potentially conflicting agendas. The shareholders' objective is to maximize the company's market value in a way that is sustainable over time. This stands in possible conflict with the objectives of a company's management, which can be to maximize their own personal wealth, to remain entrenched regardless of performance, or to manage to a different timeframe than that taken by the company's core shareholders.

The agency problem identified by Berle and Means is most relevant in situations where ownership is widely dispersed: where there is no one shareholder to exert a strong discipline on management to ensure alignment with shareholders' interests. This is characteristic of prevailing ownership structures in the United States and the United Kingdom, and has been referred to as the "outsider system," in that the governance problem is largely defined as developing structures for the small "outside" shareholder to be protected from potential abuse by the company's management.

Global Ownership Structures

In a global context, widely held ownership structures are the exception rather than the rule. Indeed, research on global ownership structures shows that most large companies have a controlling shareholder, most typically either families or the state (La Porta, Lopez-de-Silanes, and Shleifer). In continental Europe, for example, blockholders with 20 percent or higher stakes are the norm among listed companies, whereas in the United States and the United Kingdom there are few voting blocks in excess of 10 percent (Barca and Becht, 2001). And in East Asia, more than two-thirds of listed firms are controlled by a single shareholder (Claessens et al., 2000). Franks and Mayer refer to concentrated ownership structures as "insider" systems, in that the blockholder, either as a manager/owner or as a strongly influential shareholder, is in a more "inside" position to provide a direct basis of control and influence than is the case with the small minority shareholder.

The individual structures may vary but can be generally categorized in one of three ways:

  • *Family-controlled companies*: common in Asia, Latin America, and certain western European countries (Germany, Italy)

- *State ownership:* still a feature of transition economies of the former Soviet bloc and also common in Asia
- *Financial-industrial groups:* common in Japan, Russia, and less formally in western Europe. Characterized by cross-shareholdings and other financial/operational links

Each of these situations creates potentially different agency problems than the ones that stem from the "outsider" system of widely held companies. In the case of family-controlled companies, for example, issues of succession and management legitimacy are often more important governance issues than in the case of companies that have already established professional managers. Intercompany links in financial industrial groups can result in opaque related party transactions controlled by blockholders with conflicting interests. And in firms with state ownership, the company's link to governmental interests also may result in corporate actions, which may not be in the interests of shareholder value, given the public policy agenda of the state shareholder.

An example of how blockholder influence can work to the detriment of minority shareholders can be seen in the case of the Russian airline Aeroflot. Aeroflot is 51 percent owned by the Russian state, and Aeroflot's management intends to modernize and improve Aeroflot's international image. One of its strategies in this regard would be to build a fleet of western aircraft, either from Boeing or Airbus, in particular to address western concerns about safety. However, this possibility is effectively blocked by Aeroflot's majority owner, since the Russian government also has a stake in the Russian aircraft manufacturing sector and has an interest in ensuring the commercial prospects of this sector. As a result, Aeroflot can only purchase very few western aircraft without incurring a punitive import tariff. This is a point of contention that Aeroflot's management has commented on publicly. Its majority owner, the Russian state, in some ways is subsidizing its aircraft sector at the expense of Aeroflot and its minority shareholders.

Understanding Ownership Structure

It is not always easy to know who really owns a company. However, understanding the ownership structure of a company is essential, especially when there is a known blockholder or when *de facto* majority holdings may exist on the basis of collusive shareholding arrangements. It is difficult, if not impossible, to assess the influence of a company's blockholders if the identity or the exact size of the blockholder's stake is not clear. Moreover, where blockholders do exist, transparency of ownership goes beyond identifying the size of the blockholder's stake. Other pertinent information is important to assess existing or potential blockholder influence, such as the blockholder's other interests, the register of related party transactions, and the relationship of the blockholder to the individual company managers.

It is also important to understand exact amounts held by a company's senior managers and directors, regardless of whether these individuals have large equity positions.

On that basis the company's ownership structure should be transparent, and should not be obscured by cross-holdings, management-controlled corporate holdings, nominee holdings, or simply the lack of disclosure. A particular problem is getting behind the beneficial holders of nominee accounts, as it is the beneficial holders who hold the control rights in the individual company. Disclosure standards on ownership structure can vary from jurisdiction to jurisdiction. In the United States, for example, there is a requirement to disclose individual owners having 5 percent of a company's shares. Disclosure down to the 5 percent level is a good standard, and except in exceptional cases should provide the necessary understanding of a company's ownership structure, particularly with regard to the potential for blockholder influence. However, there are examples of companies that disclose ownership to even lower levels. The U.K. energy company BP Plc, for example, discloses its individual shareholder structure down to a 3 percent level.

It should be noted that even the most transparent companies in the most advanced markets cannot know all the beneficial holders behind nominee holdings. Some companies address this issue by engaging a shareholder tracking service—a service offered by proxy solicitation firms—to track down the details of the beneficial holder to the extent possible.

Blockholders: Benevolent Despots or Just Despots?

Blockholders represent a dominant form of ownership in many parts of the world. The reasons for ownership concentration are a topic of debate among economists, with factors such as the legal framework, regulation, and culture often cited as driving forces. For example, the research series by the academics La Porta, Lopez-de-Silanes, Shliefer, and Vishny (2001) suggests that weak enforcement of investor rights in certain jurisdictions results in ownership clusters. Where the rule of law is weak, shareholders are better positioned to monitor their investments through more active and direct involvement as blockholders. A conclusion of the research conducted by La Porta and colleagues is that civil law countries have weaker shareholder rights than common law countries; this, in part, is said to explain the tendency for ownership concentration in civil law countries, as compared to the United Kingdom, the United States, or other common law jurisdictions.

In situations where concentrated ownership exists, analysis of corporate governance needs to take additional steps to address blockholder influences that may not be present in widely held firms. While blockholder structures may evolve and disintegrate over time, particularly as family holdings disperse or legal environments evolve, they will remain a common ownership structure for the foreseeable future. In this context it is relatively pointless to argue whether blockholders should or should not exist. Blockholders are a reality, and the main focus should be to understand areas where the potential for abuse exists and how effectively the individual blockholder addresses the needs and interests of the minority shareholder.

Where blockholder control exists, the agency problem becomes more complex. From the perspective of the minority shareholder, it is the blockholder—and not necessarily the company's management—that is a subject of primary scrutiny from an agency perspective. In other words, the blockholder may be in a position to monitor management effectively, but how are minority shareholders able to monitor effectively the influence of the blockholder? This concern is particularly important in jurisdictions where protection of shareholder rights is weak and where transparency and disclosure standards are poor. Consequently, assessment of blockholders is a fundamental starting point in the assessment of an individual company's governance framework.

While blockholder influence warrants considerable scrutiny for potential abuse of minority shareholders, it is only fair to begin the analysis of a blockholder's influence with an agnostic perspective. The effect of blockholders can be positive, negative, or neutral. Each situation needs to be assessed on its own merits. The first instinct of the analyst should be to concentrate on potential negative influences: *expropriation* (through asset purchases or sales, transfer pricing, related party transactions) and the *entrenchment* of incompetent or corrupt managers.

However, at the same time, analysis should be sensitive to the potential positive effects of blockholder influence. Blockholders often have a strong incentive to increase the valuation of their holding and tend to be in a superior position to monitor management (through direct board seats) and ensure proper control against management abuse or incompetence. For example, the Russian telecommunications company, Mobile Telesystems (MTS), has benefited positively from the close involvement of its blockholder, the German firm Deutsche Telecom. Deutsche Telecom has not only monitored MTS's management closely, it also has had the effect of elevating MTS's governance, control, and disclosure practices to levels that in many cases are consistent with international best practices.

Indeed, in a conceptual sense, two strong blockholders can constitute an "ideal" ownership structure, assuming the two blocks operate independently from each other. In this type of structure, two independent groups are in a position to closely monitor management to ensure management is fulfilling properly its agency role. But at the same time, the two blocks are in a position to effectively monitor each other—in a check and balance context. Again, assuming there is no collaboration between the two independent blockholders, this minimizes the scope for abuse by an individual blockholder. The two keep each other honest. Consequently, the potential distortions of management or blockholder interests are removed, and the focus of the company's operations and governance is freed to focus on enhancing shareholder value. Hence, a multiple blockholder structure has the potential to mitigate some of the key agency risks by managers and individual blockholders, thus aligning the governance focus with the interests of a company's minority shareholders.

However, in most cases of blockholder ownership, there is only one major blockholder. Though bound by law, the individual blockholder in this context is in a position to act in some ways as a "despot" or dictator. But history has shown despots to be benevolent as well as malevolent. How can this be detected in external analysis? In particular, what are the characteristics of companies where individual blockholder involvement is positive or at least neutral?

Ultimately it depends not only on the commercial abilities of the blockholder, but also on the blockholder's overall integrity. This is manifest in an implicit or explicit blockholder commitment to the core principles of fairness, transparency, and accountability: to manage the company according to the interests of all shareholders, not just the blockholder's interest. Most blockholders are likely to represent that they look after the interests of all shareholders, not just their own. But this cannot be taken for granted. Stated policies and principles are a positive start. However, these need to be reconciled with a company's specific governance structures and practices.

The analytical methodology that follows outlines many of the features that can guide an analyst in determining the effects of the blockholder on a company's governance practices. While many factors are identified in this context, the keys are to ensure equality of shareholder rights, a regime of clear and frequent disclosure (particularly with regard to related party transactions), and a board structure that provides a meaningful role for truly independent directors. In this latter context, cumulative voting structures represent an important structural mechanism to provide for independent directors elected by minority shareholders.

Institutional Investors

In widely held corporations, the potential problems posed by blockholders do not exist. The risk in widely held firms is that no individual shareholder may be in a position to provide meaningful oversight and ensure management accountability. In these situations, institutional investors can play an important role in providing explicit oversight and engagement of management. In the United States, for example, CalPERS and TIAA-CREF actively monitor both U.S. and non-U.S. companies from a governance perspective, as does the pension fund Hermes in the United Kingdom. In the United States, the United Kingdom, and Europe, proxy advisory services play an important role providing specific recommendations to institutional investors as to how to vote individual company proxy items. As the focus on sustainable development gathers momentum, specialist investors also are beginning to engage company management on social and environmental issues.

The absence of a strong blockholder keeping an eye over management can therefore be filled, partially or substantially, by active institutional investors. These investors may be in a position to punch above their relative shareholding weight in terms of the influence they can have. This can be the case particularly if there is independent public research that may influence company governance policies and practices.

Other External Stakeholders

Other external stakeholders also can exert meaningful influence on a company's governance process without holding a significant equity stake—or even without a shareholding at all. These nonfinancial stakeholders may include a company's employees, the communities in which it operates, its customers, environmental interest groups, regulators, and governments. Influences can be both direct and indirect, and need to be interpreted on a case-by-case basis. For many listed companies, external stakeholder influences are benign or minimal; in other cases the influence can be more pronounced and can sway a company to act in ways that are not necessarily efficient from at least a short-term commercial perspective.

Nonfinancial stakeholders can carry a more visible influence in those countries and cultures that view the role of the corporation in a wider societal context than existing primarily to create value for shareholders. For example, in Japan the interests of the company's employees often come before those of shareholders, and hence form an important influence over the company's management and governance processes. In Germany, it is standard practice to include an employee representative on the company's supervisory board to represent the interests of the worker.

The growing movement in sustainable development and corporate social responsibility suggests further external influence from stakeholders who take what is often referred to as a "triple bottom line" perspective of "profits, people, and planet"—a measure of corporate responsibility reflecting societal and ecological impact in addition to traditional financial measures. This can play a particularly important role in specific industry sectors, notably in extractive industries and in industries whose products may be considered by some as socially irresponsible (tobacco, weapons) or whose manufacturing processes may release carbon or other toxic substances.

As the niche sector of "socially responsible investment" continues to develop as a percentage of assets under management, the influence of nonfinancial stakeholders will grow. However, that growth is starting from a very small base. To the extent that activist funds continue to grow and begin to use institutional shareholding as a basis for advocating sustainable development issues, the influence of nonfinancial stakeholders may grow more significant. This influence is more pronounced in jurisdictions such as the United Kingdom, where requirements exist for public pension funds to disclose the extent to which they consider corporate social responsibility in their investment decisions. However, until more empirical evidence emerges to link sustainable development issues more clearly to tangible claims of longevity and lesser vulnerability to litigation, operational disruption, or loss of reputation, these nonfinancial stakeholder concerns are unlikely to become a major focus of the mainstream investment community. These issues are explored further in Chapters 10 and 11.

There exist other areas in which external stakeholders may influence a company's management and governance processes. Examples can include regulated industries or companies that combine a public-interest mission in conjunction with their mission to increase shareholder value. These situations can give rise to pressures from regulators, trade associations, nongovernmental interest groups, legislators, and government officials. Such pressures or influences can be healthy in focusing corporate executives and board members on a broader societal agenda; but there is also the risk that they can distract the company from its core commercial mission.

The Hong Kong Exchange provides a good case study of indirect government influence in the company's governance process. Even though the Hong Kong government is not a shareholder in the privately listed exchange, it exerts an influence on the Hong Kong Exchange, given the company's special status as the sole stock exchange in Hong Kong and the importance of financial markets to the Hong Kong economy. In addition to its financial goals, the Exchange also carries the legal responsibility to act in the public interest to preserve Hong Kong's status as one of Asia's leading financial centers. The Hong Kong government enforces this responsibility through its appointment of 8 of the company's 15 board directors. This structure allows for the possibility that the Hong Kong Exchange could adopt a public-interest orientation that conflicts with the interests of shareholders seeking to maximize the value of their equity investment. Its shareholders, in turn, have a limited ability on influencing the company policies in this regard, given that they cannot themselves elect a majority of directors to contest such a strategy. In the particular case of the Hong Kong Exchange, this potential concern has not proven to be a problem to date in practical terms. However, the structural possibility for a divergence between public sector and private sector interests warrants ongoing monitoring.

ANALYTICAL FRAMEWORK

The analytical assessment of the influences of ownership and external stakeholders can be broken down into three subcomponents:

1. Transparency of ownership
2. Ownership concentration and influence
3. Influence of external stakeholders

Transparency of Ownership:
Analytical Framework

FACTOR *Disclosure of beneficial ownership/voting control. There should be adequate public information on the company's ownership structure, including, where relevant, information on beneficial ownership behind corporate nominee holdings.*

Analytical Instruction

Investigate the ease with which ownership structure can be understood by an outside investor.

Analytical Instruction

(i)   Provide a breakdown of shareholdings in the company, within the limits of the disclosures established above. Where possible, provide a breakdown of indirect holdings.

(ii) Review the recent evolution of the ownership structure and the nature of the process and events by which any change has been achieved.

(iii) Establish the share structure. Prepare a table that breaks down share capital according to classes of shares (where possible), identification of beneficial owner/controller, and identification of method of holding (e.g., via nominee/custodian).

Information Sources

(i)   Public reports

(ii) Share register/registrar

(iii) Directors/company secretary

Questions to guide analysis of transparency of ownership

♦ Have substantial holders been identified? (Indicate at what level of holding the company discloses substantial holders; e.g., 5 percent; 10 percent; etc.)

♦ Have all substantial/major holders been identified? If there are blockholders, is there disclosure about the blockholders' other commercial interests and the nature of any transactions between the blockholders and the company?

- Have shareholdings in the company been broken down by:
  - identity of shareholder (names of substantial/major holders including identification of beneficial ownership and voting control)?
  - nature of holding (indication of investors' holding on register as principal or through a nominee/custodian structure)?
- Have board and individual director shareholdings been disclosed?

FACTOR *Disclosure of structure of indirect shareholdings. The company's actual ownership structure should be transparent, and should not be obscured by cross-holdings or management-controlled corporate holdings. If there are nominee holdings, the company should go to some length to identify beneficial ownership of these shares, taking into account the constraints of the regulatory environment.*

Analytical Instruction

Note that here the focus is not on the *share structure*, but on the *shareholding structure*. Whereas share structure describes the different types of shares that make up the equity capital of the firm, shareholding structure refers to the beneficial ownership of equity capital, both direct and indirect. The focus of analysis in this subsection is the level of complexity of shareholdings and the extent to which this obscures actual ownership control. Note that the company's directors and officers cannot necessarily control the shareholding structure, as this is in part a function of outside investors' preferences.

Questions to guide analysis of nominee versus beneficiary ownership

- Do the reports identify indirect holdings and thereby enable investors to assess the likely impact of these on ownership structure?
- Is there evidence of indirect holdings not reported (e.g., holding company structures and/or nominees or offshore shareholders)?
- Is management involved in indirect holdings?
- Is management willing to discuss indirect holdings and its own involvement in indirect holdings, in terms of the impact on corporate control?

Transparency of Ownership: Evaluation Guidelines

Strongest Analytical Profile

♦ *Disclosure of shareholding structure*: Full disclosure of shareholding structure in public reports in terms of identifying major and majority beneficial shareholders/control-right holders.

♦ *Indirect shareholdings*: Where applicable, indirect holdings (including ADRs) have been disclosed and explained and management is willing and able to identify how shareholding structure relates to control environment, including with respect to its own shareholdings.

♦ *Identification of beneficial shareholders*: Where necessary the company has engaged a shareholder tracker service in order to identify the largest shareholder(s) who are beneficiaries behind nominee holdings.

♦ *Disclosure of block shareholdings*: Public identification of shareholdings in excess of 3 to 5 percent.

Weakest Analytical Profile

♦ *Disclosure of shareholding structure:* No reporting on ownership structure in public reports.

♦ *Disclosure of shareholding structure:* Management/directors are unable or unwilling to disclose additional information about shareholders.

♦ *Indirect holdings:* There is evidence of blockholders or indirect holdings with a material impact on the company's control and governance, but there is no clear disclosure.

♦ *Indirect holdings:* No information provided on managerial holdings in public reports, but clear evidence that there is managerial holding.

♦ *Identification of beneficial shareholders:* Shareholders are unidentifiable, privately held corporations, possibly domiciled in an offshore tax haven.

♦ *Disclosure of block shareholdings:* No public identification of individual shareholdings, or only at a relatively high threshold rate (in excess of 10 percent).

Ownership Concentration and Influence: Analytical Framework

The objective of this section is to assess the extent of actual control stemming from concentrated ownership and to evaluate the impact on the interests of minority shareholders and other financial stakeholders of any controlling influence. A key focus here is on whether the observed ownership structure provides for the actual or potential exercise of power by one shareholder or shareholder group to the detriment of other shareholders. Hence the presence of blockholders, while not intrinsically good or bad, necessitates that more questions be asked than might be required for a widely held company.

FACTOR   *Large blockholders should not exert influence that is detrimental to the interests of other stakeholders. Minority shareholders should be protected against loss of value or dilution of their interests (e.g., through capital increases from which some shareholders are excluded or through transfer pricing with connected companies).*

Analytical Instruction

Investigate the company's internal financial and operational control environment in order to assess the influence of blockholders.

Information Sources

+ Capital-raising documents of parent company
+ Minutes of shareholder meetings of the company and key operating affiliates
+ Board minutes of the company and key operating affiliates
+ Finance and accounting control plan and reports on implementation
+ Parent/holding company board minutes and (where applicable) audit committee minutes
+ Business plans

Questions to guide the assessment of ownership concentration and influence

+ Concentration of ownership

- ◆ Does there exist a majority shareholder of the holding/parent company?
- ◆ Does there exist a small number of major shareholders?
- ◆ What proportion of the company is widely held?
- ◆ Exercise of control to the detriment of minority shareholders
  - ◆ What is the relationship of any blockholder with the board of directors?
  - ◆ Is there evidence of informal cooperation among large block-holders or minority holders over important matters, i.e., in the form of capital increases, new equity issues, and share buy-backs?

FACTOR *Concentration of economic interests and the influence of controlling shareholders can negatively impact minority shareholders when these interests separately control key operating subsidiaries, customers, or suppliers. Relationships with related parties should be disclosed accurately.*

Analytical Instruction

Identify significant transactions, including both those sources and destinations within the corporate structure or wholly or partly outside of it. Evaluate company representations relating to board discussion and basic commercial conditions of key transactions.

Information Sources

- ◆ Public reports
- ◆ Share register of key affiliate companies
- ◆ Consolidated accounts/affiliate company accounts/centralized management reporting
- ◆ List of affiliated parties and related party transactions

Questions to guide assessment of blockholder influences

- ◆ Concentration of influence
  - ◆ What are key revenues or receivables and are they generated by affiliate companies? Is there evidence of nonmarket pricing of goods and services?
  - ◆ Are the controlling shareholders and/or managers of those entities associated with blockholders of parent enterprise?

- ♦ Are the controlling shareholders and/or managers of destinations of significant transactions associated with blockholders of the parent company?
- ♦ Does the company procurement policy involve tenders?
- ♦ What other interests outside the company does the majority holder have, and how may majority holders interfere with the business purposes of the company?
- ♦ Does management have actual or effective control, or a shareholding conferring significant influence, or are they affiliated with such a blockholder?
- ♦ Is the company a member of a financial-industrial group, conglomerate, or any other group with a cross-shareholding?
- ♦ If so, what are its relations with other group members (are there relationships amongst the management of cross-held companies)?
  - ♦ Business
  - ♦ Shareholding
  - ♦ Management/shared directors
  - ♦ Are there other companies with the same general management or cross-directorships?
- ♦ Does management hold preferred share interests, thereby shielding them from accountability in other respects?
- ♦ For banks: Is there any "connected lending" or financial support of any sort to outside interests of managers, directors, or shareholders?
- ♦ For all enterprises: Does the enterprise engage in certain transactions or business practices for purposes other than maximizing long-term financial performance? This could include permitting managers to enjoy economic benefits via related party transactions.

FACTOR *For widely held companies, institutional investors can play a positive role by actively monitoring and engaging with companies on governance-related issues.*

Analytical Instruction

Explore the role played by institutional investors.

Questions to guide assessment of the role of institutional investors

- Is the company actively covered by equity analysts?
- Are there asset managers who play a visible role in overseeing the company's governance processes?
- Are proxy advisory firms influential in determining institutional investor preferences in specific resolutions?
- What are the company's policies with regard to engagement with institutional investors on governance and social issues?
- What shareholder resolutions exist and how does the company address them?

Information Sources

- Company disclosure
- Broker or investor public reports
- Proxy solicitation firm reports

Concentration and Influence of Ownership: Evaluation Guidelines

Strongest Analytical Profile

- *Widely held companies*: Little potential for individual shareholders to exert undue influence over the company's governance processes. Institutional investors and regulators serve an active role of monitoring and engagement.
- *Multiple blockholders:* More than one blockholder exists, providing an effective check and balance over individual blockholder interests that may not be consistent with the interests of other shareholders. This assumes that each blockholder is acting independently of the other.
- Blockholders exist
  - They perform an effective and responsible role overseeing and controlling company management given their easier access to internal company information.
  - There is no evidence of undue blockholder influence or inappropriate related party transactions.

- There is evidence of succession policies that do not entrench existing management or their families.
- Appropriate shareholder rights structures exist to mitigate potential for negative blockholder influences. This includes equality of voting rights for all shareholders.
- The company operates a policy of continuous disclosure so as not to provide an undue advantage for blockholders with more regular access to internal information.
- Cumulative voting structures exist to enable minority shareholders to gain board representation and provide a meaningful voice independent of the company's blockholders.
- No blockholder has veto powers in key decision areas: Supermajority provisions exist in the company's by-laws to ensure the voice of minority shareholders in major corporate events.
- No cross-shareholdings with other corporates.

Weakest Analytical Profile

- *Unidentified blockholders:* Blockholder control exists *de facto* even though this is not transparent or publicly acknowledged; blockholders are concealing their ultimate beneficial ownership.
- *Blockholder influence:* Majority shareholders or cooperation among major shareholders to achieve majority control and clear evidence that majority control is being used to the detriment of minority shareholders. Evidence of cross-shareholdings with relationships among boards/officers. Major shareholders with veto powers and evidence that veto powers are being used to the detriment of minority shareholders.
- *Blockholder influence:* By-laws establish weak minority shareholder rights: unequal voting rights, no possibility for cumulative voting, no supermajority provisions.
- *Blockholder influence:* Infrequent reporting and asymmetry of information: Blockholders and management have steady access to internal information, whereas minority shareholders are given only infrequent updates (e.g., semi-annually).
- *Holdings by management:* Management holds a major stake and demonstrates an influence that is detrimental to minority shareholders.

Influence of External Stakeholders: Analytical Framework

FACTOR *Influences from nonfinancial stakeholders can distract or impair management's ability to realize commercial objectives, thereby affecting shareholder value. The influence of nonfinancial stakeholders must be scrutinized in this context for negative, as well as positive, impact. Large companies or companies that operate in regulated or environmentally sensitive areas also are exposed to important governmental and regulatory influences. Even in cases where there is no state ownership, analyst attention needs to focus on areas where governmental or political influences could prompt companies to take actions not in the best interest of shareholder value.*

Analytical Instruction

Look for evidence of influences from nonfinancial stakeholders that may cause companies to undertake actions that may have a material impact on the company's commercial performance or market value.

Information Sources

+ Company public disclosure
+ Social and environmental reporting
+ NGO reports
+ Media coverage

Questions to guide analysis of influence of external stakeholders

+ Is the company a major local force in the regional or national economy on the basis of its employment or support of other commercial or economic activities? Does the company work in a sector that makes it vulnerable to governmental/political influences?
  + Financial institutions?
  + Strategic sectors (e.g., defense, energy, public utilities)?
+ Do external stakeholders have a direct influence on the company's governance process?

♦ Is there an explicit public-interest mission?
♦ Is there government or employee representation on the board of directors?
♦ Are there golden shares (even without equity ownership)?

Influence of External Stakeholders: Evaluation Guidelines

Strongest Analytical Profile

♦ *Nonfinancial stakeholders:* No evidence of problematic influence from nonfinancial stakeholders that could impair longer-term performance and shareholder value.
♦ *Regulatory and political environment:* No (or limited) governmental or political pressures.
♦ *Public-interest agenda:* No (or limited) potential conflicts between commercial interests and a public-interest agenda.

Weakest Analytical Profile

♦ *Nonfinancial stakeholders:* History of employee disruption, environmental litigation, and conflicts with local communities.
♦ *Nonfinancial stakeholders:* Nonfinancial stakeholder interests have an influence that works materially against the company's commercial interests or detracts from shareholder value.
♦ *Political environment and public-interest agenda:* Company is directly influenced by governments or regulators to act in a way that detracts from its commercial interests.

SUMMARY AND CONCLUSIONS

The influences of a company's owners and stakeholders can play a critical role in shaping its governance practices and policies. These must be understood as a starting point before examining other components of company governance. There are pros and cons to both widely held and closely held ownership structures, and it is essential that the fundamental ownership structure is transparent and properly understood. Equally, external stakeholders have a legitimate role in influencing company governance practices. This role can be positive, but attention must be paid to ensure that such influences provide benefits to all stakeholders and do not merely address the particular interests of one stakeholder group at the expense of others.

REFERENCES

Barca, F., and M. Becht. "The Control of Corporate Europe," Oxford University Press, Oxford, 2001.

Berle, A., and G. Means. "The Modern Corporation and Private Property," MacMillan, New York, 1932.

Claessens, S., S. Djankov, J. P. H. Fan, and L. H. P. Lang. "Disentangling the Incentive and Entrenchment Effects of Large Shareholdings," *Journal of Finance*, vol. LVII, no. 6, 2002.

Claessens, S., S. Djankov, and L. H. P. Lang. "The Separation of Ownership and Control in East Asian Corporations," *Journal of Financial Economics*, 2000.

Claessens, S., J. P. H. Fan, and L. H.P. Lang. "The Benefits and Costs of Group Affiliation: Evidence from East Asia," *Working Paper*, University of Amsterdam, Hong Kong University of Science & Technology, and the Chinese University of Hong Kong, 2002.

Franks, J., and C. Mayer. "Corporate Control: A Synthesis of the International Evidence," *Working Paper*, London Business School and City University Business School, 1992.

Franks, J., and C. Mayer. "Bank Control, Takeovers and Corporate Governance in Germany," *Journal of Banking & Finance*, vol. 22, 1998, pp. 1385–1403.

Jenson, M. C., and W. H. Meckling. "Theory of the Firm: Managerial Behavior, Agency Costs and Ownership Structure," *Journal of Financial Economics*, vol. 3, 1976, pp. 305–360.

La Porta, R., F. Lopez-de-Silanes, A. Shleifer, "Corporate Ownership Around the World," *Journal of Finance*, vol. 54, 1999, pp. 471–518.

La Porta, R., F. Lopez-de-Silanes, A. Shleifer, and R. Vishny. "Investor Protection and Corporate Governance," May 2001.

Mayer, C., "Ownership Matters," Paper written for the Inaugural Lecture of the Leo Goldschmidt Chair in Corporate Governance at the University Libre de Bruxelles, 2000.

Shleifer, A., and R. Vishny, "A Survey of Corporate Governance," *Journal of Finance*, vol. 52, 1997, pp. 737–783.

CHAPTER 4

Shareholder Rights and Stakeholder Relations

Dan Konigsburg

OVERVIEW

The ability of investors to both exercise control rights and share in the financial benefits of a company's success is at the core of good corporate governance.

Most corporate governance issues relevant to modern joint-stock corporations, including those of shareholder and ownership rights, arise from the separation of ownership from control. When owners do not manage companies directly, they must ensure that the managers they hire to run the business are doing a proper job (and are not abusing their positions) and that mechanisms are in place for owners to still exert control, albeit indirectly and at a distance. Another way of looking at ownership rights has been from the perspective of property rights theory. From this perspective, the shareholder, as the owner of the shares, ultimately bears the residual risk of success or failure of the enterprise, and is compensated for this risk with specific ownership rights.[1]

Ownership rights can be thought of in two categories: control rights and cash flow rights. Cash flow rights include the right to a dividend and the right to receive proportionate payment in turn for the sale of the share. Control rights are more procedural in nature and focus on voting rights, including the right to attend meetings and the right to convene a meeting. Cash flow and control rights may or may not imply fair and equal treatment, however, and cash flow rights may not be equal among asset classes. It is more difficult to categorize takeover defenses: Shareholders should have the right to receive an offer for their shares and a right to be treated equally with other members of the same share class in the process. But takeover defenses also can affect director accountability. Takeover defenses will be discussed in more detail later in this chapter.

The extent to which control rights are given to shareholders depends on a number of things, but can be traced to fundamental decisions about how much power should be delegated to the board and how much should remain in shareholders' hands. This decision, in turn, is often based on individual markets' trust in corporate boards and, in particular, trust in concentrations of power.[2] It also is linked with the effectiveness of other institutions, like regulators, the judiciary, corporate law, and media oversight that together may compensate for companies that allow their shareholders fewer control rights.

With the exception of the United Kingdom, which combines empowered boards with extensive control rights and strong institutions, markets that have weaker boards and less effective market regulation will often compensate shareholders with more control rights.[3] In the United States, for example, almost all control rights other than the right to elect directors have been delegated to the board. Here, corporate law recognizes directors' fiduciary duties to act in the assumed interests of shareholders—and in most cases, the threat of legal liability and/or public exposure ensures this. In Russia, on the other hand, where the former threats are either absent or ineffective, and where concern exists about misappropriation of shareholders' funds, company law has recognized the need for more shareholder control rights. In other countries, there may be less recognition that these controlling institutions are absent or ineffective, so control rights might be more needed from companies.

This raises the question of the importance of control rights in different markets, and we may assume that the importance of specific control rights in the context of a company's overall corporate governance will depend to a large degree on these external factors that may compensate for their absence. A strong judiciary, or majority independent boards, may mean that more of these rights can be delegated to the board, or indeed be missing, if these broader ideas compensate or dominate. Independent boards should be singled out as a mitigating factor, for as long as these are coupled with a fiduciary duty to shareholders, they may grant ownership rights by default. This is another reason why ownership rights cannot be viewed in isolation from other corporate governance elements like board structure.

Indeed, as much as effective ownership rights may be connected to board structure, connections with who owns the company can be just as strong. An academic study of ownership rights and shareholding structures has found a significant correlation between countries with weaker ownership rights and companies where ownership was concentrated in the hands of executives.[4] This may imply that less protection for outside investors is needed when high levels of insider ownership provide incentives for management to protect their assets by running the business well. But it is advisable to be cautious: Taken to its extreme, this assumption may offer false hope and may even lead to abuse, if the recent experience of owner/managers in Russia is any guide.[5] As well, this theory is challenged by the frequent lack of diversification of the interests of owner/managers, who may have large parts of their wealth tied up in the stock of one company. At its extreme, this may represent a danger to investors in western and emerging market companies, as executives follow perverse incentives to maintain or increase the value of their wealth.

In most jurisdictions, nonfinancial stakeholders (including employees, customers, suppliers, and local communities) usually do not have distinctly articulated rights *per se*, as outlined in a company's by-laws or articles of association. Their rights are typically protected in the broadest sense by the prevailing laws in individual jurisdictions. However, the relations that a company has with its key stakeholders can be critical to its long-term financial and operational sustainability. Those companies with poor external stakeholder relations may be more vulnerable to operational disruption, lawsuits, loss of reputation, and diminution of brand value. Hence, it is also important to appreciate the nature of a company's relations with its nonfinancial stakeholders together with its protection of specific ownership rights.

VOTING AND SHAREHOLDER MEETING PROCEDURES

The right to attend and vote at shareholder meetings is a fundamental component of well-governed companies. At many companies, the annual meeting is the only opportunity for smaller shareholders to exercise their ownership rights and to meet and discuss concerns with management. Moreover, fair and equal treatment in the arena of shareholder voting is often a window into how well companies treat shareholders in other areas.

Meeting and voting procedures are relevant not only in places like Russia, where voting irregularities have received significant attention. Vivendi, in France, suffered considerable embarrassment when its electronic voting system broke down in 2001 and back-up procedures were not clear. Embattled conglomerate Tyco angered shareholders by calling its 2003 shareholder meeting in Bermuda, where it is incorporated but where few of its shareholders are located. Many companies in the United Kingdom, Australia, and South Africa still vote at meetings via a show of hands, a practice that can disenfranchise those not present, including those who vote by proxy when a poll is not called. It is relatively easy to assess the strength of shareholder meeting procedures through public sources, though in some cases, weaknesses will be made most apparent from attendance at meetings themselves or from access to meeting transcripts.

Procedures for advising shareholders of general meetings should provide for equal access to all shareholders and should ensure that shareholders are furnished with sufficient and timely information. Questions to ask include how the company advises shareholders (including beneficial shareholders) of shareholder meetings, how much notice is given, what information or papers are circulated before meetings and what kind of information is included in the notice. Meeting notices should afford shareholders a good understanding of why a meeting has been called, how to cast a vote, and the background and rationale to proposed voting items. Companies should provide any supplementary information that would be needed for shareholders to make informed voting decisions.

Beyond notices of meeting and disclosure of voting procedures, procedures themselves should ensure equal and fair participation for all shareholders. If it is unduly expensive or difficult for a large proportion of shareholders to attend, or if shareholders are required to pay fees to attend meetings, the efficacy and perhaps the legitimacy of meetings may be placed under question. Fairness and predictability are central concerns here, and if there are minimum share requirements for attendance, or if registration procedures are not transparent, convenient, and equal for all shareholders, then confidence in the company as a whole may be at risk.

Voting procedures themselves are often a window into the company's commitment to strong governance practices. Do precise voting procedures exist? Are they articulated to the market? These are a few of the questions that investors can ask to begin to assess a company's commitment to shareholder democracy. Other questions include:

- whether voting procedures are transparent;
- whether they are independently verified;
- whether voting is confidential;
- whether all votes, cast in person or in absentia, are treated equally; and
- whether the company administers voting via a show of hands.

Even how proposals are presented to shareholders at meetings can be relevant: Bundled resolutions—that is, combinations of disparate issues where one issue is favorable to shareholders but others are not—can present investors with a difficult, all-or-nothing choice. At their worst, they can be used to introduce a negative change that shareholders would not likely approve if presented on its own.

Another element in the analysis of voting procedures is how companies handle voting by those shareholders who are not able to attend. Companies may entitle shareholders to vote by post/mail, by telephone, or electronically through the Internet. Many companies facilitate these rights by allowing representatives, or proxies, to attend and vote at shareholder meetings. But there can be wide variation in the arrangements that companies make to ensure that shareholders who are unable to attend meetings can vote through proxies: Deadlines for completing and sending voting forms back to the company or its registrar can be short. Some companies take additional measures to solicit voting instructions from beneficial holders by hiring proxy solicitors to contact custodians; others encourage custodians to provide shareholders with information concerning their options in the use of their voting rights.

Companies with bearer shares instead of registered shares must find some way to ensure that those who vote at shareholder meetings are in fact current shareholders. Without a register, or list of current holders, some companies have resorted to share blocking, whereby a bearer shareholder will deposit company shares with his or her broker for a number of days before the meeting, promising not to trade the shares for the duration. This process is also called share freezing. Share blocking or freezing forces holders to decide between voting rights on the one hand, and the flexibility to sell shares on the other.

If the company has an overseas listing via a depositary facility (for example, U.S. American Depositary Receipts), the provisions of the depositary agreement can vary as well, with corresponding effects on shareholder rights. For example, some agreements allow the depositary or even a management designee to vote shares on behalf of investors who have not submitted voting instructions to the depositary bank. Other agreements have been designed to accept votes only from beneficial owners who have provided voting instructions. Similarly, in the United States, some companies allow brokers to vote in the assumed interests of beneficiaries, even if they have not sent voting instructions.

OWNERSHIP AND FINANCIAL RIGHTS

Ownership and financial rights represent the mechanisms through which shareholders remain involved with the modern corporation. An analysis of these issues will establish the level and extent to which the company has delegated powers of control and oversight to shareholders, rather than to the board or management. It will include a discussion of some specific voting rights, all control and cash flow rights, and an analysis of takeover defenses and openness to a change in control.

Some of these factors will be less relevant in developed markets where market regulation and other institutions ensure fairness and high levels of default compliance. In these markets, it will be less necessary for companies to take proactive steps themselves to ensure, for example, share transferability or secure ownership. When evaluating governance, these factors may be weighted less heavily in mature markets with effective legal enforcement mechanisms.

A central concern here is that of fairness. The comparison of public companies with democracies is a false analogy: A shareholder can generally sell out of a company more easily than a voter can leave his or her jurisdiction, and shareholders can have diversified investments. Yet strong corporate governance demands mechanisms that ensure equal contributors of capital have an equal voice, no one shareholder is privileged above others, and elected representatives are held to maximum account by owners. More fundamentally, fairness promotes confidence in the enterprise and its management. An overview of major cash flow, voting, and control rights is listed below.

Cash flow rights include the right to receive a dividend, the right to have excess cash returned if the company cannot find suitable uses for it, the right to participate in share buy-backs at a fair price, and the right to receive proportional payment in turn on a liquidation of the company. A clearly articulated dividend policy is very important for investors seeking current income in addition to long-term capital appreciation.

Voting and control rights can be more extensive and include the following:

◆ The right to secure ownership and full transferability of shares.
◆ The right to an equality of economic and voting interests in a company, or "one-share, one-vote" provisions.
◆ The right to equal treatment within share classes. There should be no classes of shares with variable rights, or if variable rights do exist these should be explicit and some form of economic

benefit should offset the lack of specific rights. This is particularly the case with regard to voting rights.

- Preemptive rights, or the right of first refusal over dilutive share issuances, including the right not to be threatened by large issuances of preferred stock (so-called "blank-check preferred stock provisions").

- Tag-along (co-sale) rights, or the right of minority shareholders to receive the same offer accepted by a majority shareholder.

- The right to receive a bid for all outstanding shares when a large percentage of shares (typically 30 percent) is bought by a larger shareholder (a mandatory bid).

- The right for shareholders to act by written consent, or to vote on an issue outside of the context of an annual or special meeting.

- The right for shareholders to convene a special shareholder meeting.

- The right for shareholders to put forward specific shareholder proposals.

- The right for shareholders to nominate directors to the board.

- The right to approve specific corporate actions subject to reasonable threshold levels: mergers, acquisitions, disposals, restructurings, changes in corporate purpose, changes to class rights, share option/incentive plans, poison pills and other defense measures, related party transactions, amendments to the corporate by-laws/articles.[6]

- The right to approve routine corporate proposals: financial statements, auditors and auditors' fees, dividends.

- The right to elect or remove all directors—executive and nonexecutive—each year.

- The right of shareholders to influence board size and board vacancies. An important question is whether the board has the right to increase or decrease its size between shareholder meetings.

TAKEOVER DEFENSES

In addition to voting, cash flow, and control rights, any discussion of ownership rights will include an analysis of takeover defenses and the market for corporate control. Investors should expect to receive a premium for their shares if there is a change in control or to see significant change in severely underperforming managements including, in the latter case, nil-premium takeovers proposed by more competent managers. Beyond the financial benefits that accrue to shareholders as they realize premiums on their shares, the possibility of an unwanted takeover can act as a short- to medium-term performance pressure on managers.

Specific takeover defenses, like poison pills, staggered boards, and greenmail payments must be treated on a case-by-case basis. Academic studies have shown mixed results as to whether defenses are ultimately positive or negative to shareholders' interests over the long term. There is little consensus, for example, on the ultimate effects of poison pills in the United States,[7] while structures like staggered boards have received more clear-cut academic review of the impact they can have on director accountability.[8]

There often may be good reasons for a takeover defense: to buy time to achieve a higher offer price, for example, or to guard against opportunistic or coercive takeover attempts—particularly in certain industries or at companies where there is significant share-price volatility or where large cash reserves make for more attractive targets. While there is room in all of this for debate about the extent to which certain decisions should be delegated to the board, the ultimate decision on a change in control, particularly if there is more than one possible bid, should be made by the shareholders. Anti-takeover provisions that unreasonably remove this decision-making power from shareholders, taking into account the board's more perfect knowledge of outstanding bids and shareholders' collective action problems, should be viewed as a negative factor.

Despite the above, specific takeover defenses must not be viewed in a vacuum, separately from other governance factors such as board independence and incentive pay for managers. Majority independent boards are likely to accept reasonable or compelling bids, despite pressure from a defensive management or the presence of a poison pill, because they will be aware of their fiduciary duties and outside scrutiny. Similarly, despite the potentially perverse incentives that may exist outside of a takeover situation, incentive compensation that pays out on a successful change in control may make managers more amenable to a takeover if they are confident of their eventual financial security.[9]

Companies where changes of control are unlikely, despite a lack of structural defenses, also must be considered on a case-by-case basis. These include companies where the industrial or strategic importance to a particular country would invite interference from the government during a takeover bid, subsidiary companies, or companies where there is an existing majority shareholder.

Examples of more common takeover defenses are listed below:

- Double voting rights for long-term shareholders (France).
- Issuance of voting preference shares to voting trusts that are friendly to management (Netherlands).
- Golden shares offering a veto to an important shareholder or stakeholder, including a government (various jurisdictions).
- Shareholder agreements offering golden share benefits to a strategic holder or holders or Syndicate Pacts (Italy, France), where two or more shareholders agree to vote together with the purpose of preventing a change in control.
- Voting or ownership caps restricting voting or share ownership to a certain percentage of outstanding shares (various).
- Staggered, or classified, boards (United States, Canada).
- Poison pills (United States, Canada; also called "shareholder rights plans"). Poison pills take many forms, but are typically provisions that give shareholders certain conditional rights, which become effective during a takeover and which significantly raise the costs of mounting a bid. Typically, a triggered pill will automatically issue new shares in some ratio (two shares for every one already held, for example) to all shareholders except the one making a bid, thereby diluting the potential acquirer's stake in the company and making it more expensive for the acquirer to buy out remaining shares. Pills are usually triggered when an acquirer's stake reaches a specified percentage of total shares.
- Dual-class capital structures designed for one shareholder or one family.
- Ability to issue a large number of shares without preemptive rights.
- Greenmail provisions, including "fair price" provisions that place limitations on a company's ability to buy back shares from a particular shareholder at higher-than-market prices (United States).
- Supermajority voting requirements, particularly for approving a change in control. Depending on a company's ownership structure, these could be used to entrench management or to protect minority shareholders (various jurisdictions).

◆ Freeze-out provisions (also called merger moratorium laws)
  restricting a shareholder from buying more than a certain percentage of shares for a period of 1 to 3 years (various
  U.S. states).

◆ Control-share provisions, blocking the purchase of more than a
  20 percent interest in a company unless the acquirer first wins
  majority approval from holders of the other shares (various
  U.S. states).

◆ Restrictions on shareholders acting by written consent (acting
  by written ballot unconnected with a shareholder meeting).

◆ Protected board seats, where no shareholder can remove a particular director as he or she never stands for re-election.

A company's best defense, of course, is often its own market capitalization—companies like IBM or Microsoft may not need traditional
takeover defenses because there are few companies with the resources to
make a serious offer for their shares.

Importantly, creditor rights do not easily fall into this category.
However, creditor rights are important from a wider perspective, as the
rights of creditors can come into conflict with those of shareholders.
Creditor rights should be examined more closely if there is evidence of
abuse of other stakeholders. These rights can be difficult to assess holisti-
cally, as they tend to be defined in specific loan or bond indentures; e.g.,
some creditors may have more or less rights than others.

RELATIONS WITH NONFINANCIAL STAKEHOLDERS

It is an aspect of the broader principle of responsibility for a company to
address and show sensitivity to legitimate nonfinancial stakeholders,
including employees, local communities, environmental interests, regulators, and governments. These are important constituencies in the near
term and the maintenance of positive relationships stands to enhance a
company's longer-term sustainability—or to lessen vulnerability to legal
challenges, operational disruption, or loss of brand or franchise value.

While the "business case" for sustainable development or corporate
social responsibility remains an ongoing debate with regard to its meas-
urability and link to financial performance measures, it is nevertheless
important for corporations to act responsibly within the jurisdictions
where they operate. Relationships with key outside stakeholders, includ-

ing regulatory and governmental relationships, should be positively and proactively maintained. For well-governed companies, this should be an area of explicit focus by both company executives and directors.

Measuring a company's environmental or social performance *per se*, can be an ambitious exercise, and metrics of these stakeholder interests may only be relevant in specific industry or cultural contexts. In many cases there may be no "absolute" answers to questions relating to responsibility. It is still challenging, but perhaps more feasible, to approach this issue by assessing the nature of the relationship of the company with key stakeholders or nongovernmental organizations (NGOs) representing stakeholders' interests. This can include assessment of the extent to which the company makes disclosure on its social and environmental performance and the extent of its engagement with investors and stakeholders relating to social and environmental performance issues.

Evaluating stakeholder relationships can be subjective. Analysts should look to a company's specific disclosure about a number of its external stakeholder relationships, including disclosure about its employees, local community, customers, suppliers, and the environment. Reporting on employees may cover training and development, issues of diversity and equal opportunity, or workplace health and safety. Community reporting may discuss the company's engagement with its community, corporate philanthropy, or the costs and benefits of how the company interacts with the local economy.

Environmental reporting covers issues including the use of energy and renewable resources, pollution, and the use of recycling within the company. Investors should expect higher levels of reporting for companies in industries that can have large effects on the environment—mining, oil and gas, and other extractive industries are good examples. While disclosure of this nature can be helpful and supportive of stakeholder relationships, analysts should be alert to the possibility of "greenwashing"—companies portraying themselves in an inaccurate or misleading way with regard to social or environmental issues.

Beyond disclosure, there may be evidence of problematic relations with key stakeholders, including lawsuits, regulatory censure, strikes, operational disruption, environmental damage, or public protest. There are also a number of clear sectoral sensitivities, like the environment and community at companies in the extractive and manufacturing industries and human resource issues in the technology sector. Other issues to examine are problematic regulatory relationships (the securities regulator, any industry-specific relationships) and relationships with key NGOs or relevant interest groups.

ANALYTICAL FRAMEWORK: SHAREHOLDER RIGHTS AND STAKEHOLDER RELATIONS

The analysis of shareholder rights and stakeholder relations can be broken into three subcomponents:

1. Shareholder meeting and voting procedures
2. Ownership rights and takeover defenses
3. Stakeholder relations

Shareholder Meeting and Voting Procedures: Analytical Framework

FACTOR *The objective here is to establish whether the voting and meeting procedures promote shareholder democracy—namely, access to the shareholders' decision process and equal rights of participation through voting. Additional considerations are: (1) equal access, (2) ease of access and registration process, (3) sufficiency of information.*

Information Sources

Company charter

Records of resolutions, notices of meeting, and proxy materials

Records of communications with shareholders

Company secretary/directors/board chairman or lead director

Company registrars

Shareholders

Back-dated minutes, transcripts of AGMs

Back-dated records of mailings to shareholders

Direct attendance at shareholder meetings themselves

Questions to guide analysis of shareholder meeting procedures

- ♦ Do the company's statutes stipulate conditions under which shareholders can call a special meeting? What are these conditions? Indicate number/proportion of shareholders required and/or percentage of the shareholdings required to be behind the call for a special meeting.

♦ Is there evidence of successful or failed attempts by shareholders to invoke these provisions in the past in calling a special meeting?

♦ What arrangements are made by the company to ensure that shareholders are able to ask questions of the board and facilitate the power of shareholders to place items on the agenda of shareholder meetings?

♦ How much Q&A time is usually set aside during shareholders' meetings?

♦ Is this sufficient to answer all shareholders' questions or is it usually necessary to cut discussions short?

♦ How does the company advise shareholders (including beneficial shareholders) of shareholder meetings?

♦ How much notice is given?

♦ Where were the last four shareholder meetings held (including the last annual general meeting and special meetings)?

♦ Is it unduly expensive or difficult for a large proportion of shareholders to attend?

♦ Are registration procedures transparent, convenient, and equal for all shareholders?

♦ What information/papers were circulated before the last four meetings?
   (a) Date and location
   (b) Agenda of general meetings, including a list of the issues to be decided at the meeting
   (c) Further background information on issues to be decided (especially nonroutine matters decided either at annual or special shareholders meeting)
   (d) Details of the rules, including voting procedures and vote tallying
   (e) Financial statements
   (f) Directors and auditors reports
   (g) Information needed to vote on large transactions, restructuring, etc. Detailed information about candidates for the board

◆ Are shareholders required to pay any fees to attend?
◆ Are shareholders entitled to send votes by post or electronically, or appoint a proxy to attend and vote at shareholder meetings?

FACTOR *A shareholders assembly should be able to control decisions through voting processes that ensure participation by all shareholders.*

Questions to guide analysis of voting procedures

◆ Do precise voting procedures exist?
◆ How are voting procedures articulated?
◆ Are voting procedures independently verified?
◆ Do cumulative voting rights exist?
◆ Do the company's statutes contain "supermajority" provisions?
  ◆ If so, do these interfere with the election of directors and ratification of corporate actions?
◆ Have there been examples of combinations of disparate issues (i.e., "bundled" resolutions—where one element of the resolution is favorable to shareholders but others are not)?
◆ What arrangements does the company make to ensure that shareholders who are unable to attend shareholder meetings can vote?
  ◆ Are proxies sent out in a timely fashion?
  ◆ Is there evidence of some effort to ensure that agreement on voting is solicited from beneficial holders by nominees and custodians?
  ◆ Are custodians required to provide shareholders with information concerning their options in the use of their voting rights?
  ◆ Is equal effect given to votes, whether cast in person or in absentia? Where an overseas listing via a depositary facility is in place (e.g., U.S. ADR), do the provisions of the deposit agreement prevent the depositary or a designee of management from voting shares on which investors do not submit voting instructions to the depositary bank? Are these procedures transparent?

Strongest Analytical Profile

◆ *Notification of shareholder meetings:* Shareholders are notified of shareholder meetings individually where possible (registered share systems) and by the company website, and there is evidence that the company has attempted to ensure that beneficial shareholders receive notices. Where appropriate, professional proxy solicitation services may be used.

♦ *Advance notice:* The notice period for meetings is at least 21 days in advance.

♦ *Accessibility:* Meetings are held in a "home city," or in a place relatively convenient to shareholders.

♦ *Quality of information provided:* Meeting information distributed to shareholders includes the date and location of the meeting, a clear agenda, background information on issues to be decided, details of voting procedures, financial statements for the year in question, director and auditor reports, and, if relevant, sufficient information to make informed voting decisions on large transactions and candidates for the board.

♦ *Proxy voting rights:* Shareholders are entitled to appoint a proxy to vote at the meeting by post or electronically. Voting standards are clearly articulated and independently verified.

♦ *Drawing rights holders:* At companies where there is an overseas listing via depositary receipts, the depositary agreement prevents the depositary or a management designee from voting shares on which they have received no instructions. Other custodians do not vote without beneficial owners' consent.

   If there are ADRs, they are voted only with instructions from beneficial owners. Proxies are sent out in good time before the meeting.

Weakest Analytical Profile

♦ *Notification of shareholder meetings:* Notice is posted in a locally read newspaper only. Or, if the notice is sent out, it is only sent to shareholders.

♦ *Advance notice:* Shareholders receive no information about shareholder meetings in advance.

♦ *Accessibility:* Shareholders (especially individual minority shareholders) have encountered difficulties in attending meetings and they have to pay for attendance. The meeting location may have changed at the last minute, or may have been called for a location particularly inconvenient to the majority of shareholders.

♦ *Proxy voting rights:* Voting procedures are not clear and there are no provisions for voting in absentia.
♦ *Drawing rights holders:* Depositary banks and other custodians routinely vote their shares without owners' consent.

Ownership and Financial Rights: Analytical Framework

General Instruction
The objective is to establish the extent to which ownership rights have been granted to shareholders vis-à-vis the board, including cash flow and control rights—and to evaluate their appropriateness given other governance factors. The objective here is to establish whether rights attached to shares are secure, fully transferable, and equal.

Information Sources
      Company charter/articles/statutes
      SEC filings
      Annual report
      Board/Corporate secretary
      Records of resolutions, notices of meeting, and proxy materials
      Shareholders

FACTOR *There should be secure methods of ownership of shares and full transferability of shares.*

Questions to guide analysis of securing ownership and full transferability of shares

♦ What methods exist for securing ownership of shares?
♦ What arrangements exist for full transferability of shares?
♦ Who is the registrar (is this a function performed in-house or contracted out)?
    ♦ How was the registrar selected?
    ♦ How is its independence ensured?

FACTOR *A company's share structure should be clear, and voting rights attached to shares of the same class should be uniform and easily understood.*

- ⬥ What is the company's share structure?
  - ⬥ Preferred versus common?
  - ⬥ Same par value?
  - ⬥ Equal rights?
  - ⬥ Voting rights?
  - ⬥ How are new shares issued?
  - ⬥ Have there been instances where new issue regulations have not been adhered to?
  - ⬥ Does each common share have one vote?
  - ⬥ Are there any multiple classes of common shares with disparate voting rights?
  - ⬥ Do arrangements exist that enable certain shareholders to obtain a degree of control disproportionate to their apparent equity ownership (e.g., multiple voting rights)?
    - ⬥ Are these disclosed? Is the board able to issue any previously authorized shares—with voting rights to be determined by the board—without prior shareholder approval for the specific intended use?
    - ⬥ Are there provisions in the company's statutes for this?
    - ⬥ Has this ever occurred?

FACTOR *A shareholders assembly or general meeting should be able to exercise decision rights in key areas, ensuring that minority shareholders are protected against dilution or other loss of value (e.g., through related party transactions on non-arm's-length terms).*

Factors to guide analysis of shareholder assembly decision rights

- ⬥ Decisions reserved for shareholders' assembly:
  - ⬥ Elect and remove directors
  - ⬥ Approve the company's accounts and directors' report
  - ⬥ Appoint and remove auditors
  - ⬥ Approve changes to the charter and major decisions involving a reorganization in the company or a change in its activities or other extraordinary transactions
  - ⬥ Approve payments of amount of final dividends
  - ⬥ Authorize additional non–pro rata issues of shares, creation of new classes of shares, or changes to voting rights
  - ⬥ Material related party transactions on non-arm's-length terms—to be approved by noninterested shareholders

+ Shareholders' ability to place items on the agenda
+ Shareholders' ability to call a general meeting

FACTOR *All shareholders should receive equal financial treatment including the receipt of an equitable share of profits.*

+ What was the company's dividend policy over the preceding 2 years?
+ Is it clearly articulated and does the company follow its policy?
+ Do all holders of common shares receive an equitable share of profits?
+ Have there been any instances of dividend payment delays?
+ Where there have been delays, were all shareholders affected?
+ Are there any "fair price" provisions and limitations on a company's ability to buy back shares from a particular shareholder at higher-than-market prices?

FACTOR *The company should create a level playing field for corporate control and should be open to changes in management and ownership that provide increased shareholder value. Shareholders should be allowed to vote or have a say over material takeover bids or the presence of anti-takeover devices.*

Instruction
The objective in this section is to determine how open the company is to a takeover that would increase value for shareholders. The presence of a takeover defense should not by itself be interpreted negatively: analysts must assess the takeover defenses with regard to the ownership structure of the company, and analyze how virulent or benign the defense is in practice.

Questions to guide analysis of takeover defenses and corporate control issues

+ Is there a presence or absence of takeover defenses? While their mere presence is not always negative from a corporate governance point of view, the number of takeover defenses should be kept to a minimum.
+ Has the company used/triggered any takeover defenses in the past 2 years? What were the circumstances of their use?
+ What is the severity of the defenses that the company has? Are they highly frustrating to a potential bidder or mildly frustrating?

- Are shareholders able to vote or have a say in takeover bids?
- Have shareholders approved, or sought approval for, a company's takeover defenses?

Strongest Analytical Profile

- *Security of ownership:* Share ownership is guaranteed by a transparent and independent registrar system. Registrars should not share corporate ownership with client companies. Where American Depositary Receipts (ADRs) are in place, the depositary bank should be reputable and beneficial owners should be able to vote their shares.

- *Equality of shares:* Reflecting the principle of fairness, there are no classes of common shares with varying rights and the charter should establish a "one share, one vote" principle. Companies with tracking stock, however, should be assessed on a case-by-case basis. The rights of preference shares are clearly articulated. There are no provisions for block voting, multiple voting powers, or supermajority requirements that can interfere with the election of directors or the ratification of corporate actions. This factor is based on the premise that shareholders' economic stake and voting interest in a company should be consistent.

- *Shareholders' ability to call a meeting:* Shareholders accounting for at least 10 percent of all shares are empowered to call an Extraordinary General Meeting (EGM). This is specified in both the company charter/by-laws and other shareholder communications, for example, on the company's website.

- *Shareholders' ability to place items on the agenda:* Shareholders accounting for at least 5 percent of all shares are able to place items on shareholder meeting agendas. This is specified in both the company charter/by-laws and other shareholder communications, for example, on the company's website.

- *Shareholders' ability to ask questions in meetings:* Both shareholders and proxies have the right and reasonably sufficient time to ask questions in a general shareholder meeting. This right can be overused, however (some companies in Germany, for example, seek such high levels of consensus that meetings can last for more than a day), and must be balanced against directors' time and shareholders' funds.

◆ *Decision rights:* A variety of decisions are reserved for the shareholder assembly in the interests of promoting shareholder
democracy. While there is room for debate about the extent to
which certain decisions should be delegated to the board, shareholders are able to vote on the following issues: election and
removal of directors; approval of the company's financial statements and reports; appointment and removal of auditors;
approval of changes to the charter/by-laws/articles, and major
decisions involving a reorganization or a change in its activities
or other extraordinary transactions; approval of dividends;
authorization of additional non–pro rata issues of shares; creation of new classes of shares, or changes to voting rights;
approval by noninterested shareholders of material related party
transactions on non-arm's-length terms.

◆ *Director elections:* This is perhaps the most fundamental ownership right shareholders have. Shareholders delegate powers to
directors they elect, and a mechanism should therefore be in
place to hold directors accountable to owners. Director elections
should be transparent, and shareholders should have the opportunity to vote on, and potentially remove, all directors, both
executive and nonexecutive, each year. In situations where
blockholders exist, cumulative voting should be in place to
ensure that minority shareholders can achieve some board representation. (In widely held firms, the argument for cumulative
voting is less compelling.)

◆ *Dividend rights:* A specific and reasoned dividend policy exists
and is articulated to the market, even if the policy is not to pay
a dividend. Companies follow their policies and make all
announced payments.

◆ *Preemptive rights:* Though this right needs to be balanced against
efficiencies in capital-raising, shareholders are not threatened
with unreasonable levels of dilution to their ownership interests.
They enjoy rights of first refusal, or preemptive rights, in proportion to their shareholdings. Shareholders are notified of this
right in company disclosures.

◆ *Presence and use of anti-takeover defenses:* While again there is
room for debate about the extent to which certain decisions
should be delegated to the board, the ultimate decision on a
change in control is made by shareholders. There should be no

anti-takeover provisions that unreasonably remove this decision from shareholders, taking into consideration the board's more perfect knowledge of bids and shareholders' collective action problems.

♦ *Virulence of defenses:* Despite the above, protection from takeovers that the company enjoys does not dissuade potential acquirers or unreasonably increase the costs of mounting a takeover.

Weakest Analytical Profile

♦ *Security of ownership:* Ownership is not secured by an independent registrar or other system.

♦ *Equality of shares:* There are undisclosed shareholder agreements and differential voting rights among common shares, without offsetting economic benefits. There are supermajority provisions inconsistent with a dispersed ownership structure.

♦ *Shareholders' ability to call a meeting:* Shareholders cannot call an EGM/special meeting.

♦ *Shareholders' ability to place items on the agenda:* Shareholders do not have the ability to place an item on shareholder meeting agendas.

♦ *Shareholders' ability to ask questions in meetings:* Shareholders do not have the ability to ask questions at shareholder meetings.

♦ *Decision rights:* Shareholders do not decide on many or most of the issues described above in "best of class."

♦ *Director elections:* Shareholders do not vote on director nominations or appointments. Cumulative voting does not exist despite the presence of blockholders.

♦ *Dividend rights:* There is clear evidence of unequal financial treatment of shareholders.

♦ *Preemptive rights:* Shareholders do not have preemptive rights.

♦ *Presence and use of anti-takeover defenses:* The company has used a takeover defense in the last 2 years that did not involve shareholder approval or involvement and was against the interests of shareholders.

♦ *Virulence of defenses:* There is clear evidence that existing defenses have frustrated a potential legitimate bid.

Relations with Nonfinancial Stakeholders: Analytical Framework

FACTOR *The company obeys the laws of the jurisdictions where it operates and maintains positive relations with key nonfinancial stakeholders, including employees, customers, suppliers, local communities, governments, and regulators.*

FACTOR *The company maintains good public reporting on key areas of employee, community, and environmental activities that address concerns of nonfinancial stakeholders and maintains an active policy of engagement with diverse investor and stakeholder interests.*

Instruction

Examine the scope and content of company social and environmental reporting along with other internal and external data (including media reports) to assess the company's relationships with key external stakeholders. Look for evidence of and reasons for problematic stakeholder relationships.

Information Sources

Annual report

Website

Social impact reports: internal and external

Media coverage

NGO reports

Questions to guide analysis of stakeholder relationships

♦ Is there evidence of problematic relationships with key nonfinancial stakeholder groups? This can include lawsuits, strikes, public protests or boycotts, defamatory employee or interest group commentary.

♦ If so, how has the company responded to these relationship problems?

♦ Does the company maintain an active policy of engagement to investor and stakeholder interest groups?

♦ Have the company or its senior officials been convicted of offenses relating to its social or environmental activities?

♦ What is the company's relationship with government regulatory bodies?

- Are there any NGOs or public interest groups that oppose the company's activities?
- What shareholder resolutions relate to social and environmental matters?
- How extensive is the company's own social and environmental reporting?

Strongest Analytical Profile

- *External relations reporting:* There is good public reporting on key areas of employee, community, and environmental activities that address concerns of nonfinancial stakeholders.
- *Evidence of harmful relationships:* There is no evidence of problematic relationships with nonfinancial stakeholders that could impair longer-term performance.
- *Proactive relations:* The company maintains proactive programs to address interests of legitimate stakeholder interest groups.

Weakest Analytical Profile

- *External relations reporting:* There is no or minimal social reporting. This is particularly negative for companies that operate in sectors that have significant social or environmental impact.
- *Evidence of harmful relationships:* There is a documented history of employee disruption, environmental litigation, and conflicts with local communities.
- *Proactive relations:* The company does not maintain proactive programs to address stakeholder interests, and there is evidence that this is harming the company's reputation or long-term performance.

CONCLUSION

Protecting the rights of shareholders and preserving important long-term relationships with external stakeholders are important fundamentals to good governance practice. In many developed markets, protection of fundamental ownership rights is almost assumed and procedures such as shareholder meetings are often viewed as a formality. However, in more emerging economies these fundamental rights cannot always be assumed as givens. Even within developed countries there are differences with regard to fundamental issues of shareholder rights such as voting rights, shareholder decision rights, and takeover defenses. These need to be analyzed on a case-by-case basis.

The importance of nonfinancial stakeholders is becoming increasingly focused on in corporate governance. While there is scope to develop more sophisticated and refined metrics with regard to social and environmental performance, the strength of these relationships can be assessed in terms of company engagement and reporting on issues relevant to key stakeholders.

NOTES

1. Not everyone agrees with even this, however. Dissenting from the theory of shareholder primacy, Georgetown University Law professor Margaret Blair has argued that stockholders are not the owners of the corporation; they are merely the owners of the shares, and they share residual ownership rights with other stakeholders. See London, Simon.

2. Levels of trust and comfort can change over time, with consequent changes in delegation of control rights. Witness the increased use of the shareholder proposal mechanism in the United States after the 2001 Enron collapse.

3. See R. La Porta, et al.

4. See C. Himmelherg, et al.

5. See D. McCarthy, et al.

6. Different companies and jurisdictions will have different rules on shareholder approval, even of similar items. Share option or incentive plans, for example, require shareholder approval in many markets only if they involve the issuance of new shares or grants to directors. In the United States, recent proposals to exchange listing rules now require shareholder approval of all share plans, even if awards will be covered by Treasury stock. See "Corporate Governance Rule Proposals," NYSE.

7. See M. Gordon.

8. See L. A. Bebchuk, et al.

9. See M. Kahan, et al.

REFERENCES

Bebchuk, L. A., J. C. Coates IV, and G. Subramanian. "The Powerful Antitakeover Force of Staggered Boards: Theory, Evidence, and Policy," *Stanford Law Review*, vol. 54, no. 5, May 2002, p. 887.

"Corporate Governance Rule Proposals," NYSE, www.nyse.com (accessed August 1, 2002).

Gordon, M. "Takeover Defenses Work. Is That Such a Bad Thing?," *Stanford Law Review*, vol. 55, no. 3, December 1, 2002, p. 819.

Himmelherg, C., R. G. Hubbard, and I. Love. "Investor Protection, Ownership and the Cost of Capital," World Bank Finance, *Development Research Group Working Paper*, 2002, p. 2834.

Kahan, M., E. B. Rock, S. A. Fox. "How I Learned to Stop Worrying and Love the Pill: Adaptive Responses to Takeover Law," *The University of Chicago Law Review*, vol. 69, no. 3, Summer 2002, pp. 871–915.

La Porta, R., F. Lopez-de-Silanes, A. Shleifer, and R. Vishny, "Investor Protection and Corporate Governance," *Journal of Financial Economics*, vol. 58, nos. 1–2, 2001.

La Porta, R., F. Lopez-de-Silanes, A. Shleifer, and R. Vishny. "Investor Protection: Origins, Consequences, Reform," *Discussion Paper 188*, Harvard Institute for Economic Research, October 1999.

London, S. "An Uprising against Stock Arguments," *Financial Times*, 10, August 20, 2002.

McCarthy, D., and S. Puffer. "Corporate Governance in Russia: Towards a European, U.S., or Russian Model?," *European Management Journal*, vol. 20, no. 6, December 2002.

CHAPTER 5

Transparency, Disclosure, and Audit

Amra Balic

BACKGROUND AND CURRENT ISSUES

Transparency is one of the core principles of corporate governance. It relates to the quality, content, and timeliness of company disclosure. The audit process is essential in this context, as is the underlying rigor and independence of accounting information that a company discloses. However, a robust transparency regime extends beyond financial disclosure to encompass other important aspects germane to investors. This includes disclosure relating to a company's broad strategy and mission, its operational and competitive dynamics, key corporate actions, its ownership structure, its shareholder rights, and its management and board structures. Increasingly, the focus on disclosure is addressing interests of nonfinancial stakeholders, particularly in the realm of social and environmental reporting.

Why is transparency and disclosure important? Transparency and disclosure are leading indicators of a company's overall governance standards, as companies that have a greater level and higher quality of disclosure tend to be more open and investor friendly. In this regard it plays a crucial role in the capital allocation process and is critical to informed investment decisions by portfolio investors, direct investors, and creditors. It is also an important tool for other stakeholders including employees, customers, suppliers, and local communities.

Transparency and disclosure have been a focal point of corporate governance debate amongst both academics and market practitioners in recent years. The information that companies have disclosed has been under close scrutiny, particularly with respect to its scope and quality. In many jurisdictions, particularly in emerging markets, relatively generic and superficial information disclosure is the norm and fails to meet the actual information needs of investors and other users.

The widening gap between statutory company disclosure and the actual needs of investors and stakeholders has become increasingly apparent as business practices have developed and as sophisticated investment and transaction tools have become more widespread. The need for improvement is clear, particularly on the heels of a number of highly publicized corporate failures for which inadequate transparency and disclosure were partly to blame. This has created an urgency regarding the need to review and create a new set of requirements relating both to disclosure and the quality of the audit process. Increasingly, leading companies have developed disclosure programs that exceed regulatory norms, particularly with regard to the use of the Internet and related technologies. The issues are broad in scope, and include topics relating to timing and methods of disclosure, accounting standards, the audit process, disclosure of management and director compensation, and accounting rules.

SOME EMPIRICAL EVIDENCE

The quality and scope of a company's transparency and disclosure is a fundamental concern for investors. A lack of transparency combined with inadequate disclosure is often cited as one of the main reasons why investors are reluctant, or unwilling, to invest in companies in certain markets. It also can explain why, in some economies, the shares of many companies trade at a significant discount to their underlying value and why their cost of capital is substantially higher than that of their peers in developed and/or more transparent markets.

Academic research into the benefits of higher transparency and disclosure has been extensive in this context. Most of the research has focused either on the connection between transparency and disclosure and the cost of capital or on the effect that different market-specific requirements have on global patterns of transparency and disclosure.

C. A. Botosan's 1997 academic study *Disclosure Level and the Cost of Equity Capital*[1] warrants attention, as it addresses diverse empirical aspects of transparency and disclosure, drawing some clear conclusions and raising further questions. The paper investigates the benefits that greater disclosure creates for companies. This study provides evidence of a connection between the cost of equity capital and disclosure. Botosan shows that a greater level of disclosure is particularly beneficial for those companies that have a low level of analyst following. The evidence suggests that for these companies greater disclosure does lead to a lower cost of equity capital. The study also provides some basic evidence that certain types of disclosure have a greater impact in reducing the cost of equity capital than others. For the companies with a low analyst following, providing forecasts and key nonfinancial statistics is particularly important. Conversely, for companies with a high analyst following providing a summary of historical information is more important.

However, the Botosan study is inconclusive in other areas, suggesting scope for further research. For example, it indicates that for companies with a higher level of analyst coverage no significant relationship between disclosure and cost of equity capital was found. Moreover, it acknowledges the fact that the real benefits of greater disclosure are not well established. Even though some asset pricing models suggest a connection between greater disclosure and lower cost of capital, there is very little empirical evidence to prove that this is truly the case.

Another important aspect of transparency is the extent to which companies operating in international markets show greater levels of disclosure than companies with a local business focus. A recent paper by T. Khanna, K. Palepu, and S. Srinivasan from Harvard Business School,[2] looked into the effect that business interaction with U.S. markets has had on the disclosure, content, and practices of foreign companies (466 companies from 13 Asia-Pacific countries). The analysis indicates that foreign companies from the sample with considerable interactions with U.S. product, labor, and financial markets show a greater level of transparency compared to companies with no such interactions. These findings suggest that the quality of a company's transparency can be an important "passport" into international markets. For companies wishing to access international markets, best practice in disclosure is not a simple matter of compliance with local norms. The development of world-class transparency and disclosure practices is an important—if not a necessary—criterion.

Standard & Poor's has conducted its own study into transparency and disclosure practices across approximately 1500 companies globally, focusing on companies that comprise its global 1200 index and its S&P/IFCI emerging markets index.[3] This study reviews a wide range of disclosure items relating to ownership structure, investor rights, financial transparency, and management and board structures, focusing on annual reports as the core unit of company disclosure. It shows that disclosure patterns vary significantly in different jurisdictions globally, with the strongest disclosure regimes occurring in the financial market–oriented Anglo-Saxon countries (e.g., the United States, the United Kingdom,

Australia, Canada), whereas disclosure in emerging markets is at a notably lower level. It also shows that nonfinancial disclosure is notably weaker in • all jurisdictions than financial disclosure. The study also suggests that regulatory disclosure requirements are a key determinant in driving disclosure patterns on a global basis, but that companies also can exercise considerable discretion in their own disclosure practices—in many cases to gain access or to "bond" with international financial markets.

Research based on the Standard & Poor's study on 400 emerging • markets companies shows that firms with higher transparency and disclosure are valued more highly than comparable firms with lower transparency and disclosure.[4] Valuation is positively correlated with transparency and disclosure—consistent with the notion that the market places a premium on companies with lower levels of information asymmetry between a firm's management and equity and bondholders. The results provide empirical support to the academic, practitioner, and regulatory focus on transparency and disclosure.

In a nonacademic study released in 2003, Sibson Consulting and recruitment firm Spencer Stuart conducted a similar study of 352 U.S. companies, testing for disclosure on 52 nonmandated disclosure items. This study suggests a relationship between disclosure levels and share price performance and also concludes that disclosure about a company's own corporate governance practices is at a relatively minimal level.[5]

It is intuitive and reasonable that investors will put a greater value on companies that are prepared to disclose more information that is of high quality and easily accessible. This allows investors to better understand the underlying issues affecting the company as well as giving them greater confidence in the appropriateness of their investment decision.

KEY ISSUES IN THE TRANSPARENCY AND DISCLOSURE DEBATE

Rules versus principles. In an accounting context this is often presented as the debate between rules-based U.S. Generally Accepted Accounting Principles (U.S. GAAP) and principles-based International Accounting Standards (IAS). This debate is often conducted simplistically, ignoring the fact that rules and principles are relevant to both accounting systems. However, it is fair to characterize the U.S. GAAP system as emphasizing compliance with extensive rules in contrast to the somewhat less extensive and exhaustive IAS system, where principles hold the ultimate trump card. Visible corporate failures in the United States, notably Enron, have demonstrated that even sophisticated rules-based accounting systems run the risk of being "gamed," and in this context the 2002 Sarbanes-Oxley Act includes a provision to explore the merits of a more principles-based approach for the United States. The advantage of the principles-based approach is that the ultimate concern is the overarching focus on a firm's status as a going concern, rather than focusing on compliance with complex rules as an end in and of itself.

Accounting standards and convergence. IAS, U.S. GAAP, and several other accounting systems are generally recognized in international financial markets as "world class" on the basis of their approach and comprehensiveness. However, there are many individual accounting standards on a global basis. These may vary widely in quality and orientation. Some are robust and comparable with world-class standards. Others may be narrow or incomplete in scope, often driven by the desire to minimize corporate income tax. Even for the most sophisticated financial analysts operating with a multinational perspective, it is difficult, if not impossible, to master the intricate details of numerous accounting systems. That is why convergence is an important trend. Many companies globally are either adapting to IAS or U.S. GAAP accounting for example; indeed, in the European Union conversion IAS is mandated for all member states by 2005. However, even for companies that do not submit accounts in one of the leading international accounting standards, it can be helpful at least to present a reconciliation of results from local standards to those of more globally recognized standards.

A remarkable case study of disclosure relating to diverse accounting standards is provided by the Indian software company Infosys. In its published accounts it provides statements of Infosys' financial performance in multiple accounting standards, including Indian, United States, IAS, French, and German. Moreover, it presents the individual statements in the native language of the accounting standard's country.

Even within well-established accounting frameworks, such as U.S. GAAP, there is room for discretion. Analysts should not relax simply on the basis that a company's accounts are compiled according to globally recognized accounting standards. Chapter 9 focuses on the concept of CORE Earnings. This is an attempt to build a more standardized approach to the reporting of key accounting parameters relating to a company's earnings performance. In this regard, controversial issues such as the expensing of options and the treatment of company pension earnings and expenses are addressed.

Fair and continuous disclosure. The concepts of fair and continuous disclosure are adopted into legislation in many jurisdictions (such as Regulation FD in the United States), and provide a framework and discipline for companies to disclose material developments on a "continuous" basis—namely, when it happens as opposed to waiting for the next quarterly or semi-annual reporting cycle to come around. For example, if a senior executive either sells shares or exercises options, this can be an important signal to investors that warrants prompt communication. The case of Enron senior management selling their own shares while encouraging its employees to buy company shares is a good example of this.

The notion of "fair" disclosure means that information should be provided to the market as a whole, via newswires or other communications platforms, and not disclosed selectively to a privileged group of analysts or other shareholders. Together, the concepts of fair and continuous disclosure in principle provide a basis for timely and equitable disclosure above and beyond normal reporting cycles. However, to the extent that materiality of what needs to be disclosed on this basis remains a matter of discretion, there is the risk that companies may choose a very high materiality threshold, with the result that the effectiveness of a fair and continuous disclosure regime may be less robust in practice than it may sound in theory.

Quarterly reporting. Frequency of reporting cycles is a hotly debated issue, particularly with regard to the question of quarterly reporting. For example, it is one of the issues that is viewed separately between the United States and the United Kingdom: The United States requires quarterly reporting and, in the United Kingdom, semi-annual reporting remains the norm. Proponents in favor of quarterly reporting speak to the notion that more disclosure is better than less. This is particularly important in companies with blockholders who may be in a position to have more frequent access to information (owing to managerial or director positions) than minority shareholders. Detractors focus on both the incremental costs involved with quarterly reporting and the fact that the time-frame of quarterly reports is too short to have great relevance and can lead to a dysfunctional, short-termist perspective by both managers and analysts. Standard & Poor's Governance Services takes a nuanced view of this debate in its governance scoring. While on balance quarterly reporting is viewed as preferable, particularly for companies with significant blockholdings by managers and directors or for companies in volatile sectors, it may be less important for widely held companies that operate with a policy of fair and continuous disclosure.

Accessibility. Timing and content of public disclosure should be viewed in conjunction to its accessibility. Disclosure that is timely and of high quality may be of little value if it is difficult to access. In some jurisdictions regulatory disclosure filed with regulatory authorities may be used for the regulator's own purposes, but not accessible to the wider public. In other cases, prospectuses may contain ample amounts of disclosure for public dissemination; however, the public may only be able to access information of this nature as and when a company makes an issue for new capital.

Role of the Web and technology. Technology and the Internet provide a means for unprecedented access to public disclosure. Regulatory websites such as the SEC's EDGAR system can provide for a comprehensive and accessible basis of company disclosure. Companies also are improving in terms of their own use of technology to communicate to the public. Increasingly, company websites contain not only their annual reports, but considerable additional information, including regulatory filings, social and environmental reports, operational discussion, and profiles of company managers and directors. The investor relations function in many companies uses the Web to provide supplemental information on the company. This can include the publication of broker reports and the use of webcasts to more directly communicate to investors and other external analysts. Many companies also employ newswire services to ensure that key corporate actions are communicated directly to a wide universe of users. A key issue for companies with international investors is the language of disclosure, both in company materials and on the Web. Websites that have a preponderance of information in a company's local language, as opposed to English (as an international standard) can create an asymmetry in favor of local investors. On the other hand, companies that provide 20F reports to the U.S. SEC, but do not reciprocate this disclosure for local investors may be creating an unfair advantage for U.S. investors.

The relevance of the annual report. Given the development of the Internet and the role of strong regulatory disclosure requirements in jurisdictions such as the United States, Canada, France, and Japan, the role of the annual report as an information tool can be a matter of company discretion. Many companies in these jurisdictions provide only minimal disclosure in annual reports, and position the annual report more as a glossy public relations document. Regulatory filings are often bound together with the annual report to make for a more complete basis of disclosure. While many companies have adopted cursory annual reports, deferring to regulatory filings as the main platform of informational disclosure, other companies opt for more complete annual reports, even if they may not be required to do so.

The argument for relying on regulatory filings is that it is ultimately less costly and avoids repetition of information in the regulatory document as well as the company annual report. For sophisticated institutional investors this is typically not viewed as a problem. However, particularly for retail investors, regulatory filings may be more difficult to access and more intimidating to read. There are counter arguments calling for more complete corporate disclosure presented in a format that is readily accessible and easier to read.

Social and environmental reporting. The main thrust of company reporting is focused on the interests of a company's financial stakeholders, in particular its shareholders. However, the growing focus on corporate social responsibility and sustainable development is resulting in increasing calls for more robust disclosure relating to broader elements of performance, particularly with regard to the company's own workforce, its involvement with local communities, and its environmental impact. The United Nations–sponsored Global Reporting Initiative represents a major effort to develop more systematic reporting practices on a company's environmental and societal impact, and is increasingly being adopted, particularly in Europe, and to a lesser extent in other parts of the world.

Executive compensation. Executive compensation is an important area of scrutiny in governance analysis, and reporting standards differ considerably on this point on a global basis. U.S. disclosure on individual executive and director compensation is arguably the most detailed on a global basis of comparison, and it is ironic that this has not prevented excessive pay and option grants or other compensation-related abuses. Disclosure in the United States includes aspects of basic salary and other incentive compensation, including equity and option grants. Other aspects of executive compensation, such as perquisites or severance packages, may be less apparent. Some companies disclose publicly the contracts of their CEO; most do not.

In most jurisdictions globally, there is scant, or negligible, reporting on executive pay practices. To the extent that executive compensation is disclosed it is often done so anonymously, either grouping management compensation as an aggregate or in bands relating to individual compensation on an unnamed basis. This can be viewed by some as an issue of cultural preference, preserving a degree of personal privacy and greater harmony between management and the workforce. Others view disclosure of senior executive compensation as an intrinsic obligation for senior executives who work for publicly listed companies. Executive compensation is viewed by many governance analysts as a unique "window" to assess how the board values its senior executives, providing an indication of how disciplined or independent the board is *vis-à-vis* its CEO and other key executives.

Internal control and risk management. The question of transparency and disclosure is not limited to those external to the company. The scope and breadth of a company's internal control and risk management systems are critical in this context. Internal disclosure is crucial in allowing the senior executives and board directors (particularly audit committee members) to perform their duties appropriately. Directors' and senior managers' ability to identify and effectively mitigate risks related to the company is often what differentiates successful companies from their less successful peers. Increasingly, operational risk management systems, particular to the nature of individual companies' own unique circumstances, provide executives and directors with information systems that define key parameters of risk relating to both financial and nonfinancial risk factors. Inadequate internal controls may well result in errors of judgment, product failures, operating losses, and legal actions, all of which can have a substantial negative effect on shareholder value.

Audit process and independence. The quality, integrity, and independence of the audit process are key focal points in recent governance reform efforts. The role of the audit committee is particularly focused on both to provide greater integrity to the preparation of the company's financial statements and to provide more generally a robust system of internal control reflecting both operational and financial risks.

A number of new guidelines on corporate governance propose more stringent rules and procedures regarding auditor independence and the audit process as a whole. As many of the recent corporate failures, to a great extent, are a result of accounting irregularities, the need for more structured monitoring of the process comes as an obvious requirement.

Both the U.S. Sarbanes-Oxley Act of 2002 and the Smith Report in the United Kingdom are prominent and extensive examples of new and tighter rules governing the audit process and ensuring auditor independence. The policies regarding the auditor independence, and the controversial issue of engagement of external audit firms for nonaudit work, are focused on prominently in both documents. While neither the U.S. set of rules and recommendations nor those of the United Kingdom completely prevent companies from using their auditors for nonaudit work, they both require a rigorous oversight of the whole process and are including the guidance on situations where use of an audit firm for nonaudit work is prohibited. With regard to ensuring the independence of the auditor, recent reforms have brought several new features, including having the independent audit committee "own" the relationship with the auditor; having the internal audit committee report directly to the audit committee chairman; ensuring a transparent and accountable process for auditor selection; and a mandatory periodic rotation of audit partners and audit firms.

Increasingly, best practice is defined as having an entirely independent audit committee, with an engaged and financially literate board team. Definitions of financial "expert" have been framed to ensure that audit committee members have requisite financial skills. In many cases, meaningful and precise definitions of financial expertise can be problematic. However, given the particular role of the audit committee in overseeing the preparation of financial statements, the committee would be strengthened by having at least one director with a background or experience in financial statement preparation. While director training is desirable generally, the need is arguably greatest for audit committee members. In addition, the effectiveness of audit committees can often be enhanced by reasonable access to external consultants or advisors.

Audit charters are important for the articulation of the specific duties of the audit committee, including the review of financial statements, the approval of the audit and nonaudit services, engaging with the auditor, and monitoring internal controls. The nature of audit committee work means that it often meets more frequently than the board as a whole, either formally or informally. Many companies have six to eight formal audit committee meetings per year, and some audit committees meet with greater frequency. Audit committee members often receive monthly reports comparing company performance measures relative to budget and internal control parameters.

ANALYTICAL FRAMEWORK

In its governance scoring methodology, Standard & Poor's breaks down the analysis of transparency, disclosure, and audit into the following subcategories:

- Content of public disclosure
- Timing of and access to public disclosure
- The audit process

Content of Public Disclosure: Analytical Framework

FACTOR   *Reporting and disclosure should be completed to a high standard. Financial reporting should be comprehensive and complemented with substantial reporting of company operations, governance, ownership rights, and social performance.*

Quality and content of public disclosure can be assessed as a function of the following variables:

1. Completeness and clarity of financial statements;
2. Scope and depth of the operational disclosure;
3. Register of minority, interfirm, and related party transactions;
4. Regulatory filings;
5. Shareholders' meeting records;
6. Investor briefing materials;
7. Company website content;
8. Communications with shareholders;
9. Company legal documentation (including its by-laws or articles of association); and
10. Social and environmental reporting.

Analytical Instructions

Instruction

Assess overall comprehensiveness of company disclosure along financial operating, governance, and social parameters. Seek to identify gaps or holes in reporting. If there are areas that are opaque or difficult to understand, these should be clearly identified.

Questions to guide assessment of scope and content of public disclosure

- What accounting standards are used? Does the company use internationally recognized accounting standards such as IAS or U.S. GAAP as well as local accounting standards?
- If the company only reports according to a local standard, is a reconciliation to a more global standard provided?
- Is there any evidence of holes in financial reporting? Are some aspects of financial disclosure opaque or unclear?

♦ Are some key aspects of reporting addressed only in a superficial manner?

♦ Does a register of related party transactions exist? What related party transactions are reported publicly?

♦ Are corporate records of shareholders meetings kept and disclosed?

♦ Are the company charter and by-laws published and readily available publicly?

♦ Does the company publish its code of ethics or a statement of its corporate mission?

♦ Does the company publish a corporate governance charter or a charter of its various board committees?

♦ What level of detail is provided about management and the board?

♦ How extensive is disclosure relating to management and director compensation?

♦ Does the company provide extensive reports relating to its social and environmental performance?

♦ Are there areas where the company's disclosure exceeds regulatory requirements?

Quality and Content of Public Disclosure: Evaluation Guidelines

Strongest Analytical Profile

♦ *Accounting standards:* Company financial statements are produced according to local country accounting requirements and according to at least one internationally recognized set of accounting standards (IAS, U.S. GAAP, or equivalent), and both the former and latter are audited. If financial statements are only prepared on a local basis, particularly in emerging market countries, a reconciliation *vis-à-vis* one of the more globally recognized accounting standards can provide value to external investors.

♦ *Ownership structures:* Ownership information is provided down to at least the identification of shareholders holding 5 percent of the company shares.

♦ *Operating information:* There is a comprehensive discussion and analysis of company strategy and operating performance.

♦ *Related party transactions:* There is an accessible register and discussion of related party transactions.

♦ *Shareholder meeting records:* Corporate records of shareholder meetings are maintained and accessible.

♦ *Company mission and ethics:* The company publishes a mission statement and a statement or code of ethics.

♦ *Company legal documentation:* Company by-laws, statutes, and/or articles are articulated and published. There is a clear articulation of voting rights and other key ownership rights.

♦ *Takeover defenses:* If poison pills or other takeover defenses exist, there is clear disclosure of these mechanisms and associated procedures.

♦ *Management and board information:* The company provides a comprehensive review of its management and board directors, including responsibilities, compensation, background, share ownership, and outside directorships.

♦ *Executive compensation:* Director and senior executive compensation is spelled out in detail by individual, including salary, bonus, share grants, options, and other perquisites. Service contract details, including severance benefits, if relevant, also are provided. Compensation policies and processes are articulated.

♦ *Corporate governance reporting:* The company produces and publishes a corporate governance report, which clearly outlines governance policies and practices including committee structures and charters, numbers of meetings, and attendance rates.

♦ *Social and environmental disclosure:* The company provides substantial reporting on its social and environmental performance.

Weakest Analytical Profile

♦ *Accounting standards:* Company financial statements are produced; however, there is clear evidence of noncompliance with local country accounting standards. An audit may not have been performed, but there is no opinion given by the auditor—or only a qualified opinion.

♦ *Accounting standards:* The company has made no attempts to produce accounts in accordance with recognized international accounting standards.

- *Accounting standards:* Company financial statements provide insufficient detail to assess off balance–sheet structures or other contingent liabilities.
- *Related party transactions:* There is no disclosure regarding related party intrafirm transactions.
- *Shareholder meeting records:* Records of shareholders meetings are not publicly disclosed.
- *Shareholder communications:* There is limited evidence of efforts to notify shareholders of major corporate events.
- *Company legal documentation:* No company by-laws, statutes, and/or articles are articulated and published.
- *Mission and code of ethics:* There is no mission statement or statement of ethics.
- *Takeover defenses:* Poison pills or other takeover defenses exist, but there is no clear disclosure of these mechanisms or associated procedures.
- *Corporate governance reporting:* The company produces no corporate governance report, and there is no or minimal disclosure regarding governance policies and practices including committee structures and charters, numbers of meetings, and attendance rates. The company provides limited or no information about its management and board directors.
- *Executive compensation:* Director and senior executive compensation is not spelled out in detail by individual, including salary, bonus, share grants, options, and other perquisites. Service contract details, including severance benefits, if relevant, are not provided. Compensation policies and processes are poorly articulated.
- *Social and environmental reporting:* No social or environmental reporting or misleading representation of stakeholder relations (e.g., "greenwashing").

Timing of and Access to Public Disclosure: Analytical Framework

FACTOR *All publicly disclosed information should be promptly available and freely accessible to the investment community and shareholders: The company operates on a policy of free and continuous disclosure.*

FACTOR *The company's by-laws, statutes, and/or articles of association should be readily accessible to all shareholders.*

FACTOR *The company should maintain a website and make company reports, summary reports, and/or other investor-relevant information available in both the local language as well as English.*

The above factors are functions of the following variables:

1. Filing records;
2. Easy access to public information;
3. Continuous and fair disclosure of public information;
4. Value-added information; and
5. Access to company legal documentation.

Analytical Instructions

FACTOR *All publicly disclosable information should be promptly available and freely accessible to the investment community and shareholders.*

Instruction

Two types of disclosure are considered in assessment of this factor: (*a*) timing and ease of access of publicly reported financial, strategic, and operating information; and (*b*) timing and ease of access to disclosures on key legal or constitutional issues, as defined by the company's governing documents.

Questions to guide accessibility of disclosure

- When is publicly available information made available?
- Has the annual report been published in advance of the share-holders meeting and with enough lead-time to allow investors to make informed voting decisions?
- Have there been any occasions when information has been filed late to the regulators?
- How is publicly available information distributed or made available?
- Does the company report quarterly?
- What internal procedures are in place for ensuring continuous disclosure of material, price-sensitive information to market participants, exchanges, and regulators?

- Do established channels exist for disseminating information to shareholders and investment professionals?

    Comment on the use of analyst presentations, conference calls to investment community, and assess the way the company ensures that information is available to small, outside shareholders and employee shareholders.

- If major corporate changes (acquisitions, disposals, restructuring, refinancing, etc.) have occurred during the last 12 months, how were these disclosed?

    How have shareholders been notified of these specific and major events?

- What records of these events are publicly available?
- How are corporate records made available to all shareholders?

FACTOR *The company by-laws, statutes, and/or articles of association should be readily accessible to all shareholders. Any changes in content of these documents should be disclosed in a timely manner and disclosure should, if necessary, provide a detailed explanation of the nature of the changes.*

Instruction
Establish the company's transparency on key constitutional issues:

Are these issues contained in the company charter and how are they applicable to board decisions?

Questions on disclosure of company legal documents and shareholder rights

- Has the company published its by-laws?
- How are by-laws, statutes, and/or articles made available to all shareholders?
- How does the company communicate changes to its by-laws or articles?
- Is there public disclosure of board and Annual General Meeting (AGM) voting rules?

FACTOR *The company should maintain a website and make company reports, summary reports, and/or other investor-relevant information available in both the local language as well as English. The website should be updated on a regular basis and should, apart from regular* *filings, include press releases and any press coverage that the company receives.*

Instruction

Establish comprehensiveness of the company website. The company should not make a difference in content of disclosure in local versus English language.

Questions to guide review of website

♦ Does the company have a website?

♦ Does the company have a separate investor relations section at its website? Or has the company devoted one or more pages to conveying investor-related information?

♦ Has the company posted any of its public reports (annual financial statements, interim reports, etc.)? Indicate which reports are posted and for what periods. Are these made available in user-friendly formats: pdf, Word, and/or Excel?

♦ Is the website regularly updated?

♦ Are investor/analyst presentations made available at the site?

♦ If more than one language is used on the site, does one language contain more information than another?

♦ Are press releases made available at the site?

♦ Has the company provided any share price/share movement information?

♦ Are there links to regulatory filings or other online government agency filings (if relevant)?

Timing of and Access to Public Disclosure: Evaluation Guidelines

Strongest Analytical Profile

♦ *Filing record:* Public reports are always filed on time.

♦ *Frequency of reporting:* The company reports quarterly. This is particularly important for companies with large blockholders or where company management holds a significant stake.

♦ *Continuity and distribution of disclosure:* The company maintains a policy of fair and continuous disclosure.

+ *Company website:* The company maintains a website which contains at the very least the following information: annual, semiannual, and quarterly reports (both the most recent and for the last 3 years); information on shareholder meetings, analyst reports, and analyst presentations; press releases, board of directors information, information on board committees including their structure and short biographies of members, the company's mission statement, and its code of ethics.

+ *Legal documents:* The company's articles of association or by-laws are freely available (without charge) and there is an accessible register of related party transactions for confidential inspection. Corporate records of shareholders' meetings are available for inspection.

+ *Shareholders' rights:* Shareholders are sent information on where and how to access corporate records of shareholders' meetings, and are sent publicly filed financial statements and reports.

+ *Value-added information:* There is also evidence of extra effort to ensure that reports reach a significant number of interested shareholders and investment professionals, e.g., via analysts' presentations, conference calls, and having an up-to-date website.

Weakest Analytical Profile

+ *Filing record:* The company has failed to file one or more of the required public reports.

+ *Access to public information:* There are no formal channels through which information is distributed to all shareholders.

+ *Continuity and distribution of disclosure:* The company does not disclose information in a continuous and regular manner.

+ *Legal documentation and shareholder information:* Company-governing documents and regulatory disclosure are difficult or impossible to obtain on request from corporate headquarters and difficult to access via government agencies.

+ *Company website:* Company does not have a website or its website is not regularly updated and it does not include pertinent regulatory filings.

+ *Value-added information:* There is no disclosure beyond regulatory minimums.

The Audit Process: Analytical Framework

FACTOR *Auditors should be independent of the board and management of the company and the company's performance and objectives.*

FACTOR *Auditors should be experienced and also should be reputable.*

FACTOR *The company's audit committee plays a key role in the oversight of financial statement preparation and in ensuring an effective, clearly articulated internal control and risk management system.*

These factors are functions of the following variables:

1. The audit is provided by an experienced and reputable audit company.
2. Clear evidence of explicit consideration is given to auditor independence.
3. Audit versus nonaudit work/fees: Nonaudit fees should either not exist or should be so immaterial as not to establish potential conflicts of interest or compromise independence.
4. Definitions of nonaudit services.
5. Selection process for auditors.
6. Audit committee and its independence.
7. Clarity of audit committee's remit.
8. Frequency of audit committee meetings and attendance records.
9. Audit committee accountability.
10. Auditor rotation.
11. Internal control and risk management systems.

Analytical Instructions

FACTOR *Auditors should be independent of the board and management of the company and the company's performance and objectives.*

Instruction
The focus here is to ascertain how the board and audit committee maintain the integrity of the audit process and the independence of the outside auditor. These processes signal the integrity of the results of the audit and, by extension, the quality of the company's reports. Auditor independence is a function not only of the reputation of the auditor for integrity and objectivity, but also of the relationship between the auditor and company.

FACTOR *Auditors should be experienced and reputable.*

Instruction

The main considerations are the competence and integrity of the outside auditor. The auditor should be an experienced and reputable audit company in the local country, or should be one of the leading international audit firms.

FACTOR *The company's audit committee plays a key role in the oversight of financial statement preparation and in ensuring an effective, clearly articulated internal control and risk management system.*

Instruction

The focus here is to assess the independence and effectiveness of the company's audit committee. The audit committee charter and minutes can highlight the frequency and the nature of the audit committee's involvement. In particular it is important to understand how the audit committee approaches its responsibilities for the company's financial statements and for the establishment of an appropriate internal system of control and risk management.

Information Sources

The audit committee charter, audit committee minutes, disclosure of nonaudit fees paid to the auditor, documentation of the company's approach to risk management and internal control, and examples of periodic financial reports supplied to audit committee members and board members are good sources of information. Interviewing audit committee chairpersons, the CFO, the internal control/risk manager, and auditor also is a beneficial means of gathering information.

Questions to guide analysis of the audit process

- What auditing company is used?
- Is it experienced and does the auditor's geographic coverage adequately match the scope of the company's operations?
- What is the history of the audit firm (and, where applicable, its associated consultancy firm) in the development of the sector?
- Does the auditor do other work for the company, including other consulting or professional services?
- Are the fees for this additional work disproportionate in comparison to audit fees?
- Could the level of audit fees be seen to compromise independence?

- What process is used to select auditors? How is the auditor's independence ensured? Does an audit committee appoint auditors?
- Are the auditors indemnified against liabilities incurred through legal action out of the assets of the company?
- What is the relationship between the audit committee and the company auditor? Does the audit committee "own" or manage this relationship?
- What is the degree of independence of the audit committee in terms of the composition of its members?
- Does the company's audit committee have a formal charter? Does this charter expressly address the audit committee's engagement regarding financial statement preparation and internal controls?

Auditor Independence and Audit Process: Evaluation Guidelines

Strongest Analytical Profile

- *Auditor competence and reputation:* The auditor is an experienced and reputable audit company in the local country, or a leading international audit firm.
- *Auditor independence:* There is clear evidence of explicit consideration given to auditor independence.
- *Nonaudit versus audit-related fees:* There are no nonaudit fee relationships with the auditor. Or to the extent that some fee relationships exist, they are minimal in scope and are logical extensions of the audit-related work. If the audit firm also is paid for consulting work or other professional services, this is made transparent and there is information on the percentage of nonaudit fee in the total fee paid to the auditor. The company has a clear definition of audit and nonaudit services, and/or adopts the accepted definition of relevant regulatory authority. The audit committee monitors and approves all audit and audit-related fees provided by the auditor.
- *Auditor selection:* There is an explicit, transparent, and accountable process for selecting the auditor.
- *Auditor rotation:* The company has a clearly articulated policy regarding rotation of auditor firm and/or lead audit partner and

(a) the senior partner in charge of the account is rotated every 5 years, or (b) the audit firm is rotated every 10 years.

♦ *Auditor relationship:* The relationship with the external auditor is managed primarily by the audit committee.

♦ *Audit committee independence:* The audit committee is made up solely of independent nonexecutive directors.

♦ *Clarity of remit:* There are clearly articulated and updated terms of reference for the audit committee.

♦ *Audit committee effectiveness:* Audit committee members have access to funds and independent advice and training. Audit committee members have an explicit right of access to company information as well as to executive directors, employees, and the external auditor, and audit committee members have the right to meet on their own.

♦ *Engagement:* Audit committee meetings are held at least quarterly with acceptable rates of attendance, and audit committee members receive reports at least monthly providing updates on financial and operating results, along with risk management reports relating company performance to defined operational risk parameters. The company will hold more frequent audit committee meetings, formally or informally, as needed.

♦ *Accountability:* The chairperson of the audit committee is present at the AGM to answer questions on the report and matters within the scope of the audit committee's responsibilities.

♦ *Internal control:* There is clear evidence that the audit committee is involved in the internal control process by helping to establish and monitor internal control procedures. The audit committee oversees the work of the internal auditor. The internal audit function has direct lines of communication and a reporting relationship with the audit committee. The audit committee has in place an ombudsman or a "whistleblowing" system that provides employees a mechanism to report irregularities or violations of operating policies.

♦ *Risk management:* The audit committee has engaged in a formal assessment of the company's financial and operational risks and has established a control and reporting system to monitor these risks.

♦ *Accounting and financial policies:* The audit committee conducts an annual review of the effectiveness of internal controls and is involved in reviewing key accounting policies and practices used by the company, in particular matters which might distort or undermine the quality or clarity of disclosure.

♦ *Skill set of audit committee:* Members of the audit committee are all financially literate and at least one member has experience in the preparation of financial statements. At least one member has experience in risk management.

♦ *Training:* Audit committee members, particularly those who are not active in the financial services or auditing sectors, receive training on technical aspects of managerial finance, control, and risk management.

Weakest Analytical Profile

♦ *Accountability:* Auditors are indemnified for liability out of the assets of the company.

♦ *Auditor selection:* Auditor is appointed via a nontransparent process over which management presides.

♦ *Nonaudit fees:* If the auditor is involved in nonaudit work, there is no clear disclosure of the level of audit fees versus nonaudit fees. Or, if nonaudit fees are disclosed, they are disproportionate relative to the level of audit fees, suggesting the potential for conflict of interest.

♦ *Auditor relationship:* The audit committee or board does not truly "own" the internal/external audit relationships.

♦ *Auditor rotation:* The company does not have a clearly articulated policy regarding rotation of auditor firm and/or lead audit partner.

♦ *Clarity of audit committee remit:* There is no audit committee, or its terms of reference are not clearly articulated.

♦ *Engagement:* The audit committee meets infrequently and these meetings have a poor attendance record. The agenda is limited in scope and audit committee members are supplied with limited information to support committee deliberations.

♦ *Accountability:* The chairperson of the audit committee is not present at the AGM to answer potential questions on the report and other matters within the scope of audit committee responsibilities. Shareholders have no direct access to the audit committee chairman.

+ *Independence:* None or only a few of the audit committee members satisfy criteria for independence.
+ *Audit committee effectiveness:* Audit committee members have no or limited access to extra funds for independent advice and training. Audit committee members have difficulty accessing company information and company management or staff.
+ *Internal control:* The audit committee has limited or no engagement with the internal control process. There are no mechanisms for the audit committee to receive inputs from the company's employees about violations of audit procedures.
+ *Risk management:* There is no formal risk management system in place, or to the extent there is, the audit committee plays a limited role in overseeing the risk management process.
+ *Accounting and financial policies:* The audit committee plays little or no role in reviewing key accounting policies and practices used by the company.
+ *Skill set of audit committee:* Limited financial experience and literacy of audit committee members. No member has experience in the preparation of financial statements or risk management.
+ *Training:* Audit committee members, particularly those who are not active in the financial services or auditing sectors, receive training on technical aspects of managerial finance, control, and risk management.

SUMMARY

Transparency, disclosure, and the audit process are fundamental to a company's corporate governance. The need for more robust, internationally comparable financial reporting is clear in the wake of many recent governance failures. But the bar is continuing to rise in the area of nonfinancial reporting as well, with an increasing focus on operating, management, governance, and social disclosure. Technology, particularly the Internet, increasingly provides the ability to make disclosure accessible, timely, and fair. However, the scope, content, and timing of disclosure is meaningless if the disclosure lacks integrity and independence. Consequently, the increased scrutiny on the audit process and the audit committee that oversees this process is one of the key focal points of current corporate governance reform.

NOTES

1. Botosan, C. A. "Disclosure Level and the Cost of Equity Capital," *The Accounting Review*, vol. 72, no. 3, July 1997, pp. 323–349.

2. Khanna, T., K. Palepu, and S. Srinivasan. "Disclosure Practices of Foreign Companies Interacting with U.S. Markets," Harvard Business School, December 2002.

3. Patel, S. A., and G. Dallas. "Transparency and Disclosure: Overview of Methodology and Study Results—United States," Standard & Poor's, New York, October 2002.

4. Patel, S. A., A. Balic, and L. Bwakira. "Measuring Transparency and Disclosure at Firm Level in Emerging Markets," Standard & Poor's, New York, May 2002.

5. Sibson Consulting and Spencer Stuart, "A Study of Corporate Governance Disclosure Practices," The Segal Group, 2003.

REFERENCES

"Audit Committee Combined Code Guidance," Report and proposed guidance by a Financial Reporting Council appointed group chaired by Sir Robert Smith, January 2003.

Botosan, C. A. "Disclosure Level and the Cost of Equity Capital," *The Accounting Review*, vol. 72, no. 3, July 1997, pp. 323–349.

Gore, P., P. F. Pope, and A. K. Singh. "Non-audit Service, Audit Independence and Earnings Management," Lancaster University, January 2001.

Gompers, P. A., J. L. Ishii, and A. Metrick. "Corporate Governance and Equity Prices," *Quarterly Journal of Economics*, February 2003.

"Improving Business Reporting—A Customer Focus," American Institute of Certified Public Accountants, Chapters 1 & 4, www.accounting.rutgers.edu/raw/aicpa/business, 1999.

Khanna, T., K. Palepu, and S. Srinivasan. "Disclosure Practices of Foreign Companies Interacting with U.S. Markets," Harvard Business School, December 2002.

Patel, S. A., A. Balic, and L. Bwakira. "Measuring Transparency and Disclosure at Firm-Level in Emerging Markets," Standard & Poor's, New York, May 2002.

Patel, S. A., and G. Dallas. "Transparency and Disclosure: Overview of Methodology and Study Results—United States," Standard & Poor's, New York, October 2002.

Sarbanes-Oxley Act, One Hundred Seventh Congress of the United States of America (at the Second Session), "An Act," www.FindLaw.com/ , 2002.

Sibson Consulting and Spencer Stuart, "A Study of Corporate Governance Disclosure Practices," The Segal Group, 2003.

"Summary of Sarbanes-Oxley Act of 2002," The American Institute of Certified Public Accountants, www.aicpa.org.

Board Structure and Effectiveness

Nick Bradley

A major problem faced by the shareholders of joint stock companies, particularly those in "outsider systems" who trust the running of the company to its managers, is the so-called agency monitoring problem. Therefore, an analysis of board structure and effectiveness addresses the role of the corporate board and its ability to provide independent oversight of management's performance and to hold management accountable to shareholders and other relevant stakeholders while ensuring that management is appropriately motivated and remunerated.

Board structure and effectiveness is a focal point of corporate governance. The board acts as a bridge between the owners, or principals, of a business (the shareholders) and their agents (management), some of whom also may sit on the board in their capacity as executive (or employed) directors. A company's shareholders provide funding for the business and, in exchange, expect a return on their investment—usually from a combination of *income* (dividends resulting from profits made by the business) and *capital appreciation* resulting from the increase in share price as a consequence of the sustainable long-term growth of the business.

The senior managers of the company are appointed by the board to run the business on a day-to-day basis and to ensure that the company achieves its strategic and financial objectives, and that shareholders and other stakeholders receive their fair share of the company's earnings and assets. In turn, director and senior executive compensation policies attempt to provide alignment between managers', directors', and shareholders' interests.

Board structure is important, as it plays a key role in framing the balance of power between company managers and directors. But ultimately, board effectiveness is more than a matter of structure or architecture. The "tone at the top" is a reflection of the integrity, independence, and teamwork of individual board members and a company's executive management.[1] For the board to be truly effective, not only must an appropriate structure be in place, but individual board members also should be engaged, well informed, and represent diverse skill sets and perspectives. The "human side" of the board process suggests that the board should demonstrate true "independence of mind" *vis-à-vis* the chairman, CEO, or other board members. The ability to work as a cohesive team also must mesh with the ability for constructive criticism of senior executives or other board members.

Effective boards bear overall accountability for the strategy, performance, and internal control of the company. An analysis of the effectiveness of boards will establish the extent to which the board determines, or influences to a significant extent, the direction of the company, sets performance objectives for management, and places limits on the discretion of management. The board also should bear overall accountability for the performance and internal controls of the company. In a more qualitative sense, the board also should ensure the proper tone at the top, to establish an overarching culture of integrity and business ethics to permeate through the entire company.

STRUCTURAL ISSUES

The size of the board can be an important governance consideration, as boards with too many directors can be unwieldy, with inefficient communication among directors affecting decisionmaking. Boards with too few directors may lack the appropriate skills and backgrounds or may be dominated by management and thus not be representative of all shareholder groups. Particularly given the tendency for increased use of individual board committees, it may be difficult for small boards to effectively accommodate a wide range of committees with independent directors.

The size of the board should be appropriate for the size and nature of the company. Although board size varies significantly from company to company and from country to country, the average size of boards in the United States tends to be smaller than in many other countries where there is stronger representation of executive directors. In the United States, the average board size of the largest companies is often well below 15 members, whereas companies in Japan have boards often in excess of 20 individuals (most of whom are employees of the company).

Boards with high accountability typically include a strong base of independent nonexecutive directors who look after the interests of *all* shareholders—both majority and minority holders. Conversely, companies with a strong majority shareholdership, or dominated by a few shareholders, may have boards with limited accountability to all shareholders. This is particularly the case when the company's management is heavily represented on the corporate board.

Board composition and independence need not only be addressed at the level of the whole board; the balance of power and the composition of key board committees can be significant. Audit committees are a particular focus in this regard, and best practice in many jurisdictions is increasingly being recognized as having 100 percent director independence in audit committees. In other key committee areas, notably nomination or remuneration committees, there is also an increasing focus on substantial or complete director independence.

DEFINITIONS OF ROLES

A key concern here is that of responsibility. Do board members and senior management clearly understand lines of responsibility and who does what? However, as recent corporate failures have shown, it is extremely difficult for outside directors to truly know what is going on in a company, particularly companies with complex operations. Therefore, an effective board delegates the day-to-day management of the company to the executive management of the company, who may include a number of executive directors. Despite this, a board should clearly articulate a set of matters reserved for its own discretion and these should be clearly understood by board members and executive management.

These reserved matters vary widely from company to company. For example, in the United Kingdom, the Institute of Chartered Secretaries and Administrators (ICSA) has produced guidance notes[2] for boards, consisting of 35 matters that should be reserved for the board's decision including:

- Clarification of which transactions require multiple signatures;
- Which matters should be delegated to board committees;
- Approval of the company's long-term objectives and commercial strategy;
- Oversight of the company's risk management strategy;
- Approval of the financial statements;
- Changes in accounting policies and dividends; and
- Board appointments.

It is also important that directors, particularly outside directors, receive regular and comprehensive information about the company's operations and important strategic issues.

ENGAGEMENT, DIVERSITY, AND TEAMWORK

Effectiveness is also a function of the level of engagement and quality of interaction at the board level. Directors must be actively involved, both at the board level and in individual committees. This requires regular attendance, keeping informed, and ensuring that the board process is conducted with the appropriate level of constructive criticism. Collegiality must be balanced with the readiness to challenge the chairman, CEO, or other directors. They learn to work as a team, and avoid fractious behavior, but not necessarily avoid conflict or expressions of differences in opinion. Increasingly, boards conduct regular self-evaluations, in addition to the evaluations of the CEO. Training also can be an effective way to ensure that board members have the appropriate skills in directorship, particularly as the roles of boards and board committees have been recently subject to new rules of compliance and best practice. Meaningful equity ownership by board directors can help to ensure personal engagement and the alignment of directors' interests with those of minority shareholders.

Board diversity is an important theme, extending beyond the issue of independence alone to consider other aspects, including range of experience, skill sets, and perspectives. "Softer" issues that are focused on increasingly include aspects of diversity by nationality, race, gender, and age, to bring vitality and diverse perspectives, and to avoid stolid and homogeneous boards that can otherwise run the risk of being myopic.

GLOBAL DIFFERENCES

The composition of boards varies widely from country to country. In the United States, a market characterized by a widely dispersed shareholder base and where shareholder primacy is widely advocated, boards typically consist of a number of nonexecutive directors (some of whom may be independent) and few executive directors (often just the CEO or sometimes the CEO and the CFO). It is common in the United States for the CEO to combine the role with that of executive chairman and president. Thus, chief executives in the United States have significant power over the boards over which they preside, as they oversee both the company's and its board's activities.

In the United Kingdom, which also has a widely dispersed shareholding structure and also adopts a shareholder primacy view, the landscape is somewhat different. Relative to the United States, U.K. boards often have more of a balance between executive and nonexecutive directors (a number of whom will be independent). However, this balance is now starting to tilt more toward the inclusion of a greater number of independent nonexecutive directors following the publication of the revised Combined Code by the Financial Reporting Council in July 2003,[3] which made a number of key amendments to the existing Code including the following:

- At least half of the board of larger companies, excluding the chairperson, should be independent, nonexecutive directors.
- There should be separation of the chairperson and CEO roles— the chairman should satisfy the criteria for independence on appointment, but should not, thereafter, be considered independent when assessing the balance of board membership.
- The criteria for independence are defined.

In some continental European countries, such as Germany, the Netherlands, and Austria, the board system consists of two separate boards—the supervisory board (the nonemployed element) and the management board (the executives of the business). Typically, the supervisory board is responsible for the approval and evaluation of strategy, the monitoring of performance, and the appointment and dismissal of the management board and the monitoring of its performance. The management board is responsible for the day-to-day operations of the business and is charged with regularly reporting to the supervisory board.

In emerging economies where many of the companies have been created from the nationalization of state-owned enterprises or in countries where family-controlled companies are prevalent, the board will typically be dominated by management directors or owner-appointed directors. This can lead to problems for minority shareholders in situations where controlling shareholders have little regard for their interests, as there are no, or few, independent directors to provide checks and balances.

Proponents of the two-tier board system claim that unitary boards lead to conflicts within the board, with one group of directors (the nonexecutive directors) supervising another group (the executive directors), and that the executive directors have far too much influence over the business to the detriment of shareholders. Opponents of the two-tier system often claim that supervisory boards frequently lack true independence, are riddled with conflicts of interest (particularly in economies where representatives of cross-shareholders are present), are often less focused on shareholder value than unitary boards, and have less contact with management.

The unitary board continues to be the dominant structure around the world. In a March 2001 guide, *"The Board Agenda"—Good Practices for Meeting Market Expectations*, PricewaterhouseCooper's Global Corporate Reporting Group made a study of 80 leading companies from around the world including Asia, Latin America, the United Kingdom, Europe, the United States, and Canada.[4] Of these, 87 percent had unitary, or one-tier, boards.

INDEPENDENCE

Independence of judgment is one of the most important contributions that directors can make to the board. Therefore, the extent to which the board is comprised of truly independent directors is one of the most distinguishing factors about a company's entire governance framework.

For purposes of this chapter we define three principal categories of director.

1. *Executive directors* (sometimes referred to as *employed directors*). These are senior employees of the company who are elected to the board. They are responsible for the day-to-day operation of the company, and by definition are nonindependent;

2. *Nonindependent and nonexecutive directors* (often referred to as *nonemployed* or *outside* directors). These directors are usually elected to the board by the shareholders but are not classed as independent of management, possibly because of close commercial ties with the company or previous employment with the company; and

3. *Independent nonexecutive directors*. These directors are usually elected to the board by shareholders and have no previous ties or commercial relationships with the company. They are often viewed as being the most objective when taking minority shareholders' interests into account.

The distinction between nonindependent and independent nonexecutive directors was highlighted in paragraph 4.12 of the U.K.'s Cadbury Code.[5] It emphasizes the point that outside directors are not necessarily independent just because they are not part of the current executive team. There may be other past or existing relationships between such outside directors, which could compromise full independence.

While the concept of independence is embraced in the abstract, it can be less clear-cut in application to individual directors. After the recent corporate governance failures in the United States, the New York Stock Exchange (NYSE) has proposed a set of tighter rules[6] governing the structure and composition of the boards of directors of listed companies. The proposals tighten the definition of independence, including specification of relationships that negate independence and cooling-off periods to allow for subsequent reclassification as independent. For example, no director who is a former employee would be considered by the NYSE as "independent" until 5 years after the employment has ended. In addition, the NYSE also is proposing to tighten the definition of independence for members of the audit committee.

These attempts to more explicitly define independence reflect an attempt to more clearly distinguish "true" independent directors from other "outside" directors. Experience has taught how prior relationships, even loose connections through families, schools, charities, or other social structures, can compromise independence, either overtly or subtly. However, even as these definitions become more sophisticated and detailed, defining "true" independence may be elusive in practical terms. An active and assertive "independence of mind," *vis-à-vis* a company's chief executive, chairman, or other senior management, is not necessarily assured by directors who simply satisfy granular independence criteria. Moreover, it also is not necessarily the case that certain directors who do not satisfy this independence criteria are incapable of exercising an independent voice.

For true effectiveness, independence must be linked with true engagement. In other words, even if a director is independent it means little in practical terms if the director makes little effort to keep informed, to be engaged, and to actively participate in the board process. It also may mean little if the independent director is vastly outnumbered on the board, with a role that is little more than a "token" of independence. Companies need to be assessed on a case-by-case basis in this context.

CHAIRMAN/CEO ROLES

The debate regarding the combined or split roles of the chairman and CEO warrants particular mention. As noted earlier, there are different

practices in place globally, and this is an area that has received considerable attention in the post-Enron era of governance reform. In the United
States, the business culture has historically placed a significant amount of
power in the hands of the CEO, who typically also holds the position of
chairman of the board as well. The PricewaterhouseCooper's study (see
note 4) found that in less than 30 percent of U.S. companies the CEO and
chairperson positions were separate, whereas there was substantial separation at U.K. companies, and notably higher levels of separation of these
two roles in Asia, Europe, Japan, Latin America, and Canada.[7]

Proponents of dividing the roles argue that combined roles concentrate too much power in the hands of the CEO and that combining two
vitally important roles risks neither role being conducted effectively.
Opponents of dividing the roles argue that the CEO is best placed to
understand the business and therefore guide other board members. The
combined role structure creates less potential for confusion of roles, and
advocates of the combined role argue that it is more efficient and allows
for more agility in the commercial arena. The debate for splitting the roles
in U.S. corporations seems to be gathering momentum. Notably the
Conference Board's commentary on corporate governance calls either for
the chairman/CEO roles to be split or for a presiding director role to be
established to provide independent directors with a more explicit voice in
the boardroom.[8]

The governance scoring criteria at Standard & Poor's does not explicitly endorse one approach or the other in this regard. The analytical
process focuses on board dynamics and seeks evidence to appreciate the
balance of power between the chairman, CEO, and other board members.
This evidence comes from director interviews and the inspection of board
papers. The split of the chairman and CEO roles is "cleaner" in many
ways. However, in such cases the analytical process seeks to identify the
existence of fractious or divisive factions. In cases where the chairman and
CEO roles are combined, the focus is on whether independent directors
can meaningfully exercise their voices. This needs to be monitored on an
ongoing basis. In structures where concentrated power exists in the form
of a combined chairman/CEO, the introduction of alternative structures,
such as a presiding director or lead director, can establish a constructive
mechanism to support the independent voice of the directors.

Presiding or lead independent director structures are a relatively
new concept, and in many ways are still being tested for their effectiveness in practical terms. Explicit presiding director or lead director structures may have their merits in building a more formalized framework for

the board's independent directors to exercise their independence. However, these structures, and the individual roles, need to be carefully considered and defined. In particular, concerns often are expressed by companies with an established combined chairman/CEO role that the enforced introduction of a presiding director system could lead to greater board fractiousness.

Why Is Executive Compensation Important to Board Effectiveness?

It can be difficult to construct executive compensation schemes so that the interests of directors and senior executives are aligned with those of shareholders—namely that senior management is motivated to deliver long-term and sustainable returns to shareholders and is compensated appropriately if they achieve this goal. Guiding principles in this context are that pay should be linked to performance and that the executive compensation should be determined with appropriate independence: Managers should not set their own pay levels.

Executive compensation is a particularly important area of responsibility for the board, and warrants analysis as a standalone factor. A key function of the board is to attract, motivate, assess, and retain able senior executives. The compensation process is at the center of this, and can be a way to observe how the company's board interacts with its senior executives. In particular executive compensation is a statement on how the board values its own senior management. It is also a way to assess the extent to which the board does—or does not—stand up to a powerful chief executive or other senior managers.

Executive compensation has to be designed to enable companies to recruit, retain, and motivate their senior staff. Increasingly, shareholders require transparency in the reporting of the remuneration of directors and senior executives—this transparency is an anathema in certain countries. For example, in many European and Asian countries, it is unusual to find disclosure of directors' and senior executives' pay in companies' annual reports or annual statutory filings. Indeed, where there is disclosure, this is often an aggregate amount covering all directors and senior executives of a company and tells the investor very little of use.

In much of the developed world and particularly in the United States and the United Kingdom, where there is greater disclosure about remuneration, many studies have shown that executive remuneration has risen at a much faster rate than average earnings for base salaries and performance-related pay (annual bonuses and equity-related rewards, e.g., share option schemes). An often cited frame of reference for the United States is that the ratio of pay for a CEO to an average employee has gone from 40 to 1 to as much as 400 to 1 over the past generation or so. It is certainly not the case that all companies, whose managers' compensation increased on this basis, also achieved similar rates of growth or value.

Historically, shareholders have supported high rewards for directors and senior executives if these rewards were linked to tangible performance outcomes, but increasingly many take great exception to the high levels of compensation paid for average and below average performance. In the United States, activist investors are increasingly turning their attention to what they see as excessive executive remuneration. In 2003, according to data by the U.S.-based Investor Responsibility Research Center (IRRC), shareholders filed 275 proxy resolutions that focused on executive remuneration—44 percent of all corporate governance issues. In 2001, executive remuneration was the subject of 19 percent of all governance-related resolutions according to IRRC.

The use of options as a component of executive pay has become the subject of considerable scrutiny, particularly following mega grants of options to CEOs and other senior executives, most notably in the United States. While options have been viewed traditionally as a mechanism to bring about alignment of interests between executive management and minority shareholders, the granting of excessive amounts of options has the potential to encourage a performance timeframe (given exercise dates) or aggressive strategies that are not always consistent with the goals of core long-term shareholders. Option repricing or the providing of corporate loans to executives to cover tax payments upon the exercise of options also have been abuses of the system. This has led many critics to call for companies to expense options in the income statement or, in more extreme cases, to reject the use of options as a form of compensation.

Standard & Poor's Governance Services views options as a legitimate component of an executive pay package, particularly if these carry shareholder approval and are issued as an ongoing program in smaller and more regular intervals—and not in one-shot mega grants. Equity, whether in the form of direct share grants or restricted stock, is viewed by many observers as a more appropriate way of senior executive incentive remuneration, particularly given that it does not cause executives to think in terms of the option exercise date, but rather to consider the long-term sustainable development of the company. To the extent that the expensing of options becomes more prevalent going forward, the benefits of option grants stand to diminish in scope, and it is likely that direct equity will become a more pronounced part of the compensation mix.

For companies that do have extensive option programs, either for senior executives or for a broader base of employees, it is important to understand the dilution "overhang" that comes from outstanding options. The overhang is the amount of dilution to occur if all options are exercised. High levels of stock overhang can contribute to low shareholder return (the dilution effect). In the United States in 2001, average levels of stock overhang exceeded 14 percent according to some studies. At technology companies the figure was in excess of 25 percent. Most investors do not express considerable concern if this dilution overhang is in the range of 10 to 15 percent over the duration of a specific plan (or plans) or in excess of 2 percent in any one year. But to the extent that the overhang rises materially above these levels or exceeds, this can be a warning bell.[9] Many companies engage in the practice of repurchasing stock on an annual basis to keep employee option grants from resulting in excessive dilution.

Option plans for nonemployed directors, common in the United States, are also controversial, particularly in the United Kingdom. Although paying nonexecutives in shares can make good sense, with options the incentives are different. As Sir Adrian Cadbury has noted, the figure for reported profits in any year is a matter of judgment, but one which influences option values. And the effect of a rise in share price on option values is, of course, leveraged. It is therefore helpful, says Sir Adrian, to have some board members whose judgment on the subjective elements of accounting is entirely disinterested. Similarly, the Association of British Insurers (ABI) has taken a similar stance arguing that being part of an option scheme could compromise the judgment of nonemployed directors.[10]

In conclusion, directors and executives should be fairly remunerated and motivated to ensure the success of the company. Directors and executives should be compensated in a fashion that rewards excellent service, not marginal performance, and enhances directors' links to shareholders. The board's role is to ensure appropriate rigor, fairness, and independence in the setting of compensation policies and in the determination of specific compensation awards.

ANALYTICAL FRAMEWORK

In its governance scoring methodology, Standard & Poor's breaks down the analysis of board structure and effectiveness into the following subcategories:

1. Board composition and independence
2. The role and effectiveness of the board
3. Director and senior executive compensation

Board Composition and Independence Analytical Framework

FACTOR   *A board should be structured in such a way as to ensure that the interests of all the shareholders may be represented fairly and objectively.*

The focus here is specifically on the observable structural features of the board. The general structural categories include board size, composition, leadership, committees, skill sets, and diversity. These are elaborated in the listing of questions below.

Questions to guide assessment of board structure

♦ How many directors are on the board?
♦ What is the composition of the board of directors in terms of
   ♦ Executive versus nonexecutive directors?
   ♦ Independent versus nonindependent directors?
♦ Is there a separation of the roles of chief executive officer and chairman (unitary boards)?
♦ Is the chairman an executive director or a nonexecutive director? If an executive director, is there some effort taken to identify an independent deputy or senior director to lead the nonexecutive element of the board?
♦ What board committees exist (audit, nomination, compensation, etc.)?
♦ Is there some consideration of the composition of committees in terms of executive and nonexecutive directors?
♦ Do any members of the board represent certain shareholder or groups of shareholders' interests (e.g., state, employee, etc.)?
♦ How does the selection process take the professional qualifications of the proposed directors into account in order to ensure that they have the required skills/experience to contribute in a meaningful way to the board's functioning?
♦ What skill sets are present? What skill sets are lacking? Do any directors have a technical understanding of or experience in the company's sector?

- Is the board sociologically homogeneous, or is there a diversity of nationality, race, gender, and professional experience?

FACTOR   *A significant proportion of the nonexecutive directors should be truly independent and act as such. Independent or outside directors should ensure that the interests of all stakeholders are being respected.*

The focus here is on the independence of individual directors and, by extension, of the board as a whole. "Independent" directors are a subset of nonexecutive directors. An independent director is a nonexecutive director who has no present or former employment by the company or any significant financial or personal tie to the company or its management that could interfere with the director's loyalty to the shareholders.

Questions to guide assessment of independence

- What is the proportion of independent to total directors on the whole board?
- What committees are comprised of a majority of independent directors?
- Are any committees comprised 100 percent of independent directors?
- Where there exist committees with independent director membership, what degree of delegation of the control functions to these committees exists? Do committee charters exist?
- What are the criteria for independent director qualification?
- How many external directorships do nonemployed directors have?
- Are there cross-directorships, i.e., directors who sit on each others' boards?
- Do any directors have contracts of longer than 1 year?
- How often do directors have to offer themselves up for reelection? Are members of the board and managers required to disclose their material interests in transactions or matters affecting the company?
- Is there true independence of directors: absence of any monetary, commercial, or social relationships with the company that might impair the duty of loyalty to shareholders as a whole? If a director has an equity stake, does it reinforce alignment with minority shareholders, or might it be of a sufficient magnitude that could create an alternative set of interests?

- Is there any evidence to suggest that nominally independent directors are not independent in fact? Where directors are not judged to be completely independent, identify how they are associated with the company or its management.
- What materials are sent to independent directors before the meeting? Are they the same as for employed directors?
- Do independent directors ever complain about insufficient information?
- Do the independent directors ever meet alone?
- How are independent directors compensated?
- Are there any other routes by which independent directors are paid other than directly for their services on the board?
- Do independent directors feel that their role on the board is valued and meaningful?

Strongest Analytical Profile: Board Structure and Independence

- *Board size:* The size of the board is appropriate for the size and nature of the company. This will vary from company to company and from industry to industry. As a standalone factor, the size of the board should not be weighted too highly in an analysis of the governance standards of a particular company. Nevertheless, for most publicly traded companies, boards of between seven and fifteen members are commonplace, although companies with two-tier board systems would be expected to have a combined total in excess of fifteen.
- *Skill mix:* There is evidence of a transparent, formalized, and clearly articulated director-selection process that considers the professional qualifications, competencies, and other commitments of the proposed directors into account in order to ensure that they have the required skills and experience to contribute in a meaningful way to the board's functioning. There is a diverse board and, in the case of companies with a significant international presence, the board has international representation. The company regularly goes through a formal process to review the balance and effectiveness of the board. The company also has a nomination committee, comprising (in the case of unitary

boards) of a majority of nonexecutive directors to consider the balance of the board and to consider whether or not directors retiring or reaching predetermined age limits are put forward for reappointment at the next shareholders' meeting.

♦ *Chairman/chief executive officer split roles (unitary boards):* The CEO's influence is balanced by the presence of a separate nonexecutive independent chairman (who is not a former CEO). If the chairman and CEO roles are combined, there is a lead or presiding independent director or an alternative way to demonstrate appropriate leadership for the board's independent directors. In the case of two-tier board systems, there is clear separation between supervisory and management boards and the chairman of the supervisory board is not a former executive of the company and meets other independence criteria.

♦ *Nonexecutive director selection:* The company has a transparent and articulated policy with respect to nonexecutive director (NED) selection, revealing a concern for the amount of time, quality, and independence of involvement that each NED is able to give to the board. There is clear evidence that these criteria have been used in making board appointments.

♦ *Directors' appointment process:* All shareholders in general meetings approve all director nominations. The nomination committee (or supervisory board, in the case of two-tier boards) proposes nominated directors to the shareholders' meeting for final approval. Shareholders are given sufficient information about the rationale for the directors' nomination and are able to vote for each director separately, not via a combined resolution.

♦ *Director shareholdings:* The interests of shareholders, executive management, and directors are aligned closely. Accordingly, directors and senior executives have meaningful shareholdings (relative to their individual financial positions) to ensure appropriate engagement. If individual director shareholdings approach the size of a material blockholding (10 percent or greater), there is no evidence that the director has an agenda that is separate from that of other minority shareholders.

♦ *Board independence:* In the case of unitary boards, a clear majority (two-thirds or more) of board members are independent. The presence of independent directors is particularly important in the case of widely held companies as they are able to look after the interests of a large number of small shareholders that individually have little influence on the company. In companies where there is a large blockholder or majority shareholder, independent directors can act as a balancing influence on management or majority shareholder-elected directors. There is also clear evidence that the role of the independent director is recognized as such, e.g., there is a separate committee for independent directors (such as the chairman's committee) and/or special meetings organized for independent directors only — enabling them to discuss control issues separately from executive directors. In the case of two-tier boards, a transparent process by shareholders appoints the supervisory board and a majority of at least two-thirds meet "independence" criteria. Independent directors have open access to company information and have the ability to engage external experts to assist in particular areas.

♦ *Role of independent directors:* Independent directors play a meaningful role on the board, and exercise true independence of mind in board discussions and decisionmaking.

♦ *Range of board committees:* In the case of unitary boards, there are board committees that address all the main control functions, i.e., audit, remuneration, nomination, and any other appropriate functions (e.g., risk and governance). The supervisory board performs at least some of the functions of these committees in a two-tier board system.

♦ *Composition of board committees:* Each of the control function committees are composed of a majority of independent directors. The remuneration and audit committees are composed entirely of independent directors. The audit committee consists of at least one member who has explicit financial expertise, and all audit committee members are financially literate.

Role and Effectiveness of the Board: Analytical Framework

FACTOR *The board should bear overall accountability for the oversight and control of the company.*

Establish the extent to which the board determines, or influences to a significant extent, the direction of the company, sets performance objectives for management, and places limits on the discretion of management. In order to do this, one should, at a minimum, interview at least two independent directors (of which one should be the chairman of the board audit committee), and the chairman or CEO. One also should request to see the board minutes, the package that the members receive before board meetings, the audit reports used by and presented to the board audit committee, and possibly the business plan.

Questions to guide the assessment of board role and effectiveness

- Does the board determine or influence:
    - Corporate strategy?
    - Major plans of action?
    - Risk policy?
    - Annual budgets?
- Does the board identify and articulate key matters reserved for board decision?
- Does the board:
    - Set performance objectives?
    - Set parameters for major capital expenditures, acquisitions, and divestitures?
    - Monitor implementation and corporate performance?
- How actively is the board involved with the review of the:
    - Company's operating performance?
    - Strategic direction and key strategic decisions?
    - Key commercial decisions and urgent matters (e.g., takeover approaches)?
    - Approval of interim and final financial statements?
    - Approval of interim and final dividends?
    - Approval of any significant changes to accounting standards?
    - Approval of auditors' remuneration?
    - Approval of appointment of auditors?
    - Review of the audit process?
    - Approval of resolutions to be put to a shareholders' meeting?
    - Review and approval of the company's medium and long-term strategy?
    - Review and approval of the company's annual operating budget?
    - Review and approval of the company's risk management policies?

- ♦ Approval of related party transactions and major transactions?
- ♦ Review and approval of board appointments and the terms and remuneration of directors?
- ♦ Does the board determine and award executive compensation?
- ♦ How does the board inform itself? How frequently are board members provided information by the company?
- ♦ Is there evidence that board meeting agenda setting, papers, and subsequent discussion of major issues are timely and complete and directly address shareholders interests?
- ♦ Does the board require disclosure of, and actively review, the terms of related party transactions and large transactions to ensure fairness?
- ♦ Does the charter provide an indemnity for directors? What is the scope of any insurance provided to directors (i.e., managerial protection mechanism)?
- ♦ Does the board review, and reserve the right to approve, the external directorships of its executive directors?
- ♦ Are nonemployed directors able to devote sufficient time to their duties? Do they have too many other directorships, activities?
- ♦ Do the board members have many outside responsibilities, including other directorships?
- ♦ What is the attendance rate at board and committee meetings? Is there an indication of an individual member having an attendance problem?
- ♦ Are there any pending lawsuits involving the company or any of its directors?
- ♦ Has the board approved all of the directorships of the CEO? If the CEO serves on more than three or so boards, has the board asked how the CEO has time for these additional responsibilities?
- ♦ Does the board conduct self-evaluations?
- ♦ What are the criteria on which the board judges the CEO's performance? Are nonfinancial criteria taken into account, along with financial performance targets?
- ♦ Does the company provide training for board members?

FACTOR *The board should be ultimately responsible for the system of internal control at a company.*

Questions to consider in assessing the internal control environment

- Is the board actively involved in providing direction to the organization with regard to internal control procedures?
- Where does the area of control exist at the board level? Is this at the audit committee or is there a separate risk management/internal control committee?
- What is the nature of board level discussion of the following:
  - Nature and extent of risks, both financial and operational?
  - Extent/categories of risk board finds acceptable?
  - How the board monitors risk: internal reporting content and frequency?
  - Likelihood of risks happening?
  - The company's ability to reduce the likelihood of these risks appearing, and the ability to reduce damage/impact if they do occur?
  - Costs/benefits of controls in relation to specific risks?

Strongest Analytical Profile: Role and Effectiveness of the Board

- *Lines of responsibility:* The board has clearly articulated for itself a set of matters reserved for its discretion. It has defined an appropriate scope of oversight and control procedures and responsibilities.
- *Adequacy of information and reporting systems:* The board receives quality information memoranda on a timely basis and is able to act on a fully informed basis always. Directors generally receive board papers, associated research notes, and explanatory notes for agenda items at least 7 days before board meetings. Audit committee members receive more frequent (monthly) updates, summarizing financial performance and key risk exposures relative to budget or policy parameters.
- *Notice of board meetings:* Directors receive adequate notice of forthcoming board meetings so that they have sufficient time for

preparation and can research specific issues. Directors receive at least 30 days' notice for regularly scheduled board meetings and have procedures in place for urgent matters. For regularly scheduled board meetings, directors generally receive information at least 7 days prior to the meeting.

♦ *Frequency of board meetings:* The board meets frequently enough so that it is able to effectively discharge its duties to shareholders and other stakeholders. Typically, most large companies have a minimum of six to eight board meetings each year. During exceptional circumstances (for example, major corporate transactions such as takeovers or bids), the board meets significantly more frequently, sometimes on a daily basis.

♦ *Strategy setting, implementation, and monitoring:* The board approves and monitors the strategic direction of the company. Individual board members understand the strategic goals of the company and review progress regularly.

♦ *Delegation to management:* The board ensures that the day-to-day running of the company is delegated to management and that clear distinctions exist between executive and board responsibilities.

♦ *Setting executive limitations—the ethical boundaries of the business:* The board ensures that senior executives adhere to ethical considerations and that these are clearly defined, articulated, monitored, and reviewed. The company has a code of ethics and enforces annual employee confirmation of adherence to the code.

♦ *Effectiveness in monitoring the system of internal controls:* The board demonstrates a strong commitment to articulating, implementing, monitoring, and reviewing internal control procedures. A sound system of internal control is in place to safeguard shareholders' investments and the company's assets. Effective financial controls are also in place, including proper accounting records to ensure that the company is not unduly exposed to otherwise avoidable financial and operational risks.

♦ *Frequency of main control committee meetings:* The main control committees meet frequently enough to enable them to conduct their business in an efficient, effective, and timely manner. Although most of the main control committees (e.g., nomination and compensation) meet less frequently than full board meetings, the audit committee meets more frequently—often more than six times each year.

♦ *Risk management:* The board is actively involved in the identification, assessment, and monitoring of key business risks to safeguard shareholders' investment and the company's assets. The board, at least annually, reviews the effectiveness of the company's annual risk management procedures. Companies with particularly complex risks such as banks, insurance companies, and other nonbank financial companies, may find the need for a separate risk committee of the board comprised of directors with relevant knowledge and experience.

♦ *Monitoring management's performance:* The board and the relevant control committee members carry out regular evaluations of the performance of the employed directors, particularly the CEO.

♦ *Succession planning:* The board and the relevant control committee meet regularly to review the succession plans for employed directors and senior level managers. The board also meets regularly with senior management to assess their capability to lead the management of the company in the future.

♦ *Evaluation of the board's own performance:* The board carries out regular evaluations of its own performance, facilitated by an independent evaluator. The board does not receive excessive indemnification of liabilities for bad faith or breaches of duty and care.

♦ *Attendance at board meetings:* All directors regularly attend board meetings in person or, if not practicable, attend via conference call if appropriate. All directors attend at least 75 percent of board meetings each year.

♦ *External commitments of external directors:* The external directorships of the CEO and other executive directors are not excessive and do not interfere with their executive duties. The board approves all external directorships held by the external directors. The nonexecutive directors are able to devote sufficient time and energy to their duties. Nonexecutive directors do not have an excess of similar positions. While it is risky to be prescriptive about the maximum number of directorships a director should have and each individual's workload and capabilities have to be evaluated on a case-by-case basis, generally, more than six to eight directorships should be considered as excessive—significantly less for the chairman of the board and audit committee.

♦ *Board cohesiveness:* While it is unrealistic to expect unanimity on every issue, the board displays no signs of habitual division. Board minutes and voting records of directors support this.

♦ *Self-evaluations:* In addition to assessing the CEO and executive management, board members also assess their own performance in a serious, but collegial, way.

♦ *Training:* Directors, particularly key committee members, receive further training into the roles and responsibilities of being directors.

Directors and Senior Executive Compensation Analytical Framework

FACTOR *Directors and executives should be fairly remunerated and motivated to ensure the success of the company.*

Analytical instruction
Establish the extent to which directors and executives are compensated in a fashion that rewards excellent service, not marginal performance, and enhances directors' links to shareholders. A significant component of total remuneration should be in the form of equity. Information sources can include: executive and director contracts, compensation policies, and compensation reports from executive recruitment firms.

Questions to guide assessment of executive compensation

♦ How are directors and executives remunerated? Indicate form of payment: cash base salary, cash bonus, shares, share options, benefits (e.g., health insurance, car, pension, etc.).

♦ Does compensation include salary and significant at-risk components? If so, does the at-risk component include performance hurdles?

♦ If compensation includes performance elements:
  ♦ Indicate performance evaluation periods.
  ♦ What performance measures are used?
  ♦ Do salaries have a defined relationship to salaries in industry peer groups?

- Are stock options and restricted stock awards integrated with other elements of compensation to formulate a competitive package?
- Is compensation appropriate in light of the current financial rewards to shareholders and employees?
- What comparator groups are used to set remuneration policy? Where does the company position its own executive remuneration relative to its comparators?
- Does a compensation (remuneration) committee of the board determine compensation? Is the committee composed exclusively of independent directors, or at least exclusively of nonexecutive directors? Is care taken to avoid interlocking compensation committee membership with other boards?
- Is there full and clear disclosure of all significant compensation arrangements in a form such that shareholders are able to assess the reasonableness of the entire compensation package? Is there any evidence that senior executives participate in decisionmaking on their own executive compensation plans?
- Do board members or controlling shareholders have a personal interest in individual transactions in which the company is engaging?
- Has the remuneration committee ever approved or discussed repricing existing options?
- Do shareholders have a right to approve equity-related plans?

FACTOR *There should be clearly articulated performance evaluation and succession policies/plans for employed directors of the company.*

Questions to guide evaluation of succession policies

- Is there any evidence that the board requires succession plans for senior management to be considered and meets senior management with a view to assessing their capability to lead the management of the company?
- What are the arrangements for the board to evaluate its performance and that of individual directors (including CEO) and the performance of other senior executives? Is there a minimum of an annual review of performance by the board that measures results against appropriate criteria defined by the board?

Strongest Analytical Profile:
Senior Executive and Director Compensation

♦ *Performance-based pay:* Clearly articulated policy linking pay to performance.

♦ *Independence of executive compensation setting:* Executive compensation is decided on by a board committee composed exclusively of independent directors. The committee receives independent advice regarding pay and salary structures and has established its own guidelines and benchmarks for senior executive compensation.

♦ *Cash versus equity balance for employed directors:* Shareholders', employed directors', and senior executives' interests are aligned; the remuneration of employed directors and senior executives consists of a significant share-based component in addition to cash. Incentives rewarding longer-term performance are given preference over annual incentives that reward short-term performance. The performance element of pay is (1) a significant portion of total compensation and (2) tied to demanding, but achievable, performance goals that are tied to profit generation and not just to share price alone. There is reasonable peer group benchmarking and some evidence of award and risk for meeting a range of financial and operational objectives.

♦ *Option plans for executive management:* If option plans exist, they are reasonable in size, phased over time, and there is no discounting. Shareholders approve these plans. Executive option plans and all other equity-related plans are approved by shareholders.

♦ *Remuneration plans for nonexecutive directors:* Directors receive enough remuneration to reward them fairly for their increasingly demanding roles. Cash payments are balanced or modest, relative to equity-based compensation. Share-based compensation is more focused on equity or restricted stock; share options are either not used or used at a minimum. The director is not in a position to receive the benefits of the equity or option grant until he or she leaves the board.

♦ *Process for determining compensation of employed directors:* Employed directors and senior executives are not involved in the determination of their own pay and do not seek to exert any improper influence over any of the members of a committee established to determine their pay. A board committee composed entirely of independent directors determines the compensation of employed directors and senior executives. External and independent remuneration consultants, where appropriate, provide advice to the board committee about suitable remuneration schemes and the committee has sole authority to choose, hire, and dismiss those consultants.

♦ *Performance-based remuneration:* For employed directors and other senior executives, there is a performance contingent element (1) comprising at least half of total compensation (if performance targets are reached), (2) based on performance measures that are related to shareholder value, and (3) that is adequately stretching (both in terms of metrics and in terms of goals). There is also at least a 3-year performance evaluation period, at least one share-based performance metric, some evidence of peer group benchmarking in assessing performance, and some evidence of award and risk for meeting "softer" objectives (i.e., environmental, ethical conduct).

♦ *Disclosure of remuneration (both senior executives and nonexecutive directors):* The company publicly articulates its compensation policies and performance targets for the payout of performance-based compensation. Compensation disclosures indicate what each employed and nonemployed director, and the most-highly remunerated executives below board level, earns broken down into all compensation components; they also document performance measures, performance targets, as well as actual performance and associated pay.

♦ *Option overhang:* Dilution overhang is not excessive and is within industry averages.

SUMMARY

Analyzing a company's board of directors is often the most important, and perhaps the most challenging, aspect of the overall corporate governance assessment. By breaking this analysis into the three subcomponents of board structure and independence, the role and effectiveness of the board, and senior executive and director compensation, we look at the board from different perspectives. There are many aspects of the board, notably structural features and aspects of compensation, which can be scrutinized objectively. These are presented in this chapter. The qualitative assessment of board effectiveness is more difficult to pin down with data from public disclosure or other outside data. While board structure is important, its assessment needs to be balanced with the more human aspects of board performance. This is where interviews with senior managers become important. These can both provide additional information and guide the weighting given to other factors in the analysis.

NOTES

1. Sonnenfeld, J. "What Makes Good Boards Great," *Harvard Business Review*, September 2002.

2. ICSA Guidance Note, "Matters Reserved for the Board," Reference Number 011104.

3. Financial Reporting Council, "The Combined Code on Corporate Governance," July 2003.

4. PricewaterhouseCoopers, " 'The Board Agenda'—Good Practices for Meeting Market Expectations," March 2001.

5. Cadbury Committee, "Report on the Financial Aspects of Corporate Governance," December 1, 1992, chaired by Sir Adrian Cadbury.

6. New York Stock Exchange, Corporate Governance Rule Proposals (reflecting recommendations from the NYSE corporate accountability and listing standards committee as approved by the NYSE board of directors), August 1, 2002.

7. PricewaterhouseCoopers, "'The Board Agenda'—Good Practices for Meeting Market Expectations," March 2001.

8. The Conference Board, "Commission on Public Trust and Private Enterprise— Findings and Recommendations Part 2: Corporate Governance," January 9, 2003.

9. TIAA CREF Policy Statement on Corporate Governance, www.tiaa-cref.org/libra/governance/index.html#app.

10. Association of British Insurers, Guidelines on Executive Remuneration, December 19, 2002.

External Influences on Company Governance: Macro Perspective

Part Three places the assessment of corporate governance at the individual firm in the context of larger macro or environmental forces. Chapter 7 discusses various macro forces, particularly how a broad range of country-related factors can affect individual company governance. This chapter provides a framework for evaluating the corporate governance environment at the country level—the framework used in the country analyses in Part Five. It also addresses the issue of whether companies domiciled in weak governance environments can transcend the constraints of their country of domicile with regard to their governance standards. Of all the external forces, law is arguably the most important force shaping corporate governance practices. Chapter 8 focuses specifically on law and its role in defining corporate governance in countries around the world. It addresses the influence—as well as the limitations—of law and legal reforms in changing company attitudes toward governance and affecting specific company governance practices.

This section also contains two chapters linked by the common themes of accounting and reporting. Chapter 9 focuses on the reporting of earnings. It discusses Standard & Poor's Core Earnings model, an attempt to objectify and provide a consistent underlying basis for computing company earnings. It explores in particular the issues of expensing options, the treatment of pension fund income, and the treatment of write-offs in this context. Chapter 10 explores a broader area of disclosure, relating to social and environmental reporting. It speaks to the importance of this disclosure to address the needs of a broader nonfinancial stakeholder base, and explores the parameters of this disclosure in greater detail.

CHAPTER 7

Country Influences on Individual Company Governance

George Dallas

Country factors can play important, and in some cases determining, roles in setting the environment for corporate governance practice at the individual company level. Attitudes toward corporate governance can vary notably from country to country. Diverse country forces—legal, political, historical, cultural—come together to shape ownership structures, stakeholder priorities, and fundamental attitudes toward the role of the firm in the economy. These, in turn, influence the structures and rules that guide both the culture and practice of corporate governance in individual firms. In particular the country environment can influence the articulation and practical protection of ownership rights, the norms of transparency and disclosure, as well as the tradition of strong, independent board oversight. However, a positive country governance environment does not ensure that all companies in a given country will demonstrate strong corporate governance standards. At the same time, it is generally possible for companies in weak country environments to adopt governance standards that transcend local practice.

PATTERNS OF OWNERSHIP AND CONTROL

Legal tradition, history, and sociological attributes can be used to explain differences in management and governance practices on a global basis. These core factors, in turn, affect ownership structures, as well as the institutions and rules of corporate control. These patterns are often placed into differing country groupings, which are outlined briefly below.

Anglo-American Governance

United States, United Kingdom, and certain commonwealth countries. These countries share a common law heritage, and are characterized by wide ownership dispersion, developed financial markets, a greater market for corporate control, and relatively strong levels of transparency. The primary governance focus is on the shareholder as compared to other jurisdictions. Ownership rights are generally well protected.

Main corporate governance problems:

♦ Ability of dispersed shareholders to control management;

♦ Lack of board effectiveness and independence;

♦ Weak internal controls and risk management;

♦ Excessive executive compensation; and

♦ Short-termism, stemming from continuous capital market scrutiny.

Continental Europe/Developed Asia

Primarily western Europe and Japan. These countries share a continental European, or civil law, influence (French, Scandinavian, and German law). Compared with the Anglo-American countries there is a greater tendency for ownership concentrations, with strong bank relationships often playing an important finance, monitoring, and control function. A somewhat lesser role is played by public capital markets. Industry groupings (e.g., Keiretsu in Japan, the *noyaux dur* in France) or significant family ownership, such as the Mittelstand in Germany, all account for the greater ownership concentrations. Boundaries of the firm also are defined differently; there is often a broader stakeholder approach to corporate governance, particularly with regard to the role of employees.

Main corporate governance problems:

♦ Inequitable minority shareholder rights;

♦ Influences of blockholders and potential for expropriation;

♦ Cronyism;

♦ Influences of external stakeholders;

♦ Less active market for corporate control;

♦ Opacity; and

♦ Lack of board effectiveness and independence.

Emerging Markets

Emerging Asia, Latin America, Middle East, and Africa. Legal influences include both common law and civil law. Previous colonial status can be an important influence on existing structures and institutions. Family ownership is the predominant model, combined, in some cases, with lingering state ownership and financial industrial groupings. There is relatively limited separation of ownership and control, compared to the Anglo-American environment. In certain countries the state plays an overt role in the governance of individual companies. In China, for example, state-owned enterprises warrant special attention with regard to how their governance balances interests of the state with those of private investors.

Main corporate governance problems:

♦ Influence of family blockholders;
♦ Entrenchment of family members in management and board structures;
♦ Susceptibility to government influence;
♦ Cronyism;
♦ Lack of protection of minority shareholders' rights;
♦ Limited market for corporate control;
♦ Poorly enforced accounting standards;
♦ Lack of independent directors; and
♦ Weak board effectiveness.

Transition Economies

Former Soviet bloc, including Russia, Poland, other countries of central Europe and the CIS. State ownership is still important, but diminishing. Other new companies are taking shape or local firms are adapting to governance structures imposed by foreign company direct investment. The legal infrastructure in many transition countries has been affected by its relative inexperience with a free market environment. Most transition economies, perhaps most visibly Russia, have experienced corporate governance-related problems during the process of transition to a market economy.

Main corporate governance problems:

♦ Lack of effective definition and enforcement of ownership rights;
♦ Strong blockholder influences;
♦ Influences of the state that detract from shareholder value;
♦ Limited free float/capital market liquidity;
♦ Weak internal controls;

⧫ Poorly enforced accounting standards;

⧫ Weak board effectiveness; and

⧫ Lack of independent directors.

The above classifications may be helpful in understanding some key drivers of comparative corporate governance structures at the country level. However, such general groupings also require some caution. In particular these individual groupings are so broad that important differences can exist within these categories. For example, there are several notable distinctions in the practice of corporate governance in the United States *vis-à-vis* the United Kingdom, even though the United States and United Kingdom are often grouped together in global comparative analyses. (These similarities and differences will be explored in greater detail in Chapter 16.)

One message from the above description of differing regional governance environments should be underscored: *These differing regional governance systems all have their individual strengths and weaknesses.* In particular, it should be noted that *no one system is without its flaws*; each has actual or potential weaknesses that reflect its underlying structures and circumstances. Hence, even though protection of shareholder rights and transparency standards have been regarded by some as highest in the Anglo-American grouping, the recent governance failures at prominent U.S. and U.K. companies show that no one region or country can be considered to be insulated from corporate governance problems.

UNDERLYING DETERMINANTS OF COUNTRY GOVERNANCE ENVIRONMENTS

The question as to what determines ownership structures and country-specific corporate governance environments is the subject of considerable research. There are many potential explanatory factors, which can vary in importance in individual countries, ranging from "hard" issues of economics and law to "softer" issues of culture, psychology, and religion. The country assessment framework, discussed later in the chapter, is built around four key components: *market infrastructure, legal infrastructure, regulatory infrastructure, and informational infrastructure.* However, before addressing this broad country framework, it is helpful to consider some of the key underlying factors that help to shape a country's governance environment. These factors are interlinked, and form the foundation for the country environment diagnostic framework at the end of this chapter.

Legal Origins

The legal environment is arguably the most important external factor affecting individual company governance. At a fundamental level, it is important to understand both the scope of relevant written law and the effectiveness with which it is enforced.

The "law matters" school of thought is well represented in academic literature relating to comparative corporate governance systems. Among the most referenced recent research in this context is the series relating to law, ownership, and shareholder rights by the academics La Porta, Lopez-de-Silanes, Shleifer, and Vishny (LLSV). A key theme that is highlighted by this team is that ownership patterns are linked to the relative strength or weakness of investor protection at the country level. In other words, in jurisdictions where shareholder rights are strong, there will be more diverse ownership because minority investors can have greater confidence in the prevailing legal system to protect ownership rights. However, in countries with weak investor protection, concentrated ownership is required to provide greater controls and oversight to the controlling block-holder. Protection of ownership rights reflects a country's ability to operate a legal system, which is fair, efficient, consistent, and incorrupt.

The LLSV research focuses in particular on issues relating to legal family origin, and draws particular distinction between *common law* (English origin) and *civil law* (Continental European origin). A provocative conclusion of this research is that civil law is less effective in protecting shareholder rights than common law. While the distinctions between civil and common law have their own historical and political roots, the practical effect today can be expressed in the context of differing degrees of greater "procedural formalism." This concept relates to how effectively or efficiently the prevailing legal system, its court system in particular, is in enforcing the law. In an index constructed to reflect procedural formalism (Djankov, La Porta, Lopez-de-Silanes, Shleifer, 2002) for 109 countries, civil law countries were found to be more formalistic than common law countries, and richer countries were found to be less formalistic than poorer countries.

Looking at legal families alone, however, is too narrow. Whether or not further research supports or invalidates the claims regarding the merits of common law versus civil law, the influence of law also must be viewed in a wider context. Certainly in the case of many emerging economies operating with British common law systems, it is clear that common law alone is not a determinant of an effective legal environment—nor does it necessarily result in widely held ownership structures. Other factors including the stage of economic development, political environment, and even broader cultural issues may be relevant in shaping legal and governance systems.

Culture/Historical Legacy

A country's history, value system, and cultural norms also can affect how business is perceived and conducted. These are often viewed as "soft" issues, inasmuch as they are less subject to precise measurements or metrics. Nevertheless, these factors can be significant forces. Confucian philosophy in Asia, for example, with its emphasis on hierarchy and family loyalty, complements the ethos of the family ownership structures that are pervasive in the region. Conversely, the more aggressive capitalist culture in the United States is consistent with the spirit of individualism that is linked to American history.

Cultural profiles can be developed from aspects of history, religion, language, geography, sociology, and psychology. Studies have attempted to express individual cultures in terms of psychometric attributes. For example, the researchers Hampden-Turner and Trompenaars (*The Seven Cultures of Capitalism*, 1993) surveyed executives in seven distinct countries to identify underlying values that shape the individual country's commercial culture. The explanatory values included individualism versus communitarianism; equality versus hierarchy, time horizon, social status, and the like. Research of this nature can help to explain why some cultures are more individualistic or short termist, whereas others may place greater emphasis on social harmony or have longer-term time horizons.

A particular cultural issue that is important in comparative corporate governance analysis is the prioritization of stakeholder interests. In the Anglo-American world, corporate governance is often viewed exclusively around the interests of the shareholder. And even though much economic theory is built on the basis of the shareholder-dominated model, this does not reflect reality in other jurisdictions, where broader stakeholder interests are more prominent. Japanese corporate governance, for example, places strong emphasis on the employee as a stakeholder. In Germany a similar orientation toward the employee has institutionalized labor representation on company supervisory boards. The continued development of environmental and social reporting and the related agenda for greater attention to issues of corporate sustainable development may lead to further differentiation from country to country based on the relative priorities given to non-financial stakeholder interests.

Political Economy

No company is wholly insulated from its political or economic environment. This is particularly the case in countries with significant state involvement in the economy or in countries with troubled or developing economies. These factors can distract managers and directors from a governance focus on building sustainable shareholder and stakeholder value.

There are relatively few sovereign states active in global financial markets that still espouse explicit communist or socialist structures. Even China, which is both the world's largest country and its largest communist state, is developing a much more market-oriented focus to its economy. However, in both socialist and nonsocialist states, government ownership or influences can be an important dimension to individual company governance practices.

State ownership in particular can raise concerns about the alignment between the public interests of the state and private interests of shareholders—a dual agenda that potentially deviates from the pursuit of financial stakeholders' interests. State ownership also in many cases results in a limited or negligible market for corporate control. Hence, there is greater risk for entrenchment of executives and directors with a bias for state interests relative to minority shareholders.

Even in liberal economies, where largely private forces guide markets, governmental or state interests can affect company governance—particularly for large employers in local communities or companies operating in strategic sectors. State or political influences also can be very important in the setting of regulatory and disclosure standards. Both the regulatory and informational infrastructure environments are fundamental to shaping individual company governance practices, and will be elaborated on in greater detail in the discussion of the country governance analytical framework later in the chapter.

COUNTRY INFLUENCES ON INDIVIDUAL COMPANY GOVERNANCE

Can Macro Governance Environments Be Benchmarked or Rated?

The framework in this chapter can be used to develop a system to benchmark the country influence on corporate governance. The individual country reviews presented later in the book follow this framework, and could be adapted to a country governance ranking or benchmarking exercise. Multinationals, including the World Bank, as well as other organizations, such as Transparency International and the World Economic Forum, have begun to benchmark country governance environments, as have financial institutions such as CLSA and Deutsche Bank. Standard & Poor's has yet to develop an explicit country governance environment score or benchmark to date, but conducts environmental analyses of the countries where it is active in scoring individual companies. Country studies of this nature are presented in Chapters 16 through 18.

Conducting rigorous comparative analysis of differing market, legal, regulatory, and accounting systems in practice is a challenging undertaking requiring diverse perspectives. Particularly with regard to the important, but subjective, interpretation of effectiveness of legal and regulatory regimes, it can be difficult to substantiate differences in the form of a rating system. However, country research continues to build in this direction.

Table 7-1 summarizes the examinations of various country perspectives on corporate governance. For each country we examine several country benchmarks outlined below that speak in different ways to an individual country's governance environment:

- *Standard & Poor's Sovereign Credit Ratings.* This focuses on a national government's financial strength in terms of its ability to meet current and future financial obligations at the macro level. The financial analysis in sovereign credit rating is also complemented with more qualitative assessments of a country's general macro- and microeconomic performance, since these factors can indirectly influence the government's willingness and ability to service its financial obligations. A weak governance environment can negatively influence the assessment of financial market institutions and the corporate sector in the overall sovereign credit analysis. The sovereign credit ratings in this sample run a wide range, from AAA for the United Kingdom, United States, Germany, and France, down to B− for Indonesia. Sovereign credit ratings can be used in a governance context as a general proxy for fundamental economic stability and the robustness of market institutions.
- *World Bank Rule of Law and Regulatory Quality Indicators.* As part of a World Bank project evaluating determinants of country governance environments, World Bank researchers assembled indices of key governance indicators for a wide range of countries

TABLE 7-1

Macro Governance Indicators

Ranking	Country	S&P Long-Term Credit Rating	Rank by S&P Long-Term Credit Rating	WB Regulatory Quality (Scale -2.5 to +2.5)	Rank by WB Regulatory Quality	WB Rule of Law (Scale -2.5 to +2.5)	Rank by WB Rule of Law	Corruption Perceptions Index (CPI) Score (1 to 10)	Rank by Corruption Perception Index (CPI)*
1	UK	AAA	1	+1.32	1	+1.61	1	8.7	1
2	USA	AAA	1	+1.19	2	+1.58	3	7.7	2
3	Germany	AAA	1	+1.08	3	+1.57	4	7.3	3
4	Japan	AA–	7	+0.64	5	+1.59	2	7.1	4
5	France	AAA	1	+0.59	6	+1.22	5	6.3	6
6	Spain	AA+	5	+1.08	3	+1.12	6	7.1	4
7	Italy	AA	6	+0.59	6	+0.72	7	5.2	7
8	South Korea	A–	8	+0.30	9	+0.55	8	4.5	8
9	Poland	BBB+	9	+0.41	8	+0.55	8	4.0	9
10	China	BBB	10	-0.13	12	-0.19	12	3.5	11
11	Brazil	B+	13	+0.13	10	-0.26	13	4.0	9
12	India	BB	11	-0.16	13	+0.23	10	2.7	13
13	Turkey	B–	14	+0.04	11	-0.16	11	3.2	12
14	Russia	BB	11	-1.40	15	-0.87	14	2.7	13
15	Indonesia	B–	14	-0.43	14	-0.87	14	1.9	15

Sources: Standard & Poor's (Note: sovereign credit rating effective as of June 2003); Transparency International (2002), www.transparency.org/cpi; and World Bank (2001).
* The Transparency International rankings here are not the rankings in its CPI 2002, which features 102 countries, but the relative ranking of these 15 selected countries in the CPI, corresponding to rankings ranging from 10th for the United Kingdom to 96th for Indonesia in the full CPI 2002.

around the world. Two of the World Bank indicators presented
in Table 7-1 on rule of law and regulatory quality can be used as
proxies for the legal environment.

♦ *Transparency International Corruption Perceptions Index*. The
Transparency International Corruption Perceptions Index is an
annual poll of polls, reflecting the perceptions of business people
and country analysts, both resident and nonresident, of corruption levels in individual countries around the world. It is produced annually by the Berlin-based organization, Transparency
International (TI). The organization's mission is to fight corruption around the world, in part by making levels of corruption
more transparent. Though indicators that are based on individual perceptions run the risk of subjectivity, the robustness of the
TI Corruption Perceptions Index (CPI) is reflected in the fact that
there is a high degree of correlation between surveys of both residents and nonresidents. The CPI provides an interesting perspective on transparency and corruption standards globally.

Combined together, these various indices show broad correlations
from country to country, even though they address somewhat different
issues. Taking these four factors alone, and grouping them by their relative rank ordering, a composite ranking result shows the leading countries in the sample to be the developed markets of the United Kingdom,
United States, Germany, Japan, France, and Spain. On the other hand, the
emerging and transition economies of Indonesia and Russia ranked consistently in the lower grouping of these individual ranking systems.

Table 7-1 is not presented as a definitive guide to ranking countries
by their corporate governance parameters. To do that properly would
require much more detailed analyses. However, it does provide some
indication of how countries can differ along a range of factors that are
governance related, and perhaps provides at least a starting point to make
more substantive distinctions.

Will Country Governance Standards Converge?

In countries around the world there has been a spate of corporate governance codes and reforms introduced in recent years to raise governance
standards in individual markets. Many of these reform efforts have common themes relating to shareholder rights, transparency, greater board
independence and accountability. Globally focused codes and standards,

such as those promulgated by the OECD or the International Corporate Governance Association, speak to a governance architecture that can be adopted as a global standard.

This raises the issue of global convergence of corporate governance standards. While in many ways there is a growing consensus on broad principles of corporate governance, significant differences in individual governance systems still exist. The differences reflect the market, institutional, and legal environments of individual countries, and result in differences in both interpretation and implementation of corporate governance standards.

Hence, while common themes are beginning to take shape on a global basis, many countries will be approaching these common standards from different starting points. Some countries may be actively trying to adapt to global standards with success; some may be trying, but without success; some may be pretending to try on the surface, but not in earnest; others may not be trying at all. Even for those countries that are pressing seriously for systematic change and improvements, this has to be taken in the context of the country's current political and economic situation, including the legal system, market institutions, and ownership structures. Resulting governance standards for individual countries may only evolve with the pace of change in these larger country structures. This could be a very slow process, with pockets of resistance to change.

Governance scholars (Bebchuck and Roe, 1999; Coffee, 1999) speak to the concept of "path dependency" in this context. This effectively means that historical governance structures and institutional arrangements have large influences on shaping governance structures and rules. This implies a "stickiness" to change on the basis of the costs that would be incurred to overhaul prevailing laws and governance structures, but also on the basis of resistance from those with entrenched interests in the prevailing system. Particularly for companies dominated by blockholders, the private benefits of control may offset any benefits in market valuation that may come through offering shareholders more rights and control.

So while some movements toward convergence are occurring, the pace of change on a global basis is likely to remain slow and uneven. Governance standards are not likely to evolve radically ahead of prevailing ownership structures. And changes in ownership patterns will either take a long time, or in some cases may not happen at all.

On that basis, we can anticipate that countries might act to change and improve their governance environments over time. But this might only be a gradual process. Hence, it is important to remain aware of national differences that affect the governance environment in individual countries. That in some ways may be a constraining factor. But we also need to be alert to companies that seek to transcend their own country's governance environment.

Is a "Sovereign Ceiling" a Relevant Concept for Governance Analysis?

In credit analysis, the concept of a sovereign ceiling means that the credit rating of an individual company can be constrained by the credit rating of its country of domicile. While the approach to sovereign constraints is becoming more nuanced in credit analysis, it is relevant to pose the same fundamental question when evaluating corporate governance in different countries around the world:

♦ Are the various macro/country forces sufficiently strong so as to create an explicit ceiling or limit on the governance rating/evaluation of an individual company?

or,

♦ Can individual companies take specific measures to transcend their domestic corporate governance environment such that their analytical assessment is unconstrained?

While it is important to appreciate country risk factors when looking at individual companies, *it is inappropriate to mechanically limit individual country assessments by some form of sovereign ceiling*. Corporate governance analysis at the company level focuses on what the company does, rather than what is required by law and regulation. Companies can adopt practices that exceed local standards or they also can fall short of prevailing standards.

Particularly in the context of developing an effective governance rating or scoring system, a sovereign ceiling would be self-defeating. Part of the logic of a governance rating system is to provide a positive incentive structure for individual firm improvement. To imply that an individual firm in a weak country environment cannot have anything but weak corporate governance itself is not only wrong, but it also could have perverse implications. Namely, an artificial ceiling might de-motivate a firm from making positive improvements in its own governance standards if such improvements were not reflected in its standalone governance rating assessment.

To address the notion that company governance standards need not be constrained by its country's overall environment, it may be useful to consider a concept that is referred to in financial literature as the "bonding" hypothesis (see Coffee, 2002). This is most often referenced in the context of firms, often from emerging markets, seeking to "bond" themselves with exchanges of higher standards, adapt voluntarily to more stringent listing requirements—and expose themselves to greater legal obligations and penalties. The reasons why firms list on exchanges outside their home countries can be varied. For some companies it may simply be a question of seeking to access multiple sources of capital to lower funding costs or to develop new growth opportunities. For other companies, the motivation for a foreign listing may be more nuanced; product market and labor market forces also can play a role. The Indian software company Infosys is an example of a company that uses governance as a basis of strategic differentiation in its industry and as a way to attract world-class technological talent. In this regard the motivation may lie just as much as a "signalling" mechanism for companies seeking to build brand or reputational equity—to signal to both global investors and their domestic investors that they are world class, and not just provincial, with regard to their governance standards.

Whatever may motivate companies domiciled in weak governance environments to bond with financial markets with a reputation for stronger governance standards, the fact of foreign listing often imposes new disciplines for these companies, effectively "raising the bar" of the company's governance standards. These disciplines can include greater regulatory oversight, tougher disclosure requirements, and the presentation of accounts in accounting standards with international recognition. It also involves submission to the laws and the law enforcement procedures of the market's governing country. Researchers (Coffee) also speak to the notion of "reputational intermediaries," such as lawyers, bankers, and accountants that tend to be involved with foreign companies listing on major global exchanges.

For example, for an Asian, Russian, or Latin American company listing on the New York Stock Exchange, this process typically will involve compliance with SEC disclosure requirements (a 20F filing), presentation of U.S. GAAP accounts, and exposure to arguably more aggressive law enforcement authorities. Particularly following the adoption of the Sarbanes-Oxley Act, those foreign companies listing in the United States will be under pressure (both civil and criminal penalties) to adopt certain governance practices to conform to those that were prescribed in the Act. In most cases, this will result in foreign companies with U.S. listings having more stringent governance requirements than those that prevail in their local markets (though in some cases there may be conflicts of law).

This example of bonding shows the effect that foreign listings can have on a company's governance structures and standards. Many, though not necessarily all, of these effects can exert positive pressure on a company's governance profile. It does suggest that a company can indeed "transcend" the potentially weak governance environment in its country of domicile by adapting to global standards found in leading international capital markets. Listing on foreign exchanges is not the only way that companies in weak governance jurisdictions can demonstrate strong governance standards. But foreign listings, and their incumbent financial and reputational benefits, often do provide a positive discipline in this context. Foreign listings in particular can demonstrate the point that a rigid sovereign ceiling is inappropriate for governance rating or scoring. It is necessary to be aware that the country environment can affect the degree to which shareholder rights are enforced. But it is also important to understand the individual company's firm-specific governance profile in a way that is not mechanically limited by its country of domicile.

Interplay of Country and Company Governance Forces

To reflect the interplay of the country and company forces, consider the series of diagrams that follow. These country and company forces are expressed in the form of a two-dimensional matrix, disaggregating systemic country forces from firm-specific practices. The vertical axis represents the governance environment at the country level: the degree to which the market, legal, regulatory, and informational environments provide a supportive infrastructure for effective corporate governance. The farther away from the origin point, the stronger the country governance influence becomes.

The horizontal axis focuses specifically on the individual company, concentrating on firm-specific factors as outlined in the corporate governance criteria: ownership influences, investor rights and stakeholder relations, transparency and disclosure, and board effectiveness. Again, the farther away from the origin point, the stronger the individual company governance becomes.

F I G U R E   7 - 1

Country Governance Risk versus Firm-Specific
Governance Risk

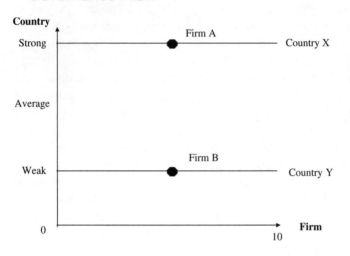

This can facilitate the comparison of individual companies within a national context, as well as comparisons of companies in different jurisdictions. While Firm A and Firm B may have a similar level of overall governance standards, Firm A is in a stronger country environment than Firm B. This suggests that the greatest investor protection is for Firm A, given its country of domicile. Country X presents a more attractive environment than Country Y. Among other things, shareholder rights would be more likely to be enforced more fully in countries with stronger country governance profiles. However, Figure 7-1 also makes clear that a "strong" country support classification does not mean that an individual company from that country necessarily will be highly rated itself. Just as there is no sovereign ceiling, there is also no "floor": An individual company in a positively assessed country can receive a low corporate governance score if so warranted.

At this point in time there is limited empirical evidence linking individual company governance scores with country environments. However, it is reasonable to assume that the two are positively correlated. In other words, one would expect to see high governance standards in countries that reflect strong legal, regulatory, and informational infrastructures; the opposite would be the case in countries that score poorly in this macro assessment. This is reflected in the "hypothetical distribution" reflected in Figure 7-2. This hypothetical distribution is broadly consistent

FIGURE 7-2

Hypothetical Distribution of Corporate Governance Scores

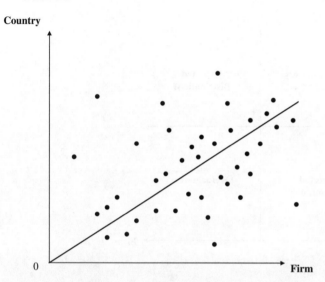

with the experience that Standard & Poor's has had to date in providing corporate governance scores to companies in diverse jurisdictions.

While this distribution does suggest a clear and positive general relationship between country and company governance standards, it also suggests that there will be "outliers"—i.e., cases of strong firm governance in weak country environments, and vice versa. In many ways these "outliers" are the most interesting situations to assess, and need to be properly identified.

In this context, this two-dimensional matrix can be further subdivided into four quadrants, as reflected in Figure 7-3. In so doing, a broad categorization of companies' international governance profiles can be made.

The northeast and southwest quadrants might be labeled the "Expected Distribution" inasmuch as they reflect the broad assumption of a positive correlation between company governance standards and the overall country governance environment. The northwest and southeast quadrants reflect the "outliers," and can be divided into two very different groups:

- ◆ *Underachievers:* Companies in strong country environments whose own governance practices do not meet high standards. Examples include Enron and WorldCom.

FIGURE 7-3

Governance Profiles by Distribution

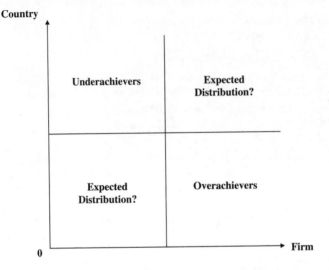

- ♦ *Overachievers*: Companies in weak country environments whose own governance standards can be viewed as high, relative to their country of domicile. Examples could include MobileTelesystems in Russia or Infosys in India.

In this schema, clearly the "underachievers" will have little or no incentive to have their governance standards publicly evaluated or scored. However, the "overachievers"—mostly from emerging economies—are likely to have the greatest interest in receiving governance scores so as to differentiate positively their firms from local peers with lower governance standards. In many cases the overachievers will be bonding with capital markets of the highest standards by listing on these markets, and hence will want to signal to investors that their own governance standards are world class and not merely local best practice.

COUNTRY GOVERNANCE ENVIRONMENT: BASIC CRITERIA AND ANALYTICAL APPROACH

The framework in this chapter can be used to benchmark the country influence on corporate governance along four major components: *market infrastructure, legal infrastructure, regulatory infrastructure,* and *informational infrastructure.* The individual country reviews presented later in the book follow this structure. This provides an important context for assessing governance practices in individual companies.

Market Infrastructure

Country-specific aspects of how markets function can influence the practice of corporate governance. As has been discussed, prevailing corporate ownership structures play a key role in shaping country-specific market institutions and practices. The fundamental distinction between markets with widely dispersed ownership and markets with concentrated ownership structures is particularly important in this context.

The functioning of public capital markets is linked to ownership patterns, and reflects the extent to which companies are publicly listed. This also affects the liquidity and transferability of shares and ownership rights. Corporate governance codes increasingly have been introduced in many different financial markets to guide local governance practices. Differing approaches to public versus private capital markets can be important in understanding the roles of institutional asset managers and banks as investors. In particular, the presence—or not—of a robust market for corporate control can have an important influence on a country's overall governance climate. It also can help the understanding of how bank influence or ownership can affect public transparency and disclosure. This is particularly the case when financial-industrial groups play an important part in the functioning of the market.

The political and general economic environment is in the background in all governance structures, but is likely to be more of a factor in cases where the state plays an active role in the economy or when the overall economy is still developing. In western markets, more liberal government structures and more developed economies often result in less direct state involvement in the private sector. It is also important to be sensitive to cultural factors that might influence the governance environment, which can include differing interpretations of the role of companies in society, the rights of employees, and the rights of other nonfinancial stakeholders.

Certain fundamental governance practices and structures can be seen to differ from country to country. Traditions of board independence, the Chairman/CEO role, usage of takeover defenses, and executive compensation can take very different shapes in countries around the world. Board structure is a good example in this context, particularly with regard to the approach of one- versus two-tiered board structures. These inevitably must be appreciated in the context of local norms. While either structure can accommodate a healthy governance process, the structure should be understood in the context of how the board acts to promote the interests of its financial stakeholders.

Factors to be considered when evaluating a country's market infrastructure

♦ Are there significant ownership blocks/concentrations?
  ♦ State ownership
  ♦ Financial-industrial groups
  ♦ Family/private blocks
♦ Are most major firms listed on public stock exchanges?
♦ Is there ease of access to public exchanges?
♦ Is there an active market for corporate control?
♦ Are nonfinancial stakeholders (employees, community, environmental interest) important governance forces?
♦ Is there a country code of governance that is generally adhered to?
♦ What is the importance of institutional investors (mutual funds, pension funds, insurance companies, etc.)?
♦ Do institutional investors play an important role in advocating governance change or engaging companies on broader stakeholder issues?
♦ Do nongovernmental organizations play an important role in influencing opinion and public policy on governance-related issues?
♦ Is there a universal banking system versus separation between commercial and investment banking?
♦ Do banks commonly hold significant equity stakes in industrial companies?
♦ Are financial-industrial groups prevalent? What is the degree of transparency in their intercompany relationships?
♦ For transition economies and other countries with state-owned enterprises: What methods of privatization exist and what impact do these have on ownership structures?
♦ Do market distortions exist in the form of uncompetitive industry structures or government protection of individual companies or sectors?

♦ Are there signs of macroeconomic stability or stress?
♦ What is the nature of the political environment? Is this relevant to the practice of corporate governance in the country?

Legal Infrastructure

An effective legal environment is essential to good corporate governance. Stakeholders' legal rights should be clearly defined. The judicial process should allow for consistent and effective law enforcement in the event that stakeholder rights are abused. In a broader context, the general rule of law and order is also important. As has been discussed earlier, a country's legal family—particularly between the broad traditions of common versus civil law—can be an important determining factor, possibly affecting the protection of ownership rights and the degree of inefficiency or formalism in the legal structure.

Of the various types of law, *corporate law* is perhaps the most important. Corporate law covers fundamental issues, including how companies are formed, what rights exist for shareholders and other stakeholders, how shares are registered, and the responsibilities of board directors and management. In cases where majority and minority shareholders exist, it is important to understand how minority shareholder rights are defined and protected. *Securities law* ranks prominently with corporate law in assessing a country's legal infrastructure—particularly for listed companies.

Other important areas of law include *bankruptcy and pledge law.* While these are less central, *per se,* to the practice of corporate governance than company law, they nonetheless form an important part of the commercial legal infrastructure. Particularly in the case of bankruptcy law, it is important that creditors and shareholders are in a position to reach settlement on whether to liquidate or restructure an insolvent company.

The effectiveness of *law enforcement* will affect the extent to which financial stakeholder legal rights are relevant in a practical sense. This analysis addresses the fairness and consistency with which laws and regulations are administered. Again, the effectiveness of enforcement for minority shareholders and creditors is a particular focus. The degree of effectiveness of a country's legal system can be assessed through positive and negative practical examples of governance cited in discussions with lawyers and investors.

Factors to be considered when evaluating a country's legal infrastructure

- What are the relevant laws that address corporate governance in the country and its various jurisdictions?
- What legal family: Is there a clear common law or civil law heritage?
- How are shareholder and other stakeholder rights defined?
- What laws exist that govern:
  - Insider trading
  - Reporting and disclosure
  - Duties and composition of boards of directors
  - Shareholder registry and share depository
  - Proxy rights at shareholder meetings
  - Voting procedures
  - Minority shareholder rights
  - Rights of foreign creditors and shareholders?
- Is a shareholder registry necessary to prove ownership?
- Are outside directors required?
- Does a licensed registrar keep the shareholder registry?
- What is the nature of the judicial system in law enforcement?
- Is rule of law weak or corruption high?
- Do examples exist that point to judicial success in promoting and enforcing corporate governance?
- Are there examples of poor corporate governance where the law is not effective in principle or in practice?
- Are there many investor lawsuits involving corporate governance-related disputes?
- What is the track record of these legal processes? What is the timeframe?

Regulatory Infrastructure

The legal and regulatory environments are closely interlinked, with regulatory bodies often being charged with regulating markets to conform to existing laws. Regulatory bodies also attempt to ensure orderly and efficient market environments, and can play a key role in setting and enforcing standards for public disclosure. Regulatory regimes differ on a country-to-country basis, and the system in each country should be understood and evaluated on its own. Regulatory bodies governing specific industries and markets may exist within individual government ministries, a central bank, or may have a more autonomous structure. For investors, the role of securities regulators in supporting effective corporate governance is highly important. Other important regulators may focus on specific interests of financial institutions, insurance, pensions, and on general competitive practices. In many countries, Self-Regulatory Organizations (SROs) or Non-Governmental Organizations (NGOs) exist to complement the regulatory process established by formal government bodies.

Though typically not part of a governmental apparatus, stock exchanges in particular can play an important regulatory role through the listing requirements they impose and the discipline they can exert in terms of public censure and delisting. Listing rule reforms, such as the ones put forward by the New York Stock Exchange and Nasdaq in 2002, can be seen in the context to be a leading force in shaping governance practices and structures in the United States.

Factors to be considered when evaluating a country's regulatory infrastructure

+ What regulatory bodies exist and what is their purview?
+ Are there regulatory gaps or areas in which regulatory responsibility overlaps among bodies?
+ Do the different regulatory bodies work in cooperation or conflict with one another?
+ Are specific regulations commonly viewed by market participants as inappropriate?
+ Do SROs, NGOs, or other interest groups play a role that is relevant from the perspective of corporate governance?
+ What new legislation is on the regulatory agenda?
+ What are the information and timing requirements for public disclosure?
+ How effectively are securities and disclosure regulations followed and enforced?
+ Do regulators have sufficient resources and practical enforcement tools to achieve their mission?
+ Is there a securities regulator? How long has it been in place?

- ◆ What is the relationship of securities and other regulators to stock exchanges?
- ◆ What are some examples of regulatory successes and failures?
- ◆ What are the key stock exchange listing rules? How have these rules evolved since 2000–2001?

Informational Infrastructure

Accounting principles differ from country to country, with differences often reflecting varying business practices, reporting practices (managerial versus tax), and disclosure preferences. The auditing profession also can take different structures. In many key markets, major global accounting firms cover the majority of the listed companies. In other markets local firms, operating on domestic standards, produce and audit financial statements. Standards relating to audit versus nonaudit services from the same auditing firm also can differ on a comparative basis.

For corporate governance to be effective, official regulation of public disclosure should produce company information that is accurate, complete, and timely. Public information should be useful enough to enable existing and potential financial stakeholders to monitor a company's governance, as well as its operating and financial performance. Where information standards are poor, proper corporate monitoring can be either difficult or impossible, leaving open possibilities for corporate governance abuses.

Accounting standards. It is not necessary to endorse one particular accounting system over another, but rather to assess the degree to which standards in individual countries provide meaningful and timely disclosure. In some countries, however, and particularly in emerging economies, accounting standards may be incomplete. In such cases, the use of International Accounting Standards (IAS), U.S. GAAP, or other internationally recognized standards of accounting, can be regarded as a positive feature.

The differences in approach taken by IAS as compared to U.S. GAAP have been characterized increasingly as a debate between the IAS principles-based approach and the more rules-based approach of U.S. GAAP. In particular, the accounting abuses that were associated with Enron and other large-scale U.S. collapses have challenged the leadership status that U.S. GAAP has long held on a global basis. Detailed rules run the risk of being both very technical and also perhaps more subject to "gaming," i.e., living by the rule, but not the spirit, of the law. In this regard, U.S. accounting is now under review with regard to whether a greater emphasis on principles might have a positive impact on preventing further abuses.

Another key issue is that of *fair or continuous disclosure.* This is often reflected in national reporting standards that call for continuous, or more immediate, disclosure of key corporate actions outside the normal annual or semi-annual reporting cycle. The dimension of fair disclosure means that company disclosure is made to the public at large, not to a selected subset. To the extent a particular jurisdiction does not have quarterly reporting requirements, a continuous reporting regime can serve to some extent as a counterbalance or mitigant.

Executive compensation is an important area of scrutiny in governance analysis, and reporting standards differ considerably on this point on a global basis. Notwithstanding a recent history of compensation-related abuses, U.S. disclosure on individual executive and director compensation is arguably the most detailed. In other jurisdictions, there is scant, or negligible, reporting on executive pay practices. This can be viewed by some as an issue of cultural preference, preserving a degree of personal privacy and greater harmony between management and the workforce. Others view disclosure of senior executive compensation as an intrinsic obligation for senior executives who work for publicly listed companies.

A final area of consideration is in the area of *nonfinancial reporting.* This can relate to company-specific areas, including ownership structures, investor rights, voting procedures, business operating performance, and management and board structures. *Social and environmental reporting* also is emerging as new areas of focus. The United Nations–sponsored Global Reporting Initiative represents a major effort to develop more systematic reporting practices on a company's environmental and societal impact.

Factors to be considered when evaluating a country's informational infrastructure

- What is the number, quality, and independence of public auditors?
- Is there a requirement for independent financial audit?
- How do the following accounting standards versus international accounting standards compare?
  - Basis of consolidation
  - Financial position of subsidiaries whose health is material to the interests of the company and individual shareholders

- Segment data: financial performance of individual business or business units
- Methods of asset valuation
- Definitions of revenues, expenses, profits and losses
- Cash flow: sources and uses of funds
- All real and contingent liabilities
- Related party transactions
- Special purpose vehicles
- Evidence of transfer pricing, hidden transfers, or subsidies
- Operating disclosure (e.g., management discussion and analysis)

- Do local reporting standards typically require disclosure relating to ownership structures, investor rights, management structures, business information, and board structures?
- What social and environmental reporting requirements exist?
- What is the frequency of reporting? Is quarterly reporting required?
- Is there ease of access to independently audited financial statements?
- How accessible are regulatory filings to the general public?

SUMMARY

The country environment is a key determinant in shaping governance practices and policies in individual companies. It is important to understand these forces and the extent to which individual companies are shaped by the legal, regulatory, and cultural influences of its country of domicile. However, given the globalization of capital market and a trend toward convergence on many aspects of governance practices, it is also important to recognize that a company's governance practices need not be tied or constrained by its local environment.

REFERENCES

Bebchuck, L. A., and M. J. Roe. "A Theory of Path Dependence in Corporate Governance and Ownership," *Working Paper No. 131*, Columbia Law School Working Paper Series, 1999.

Beers, D. T., M. Cavanaugh, T. Ogawa. "Sovereign Credit Ratings: A Primer," Standard & Poor's *Ratings Direct*, 2002.

Claessens, S., and J. P. H. Fan. "Corporate Governance in Asia: A Survey," *International Review of Finance*, 2002.

Coffee, J. C. "Competition among Securities Markets: A Path Dependent Perspective," Columbia University School of Law, 2002.

Coffee, J. C. "The Future as History: The Prospects for Global Convergence in Corporate Governance and Its Implications," *Northwestern University Law Review*, vol. 93, 1999, pp. 641–657.

Djankov, S., R. La Porta, F. Lopez-de-Silanes, and A. Shleifer. "Courts: The Lex Mundi Project," *Working Paper 8890*, National Bureau of Economic Research, 2002.

Franks, J., and C. Mayer. "Corporate Control: A Synthesis of the International Evidence," *Working Paper*, London Business School and City University Business School, 1992.

Hampden-Turner, C., and F. Trompenaars. *The Seven Cultures of Capitalism,,* Judy Piatkus Ltd, London, 1993.

Ho, S. "Corporate Ownership and the Governance of Listed Firms in China," *Corporate Governance International*, vol. 5, no. 1, March 2002.

La Porta, R., F. Lopez-de-Silanes, A. Shleifer, and R. Vishny. "Investor Protection and Corporate Governance," *Journal of Financial Economics*, vol. 58, 2000, pp. 3–27.

La Porta, R., F. Lopez-de-Silanes, A. Shleifer, and R. Vishny. "Legal Determinants of External Finance," *Journal of Finance*, vol. 1131, 1997.

La Porta, R., F. Lopez-de-Silanes, and A. Shleifer, "Corporate Ownership around the World," *Journal of Finance*, vol. 54, 1999, pp. 471–518.

Licht, A., C. Goldschmidt, and S. H. Schwartz. "Culture, Law, and Finance: Cultural Dimensions of Corporate Governance Laws," *Working Draft*, Interdisciplinary Center Herzliya and Hebrew University, Israel, 2002.

Transparency International, "Transparency International Corruption Perceptions Index 2002," www.transparency.org/.

World Bank, "Governance Research Indicator Country Snapshot 2000/01," www.info.worldbank.org/governance/kkz/sc_country.asp.

CHAPTER 8

The Legal Environment of Corporate Governance

Stephen Wallenstein and Robert Milbourne

Until very recently, investors viewed the United States as the gold standard for corporate governance law and regulation. Times have changed. Infamous governance failures like Enron, WorldCom, Tyco, Global Crossing, and HealthSouth have prompted the U.S. Securities and Exchange Commission (the SEC), the New York Stock Exchange (the NYSE), and others to launch significant reform efforts intended to rebuild investor confidence. Corporate governance failures and their potentially disastrous effects on the marketplace also have affected other markets, contributing, for instance, to the Asian financial crisis of 1997.[1] These failures have led to intense international scrutiny of the legal and regulatory foundations for corporate governance. New laws, regulations, and listing standards are being contemplated on every continent. The resulting reforms and their implications are only beginning to be felt as investors question the effectiveness of legal institutions in protecting shareholder interests.

There are many challenges in evaluating the legal environment upon which investors must rely. Even a well-developed legal system does not necessarily translate into good corporate governance. Indeed, while the U.S. system may be well developed, some investors may nonetheless "suffer" from certain aspects of this development. For example, the emergence of sophisticated techniques, such as the poison pill, and other elaborate corporate anti-takeover protections may in fact harm some investors. And, even though the governance system in the United States is well developed, it failed to prevent the recent corporate disasters or punish the vast majority of those guilty of abuse.

This chapter describes the legal environment impacting corporate governance of publicly traded companies, identifies fundamental legal issues at the heart of reform efforts, and addresses some of the enforcement mechanisms upon which investors must rely. The first part sets forth a general overview of the legal landscape. Next, we describe the role of corporate (or company) law and securities law in the corporate governance system, as well as the regulatory institutions that govern corporate oversight and impact corporate governance. We then describe three key areas that must be addressed by a corporate governance regime—disclosure and transparency, protection of shareholder and other stakeholder interests, and board role and constitution. Finally, we conclude with a discussion of enforcement mechanisms necessary to promote adequate corporate governance practices.

AN OVERVIEW OF THE LEGAL LANDSCAPE

The concept of "corporate governance" as a distinct field within corporate or company law is relatively new. Indeed, countries have generally not developed single unitary bodies of law to address corporate governance, but rather corporate governance practices have emerged from overlapping concerns arising under corporate and securities laws and regulatory and administrative concerns of market institutions such as the securities exchanges. Only recently have regulators, academics, and practitioners begun to pay attention to the adequacy of the regulatory environment in promoting effective corporate governance practice. Indeed, some would argue that the very premises of what constitutes effective corporate governance remain subject to dispute. For example, should the applicable legal framework be designed solely to address the concerns of the shareholders who invest in a corporation, and if so, how should it balance the competing needs of minority and majority shareholders? Should the corporate governance standards explicitly require consideration of the public interest and other stakeholders, such as labor, creditors, customers, or other "outsiders"? Does sound corporate governance require the board to focus on long-term shareholder value or short-term value? While there may not be consensus with respect to the objectives of corporate governance regulatory systems, nevertheless countries have begun to develop sophisticated regulations aimed toward protecting the varied interests at risk from failures in corporate management.

Divergences in corporate governance standards may be explained by a country's stage of economic development, cultural and political factors, the strength of various market participants, and the unique patterns of capital accumulation in different societies. For example, the regulatory structures of countries in which securities are held broadly may be distinct from societies in which securities are held by a small elite. Investors must consider whose interests are being protected by a given country's laws, as well as how the interests of minority and majority shareholders and other stakeholders are balanced. For example, are the interests of labor particularly protected (as in Germany)? Is there a unique role for the state in corporate governance (as in China)? Or do entrenched economic forces dominate the legal environment (as in Germany, Japan, and Korea, with their banking and industrial conglomerates), thereby undermining some investor protections?

The legal framework also will vary depending on whether the country has a common law or civil law tradition. In common law countries, corporate governance has been largely based on broad principles of appropriate conduct. Courts in such countries have often granted liberal discretion to directors and officers when evaluating corporate conduct, choosing not to second-guess business judgment. In civil law countries, corporate governance conventions have been more codified. As corporate failures have emerged throughout the world, regulators in both civil and common law countries are adopting lessons learned by their counterparts. Intriguingly, some civil law countries appear to be adopting more broad based principles, while some common law jurisdictions appear to be moving in the direction of more codified rules and standards.

International Standards
for Corporate Governance

Several recent initiatives have explored the establishment of international standards for corporate governance. The OECD's Principles of Corporate Governance (the OECD Principles), released in 1999, was the first major multinational effort to establish a benchmark for best practices in corporate governance.[2] The OECD Principles recognized that while there is no single model of good corporate governance, there are core standards which all regulatory regimes should seek to address. In the wake of the recent business scandals that have shaken public confidence, the OECD has launched a review of the OECD Principles, which it expects to complete in 2004 after surveying corporate governance developments around the world.[3] In addition, the OECD's Steering Group on Corporate Governance, in conjunction with the World Bank Group, has established regional roundtables in Asia, Russia, Latin America, southeastern Europe, and Eurasia (the Roundtables), which serve as forums to promote better governance, monitor practices, and will issue white papers targeting corporate governance priorities. The Russia region has already issued its white paper.[4]

The International Organization of Securities Commissions (IOSCO) recently recommended that member countries adopt the OECD Principles.[5] Many systems have been evaluated in light of their compliance with the OECD Principles. For example, the World Bank and the IMF have been conducting country Reports on the Observance of Standards and Codes covering 11 internationally recognized core standards for economic stability and private and financial sector development, which rely on the OECD Principles as the corporate governance benchmark against which country compliance is assessed.[6] In a recent review of 15 emerging market countries, the World Bank concluded that "none of the assessed countries comply with the OECD Principles in all respects," though the study noted that all of the countries had begun to undertake reforms intended to bring legal and regulatory frameworks into compliance with the OECD Principles.[7]

The European Union (the EU) recently commissioned a wide-ranging report on corporate law, including corporate governance standards, chaired by Jaap Winter (the Winter Report), which cautioned against creating a unified European code of corporate governance, and instead advocated that each country designate a national corporate governance code which would be based on some fundamental EU recommendations, with the EU providing coordination of guidance on best practices.[8] Each country's code, the Winter Report argued, should be driven by the market and by local customs and concerns, and companies in a country's jurisdiction would be required to either comply with the local code or explain divergent practices. The Winter Report includes such U.S.-based principles as relying on general disclosure requirements to achieve transparency rather than substantive rules. Conversely, in the Sarbanes-Oxley Act of 2002 (Sarbanes-Oxley),[9] the United States has adopted certain rules (such as certification requirements for financial reports) which had their origins in civil law jurisdictions. These ongoing corporate governance reforms may evidence a movement toward convergence across regulatory regimes. Furthermore, the recent governance failures may encourage a new harmonization between corporate and securities laws to create more uniform and coordinated corporate governance controls.

In addition to the EU, IOSCO and the OECD, other international institutions such as World Bank and the IMF, and private, nongovernmental organizations have significantly advanced the efforts toward establishing international corporate governance standards. The Institute of International Finance established an advisory group consisting of leading fund managers, which issued a code of corporate governance best practices for emerging markets (the EAG Code).[10] Other organizations, such as the Conference Board, the Financial Stability Forum, the Pacific Economic Cooperation Council, and the Business Roundtable also have conducted extensive reviews of corporate governance practices with the intent of identifying international best practices.

Efforts to define global standards are very challenging. Standards which provide for a balance between corporate independence and oversight are difficult to legislate, and must accommodate local institutions and cultures. Nevertheless, countries are experimenting with revising their standards to comply with benchmarks such as the OECD Principles, and what may be perceived as international best practice, such as separating the roles of chairperson of the board and CEO, determining the requisite number of "independent" board directors, and clarifying the definition of "independence," and requiring the CFO, CEO, and/or board members to personally certify financial reports.

Cross-Border Aspects of Corporate Governance

Corporate governance reform is primarily a domestic undertaking. Nonetheless, while an investor's sound understanding of an issuer's country's corporate governance framework is crucial, his or her rights also may be subject to the legal regime of other countries, for example, if the issuer's securities are listed and traded abroad. The corporate governance regimes of Brazil and China may be less significant than the U.S. regime for investments in Brazilian or Chinese companies whose securities are listed on U.S. exchanges. Indeed, investors may have more success enforcing rights in the United States against a company whose securities are listed on a U.S. stock exchange, than might be realized by seeking to enforce such rights in the company's country of incorporation.

Indeed, because of the perception that legal protections may be greater in the United States, non-U.S. companies that raise capital in the United States and list on the NYSE may be able to rise above less robust corporate governance regimes in domestic markets through their adoption of new U.S. requirements. However, although formalistic compliance with the requirements of Sarbanes-Oxley may give investors some comfort when investing in non-U.S. companies listed on U.S. exchanges, investors must still pay close attention to the public and private enforcement regimes in particular countries when considering the extent to which the non-U.S. issuer has effectively bridged the legal regime through its adoption of U.S. corporate governance standards.

The Sarbanes-Oxley Act and the NYSE listing standards have already had substantial practical implications for foreign issuers that list and sell securities in the United States. For example, the SEC final rule implementing Section 301 of Sarbanes-Oxley requires such foreign issuers to comply with the new listing standards by July 31, 2005.[11] Prior to Sarbanes-Oxley's enactment, foreign issuers were already subject to increased disclosure requirements and U.S. GAAP reconciliation. In some cases, Sarbanes-Oxley conflicts with comparable corporate governance requirements of the issuer's home jurisdiction.

Responding to concerns expressed by companies operating under different corporate governance systems, the SEC has shown flexibility. For example, under German law, German companies are required to include employee representatives on their supervisory board and audit committee, but such employees do not meet the independence requirements for directors under Sarbanes-Oxley. In a move toward accommodation, the SEC has allowed nonmanagement employees of non-U.S. issuers to serve as audit committee members. Other exemptions from the independence requirements also have been provided to accommodate local practice, such as allowing affiliated parties to serve as nonvoting observers on audit committees where certain criteria are met, and where such parties do not receive consulting or compensatory fees. Companies also may have alternative structures like boards of auditors or statutory auditors to perform auditor oversight where provided under local law, and shareholders may elect, approve, ratify, terminate, and determine compensation of outside auditors if provided under home country law. Other examples of SEC flexibility include the safe harbor for non-GAAP financial information distributed by certain foreign companies, the applicability of pension fund blackout rules only to foreign companies with a large U.S. employee base, and an exception for many foreign lawyers from the attorney conduct rules.[12]

In other areas, Sarbanes-Oxley has proven less accommodating. Despite some efforts to carve out exceptions for non-U.S. issuers, the SEC has not accommodated the request of many foreign issuers to exempt them completely from the requirements of Sarbanes-Oxley. Many foreign regulators, issuers, and media representatives have questioned the right of the U.S. Congress to change the rules for foreign issuers listed in the U.S. capital markets "in the middle of the game." Critics further complain that the extraterritorial application of U.S. corporate governance requirements to non-U.S. listed companies sharply contrasts with the prior reliance on home country law, regulations, and practice. Some foreign corporations have withdrawn applications to list their securities in the United States, citing increased corporate governance burdens resulting from the recent reforms.[13] Indeed a recent study has shown that the costs of compliance with U.S. securities laws for certain companies listed on the U.S. exchanges has nearly doubled since the passage of Sarbanes-Oxley.[14] But, despite these costs, non-U.S. issuers will likely remain interested in listing on a U.S. exchange to send the signal that they can handle stricter governance standards, which is important for their capital-raising efforts.

Cross-border mergers also force convergence of governance practices, resulting in better investor protection and ultimately increasing the value of a company. Target firms import corporate governance systems of acquiring companies from countries with strong shareholder protection, or, acquiring companies from countries with less protective regimes adopt a target company's governance regime through private contracting. Indeed, there is now evidence that some investors may target acquisitions with poor corporate governance standards with the intent that by raising corporate governance practices the value of the target company would increase.[15]

THE LAW OF CORPORATE GOVERNANCE

Corporate governance regimes are founded upon the basic building blocks of *corporate laws* (also known as "company laws") governing how companies are formed and managed, which specify the rights and duties of shareholders, directors, and managers, and *securities laws*, governing the issuance and exchange of securities, which specify, among other matters, disclosure and filing requirements. In addition to corporate and securities law, bankruptcy and insolvency law and the general commercial law regime of a country are critical in assuring the rights of owners, creditors, and other stakeholders, as is the effectiveness of the enforcement regime. Corporate governance laws may be promulgated at the state, regional, or national level. This legal foundation is typically supported by regulations adopted by a country's securities commission and rules and listing standards issued by securities exchanges. This section discusses corporate and securities laws and the regulatory structures that support them. The next section discusses several critical areas that must be addressed by a corporate governance regime, and the last section focuses on enforcement.

The Role of Corporate or Company Law

Laws governing company formation and the conduct of corporations involve regulation of internal operations, including matters such as the permissible scope of corporate activity; board and shareholder meeting requirements; voting procedures; and the powers, constituency, and qualifications of the board of directors. General corporation law may specify such things as the number of inside versus outside directors required on a board and the definition of an "independent" director. The General Corporation Law (GCL) of Delaware,[16] for example, provides for basic corporate structural and procedural matters like shareholder voting requirements for fundamental corporate decisions and calling shareholder meetings, as well as very broad governance principles, such as the business judgment rule and the duties of care and loyalty. Corporation laws may permit companies to issue different classes of stock with different voting rights (and even no voting rights). Corporate laws may vary widely across jurisdictions. Some countries, such as Mexico and Brazil, for example, expressly limit the number of shares that may be issued with restricted voting rights, while other countries, such as the United States, often provide greater flexibility in this regard.

The Role of Securities Laws

Corporate governance standards also are imposed through the various laws governing the issuance and exchange of corporate securities. In the United States, the Securities Act of 1933 and the Securities Exchange Act of 1934 comprise the foundation of securities regulation. These regulations, which focus heavily on disclosure obligations and transparency principles for public corporations, indirectly form the foundation for a separate prong of legal regulation over corporate governance. In addition, in the United States, each state has separate securities regulations.

Securities laws should be evaluated by how well they provide for timely disclosure of information material to determining the real health of a company to enable informed investment decisions. Internationally, disclosure and transparency regimes vary significantly, and accordingly, the playing fields with respect to fair, equal, and timely access to market information may not always be even. For example, in Japan, although its securities laws may be patterned after those of the United States in terms of financial disclosure, investors may nonetheless be unable to fully comprehend the complex intercompany linkages to which a given company may be subject.[17] Furthermore, in many countries, investors may be able to hide behind shell companies to withhold their true identity, permitting undisclosed control.

Securities laws address certain conflict of interest concerns between shareholders and management, such as insiders acting on information not readily available to all constituencies. Yet insider trading regulations vary as well. While U.S. insider trading laws require disgorgement, or return of any profits made on an insider trade, many countries do not have the rules and systems in place to adequately combat insider trading. Even when countries have an adequate system of regulation, enforcement can be lax. For example, until recently, Japan and Germany were not aggressive in combating insider trading. An investor also should be aware that a country's securities law could be a paper tiger. In Hong Kong, for instance, recent fines levied against insiders for successful prosecutions by the Securities and Futures Commission have been so small as to not serve as an effective deterrent.[18]

The Role of Securities Regulatory Commissions

Many corporate governance reform efforts have been driven by national securities commissions. Often countries confer rulemaking authority upon national regulatory bodies, such as the Financial Services Authority (FSA) in the United Kingdom, the Commissao de Valores Mobiliares (CVM) in Brazil, or the Chinese Securities and Exchange Commission in China (CSRC). In addition to promulgating standards, national securities regulatory commissions frequently have substantial enforcement powers. Furthermore, active regulatory commissions, through their investigative powers, can do much to compel compliance with governance standards. Securities commissions also develop and monitor corporate disclosures to prevent misleading information from entering the marketplace.

In 1998, IOSCO issued the Objectives and Principles of Securities Market Regulation (the IOSCO Principles) which established guidelines for creating regulatory structures that can effectively police corporate governance violations.[19] These include the need to provide regulators with comprehensive inspection, investigative, surveillance, and enforcement powers. Even with the grant of such powers, however, securities regulators in any given country may not be prepared to adequately perform their surveillance and regulatory duties. As the World Bank recently noted, many countries "are not generally equipped to carry out their surveillance activities efficiently and depend on an often overburdened, weak or slow court system for enforcement."[20]

The Role of Securities Exchanges

The self-regulatory organizations (SROs) that run exchanges are another essential feature of the corporate governance landscape. Although these institutions do not promulgate laws, exchanges may be the most direct player in establishing corporate governance standards. SROs in some countries like the United States have substantial rulemaking authority with respect to listing standards, and are empowered to establish corporate governance benchmarks, requiring compliance by listed companies in exchange for access to capital markets. The threat of public censure and/or de-listing provides an incentive for listed companies to abide by these standards.

In the United States, the NYSE has embarked on a major reform of its listing standards. The NYSE's proposed changes to its listing standards include (1) recommendations to require listed companies to have a majority of independent directors, (2) a tightening of the definition of "independence" with respect to board directors, (3) efforts to empower nonmanagement directors, (4) reforms in the management and constitution of audit and compensation committees, (5) heightened disclosure standards, and (6) CEO/CFO financial disclosure certification requirements. Many of these and other initiatives have been codified into law with the passage of Sarbanes-Oxley. NYSE proposals also have emphasized a shift in the role of corporate boards from management resource to management oversight.[21]

Many exchanges, including the Tokyo Stock Exchange, have refrained from creating a mandatory set of corporate governance standards that listed companies must meet. In the United Kingdom, the London Stock Exchange, as part of its listing rules, issued the Combined Code, setting forth both good governance principles and a detailed "Code of Best Practice" for the structure of company boards, the role of directors and shareholders, executive remuneration, and accountability and audit.[22] Listed companies are required to disclose, in their annual reports, how they apply the principles, and to confirm that they comply with the Code, or provide an explanation for why they fail to do so.

Some exchanges have begun to adopt corporate governance standards that are specifically designed to meet or exceed standards of exchanges such as the NYSE. One such recent initiative was the Novo Mercado in Brazil. The Novo Mercado,[23] established by the Brazilian stock exchange Bovespa in 2001, is accessible only to companies that, among other requirements, (1) only issue shares with voting rights, (2) have outside directors on the board, and (3) comply with international accounting standards. Importantly, in the event of a takeover, minority investors of these companies must receive the same treatment as controlling shareholders. Listed companies also agree to resolve corporate disputes through arbitration. While it is still too soon to assess the success of the Novo Mercado, its development shows that exchanges are capable of taking a significant leadership role in developing corporate governance standards far beyond those required by the applicable law of the host country.

CRITICAL AREAS IN CORPORATE GOVERNANCE

Investors must focus attention when evaluating any given corporate governance system on certain critical corporate governance concerns. These include (1) auditing, disclosure, and reporting requirements of companies; (2) legal requirements with respect to balancing interests among competing stakeholders; and (3) responsibilities and duties of the corporate board.

Auditing and Disclosure Requirements

Investors ultimately rely on the truthfulness, accuracy, and completeness of a company's published financial statements. Determining what constitutes truthful and complete disclosure is an ongoing challenge for securities regulators. Under the OECD Principles, information should be prepared, audited, and disclosed in accordance with high-quality standards and should be easily accessible to users, and an annual independent audit should be performed. The OECD Principles provide that the corporate governance framework should ensure timely and accurate disclosure of all material matters, including the financial situation, performance, ownership, and governance of the company.

As a general matter, companies should disclose any material information. This would include, at a minimum, anything that may affect a company's share price—earnings results, asset disposition, board changes, related party transactions, insider shareholdings, changes in controlling shareholders, changes to ownership including accumulations over a set percentage (which may trigger buyouts), remuneration matters, corporate strategy, off-balance sheet transactions, and business risks, among other matters.

The robustness of the disclosure environment depends on a number of things, including disclosure requirements in exchange listing requirements as well as securities regulations. Also important is the regulation of accountants and auditors, and the standards and obligations of audit committees of corporate boards. Even the most effective disclosure regimes may not adequately prevent fraud or deception within the company, and therefore the applicable standards required for who may sit on the audit committee of the board is particularly important. There seems to be a growing international consensus that best practice means most, if not all, of a board's audit committee members should be independent, at least one audit member should have a financial background, and communication between the audit committee and external and internal auditors should exclude management. It is also desirable that the whole board approve the audit process and disclose departures from accounting standards in the company's annual report. While the United States establishes certain requirements for independent board audit committees, other countries, including Japan and Italy, provide for auditor oversight through a board of auditors, or groups of statutory auditors, that are separate from the board of directors. Some countries appear to have few regulatory requirements for board review of audit compliance, such as Korea, where boards may not even have audit committees, or if they do, whose audit committees may be "neither effective nor adequately equipped to discharge their oversight responsibilities."[24]

The legal regime for oversight of accountants and auditors is evolving. The Winter Report recommends that EU law require the accuracy and truthfulness of financial statements and all statements about a company's financial situation to be the collective responsibility of all of the company's board members. In the United States, the Public Company Accounting Oversight Board recently has been established with broad authority to improve standards, although this entity has not yet begun its full-scale operations, and its role in reforming corporate governance in the United States remains untested.

Balancing the Interests of Stakeholders

Some commentators have suggested that the primary purpose of corporate governance regulations should be minority shareholder protection. Others have suggested that corporate governance regulations should require corporations to consider public interest concerns. Corporate governance regimes often respond to a wide spectrum of competing demands of shareholders, creditors, customers, employees, and the broader public interest, and may do so in a way that disproportionately favors one over another. In the U.S. legal system, for example, the interest of owners is intended to be paramount. Notwithstanding some recent spectacular failures in this regard, directors are legally required to conduct themselves as fiduciaries of shareholders, and managers are required to conduct themselves in compliance with a duty of care requiring reasonable investigation and care in managerial actions and a duty of loyalty prohibiting actions benefiting management at the expense of the corporation.

Corporate governance rules address the relative rights of corporate stakeholders differently. While some countries allow managers to explicitly consider the effect of corporate decisions on multiple constituencies, others may provide for statutory preferences for certain groups. For example, in Germany, the supervisory board of large companies (those with greater than 2000 employees) must be made up of 50 percent labor representatives.[25] In Malaysia the regime has been characterized as "an insider-system of corporate governance, with high levels of corporate ownership concentration, cross holdings and significant participation of owners in management."[26] Similarly, in China, corporate governance reforms may be dominated by the state, as the state is the largest shareholder in more than half of all listed firms on Chinese exchanges.[27] Some countries provide for particular rights of creditors and allow for creditors to serve as external monitors of corporate performance. For example, in Poland creditors often sit on the boards of their debtor companies.

Investors must examine how local laws balance the interests of the various stakeholders. For example, does the law require board directors and senior management to disclose related party and conflicts-of-interest transactions, or is management able to avoid publicly accounting for such transactions? While most countries require related party transactions to be disclosed, some, such as Morocco, do not. Moreover, investors also must recognize that corporate governance rules do not treat all shareholders equally; foreign and domestic shareholders may have different rights, and minority and majority shareholders also may have different protections, especially in takeover situations.

The OECD Principles include three general areas addressing stakeholder rights that a corporate governance framework must ensure:

1. *Protection of shareholders rights.* Basic shareholder protections under the OECD Principles include secure ownership registration, conveyance and transfer of shares, the right to receive timely and regular relevant information, the right to participate in general shareholder meetings in person or by proxy and to receive sufficient advance information on the agenda, the right to raise issues, elect board members, share in corporate profits,

participate in and be informed of fundamental corporate actions or changes, and the right to be informed of disproportionate voting arrangements. Corporate control rules should be transparent and protect shareholders according to their class, and limit anti-takeover devices so that management is not shielded from accountability.

2. *Equitable treatment of all shareholders, including minority and foreign shareholders, and the opportunity for effective redress for violation of rights.* All shareholders of the same class should be treated equally, and any changes to rights should be subject to shareholder vote; votes should be cast by nominees in a manner agreed on by beneficial owners; barriers to voting and shareholder participation should be removed; insider trading and self-dealing should be prohibited; and members of boards should be required to disclose interested transactions.

3. *Recognition of the rights of stakeholders as established by law and encouragement of cooperation between stakeholders and corporations in creating wealth, jobs, and the sustainability of financially sound enterprises.* The OECD Principles provide that laws protecting rights of stakeholders should provide for redress for violations of rights, and the corporate governance framework should provide mechanisms for stakeholder participation and access to information.

Internal corporate governance standards for companies are controlled by shareholder voting procedures. Countries vary in the degree to which they facilitate shareholder voting. For example, some countries permit shareholders to cast their votes electronically, while others require physical attendance. The Winter Report called for shareholders to be permitted to vote in absentia, and encouraged the use of electronic means to permit shareholders to participate in general meetings. Likewise, the GCL also allows for proxy voting and electronic participation, permitting shareholders to express preferences with minimal inconvenience. More formal voting procedures often serve as an impediment to shareholder control over corporate policies. The absence of a proxy voting system is likely to discourage participation in the voting process, and allow greater control by holders of large blocks of shares. Such influence creates more opportunities for management to collude with specific parties or have managerial actions go relatively unobserved. As discussed earlier, proxy voting systems are particularly important in the exercise of foreign shareholder rights. Also important are rules that prevent uncast proxy votes from automatically being voted on behalf of management or by a nominee.

The EAG Code has gone farther than the OECD Principles in its recommendations for protection of minority shareholders, including limiting capital structures to one share, one vote issues, so that shareholder rights are proportional to ownership. The EAG Code eliminates supervoting and nonvoting shares, and views multiple voting rights as inconsistent with good governance and providing the potential for abuse. While this is not a universally held sentiment, the EAG Code does take a strong position in addressing a potentially problematic area for minority shareholders. Similarly, the EAG Code also would allow cumulative voting rights to enable shareholders to concentrate voting power on issues of particular importance to them.

The Corporate Board

The structure of corporate boards, and specific regulatory requirements which boards must comply with, form a key component of corporate governance laws. Company laws often specify the number of board members required and lay out the appointment and removal process. Securities laws may include additional related regulation. For example, Sarbanes-Oxley specifies composition, function and qualifications, and independence of the members of board audit committees.

The OECD Principles state that the corporate governance framework must ensure practices that promote the board's role in the strategic guidance of the company, effective monitoring of management, and accountability to the company and its shareholders. The OECD Principles establish standards that should be reflected in a country's laws, including that board members must be required to act on an informed basis, in good faith, with due diligence and care, in the best interest of the shareholders and the company, taking into account the interests of all stakeholders, treating all shareholders fairly, and ensuring compliance with applicable law.[28]

The ability to exercise these responsibilities and to facilitate corporate transparency that will enable accurate assessment of a company requires appropriate levels of independence. How this is defined varies from country to country. Issues to consider in this area include whether a director has been a recent employee or has current business relationships with the company, whether term limits should be imposed, and the proportion of directors that must be independent on vital committees where conflicts of interest are likely to arise (such as the audit, compensation, and nomination committees).

Many countries permit both one-tier and two-tier board structures. Under a one-tier board structure, the board is elected by the shareholders at the annual shareholder meeting. The board owes fiduciary duties to the corporation principally for the benefit of shareholders. The size of the board is relatively small and is usually comprised of both senior executives and outside directors. The board is designed to manage and supervise the corporation and in particular the senior management. In two-tier boards, the supervisory board is elected, sometimes only in part, by the shareholders. The supervisory board also may be comprised of other stakeholders including employee representatives and/or creditors. The supervisory board then controls the management board that is responsible for the day-to-day operations of the firm, a role similar to that of executive officers in a one-tier board structure.

U.S. and U.K. boards follow a one-tier structure, but they differ in their application in a number of respects. U.S. boards typically consist of a majority of independent directors, a unified CEO/chairperson position and few senior executives, and much of the supervisory or oversight function of the boards are delegated to committees filled by independent directors (in particular the audit committee). Nonexecutive directors of U.S. boards must hold meetings without executive directors present. In the United Kingdom, the Combined Code supports the separation of the positions of CEO and chairperson; does not require a majority of independent directors on corporate boards; and continues to reflect the belief that significant if not majority participation on the board by senior management is a best practice.

Japanese boards are typically large and homogeneous.[29] Insiders, most of whom are employees of the company, dominate the board. The promotion of employees can create a hierarchy within the board. The balance of power is usually tilted toward senior management. If there are "outside" directors present, they are usually affiliated with a parent company or large institutional banks. Japanese companies typically also have a separate board of auditors also composed of insiders (normally retired board members). The board of auditors exercises influence but does not have voting rights or the power to dismiss a director.

Unlike Japan, German supervisory boards usually play a more integral role in the supervision of the corporation and represent a broader constituency. The supervisory board acts much like the board of directors in a one-tier system with the right to audit, call shareholders' meetings, control the annual report, and dismiss the board of management. By law, the supervisory board must consist of not only those directors elected by the shareholders but also those that represent labor.

Both one-tier and two-tier structures can meet the needs of good corporate governance provided there is a supervisory body distinct from and independent of management. The Winter Report concluded that, at least with respect to the EU, no particular form of board structure "is intrinsically superior; each may be the most efficient in particular circumstances."[30] The Winter Report did not make recommendations with respect to board composition, other than to further promote the role of nonexecutive, independent supervisory directors. The Report did recommend, however, that the nomination, audit, and compensation functions of boards should be handled exclusively by a majority of independent nonexecutive or supervisory directors.

ENFORCEMENT MECHANISMS

When evaluating the legal environment of corporate governance regimes, it is critical to assess how rights are enforced. Indeed, as the World Bank recently noted, there is a general "discrepancy between the letter of the law and actual practices" with respect to enforcement.[31] As seen recently in the United States, only a handful of the corporate directors who sat on the boards of the companies involved in the recent spectacular failures of corporate governance have faced criminal sanctions, and few have been found personally liable in civil actions.

In broad terms, enforcement may occur through civil actions by shareholders or other stakeholders against corporate malfeasance, or, through criminal or administrative actions prosecuted by the state. Criminal punishment or regulatory fines and sanctions may indeed provide the ultimate deterrence to corporate malfeasance, but such a deterrent may be compromised by lack of political will, legal infrastructure, and the resources to prosecute white collar crime. Furthermore, individual shareholders rarely recover from enforcement actions by the state. In this section, we will examine several mechanisms commonly employed by investors in protecting their rights against corporate governance violations.

Investors must first question whether host country enforcement mechanisms are effective in securing compliance with local corporate governance regulations or duties. The ability to pursue claims may turn on the efficiency and impartiality of the local courts, on how local regulations treat foreign investors (for example, whether there are barriers to enforcement of shareholder rights by foreign nationals), and on the sophistication of the local bar, among other factors. In common law countries, courts analyze and interpret the laws that form the foundation of corporate governance practice, and may thereby bring clarity to legislation enactments. Courts also may serve as a bulwark against overreaching regulatory action, and thereby provide a critical counterweight to government regulations. However, courts viewed as corrupt, inefficient, or ineffective may fatally undermine even the most carefully designed corporate governance laws.

Investors also must recognize the fine balance between legal systems that facilitate shareholder litigation and those that also permit spurious litigation that can ultimately erode shareholder value. As the OECD notes, there is a "risk that a legal system which enables any investor to challenge corporate activity in the courts, can become prone to excessive litigation."[32]

Shareholder litigation may be prosecuted by individuals, or more commonly, by classes of shareholders acting together. Individual private litigation rights are weak enforcement tools. Few individual shareholders choose to go through the expense and trouble of litigation where only small recoveries are likely. In many countries, shareholder actions may be prohibitively expensive. For example, in Korea, a joint IMF/World Bank study recently concluded that few individual suits had been filed because of the prohibitive costs involved.[33] Private enforcement regimes may therefore be effective only when they permit the economies of scale of allowing large numbers of individuals to aggregate claims into a single litigation. The most common vehicles for such aggregation are the shareholder derivative suit and the class action suit.

Class actions are fairly straightforward; they allow multiple plaintiffs whose claims involve approximately the same facts and legal theories to pool resources and litigate as a group. Shareholder derivative suits, while a powerful tool for enforcing corporate governance, are more complex. If directors and/or officers harm the corporation through actions inimical to the good of the corporation, then the corporation has a right of action against those directors or officers. This is directly analogous to the right of action an individual would have against any tortfeasor. However, normally, a corporation sues through its agents, usually its directors or officers. Presumably, in a derivative suit, these agents are now compromised. To solve this problem, the law allows any shareholder to act in the name of the corporation and sue directors or officers for the corporation's benefit. In other words, the shareholder derivative suit is an action brought by a shareholder against a corporation's directors or officers on behalf of the corporation.

Countries address the various tradeoffs between liberal and conservative approaches to class action and derivative suits differently. Germany, for example, severely restricts shareholder derivative suits. Accordingly, Germany has evolved a far different set of governance practices reflecting a lower level of concern for shareholders, which may have resulted in reduced shareholder willingness to invest in securities. Individual stock ownership is extremely low in Germany relative to the United States, with the vast majority of stock held by large financial institutions that hold greater leverage.[34]

Similar to Germany, the use of class action suits in Japan has been limited. While Japan's shareholders have theoretically been able to bring derivative suits since 1950, such recourse was severely limited by the requirement of exorbitantly high litigation fees. It was not until 1993 that the fees were reduced to an affordable rate. The number of class action suits has increased significantly over the last ten years, but the reality remains that the derivative suits are not broadly used. Moreover, Japan has evolved a set of non-legal norms that provide considerable deference to the interests of employees, creditors, and affiliates over interests of shareholders. This may have arisen from the domination by insiders, the presence of employee stock ownership plans as significant shareholders, and the close relationship most companies have with large institutional banks.[35]

The structure of a derivative suit creates a dilemma in determining who should pay for and who should receive compensation. While the corporation suffered the harm, the plaintiff is nominally the shareholder and the corporation nominally the defendant. In theory, if the shareholder wins the suit, he or she does profit as a residual claimant of the award. In reality, any compensation is directed back to the corporation. Granting awards to shareholders directly may overly incentivize shareholder litigation, leading to frivolous suits. Furthermore, plaintiffs' lawyers generally take some percentage (often a third) of the total recovery in a suit. This payment structure also can lead to excessive litigation.

Directors or officers accused of improper conduct will nominally pay the damages. However, the fear of potential liability creates a powerful disincentive from serving as a corporate board director. As a result, corporations and directors have increasingly turned to directors' and officers' insurance products, but such coverage has become increasingly expensive in recent years. Companies also may indemnify directors against legal costs and damages assessed, though such indemnification is often limited to cases not involving some egregious level of conduct, such as disloyalty to the corporation, crime, or fraud. Either way, the end result is an odd circularity: In some circumstances, the theoretical plaintiff, i.e., the corporation, pays (through indemnification and insurance premiums) for the legal costs and damages assessed against the defendants, who stand accused of failing to appropriately protect the corporation. Some criticize the indemnification system as weakening existing compliance incentives.

CONCLUSION

Corporate governance laws and regulations will continue to evolve and may in fact be converging toward some globally recognized best practices. While regulators and legislators contemplate structural change, investors will continue to demand reform, and corporate governance regimes that are less effective in protecting shareholder rights should ultimately find it more difficult and more expensive to attract capital. The OECD Principles were a significant "first step" toward defining best practices, but they were a starting point that is subject to evolution and review. Major corporate events also cause reevaluation; indeed, the mandate of the Winter Report was specifically expanded as a direct reaction to the Enron collapse. As these analyses are done and best practices are identified, it should be recognized that international standards may increasingly conflict with local practices and institutions, and total convergence may not be possible or desirable.

During this process of ongoing reform, investors should continually question whether new legal and regulatory requirements are adequately addressing the fundamental problems in corporate governance, and whose interests are in fact being protected. For example, many of the recent legislative reforms have failed to grant shareholders the right to directly nominate directors, and there has been a general failure to address the excessive compensation packages routinely granted in certain countries such as the United States. Finally, it should be noted that law might not be the primary driver in continued reform efforts. Indeed, many commentators have expressed the view that at least part of the current corporate governance problems in the U.S. capital markets result from economic factors such as years of perverse stock-based compensation incentives and other practices that encouraged short-term economic manipulation at the cost of longer-term growth.

Ultimately, the legal environment needs to be viewed in the context of the human actors who must comply with the relevant rules and regulations. Even the most stringent corporate governance standards may be insufficient to protect against complex fraud. Indeed, many commentators have noted that the failure of Enron had little to do with inadequate corporate governance standards and procedures, but everything to do with the culture and environment of the people at Enron; indeed, Enron was voted as having one of the best boards in America before its collapse and was recognized for its commitment to corporate governance practices. In that light, the investor must recognize the basic limitations of the law as a necessary but not sufficient factor in compelling corporate actors to act in a manner that achieves good corporate governance.

NOTES

1. *See* Welcome Remarks at The Fourth Asian Roundtable on Corporate Governance, by Myoung-Ho Shin, Vice President Asian Development Bank, November 11, 2002, *at* www.adb.org/Documents/Speeches/2002/ms2002127.asp. *See also* Y. Khatri, L.E. Leruth, and J. Piesse. *Corporate Performance and Governance in Malaysia*, IMF Working Paper 02/152, September 2002, Asia and Pacific Department *at* www.imf.org/external/pubs/ft/wp/2002/wp02152.pdf.

2. *See* OECD Principles, Section V(a), (b), and (c), at p. 22 (April 1998) *at* www.oecd.org/EN/document/0,,EN-document-77-3-no-24-35553-77,00.html.

3. *See* Policy Measures and Industry Initiatives to Rebuild and Maintain Confidence in Publicly Traded Companies and Capital Markets in the OECD Area, OECD (April 25, 2003) *at* www.oecd.org/EN/document/0,EN-document-0-nodirectorate-no-3-40345-0,00.html.

4. *See* White Paper on Corporate Governance in Russia (April 15, 2002) *at* www.oecd.org/pdf/M00028000/M00028789.pdf.

5. *See* Final Communiqué of the XXVIIth Annual Conference of the International Organization of Securities Commissions, May 24, 2002 *at* www.iosco.org/news/pdf/IOSCONEWS5-English.pdf.

6. For example, *see* Republic of Korea: Financial System Stability Assessment, including Reports on the Observance of Standards and Codes on the following topics: Monetary and Financial Policy Transparency, Banking Supervision, Securities Regulation, Insurance Regulation, Corporate Governance, and Payment Systems, IMF Country Report 03/81, *at* ww.imf.org/external/pubs/ft/scr/2003/cr0379.pdf.

7. *See* O. Fremond and M. Capaul, *The State of Corporate Governance: Experience from Country Assessments*, World Bank Policy Research Working Paper, June 2002 *at* www.worldbank.org/wbi/banking/finsecpolicy/domestic2003/pdf/WB_Fremond WP2858.pdf.

8. *See* Report of the High Level Group of Company Law Experts on a Modern Regulatory Framework for Company Law, *at* 1 (November 4, 2002) *at* www.europa.eu.int/comm/internal_market/en/company/company/modern/consult/report_en.pdf. *See also* J. Winter, "Why Laws Alone Cannot Prevent Bad Corporate Governance," *International Financial Law Review*, February 2003, pp. 42–43.

9. Sarbanes-Oxley Act of 2002, Pub. L. No. 107-204, 116 Stat. 804, 2002.

10. The Institute of International Finance, Inc., "Policies on Corporate Governance and Transparency in Emerging Markets," *Report of the EAG Working Group on Corporate Governance and Transparency,* February 2002 *at* www.iif.com/ipi/reports.quagga.

11. SEC Release No. 33-8220, Standards Relating to Listed Company Audit Committees, April 9, 2003 *at* http://www.sec.gov/rules/final/33-8220.htm. U.S. issuers must comply with the new listing standards by the earlier of their first annual meeting after January 15, 2004 or October 31, 2004.

12. SEC Adopts Final Rules Regarding Audit Committee Financial Experts and Code of Ethics for CEOs, CFOs, and Other Senior Financial Officers, February 5, 2003 *at* www.weil.com/wgm/cwgmhomep.nsf/Files/auditcommitteeethics/$file/auditcommitteeethics.pdf.

13. *See, e.g.,* "U.S. Listing Burdens Partly Blamed for Chinese IPO Withdrawal," *International Financial Law Review,* February 2003, p. 7.

14. Loomis, T., "Costs of Compliance Soar After Sarbanes-Oxley," *New York Law Journal,* May 5, 2003.

15. Burton, J., and A. Jack. "Brothers Emerge as SK Corp Investors," *Financial Times,* May 1, 2003.

16. *See* Del. Code Ann. tit. 8, §§ 1–398, 2002.

17. *See* H. Kanda, "Japan," *The Legal Basis of Corporate Governance in Publicly Held Corporations* (eds.) A.R. Pinto and G. Visentini, pp. 111–123.

18. *See* Press Release, Hong Kong Securities and Futures Commission, SFC Prosecutes Yu Pun Hoi for Contravening the Securities (Disclosure of Interests) Ordinance, July 31, 2001 (on file with author).

19. Objectives and Principles of Securities Regulation, International Organization of Securities Commissions, February 20, 2002 *at* www.iosco.org/pubdocs/pdf/IOSCOPD125.pdf.

20. *See* Fremond and Capaul, at 16.

21. Corporate Governance Rule Proposals Reflecting Recommendations from the NYSE Corporate Accountability and Listing Standards Committee, August 1, 2002 *at* www.nyse.com/pdfs/corp_gov_pro_b.pdf.

22. See The Combined Code Principles of Good Governance and Code of Best Practice, May 2000 *at* www.fsa.gov.uk/pubs.

23. *See* Novo Mercado Listing Rules, June 2002 *at* www.bovespa.com.br/pdf/regulamento.pdf.

24. *See* note 9, *IMF Country Report,* at pp. 60–65.

25. Birk, R. "Germany," *The Legal Basis of Corporate Governance in Publicly Held Corporations: A Comparative Approach,* (eds.) A. R. Pinto and G. Visentini, Kluwer Law International, Boston: 1998, p. 59.

26. *See* Y. Khatri, L. E. Leruth, and J. Piesse, "Corporate Performance and Governance in Malaysia," *IMF Working Paper,* September 2002, p. 6.

27. Ho, S. S. M. and X. Hai-Gen, "Corporate Governance in the People's Republic of China," *Corporate Governance: An Asia-Pacific Critique*, (ed.) Low Chee Keong, Swee & Maxwell, Hong Kong, 2002.

28. *See* OECD Principles, Section V(a), (b), and (c), April 1998, p. 22.

29. *See* H. Kanda, "Japan," *The Legal Basis of Corporate Governance in Publicly Held Corporations: A Comparative Approach*, A. R. Pinto et al. (eds.), 1998, 117.

30. *See* Winter Report, p. 8.

31. *See* O. Fremond and M. Capaul, p. 2.

32. *See* OECD Principles, Annotations, p. 31.

33. *See* note 9 , IMF Country Report, p. 63. In addition to concluding that costs effectively bar shareholder litigation in Korea, the IMF/World Bank study advocated the enactment of a pending draft law facilitating class action suits.

34. Boehmer, E. *Who Controls German Corporations in Corporate Governance Regimes: Convergence and Diversity*, J. McCahrey et al, (eds.), Oxford University Press, New York , 2002, p. 283.

35. *See generally* H. Kanda, "Japan," *The Legal Basis of Corporate Governance in Publicly Held Corporations: A Comparative Approach*, A. R. Pinto et al, (eds.), 1998.

CHAPTER 9

Core Earnings

David M. Blitzer, Ph.D.

INTRODUCTION

One of the key responsibilities of management in any modern corporation with shareholders outside of the senior management group is to provide essential financial information and keep shareholders informed of the corporation's financial results and progress. This responsibility lies at the heart of the manager-owner relationship where owners provide capital but the managers run the corporation and invest—or waste—the capital. As the management's constituencies have grown from partners to more numerous shareholders and then to include other "stakeholders" such as employees, labor unions, customers, and the communities where a corporation is located, the demand for reliable financial information has grown.

In most nations this responsibility for financial reporting is recognized in laws and regulations. In the United States, companies are required to publish financial reports on a quarterly and annual basis and the content of the reports is governed by a complex set of government regulations and accounting standards. These regulations can be traced back to legislation passed in the 1930s as a result of investigations into the stock market crash of 1929. Moreover, the recent investigations into the financial scandals and failures of the 1990s and the 2000s have included significant changes to these regulations. As this volume goes to press, debates continue over some key aspects of these regulations, including the treatment of employee stock options.

The regulations, principles, and practices of financial reporting leave a fair amount of room for companies to exercise judgment in precisely how they present their financial results. Some flexibility is necessary to allow for unforeseen events and changes in business practices as well as variation across industries and companies. However, in the last ten years this flexibility has expanded to the point where financial data is less transparent, reliable, or useful. In response to these developments and to the increasing difficulty of comparing the performance of one company to another, Standard & Poor's published a suggested corporate reporting standard, *Standard & Poor's Core Earnings*, in May 2002. This chapter discusses the developments that made the publication of *Standard & Poor's Core Earnings* necessary, its key components, how it has been received in the investment community, and the financial impacts of three key adjustments in Standard & Poor's Core Earnings. New developments in financial reporting continue at a rapid pace. At the end of the chapter, recent changes at the Financial Accounting Standards Board (FASB), the key U.S. accounting regulator, and the prospects for coordination between FASB and the International Accounting Standards Board (IASB) are reviewed.

THE BULL MARKET AND THEREAFTER

The 1990s bull market and the economic and social climate surrounding it will go down in history as one of the great booms of the twentieth century, if not any century. Stocks surged, turning in the second-best five consecutive years of the twentieth century, only surpassed by the rebound from the crash of 1929 and the Great Depression. But more soared than just stock prices. Salaries and bonuses for business executives reached unheard of levels. Million dollar annual base salaries became commonplace and option-driven bonuses 50 or 100 times that large were seen surprisingly often.

Booms and bull markets usually breed a happy-go-lucky environment where traditional warning signs are ignored, rules can be bent, everyone seems to win, and no one apparently ever has to lose. The 1990s were no exception. Moreover, as this environment grew full, complete, and transparent financial reporting seemed to fade into the background. Looking back, there were a few developments that encouraged creative accounting and reporting.

In the mid-1990s, before the bull market really took off, FASB fought the "option wars" over how to treat the cost of employee stock options. Under the rules adopted then, FASB 123,[1] declared that companies may either charge the cost of employee stock options against income or may charge the "intrinsic value" of the options against income and report the true value in the footnotes included in their annual report. The intrinsic value of the option is the difference between the price of the stock and the strike price of the option—it ignores the time value of the option, the volatility of stocks, and the likelihood that the stock price may move higher, making the option very valuable. Since most employee stock options are issued with the strike price equal to the stock price on the issue date, the intrinsic value, and the cost charged against income, are zero. When typical option grants to executives were 5 to 10 percent of total compensation, options were a modest bonus. However, once the debates surrounding FASB 123 were settled, the idea that stock options were costless spread. As the competition for talent arose in the 1990s boom, options became the weapon of choice in attracting staff, especially in technology companies. Soon stock options climbed from 10 percent bonuses to payouts that could be 10, 20, or 50 times annual compensation. All of a sudden anything that could keep those options in the money was critically important.

No one likes to see the good times end. Certainly, after five years of soaring stock prices it was hard to realize and understand that the game was over. The stock market peaked in late March 2000, and then began to slide. Initially everyone had an explanation for why the damage was only to the other fellow's portfolio or why his or her own employer's stock would continue to climb. The market slide was more than just softness in stock prices—business, especially in technology and telecommunications—slowed, earnings softened, and the economy weakened and then slid into recession. As the weakness in the stock market and the economy reached profits, some companies sought to paint rosier pictures of their results than traditional GAAP net income might suggest. The huge option grants were certainly not a deterrent to creative earnings releases that played up the good news and ignored the bad results. Moreover, pressures on stock analysts in some of the large investment banks meant less scrutiny and occasionally even some cheerleading greeted earnings releases.

As the bull market in stocks ended in March 2000, it was quickly replaced with a bull market in creative accounting and imaginative earnings releases.

OPERATING EARNINGS, PRO FORMA EARNINGS, AND OLD-FASHIONED GAAP

From all this, sometime in the late 1990s, the idea of operating earnings as a "better" measure sprang forth. Originally, a reasonable approach to focusing on ongoing earnings, the lack of any rules or standards meant that companies could redefine earnings measures from quarter to quarter, always keeping the pretty pictures one step ahead of the bad news. A combination of factors built up pressures for upbeat and optimistic earnings reports which in turn encouraged companies to keep adjusting the definitions of "operating earnings" or "pro forma earnings" to make quarterly earnings releases look even better than a consistent measure like GAAP net income would have.

One factor pressuring the earnings definitions and releases was the market and economic slide that began in early 2000 and became a recession in 2001. However, on top of that were the out-sized option grants of the 1990s, which meant that many senior executives had multimillion-dollar stakes in keeping the earnings picture bright and the stock price high. It was not unusual for all the senior executives in a company to have unexercised in-the-money options worth $10 million or more each at a time when one disappointing earnings release could have collapsed the stock price and erased the options' worth completely. As the current decade opened, companies were increasingly abandoning GAAP net income as a profit measure and replacing it by vaguely defined measures called *operating earnings* or, when operating earnings got a bad name, *pro forma earnings.*

For analysts and investors, this shift presented significant difficulties. A large part of equity analysis and selecting stocks for investment consists of comparing different companies to one another or examining how a single company changes over time. When an analyst is reviewing five or six companies to choose the one or two that have the best prospects it is essential to use the same accounting definitions across all the companies. However, if each company creates its own definition with each quarterly report, there is no comparability and the analysis is either difficult, misleading, or almost impossible to do correctly.

On top of the company-by-company difficulties caused by the use of ever changing definitions of operating earnings, none of these measures was used widely enough or had enough history to support valuation measures for the overall stock market. Traditionally, the two metrics most often used to determine if the market is over- or undervalued are the dividend yield (dividend-price ratio) and the price-earnings (P-E) ratio. Dividends fell out of fashion in the bull markets as the excitement focused on technology companies that rarely pay dividends and stock prices climbed so fast that dividends became a miniscule portion of the total return. As operating earnings proliferated as the profit measure of choice, some market strategists and analysts began to calculate the P-E ratio for the S&P 500 using operating earnings. The limited history for a P-E on the S&P 500 based on operating earnings extends back to only 1988. Further, since there are no standard definitions, there is some disagreement about the actual numbers. The real problem is that many investors compared

P-E ratios of 18 or 20 times on the S&P 500 to the long-term historic aver-age P-E based on As-Reported earnings (GAAP Net Income excluding discontinued operations and extraordinary items) over the last 50 years, a figure of about 16. On these numbers a market P-E of 18 suggests the market is reasonably valued. The proper comparison in 2001–2002 was between a long-run average of 16 and a current value based on As-Reported in the high 20s or low 30s and told a far different story: The mar-ket was overvalued.

This is the situation that analysts and investors found themselves increasingly facing in 2001 and 2002 as the market continued to slide and the true profits picture departed farther and farther from the image.

STANDARD & POOR'S CORE EARNINGS

While the creativity in redefining profit measures began with company earnings reports, it was not actively discouraged by regulators, account-ants, or analysts. There was general agreement that the growing use of nonstandard earnings measures was making good investment analysis more difficult. At the same time, no one seemed to want to tackle the issue head-on. Most observers recognized that defining earnings would require reopening some of the major accounting debates of the previous five to ten years including the treatment of stock options, pension expenses, goodwill, write-offs, and similar issues.

Standard & Poor's began exploring some of these issues internally in early 2001. It quickly became clear that there were very few organiza-tions with either the inclination or position to take on the issue of how earnings should be measured and reported. The equity research depart-ments of the large investment banks were too directed at competing with one another that none of them could hope to establish an approach that would be adopted by others. FASB, having fought a brutal battle over stock option expensing in the mid-1990s, was not inclined to reopen the same issues. Further, few organizations were in a position to draw atten-tion to accounting issues or earnings measures.

Standard & Poor's initial public announcement of a project to develop an improved earnings measure was published in early November 2001. Mostly due to lucky timing, it garnered some attention and struck a responsive chord with the financial press.[2] But, despite the slumping market, gaining interest to discuss profits and accounting was difficult. However, by the end of the same month, conditions had changed dramat-ically. At the end of the month the Enron Corporation collapsed completely in a complex accounting fraud. By the end of the following month, Tyco International's (now former) CEO was involved in an investigation surrounding both the company's accounting and the CEO's personal finances.

As 2002 dawned, the flow of news continued to draw attention to accounting issues and profit measures. In early 2002, the federal government began legal action against Arthur Anderson & Co., one of the "Big 5" auditing firms and the accountants for the Enron Corporation.

Stock options began to be more widely discussed as some commentators questioned just what incentives stock options gave to managers. Since the debates over stock options in the mid-1990s, when FASB published FASB 123 that allowed companies to elect not to treat the full value of stock options as a charge against net income, the dominant opinion was the stock options held by senior managers would align the managers' goals with the shareholders' desire for higher stock prices. In the first few months of 2002 both Federal Reserve Chairman Alan Greenspan and Warren Buffett, Chairman of Berkshire-Hathaway, spoke out against the stock options.[3] At the same time, some academic researchers also were beginning to question the true incentive effects of stock options.[4]

In this atmosphere of increased discussion and concern with corporate accounting and growing talk about accounting practices as a failure of corporate governance, Standard & Poor's published the details of its *Standard & Poor"s Core Earnings* approach in May 2002.[5] The details of the proposal are included in the materials releases on that date and a technical bulletin published in October 2002. This section will describe the response from the press and the investment community; the next section discusses the three most important provisions of Standard & Poor's Core Earnings.

The response to Standard & Poor's Core Earnings varies from group to group across the financial community and the financial press. As expected, none of the major investment banks have been willing to formally adopt Standard & Poor's Core Earnings. The biggest question is competitive rather than analytical—major institutions are unlikely to adopt an analytical approach closely linked to another organization's name.

In sharp contrast, accounting analysts at a number of major investment banks generously gave a lot of time, support, and assistance to Standard & Poor's development of Standard & Poor's Core Earnings. Second, one company has incorporated the Core Earnings into its 2002 annual earnings release. At the same time, a number of companies have explored Standard & Poor's Core Earnings and compared their results measured with GAAP net income, with Standard & Poor's Core Earnings, and with operating earnings. One factor here is that for companies with significant stock option grants or large defined benefit pension plans, Standard & Poor's Core Earnings normally results in a lower number than either operating earnings or GAAP net income. This area is likely to see some further developments under newly issued SEC Regulation G, which covers the use of any non-GAAP measures in earnings releases.

The two groups that most closely reflect investors and the public are the financial press and investment and securities analysts. In these groups the reception to Standard & Poor's Core Earnings has been very strong and very positive. Press coverage in May 2002, and with subsequent announcements has been very heavy and very favorable. There is strong agreement that a better, more consistent, and widely understood measure is important. There is also growing agreement that the issues highlighted by Standard & Poor's—options, pensions, and write-offs—are important issues. Among securities analysts there is growing recognition and agreement that a complete review of almost any equity requires a review of these same three items. Analysts acknowledge that investing was too easy in the 1990s—almost any stock one recommended went up. In the nastier reality of the bear market, good securities analysis means a lot more work and that work needs to focus on what goes into earnings.

BIG THREE ADJUSTMENTS

Stock Options: Standard & Poor's position on stock options, as presented in May 2002, is straightforward. Employee stock options are a form of compensation just like salaries, health benefits, bonuses, or anything else. As such, the cost of stock options is a charge against Standard & Poor's Core Earnings. The cost of the options should be calculated with a widely recognized option pricing model, as described in FASB 123. Second, Standard & Poor's noted that under FASB 123, companies are required to publish options data annually; S&P expressed a preference for quarterly release of the data.

In discussing stock options, Standard & Poor's noted that there is nothing inherently wrong with stock options or with using them as part of a compensation package for either senior executives or other employees. The difficulties arose when management and boards of directors treated options as free goods and made huge grants. This meant that corporations incurred significant expenses, which were borne by shareholders and which were not recognized in the corporation's income statements. Further, the dilution this often imposed on shareholders further damaged their positions.

Arguments fell into two areas—options did not really have value and therefore could not be an expense and option values are impossible to estimate. Options do have value. If options didn't have any value, they wouldn't be an attractive part of a compensation package. More significantly, a corporation could have sold the same stock options on the open market to raise funds for new investments or other corporate uses, so clearly the options do have value. The fact that employee stock options are typically issued "at the money" with the strike price equal to the stock price does not mean they are worthless. Rather, the volatility of the stock and the length of time during which the option may be exercised are critical to determining its value.

Few models or analyses in modern finance are more frequently used and tested against real data than option pricing models. Options traders and investors routinely use Black-Scholes and other option pricing models as the basis for trading. Real money is one of the best available ways to test a financial model. The growing body of opinion that stock options can be valued and should be expensed supports the positions taken in Standard & Poor's Core Earnings.[6]

Pensions: This is a common element in many U.S. corporations. About 350 of the 500 companies in the S&P 500 offer defined benefit (DB) plans to their employees. Accounting for these plans under FASB 87[7] was designed to smooth the impact of financial market shifts on corporate pensions. Its result is different—it allows a corporation to include as income funds that are not available to the corporation and may not even exist. Standard & Poor's Core Earnings' treatment of pensions is designed to correct this.

A very brief summary of pension accounting under the current FASB rules is needed to explain how the Standard & Poor's Core Earnings adjusts the current approach. Under FASB, a company calculates gross pension income as the pension fund assets at the start of the year multiplied by the expected return on plan assets. Gross pension income is then reduced by pension expenses, including certain calculations designed to smooth the impact of pension costs. What remains—net pension income— is part of the company's net income. In most cases, net pension income is positive and increases the reported net income.

Standard & Poor's Core Earnings notes two key concerns. First, the pension plan assets are not corporate funds. Rather, they are held in trust for current and future beneficiaries of the retirement plan. Therefore, earnings on these funds should not be treated as corporate income. Second, the net pension income is based on the expected rather than the actual return.

In years like 2002 when the market slid 22 percent, the actual returns were probably negative. Not only is net pension income not the company's money, the money itself may not even be there.

Standard & Poor's Core Earnings would treat pension expense as a cost as if the pension plan were being outsourced and exclude net pension income. Under FASB there are two components of pension expense—service cost and interest expense. Service cost is the increase in future pension liability due to another year of employment or "service." Essentially, this is deferred compensation. Interest expense is the growth in the assets required to keep pace with the expected future liabilities. Under the Standard & Poor's Core Earnings, service cost is a charge against income. If the plan's actual returns cover the interest expense, then the plan covers the interest expense and there is no charge to the company. If, due to market conditions or investment management, the interest expense is not covered by actual returns, the company makes up the difference and there is a charge for interest expense.

One comment about the Standard & Poor's Core Earnings approach is that pension costs are more volatile than under FASB accounting because Standard & Poor's Core Earnings uses only the actual returns and ignores the wishful thinking of expected returns. This volatility is always present in reality; it is hidden by FASB, and therefore, is often hidden from investors and analysts.

The 2000–2002 period challenged pension plans and saw a sharp deterioration in their funding status. As of early 2003, numerous organizations, including FASB, are paying renewed attention to pension accounting and related issues. It is too early to tell how this unfolds, but there are increasing questions about the existing FASB approach.

Write-offs: Write-offs occur when a company closes down an operation and takes a charge for expenses related to the closing such as severance. There are two related issues here, one with operating earnings and one that was addressed by FASB in 2002. Write-offs are typically excluded from operating earnings. They should not be—a write-off represents an investment in a company's core business that did not work out. Not all investments succeed, but when they fail the costs should not be hidden or ignored. One reason why operating or pro forma earnings often give misleading results is the exclusion of write-offs.

Second, a practice among many companies is to estimate the costs and take a large write-off when an operation is closed down, only to discover a year later that the costs were less than estimated. In the second year, the difference between the write-off and the true costs is then taken back into income as a credit. This may make two slow, soft years look like a short, sharp downturn followed by a stunning recovery. It distorts the picture of what really happened.

Standard & Poor's Core Earnings includes all write-offs as charges against income when the write-offs are taken. FASB 146[8] restricted write-offs to costs actually incurred, not just to expected or planned expenses. This is a step toward reducing the abuse of write-offs and is most welcome. Between these two—including write-offs in Standard & Poor's Core Earnings rather than hiding them from operating or pro forma earnings and requiring that write-offs track actual liabilities—difficulties in this area should be reduced.

ACCOUNTING GOVERNANCE ISSUES OUTSIDE THE UNITED STATES: IASB VERSUS FASB

Standard & Poor's Core Earnings was developed in response to issues in the United States and issues with U.S. accounting as guided by FASB. FASB differs in many ways from other national accounting oversight groups and from the International Accounting Standards Board (IASB). Some of these differences relate to specific issues, but a larger one relates to the overall approach and the relationship between accounting and corporate governance.

FASB follows a rules-based approach and publishes detailed, often exhaustive, rules covering specific accounting practices. The rules attempt to specify exactly how issues should be treated and leave relatively little discretion to a company or its auditors. The IASB takes a principles approach—it specifies relatively brief general principles and leaves more room for interpretation to the company reporting and the companies' auditors. This distinction is not absolutely black or white—FASB does leave many factors to interpretation and the IASB does specify details at times. But the differences remain and raise some questions for corporate governance.

Accurate and reliable financial reporting is a responsibility of a corporation and an aspect of good corporate governance. Moreover, accurate reporting is more than just the accounting rules or principles—it is understanding the company's financial condition and explaining it to shareholders, employers, and the public. The rules-based approach has some attractions—it should be straightforward and should assure that similar companies in similar circumstances are treated the same way. In practice, when corporate governance breaks down, the rule book is interpreted, and abused, as a guide book on how to meet the letter of the law while sabotaging its intent. The same can be argued of a principles-based accounting system—when corporate governance fails, accounting will fail as well.

However, the American experience suggests that these failures may escape notice more easily and for much longer periods when companies appear to be playing by the rules. No system is fail-safe and no system can replace diligent investors, responsible company accountants, and alert regulators. Moreover, any set of accounting reports depends on some interpretation. The celebrated—and record breaking—WorldCom fraud and collapse was based on simple decisions to classify some expenses as capital items with long service lives to reduce the annual costs charged against income. Moreover, the discovery of the fraud depended on a handful of internal accountants who discovered the wrongdoing.

Although no system is foolproof, the principles-based approach has some clear advantages. First, the accounting rulemakers, FASB or the IASB, can focus on the overall approach and principles rather than try to craft rules that cover every possible foreseen, or unforeseen, event. This should support faster, simpler, and more understandable regulations and rules. Second, when the unforeseen situation arises, as it inevitably will, the company and its auditors have some specific principles to fall back on in developing a response and reporting the results.

There are differences between FASB and the IASB on some key issues. The most discussed one is employee stock options. The IASB has taken a firm stand in favor of expensing stock options; this differs from FASB's current rules under FASB 123. However, recent announcements from FASB indicate that the options question is under review and most observers expect FASB to move very close to the IASB position by the end of 2003. Pensions are currently an area of debate for both organizations, but there seems to be a good chance that they will move to agreement on how to treat defined benefit pension programs.

Beyond the differences in approach and in some specific items, the goal of both FASB and the IASB is to bring their regulations closer and closer together so that eventually there is no difference. As equity investing becomes increasingly global there is increasing demand from investors for a common system of accounting. Such a system is within reach, but its success will depend on responsible corporate governance as well as clear principles and understandable rules.

THE INVESTMENT COMMUNITY'S RESPONSE TO STANDARD & POOR'S CORE EARNINGS

Standard & Poor's Core Earnings was initially announced in November 2001; it was presented in complete detail in May 2002 and an effort to reach out to the financial community and discuss the ideas behind Standard & Poor's Core Earnings was begun at that time. In the year since May 2002, Standard & Poor's has met with financial analysts, investment banks, financial advisors, regulators, exchanges, and others on numerous occasions. A natural question is how has Standard & Poor's Core Earnings been received.

The response differs between individual analysts, journalists, and regulators on one hand and organizations on the other. Large organizations, with concerns about their competitive or legal positions, are reluctant to adopt a new nonofficial approach to financial reporting or financial analysis. No major investment bank is willing to pin another organization's name on its own analytical methods. Rather, they see developing their own approach as a better way to enhance their brand, their marketing image, and their business. Likewise, regulators and exchanges have responsibilities to their own constituencies that prevent them from accepting a solution from outsiders. Both economics and politics argue in favor of a "not invented here" approach to solutions of financial reporting.

The response from individuals is very different. The vast majority of financial analysts, regulators, investment banking managers, and others with whom S&P has discussed the Standard & Poor's Core Earnings strongly endorse the ideas. The message Standard & Poor's Core Earnings tends to give to financial analysts is not the message one might expect to be favorably received. In effect, it is telling securities analysts and stock pickers that the easy days of the 1990s are long gone. No more can one choose any stock and watch its price soar. Now it is time for analysts to do their homework. Doing their homework means understanding and researching a lot of accounting issues including options, pensions, and write-offs. Securities analysis takes real work in the 2000s, unlike the 1990s. Yet, this message is met with agreement virtually all the time.

In the year since the May 2002, full release of Standard & Poor's Core Earnings, there have been some changes in the topics and tone of the discussion. The most notable change is with the question of stock options. In May and June 2002, the dominant argument was that stock options could not be valued and were not really worth anything anyhow, so why bother.

Now the discussion has shifted: Options have a value and the value can be measured. The arguments that remain turn on the details on various option pricing models, not on the principle that options are compensation and, as such, are a legitimate charge against Standard & Poor's Core Earnings.

These rigorous and consistent definitions of core operating earnings can add value to market participants by establishing an independent standard and benchmark for comparison. As this approach becomes more institutionalized, the presence of credible earnings benchmarks can facilitate robust independent research and valuation analysis. Progress can be made.

NOTES

1. FASB 123: Accounting for Stock-Based Compensation, Financial Accounting Standards Board, October 1995.

2. Cite to *Wall Street Journal* article, November 8, 2001, p. C-1.

3. Greenspan, Alan. *Corporate Governance*, speech at the Stern School of Business, NYU, March 26, 2002, *available at* www.federalreserve.gov/boarddocs/speeches/2002/200203262/default.htm. Warren Buffet, Berkshire Hathaway 2001 Annual Report *at* www.Berkshirehathaway.com.

4. Kahle, Kathleen. "When a Buyback Isn't a Buyback: Open-Market Repurchases and Employee Options," *Journal of Financial Economics*, vol. 63, January 2002, pp. 235–261.

5. *See* D. M. Blitzer et al. *Measures of Corporate Earnings*, May 14, 2002 *at* www.coreearnings.standardandpoors.com.

6. Bodie, Z., R. S. Kaplan, and R. C. Merton. "For the Last Time: Stock Options Are an Expense," *Harvard Business Review*, March 2003.

7. FASB 87, Employers Accounting for Pensions, Financial Accounting Standards Board, December 1985.

8. *Accounting for Costs Associated with Exit or Disposal Activities*, FASB 146, Financial Accounting Standards Board, June 2002.

CHAPTER 10

Social and Environmental Reporting

John Elkington and Peter Zollinger

As the corporate governance, corporate social responsibility, and sustainable development agendas converge, reporting and assurance are emerging as key bridgeheads. Business faces an increasing number of nontraditional and often, at least to begin with, nonfinancial risks which are not captured by traditional reporting, ranking, and rating systems. One reason: Most of these systems look backward rather than forward. Meanwhile, particularly in the wake of the disasters that hit companies like Enron and Arthur Andersen, investors are keen to find ways to avoid unpleasant surprises.

By early 1993, the whole issue of trust in capitalism, in companies, and in the processes of corporate governance was very much on the agenda. So, for example, the theme of the World Economic Forum's event in Davos was "Building Trust." WEF founder Klaus Schwab stressed that "never before in the 33 years of the Forum's history has the situation in the world been as fragile, as complex and dangerous as this year." Trust, he said, "is the foundation of all personal relationships. It is the foundation of all business. It is the foundation of all international relations. In our increasingly interconnected world, trust is the rock on which we all depend. Without trust, there can be no respect, no security, and no spirit of partnership or cooperation."[1] Against this background, corporate social responsibility (CSR) and sustainability reporting have become the most developed forms of nonfinancial reporting. At their best, they aim to capture, measure, and value performance across the triple bottom line (TBL) of economic, social, and environmental value added—or destroyed.[2] A growing range of socially responsible investment (SRI) and mainstream analysts see the quality of reporting across the triple bottom line agenda as a proxy for good management generally.

Corporate and market transparency is increasingly seen to be central to any attempts to rebuild trust. At its best, triple bottom line reporting spotlights several key areas:

- The governing principles a company is committed to;
- The wider context in which a company sees itself operating;
- The dilemmas it faces;
- The ways in which it sees its markets evolving as a result;
- Its strategies for dealing with all of the above;
- The nature, scale, and outcomes of stakeholder engagement processes; and
- Progress against targets set.

One critical success factor is the quality and credibility of the assurance processes used. All of these areas are covered by the report benchmarking methodology developed over the past decade by SustainAbility, working with the United Nations Environment Programme (UNEP) and more than 30 leading companies.

PRESSURE WAVES

Scandals, disasters, and controversies provide useful clues on where the corporate risk and governance agenda is —and on where it is headed. From 1994, using a range of indicators, three great waves of societal pressure on business can be plotted, tracking the key trends from 1961 to the present day. All three pressure waves have had profound impacts on the business world, influencing which issues have come to dominate the political agenda and —the focus of this chapter—the ways in which companies evaluate political, economic, social, and environmental risks and are held to account in these areas.

In retrospect, it is clear that these waves have paralleled—and increasingly been fuelled by—powerful economic and technological trends. These have included the globalization of markets, investment, and the media and, a strongly linked trend, the evolution of the Internet. Taken together, these trends have helped drive the linked corporate responsibility, accountability, transparency, disclosure, reporting, assurance, and stakeholder engagement agendas.

The first wave, as shown in Figure 10-1, peaked between 1969 and 1973, focused on environment and catalyzed new government agencies and regulations across the OECD region.[3] We call this the "Limits" wave, because of the strong focus on potential environmental and natural resource limits to economic growth.

FIGURE 10-1

Pressure Waves, 1961–2001

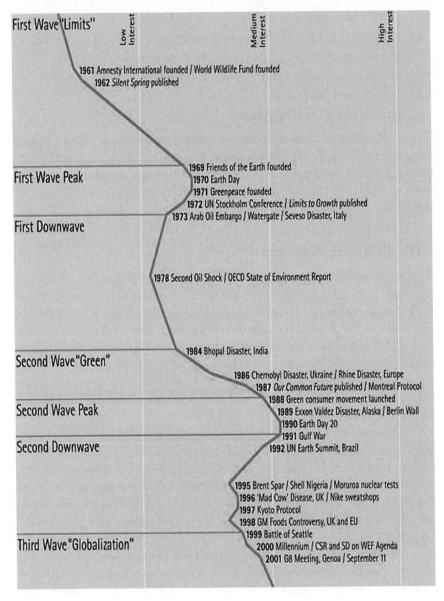

First Wave "Limits"

Low Interest   Medium Interest   High Interest

1961 Amnesty International founded / World Wildlife Fund founded
1962 *Silent Spring* published

First Wave Peak

1969 Friends of the Earth founded
1970 Earth Day
1971 Greenpeace founded
1972 UN Stockholm Conference / *Limits to Growth* published
1973 Arab Oil Embargo / Watergate / Seveso Disaster, Italy

First Downwave

1978 Second Oil Shock / OECD State of Environment Report

Second Wave "Green"

1984 Bhopal Disaster, India

1986 Chernobyl Disaster, Ukraine / Rhine Disaster, Europe
1987 *Our Common Future* published / Montreal Protocol
1988 Green consumer movement launched

Second Wave Peak

1989 Exxon Valdez Disaster, Alaska / Berlin Wall
1990 Earth Day 20
1991 Gulf War

Second Downwave

1992 UN Earth Summit, Brazil

1995 Brent Spar / Shell Nigeria / Moruroa nuclear tests
1996 'Mad Cow' Disease, UK / Nike sweatshops
1997 Kyoto Protocol
1998 GM Foods Controversy, UK and EU
1999 Battle of Seattle

Third Wave "Globalization"

2000 Millennium / CSR and SD on WEF Agenda
2001 G8 Meeting, Genoa / September 11

The second wave, the "Green" wave, peaked between 1988 and 1991, increasingly focused on big picture environmental risks (including ozone depletion and climate change), resulted in new levels of reputational risk for companies, catalyzed new corporate strategies targeting competitive advantage, and resulted in a range of new market standards.

The third wave, the "Globalization" wave, has been very different from its predecessors. It picked up a real head of steam in the streets on Seattle in 1999, during the protests against the World Trade Organization (WTO). It placed a highly critical spotlight on the various processes of globalization, and helped catalyze profound debates on both corporate and global governance. It has been less visible, largely because much of the action is taking place in boardrooms, behind the scenes. The peak period of this third wave, we believe, ended late in 2002.

Paradoxically, that means that the challenge for business—including both risks and opportunities—is only just beginning to surface. In retrospect, at least, it turns out that much of the really important work, with major implications for business, happens after a given wave's peak period has passed. So, across the OECD region, the mid-1970s saw the most intensive efforts to set up new environment agencies, enact new legislation, and ensure corporate compliance. Similarly, the mid-1990s saw a proliferation of voluntary standards in areas such as management systems, accountability, and reporting. We expect the third "downwave" period to see intensive efforts to address issues raised by the anti-globalization, security, and governance debates of recent years. Since 1993 the early interest in corporate environmental reporting has expanded into a much wider focus on the triple bottom line of sustainable development (SD).

A DECADE OF PROGRESS

From the perspective of 1990, progress in corporate disclosures against the triple bottom line has been remarkable. This is documented in the results of Trust Us,[4] the latest in a series of international benchmark surveys produced since 1993[5] by SustainAbility for UNEP. This survey built directly on the work reported in SustainAbility's first Global Reporters survey, published in 2000. Once again, we identified 50 top reports from around the world (the Top 50), analyzing them in depth. We also spotlighted another 50 reports (the Other 50) offering further insights into where best practice in sustainability reporting is headed.

As it turned out, 2002 was a watershed year in a number of respects, particularly in relation to the corporate responsibility agenda. The fate of companies like Enron and Arthur Andersen once again signaled a growing need to focus on issues related to financial accountability and corporate governance.

The early years of the twenty-first century have seen seismic shifts in relation to corporate transparency, accountability, and reporting—suggesting to us in 2002 that we were seeing the start of what we dubbed the "Trust Decade." Companies like Shell, Monsanto, Nike, Enron, and Andersen have been exposed to the disorienting pressures of the CNN World—some deserving the treatment more than others. But most major multinational companies now acknowledge that new forms of accountability are emerging at a rapid pace.

The year 2002 also saw the inauguration of the Global Reporting Initiative (GRI), after a five-year gestation period from 1997. A progress report on the GRI can be found in the following section. The GRI aside, and from the perspective of 2002, the most striking changes in reporting over the previous decade included the:

- Growth in the number of reporting companies from a few dozen to a few thousand;
- Evolution of the reporting agenda from environmental to wider triple bottom line disclosures; and
- Huge leap in the volume of information available—both printed and online.

That said, the total number of companies reporting by 2002 was still very small when compared with the estimates of more than 60,000 multinational corporations, let alone the millions of smaller companies operating in different parts of the world. Interestingly, too, best practice in reporting shows some evidence of the usual suspects syndrome, although these surveys also have picked up a range of smaller or less well-known reporters. Figure 10-2 shows the top reporters in SustainAbility's 1994, 1996, 1997, 2000, and 2002 benchmark surveys.

From 2002's perspective, the most striking challenges still remaining were the:

- Widespread failure to link company sustainability issues with brand and corporate identity;
- Continuing disinterest of most financial institutions and analysts in most of the data and information currently being reported for application in lending and underwriting decisions; and

F I G U R E 1 0 - 2

Top Reporters, 1994–2002

1994	1996	1997	2000	2002
Body Shop	Body Shop	Body Shop	BAA	Cooperative Bank
Bristol-Myers Squibb	Phillips Petroleum	Baxter	Novo Nordisk	Novo Nordisk
British Airways	Monsanto	Nestlé	Cooperative Bank	BAA
British Gas	Bristol-Myers Squibb	Novo Nordisk	BT	British Telecom
British Telecom	Dow Europe	British Airways	BP	Rio Tinto
BSO/Origin	IBM	Volvo	Shell	Shell
Dow Chemicals	Ontario Hydro	General Motors	WMC	BP
Kunert	Polaroid	Sun Company	ESAB	Bristol-Myers Squibb
Noranda	Waste Management Inc.	Bristol-Myers Squibb	Bristol-Myers Squibb	South African Breweries
Ontario Hydro	DuPont	Polaroid	Volkswagen	BASF
Shell Canada			ING	
Thorn-EMI				
Union Carbide				
Waste Management Inc.				

◆ Widespread and growing syndrome, dubbed "carpet bombing": that is, bombarding readers with ever-more information, without providing insight as to relevance, meaning, or, above all, materiality.

GLOBAL REPORTING INITIATIVE

One clear message from 2002's Top 50 was just how significant a role the Global Reporting Initiative (GRI) Guidelines have played in stimulating reporting in the previous year or two. A large proportion of the leading companies were first-time reporters, many from sectors not frequently seen in reporting circles. Of these, 52 percent were identified as having been developed using the GRI Guidelines —as are a full 60 percent of the Top 50. Furthermore, it is clear that these reporters have tended to enter the game at a higher level than many of their predecessors which we think speaks volumes for the quality and robustness of the GRI as a reporting framework.

The GRI was created as a joint initiative of the U.S.-based Coalition for Environmentally Responsible Economies (CERES) and UNEP in 1997. It was born of the desire to make sustainability reporting a serious issue for companies and a real basis of engagement and decisionmaking for stakeholders.

Five years later, the GRI was off to a flying start. Its Sustainability Reporting Guidelines—by then in their second version—are now recognized as setting the pace in this emerging field. By 2002, a new board of directors, including international thought leaders on corporate responsibility, had taken the helm of the newly inaugurated independent institution.[6]

The GRI Guidelines aim to define real, usable parameters for sustainable development and corporate performance—in many cases where such parameters have never before existed. They are marketed as a serious, strategic, professional tool. At the same time, they are a perpetual work in progress, to be continuously refined in light of experience and new knowledge, and every report built on them has been something of an experiment.

The Guidelines, last revised in 2002, provide an international framework for triple bottom line reporting. They are supported by technical protocols, by sector supplements, and by issue guidance documents. Each protocol addresses a specific performance indicator, for example, energy use or child labor, by providing detailed definitions, procedures, formulas, and references to ensure consistency across reports. The sector supplements aim to address the inherent weaknesses of any one-size-fits-all approach to reporting. They are designed to capture the unique set of sustainability issues faced by different industry sectors, for example, automotive, banking, and mining. These supplements are at an early stage of development, but will develop in scope and rigor over time. The issue guidance documents are designed to help reporters work out what is meant by specific terms like *diversity* or *productivity*.

Crucially, the GRI has embraced a balance of stakeholder and regional perspectives as fundamental—its various governance bodies and working groups must include representation from business, civil society, accountancy, and labor, from various world regions. No one group can be permitted to dominate at the expense of others' perspectives.

THE FINANCIAL ANALYSTS

The $64,000 question, as they used to put it before inflation took hold, is what do the financial analysts make of all this disclosure and reporting. SustainAbility originally addressed this question in 1996 in *Engaging Stakeholders*, focusing on the rating agencies, socially responsible investment (SRI) funds, and the Stock Exchange of Thailand. We found that a small number of organizations were starting to build environmental criteria into their stock screening processes—and a slightly larger number were looking at corporate environmental reporting as a proxy both for performance and for quality of management.

But what progress has there been since? To find out, we reviewed the Top 50 reports in the 2002 survey. As context, and to put it bluntly, most of these reports are not yet written with financial analysts, shareholders, or other financial actors in mind. Paradoxically, however, while analysts still see most of the information reported as failing their financial materiality tests,[7] some reports now contain a potential goldmine of information which switched-on analysts are beginning to turn into competitive ratings and future market assessments.

There are three general phenomena we have noted, which indicate where sustainability reporters are moving to meet financial audiences' needs.

- Shifting language to take account of newly recognized connections between sustainability issues and financial performance;
- Affiliation with well-known analyst recommendations or ratings; and

♦ Cross-linking sustainability with more mainstream notions of "good business practice."

Although the language used in most reports is not yet truly tuned to financial market needs, it is beginning to pick up on financial concerns, such as risk management. For example, the foreword from Deutsche Telekom's chairman, Dr. Ron Sommer, and Gerd Tenzer, management board member responsible for production, technology, and the environment, makes the link between CSR and SD on the one hand and risk management on the other, with risk areas including "potential environmental damage just as much as the Company's image in society."

Another good example is that by SCA Svenska Cellulosa, the Sweden-based international forestry, packaging and hygiene products company. In its *Environmental Report 2001*, it notes that SCA's objective is "to create value for its shareholders." It achieves this objective by combining profitability and growth with its corporate responsibility toward environmental and social issues, and adopting a low-risk strategy in these key areas. In its case, SCA argues, "shareholder value is inextricably linked to corporate, social and environmental responsibility."

Corporate reporters are increasingly using phrases like "sustainable growth." Take Suncor, the Canadian oil sands company, for example. Its CEO, Rick George, talks of pursuing "parallel paths to value creation." One path, he says, "leads to the responsible development of hydrocarbon resources, such as oil sands and natural gas," with over half of Canada's crude oil production expected to be from oil sands by 2007. "The second path," he continues, "involves developing alternative and renewable sources of energy." Thus, the company's sustainability strategy is directly linked to long-term shareholder value—tellingly, at least for mainstream financial analysts, the company's common share price rose 170 percent between 1996 and 2000.

One reason why analysts should be paying attention is that most of these reports are still being produced by companies with major risk profiles—for example, the Swiss-Swedish engineering group ABB, whose asbestos liabilities (which were bought in during an acquisition in the United States), reemerged with a vengeance in late 2002. Indeed, very few of the Top 50 reporting companies have business models that are currently and automatically aligned with SD principles.

Some companies say explicitly that they are using their sustainability reporting to raise their profile among financial analysts. For example, Suez, in addition to trying to give shareholders an adequate return, also tries to use its reporting to increase its shares' visibility. They are clearly pleased with their listing in such indexes as ASPI and the Dow Jones STOXX Sustainability Index. Similarly, SCA notes that it now appears in the Dow Jones Sustainability Group Index, the Dow Jones STOXX Sustainability Index, and the FTSE4Good Index. It also reports that the New York–based strategic value advisory firm Innovest recently awarded SCA a AAA rating, the top rating for social and environmental performance.

Meanwhile, just as nongovernmental organizations (NGOs) engaging in corporate stakeholder processes are often seen as trophies by reporting companies, who profile them and their involvement as a form of assurance, so companies increasingly see socially responsible investment and mainstream analysts as trophies. Some reports feature individual analysts. To date, however, their comments have more to do with the issues than the implications for shareholder value added.

But financial implications there are. "There is no danger of us running out of environmental issues to address in industry," as Professor Edward Krubasik, a member of the Siemens Managing Board, put it. In 2001, for example, Siemens had spent almost 75 million EUR on the environment, using strict definitions of what qualified, including 61 million EUR in operating costs and 13 million EUR in capital spending. These figures compare with 2001 net sales of 87 billion EUR, net income of over 2 billion EUR, and R&D expenses of 6.7 billion EUR.

Another interesting report in this area is that from the U.K. water company AWG, which among other things contains a preliminary set of environmental accounts. The accounts seek to identify and put a value on the most significant environmental impacts caused by AWG's operations—and what the impact on AWG's profits would be if these externalities were to be internalized. And, interestingly, the potential negative impact on profits increased from 8.1 percent in 1999 to 11.9 percent in 2001, because of the growing use of energy derived from fossil fuels, some of which was linked to higher water and waste treatment requirements.

AND, FINALLY, GOVERNANCE

In *Engaging Stakeholders*, published in 1996, ten transitions were forecast, one of which was a shift from the then-current focus on public relations to a new focus on corporate governance.[8] Some limited progress had been made by the time of our 2000 *Global Reporters* survey, in the sense that we could cover some interesting CEO forewords, but most of the 2000 reports still had very little to say on corporate governance. By the 2002 crop of reports, however, that position had changed significantly.

With major corporate scandals raising fundamental questions over the way companies are organized and whose interests they serve, this progress is timely. With our report benchmarking, we allocate a total of 196 points, distributed across 49 criteria. In terms of governance, where we allocated 4 points, 19 of the Top 50 scored 3, and one (South African Breweries) scored a full 4. SAB provides an excellent overview of its governance and accountability processes. "Corporate governance is essentially about efficient, honest, responsible and accountable leadership," it explains. "As such it makes sense from a corporate perspective that governance is the lead agent—not only in consolidating aspects of corporate citizenship, corporate social responsibility and sustainable development— but also in integrating these agendas into mainstream business activities."

This last issue—ensuring that SD agendas are absorbed into and supported by a company's normal business activities—is why strong board leadership is so key. Which is why it is so surprising (and disappointing) to see British Petroleum's report include the specific disclaimer that its report is not "subject to review by the board of directors or its committees." For a company with a relatively sophisticated understanding of the SD agenda, such a statement amounts to a complete disavowal by BP's board for this, the company's key public statement on sustainable development.

Apart from this disturbing message, BP turns in an otherwise respectable performance on governance reporting. In addition to clear listings of who's who in terms of board and board committee members, there are clear, short statements on such areas as the board's governance policies (adopted in 1997), board-executive relationships, board processes and compliance with the Combined Code on Corporate Governance of the London Stock Exchange. Specific links to the CSR and SD agendas, however, are not as clear as they might be.

Perhaps the existence of the aforementioned Combined Code is one reason why a number of U.K. companies make a good appearance in this area, including British Telecom and British Airports Authority. British Telecom's new main strategy committee, the Management Council, is made up of business and functional leaders from across the group. The main focus areas include ethics and values, CSR, human resources, pensions, technology, branding, and health and safety. The Council also provides advice on critical areas such as regulation, media relations, public policy, and public affairs. Interestingly, BT mentions that "social, ethical and environmental matters have been incorporated into the Directors' induction program."

It's not only U.K. companies that make the grade here, though. "Corporate governance," says the U.S. corporate Baxter International in its 2001 report, "provides an essential framework for the board of directors, management and shareholders to define, measure and balance critical performance measures that go beyond the company's financial bottom line, making sure the corporation is conducting itself in a manner that meets shareholder approval." Interestingly, the company's chairman and CEO is the only inside director on the Baxter board. There is a timely section on integrity in financial reporting.

And South Africa's Eskom also provides a leading example. After a clear mapping of the people involved in South Africa's Electricity Council and in Eskom's regulated business, Eskom offers a further six pages on corporate governance. Stakeholder relations are spotlighted, as is the fact that the company "strives to align with international sustainability initiatives such as the Global Reporting Initiative." The Eskom eye is clearly on world-class best practice.

Finally, here, Swiss Re offers an interesting discussion of the ways in which its environmental, corporate governance, and risk management guidelines are converging—with its top-level sustainability committee chaired by the Chief Risk Officer (CRO). This suggests an approach to sustainability analysis which focuses on a risk management perspective— one that is more likely to capture the attention of mainstream investors that operate without a specific social agenda. But a key challenge over the next decade will be to identify and value the opportunity spaces that sustainable development will create. In addition to the obvious areas of infrastructure provision (e.g., for clean water and affordable, renewable energy) in the poor world, there is the huge task of beginning the conversion of rich-world economies to some form of hydrogen economy.

CONCLUSION

Looking forward, two main areas of research warrant focus. The first is materiality, the second integration.

Materiality

Reporting more information is, of course, not a bad thing in itself and, in fact, stretching the reporting boundaries to cover new issues and new aspects of company operations not previously treated has been a major

priority for many stakeholders for many years. But the average page
length of reports increased by almost 50 percent between 2000 and 2002,
yet the scores against our methodology hardly moved. Clearly the time
has come to focus on the really critical issues, on materiality.[9] Without
clear issue identification—and ideally, stakeholder involvement in this
process—readers cannot evaluate the nature, extent, and seriousness of a
company's triple bottom line priorities.

We would hope to see more companies explaining how they have
used stakeholder engagement to refine their strategic priorities. This
needn't always involve major, high-profile stakeholder events—indeed,
industry federations and umbrella groups like the World Business Council on Sustainable Development (WBCSD) have a central role to play in
crystallizing the agenda for their members, large and small.

Integration

The current crop of reports shows a continuing—and unacceptable—
siloing of sustainability issues. The plateau in scores—the "glass ceiling"—can only be broken with companies showing evidence of how
each of the sustainability issues, management programs, and performance trends is directly and actively integrated into normal business
operations. The most important of these have to do with governance
and brands.

The next phase of the debate will increasingly focus on the highest-
order manifestations of corporate sustainability thinking, that is, *integration* (processes that build triple bottom line factors into existing
businesses) and *incubation* (which involves building sustainability into the
very DNA of new business ventures).[10]

The challenges we now face, and the opportunity spaces now
emerging, are indicated in Figure 10-3. To date, the focus has largely been
on balance sheets, that is, on a range of activities designed to produce
financial and nonfinancial statements. These include accounting, reporting, and assurance. This has been one part of a broader process by which
the CSR and SD agendas begin to overlap with the global and corporate
governance agendas. The next stage will be to actively and successfully
engage a growing number of corporate boards, to trigger the strategic
investments necessary.

But the really big challenges of the next decade or two will have less
to do with questions of how we report better, or govern companies better,
and more to do with how we use and change market mechanisms to

F I G U R E   1 0 - 3

The 4Bs of Integration and Incubation

	Governance	Markets
Emerging	Boards	Business Models
Existing	Balance Sheets	Brands

Source: SustainAbility 2002.

define, develop, and deliver sustainable business solutions. This will involve more work in the area of brands, to build new conversations with customers and consumers. And, more fundamentally still, we need to build the next decade's equivalent of the 1960s space race to evolve new, more sustainable business models. The key question here is: How can we create enough value and wealth to meet the needs of 9 to 10 billion people, while protecting the values embedded in the CSR and SD agendas? It seems clear that the continuous-improvement model of future sustainability, as embodied by most corporate reporters, is simply incapable of getting us there.

Given the latest crop of corporate sustainability reports, there remain questions to be answered. As far as the Global Reporters agenda is concerned, they relate to boards, brands, and business models. These, then, must be our main areas of focus in the coming years.

NOTES

1. Elkington, J. "Trusting Value," *Director Magazine*, April 2003.

2. Elkington, J. *Cannibals with Forks: The Triple Bottom Line of 21st Century Business*, Capstone Publishing, Oxford, 1997/1999; New Society, North America, 1998.

3. *Good News and Bad: The Media, Corporate Social Responsibility and Sustainable Development*, SustainAbility with Ketchum and the United Nations Environment Programme, 2002.

4. *Trust Us:* The Global Reporters 2002 Survey of Corporate Sustainability Reporting, SustainAbility with the United Nations Environment Programme, 2002.

5. SustainAbility, Deloitte Touche Tohmatsu International, International Institute for Sustainable Development, *Coming Clean: Corporate Environmental Reporting— Opening Up for Sustainable Development*, 1993. This was followed by a series of SustainAbility/UNEP reports, including: *Company Environmental Reporting: A Measure of the Progress of Business and Industry Towards Sustainable Development,*

1994; *Engaging Stakeholders,* in two volumes (*The Benchmark Survey* and *The Case Studies*), 1996; *The 1997 Benchmark Survey: The Third International Progress Report on Company Environmental Reporting,* 1997; and *The Global Reporters: The First International Benchmark Survey of Corporate Sustainability Reporting,* 2000.

6. A critique of the GRI can be found in *Trust Us.* For further details on the GRI and its Guidelines, visit www.globalreporting.org.

7. *Materiality* is centrally about information that is relevant to stakeholders in forming their understanding of the organization to make practical judgments that support well-reasoned decisions and actions [AccountAbility (2002) AA1000 Assurance Standard]. For more information on emerging definitions of materiality in this area, *see* the AA1000 stakeholder engagement-based assurance standard produced by the Institute of Social and Ethical AccountAbility *at* www.accountability.org.uk.

8. *Engaging Stakeholders,* in two volumes (Volume 1: The Benchmark Survey; Volume 2: The Case Studies), SustainAbility for the United Nations Environment Programme, 1996.

9. See note 7.

10. Elkington, J. *The Chrysalis Economy: How Citizen CEOs and Corporations Can Fuse Values and Value Creation,* Capstone Publishing/John Wiley, Oxford, 2001.

Wider Themes of Governance

Part Four includes a range of chapters that address governance in a broader and more diverse context. Chapter 11 on sustainable development addresses the concept of "sustainable governance," a fusion of traditional shareholder-focused approach to corporate governance with an additional focus on social and environmental issues—the concerns of nonfinancial stakeholders. The specific theme of directors' and officers' liability insurance is focused on in Chapter 12, illustrating the dynamic market for this form of insurance and its links to corporate governance. Chapter 13 addresses the governance of mutual funds and other collective vehicles, outlining key areas of governance risk in the managed fund area and discussing governance mechanisms to address these risks. Governance extends from the private to the public sector in Chapter 14, where governance issues are addressed for governmental organizations, both at the sovereign and regional levels. The approach taken is one that is relevant in the analysis of governmental credit quality; along with the general citizenry, the creditor is one of the key stakeholders affected by government governance. Chapter 15 concludes this part with a view on governance from a "human" perspective. In particular this relates to the interpersonal dynamics that clearly influence the effectiveness of managers and directors in the operation of the board and the overall governance of the company. The human side is a relevant factor in all forms of governance: corporate, fund, or public sector.

CHAPTER 11

Sustainable Development

Dr. Matthew Kiernan

SUSTAINABLE GOVERNANCE: THE "SUSTAINABILITY" AND CORPORATE GOVERNANCE AGENDAS CONVERGE

Social and environmental (i.e., "sustainability") issues and corporate governance historically have been viewed as quite separate concerns, of interest to two largely unrelated constituencies. Today, however, the two are becoming increasingly intertwined. The convergence of the corporate governance and sustainable development agendas is a compelling and seemingly irreversible trend, and over time it will require dramatic changes in both the thought processes and actions of company directors, executives, and institutional investors alike.

There are at least ten powerful, global "mega-trends" which can be expected to accelerate this convergence between sustainability and corporate governance to an even greater degree in the future:

- ◆ A growing appreciation of the nexus between companies' performance on environmental and social issues and their competitiveness, profitability, and share price performance.

- ◆ A tightening of national, regional, and global regulatory requirements for stronger environmental and social performance.

- ◆ The globalization and intensification of industrial competition, particularly into emerging markets, exponentially increasing the level of environmental and social risk for major corporations and investors.

- ◆ A substantial broadening of the purview of what is considered to be legitimate fiduciary responsibility to include companies' social and environmental performance.

- ◆ Tougher legal requirements for the disclosure of "nonfinancial" risks by both companies and institutional investors.

- Growing pressures from international nongovernmental organizations (NGOs), armed with unprecedented resources, credibility, and global communications platforms.

- The accelerating globalization of institutional investment, particularly by major pension funds.

- A growing inclination—and capability—among major institutional investors for shareholder activism in the governance of their portfolio companies.

- Changing demographics for both consumers and investors, substantially increasing the saliency and financial stakes of companies' environmental and social performance.

- A greater appreciation by senior executives of the competitive and financial risks and benefits of sustainability factors.

Each of the ten mega-trends is presented in turn.

The Growing Nexus Between Sustainability and Financial Performance

Leading-edge—but nonetheless mainstream—financial analysts and investors are recognizing in growing numbers that there is a strong, positive, and growing correlation between industrial companies' sustainability performance and their competitiveness and financial performance, whether measured as return on investment, return on equity, or total stock market return.[1]

Perhaps the most recent and definitive confirmation of that out-performance potential was provided in an analysis conducted in 2002 by the independent quantitative analysis specialist firm QED International in New York City. The study used a sophisticated "optimized time-series" methodology to examine the financial performance of an "eco-enhanced" Standard & Poor's 500 U.S. equities index portfolio.[2]

For purposes of that study, all of the other known investment risk factors, which could have otherwise explained performance differentials, were normalized away. The potential financial impact of differences in companies' industry sector, market capitalization, price/earnings ratio, interest rate sensitivity, volatility, and exposure to oil price shocks were among the traditional investment risk factors eliminated through sophisticated portfolio optimization techniques. The objective was to isolate that portion of the financial return that could be attributed solely to the quality of the companies' performance on sustainability issues.

As Figure 11-1 demonstrates, it does indeed appear possible to enhance risk-adjusted shareholder returns by overweighting companies exhibiting superior environmental management and underweighting their industry competitors with inferior performance in that area.

Each of the four different lines on the graph represents a different level of "tracking error," or the degree to which environmental management considerations were allowed to "tilt" the conventional baseline index portfolio. Depending on the level of emphasis given to environmental factors, the out-performance margin ranged from 180 to 440 basis points (bps) (1.8 to 4.4 percent). Significantly, the greater the emphasis, the greater the financial return. None of this out-performance can be explained by traditional securities and risk analysis; it appears to be driven entirely by sustainability factors.

Similar findings emerged in a 2002 study of European stocks by the German bank West LB Panmure. The researchers found that, "The find-

FIGURE   1 1 - 1

Ratings Normalized by Industry: Relative Performance Since 12/31/98 vs. S&P 500

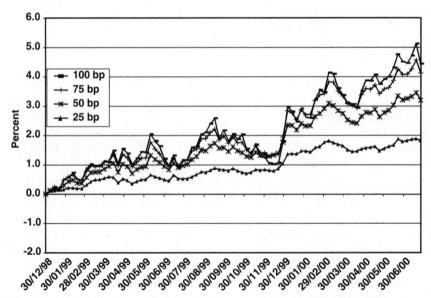

This chart shows four portfolios constructed to maximize EcoValue'21 ratings subject to tracking error limits as shown (25 bp to 100 bp). Over an 18 month period, the 25 bp TE portfolio outperformed the S&P by 181 bps while the 100 bp TE portfolio outperformed by 444 bps. Optimization techniques were used to neutralize twenty different tilts or "bets" on factors such as market capitalization, P/E, beta industry sector, and value/growth. The analysis was undertaken by external consultants to maximize objectivity.

ings of our study clearly suggest that it can pay to take the 'sustainability factor' into account when selecting stocks; there is an additional return even after risk adjustment. We estimate the 'style' alpha at 2.1 percent per annum. Another important finding of our analysis is that sustainability filters can create added value regardless of whether one is a value investor, a growth investor, or an investor opting for the small, mid, or large-cap style. We are convinced, therefore, that sustainability filters will be used as a matter of course in equities investments in only a few years' time."[3]

But what is driving this growing nexus between companies' performance on social and environmental issues and their competitiveness, financial success, and share price performance? Briefly put, they can affect both the risk and return sides of the investment equation. On the risk side, they can create a wide variety of financial exposures:

♦ *Balance sheet risks:* Historical and contingent liabilities can exert a tangible negative influence over a company's net asset value and even, under certain circumstances, its market value. The decommissioning of mines and the cleanup of derelict industrial sites, for example, can be a serious financial burden if appropriate preparatory measures have not been taken in advance. The threat of litigation on a large scale due to past business practices also can damage a firm's stock price severely. Halliburton, Dow, and ABB recently each lost roughly 40 percent of their total market capitalization over investor fears of retroactive asbestos litigation in the United States.

♦ *Operating risk:* Managing emissions and waste product discharges, coping with product liability risk, dealing with permitting issues and "eco-taxes," and handling delayed or canceled acquisitions or divestitures can draw substantial financial and management resources away from more productive business endeavors. Typically, resource extraction companies record environmental expenditures totaling between 10 and 30 percent of total annual operating costs, which is especially significant in today's environment of turbo-charged competition, falling stock prices, and razor-thin profit margins.

♦ *Capital cost risk:* Pollution control expenditures, product redesign costs, and other capital outlays due to environmental standards and regulations can be significant budgetary items. During the 1990s, the oil refining industry spent roughly $30 billion to comply with government regulations, a trend which looks set to continue, thanks to ever-tightening fuel quality standards.[4] In some cases, investor concerns about the company's sustainability performance can increase its cost of both debt and equity capital, or even make the capital unavailable altogether.

♦ *Business sustainability risk:* Companies in many industries face risks arising from the intrinsic lack of sustainability of their products and services. For example, government intentions to address climate change concerns, both through the Kyoto Protocol as well as national and regional regulations, could disrupt coal markets and significantly curtail demand, particularly for bituminous thermal coal types. The Japanese government's recent public musings about imposing a carbon tax to reduce climate change provide a sobering example. Those musings cut the market value of one major European coal company (X Strata) sufficiently to drop it out of the FTSE 100 index in the United Kingdom, thereby depriving the company of hundreds of millions of pounds worth of "automatic" investment capital from indexers.

♦ *Market and "reputational" risk:* This may be the most important risk factor of all. Major corporations remain heavily dependent on their "social license to do business," a license which can be revoked summarily over perceived environmental or social transgressions. The Brent Spar North Sea oil platform incident in 1995, for example, cost Royal Dutch/Shell fully 30 percent of its market share in Germany within 1 month, and it took more than 18 months to recover it. The company suffered similar commercial damage when its critics claimed that it was complicit in human rights abuses in Nigeria. The current "Stop Esso" boycott campaign in the United Kingdom and elsewhere—triggered specifically by ExxonMobil's obstructionist stance on climate change—provides a more recent example, as does the backlash against several major pharmaceutical companies for refusing to provide HIV/AIDS medicines at or below cost in Africa. Indeed, brand or reputational value can be so large—measured in billions of dollars for some firms—that the Financial Accounting Standards Board in the United States is currently considering a proposal that would recognize this vital "intangible asset" on corporate balance sheets.

By the same token, of course, companies achieving sustainability performance leadership also can create competitive advantage, reinforce "brand equity," and boost profits and shareholder value on the positive side. They do so by enhancing a number of key "value drivers," including:

- Improved relations with regulators, local suppliers, local communities, and other key stakeholders
- The ability to attract, retain, and motivate top talent
- Securing, retaining, and enhancing a "social license to do business," particularly in emerging markets countries
- Reducing operating expenses, through measures such as improved energy efficiency and waste minimization
- Reducing the risk of legal liabilities and fines
- Providing greater access to and affordability of investment capital
- Generating top-line revenue growth through new products, services, and technologies
- Increasing customer, and investor, loyalty
- Improving the company's corporate culture of innovation and adaptation

Companies such as DuPont, Johnson Matthey, and Interface, for example, are already generating top-line revenue growth with new products and services predicated on sustainability out-performance. Executives at companies as diverse as Merck (pharmaceuticals), Suncor (energy), and Intel (semiconductors) are convinced that their superior sustainability performance and reputations have generated concrete shareholder value through improved relations with regulators, customers, suppliers, and employees. In the case of Intel, for example, executives credit their improved sustainability performance for enhancing their relationship with their regulators. They were able to shave months off the time required for environmental permits for a new billion-dollar fabrication plant. This allowed Intel to reduce its time-to-market for its next generation of computer chip by a similar amount. This in turn translates into a few additional points of market share, which in turn represents millions of dollars in new revenue. In terms of generating a culture of innovation, STMicroelectronics in France, Aracruz in Brazil, and Royal Dutch/Shell in the United Kingdom are only three of the leading global companies where environmental innovations have helped create an entirely new corporate ethos and have elevated the companies' overall "innovation quotient" considerably.

In short, the weight of evidence appears clear: companies' environmental and social performance can indeed affect the expected levels of risk and return, both from individual companies and from entire investment portfolios. This by itself makes these issues of direct focus to those concerned with corporate governance and fiduciary responsibility. What will make environmental and social issues of even greater concern to directors, executives, and investors going forward is the confluence of nine additional "mega-trends" which can only increase their importance going forward.

Tightening Regulatory Requirements for Environmental and Social Performance

Performance standards for companies are, with very few exceptions, being raised at the national, regional, and even global levels. Examples at the national level include amendments to the U.S. Clean Air Act to raise air quality standards; tougher vehicle emissions laws in China, India, Singapore, Mexico, Thailand, and South Africa; and stricter controls over water pollution in the Philippines and Indonesia.

At the regional level, the most conspicuous generator of more exacting requirements for environmental and social performance is the European Union (EU). Virtually every year, the EU generates dozens of directives governing everything from automobile exhaust emissions and permissible fuel types to mandatory investments in renewable energy sources.

At the global level, the Kyoto Protocol is expected to come into force before 2004. That Protocol creates national quotas and limits the production of the so-called "greenhouse gases" most closely linked to climate change. Similar international conventions have already been signed and implemented to limit and reduce the emissions of ozone-depleting substances, transboundary water pollution, and a number of other sustainability concerns.

The trend is unmistakable and inexorable: All over the world, government regulators are "raising the bar" for companies' sustainability performance higher and higher. This clearly increases the competitive and financial premium for superior performers, and creates additional fiduciary risk for those associated with underperforming companies, whether they be directors, executives, or institutional investors. Once again, the imperatives of sustainability and good corporate governance converge.

The Globalization and Intensification of Industrial Competition, Particularly into Emerging Markets

The intensification of competition among major transitional companies has had at least one important corollary: the extension of that competition into emerging markets. This has exponentially increased the level of environmental and social risk for transnational companies. While the globalization phenomenon itself is intuitively relatively well understood (if not accepted), its true dimensions may be less so. One important proxy for its extent and velocity is the dramatic growth of foreign direct investment in emerging markets countries. If one examines just seven of the world's most important emerging markets (Argentina, Brazil, Chile, China, Indonesia, Korea, and Mexico), investment in those countries from OECD countries increased by an average of 680 percent in the decade between 1990 and 2000.[5]

The connection among the globalization of industrial competition, sustainability, and corporate governance is simply this: It is precisely in the emerging markets where companies' exposure to sustainability risks is greatest, yet their capabilities to deal with those risks are generally the least well developed.

Pick your business risk: consumer boycotts of products allegedly produced with child labor in Malaysia or Indonesia; human rights abuses in China and Africa; mining licenses revoked in the Philippines after an environmental "incident"; the list goes on and on. As a rule, company directors and other fiduciaries are ill equipped to monitor and manage those risks, although many are currently receiving accelerated, hands-on training.

It would be disingenuous to argue that similar, sustainability-driven business risks do not exist in developed markets; they clearly do. But in today's increasingly transparent, globally "wired" world, companies' performance on social and environmental issues in emerging markets is subject to unprecedented scrutiny, and therefore to potential business risk.

World-class corporate governance requires at the very least that company directors and other fiduciaries be aware of those risks, and put in place appropriate mechanisms to monitor them and, if necessary, intervene. There is every indication that industrial competition in emerging markets will only intensify in the years ahead. This trend, coupled with tougher local performance standards and enforcement regimes, will be another factor accelerating the convergence of corporate governance, fiduciary responsibility, and sustainability.

An Expanding View of Fiduciary Responsibilities

Conventional wisdom among investment professionals has held for decades that any measures taken to improve companies' environmental or social performance would be injurious or at best irrelevant to their financial returns, and therefore strictly beyond the legitimate purview of fiduciaries. This ethos has now begun to shift dramatically: As we have seen earlier in this chapter, a growing body of empirical research is making it clear that superior sustainability performance does indeed improve companies' risk-adjusted financial returns. As a consequence, sustainability is becoming a wholly legitimate if not mandatory concern for fiduciaries. Indeed, the fiduciary/governance equation is now effectively being turned on its head: Given the demonstrable impacts of sustainability performance on companies' risk/return profiles, fiduciaries are increasingly viewed as derelict in their responsibilities if they do *not* take them into account. Reforms of pension legislation in the United Kingdom, France, Germany, Australia, and elsewhere are already codifying this new ethos into legal requirements.

In the United States, the fiduciary duties of pension fund trustees—and, by extension, their money managers—are set out in the Employee Retirement and Income Security Act (ERISA). Those responsibilities are essentially twofold:

1. *The duty of care:* fiduciaries must act in a "prudent" and "reasonable" fashion; and

2. *The duty of loyalty:* they must act *solely* in the interests of the institution's beneficiaries.

In short, U.S. fiduciaries are legally obligated to have the long-term interests of their beneficiaries as their *sole* objective. In practice, it has been the evolving interpretation of the ERISA legislation, rather than any specific prescriptions in the legislation itself, which has determined what is and is not "reasonable," "prudent" behavior by fiduciaries. Unfortunately, until recently that interpretation was both excessively narrow and based on what turns out to be seriously mistaken assumptions. There is increasing reason to believe, however, that in the emerging era of "fiduciary capitalism,"[6] the practical interpretation of what is reasonable and prudent for fiduciaries will continue to evolve and expand, and the corporate governance and sustainability agendas will continue to converge.

Tightening Regulatory Pressures for Improved Disclosure of Nonfinancial Risks

The spectacular implosions of Enron and WorldCom in 2001–2002 were unquestionably the immediate precipitants for tougher disclosure requirements of investment risks in the United States, but in Europe the momentum had begun to build even earlier.

In July of 2000, the U.K. government passed major amendments to the Pensions Act requiring occupational pension scheme trustees to disclose in their Statements of Investment principles their approach to socially responsible investment (SRI). If their approach was to ignore SRI altogether, that, too, had to be disclosed. While social activists in the United Kingdom have argued that the amendments have had only a minimal practical effect to date,[7] their impact on pension fund trustees and their advisors and money managers arguably has already been substantial, and will continue to grow over time. The new regulations have literally placed sustainability concerns onto the agendas of dozens of pension fund trustees and money managers who had previously given them no apparent thought whatsoever. What is more, in addition to its effects within the United Kingdom itself, the new regulations have spawned similar changes in France, Germany, Switzerland, and Australia, among other countries. Indeed, in Australia, the Financial Services Reform Act of 2001 has gone even further, also requiring money managers in the private sector to substantiate in detail any claims to take account of social, environmental, and ethical factors.

In the United States, the post-Enron pressure for improved disclosure reached its apotheosis in the much discussed Sarbanes-Oxley Act of 2002, which requires much quicker and more comprehensive disclosure of material business risks. These tougher disclosure requirements were then extended squarely into the realm of social and environmental risk factors by a January 2003 ruling by the U.S. Securities and Exchange Commission that mutual funds and investment advisors would henceforth be required to disclose both their procedures for voting shareholder proxies *and* their actual voting records.

Taken together, these developments create a momentum which is both unmistakable and irreversible: Companies and their investors will both be forced to disclose a broader range of business risks, including social and environmental ones. This too will force sustainability issues onto corporate board agendas, and accelerate the convergence of the corporate governance and sustainability concerns even farther.

Growing Pressures from Nongovernmental Organizations and Other External Stakeholders

Armed with the tougher disclosure requirements just discussed, and having greater resources and much more comprehensive, real-time information about companies, these external organizations can and do now apply enormous pressure on companies. Some of the most effective nongovernmental organizations (NGOs) in the sustainability sphere are "campaigning" organizations such as Greenpeace, Friends of the Earth, the Sierra Club, and the World Wildlife Fund. While their philosophies and tactics differ, all four have had a discernible impact. In addition, more mainstream, "business-friendly" organizations such as the Geneva-based World Business Council for Sustainable Development and the World Resources Institute in Washington, D.C. have had and continue to have a significant impact as well.

In addition to their access to better and faster company information, these NGOs have two additional advantages: widespread credibility and an unprecedented ability to amplify and broadcast their views around the world instantaneously through the Internet. Anyone who doubts the strength of an NGO's credibility should consider this: In a survey by Edelman Public Relations of 2500 "opinion leaders" in five different OECD countries in 2000, the most highly regarded NGO in each country was considered to be at least twice as "trustworthy" as the most admired corporation in that same country. On some sustainability issues such as genetically modified foods, the NGOs were *six* times more credible.

In today's increasingly transparent "CNN world," companies and investors alike can expect unprecedented scrutiny on sustainability issues, and with it the continuing convergence of corporate governance and sustainability.

The Globalization of Pension Fund Investment

During the 1990s, global pension funds' total assets grew, on average, 15 percent a year, from $4.6 trillion to $15.9 trillion. Over this same period, their equity holdings increased from $1.6 trillion to $8 trillion—or from 35 to 51 percent of their total assets. By 1999, pension fund equity holdings represented fully 22.9 percent of global equity market capitalization, up from 17 percent in 1990. This growth was driven mainly by the four biggest pension markets—the United States, Japan, the United Kingdom, and the Netherlands—which together account for over 80 percent of global assets.

In 1990, only 3.3 percent of U.S. pension funds' equity investments were in the securities of non-U.S. companies. By the end of 2001, that proportion has more than tripled to over 11 percent.[8] A similar internationalization of pension fund investing is occurring in virtually every OECD country, albeit at different rates. This globalization process parallels and reinforces the expansion of industrial competition into international markets. In both cases, it increases the level of exposure to environmental and social risks which, by their very nature, are that much more difficult to manage on a global basis. This in turn creates new and unfamiliar business risks with which boards of directors must contend. Once again, sustainability and governance concerns become intertwined.

Growing Shareholder Activism

Since the late 1980s, shareholder activism has played an increasingly important role in attempts to influence the quality of companies' corporate governance. More recently, the increase in shareholder activism has coincided with and been augmented by two other powerful investment trends: the dramatic increase in the proportion of company shares held by institutions, and the rapid growth in the attention paid to corporate social responsibility and sustainable development issues. Fund managers are increasingly using shareholder activism rather than the threat of divestiture to improve the performance of their portfolio companies. In some cases, the emphasis on shareholder activism has become so strong that it has essentially become the fund managers' principal strategy for generating financial out-performance. Hermes' Focus and European Focus funds in the United Kingdom, Relational Investing in the United States, and the Sparx fund in Japan are prime examples; each of them seeks out companies where they believe improvements to deficient corporate governance practices can unlock hidden value, and then use their power as investor/shareholders to effectuate those changes.

A recent study released by the Investor Responsibility Research Center (IRRC) and the Social Investment Forum (SIF) confirmed the growth of shareholder advocacy in the United States. It also highlighted a new and significant phenomenon: the expansion of the advocacy base beyond its traditional constituency of environmental, social, and religious activists to include conservative, *mainstream* institutions such as the City of New York and the States of New York and Connecticut. The report stated that, "filers of traditional corporate governance resolutions and so-called 'social' resolutions are finding common ground to an unprecedented extent this year as they work to head off Enron-like problems at other corporations." [9]

The study reported that over 860 shareholder resolutions had been filed in the 2003 proxy season as of February, an increase of 8 percent from the previous year. Of that number, over 260 directly addressed sustainability issues of one kind or another, a year-over-year increase of over 20 percent. The range of sustainability-driven resolutions was broad: There were resolutions proposing to link executive compensation directly with companies' social and environmental performance (Boeing, Coca Cola, Unocal); ones exhorting pharmaceutical companies to become more proactive on global health issues such as HIV/AIDS (Bristol-Myers Squibb, Merck, Pfizer); proposals demanding higher company labor standards in emerging markets (Nike, Hudson's Bay Company); and resolutions on the fastest-growing category of all—climate change (Exxon Mobil, AEP, Pacific Gas & Electric).

Not only is there greater shareholder activism on sustainability issues from an increasingly broad, mainstream constituency, but the shareholder resolutions themselves are meeting with greater success. In 2002, sustainability-oriented resolutions achieved an average support vote of 9.4 percent, the highest level in a decade. What is more, in many cases they achieve even greater success: At the 2003 annual general meeting of the Bank of Montreal, a resolution requiring the bank to evaluate its money managers on their handling of environmental and social portfolio risks captured 30 percent of the votes. A resolution condemning "sweatshop" conditions in the supply chain at the Hudson's Bay Company achieved 36.8 percent of the shareholders' vote. These numbers are simply too large for boards of directors to ignore.

Perhaps the most dramatic contemporary illustration of the convergence between the sustainability and corporate governance agendas is a recent initiative called the Carbon Disclosure Project (CDP). The CDP is an unprecedented collaboration among 35 institutional investors representing assets of over $4.5 trillion. Significantly, the investors group was far from a collection of radical activists; it included such prominent mainstream names as Merrill Lynch, Allianz Dresdner, Credit Suisse, UBS Global Asset Management, the State of Connecticut, and one of the United Kingdom's largest pension schemes, the Universities Superannuation Scheme. In May of 2002, the CDP signatory institutions wrote to the chairmen of the 500 largest corporations in the world, expressing their concern as fiduciaries and investors about climate change, and requesting disclosure of what, if anything, the companies were doing to identify and manage any resulting business risks.

The report on the CDP's findings was launched in London and New York in early 2003, and received considerable attention from the financial press.[10] The CDP signatories subsequently announced their intention to repeat and expand the exercise again later in 2003, thereby virtually assuring the ongoing, high-profile linking of corporate governance and broad-based shareholder activism with what is arguably the single most important sustainability issue of our times.

Changing Consumer, and Investor, Demographics

It is almost a truism to say that today's consumers and investors are far more conscious of environmental and social issues than their predecessors ever were. In part, this represents a generational shift in the locus of purchasing power; in part it is a function of having unprecedented, nearly universal access to real-time information about companies' activities in virtually any part of the globe. Whatever its cause, evidence of the phenomenon abounds.

On the consumer side, we have witnessed everything from 25 percent annual growth rates in the sales of organic foods to highly successful boycotts of major companies such as Nike ("sweatshop" labor), Monsanto (genetically modified foods), and Exxon Mobil (climate change). This anecdotal evidence also can be supplemented by a consumer survey of unprecedented scope. In the year 2000, the polling company Environics and its affiliates interviewed 25,000 citizens in 23 countries on 6 continents. The survey, sponsored by the Conference Board in the United States and the Business Leaders Forum in the United Kingdom, provides compelling documentation of just how deep and widely shared sustainability concerns have become. One of the study's most striking findings was that companies' performance on social and environmental issues was the single most important factor governing people's purchasing decisions. As the top choice of 56 percent of the respondents, sustainability appears to be substantially more important than the two next most important factors: brand quality (40 percent) and company business fundamentals (34 percent). In addition, fully 40 percent of the sample had actively considered avoiding the products of sustainability laggards, and over 20 percent had actually done so during the previous year.

The study also found that "opinion leaders" within the survey had even stricter standards than most, and concludes: "These findings suggest that companies will come under even greater public pressure in coming years to deliver on their broader social responsibilities, as the stronger views of opinion leaders become more widely shared."[11]

Similar growth in the importance of sustainability considerations also can be seen on the *investment* side. The most obvious evidence is the accelerating increase in "socially responsible" investing (SRI). One recent and authoritative estimate placed the size of the global SRI market at nearly $2 trillion, with an annual growth rate of over 20 percent over the past few years.[12] And, while these growth rates of the SRI "asset class" are indeed impressive, what will ultimately prove even more significant is the progressive integration of many of the SRI and sustainability concerns into the $30+ trillion *mainstream* investment world.

Growing Awareness among Corporate Executives

Given the nature, direction, and power of the mega-trends we have discussed above, it is scarcely surprising that senior corporate executives are becoming more aware of the competitive and financial significance of sustainability issues. At present, awareness seems to be highest among European CEOs, but it is growing in virtually every country. A survey by

PriceWaterhouseCoopers in 2002 questioned over 1100 chief executives from 33 countries. Fully 70 percent of the respondents agreed that, "corporate social responsibility is *vital* to the profitability of any company."[13]

These findings were consistent with the results of a smaller but even more recent survey conducted by the World Economic Forum.[14] That study, conducted in 2003, questioned CEOs from 16 different countries and 18 different industry sectors. Fully 80 percent of the executives surveyed viewed their companies' sustainability performance as inextricably bound up with their overall reputation and brand value.

Thus, it seems clear that there is yet another set of drivers accelerating the convergence of the corporate governance and sustainability agendas: an increasingly aware and concerned cadre of global chief executives. Indeed, over 130 of them now participate regularly in the Geneva-based World Business Council for Sustainable Development, arguably the most influential global business forum for advancing and articulating the case for sustainability.

THE WAY FORWARD: SUSTAINABILITY, CORPORATE GOVERNANCE, AND INTANGIBLE VALUE

As recently as the mid-1980s, financial statements captured at least 75 percent of the true market value of major corporations. According to New York University accounting professor Baruch Lev, however, in the intervening years that figure has dropped to a paltry 15 percent on average.[15] That leaves roughly 85 percent of a company's value which cannot be explained by traditional, accounting-driven financial analysis. (In the case of Microsoft, the figure is actually over 99 percent.) This yawning disconnect between companies' book value and what they are really worth—their market capitalization—is now at an all-time historic high. This leaves institutional investors and fiduciaries with a severe information deficit.

As we move deeper and deeper into the era of knowledge-value and intangibles, conventional balance sheets and profit and loss statements will capture and reflect less and less of a company's true value and competitive potential. What is needed instead is a new, more dynamic "iceberg balance sheet" approach, which focuses investor and senior management attention where it belongs: on the 80 to 85 percent of companies' true value which cannot be explained by traditional, accounting-driven securities analysis. In point of fact, it is the unseen part of the "value iceberg" that contains the primary drivers of the company's future value-creation capabilities and unique comparative advantages.[16]

These intangible value drivers are of course notoriously ethereal and difficult to measure, but they will be absolutely central to companies' competitiveness and profitability going forward. Corporate governance and sustainability are two of the most potent of these nontraditional, intangible value drivers. Fiduciaries, financial analysts, and investors would all be well advised to remember that, and ensure that both sets of issues receive careful and continuous scrutiny at board level.

NOTES

1. West LB Panmure (November 2002) and May 2002; UBS Warburg (2001); Bank of Sarasin (1998 and 1999).

2. Blank and Carty, 2003.

3. West LB Panmure 2002, p. 1.

4. Innovest Strategic Value Advisors. *Global Integrated Oil and Gas Sector Report*, 2002.

5. The World Bank Group. *World Development Indicators*, 2002.

6. Hawley and Williams, 2000.

7. Just Pensions. *Do U.K. Pension Funds Invest Responsibly?*, A Survey of Current Practice on SRI, 2002.

8. Monks, 2001.

9. IRRC/SIF Study, available online at www.shareholderaction.org *and* www.irrc.org.

10. Innovest Strategic Value Advisors. *The Carbon Disclosure Project: A Report of Findings*, 2003.

11. Conference Board and Environics. *The Millenium Poll on Corporate Social Responsibility*, 2000.

12. Cerulli Associates. *The Cerulli Edge: SRI Issue*, November 2002, p. 2.

13. PriceWaterhouseCoopers. "Uncertain Times, Abundant Opportunities," *5th Annual Global CEO Survey*, 2000.

14. World Economic Forum. *Responding to the Leadership Challenge: Findings of a CEO Survey on Global Corporate Citizenship*, 2003.

15. Lev, 2001.

16. Kiernan, February 2003.

REFERENCES

Bank of Sarasin. *Environmental Shareholder Value*, 1998; and *Sustainable Investments: An Analysis of Returns in Relation to Environmental and Social Criteria*, 1999.

Bauer et al., "The Eco-Efficiency Premium in the U.S. Equity Market, " *Journal of Investing*, forthcoming, 2004.

Blank, H., and M. Carty. "The Eco-Efficiency Anomaly," *Journal of Investing*, forthcoming, 2004.

Camejo, P. "The SRI Advantage," New Society Publishers, 2002.

Forum for the Future. *CIS Sustainability Pays*, 2002.

Hawley, J. P. and A. T. Williams, *The Rise of Fiduciary Capitalism*, Philadelphia: University of Pennsylvania Press, 2000.

Investor Responsibility Research Council and Social Investment Forum. "Towards a Shared Agenda: Emerging Corporate Governance and Social Issue Trends," 2003.

Kiernan, M. "What Lies Beneath: Intangible Value and the Iceberg Balance Sheet," *Investments and Pension Funds Europe*, February 2003.

Kiernan, M. *The Eleven Commandments of 21st Century Management*, Prentice Hall, New York, 1996.

Lev, B. *Intangibles: Management, Measurement and Reporting*, Brookings Institution: Washington, D.C., 2001.

Monks, R. A. G. *The Emperor's Nightingale*, Capstone, 1998.

Monks, R. A. G. "The New Global Investors: How Shareholders Can Unlock Sustainable Prosperity Worldwide", 2001, full text available online at www.ragm.com.

UBS Warburg. "Sustainability Investment: The Merits of Socially Responsible Investment", L. Chen, August 2001.

West LB Panmure. "From Economics to Sustainomics: SRI—Investment Style with a Future" (West LB AG. analysts: H. Garz, C. Volk, and M. Gilles), May 2002.

West LB Panmure, "More Gain than Pain: Sustainability Pays Off," November 2002.

CHAPTER 12

Directors' and Officers' Insurance and Corporate Governance Risk

Ian Byrne

INTRODUCTION

In the traditional literature on corporate governance, the role of directors' and officers' (D&O) insurance is rarely dealt with in any detail, if at all. In standard textbooks on corporate governance it barely rates a mention and until recently it has been relatively underresearched. However, in certain key markets, particularly the United States, the existence and terms and conditions of D&O insurance policies have a significant effect on the behavior of market participants, and in a world that is becoming increasingly global, its use and impact cannot be ignored no matter where one is conducting business.

D&O insurance is intended to protect the directors and officers of a company against losses which arise from any actual or alleged wrongful acts that were carried out by those directors and officers acting in their corporate capacities. Directors and officers can be sued by a variety of interested parties—creditors, employees, competitors, suppliers, or customers. However, in recent years it has been the shareholders, particularly in the United States, who have initiated the largest suits; and the majority of these have been class action suits alleging securities fraud.

Corporate governance and D&O insurance affect and are affected by each other in a variety of ways. One facet of corporate governance deals with the way in which the senior executives ("officers") and directors interact to ensure that the assets of a company are used to the benefit of all the financial stakeholders. As directors and officers can obtain insurance to cover themselves against the consequences of their actions, this could have impacts on their decisions. Naturally, therefore, an analysis of corporate governance of a company forms a part of the due diligence undertaken by D&O underwriters. Importantly, the development of investor activism in the United States and the use of class action suits since the early 1990s, especially relating to securities fraud, have sent shock waves through the D&O industry. Further, a company's corporate governance is crucial to each individual director and executive.

In this chapter we will look at the development of the D&O insurance market, focusing on the link between corporate coverage and the "full compensation" ethos of the U.S. legislation covering securities fraud.[1] Although D&O insurance is now becoming available around the world, most research has been conducted on the two most developed D&O markets—the United States and the United Kingdom. This chapter focuses on those two markets. We will also look at the links between D&O insurance and other factors in the corporate governance mix. In particular, we look at the research that has been conducted on insurance premiums.

DEVELOPMENT OF THE D&O MARKET

Although individual coverage for directors had been available since Lloyd's of London introduced the first policies in the 1930s, these were not in great demand in the United States until the 1960s, and the 1980s in the United Kingdom. Even then, until the latter part of the 1980s the policies had to be funded by the directors themselves, again curtailing demand. By the end of the decade, however, legal changes in both the United States and the United Kingdom enabled corporations to pay for the coverage of individual directors and officers. This was a result of the increased litigation seen especially in the United States. Further, in a crucial development, through the 1990s the D&O industry expanded to include writing policies not only for individuals, but also for the corporations themselves ("entity coverage"). Some of the consequences of this development are dealt with later in this chapter.

Conceptually D&O insurance is simple; however, in practice the policies can be extremely complex with different inclusions, exclusions, and different levels of co-insurance (where the corporation takes on part of the variable risk), each dependent on the particularities of any given claim. However, in simple terms, the basic types of insurance are as follows.

1. Individual coverage. Primarily for nonexecutives who sit on multiple boards and who need coverage under one policy; paid for by the individual.

2. **Professional indemnity.** For those who sit on boards of companies in their professional capacity (as a lawyer, accountant, etc.); paid for by the individual.

3. **"A-side coverage"** is normally provided directly to individuals (i.e., the directors and officers themselves) where the company does not indemnify those individuals (e.g., it chooses not to, it is financially unable to do so, or it cannot do so by law); normally paid for by the corporation.

4. **"B-side coverage"** provided to (and paid for) by the company, which in turn indemnifies its directors and officers. Both A- and B-side policies cover the individuals concerned for loss arising from claims made against them for "wrongful acts" committed in their capacity as directors and officers of the company.

5. During the late 1990s the concept of entity coverage, sometimes known as "C-side coverage," was developed to cover corporations against securities claims. This is paid for by the company.

6. Employment practices liability is sometimes added to entity coverage in order to protect the company against claims for wrongful dismissal and other employment practice issues (paid for by the company). However, although very relevant to a company's corporate citizenship, this particular piece of D&O insurance has less relevance for mainline corporate governance.[2]

From a corporate governance point of view there are arguments both for and against the corporate purchase of D&O coverage—whether for individual directors or the company. The fact that the individuals are "covered," to a greater or lesser extent for the consequences of their actions could reduce the threat of litigation by shareholders, therefore reducing the effect of one of the tools of management control. Alternatively, one can argue that without such cover rational directors and officers would not take on such a role, especially in an environment of shareholder activism. Therefore, to attract good directors a company needs to offer such cover.

Further, if directors and officers were to take on such responsibilities without cover they could become unduly risk averse in the way they run the business, which may negatively affect shareholder value. Reputation risk and an efficient market for corporate control are other factors that argue in favor of indemnification. If the potential financial effects of personal litigation are eliminated as one method of ensuring that the actions of directors are in line with the interests of the other financial stakeholders—due to D&O insurance—then it is important that other methods are in place. An efficient market for corporate control is one such alternative. Takeover provisions are therefore clearly an important issue when looking at the governance practices of a company. The few empirical studies carried out in this area have tended to support the hypothesis that, on balance, D&O insurance does not have a negative impact on shareholder wealth.[2]

CLASS ACTION SUIT

The class action suit is by far the most common way in which shareholders seek compensation from a company and its directors and officers for alleged wrongdoing, and therefore the most common way that there is a claim against a D&O insurance policy. Originally included in the U.S. Securities Act of 1933[3] class actions have become very common in the United States, and are starting to be seen in other jurisdictions. Further, in recent years securities fraud has been the most prevalent type of claim.

A drop in the company share price is one of the more common reasons given by companies for being sued, and the damages calculation often related directly to the size of the fall and the consequent "lost wealth." Following such a fall a series of claims may be made against the company. Within 90 days of the initial notification a lead plaintiff (and lead council) are appointed from members of the class—the "most adequate plaintiff"—to pursue the case on behalf of all the members of the class.

At this point the company has the opportunity to apply for a dismissal of the case. In the United States, since the passing of the Private Securities Litigation Reform Act, December 1995 (PSLRA) plaintiffs must specify with "particularity" exactly what the subjects of their case are. In 2002 for example, 85 percent[4] of the total number of U.S. claims made involved citing Rule 10b-5 of the Securities Exchange Act of 1934: "Employment of Manipulative and Deceptive Devices."[5] This rule covers attempts to defraud, making untrue statements, or omitting to state a material fact in connection with the sale or purchase of a security. The PSLRA, which is discussed in more detail later in this chapter, has had the consequence that there is a requirement for "hard evidence" to be identified at the early stages of the claim. This requirement has meant that much attention is focused on demonstrable accounting issues. Earning restatements, false forward-looking statements, and GAAP violations are currently the most cited issues. Sections 11 and 12(2) of the act, relating to insider trading, were cited in 13 and 10 percent of cases in 2002. (In certain cases these sections were cited along with Rule 10b-5.) These three rules currently form the basis of the vast majority of securities fraud class action suits in the United States. If the plaintiff cannot exactly specify what the complaint is, then the case may be dismissed. (However, often the plaintiffs are given leave to appeal.) If the points raised by the plaintiffs are clearly not illegal, then, again, the case may be dismissed.

Since the PSLRA was passed in December 1995, the number of claims has risen but so too has the number of dismissals. Interestingly, although "particularity" was expected to reduce the number of "nuisance suits" (those suits below $1 million), the proportion of these suits has stayed basically the same at around 10 percent of the total.[6] If a claim is not dismissed, then the process moves to the "discovery stage"—which means that the plaintiffs obtain access to the company's documents and the company to the plaintiffs'. The case will then move toward trial. However, the vast majority will settle before going to court—the sum normally being determined in relation to the shareholders' "wealth loss." A proportion of this cost is covered by the D&O insurance, and the remainder by the corporation. The proportions are defined by the D&O policy document.

D&O INSURANCE MARKET

The D&O industry is faced with a number of significant issues.

1. Increased number of claims
2. Larger settlements
3. Compensation focus of U.S. legislation
4. Exposure of non-U.S. companies to U.S.-style litigation
5. The problems associated with entity coverage and other policy changes

Further, in the United States in particular, there have been three major influences that have altered behavior.

1. Private Securities Litigation Reform Act, December 1995
2. The boom and bust of the stock markets in the 1990–2002 period
3. The competitive situation in the industry

Claims

There has been a good deal of research conducted into the effect of the Private Securities Litigation Reform Act (PSLRA) on the number and size of the claims made. The PSLRA was passed by Congress in December 1995, overriding President Clinton's veto. Those who crafted the Act designed it to "reduce abusive litigation and coercive settlements." It was seen by the D&O insurance industry as a victory for corporate America and also for the D&O industry itself. The PSLRA also was intended to reduce the number of "nuisance" claims that were being filed in the federal courts. The Act does require much more detail from plaintiffs at the start of a case. It requires plaintiffs to highlight specifically any and each misleading statement made by the target company and the reasons why the statement is misleading.

There was a strengthening of the "scienter" rule, which meant that plaintiffs also must demonstrate that the company/director/officer acted with the "required state of mind"—i.e., they clearly intended to mislead. Further, as long as any projections are "not knowingly false," meaningful cautionary language will protect the company (the so-called "safe harbor" for forward-looking statements). The Act also introduced a "stay of discovery," which means that the plaintiffs cannot get sight of the company's documents until after the company's motion to dismiss has been heard and itself been dismissed. This has restricted the use of a claim as a device to investigate a company, while the financial sanctions imposed on those who are judged to have filed a frivolous claim are a disincentive to filing.

The Act also was designed to reduce the preference given to the position of lead plaintiff and lead council—promoting a more considered approach to litigation. Joint and several liability of defendants was replaced with proportionate liability—intended to protect co-defendants (e.g., accounting firms) who now would pay only their share of the settlement, irrespective of the situation of their client company. Previously, if a company was bankrupt and unable to pay their share of the settlement, the full cost could be attributed to the co-defending accounting company.

One clear effect of the PSLRA has been that, whereas before the Act claims would be more general in their nature citing "misleading forward projections" or similar, since the end of 1995 these were replaced by those citing specific issues (such as earnings restatement or insider trading, a reaction to "particularity" in the claims process).

Figure 12-1 shows claims data from the Stanford Securities Class Action Clearinghouse.[7] Given that the Act was supposed to reduce the number of claims being made, it is a little surprising to see what actually

Number of class action filings

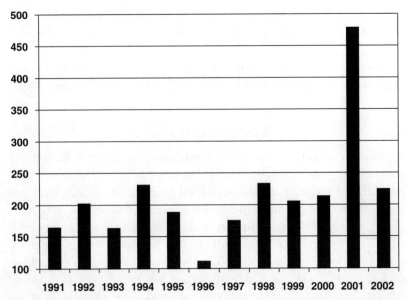

Source: Stanford Class Action Clearinghouse

happened. Comparing the years 1991 through 1994 with 1997 through 2002, the average number of claims in fact rose from 190 to 254. However, in 2001, of the 478 claims shown, over 300 were so-called "laddering" claims. Plaintiffs who have brought "laddering," or more properly "underwriter laddering," claims assert that broker/dealers acting on behalf of companies coming to the market for initial public offerings (IPOs) would provide generous allocations of low offer–priced stock on the condition that the same buyers would commit to buying the same stock after the IPO at predetermined prices. Thus, the price of the stock would continue to rise until the preferred clients took their profit. The cases most often revolve around Section 11 of the 1933 Securities Act, which prohibits material misrepresentations or omissions in prospectuses, and were particularly associated with the "dotcom" bubble. If one excludes the laddering claims from the figures, then the average number of claims in the 1997–2002 period was only slightly higher than the early years of the decade at 203—though not the expected fall in claims.

Research has shown that around the time that the Act was being prepared claims were brought forward, as plaintiffs' believed it would be harder to bring actions successfully under the new Act—due to the requirements for particularity—thus distorting 1995 and 1996 statistics.[8] Further, although following the introduction of the Act there was a large spike of activity in the state courts, possibly indicating attempts by the plaintiff bar to circumvent the federal courts, this has returned to its pre-Act level.[9]

Class action filings against non-U.S. companies also have risen from only 6 per year in the mid-1990s to around 25 per year in 2001 and 2002.

Settlements

The number of claims has risen, if not significantly. As shown in Table 12-1, the evidence suggests that the size of settlements has indeed increased and that a significant majority of the claims filed (and not dismissed) have yet to settle. The average (mean) settlement size during the period 1996–2001 was $24.9 million, which compares with $7.8 million for the period 1991–1995; however, the 1996–2001 figure includes one settlement (Cendant Corp.) which was for over $3 billion itself. Cendant is a provider of travel, real estate, vehicle, and financial services which was sued, along with its predecessor CUC International Inc., and three of its officers, in

TABLE 12-1

Recent Class Action Suits

Issuer	Maximum Asserted Valuation ($ millions)
Cendant	3527
Bank of America	490
Waste Management (II)	457
3 Com	259
Waste Management (I)	220
Rite Aid	193
MicroStrategy	192.5
Informix	136.5
Sunbeam	125
Conseco	120
Ikon	111
Prison Realty	104.1

Source: Stanford Securities Class Action Clearinghouse

1998. The complaint alleged that Cendant violated the Securities Exchange Act of 1934 by publishing false and misleading financial statements by overstating its income by over $100 million. The plaintiffs alleged that the market price of Cendant stock was artificially inflated during the class period as a result of the misrepresentations.[10] The suit was settled in 2000.

Excluding Cendant, the average (mean) for the period 1996–2001 is $14.4 million. Interestingly, if one compares the median of the two sets (an average unaffected by outliers) the results are even closer—$4.0 million between 1991–1995, $5.5 million during 1996–2001. In recent years however, there have been a greater number of "mega" settlements.[6]

N.B. Values in Table 12-1 may include securities as well as cash. Securities are valued as of the highest value asserted by any party and the values include proceeds from all sources. Not all settlements have received final court approval, and settlement values in some cases may still increase as additional defendants settle claims. The Cendant figures include settlements for the common stock litigation plus settlements for the litigation concerning Cendant's Preferred Redeemable Increased Dividend Equity Securities (PRIDES).

F I G U R E   1 2 - 2

S&P stock prices indices.
December values rebased to Dec. 1989 + 100.

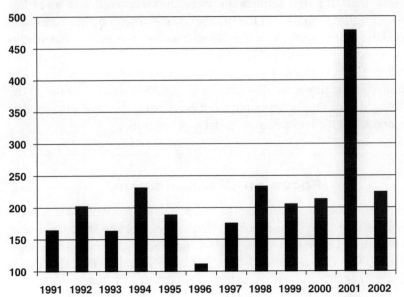

According to several pieces of research, the market—the 1990s boom followed by the crash from the end of 1999 (shown in Figure 12-2)—has played its part in determining the trend toward greater claims and settlements. During the boom it is alleged that oversight took a less important role as the dash for growth occurred. Expectations were set at high levels and managers strived to meet those expectations on a quarterly basis.

Mechanistically, there should be a clear relationship between the size of settlements and the market. U.S. securities legislation focuses on compensating investors who have lost wealth as a result of a company breaching that legislation. Once a claim has passed the dismissal stage and discovery is ongoing the parties to the case will each calculate the likely settlement figure. Normally in securities fraud cases (the vast majority of cases) the expected settlement value will be a function of several factors, including the type of allegation, whether the company's accountants and/or underwriters are also being sued, and the size of the loss. The size of the loss is normally calculated using a plaintiff-style model in which the price of the stock "but for" the alleged fraud is calculated. This is then compared to the price of the stock after disclosure of the alleged fraud. Various models are used to take account of market, industry, and even company events over the period of the alleged fraud. With the stock market continuing to post at all-time highs during the 1990s one would expect the nominal value of the implicit "but for" price to be inflated, thus increasing expected settlements. It is interesting to note therefore that although settlements were higher overall and there has been a significant increase in the number of mega settlements, when one looks at the ratio of settlement sizes to estimates of plaintiff-style damages for the two periods 1991–1995 and 1996–2001, the ratio is smaller for the second period.[6] Further, this research suggests that once the effects of plaintiff-style damages are taken into account, the existence or not of the PSLRA adds nothing to explaining settlement size; i.e., this implies that the market, not the legislation, was driving behavior.

Focus on Compensation

Researchers have commented on the compensation focus of the U.S. securities legislation. The 1934 Securities Exchanges Act allows for investors who have lost wealth due to a securities fraud access to appropriate compensation. This compensation is at least partially paid by the D&O insurance coverage. Thus even though, in the absence of insider-trading, a group of shareholders may have gained during the period of alleged fraud (by selling the security) while a second group has lost (by buying the security), the second group still has the fall-back of a class action suit (whereas some commentators suggest they should have a sufficiently diversified portfolio to protect against this risk).[11]

The requirement of particularity in the PSLRA has caused the plaintiff bar to focus on key "hard facts" in the pursuit of compensation. In the cases where there is evidence of insider trading, there is direct evidence of a transfer of wealth from shareholders to the managers as a consequence of inappropriate information being communicated. Where the cases are based purely on Rule 10b-5 the managers may have made knowingly false statements or omitted statements and gained in more indirect ways —executive job protection and incentives, including keeping stock options in the money (or bringing them back into the money), are high on the list.

Some commentators have made the argument that the current system in the United States as it is currently played out does not in fact deter fraudulent behavior. The normal method of calculating damages in a securities class action case, described in this chapter, takes account of the losses of one set of investors, but these are not offset by the gains of those investors that sold the securities before disclosure of the fraud. It is a one-sided bet. For a liquid stock, therefore, the potential costs of a suit are significant and consequently the incentive to settle great. The D&O insurance policy will cover a significant proportion of the settlement costs and the corporation will cover the rest.

In the worst case the directors and officers are protected against their wrongdoing, the shareholders who gained over the fraud period keep their gains, and the shareholders who lost are compensated— partly by the D&O insurance and partly by the corporation (which is owned by the shareholders). There is little clear incentive for the managers of a company within this framework to act lawfully, apart from normal honesty and the stigma of undergoing a law suit. However, in situations where it is difficult, if not impossible, to discern whether the symptoms causing a suit to be brought were because of fraud or bad luck, the deterrent effect of stigma and reputation loss is reduced. It would seem appropriate that if managers have indeed fraudulently transferred wealth from the shareholders during the period of the fraud they should repay this.

Section 305 of the Sarbanes-Oxley Act 2002[12] is a step in that direction. Namely:

If an issuer is required to prepare a restatement due to "material noncompliance" with financial reporting requirements, the chief executive officer and the chief financial officer shall "reimburse the issuer for any bonus or other incentive-based or equity-based compensation received" during the twelve months following the issuance or filing of the noncompliant document and "any profits realized from the sale of securities of the issuer" during that period.

One crucial governance point arises from the discussion of current practice. The most common reason cited for the initiation of a class action suit is a drop in the company's share price. At the outset of such a case, before discovery, it is very difficult to distinguish between intentional fraud and a case of bad business luck or honest misjudgment. The plaintiff's bar must use all publicly available information at their disposal to decide on the likelihood of a fraud. The growing availability of corporate governance assessments of companies will help in this process.

For a company to be able to demonstrate to the marketplace that it is well governed should, in a rational world, help in removing some of the risk that the company will be sued for making an honest business mistake. This is important. The current dynamic in securities class actions is that, once a motion to dismiss has failed, there are significant cost and time pressures favoring a settlement rather than a fight. It is important to do the utmost to protect against getting sued in the first place.

Internationalization

The international dimension impacts D&O insurance from two main directions. The first are non-U.S. companies who, through their American Depositary Receipt (ADR) programs, have access and exposure to U.S. investors. An ADR is issued by a U.S. bank on behalf of a non-U.S. company. The bank buys shares in the non-U.S. company on the non-U.S. market and then issues the ADRs in some proportion (one for one, two for one, etc.) either over the counter, by private placement, or on a U.S. stock exchange. If the ADR is so listed (a Level III ADR), the company must file its accounts with the SEC. With certain exemptions it also must comply with U.S. regulatory requirements. The ADRs are traded just like normal stocks and therefore the non-U.S. company also is exposed to potential law suits. Although the non-U.S. world is by no means as exposed to law suits as the United States, companies that are not exposed directly to U.S. investors also are finding it important to cover their directors and officers for the consequences of their actions.

Entity Coverage and Other Policy Changes

In the United States, the reaction of the insurers to the passing of the PSLRA and the resultant competitive situation in the D&O business also contributed to the recent problems. Following the Act, D&O insurers believed that claims and settlements would be significantly reduced.[13] Existing suppliers of insurance to the market allocated more capital to what they believed would be an even more stable business and the market saw a group of new suppliers enter. With increased supply and no real change in demand the premiums charged fell by 50 percent.[13] Further, suppliers also increased the coverage of policies and multiyear contracts were introduced. However, the introduction of entity coverage is perhaps the one change that caused the most behavioral alterations. Under normal A-side or B-side coverage, although the corporation paid for the D&O insurance of its directors and officers, the corporation itself was not covered. As claims and settlements heated up in the late 1990s there was a series of disputes between corporations and their insurers. Companies argued that the D&O insurance policy should pay all settlement and defense costs, while insurers argued that there should be an "allocation" of costs to the company, which would need to be paid out of the company's bottom line. Various U.S. court circuits allocated costs differently causing uncertainty and confusion. The industry therefore came to market with a product that was intended to align the interests of both parties.

The introduction of entity coverage itself has had some very interesting behavioral consequences and has had a significant impact on the D&O industry. This is partly due to the fact that D&O insurance covers damages, judgments, awards, *plus* settlements *and* defense costs. Thus, a company and its directors and officers can be covered whether they settle or fight a claim. Further, a key exclusion in D&O insurance policies is *proven fraud*. However, to prove fraud there must be a final judgment. If the case is never finally judged, this exclusion will never be acted upon.

Hence, even if the defendants believe that they have a reasonable chance of getting a judgment in their favor, the risks of getting a final judgment against them and the consequent loss of their D&O coverage provides a significant incentive for companies and individuals to settle rather than fight. This pressure is increased by the high (and growing) costs of mounting a defense. On the other hand, directors as *individuals* have a further issue to consider—in that if they settle, their reputations may be tarnished. Situations can arise therefore where individual directors wish to fight the case and the corporation wishes to settle. Clearly the interests of the participants are not aligned in this case.

A further complication can arise because entity coverage policies are sometimes treated as assets of the company—particularly important in cases of bankruptcy. Rather than protecting the directors and officers the D&O insurance may become a target for recovery for the settlement of creditor demands. This too was not an expected consequence of the introduction of this product.

CORPORATE GOVERNANCE AND D&O INSURANCE

Practitioners in the D&O industry are actively looking for new information and new tools to help them conduct their business more efficiently, in a market environment, which is becoming increasingly more difficult. Some have focused solely on the accounting issues—mainly because the PSLRA forces plaintiffs to look for tangible evidence. However, if one looks at examples of the many claims over the past ten years, often there were transfers of wealth from shareholders to management for years before the problems surfaced in the accounts. This suggests that a more holistic corporate governance approach is appropriate. Further, to conduct a forensic accounting review of each potential D&O candidate company, as many commentators have pointed out, would be extremely expensive.

Due to the lack of hard data the amount of empirical research into the links between D&O insurance and corporate governance is relatively sparse. One line of work, for example,[14] looks at D&O insurance as part of the corporate governance mix. Examining D&O insurance alongside the market for corporate control, oversight by large shareholders, boards of directors, and the incentive effect of managerial ownership (aligning the interests of the managers with the shareholders) has highlighted some questions over the role of D&O insurance. For a given level of required oversight, D&O insurance, assuming that the insurers conduct the appropriate level of due diligence, could be a substitute for other types of oversight (such as increasing the number/quality of the nonexecutives on the board). However, D&O insurance itself is used as an incentive to attract nonexecutives.

The fact that nonexecutives are covered by insurance, however, may make them less diligent than if their own assets were at risk. Therefore, further tools to ensure oversight are required. The use of D&O insurance and the use of nonexecutives and other forms of oversight may indeed be complements. Similarly, in the case of executive ownership—as the managers' interests become more aligned with those of the shareholders through equity ownership. Their demand for insurance coverage for not only themselves but also for the corporation will increase. This tendency itself may be offset by other effects, such as the size of the company.

Two points emerge from this line of thinking. First, it is inappropriate to argue that D&O insurance per se is a pure substitute for other forms of corporate governance control—and that a company taking out D&O insurance is quite consistent with that company being "well governed." Second, to understand the mix of governance effects in a company one truly does need to find a way of looking at all the offsetting or exaggerating governance issues.

Research in the United Kingdom published recently[15] based on data from the early 1990s, shows that insured companies tend to be larger, have a more volatile stock price, have greater exposure in the United States, and have a larger proportion of nonexecutives on their boards. They do not tend to have a larger managerial ownership—however, this could be a function of the size of the companies.

If we accept that a company taking out D&O insurance is consistent with and a complement for other forms of governance oversight, then what of the supply of and demand for such insurance—and therefore the price? Research in Canada[16] on corporate governance and D&O insurance has suggested that companies with less management oversight are more likely to be sued; while the same research indicates that the effect on settlements of having insiders (including directors) own shares may be ambiguous. Although being shareholders they have an incentive to protect the interests of shareholders, they also have more wealth at risk during litigation and may wish to settle early. Further, the research suggests that companies with "better governance" indeed pay a lower D&O insurance premium. This type of research is useful; however, without being able to examine the companies' governance from within the company it is handicapped. The use of only external corporate governance indicators such as the proportion of insider equity holdings, the number of external directors, and other measures can only represent proxies of what is actually happening within a company.

CONCLUSION

In the United States, the D&O industry therefore finds itself in the first years of the new century right in the middle of a bear market, with significant numbers of their clients facing securities class action suits brought by a strong plaintiff bar representing shareholders who are facing unprecedented stock price losses. They are being required to cover claims at historically high levels, both against individuals and corporations. Outside of the United States, companies with exposure to the U.S. market also are finding that access to the largest capital market in the world means exposure to the most active shareholders in the world, and consequently significant requirements for D&O insurance. Coverage, too, for individuals and corporations not exposed to the U.S. market also has grown considerably, not only in average size but also in the number of policies written.

The boom and bust of the 1991–2002 period provided the background for the largest number of U.S. corporate accounting restatements ever recorded (running at almost 300 a year). The "dotcom" bubble provided the background to a series of laddering and insider trading claims. The period provided a culture in which oversight was minimized and growth maximized. The D&O insurance industry in the United States believed that the PSLRA of 1995 would provide the basis for a stable and secure business going forward. The product innovations and competitive situation in the industry along with the waves of accounting and insider trading issues that they had to cover has made the industry very difficult. The PSLRA does seem to have kept some check on the number of claims filed and on the quality of those claims, but the industry toward the end of the twentieth century was all but overrun.

We now have a situation where there needs to be a way of separating companies that are demonstrating good governance practices from those that are not. Some market participants suggest that well-run companies that make an honest business mistake or hit bad luck are as equally likely to be sued as those that are actively behaving fraudulently. It is suggested by some commentators that it is unclear whether there are sufficient incentives and punishments within the full compensation system currently operating within the United States to change behavior—although the effects of the Sarbanes-Oxley legislation have yet to be seen. Although the main impact of corporate governance and D&O insurance has been in the United States, and to some extent in the United Kingdom, the exposure of major European and Asian companies to litigation risk through dual listing or ADR programs is real. Further, growing investor activism globally will increase the risks for directors and officers and provide additional reasons why their companies should adopt and demonstrate good governance practices.

NOTES

1. Pritchard, 2003.

2. Gische, and Fishman, 2003. Provides a good summary of the fundamentals of D&O insurance.

3. The Securities Lawyer's Deskbook, 2003.

4. Cornerstone Research, 2003.

5. U.S. Securities Exchange Act of 1934, 2003.

6. Cornerstone Research, 2002.

7. Cornerstone Research, 2003. Earlier data reproduced in Painter et al., 2002.

8. Woodruff-Sawyer Report January 2002, quoted in Painter et al., 2002.

9. Foster et al, January, 2002.

10. Stanford Law School. Securities Class Action Clearinghouse, www.securities.stanford.edu/1002/CD98/2003.

11. Pritchard, 2002.

12. The Corporate Auditing and Accountability Act, July 30, 2002.

13. Cotter and Barbee, 2002.

14. O'Sullivan, 1997. This work provides an excellent introduction into these studies.

15. O'Sullivan, 2002.

16. Core, 2000.

REFERENCES

Bajaj, M., S. C. Mazumdar, A. Sarin. "Securities Class Action Settlements: An Empirical Analysis," www//business.scu.edu/asarin/WorkingPapers/Settlement.pdf, November 16, 2000.

Core, J. " The Directors' and Officers' Insurance Premium: An Outside Assessment of the Quality of Corporate Governance," Oxford University Press, 2000.

Cornerstone Research (L. E. Simmonds). "Post-Reform Act Securities Case Settlements 2001: A Year In Review," www.cornerstone.com, 2002.

Cornerstone Research. "Securities Class Action Case Filings: 2002: A Year in Review," www.cornerstone.com, 2003.

Cotter, W. (Chief Underwriting Officer National Union Fire Insurance Co.) and C. Barbee (PwC). "2002 D&O Insurance White Paper," American International Group Inc. monograph provided by the authors, 2002.

Ferris, S. P., M. Jagannathan, and A. C. Pritchard. "Too Busy to Mind the Business? Monitoring by Directors with Multiple Board Appointments," *Journal of Finance*, vol. 58, 2003, p. 1087.

Foster, T. S., D. N. Martin, V. M. Jueja, F. C. Dunbar, and L. P. Allen. "Recent Trends VII: PSLRA, Six Years Later," National Economic Research Associates Inc.; monograph provided by the authors, January 2002.

Foster, T. S., D. N. Martin, V. M. Jueja, and F. C. Dunbar. "Trends in Securities Litigation and the Impact of the PSLRA," National Economic Research Associates Inc.; monograph provided by the authors (2001).

Gische, D. M., and V. Fishman. "Directors' and Officers' Liability Insurance Overview," www.cnapro.com/pdf/DavidG.PDF (2003).

Grudfest, J. A., and M. A. Perino. "A Statistical and Legal Analysis of Class Action Securities Fraud Litigation Under the Private Securities Litigation Reform Act of 1995," Cornerstone Research, www//securities.stanford.edu/research/studies/19970227firstyr_firstyr.html (1997).

Johnson, M. F., K. K. Nelson, and A. C. Pritchard. "Do the Merits Matter More? Class Actions Under the Private Securities Litigation Reform Act," unpublished monograph provided by A. C. Pritchard, acplaw@umich.edu (September 2002).

O'Sullivan, N. "Insuring the Agents: The Role of Directors' and Officers' Insurance in Corporate Governance," *The Journal of Risk & Insurance*, vol. 64, no. 3, 1997, pp. 545–556.

O'Sullivan, N. "The Demand for Directors' and Officers' Insurance by Large U.K. Companies," *European Management Journal*, vol. 20, no. 5, 2002, pp. 574–583.

O'Sullivan, N. "The Impact of Directors' and Officers' Insurance on Audit Pricing: Evidence from Large U.K. Companies," unpublished monograph provided by the author, c.n.osullivan@lboro.ac.uk (1997).

Painter, R., M. Farrell, and S. Adkins. "Private Securities Litigation Reform Act: A Post Enron Analysis," *The Federalist Society for Law and Public Policy Studies* (2002).

Perino, M. A. "A Census of Securities Class Action Litigation After the Private Securities Reform Act of 1995," Written Testimony Before the Subcommittee on Securities of the Committee on Banking, Housing, and Urban Affairs United States Senate, www//securities.stanford.edu/research/articles/19970723sen2.html (July 24, 1997).

PricewaterhouseCoopers. "PricewaterhouseCoopers LLP 2001 Securities Litigation Study," www.10b5.com (2002).

Pritchard, A. C. "Should Congress Repeal Securities Class Action Reform?," unpublished monograph provided by the author, acplaw@umich.edu (2002).

Pritchard, A. C. "Who Cares?," www.law.wustl.edu/WULQ/80-3/p883Pritchard bookpages.pdf (2003).

Simmonds, L. E., with Cornerstone Research. "Post-Reform Act Securities Lawsuits: Settlements Reported Through December 2001," www.cornerstone.com (2002).

Simmonds, L. E., with Cornerstone Research. "Post-Reform Act Securities Lawsuits: Settlements Reported Through December 2002," www.cornerstone.com (2003).

The Corporate Auditing and Accountability Act (The Sarbanes-Oxley Act), www.sarbanes-oxley.com/ (July 30, 2002).

The Securities Lawyer's Deskbook, Section 27 Private Securities Litigation, www.law.uc.edu/ccl/33act/sec27.html (2003).

U.S. Securities Exchange Act of 1934, www.law.uc.edu/ccl/34actrls/rule10b-5.html.

CHAPTER 13

Managed Fund Governance

Meyrick Payne

This chapter tackles the risks associated with governance from a different angle—that of collective investment schemes (CISs). In most countries these take the form of contractual deposits held by a bank, or other financial institution, for the benefit of the depositors; in others, CISs take the form of trusts and still in others, notably the United States, they take a corporate form, where the shares in the CISs are owned by the depositors. The governance of each is quite different with different risks for each.

Over the past decade CISs have garnered an ever-larger proportion of the savings and investments of developed countries. In 1992, the OECD estimated that there was $3.4 trillion in the CIS of the largest 16 developed countries. By 2002, this is estimated to have risen to $14.0 trillion.[1] This amount was dramatically impacted by the increase in personal savings for retirement and by the rapid growth in stock market values during this time period. Furthermore, retail investors increasingly moved away from savings and other forms of bank deposits to collective investment schemes.

To make CIS offerings more attractive, plan sponsors packed an ever-greater range of financial products, from equities to bonds to money market deposits, further blurring the differences between conventional banks and other financial institutions. In addition, technology has been well used to market and service CIS products. In particular, the Internet has been an effective sales and distribution device.

This chapter is divided into two sections: (1) how collective investment schemes are governed, and (2) how collective investment schemes can impact the governance of the companies in which they invest.

GOVERNANCE OF COLLECTIVE INVESTMENT SCHEMES

The term *CIS* includes several forms of open-ended instruments such as investment companies, mutual funds, unit trusts, and investment trusts.

A CIS is an instrument that (1) invests in transferable securities, (2) is publicly traded, and (3) is open-ended. An open-ended CIS is one in which the net asset value (NAV) is calculated periodically and investors may buy or redeem shares at NAV, net of certain charges, at regular intervals.

To all extents and purposes CISs fall into three categories; the contractual form, the trust form, and the corporate form. Typically, the form of CIS has evolved over time from contractual to corporate. The countries with the largest investment base tend to have evolved from the contractual form through the trust form to the corporate form.

CISs are organized under the laws of each developed country. Not surprising, these differ quite substantially. In Europe, CISs are governed by the European Commission's Undertakings for Collective Investment in Transferable Securities (UCITS) directive of 1985. This directive was intended to bring some consistency to the various forms of CISs that had evolved all over Europe. In the United States, the Investment Company Act of 1940 and subsequent modifications primarily govern CISs. The exact form of CIS adopted in individual countries is often determined by local tax policies.

Contractual Form

In the contractual form the depositor places his or her money with another under a contract, either explicit or implicit, that the financial institution will safeguard it and, in most cases, invest the money in a way that yields a return to the depositor. The depositor places great trust in the financial

FIGURE 1 3 - 1

Investor places assets with bank or financial institution under a contract. Governance is provided by bank's board.

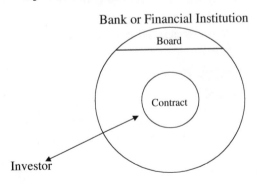

institution and has no specifically designated independent watchdog or guardian. Of course, the trust is typically recognized in the law of the land and regulations define the responsibility of the financial institution. Deposits of this nature do not have to be with a bank; they could equally be made with an investment club or collective investment pool.

Figure 13-1 illustrates the simple nature of the contractual form. An investor deposits his or her money into a financial institution with no separate mechanism or legal entity distinguishing the deposit from others. Of course the financial institution is obliged to keep track of the individual deposit. The directors of the financial institution itself are responsible for safeguarding the deposit.

Trust Form

In the trust form, the depositor places his or her assets in a specifically designated trust. As such the law recognizes that the depositor has certain legal rights and the trustee has very specific responsibilities. The trustee, or trustees, has the primary responsibility to safeguard the assets. Typically they work for and are paid by the financial institution that operates the trust. Governance of the trust does not typically rest with an independent third party. Nonetheless, the degree of safeguard that the depositor enjoys is typically greater than in the contractual form.

Figure 13-2 illustrates the nature of the trust form. Note that there is a distinct legal entity into which the depositor's money is placed and trustees safeguard this pool. However, since the trustees almost always

FIGURE   13 - 2

Investor places assets with a trust which is managed by a bank or financial institution. Governance is provided by bank's board.

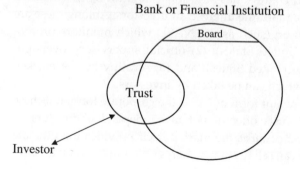

Bank or Financial Institution

work for the financial institution, oversight of them rests again with the board of directors of the financial institution.

In Europe, these trusts are usually known as "unit trusts." In these, investors pool their assets into a trust that is managed by a trustee. This trustee is typically independent of the investment manager. The trustee does surveillance of the investment manager, computes NAV, keeps the books, keeps records of shareholder purchases and sales of fund shares, and often is the custodian of the fund's securities.

The trust system is found in the United Kingdom, Ireland, Australia, New Zealand, Canada, Singapore, and Hong Kong, China.[2]

Corporate Form

In the corporate form, the depositor places the investment in a corporation, typically called an investment company, in exchange for shares. This investment company is independent and distinct from the manager that invests and otherwise handles the investment. Its own board of directors, a majority of whom, in most countries, has to be independent of the manager, governs the company. The manager is retained by the board under a contract to invest and process the assets of the fund's shareowners.

Figure 13-3 illustrates the corporate form. Note that the board, consisting of a majority of independent directors, hires and pays the manager on behalf of the investors. Note that the directors, sometimes called trustees in recognition of their evolution from the trust form, are very influential. The degree of their authority and responsibility varies by jurisdiction, but suffice it to say that financial management firms prefer the contractual or trust form, as there are fewer sources of unpredictable behavior. In addition, the corporate form tends to be less expensive to operate precisely because there are fewer interveners.

The internal governance procedures are the primary form of governance. Every developed country has additional monitoring mechanisms that are intended to safeguard the interests of investors. Among these are (1) industry self-regulation (such as the NASD which monitors promotional material in the United States); (2) official supervisory oversight (such as the SEC in the United States); and (3) scrutiny by the market, including legal action which can be taken by investors.

In Canada the dominant form of CIS is the corporate form, but these entities, typically called trusts, often do not have independent directors.

In every developed country, the market itself provides the ultimate safeguard. The investor can sell his or her shares or interest and invest else-

FIGURE 13-3

Investor places assets in corporate form mutual fund with its own board of directors.

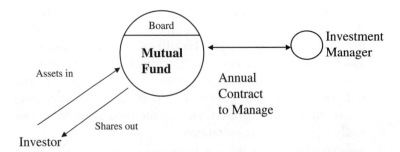

where. In some countries the laws and regulations rely heavily on this capability. In others, the right to sell and move on is not seen as the ultimate protection because there are tax implications and because the average retail investor may not have the knowledge to do so in a timely manner.

RISK TO INDIVIDUAL INVESTORS

The overall thrust of this book is risk. As such, the risk to an individual investor from each type of CIS differs. Before we analyze the comparative risks of each form, let us isolate the typical risks faced by an investor. The following is a listing of the six most common risks.

1. *Institutional failure or credit risk:* The financial institution may fail. In most developed countries the government has some sort of deposit insurance for banks so that people are not afraid to deposit their money. However, many financial institutions are not insured. At the least-sophisticated end of the spectrum, investment clubs or informal schemes provide no legal protection. Typically contractual forms of CIS, especially if they are made with banks, are insured up to a certain amount. In exchange for the government-provided insurance on deposits up to a certain limit, banks typically have to place a certain percentage of their assets with the central bank and accept strict limitations on what they do with their investors' money. As a result, the return to the investor is typically low and certainly less than

expected than from an uninsured institution. Deposits with any other form, whether trust or corporate, are not protected.

2. *Theft:* Whenever a depositor trusts another with his or her assets, there is an element of trust that the recipient will not abscond with the assets. The fiduciary has custody of the depositor's money. The laws in all developed countries place a burden on the fiduciary that he will safeguard the depositor's assets as if they were his own. Most fiduciaries have insurance coverage to indemnify the depositor if an employee absconds with the money. Most CISs in developed countries have laws to ensure that the securities owned by the fund are held by financially responsible organizations.

3. *Investment loss:* All CIS carry investment risk. Typically, the greater the risk, the greater the possibility, but not promise, of return. In most developed countries the name of the fund bears some relationship to the level of investment risk. For example, a "government bond fund" by implication carries less risk than an "aggressive growth fund." There is usually no guarantee that a particular fund will not lose money for an investor. Even funds that carry the tag "principal protected" will only guarantee a return if held to maturity. Intermediate swings in interest rates can cause such a fund to vary widely in value.

4. *Inflated expenses:* A more sophisticated form of risk for the CIS investor is that the manager deliberately, or inadvertently through inattention or carelessness, inflates the expenses of the fund. In most cases these inflated expenses are borne by the CIS investor. Diligent oversight of potentially inflated expenses is difficult and not particularly credible when oversight rests with the fund manager, rather than an independent third party such as a board of disinterested directors or trustees.

5. *Conflict of interest:* A real form of risk to the investor is that there is a conflict of interest between the CIS manager and the investor. When a portfolio manager knows that he or she is about to buy a large block of stock for the fund he or she manages, there may be temptation to front-run (that is, buy shares personally before the inevitable run up in price). A CIS manager usually operates numerous funds and often invests money for his or her own account. Ensuring that an individual investor in one fund is not disadvantaged by a potential conflict of interest is not credibly accomplished without an independent watchdog or board.

6. *Inappropriate allocation of benefits:* The investor is primarily interested in what is returned; the manager is primarily interested in the fees he or she can earn from managing the portfolio. Sometimes the manager is interested in the ancillary benefits that he or she can accrue. For example, the allocation of rights to valuable initial public offerings (IPOs) or offsetting favors from brokers and research houses. Without an independent watchdog in the form of an independent board of directors or trustees, the investor can have little assurance, other than the word of the manager, that he or she is getting all the benefits produced by their assets.

These six types of risk do not impact all classes of investors equally. Generally speaking the more sophisticated the investor, the less need there is for constant and detailed governance. On the other hand, when a relatively low-income worker places his or her savings in a CIS, there is a greater need for diligent oversight because the risk of loss from some sophisticated form of misappropriation is greatest to the least sophisticated investor (Figure 13-4).

FIGURE   1 3 - 4

The risk of sophisticated manipulations is greatest to unsophisticated retail savers.

Risk to ⟶ Risk of ↓	Financial Institutions	Sophisticated Investors	Retail Investors	Retail Savers
Failure or Credit Risk				
Theft				
Investment Loss				
Inflated Expenses				
Conflict of Interest				
Misallocation of Benefits				

DIFFERENT RISK TO VARIOUS CLASSES OF INVESTORS

The laws of developed nations usually recognize that different classes of investors require different levels of protection from the multitude of risks that are implicit in collective investment schemes.

Financial institutions, often the same as institutional investors, require the least protection. As professionals, the management of financial institutions are well acquainted with the risks of investing. They would rather have the opportunity of choosing greater returns than the assurance of principal preservation. For those who have principal preservation in mind, there are a multitude of investment options. For those who wish to "chance it all on one turn of pitch and toss," there are other investment vehicles.

For sophisticated investors, typically those with large sums to invest and a high net worth or income, the risks are also well known and understood. They do not truly need the protection afforded by an independent third party or board of directors. Similarly, speculators want to play high stakes poker and do not require, or want, to pay for independent governance.

Retail investors, typically the middle class who are trying to accumulate assets for retirement or to educate their children, are not sophisticated. These consumers, who typically make up the bulk of investors in collective investment schemes, rely on the laws and interpretative regulations to safeguard their interests. As this is such an important job, and the amount of assets so significant, the oversight provided by an independent board of directors is vital.

Retail savers, typically working people who need to accumulate savings for their future well being, often do not understand the complexities of collective investing. Their assets often are accumulated in a job-related savings plan and invested in a privately managed investment pool to provide a better-than-inflation return. They need diligent and consistent vigilance. As a result, pension plans and employment-related plans, are typically subject to the most exacting rules and regulations.

If a developed country is to provide a way for ordinary citizens to save for their retirement and for capital investment, the laws need to recognize that the six types of risk discussed above need to be ameliorated for the different classes of investors. Collective investment schemes tend to be used by the mass market to accumulate capital. As such the governance of mutual funds, trusts, and other collective investment schemes is the linchpin of the financial structure of a developed country.

ALTERNATE FORMS OF SAFEGUARDING CIS INVESTORS

Making the risk associated with collective investing acceptable to the person on the street is a fundamental driver in the development of laws and financial structure of developed nations. Generally speaking there are five alternatives, which may be applied individually or collectively.

1. *Code of ethics or conduct:* Probably the oldest form of ameliorating the investor's risk or misappropriation is the adoption of a code of ethics or conduct. The investor is supposed to take away from this assurance that the fiduciary will indeed safeguard the client's money as his or her own. The code of ethics typically lays out the conduct that is unacceptable, such as front-running or using inside information. The difficulty is that without an enforcement mechanism, such as an independent board, the adoption of a code of ethics does little more than codify the duties of a contract fiduciary.

2. *Law:* While the law of the land may be the ultimate sledgehammer for safeguarding the interests of the CIS shareholder, it is by no means subtle or precise in its application. By definition, laws tend to prohibit certain acts implying that any other behavior is acceptable. Through such loopholes pass a great many injustices because the law, by itself, cannot be detailed or timely enough to monitor day-to-day behavior accurately enough to credibly prevent fraud or malfeasance.

3. *Regulations:* Laws have to be interpreted for individual situations; in the United States the SEC performs this function. For mutual funds, the Division of Investment Management is the operative section of the SEC. This division has about 300 professional personnel who oversee, assisted by the independent directors, about $7 trillion in mutual fund assets. Contrast that number with about 30,000 regulators at the federal and state levels, who oversee various types of banking with an aggregate asset base of about the same amount. The U.S. mutual fund industry has never had the same degree of meltdown as the savings and loan or banking industry has had.

4. *Independent directors (majority or minority on board):* Supplementing regulation of CISs with independent directors clearly makes the oversight function more efficient and effective. This is because the directors are extremely knowledgeable

and diligent in monitoring the application of laws and regulations. In addition, independent directors can closely monitor the six types of risk faced by investors; credit, theft, investment loss, inflated expenses, conflict of interests, or misallocation of benefits. Law, regulations, and whether or not they hold a majority on the board determine the degree of power exerted by the independent directors. Different models of their authority are discussed below.

5. *Plaintiff's lawsuits:* The ultimate form of safeguarding the investor's rights comes from the plaintiff's bar. In the United States, for example, investors who believe that they have been wronged can come together in a class action lawsuit and sue the CIS if it is a corporate mutual fund or the fiduciary if the CIS is a trust or contractual investment pool. The attorneys who bring this type of lawsuit are often paid on contingency; if they lose they collect nothing, if they win they can collect as much as a third of the damages. Some say that plaintiff's lawsuits are expensive and unnecessary; some even say that the fear of them impairs innovation. On the other hand, most CIS managers recognize that the potential for enormous awards, such as has occurred in the tobacco and asbestos industries, provide for a real check and balance on malfeasance. Plaintiff's lawsuits are brought not only against the fund managers, but also against fund directors. This pressure goes a long way toward keeping the directors' attention focused on safeguarding the investor.

The five methods of protecting the investor work best when they are all applied. Furthermore, the level of confidence that the investor feels is greatest when his or her interests are protected by professional fiduciary conduct, well-crafted laws, timely regulations, a board with a majority of independent directors, and the threat of class action law suits. This consumer confidence is what allows people with relatively low incomes to save for their future. The less sophisticated the investor, the more significant the basic building blocks of governance and safeguards become (Figure 13-5).

All forms of investor protection require transparency and good disclosure. There is always an ongoing debate about how much disclosure is necessary. What is certain is that poor or inadequate disclosure impairs the ability of an individual investor to act in his or her own best interest.

The most important aspects of disclosure in any CIS include past performance, accurate description of the type of securities included in the

The less sophisticated the investor, the more significant the basic building blocks of governance become.

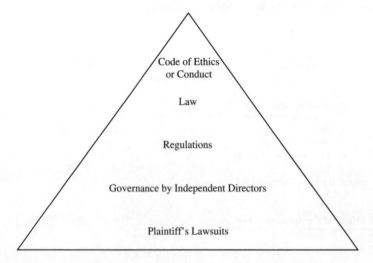

CIS, expense levels, sales charges, and the names and backgrounds of senior fund managers and directors. In addition, any transactions that take place between the CIS and affiliated parties, such as shareholder and brokerage services, should be quantified and disclosed. The independent directors are usually responsible to see that this is accurately done on a timely basis.

DIFFERENT AUTHORITY LEVELS FOR INDEPENDENT DIRECTORS

Even when a majority of independent directors exists on a CIS board, there are substantial differences between levels of authority. Generally speaking, the authority level of CIS independent directors can vary from a low level of authority—ability to only ask probing questions—to a high level of authority—the ability to hire and fire the fund manager (Figure 13-6).

1. *Authority only to ask questions:* The most basic, and least intrusive to the manager, authority level for independent directors is to be empowered solely to ask probing questions without the accompanying power to cause change. The limited version of authority is sometimes compounded by a lack of specific laws

The authority to ask probing questions is the least
effective form of governance. The greatest is the ability
to hire and fire the investment manager.

and regulations for the directors to follow. In a fast-moving
environment, such as the securities markets, where new types
of derivatives and structured instruments are constantly being
invented, this limited authority level for independent directors
provides little or no protection for investors.

2. *Authority to monitor the application of appropriate laws and regulations:* Where the laws and regulations do provide a reasonable
framework in which the independent directors operate, the
authority to monitor the application of the rules does provide
improved protection for the investor. However, this can be illu-
sory if the independent directors do not have the power to take
corrective action. Sometimes, the basis on which the directors
monitor compliance is distorted by the fact that the information
provided to the directors comes almost exclusively from the
manager, with little or no outside checks and balances.

3. *Authority to secure economic information from the investment
adviser:* In the laws and regulations governing U.S. mutual
funds, the manager is obligated to provide whatever information is requested by the independent directors. Sometimes this
seemingly simple requirement is problematic. For example,
fund managers are loathe to provide information about their

own profitability. That is often required as a way for independent directors to gauge the reasonableness of the management fees levied by the manager. Fund managers are also loathe to provide compensation data for their star portfolio managers, even though the directors may want to ensure that the portfolio manager in question is being paid appropriately for the performance achieved. In some cases the directors also retain third parties to obtain an independent perspective as a check and balance mechanism.

4. *Authority to change the terms of the investment advisory agreement (particularly the management fee as asset levels rise):* Even more authority is vested in the independent directors if they have the right to change the terms of the advisory contract. The argument against this level of authority is that the investors know from the prospectus what the costs associated with managing the fund are and have agreed to those charges. Why should the independent directors have the right to intervene? The case in favor of such authority derives from the economic assertion that as assets rise, there are economies of scale in managing the portfolio. In other words, it does not cost proportionately the same to manage $1 billion as it does to manage $100 million; and these savings should be passed back to the shareholders— particularly if the present shareholders are being asked to pay for marketing the fund to future investors.

5. *Authority to hire and fire the fund adviser:* The most powerful level the independent directors can have is the authority to hire and fire the investment adviser. In the United States, this is referred to as the *nuclear option* as it has the potential to destroy the fund. The fund investors purchased shares in a particular fund, presumably because they had faith that the manager, who sponsors and promotes the fund, has the capability to invest fund assets in the manner prescribed by the prospectus.

     Certainly, no investor acquires shares because he or she anticipates the independent directors intervening in the compact between themselves and the investment manager.[3] There also are very practical considerations. The fund is distributed and sold as part of a family of funds. In most cases, a shareholder can transfer his or her investment from one fund within the family to another. It is enormously valuable for an investor to be able, at essentially no cost, to move from an equity fund to a bond fund to a money market fund within the same family. Should the directors decide to pull one fund from a manager and transfer it to another, the shareholder would be deprived of this convenience. As a result, it even occurs in countries like the United States where the directors have the "hire and fire" authority.

Several Canadian provinces are debating among themselves about this very subject. Ontario, for example, has decided that there should be independent directors but that they should not have the authority to terminate the adviser nor change the terms of the advisory agreement.

The investment management industry prefers that the directors exercise their power sparingly. The industry perceives that it carries the risk of creating new funds and the obligation to keep them innovative and attractive. As such, investment managers tend to dislike the idea that independent directors can change the terms of their customer compact. Such authority tends to make the fund business less predictable. On the other hand, individual investors, particularly middle-income savers, may want the added protection afforded by truly independent and powerful directors. Certainly politicians and economic policymakers want the directors to have sufficient authority to represent a credible and proactive safeguard. Many argue that if a country is to have a viable private-sector savings and investment program, strong governance is mandatory.

When CIS directors have the full range of powers described in Figure 13-7, they become extremely important to the financial infrastructure of a

FIGURE   13-7

The board of a mutual fund usually serves multiple boards.

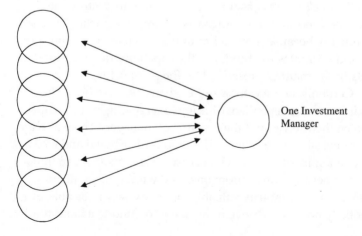

One Investment
Manager

nation. Consider that there are about 3000 independent mutual fund directors in the United States. Together they oversee about $7 trillion in assets—just about the same amount as all the personal domestic banking deposits, and slightly less than the value of all the shares traded on the New York Stock Exchange. Then compare the influence of these 3000 with the influence of 700,000 lawyers or 650,000 doctors in the United States.

CIS DIRECTORS AND PERSONAL LIABILITY

CIS directors, especially in countries that have accorded them considerable authority, are increasingly aware of their responsibility. Indeed in the United States, mutual fund directors now have to disclose their aggregate compensation that can, in some of the larger complexes, exceed $200,000 per year. Oddly enough, the compensation of portfolio managers, who are often paid in the millions, is not disclosed. As a result, dissatisfied investors often focus their anger on the directors who can be readily identified. In addition, the recent spate of legislation designed to improve corporate governance, has impacted fund governance as well. The 2002 Sarbanes-Oxley Act has elevated directors' liability from civil to potentially criminal. The combination of these factors has greatly increased the sensitivity of directors to be perceived as doing a good job for shareholders.

Some of the ways in which independent CIS directors can lessen their exposure to personal lawsuits include:

- *Be prepared and well informed:* Being prepared means much more than reading the material and participating in the discussion. It implies that relevant information about the issue is credibly produced in sufficient time for the directors to debate the ramifications among themselves and to reach consensus about corrective action when appropriate.

- *Be truly independent:* CIS directors rarely get to see investors. Over time they may find themselves identifying more with the problems and opportunities of the manager, with whom they work regularly. CIS directors should not have any business or personal relationship with the fund manager. In the United States, if it could be proved that the directors were not independent, the entire management agreement might be considered void. In such a case, the full amount of management fees might have to be returned. As a result, the fund manager is anxious that directors actually are, and are perceived to be, independent.

- *Have independent counsel and access to third-party industry and economic consultants*: To help the directors exercise their responsibilities and to ensure that they receive accurate and timely information, many CIS directors retain legal counsel. In addition, they also retain third-party experts to provide unbiased comparisons and trends.

- *Have an independent audit committee and retain the audit firm directly*: The directors want to assure themselves that information they receive from the independent auditors is unvarnished and timely. As a result, recent legislation in the United States and Europe calls for auditors to be retained by an audit committee made up solely of independent directors. The outside auditors are one of the bulwarks of investor protection, and their report, together with any concerns they have about systems and internal controls, must be made known to the independent directors without the reality or appearance of interference.

- *Have access to investor aggravations and complaints*: Fund directors can become detached from the day-to-day aggravations of fund ownership. In the United States, the Investment Company Institute (ICI) has adopted a best practice that fund directors should own shares in the funds they govern. In addition, many directors establish a mechanism by which they receive at least an aggregation of shareholder complaints.

- *Secure directors' and officers' insurance:* Not only should CIS directors secure D&O insurance, but they also should ensure that coverage is adequate and covers action against the fund manager. Furthermore, the coverage should advance funds for legal defense before a verdict is rendered. The extent of damages, which can be alleged in the United States under the new Sarbanes-Oxley legislation and by plaintiff's bar, is so large that even defending oneself is a very expensive undertaking.

- *Have the CIS assets indemnify the reasonable actions of the directors*: Since the directors perform a valuable function for a corporate form fund or for the trust, often the underlying documents provide that fund assets indemnify the directors, absent gross negligence or malfeasance.

The combination of these actions provides sufficient protection for CIS directors to do their jobs well. As a result the interests of CIS investors can be safeguarded so that the private sector is able to supplement whatever government-sponsored programs are available for retirement.

CIS IMPACT ON GOVERNANCE OF CORPORATIONS

Mutual funds, trusts, and other forms of collective investments constitute over 50 percent of the institutional assets in the developed world. Generally, the laws under which CISs are formed preclude use of CISs as a mechanism to control the actions of companies whose shares are owned by the fund. This is because the intent of CISs is to provide a relatively conservative investment vehicle in which many investors can share and manage risk. If CISs were used as vehicles to control companies, they would become, de facto holding companies and lose the very essence that makes them attractive to so many investors.

Nonetheless, CISs are major institutional shareholders and, as such, have the potential to exert enormous influence over the conduct and governance of the organizations in which they invest. Generally, this is done by:

- *Recognizing that an investment made with fund assets is made solely for the benefit of the fund investors:* CIS directors intuitively understand that the dividend and investment gains from fund investments, after expenses, belong to the fund shareholders. It is harder to remember that all the other benefits that flow from the portfolio holdings also belong to the fund's investors. The most important of these include brokerage commissions, research credits, IPO allocations, and proxy voting rights.

- *Voting proxies in the interest of the fund shareholder:* Since the beneficial ownership of proxies lies with the fund investors, the CIS directors should ensure that they are voted in the fund's best interests. This responsibility provides CIS directors with considerable authority to impact the behavior and governance of corporations. For example, the fund directors can refuse to vote in favor of a shareholder proposal which is dilutive, or which compensates executives disproportionately. Similarly, CIS directors have the ability to influence the economic, accounting, and social policies of corporations. CIS directors could specify, for example, that the fund they govern would not invest in companies that fail to expense stock options. Alternatively, the fund could pressure companies to merge or accept a favorable takeover bid even though the management was against such a transaction.

- *Publishing the guidelines to be followed:* The Investment Company Institute (the trade association for American mutual fund managers) recently came out with a governance best practice that states that independent directors should have written guidelines to determine how the proxies of their funds should be voted.

♦ *Disclosing how the fund shares actually vote:* Following the ICI's lead, the SEC has recently ruled that mutual funds should disclose how they voted on proxy issues. This disclosure gives the fund shareholder the right to ascertain for him- or herself that the fund's shares were voted.

Collective investment schemes can have the same level of influence as any institutional shareholder. Historically, most CIS directors have believed that if a fund investor does not like the conduct or investment policy of a fund, he or she is easily able to sell their position and invest in something they prefer. However, the tax implications of doing so, combined with the practical lethargy of the marketplace has changed CIS directors' feelings about exercising this authority. Not only are they now more inclined to do so, but also are obliged under SEC rules to disclose how they voted.

In conclusion, CISs have emerged as the preferred form of personal capital accumulation in the developed world. As such, good governance is mandatory to reassure investors that their assets will be safe and productive. The directors of CISs have a responsibility to be diligent and single minded in the pursuit of the fund's shareholders interests.

NOTES

1. Thompson, J. K., and S-M. Choi. "Governance Systems for Collective Investment Schemes in OECD Countries," *Organization for Economic Co-operation and Development (OECD)*, 2001.

2. Ibid.

3. Story, J. M., and T. Clyde. "The Uneasy Chaperone—A Resource for the Independent Directors of Mutual Funds," *Management Practice Inc.*, 2001.

RELATED WEBSITES

Institutional Investor Newsletters, www.funddirections.com
Investment Company Institute, www.ici.org
Investment Funds Institute of Canada, www.ific.ca
Management Practice Inc., www.mfgovern.com
Money Media, www.ignites.com and www.boardiq.com

CHAPTER 14

Public Sector Governance

John Chambers and Monica Richter

This chapter examines governance as it relates to the creditworthiness of governments.[1] Following the approach set out for corporations in Chapter 2, the analysis of governmental governance focuses on its effects on key stakeholders: those whom it taxes, creditors, and those for whom it provides goods and services. In most countries there is substantial overlap between these three categories of stakeholders, with their related interests usually best served by governance that supports an environment conducive to sustainable economic growth, which in turn underpins improvements in living standards in a broadly equitable manner.[2]

Creditworthiness is defined as the capacity and willingness to service debt in full and on time, without recourse to involuntary exchanges or other forms of debt relief. This chapter draws from the framework used by Standard & Poor's to assign its credit ratings to governments.[3] At the sovereign level, that framework examines political institutions, the real economy, fiscal policy, monetary flexibility, and external vulnerabilities to determine the probability of a government default on its financial obligations. At the regional and local government level, the framework focuses particularly on the real economy and fiscal policy, as well as intergovernmental relations. Governance issues that speak both to the capacity and willingness to service debt are a factor in all of these categories.

It also may be useful to state what this chapter does not cover, as its scope differs from other chapters of this book, which are more proscriptive in nature. This chapter does not replicate the work of the International Monetary Fund, the World Bank, the United Nations, or other organizations in setting out what constitutes best practice in political and governmental organization, accountability, rule of law, control of corruption, or other issues of governmental effectiveness. Readers interested in this subject may refer to a selection of works cited in the References.

POLITICAL STABILITY

Political stability rests on the strength of public backing for its political institutions or, to use Rousseau's formulation, it is founded on the strength of the social contract. Governments that enjoy the greatest political stability are those that possess stable, predictable, and transparent political institutions. Checks and balances between branches of government and between the government and its citizens help assure stability and predictability. Without good governance, the checks and balances among a government's institutions will not function properly.

Good governance begins with a country's legal system. Often, but not always, the legal system is based on a constitution. It encompasses a legal code or a history of jurisprudence. A country with a long tradition of respecting the rule of law, of maintaining the competency and integrity of judges, of exercising prompt and fair justice, and of respecting property rights will obtain a high degree of order in its society and public trust among its citizens. Such an environment will allow the greater freedom of commerce, one based on contracts rather than personal relationships. It facilitates the deepening of financial markets, due to the greater confidence in collateral values and financial covenants.

Similarly, countries benefit from strong regulatory regimes that establish clear rules for conduct in matters of public interest without stifling innovation. In the financial world, these include the regulation of financial markets and of banking. More broadly, they include public health, consumer protection, and environmental safety, among others. A strong governance culture sets high expectations for honest, open, ethical behavior in tandem with a low tolerance for deviation with explicit and respected sanctions for negligence, fraud, misconduct, and corruption.

More will be said in a moment about governance within a central bank as it pertains to monetary policy or within a ministry of finance as it pertains to fiscal policy. However, an element of good governance consists of the branches of government (executive, legislative, and judiciary, be it at the central, regional, or local level) and the various independent offices of government interacting according to established rules, with clear reporting lines, sufficient independence, and proper accountability. Preferably, heads of autonomous government agencies operate with fixed terms and can be removed only for cause. Their budgets should be a matter of public record.

With checks and balances, power is diffused. With levels of government, departments of government, and autonomous agencies invested with authority and autonomy, decisionmaking is spread out and brought closer to those with specific expertise. With a long tradition of respect for the rule of law and respect for intergovernmental relations, precedence takes more importance and the risk of policy reversals is diminished.

For example, the candidate countries for membership in the European Union would illustrate rising creditworthiness due to improved governance. The qualification process includes harmonizing national laws in 31 areas (or "chapters") with EU laws. The corpus of EU law and regulation is well elaborated. The benefits of EU membership provide a powerful incentive for applicants to adapt their national laws and to respect their enactment. The EU policy anchor sharply reduces the chances of policy reversals.

On the other hand, Venezuela under the administration of Hugo Chávez would be an example of where weakening standards of governance increased political risk and in turn impaired creditworthiness. With the passage of a new constitution in December 1999, Chávez concentrated decisionmaking in the executive branch. Checks and balances between branches of government and autonomous agencies—especially the national oil company Petroleos de Venezuela, which up until then had been a model of good corporate management for a public enterprise—were eviscerated. The ability of the population to express their views through their public institutions was reduced. The result was an estrangement of a majority of the population, debilitating general strikes, urban violence, and a sharp economic contraction, despite very positive terms of trade.

Another example of poor governance can be seen in Russia, where interbudgetary arrangements between regional and local governments are so variable as to make planning difficult. Many regional governments unilaterally change tax sharing rates with localities on an annual basis and with little advance notice.

For the State of Nayarit in Mexico, poor governance was inherited when in 2000 the recently inaugurated administration had problems locating historic financial information. The prior administration—from a different political party—had destroyed almost all the financial records, adding to institutional weakness and managerial difficulties.

INCOME AND ECONOMIC STRUCTURE

Although the starting position of a government's income and economic structure is predicated on its endowment factors (geography, natural resources, and climate), its capacity to grow rests on the ability of economic agents to allocate resources efficiently. In most economies, this allocation takes place outside of the activities of the public sector. However, public sector governance has a role to play. If commercial regulations are well drafted and enforced, the opportunities for rent-seeking activities are lessened. If labor laws are flexible and incentives are focused on keeping individuals productively employed, unemployment will be reduced and labor mobility will help smooth out regional employment disparities. If financial regulators permit innovation while insulating the government from contingent risks, financial markets will deepen without moral hazard.

Kaufmann and Kraay at the World Bank have tried to quantify governance and chart its correlation to growth. They measure the individual's ability to express his or her opinion; public accountability; political stability; government effectiveness; regulatory quality; rule of law; and control of corruption. They discuss the impact of a country's elite "capturing" the instruments of the state to preserve their economic privileges. They conclude that good governance promotes growth but that economic development does not automatically engender improving public sector governance.[4]

The more the state is involved in economic activity, the more opportunities vested interests will have in appropriating gains to themselves at the expense of the population at large. William Easterly argues along the same lines as do his former colleagues at the World Bank when he writes "in an economy with many government interventions, skilled people opt for activities that redistribute income rather than activities that promote growth."[5] Governments that excessively regulate economic activity create opportunities for individuals or interest groups to limit competition through lobbying or through corruption of bureaucrats.

Nigeria would be an example where an elite has aggrandized public wealth for private benefit. Nigeria scores poorly on lists of perceived corruption, such as those published by Transparency International or the World Bank. Government regulation is capricious and vested interests excel in protecting their entrenched interests. Partly as a result, per capita GDP has grown little since independence.

On the other hand, Singapore is an example where corruption of public officials has been routed out since its colonial days. Singapore consistently receives high marks on the ethics of its public officials. Although its resource base is poor, it has enjoyed among the highest rates of per capita GDP growth and the most improvement of social indicators in education and health of any developing country in the past 40 years.

FISCAL POLICY

The fiscal transparency code of the International Monetary Fund (IMF) opens with the following:

> The Code is based around the following key objectives: roles and responsibilities in government should be clear; information on government activities should be provided to the public; budget preparation, execution, and reporting should be undertaken in an open manner; and fiscal information should attain widely accepted standards of data quality and be subject to independent assurances of integrity.[6]

The connection between public sector governance and creditworthiness is most easily seen when it comes to fiscal policy. Taxpayers are more supportive of government fiscal policy and less likely to avoid or evade taxes when they believe their money is well spent. In the process, public support for public institutions will grow and political risk will fall in tandem.[7]

Policy formation improves when the demarcation is clear between the branches and levels of government. Moral hazard is reduced when there is less ambiguity between the responsibilities of the public and private sector as well as between the central and local governments. It is on the belief that money is more effectively spent when there is closer contact with the citizens that the subsidiarity principle promoted by the European Union was affirmed and that contributed to the gradual decentralization of powers from the central to the local governments over the last 20 years.

Governance is also an important element in measuring government performance. At one level, governance includes the timely publishing of a comprehensive government budget and multiyear investment plan as well as auditing of government fiscal outturn. At another level, governance encompasses measuring the effectiveness of government spending, be it for supporting scholastic achievement, reducing toxins in the environment, or promoting public health, to cite three examples.

Good governance at the regional and local levels also focuses on the continuous improvement in economic potential and prosperity via efficient, unbiased procedures for attracting investment, collecting revenues, and expending public funds on maintaining and developing infrastructure. The municipality of Mérida has procurement practices among the most transparent in Mexico. All of the city's major purchases and infrastructure projects are done through public bids. The information on the contractors and suppliers is updated and published on a regular basis.

Finally, Mérida places all of its information on the Internet and in major local newspapers.

The same is true of the City of Venice in Italy, which has posted all its administrative tasks—procurement, administrative procedures, payment of taxes, invoices, and payments—on the Internet as well.

Examples of poor fiscal governance are frequent at the local level where reliance on a regional or national government to bail out a troubled municipality has sometimes led to complacency. For example, the municipality of Leukerbad, Switzerland, is currently in default. The Wallis Cantonal government concedes that it made mistakes in supervision, but blames creditors for lax lending policies. The courts are expected to rule that the cantonal government was remiss in its monitoring from 1996 and should have stopped the mayor from limiting the disclosure of negative trends much earlier.

In September 1993, Málaga, Spain, defaulted when one of its financial obligations came due, delaying 20 days the repayment of a bank loan. While the city could have drawn on bank lines to meet the obligation, which only represented 2 percent of Málaga's operating expenditures, the mayor decided to default as a political tool to pressure the central government. Although the outcome was relatively positive for all local governments in Spain, since the central government finally started to transfer funds on a timely basis, Málaga has had to take painful measures to restore its credit standing as the stigma of default tarnished the government's reputation for several years after the missed payments.

In laying out a description of the IMF's perspectives on the subject, Peter Heller lists it as the last of six elements.[8] Governance is just one part of sound fiscal policy. Good governance will not alone correct for procyclical, inflexible, or unsustainable fiscal policies, policies oriented to short-term objectives, or policies that encourage nonproductive behavior. It will, however, bring greater scrutiny to bear and perhaps intelligent debate.

Governance issues are also at play in the management of public debt. The ethical standards that apply to any issuer *vis-à-vis* its investors apply for governments. The matter is not simply one of timely and full disclosure of relevant debt and contingent liability data. It entails equal treatment of investors in dissemination of information on debt issuance strategies. It includes the establishment of clear rules for debt issuance, such as set auction times and procedures. It requires that the state maintain and supervise well-functioning systems for payments, settlement, custody, and financing through repurchase agreements. It requires a strong repayment culture and contingency planning.

Several governments have embraced the IMF's efforts to improve fiscal governance by adopting the IMF's data dissemination standards and by engaging the IMF for a review of their regulations, standards, and codes. Currently, 53 governments adhere to the IMF's Special Data Dissemination Standard and 47 governments have permitted the IMF to publish fiscal Reports on the Observance of Standards and Codes.

Australian states' financial disclosure and transparency are examples of good regional practices. The states produce fully articulated financial statements with an accrual operating statement, balance sheet, and cash flow statement for each of the general government sector, the state-owned trading enterprise sector, the state-owned financial enterprises sector, and a consolidated statement for all of these sectors (i.e., the regional public sector). The general government sector accounts also have estimates for each of the three years beyond the current budget year. In addition, there is a consolidated financial statement produced a few months after the conclusion of the financial year containing full audited accounts for the just-completed financial year. These accounts resemble financial statements prepared for commercial companies. They provide information on contingent assets and liabilities, forward expenditure commitments, interests in joint ventures, post-balance date events, derivative exposures, interest rate risks, counterparty credit risks, foreign exchange risk and liquidity risk, and information about off-budget liabilities such as public/private partnerships.

Other governments, however, still have progress to make on improving the transparency of their fiscal affairs. In Panama for example, cash movements between different levels of government are difficult to reconcile, data are released with long lags, and proposed budgets often differ greatly from executed budgets. Similarly, many local and regional governments poorly account for guaranteed debts or other contingencies. Gaps in information on financial assets and liabilities are still common for many localities.

In some instances, there is transparency in reporting, but the payment culture is weak. Common to most Italian regions and some Spanish ones are delays in payments to health care suppliers because of revenue and expenditure mismatches. Payment delays of more than one year are not uncommon. The result is a cycle of increased costs for the regional governments as suppliers charge a premium, which, in turn, exacerbates the mismatch. The local implementation of EU regulations to reduce and standardize payments delays to an acceptable level are pushing the public sector to increase governance standards.

Legacies of poor governance in the public sector unfortunately are often passed on to future generations with unsustainable debt levels and unfunded pension liabilities being two common examples. Many local and regional governments are prudently avoiding these pitfalls—with or without the leadership of their central governments. The State of Rhineland-Palatinate in Germany pays specific supplemental amounts into a pension fund without legal obligation in order to meet looming future pension liabilities.

MONETARY POLICY

The motives for seeking good governance in fiscal affairs apply equally to monetary policy. Good governance for monetary policy includes setting clear objectives for the central bank, preferably in law; establishing lines of accountability to elected figures; and insuring independence, usually through fixed terms of directors.

Governance in monetary policy takes on a special importance in that the average citizen often does not easily understand its effects. Whereas citizens feel immediately the impact of changes in tax rates or observe directly the effectiveness of government services that they individually consume, they may not immediately link the conduct of monetary policy with the indirect tax of inflation or the loss of purchasing power of tradeable goods by real depreciation of their currency. Nor would average citizens immediately grasp the implications of different forms of financial suppression, such as negative real interest rates, exchange controls, directed lending, or high reserve requirements. As in fiscal policy, governance alone cannot right these wrongs, but bringing them to light can help spur public policy debate.

Several emerging market sovereigns have strengthened the laws regarding central bank independence and thereby helped improve the credibility of future monetary policy. In the Dominican Republic, for example, legislation passed in December 2002 that permitted the central bank to divest its commercial assets, fixed the term of the governor, and recapitalized the bank.

On the other hand, the efforts of the Abdurrahman Wahid administration in Indonesia in 2000 to gut the central bank law as part of an attack on the central bank president who had been appointed by the previous administration, seriously disrupted its relations with the IMF, and put at risk its entire official creditor program.

EXTERNAL SECTOR

Issues of public sector governance that are relevant for credit aspects of a country's external position pertain to reserve management and management of public sector external debt. The holder of a country's international reserves should be clearly identified, be it central bank, central government, or monetary authority. Reserves should be available for use and their amount regularly disclosed. Disclosures also should be promptly made of any reserves that are placed with foreign branches of domestic banks that are pledged as security for loans, that are sold forward in the foreign exchange market, or that are otherwise encumbered.

The issues of governance for management of public sector external debt draw from the same principles that apply for domestic debt management. Again the issue of fairness should be central. Voting rights on government securities held by domestic public sector entities should be voided. Foreign currency denominated securities repurchased in the open market or by tender by the government itself should be retired and not held for reissue.

In the event that sovereign foreign currency denominated debt needs to be renegotiated, the renegotiation should entail as much debt as possible, including that debt held by residents, to achieve more equitably a sustainable level of debt.

Errors in reserve management contributed to the balance of payment crisis for Korea and Thailand in 1997. In the case of Korea, the Bank of Korea lent almost all of its usable reserves to foreign branches of Korean banks when they themselves faced rising cross-border interbank lending rates. When the Bank of Korea's reserves were revealed to be almost entirely immobilized, the crisis of confidence forced the government to help the banks to strong-arm their creditors into providing extended terms for their advances under a government guarantee. In the case of Thailand, the Bank of Thailand had sold dollars against baht to nonresidents in an amount comparable to its reserve base. Although the balance of payment impact was not potentially as damaging as in Korea, the impact on confidence was similar when the clandestine transactions were uncovered. In Russia in 1998, some regional governments suddenly found put clauses on foreign borrowings triggered after the sharp depreciation of the ruble. High-profile restructurings occurred and the central government has since curtailed foreign currency borrowing approval.

Examples of good governance are less dramatic in this area. Several OECD governments and emerging market governments are members of the World Bank's government borrowers forum. The forum seeks to pool knowledge about techniques of debt management to reduce issuing costs and to render the debt markets more liquid. Maintaining orderly and efficient debt markets is a necessary condition of good credit standing.

In conclusion, governance affects creditworthiness of a governmental entity just as in the corporate sector. The evolution of political institutions, trends in economic policy, and shifts in revenue-raising authority and expenditure responsibilities make the dynamics of good governance for each level of government a challenge.

NOTES

1. The authors would like to thank Marie Cavanaugh and Carol Sirou for commenting on this article in draft.

2. Central to effective government governance is that governing has to be organized in such a way as "to enhance the independent adaptive, reactive and problem-solving capabilities of societal actors, which means to motivate and to enable them to react purposefully at any moment to changing conditions." B. Kohler-Koch, "The Strength of Weakness: The Transformation of Governance in the EU," 1996.

3. Beers and Cavanaugh, 2002; Eddy, 2003.

4. Kaufmann and Kraay, 2002.

5. Easterly, 2001.

6. "Code of Good Practices on Fiscal Transparency," 2001.

7. It is with a view to improve accountability and efficiency that the European Union, World Bank, and others promote the devolution of spending powers to the level of government closest to the population consuming the expenditure, consistent with obtaining economies of scale.

8. Heller, 2002.

REFERENCES

Beers, D., and M. Cavanaugh. "Sovereign Credit Ratings: A Primer," Ratings Direct, April 3, 2002.

Blinder, A. "Central Banking in Theory and Practice," MIT Press, 1998.

"Code of Good Practices on Fiscal Transparency," IMF, March 23, 2001.

Easterly, W. "The Elusive Quest for Growth," MIT Press, 2001.

Eddy, J. "Rating Regional and Local Governments," RatingsDirect, January 17, 2003.

"Fiscal Decentralization in Emerging Economies: Governance Issues," OECD, April 1999.

Heller, P. "Considering the IMF's Perspective on a 'Sound Fiscal Policy,'" IMF Discussion Paper, IMF (July 2002).

Kaufmann, D., and A. Kraay. "Growth without Governance," World Bank (2002).

Lienert, I. "A Comparison Between Two Public Expenditure Management Systems in Africa," IMF Working Paper 03/2.

Lubbers, R. F. M., and D. Watts. "Government, Governance and International Business: Seeking Conditions of Sustainability among Government, Economy and Society," Globus, February 1997.

"Manuel on Fiscal Transparency," IMF, March 23, 2001.

Rawls, J. "A Theory of Justice," Oxford (1976).

"Recommended Practices for State and Local Governments," Government Finance Officers Association, May 2001.

Rousseau, J. J. "The Social Contract," translated by M. Cranston, Penguin Books 1975.

Stiglitz, J. "Globalization and Its Discontents," W.W. Norton, 2002.

CHAPTER 15

The Human Side of Corporate Governance

Lynn McGregor

This chapter focuses on the importance of the human side of corporate governance for sustained success. It is a neglected area, ignored at peril. A more professional approach to the subject would benefit analysts and fund managers as much as boards, CEOs, and directors. A conceptual understanding of the basic principles—principles that span international boundaries—is offered as a starting point for better evaluating the human elements of governance. The importance of better risk management is stressed, both as opportunity management and risk avoidance.

RISK GOVERNANCE AND THE HUMAN FACTOR

As humans, we seek to manage risk by anticipating it and outmaneuvering it or responding to situations through crisis management. Different circumstances evoke their own types of risk.

Taking the stock market as an example: We distinguish two states—Bull and Bear—and recognize the need for different trading strategies according to the state. A new crisis has been defined, because the transition from Bull to Bear or vice versa now demands a change of mindset and a whole new rulebook. The trader who survives best in these conditions is the one who keeps his or her cool, and does not lose track of their broader human skills based on experience, intuition, and the understanding that market movements form a continuum rather than a binary series.

The present sharp focus on governance is largely a reaction to such a change of state—from a boom-time of optimism and growth, to a time of doubt and shrinking fortunes.

When things are going well we focus on the individual, asking: Who are the stars driving this growth? What is the star quality that they possess? But when the business climate turns sour, reputations that were built up over years can be destroyed in minutes. Attention then moves from the individual to the system. The bigger questions are now: What is wrong with the system? How can we police it better? What new rules will stop this from happening again?

The trouble is again that this swing of attention—from star quality in times of boom to the faults of the system in times of bust—is a distraction that obscures the continuum of human factors linking these two extremes.

Four levels of governance are recognized in the book *The Human Face of Corporate Governance:*[1]

+ *Systemic governance:* the rules, the culture, and the system under so much present scrutiny;

+ *Intergroup governance:* for example, the relationships between board and executive, board and shareholders, executive and stakeholders, and so on;

+ *Interpersonal governance:* including leadership and communication skills, as well as functioning well within a group; and

+ *Personal governance:* which has a lot to do with "star quality" but addresses broader issues as well.

These four levels were defined for convenience, and they have proved their usefulness, but they are, of course, interrelated and we are dealing with a whole continuum of human experience between "box-ticking" and individual human potential.

The organizations that survive and flourish in the longer term are the ones that get the human side of governance right.

And what we forget when we re-write the rulebook is that, however good the new regulations, they will need to be accepted and operated by humans and human groups. A brilliant constitution will not work without wise intergroup governance between the rulemakers and those putting the rules into practice. To quote Derek Higgs's introductory letter to the U.K. Chancellor and Secretary of State: "The brittleness and rigidity of legislation cannot dictate the behavior, or foster the trust, I believe is fundamental to the effective unitary board and to superior corporate performance."

The title of this chapter "The Human Side of Corporate Governance" is therefore an understatement—for the purely regulatory box-ticking mechanisms of corporate governance are no more than the tip of an iceberg that is wholly created by humans, administered by humans, applied to humans, and sustained by humans. We do our best to tackle such complexity by analyzing, categorizing, and defining simple rules, but the more successful the model the greater risk that we will forget the under-lying reality and trip over the next-step change.

The more financially numerate we are, the greater the temptation to forget the human factor, to dismiss it as "fluffy stuff" or to place it outside the category of measurable and manageable business factors. Directors' academic qualifications in finance, law, and business are taken carefully into account, but their personal judgments may be entrusted to "gut feeling."

The fact is that there are social science disciplines for which people receive academic qualifications that provide deeper and more accurate insight into the human side of corporate governance than these amateur-ish hunches. The human side needs to be taken seriously, and its status and professionalism raised to compare with those of financial or techno-logical competence.

THE COST OF IGNORING THE HUMAN SIDE

Recent years have seen massive scandals leading to the demise of promi-nent firms in the United States and Europe. The reasons for these several disasters and lapses are primarily human, not structural or financial. They relate to human values, behavior, and the quality of decisionmaking. Dishonesty, negligence, and lack of intelligence have cost companies and investors billions of dollars, yet although the human side is always pres-ent in the minds of the chairman and the board, not many boards will invest in professional expertise to check whether the quality and mix of directors is adequate and how effectively the board functions.

Poor corporate governance takes many less dramatic forms than these well-publicized criminal lapses. One dominant CEO, chairman, or director can cause the board to become dysfunctional and prevent other directors from contributing. Or a chairman or CEO, however good in other circumstances, may not be right for the immediate situation and business characteristics of a company. If they deny this, or refuse to let go, retire, or move on, the quality of governance will be at risk. Poor succes-sion planning compounds the error.

A company can be doing very well but, if the board and executives become arrogant and complacent, there will be risk. They may be good performers who have proved themselves, but they might still not be the right team to lead the next stage of growth. The same is true of accepted practices: whether it is sheer conservatism or respect for some proven "formula for success," there is no guarantee that it will hold up under the winds of change and still deliver competitive advantage.

Unrealistic pressure by investors to grow, coupled with promises that the CEO fails to keep, is a sure recipe for disaster. Boards that resist codes of conduct, or merely pretend to conform to guidelines, betray poor understanding of corporate governance. Add negligence on the part of nonexecutive directors to speak out when they feel something is not right, and you are on a slippery slope. And when things do go wrong, there may be buck-passing and political games rather than willingness to learn from mistakes. These tensions and interpersonal conflicts will only distract the board from doing its real work.

The chairman may be highly skilled, but not trained in human interaction, using structural solutions to solve "human" problems and not recognizing the conditions for good decisionmaking. Without access to the right kind of information, boards cannot do their work properly; and even if the information is good, if directors are not given it in time to read or think it over, they cannot do their job well.

People rely on intuition and experience to judge others and are surprised when it does not always work. Getting a senior recruitment wrong can cost a fortune in litigation and head hunter fees. Even worse, a leaderless company can lose profitability over a period of years.

RISK MANAGEMENT

Risk management is understandably high on the agenda but, unless we find ways of integrating the human side, it cannot be truly effective. The problem is that it is not easy to anticipate hidden risks, particularly if there is a conspiracy of silence or the board itself is ignorant about what is going on. Often what happens is that directors are reluctant to speak up when they feel something is wrong, but cannot prove it at the time.

The art of governance requires more than checking boxes. It depends on the integrity, composition, alertness, intelligence, creativity, and quality of communication of both nonexecutive and executive directors on the board, together with the ability and willingness of internal and external auditors, analysts, and fund managers to flag danger signs before they become problems. This means a major shift in the way the "risk game" is currently played, toward a preventative rather than a punitive culture.

The current reaction to failure is to axe people, cut costs, and focus on counting the pennies. While important, it is not the whole picture. Extreme cost cutting limits the capacity of a company to grow and function. If monitoring is too heavy handed, executives grow defensive and economical with the truth. Such defensive measures require a balance, and it is vital that the board also supports those willing to optimize opportunities. There needs to be a good balance in the board between those good at avoiding risks and those who are entrepreneurial—and there are indicators of a company's ability to handle both risk avoidance and opportunity management.

Certain industries have a way of cloning their boards to reflect a pre-existing bias in the industry. For example, pharmaceutics demand a detailed, analytical approach with fail-safe production and everything carefully tested. This very culture can shape the handling of risk—pharmaceutical companies tend to select directors who are careful about detail, but are not necessarily good at generating alternatives or insisting on contingencies if things go wrong. While directors of fund management companies usually know their finances, they often can be weak in succession planning or sustainable development of the company.

In addition, every company has its own specific risks, financial and nonfinancial. The board itself can constitute a risk—it has intrinsic strengths, weaknesses, and habitual solutions, which may or may not be appropriate to certain types of risk. The personalities and styles of the chairman and CEO will determine the board's approach to risk—they too have their strengths and blind spots. Nonexecutive directors need to address these factors consciously in order to know what questions to ask and where to apply checks and balances.

The greater the trust and understanding between board members, the more effective nonexecutive directors can be. Likewise, the more information the chairman has about the board members and their interactions, the more effectively he or she can use specific strengths to manage risk effectively. It also helps the chairman to ascertain which new skill sets and processes are most needed to keep ahead of best practice—what worked in the past may not be good for tomorrow.

"By the time we realized, it was too late" is a frequent claim, but after the fall it sounds so very feeble. It reflects an equally common error—forgetting that the ability to listen is as important as making sure one is heard. It is not uncommon to "shoot the messenger who brings bad news"—but if taken seriously, expensive mistakes can be avoided. Quality of information is a vital factor in board meetings, for nonexecutive directors only have limited time and there are often long intervals between board meetings. When they consciously take responsibility for asking penetrating questions and requesting relevant information, many expensive mistakes can be avoided. When the CEO provides the right information and flags important issues on time, the chances of risk being well managed before disaster are considerably improved.

The old roles of the nonexecutive director are changing and new roles are more demanding, and need to include higher levels of awareness, particularly of the human side. How then can this be achieved?

GETTING IT RIGHT

Definitions of best board practice are not hard to find. There have been a number of reports, codes of practice, and guidelines generated in countries across the world. The King Report in South Africa is an excellent example of the quality of thinking about this subject. It is very clear about defining principles and the structural requirements of governance and at the same time stating that the quality of governance is related to values, culture, ethics, and behaviors.

Such reports set high standards, but the problem is how to implement and embed some of the suggested practices in already existing boards. Apart from reducing the whole matter to some unsatisfactory box-ticking exercise, it is not easy for those without specific training to assess whether real improvement has been made, particularly in terms of the so-called "soft" aspects. How is it possible to assess the human capital of boards and executives?

A good board is likely to score highly on the following characteristics:

♦ *A culture of integrity and respect,* to build on each others' strengths, while recognizing and dealing with intrinsic weaknesses, conflicts of interest, or personality problems

♦ *A collegiate atmosphere with high-level debate,* freedom to ask the right questions and warn of potential risks—plus a waiting list of good directors to join the board

♦ *The right composition* reflecting a balance between decision-making skills, expertise, and experience; supported by a sound succession strategy, induction and integration of new nonexecutive directors, plus continuous training and development for all directors, including the chairman

♦ *Constructive and effective relationships* between the chairman, CEO, key fund managers, and other stakeholders

♦ *A highly competent chairman* who understands both the business issues and the directors' needs; who is able to support or challenge the CEO as appropriate, or to make unpopular strategic decisions when necessary

* *A highly professional company secretary's office*, with good, quality information delivered on time and in the right amount
* *Regular internal and external board reviews*

There has been increasing interest in this area of board assessment and review by "management," some analysts, and proactive fund managers. The starting point is a conceptual framework including the key factors that need to be taken into account when evaluating the human side of corporate governance.

A CONCEPTUAL FRAMEWORK FOR THE HUMAN SIDE

In our experience and the views of board members we have surveyed, there appear to be a number of universal principles that are fundamental to good corporate governance:

* Rules, codes, and regulations have a legitimate and vital place in governance
* Good governance also must focus on wealth generation
* Integrity and trust are vital for sustainable financial success
* Structural solutions are not enough; they only work if people are effective
* It is vital to have the right people in at the right time
* Undisclosed or unresolved conflicts of interest always cause trouble
* The quality of decisionmaking is central to good governance
* Good governance relies on effective working relationships

Given these principles, how does one assess the human side? It is a complex combination of factors and not easy to formulate, given that no board or company is the same as any other. It is, however, possible to identify key indicators as to whether a board or executive is more or less likely to succeed—though the quality of evaluation will depend on who does the assessment and the required depth of analysis.

The following eight factors are those relevant in this context:

1. The context in which governance is taking place
2. Whether there is a workable culture that encourages integrity
3. Whether the composition is right and personalities integrate

4. Whether there is a good succession process in place
5. The quality and timeliness of decisionmaking
6. Whether the board and committee dynamics are effective
7. Whether governance systems and processes support the board
8. How well the board manages risk

These factors make a real difference, and are best illustrated by presenting under each heading some of the leading questions we address when assessing the quality of boards or management. Sometimes they are answered directly; other times the answers reveal themselves through diplomacy, a constructive approach, and mutual trust.

Context
What are the key business drivers for the company at the moment and for the next three years? How well are these understood by the board and the executive?

By "context" we mean the current economic, market, political, and social climate plus the specific financial and organizational issues of the company. The board is an important bridge between the outside world and the inner world of the organization, ensuring that the company is not too inward looking.

We also take into account the company's type and stage of development. The very people who excel with start-up companies and high-growth conditions may not be at all good for helping a company survive a bear market. Equally, successful well-established companies where the same directors have held the reins for many years may forget that new energy and skills are sometimes needed to wake up the organization.

A general understanding of the context is the basis for setting performance criteria for board members in terms of their set targets. It helps to determine whether those targets are humanly realistic and how best to achieve them.

Culture
Are there any concerns about the integrity of the chairman and board members? When a merger is considered, will the corporate cultures integrate? What do we know about the track record of the directors of this board? What questions do we ask to test for integrity? How well can we read human signals to tell whether we are being misled? The same questions apply for the senior executive team.

The cultural tone on the board is set by the chairman's own behavior. If the chairman is dominant, it is harder for directors to contribute. On the other hand, a good chairman provides a cultural environment in which high-level, open, and honest debate can take place and where each director feels free to add value. A constructive and effective culture is a corporate asset—the opposite, as in the case of Enron, can bring a company to its knees.

The extent to which a board is open and honest can be partly tested through the quality of disclosure—what the annual report does and does not say, and what board members admit about the way the board operates. Often the integrity of the CEO and his or her team can be tested by direct questions or by examining documents they put forward to the board.

For nonexecutive or independent directors, or external auditors who do not feel comfortable about the way the chairman or CEO is operating, it is important to speak up as early as possible—even if only to request further information or a quiet word. The problem is that people are reluctant even to ask simple questions when they have a gut feeling that something is wrong but cannot prove it, or feel disloyal to an old friend. Some dishonest people are extremely good at covering their tracks, yet it is also possible to sense that something is wrong in a board meeting. This is often admitted in confidence—but the challenge is to follow the scent until either the miscreant backs off, or firm evidence of wrongdoing emerges.

Nor is the question of culture purely a matter of ethics. In the case of acquisitions and mergers, cultural differences and misunderstandings about value and behavioral expectations are often overlooked while everyone is dazzled by the potential business and financial benefits. But how many acquisitions really deliver those benefits in the long term? Unacknowledged cultural differences are a major factor in so many failed mergers.

Composition

What skill sets, knowledge, and expertise are needed for the particular board and executive team? Does the board have the right balance of power, expertise, and types of decisionmaking? And are these well integrated? How good is the current nominations committee, and what track record does the board have for getting the people right?

Good board composition is the cornerstone to good governance. The board or nominations committee need to set up their own criteria for directors and the standards needed for effective performance, and this is seldom done. The chairman is key—his or her style of leadership sets the tone, quality, and working habits of the board. The same applies to the CEO, although the roles of chairman and CEO are totally different and it should not be assumed that a good CEO would make a good chairman.

There is controversy about whether the roles of chairman and CEO should be separated, or the role of nonexecutive directors and senior nonexecutive director, and whether nonexecutive directors should have a financial stake in the company. Prescriptions about these derive from the fact that certain combinations are less likely to provide successful governance. While principles are important, caution should be exercised about prescribing too precisely given that each board is unique. With that caution, however, it can be suggested that the board composition should address:

+ Appropriate skill sets, knowledge, and experience to ensure that the company adds value for shareholders; and
+ The right values of integrity, emotional maturity, and honesty.

Attention also should be paid to creating a good balance in the following areas:

+ Power: so all board members are strong enough to contribute;
+ Decisionmaking: without blind spots in thinking;
+ Externally or internally focused directors;
+ Differences between cautious monitoring and encouraging entrepreneuralism,
+ Differences between bright ideas and sound implementation plans; and
+ Short-, medium-, and long-term thinking.

Remember also that there must be sufficient talent to fulfill all the necessary board and committee functions. Although the chairman should play a large part in establishing performance standards and be involved in discussions about composition, the quality of the nominations committee is vital.

Succession

Is there an effective succession process? Is there a good track record for appointing key people? How good is the nominations committee?

Board succession often is not managed successfully—usually because of emotional difficulties around the chairman and CEO not wanting to move on when they should. However good, they may no longer be ideal for the current stage of development. When someone does go, with no one groomed to fill their place, governance is equally at risk—a leaderless board or executive cannot function properly and the company can be set back years.

Apart from the case of a start-up company, most chairpeople inherit a board and then decide whether to make changes. When a chairman or CEO plans to retire, it is wise to pass on to a successor an understanding of the principles and values of their legacy so that work built up over years is not wasted.

Good succession planning and processes are essential for continuity, and they should be supported with transitional management and induction programs for new arrivals.

Quality and speed of decisionmaking

What is the quality of strategic thinking on the board? How independent is the thinking on the board? Is the level of contribution by individual directors adequate?

The quality and timeliness of decisionmaking is one of the oft-neglected functions of governance. High-level decisionmaking requires high-level thinking and debating skills, the ability of the chairman to understand and play to the strengths of the directors, to find ways of dealing with weaknesses and blind spots, and the ability of directors to contribute in a meaningful and timely way. It also entails an ability to process complex information, to gain an overview of how the company works, and to ask the right questions.

Most board meetings are run to the same formula and do not fully harness the real value that directors can add. Greater understanding and mastery of the decision process and more advanced facilitation skill sets can transform the quality of board performance, particularly in the ways of working as a board as they are geared to a knowledge of how each director prefers to work, their unique contributions, and what they need in order to make intelligent decisions.

Board dynamics

How good are the working relationships between the chairman and CEO? How good are the working relationships between the board, shareholders, and executives? Is the chairman good at harnessing the strengths of each director at the right times?

Good decisionmaking also depends on the quality of board dynamics, i.e., how the board operates, and especially the effectiveness of the working relationships between board members, with the executive and other significant groups. Board dynamics must be good at each level.

At the personal level, it has to do with how well each director fulfils his or her function, participates in board meetings, and exercises interpersonal skills. The most important factor is how effective each is at managing his or her energy, abilities, and time.

At the interpersonal level, the following relationships are core to good performance:

♦ between the chairman and the CEO;

♦ between board members and the executive group;

♦ with shareholders, key fund managers, or investors; and

♦ with the media and other stakeholders such as government and pressure groups.

If relationships are dysfunctional, people cannot concentrate on what really matters. Ego games and point-scoring can be destructive. Lack of respect and trust causes secrecy and defensiveness.

Good dynamics require high-level facilitation from the chairman. Most directors work at considerably below their potential and the chairman needs to be able to tap their potential. Directors also need the ability to communicate, listen, and be heard in order to participate, influence, persuade, or lead as necessary. The skills required for excellent board communication are not evident in most boards; many just muddle through.

At the intergroup level a deeper understanding of how fund managers, boards, and companies work and the development of better working relationships between them can significantly enhance the quality of governance. Directors often complain that analysts and fund managers have superficial views of how they operate and how their company works, but executives seldom scan a range of analysts' reports to see what predictions may be made in the context of the industry.

In a situation where sustainability is encouraged and fund managers or investors are involved, the relationship between the fund manager and the board or CEO and CFO is important. Because active fund managers tend to be analytical and not emotionally sensitive, they come across as more interrogatory, aggressive, and disrespectful than they intend. The reaction is defensive and power games result. If a director sacrifices his or her reputation for personal pride, it is neither within the interests of the company nor the shareholders.

Systems and processes

Is the infrastructure adequate for the needs of shareholders and the board? Are there good processes for the provision of and access to information? How good are the communication processes between the board and its committees?

Effective systems and processes need to be in place. These should include attention to the presentation of written material, processes for alerting board members to new laws and regulations and their implications, and systems for enabling committees, meetings, and the AGM to function smoothly. This is the territory of the company secretary.

How well the board and executives manage risk

How much time does the board spend discussing risk? Does the board have a strategy for managing risk? Is there the right balance on the board for different kinds of risk?

While certain risks can be anticipated and averted ahead of time, the board must equally be able to react promptly and creatively to unexpected global, political, and social crises, or preemptive strikes by competitors. This requires flexibility and swift reactions, and it is important that nonexecutives have the time to be available at short notice. If boards have been doing things in the same successful manner for years, they may no longer possess this flexibility, creativity, and speed of response. Unless they benchmark against best practice elsewhere, they could find themselves overtaken by events.

Most importantly, the board must provide the CEO and his or her team with quick, constructive feedback, and suggestions for alternative action when appropriate. The added value that nonexecutives can bring by increasing their input without interfering in executive responsibility is considerable, and has significant bottom line implications.

To manage risk properly, directors need to be informed, trained, and have time to deal with important issues. It is broadly assumed that directors should be informed about ethical issues and up to date with national and global regulations; they also are expected to be in tune with new business thinking and technologies. However, risk management as a human process is seldom formally addressed, nor is there much consideration given to the board's ability to simultaneously respond in time, maintain integrity, and not sacrifice competitive advantage. How much time is actually spent on discussing how the board itself manages risk?

Given the limited time available to nonexecutive directors, their approach to risk needs to be streamlined. Boards can no longer afford to be amateur about risk, as insurance companies reluctant to pay for expensive mistakes increasingly opt to accuse directors of negligence. One slip can lose a personal reputation built over many years.

Taking all these key factors into account, how easily can they be assessed in a more credible way than "gut feel"? Is it feasible?

SOME EXAMPLES

The following examples are intended to give an idea of the importance of the human side. These are taken from real companies we have worked with but are not ascribed to honor confidentiality agreements.

Dominant Chairman Gets More from His Board

A chairman in a major global company knew that two eminent board members were about to retire. He wanted to use this as an opportunity to not only recruit different people but also to improve his own performance and that of the board. So he commissioned an external board review.

One of his complaints was that his nonexecutive directors did not contribute to debates, while they claimed that he dominated meetings and came to conclusions before they had a chance to speak. The external review helped him to understand the effects of his style, and he changed the way he ran meetings and was delighted by the quality of debate that resulted. Two new high-level directors were recruited to fill gaps that had been left. They spoke highly of the quality of the board, and it acquired such a reputation that, within a year, prestigious nonexecutive directors were applying to join it.

He also asked for an evaluation of the CEO and her executive team, which was shared with the board so that members could gain a better understanding of the executive. One of the strengths of the CEO was that she was able to persuade the board to adopt certain strategies. However, one nonexecutive director picked up from his profile that she was good at strategy, but not good at seeing things through. The nonexecutive director asked a series of questions and visited the company. It was discovered that the capacity of the company to deliver the proposed strategy was severely limited. If the board had agreed to the strategy without the information, they would have shown a huge loss. This would not have made the shareholders happy.

Need for a New Board in a Family-Owned IT Company

A company founded by an entrepreneurial father had grown both in profits and size over a period of 20 years. The board comprised only family members, some of whom had no previous board experience and did not fully understand their governance responsibilities.

The company was taken over by the son who had a radical vision of how to change and expand the company. There was considerable tension and disagreement as members of the family were asked to stop regular withdrawals of large sums of money. For the board to achieve agreement, it was necessary for a detached facilitator to help them work through the issues without being destructive. It became clear that the company would have to go outside for capitalization. This meant that the board had to meet certain requirements and standards, including organizing a new board that had more experience of growth and was better suited to deal with the next stage.

After a specification was agreed, candidates were screened to check them against the personalities and abilities of each director and the deeply felt values. When the right board was in place and the chairwoman had been trained to facilitate a larger board, the new members settled in rapidly. They were strong enough to challenge an idealistic president and to help him avoid obvious mistakes. Because of this he was able to take a calculated risk in a tough economic environment—and it paid off.

Production Company Needing to Get a Merger Right

A large international production company merged two external companies with one internal one to gain greater market control and economies of scale. One of the companies was bought at a higher price than the CEO expected, and he told the board they would have to wait longer for their returns. However, the board insisted that he come up with the original results within the same time period.

When he started with his new team, there were horrific cultural clashes, power struggles, and personality problems. This was slowing down the progress that the board badly needed. A nonexecutive director suggested that this needed to be sorted out as soon as possible, and the CEO—who had been totally preoccupied with the financial situation—realized that he had a people problem.

He had his individual directors and the team as a whole profiled and worked with the team over a period of two years to resolve conflicts, power games, and to optimize their performance. Despite all the pressures, they reached their targets on time to the delight of the board and the shareholders.

SUMMARY AND CONCLUSIONS

This chapter should serve as a reminder that the only way all the elements of this book can be applied is by the agreement and determination of human beings. Governance can only be done well if the human side is truly valued and taken seriously. There are techniques and approaches available but, in most companies, they could be better tuned. The more professionally chairpeople, CEOs, analysts, and active fund managers approach this subject, the better the quality of governance.

There is still need for more research concerning the correlations between aspects of the human side and financial results. However, the fact remains that the way companies are governed depends on the quality of the people and the extent to which they care about the implications of their decisions.

NOTE

1. McGregor, 2000.

REFERENCES

Carlsson, R. H. "Ownership and Value Creation," Wiley, 2001.

Dekker, C. "King Report on Corporate Governance for South Africa," www.mbendi.co.za, 2002.

Fukuyama, F. *Trust*, "The Social Virtues and the Creation of Prosperity," Hamish Hamilton Ltd, 1995.

Higgs, D. "Review of the Role and Effectiveness of Non-Executive Directors," www.dti.gov.uk/cld/non_exec_review, January 2003.

Isles, N. (ed.), "Enterprising Europe," Spiro, 2002.

McGregor, L. "The Human Face of Corporate Governance," Palgrave, 2000.

McGregor, L. "The Value of Board Reviews in an Uncertain Climate," Hermes Conference on Corporate Governance, www.governance.co.uk, September 2001.

McGregor, L. "Improving the Quality and Speed of Decision Making," *Journal of Change Management*, Henry Stuart Publications, U.K., April 2002.

Monks, R. A. G. "The Emperors Nightingale—Restoring the Integrity of the Corporation," Capstone, 1998.

Country Reviews

Part Five explores the country governance environments in 12 diverse countries, following the general framework that was developed in Chapter 7. In that chapter, the macro forces shaping the corporate governance environment in individual countries were placed in the categories of *market infrastructure, legal infrastructure, regulatory infrastructure,* and *informational infrastructure.* Each of the country reviews in Chapters 16 through 18 will follow the common template of examining country governance environments on the basis of these four macro forces, and also will highlight the key governance issues that each country is currently facing.

These countries are placed in three broad groupings.

Chapter 16: *Anglo-American*: The United States and the United Kingdom. These are the so-called "outsider" systems where ownership is dispersed and where stock markets and institutional investors play important roles. The United States and the United Kingdom share many common governance features, including a common law heritage. As such they are appropriately lumped together in many global comparative studies. However, the two countries have notable differences as well. As such Chapter 16 also includes an analysis of the key areas of difference between the United States and the United Kingdom.

Chapter 17: *Continental European/Japan*: The European Union, France, Germany, and Japan. Most of these are "insider" systems in mature markets characterized by more concentrated ownership patterns, including financial-industrial group holdings, and have more of a civil law heritage. Compared to the Anglo-American countries there is often a more explicit recognition and focus on nonfinancial stakeholders, particularly from an employee and social perspective. The European Union, which obviously covers the United Kingdom, France, Germany, and other Member States, is analyzed separately with regard to its pan-European approach to governance.

Chapter 18: *Emerging/Transition Economies:* Brazil, China, India, Korea, Russia, and Turkey. Many of these countries are still relatively poor on a GDP/capita basis and in many cases are still developing strong market infrastructures. The effectiveness of the legal and regulatory environment in these economies can be limited, either due to the quality of law or to its enforcement. Concentrated ownership is the norm, and particularly in transition or socialist economies, the state still can play an important role in individual company governance.

Anglo-American Governance: The "Outsider" System

United States

Andrea Esposito, George Dallas, and Gurinder K. Badial

INTRODUCTION

Despite the spate of corporate failures in the 2001–2003 period, the United States (U.S.) is the home of many of the world's largest and most powerful corporations, and has traditionally been considered as a global leader in corporate governance. The U.S. has had a long—and broadly successful—history of a free market system, dating back to the foundation of the New York Stock Exchange (NYSE) in 1792. To support this development, the U.S. has been effective at building and strengthening the legal and regulatory framework to govern the financial marketplace. Its capital markets are the broadest and deepest in the world in terms of both market capitalization and the number of listed companies, suggesting an historical trust by investors in the legal and regulatory architecture as well as a robust body of nongovernmental groups that provide a clear focus on U.S. business, governance, and disclosure practices.

Despite this historical foundation, the recent failures of some major U.S. corporations have shaken public and investor confidence, and have raised questions about U.S. corporate governance standards. First came the collapse of Enron (2001), one of the largest listed U.S. companies by market capitalization. Following this, there have been a host of other companies reporting governance-related problems of varying orders of magnitude. Names on this increasingly familiar litany include WorldCom, Qwest, Adelphia, Tyco, Global Crossing, Xerox, and HealthSouth. These corporate failures, to name only a few, have had significant implications across the legal and regulatory framework within the U.S., all aimed at enhancing corporate governance.

Key features and current issues of the U.S. corporate government environment include the following:

- *Regulatory reform:* In response to these corporate scandals, the U.S. adopted the Sarbanes-Oxley Act into law in July 2002 (as mentioned in previous chapters), and new stock exchange listing rules also were redrafted by the NYSE and the National Association of Securities Dealers Automated Quotation (NASDAQ). Collectively, these initiatives represent attempts to address the need for more independent and effective boards and for greater accountability and integrity in the reporting and auditing process. Relative to other jurisdictions, the new U.S. governance initiatives are more prescriptive and carry stiff penalties, including criminal liabilities. Many European countries, for example, adopt a more voluntary approach to governance standards, focusing on disclosure of non-compliance rather than forcing compliance.

- *Ownership structure:* Relative to most other countries in the world, the U.S. equity market is characterized by a widely dispersed ownership structure, with relatively few blockholders among the largest listed firms. This results in U.S. corporate governance being shaped by the "classic" Berle/Means agency problem of separation of management from a wide range of small shareholders. This also suggests a key role for institutional investors who manage funds as nominees on behalf of small investors, and whose aggregate holdings total over 50 percent of the market capitalization of U.S. equities. To the extent institutional investors operate with a collective voice, their influence in the proxy and shareholder proposal process, and in general corporate oversight and engagement, can be very important. Current areas of focus in shareholder proposals include: poison pills, classified boards, and executive compensation.

- *Corporate law and governance regulation:* Reflecting the United States' preference for decentralized power, U.S. companies are not subject to any federal body of corporate law. While there are extensive federal securities laws enforced by the Securities and Exchange

Commission (SEC), these govern the functioning of the securities markets themselves and leave fundamental decisions about power within individual companies (board power versus shareholder power, for example) to the individual states. As companies can incorporate anywhere, this has resulted in some corporate law competition among the 50 states, with Delaware attracting the majority of S&P 500 incorporations with its extensive case law and established court system. However, other states can still attract companies with defense-friendly takeover laws. In addition to the states and the federal securities laws, the national stock exchanges are the third leg of American governance regulation. Through their listing rules, the NYSE and NASDAQ require specific governance policies of companies, regardless of state incorporation. Exchange listing rules tend to complement, rather than contradict state statutes, and while they cannot contradict federal securities laws, the SEC cannot impose changes onto the rules themselves.

♦ *Shareholder rights:* Compared to some other jurisdictions, U.S. shareholders have relatively fewer direct rights, effectively deferring many ownership rights to the company's directors—who, in turn act in a fiduciary capacity on behalf of the company and its shareholders. Preemptive rights and the ability to call shareholders' meetings are examples of ownership rights that shareholders of many U.S. companies do not have. The takeover environment in the 1980s also resulted in anti-takeover devices, or poison pills, being adopted by many companies to avoid—or at least inhibit— a sometimes overaggressive free market for corporate control. Many U.S. companies retain these structures, which remains an area of debate by the growing shareholder activist community. A specific right that has been focused on by the shareholder community is the right to approve equity-related plans (including options)—both to have a stronger voice in the remuneration of key executives and to avoid schemes that may be overly dilutive or excessive. This latter proposal is included in the NYSE listing rule amendments.

♦ *Board structure and effectiveness:* U.S. boards are unitary in structure, and typically are well represented by independent directors. Much work is often done in board committees. The listing rule reforms place emphasis on specific committee structures, including the audit, compensation, and nomination/corporate governance committees. Reforms point to U.S. boards having a majority or substantial majority of independent directors, with the definition of independence being increasingly tightened. One hundred percent independent representation on key committees has been established as a best practice in some cases and is a requirement for audit committees under the Sarbanes-Oxley Act. Greater board effectiveness also is being promoted by ensuring proper skill set mix, training, information flow, resources, CEO evaluations, and self-evaluations.

♦ *Combined chairman/CEO:* In the U.S., the roles of the chairman and chief executive often are held by the same individual. This combined role is under considerable scrutiny in the U.S. and abroad, with strong voices on both sides of the debate as to whether these roles should be combined or separated. This debate has led to the promulgation of alternative roles, such as that of lead or presiding director, to provide independent directors with a more explicit spokesperson to offset a potentially powerful combined chairman/CEO.

♦ *Audit process and committee:* The occurrence of multiple accounting scandals has resulted in the audit process and audit committee being a particular area of focus of the Sarbanes-Oxley Act. This specifies direct audit committee engagement and relationship control with the company auditor, as well as the requirement for financial expertise on the audit committee. Internal controls and operational risk management also are becoming key areas of focus, with company CEOs and CFOs having to submit individual certifications relating to the company's accounting integrity.

♦ *Accounting:* U.S. Generally Accepted Accounting Principles (U.S. GAAP) are generally recognized as a leading global standard for accounting quality, notwithstanding scrutiny stemming from the recent U.S. corporate failures. U.S. GAAP is characterized by extensive and sophisticated rules relating to specific accounting issues, compared with the more general principles-based approach found in International Accounting Standards (IAS). Part of the Sarbanes-Oxley process will be to review the basis for a more principles-based approach to accounting in the United States. The Sarbanes-Oxley Act also establishes the Public Company Accounting Oversight Board (PCAOB) to monitor the accounting profession, with a view to enhancing the quality and independence of the audit process. With regard to timing of disclosure, the U.S. is noted for its quarterly reporting requirements. While this provides a greater amount of disclosure, critics also report on the short-termist orientation that quarterly reporting can foster among both investors and company managers.

MARKET INFRASTRUCTURE

Ownership Structure

Relative to most other jurisdictions globally, the U.S. is characterized by a widely dispersed shareholding of its major companies. Family structures, state ownership, or financial-industrial groups are not important features of the U.S. market. In comparing European ownership structures with the U.S., the academic Marco Becht[1] notes that 92.2 percent of listed companies on the NYSE and 83.3 percent of companies listed on NASDAQ do not have blockholders (defined as single shareholdings in excess of 25 percent). This is very low compared with Europe, where it is very common for the largest liquid companies to have significant blockholders. This limits the main agency problem in the U.S. to the classic separation of a company's management from a large and diffused shareholding base. Specifically, without a strong blockholder keeping close tabs on company operations, there is the potential for limited or less rigorous board oversight by small investors. This frames the debate in the United States.

Institutional Investors and Activism

The role of institutional investors has grown steadily in importance in the U.S. On the website of the NYSE, a tracking of ownership patterns of U.S. equities shows the share of U.S. equities held by institutional investors has grown from 7.2 percent of all equities in 1950 to 46.7 percent of all equities for a total of $6.4 trillion as of year end 2001.[2] The largest groups of institutional shareholders include both private and public pension funds, as well as privately managed investment funds.

Pension funds play an important role due to their size and their long-term investment horizon. Private, state, and local pension funds account for roughly 20 percent of all U.S. holdings of equity securities. Many pension funds are forced by their size to spread their investments widely. As a result, many pension funds are guided by indexes, such as the S&P 500, and are therefore disinclined from active trading. The passivity in portfolio selection that comes from an index-led strategy can, however, translate into a more active investor strategy with regard to shareholder activism and management engagement. Since these funds are ill positioned to sell companies whose management and governance they do not like, they often seek to bring about change through the corporate governance process itself by exercising their ownership rights.

The rise in shareholder activism in the U.S. stems back to the early 1980s, and has been led by public pension funds. The California Public Employees' Retirement System (CalPERS) and the Teachers Insurance and Annuity Association College Retirement Equities Fund (TIAA-CREF) are noted in particular for their active engagement in the area of corporate governance through various activities which include proxy voting, publishing commentary, and engaging in research on U.S. corporate governance practices. Many of the U.S. labor unions also are active with regard to their public pension funds and are particularly active in presenting shareholder proposals at annual meetings. Increasingly, institutional investors across the spectrum are expressing more active interest in U.S. corporate governance. An industry organization, the Washington, D.C.–based Council of Institutional Investors, serves as a coordinating body expressing institutional investor interests. While its membership includes a wide range of public and private investors, the most active investor groups remain the public pension funds.

Private investment firms have been shown to be less overtly activist, in part reflecting the fact that these investment firms also solicit investment business (including the management of 401k programs) from the companies they invest in. In many cases, private investment funds have not disclosed their votes on proxy issues, making it impossible for beneficial shareholders to know how the funds had voted their shares. In January 2003, the SEC acted to enforce this disclosure with its mandate that all mutual funds making proxy votes must disclose their votes and proxy voting policies.

Other Governance Commentators

The U.S. benefits from an open and free debate on governance standards, involving not only regulators, exchanges, and investor groups, but other commentators as well. Two prominent organizations in this context include The Conference Board and the Business Roundtable (BRT). The Conference Board is an independent not-for-profit organization comprised of senior representatives from the public and private sectors and from academia. It has issued a series of statements on corporate governance, executive compensation, and auditing/accounting. Among its proposals is the pro-vocative contention (at least in the U.S.) that the chairman and the chief executive officer roles should either be separated or that a lead or presiding director should be formally appointed to balance power between the board and a powerful combined chairman/CEO.

The BRT is an association of CEOs with a combined workforce of more than 10 million employees in the United States. The BRT published *Principles of Corporate Governance* in May 2002, which recommended best practices in a range of areas such as the responsibilities of the board of directors, board composition, and the role of audit committees.[3] While the BRT by nature takes a more management/corporate perspective in the governance debate, many of its recommended practices are consistent with the recent listing rule changes put forward by the major stock exchanges. Other important interest groups with a corporate perspective on the governance debate include the National Association of Corporate Directors, the American Society of Corporate Secretaries, and the National Investor Relations Institute.

Proxy solicitation firms such as Georgeson Shareholders and Morrow & Company, play an important institutional role in identifying nominee shareholders for the proxy voting process, and other firms, including Institutional Investor Services (ISS) and the Investor Respon-sibility Research Center (IRRC) provide the institutional investment com-munity with information and recommendations on proxy votes and other shareholder proposals. The Corporate Library is a website and informa-tion service that also serves as a strong voice in the U.S. corporate gover-nance debate from the investor perspective.

The development of corporate governance ratings or scores in the U.S. is beginning to take shape, including firms such as Standard & Poor's, ISS, IRRC, and The Corporate Library, as well as newer firms, including Governance Metrics. This also should serve to raise the visibil-ity standards of governance practices of many U.S. companies through the process of providing public analytical benchmarks.

LEGAL ENVIRONMENT

The U.S. legal framework includes two very significant acts, the Securities Act of 1933 and the Securities Exchange Act of 1934, which play major roles in governing the issuance and trading of public securities and performance of stock exchanges. There are also other acts, such as the Investment Company Act of 1940 and the Investment Advisers Act of 1940, which regulate the activities of investment companies and advisers who are involved in investing, reinvesting, and trading in securities.

Corporate governance standards in the U.S. are not dictated by one specific statute or ruling body. With 50 states in the U.S., each state has a variety of laws affecting the firms incorporated in that particular state. Delaware is the state of incorporation for many large U.S. corporations, and its corporate law is often cited more frequently than that of other states as a basis of reference. U.S. federal securities law and U.S. stock exchange listing requirements do codify certain national standards, and it is the case that the Securities Act of 1933 and Securities Exchange Act of 1934 preempt the creation of individual state securities laws.

Generally, the federal government has tended to play a lesser role in the authority over corporate governance mainly because the state and stock exchange regulations have had a significant role in this arena. However, since corporations engage in business in many states, and therefore register as "foreign corporations" in those states, the "core" of corporate law is uniform in the U.S. in many aspects. Some states may give more minority rights and provide for different governance procedures. But all states have an interest in attracting business to the state and this creates some basis of uniformity in the context of multiple jurisdictions. Moreover, the emergence of the Sarbanes-Oxley Act shows that the federal government is becoming more involved in corporate governance issues.

The U.S. legal framework has provisions in place to protect the rights of investors, and ranks highly on indicators of legal enforcement, such as the World Bank Rule of Law indicator.[4] There are effective law enforcements in place if stakeholder rights are abused and even tougher criminal penalties coming into effect through Sarbanes-Oxley.

Securities Act of 1933

The Securities Act of 1933 (Securities Act) has two key objectives: to ensure investors receive relevant information regarding securities being offered for sale and to ensure securities are sold without misrepresentation and fraud. This requires the disclosure of relevant financial information for the registered securities. Securities that are sold in the U.S., with some modest exceptions, must be registered and the information made public includes:

- Financial statements that have been certified by independent accounts;
- Information regarding company management;
- Information on the company property and business; and
- Details of the securities that are on sale.

Securities Exchange Act of 1934

The Securities Exchange Act of 1934 (Securities Exchange Act) led to the creation of the SEC, which oversees the securities market. The Act enables the SEC to ensure that companies with publicly traded securities conduct periodic reporting of relevant information. Any company that has more than $10 million in assets and whose securities are held by more than 500 owners are required to file annual and other periodic reports, which are filed on the SEC's EDGAR database for public disclosure.

The Act monitors the material that is disclosed to shareholders to solicit their votes in both annual and/or special meetings held for the appointment of directors and any other corporate matters requiring shareholder approval. The Act also deals with issues surrounding insider trading, tender offers, registration of exchanges and associations.

Investment Company Act of 1940

The 1940 Investment Company Act regulates the organization of investment companies, including mutual funds that offer securities to the public and are involved in investing, reinvesting, and trading in securities. In accordance with the Act these companies are required to make available to investors the fund's financial statements and investment policies.

Investment Advisers Act of 1940

The Investment Advisers Act of 1940 regulates investment advisers and requires that advisers who have a minimum of $25 million of assets under management or advise a registered investment company register with the SEC and conform to the regulations created to protect investors.

Sarbanes-Oxley Act of 2002

The Sarbanes-Oxley Act of 2002, which became law on July 30, 2002, was drafted in response to various corporate failures in the United States. The Act applies to any company or legal entity that has securities listed on a U.S. exchange or is registered with the SEC. Foreign private issuers are subject to the Act with exemptions from certain rules if those rules conflict with the laws of the issuer's home country. The Act aims to enhance corporate governance and the accountability of board directors, corporate directors, and company auditors.

The Sarbanes-Oxley Act is a detailed document addressing a very wide spectrum of issues, including the PCAOB, auditor independence, corporate responsibility, financial disclosure, corporate and criminal fraud accountability, and white-collar crime penalty enhancements. A particular focus is on the audit process and on ensuring appropriate accountability at the board level; audit committees are focused upon in particular. While the legislation was enacted in 2002, the SEC is still working through specific aspects of the regulation. For example, the SEC has indicated that it will review its applicability for foreign companies whose own laws or governance structures may run into conflict with aspects of the Sarbanes-Oxley Act. Relative to other jurisdictions with voluntary governance codes, Sarbanes-Oxley represents a more prescriptive and legalistic approach to corporate governance reform.

Corporate Law

The U.S. has had a long and extensive history of state versus federal rights. It is state law and regulation, however, that has developed the greatest authority over corporations, not federal law. Since companies can choose to be incorporated in any state regardless of where they do business this further complicates corporate oversight, as each state's corporate laws vary. However, the state of Delaware has registered the majority of incorporated firms including over 40 percent of the NYSE listed corporations. The attractiveness of Delaware is due mainly to the state's long-established and judiciously tested corporate body of laws that increases legal precedent and stability, limits unexpected judicial outcomes, and enables the court to handle disputes expeditiously.

Shareholder Rights

Shareholder rights are impacted by state corporate laws, the U.S. federal securities laws, and the national stock exchanges—all of which promote effective corporate governance practices. The U.S. federal securities laws regulate the submission of shareholder proposals for shareholder meetings and proxy voting while requiring companies to regularly disclose relevant information. The national securities market also affects corporate governance practices since issuers of securities traded on the markets are subject to specific listing requirements.

However, as stated above it is state incorporation law that is responsible for establishing the shareholder rights of U.S. public companies. Although state laws differ they generally govern matters involving shareholder voting rights and board functions. Companies also may create their own additional governance practices in their corporate charter and by-laws, as long as they fall within legal and regulatory frameworks.

Compared to many other jurisdictions, U.S. shareholders have relatively fewer direct rights, effectively deferring many ownership rights to the company's directors—who, in turn, act in a fiduciary capacity on behalf of the company and its shareholders. The "business judgment rule" is a legal concept in the U.S., allowing for directors to make significant decisions on their own that directly affect shareholders' interests. This rule keeps the courts from second-guessing directors; even if the shareholder can show that the resulting action was in fact detrimental, the director would not be liable to the shareholders or criminally liable, as long as director decisions are shown to be made in good faith and on an independent and well-informed basis.

Preemptive rights and the ability to call shareholders' meetings are additional examples of ownership rights that shareholders of many U.S. companies do not have. Or to the extent that shareholders are given the right to call for a shareholder meeting, the threshold is often higher than in other jurisdictions. The proxy contest process is regarded in some ways as an alternative mechanism to ensure shareholders have direct input on company management and operations. Offering a dissident slate of directors for election is an example of this. However, this is an expensive process that will preclude many small shareholders from directly participating in the company governance process outside the annual general meeting.

Takeover Defenses

The U.S. also is noted for the presence of takeover defense structures in many companies, often in the form of prohibitively expensive rights offerings that would be triggered upon a hostile bid not supported by the company. In more severe cases, "dead hand" provisions limit control decisions to an existing group of board directors, even if they may have since left the board of the company.

Many of these anti-takeover provisions or "poison pills" were put in place in response to the excesses of the hostile takeover movement in the 1980s. Advocates of these structures emphasize that poison pills enable company managements to focus on more medium-term objectives without having to continuously dwell on short-term performance to ward off opportunistic corporate raiders. They also emphasize that in the event of a legitimate takeover bid, these structures provide company boards with greater flexibility to negotiate for a more generous bid valuation.

However, it remains the case that anti-takeover devices inhibit the free market for corporate control and thereby limit a fundamental shareholder right to sell shares to legitimate buyers at a market-driven price. As such, their ongoing presence remains a source of controversy. Delaware courts preserve the right for poison pill structures to exist without shareholder approval. However, this is an area where activist shareholders are pressing for more direct shareholder input. This is one of the main areas of shareholder proposals that are put forth in U.S. company annual meetings.

REGULATORY ENVIRONMENT

The U.S. regulatory framework supports the legal infrastructure through a range of federal departments, agencies, state securities regulators, and self-regulatory organizations. The SEC is a key player in promoting stability in the securities markets. It oversees the U.S. securities markets where it enforces law, establishes and modifies regulations, and requires public companies to disclose financial information to all investors. The major stock exchanges also play an important role in shaping U.S. governance practices outside the formal regulatory framework.

The Securities and Exchange Commission

The SEC oversees and regulates the U.S. securities industry as well as enforces securities law to protect investor interests and promote stability in the securities markets. The commission sets the disclosure standards publicly traded securities must meet.

The commission was established in 1934 and relies on The Securities Act of 1933, Securities Exchange Act of 1934, the Investment Company Act of 1940, and the 2002 Sarbanes-Oxley Act to enable it to oversee the securities markets, and conduct civil enforcement action against companies and individuals who violate the securities law—including accounting fraud, insider trading, and providing misleading or false information about companies and securities. The SEC also will oversee the recently established PCAOB.

The SEC works with various private sector organizations and institutions including federal departments and agencies; state securities regulators; and self-regulatory organizations such as the NYSE, American Stock Exchange (AMEX) (AMEX merged into NASDAQ in 1998 but still operates independently), and the NASDAQ.

U.S. Stock Exchanges

The NYSE, AMEX, and NASDAQ are self-regulatory organizations, which create their own rules subject to the approval of the SEC. Companies that are listed on these stock exchanges are subject to continuous regulatory and disclosure requirements. The recent revisions of the listing rules of the NYSE and NASDAQ show a convergence of governance standards for both institutions in many cases. But each retains its own identity and own specific rules, in part reflecting the different characteristics of the companies that list on these exchanges.

New York Stock Exchange

The NYSE, also known as the "Big Board," is the largest global equity market with approximately 2800 listed companies; as of March 2003, its website reported an aggregate market capitalization of about $15 trillion. These include most of the largest and most liquid U.S. companies. Its regulatory responsibilities entail checking on brokers' sales practices, monitoring specialist operations, and overseeing firms to ensure they are abiding by the financial and operational rules.

In response to the Sarbanes-Oxley Act, the NYSE proposed new corporate listing standards in August 2002, with the aim of increasing reliability, transparency, and accountability. The key proposals include the following:[5]

- ♦ The company board should consist of a majority of independent directors.
- ♦ A tightening of the definition of an "independent" director.

♦ The authority and responsibility of the audit committee is strengthened, including requirements for financial literacy and at least one financial "expert," as defined by the SEC. Audit committees also are responsible for maintaining the primary relationship with the company's auditors and review internal control processes.

♦ The board of directors must have a compensation committee and a nominating/corporate governance committee each comprised entirely of independent directors.

♦ A requirement for companies to adopt and disclose their corporate governance guidelines, including the charters of key committees, director qualifications, codes of conduct, and ethics.

♦ Greater shareholder participation in the governance process through voting on all equity-based compensation plans with limited exceptions. Moreover, brokers may only vote as nominees for beneficial shareholders with explicit shareholder instructions.

NASDAQ

The NASDAQ has nearly 4000 companies listed, making it the largest stock market in the U.S. in terms of number of issuers.[6] Relative to the NYSE, its constituents tend to be smaller, younger companies. However, it also includes Microsoft, one of the world's largest corporations. As with the NYSE, NASDAQ also proposed new listing rule requirements in response to the Sarbanes-Oxley Act. These rules differ in some ways from the NYSE rules, but are similar in content and purpose on many points relating to improved board effectiveness and independence, a strengthened disclosure and audit committee process, and a greater role for shareholder input into the governance process. Though the SEC is encouraging convergence of NYSE and NASDAQ listing rules, some differences are likely to remain. For example, since NASDAQ companies and boards tend to be smaller than NYSE companies, the requirements for three separate committees with independent directors can present challenges in practical terms. In this case, while NASDAQ also has a requirement for a fully independent audit committee, it also provides for the board as a whole assuming certain functions typically reserved for nomination or compensation committees.

INFORMATIONAL INFRASTRUCTURE

The informational infrastructure in the U.S.—combining accounting standards, the robustness of the audit profession, and standards of information disclosure—is generally regarded as of a very high standard on a global basis of comparison. That notwithstanding, this system has been proven to be vulnerable by the visible U.S. corporate failures having at their core financial data that are undisclosed, misleading, or fraudulent.

Accounting Standards

U.S. GAAP is a sophisticated and well-established system of accounting, often serving as a model for high accounting standards on a global basis. However, U.S. GAAP came under great scrutiny when the Enron scandal and the related actions of its accounting firm Andersen occurred. A specific criticism that has surfaced relates to U.S. GAAP's focus on rules versus principles. While this characterization is somewhat simplistic, the relative emphasis on rules suggests that however sophisticated and well drafted these rules may be, they remain subject to manipulation in a way that might be technically correct, but in a way which may run counter to the broader principle of a going concern enterprise. In this regard, the Sarbanes-Oxley bill will result in a review of the rules-based nature of U.S. accounting practices, and there is scope for growing convergence of U.S. GAAP with principles-based International Accounting Standards.

The Financial Accounting Standards Board (FASB) is a self-regulatory organization that is responsible for establishing financial accounting and reporting standards. These standards govern the preparation of financial reports and are regarded as reliable and credible by the SEC and the American Institute of Certified Public Accountants (AICPA).

The AICPA is the national and professional organization for certified public accountants. It ensures its members have the knowledge they need to provide professional services to their clients. It collaborates with state accounting organizations and influences the form and content of pronouncements of the FASB and other bodies that have influence over financial accounting and reporting standards.

In addition to the debate on rules versus principles, other key accounting issues have been the subject of considerable attention in the United States. A particularly sensitive issue relates to whether or not options should be treated as an expense item in a company's profit and loss account. This issue has arisen in part given the visibility of very large option grants to U.S. corporate executives, with no impact on the income statement. Some U.S. companies have addressed this issue by beginning, at their own discretion, to expense options. Other U.S. companies have not done so. In particular young firms and high tech firms often rely on options as a key method of compensation in lieu of limited budgets for large cash compensation. Such companies often oppose the expensing of options on the basis of its potentially devastating impact on both the company income statement and balance sheet.

Another potentially important issue is whether or not income derived from company pension plans should be included in a company's income statement, given that earnings of this nature are not part of the company's core business operations. Pension income is regularly included in U.S. income statements.

Standard & Poor's Core Earnings methodology, explained in greater detail in Chapter 9, represents an attempt to identify more clearly aspects of a company's income statement reporting that consistently and accurately reflect a company's "core" ongoing operating profitability. Particularly in the U.S., this methodology demonstrates how the treatment of several key discretionary accounting issues can significantly impact a company's reported performance. The core earnings approach provides a measure against which more discretionary aspects of reporting, including a company's statement of its "as reported" earnings, operating earnings, or pro forma earnings can be compared.

Auditors

The demise of the once prominent accounting firm Arthur Andersen reduced the number of the major U.S. accounting firms down to what is now the "Big Four": Deloitte Touche, Ernst & Young, KPMG, and PricewaterhouseCoopers. Audit partner and audit firm rotation are areas of focus in Sarbanes-Oxley to preserve the independence and integrity of the auditing process. However, given the reduced number of world-class accounting firms, this creates a potentially narrow market for rotation—unless smaller accounting firms begin to demonstrate greater prominence.

Auditor relationships are subject to further change given the limitation of specified nonaudit services that the auditor can provide, as a result of the Sarbanes-Oxley limitation. Traditional areas of ancillary consulting work—including information technology, valuation, and risk management—are now out of bounds to auditors, again to ensure independence and auditing rigor.

Under the Sarbanes-Oxley Act, auditors will have their primary business engagement with the company's audit committee, not with the company's management. While this serves to reinforce the audit committee's accountability for the audit process, in practical terms it is not clear how this will change day-to-day interaction between company management and its auditors. Given that the role of the audit committee is to provide oversight and not to manage the audit process itself, it is not practical for audit committee members to have the same level of auditor interaction as the company's financial managers.

Transparency and Disclosure

Timeliness and content of regulatory filing

In response to the Sarbanes-Oxley Act, the SEC has requested that quarterly reports on Form 10-Q and annual reports on Form 10-K be filed on an earlier basis. This is in order to provide investors with more timely access to company reports. The amendment in filing company reports will be phased in over a 3-year period. The annual report–filing deadline will be altered from 90 days to 60 days and quarterly reporting from 45 days to 35 days. The SEC also has adopted new disclosure practices regarding access to reports on company websites.

The Act aims to enhance financial transparency by implementing specific disclosure requirements. All financial reports are filed with the SEC and have been created in line with GAAP and are expected to reflect material correcting adjustments. Annual and quarterly reports filed with the SEC should disclose material off-balance sheet transactions, contractual obligations, contingent liabilities, and other arrangements that could have a material effect on the financial condition or other aspects of the company such as liquidity and capital expenditure.

The SEC also requires companies to disclose whether they have a code of ethics, which their financial officers should adopt such as complying with relevant government rules and regulations. If the code has not been implemented or adopted, an explanation must be presented. In the area of nonfinancial information, the SEC's requirement for a management discussion and analysis (MD&A) report is an important basis of disclosure with regard to an analysis of a company's overall strategy, operation, and performance.

The NYSE requires companies to distribute an annual report on a yearly basis to its shareholders or distribute to shareholders the Form 10-K

(Form 20-F for non-U.S. issuers) filed with the SEC. The annual report should be provided to shareholders no later than 120 days after the close of each fiscal year (225 days for non-U.S. issuers) and at least 15 days before the annual meeting.

The 2002 Standard & Poor's global Transparency and Disclosure study[7] demonstrates that the U.S. is a global leader in terms of its disclosure practices, driven largely by regulatory filing requirements by the SEC. U.S. annual reports, on the other hand, are often less comprehensive documents. Increasingly U.S. companies also are using their company websites as a tool to disclose information to investors. In addition to annual reports and regulatory disclosure, it is increasingly common for investor guides containing relevant company information to be found on company websites.

Information Dissemination

The U.S. generally can be regarded as having high levels of public disclosure in which all U.S.-listed companies must file and disclose their registration information statements, proxy, and annual reports through the SEC EDGAR system, which allows online access to company regulatory disclosure. This information should include the governance structure and policies adopted by the companies, any material issues regarding stakeholders, company objectives, and any major shareholder and ownership and voting rights.

Regulation Fair Disclosure (or Reg FD) was introduced by the SEC in 2000. It addresses the issue of company information disclosure being first directed to all market participants, rather than to a select group of insiders or investors with privileged access to company management. Linked to this is the concept of continuous disclosure, referred to by the NYSE as a Timely Alert Policy. This means that a company should disclose information that could have a material impact on the markets for the company's securities on a "timely" basis, i.e., without waiting for quarterly reporting cycles to report material events or corporate actions. Some of the examples of information that should be released on an immediate basis include quarterly earnings, dividend announcements, mergers, acquisitions, and tender offer stock splits.

Executive Compensation

Relative to other jurisdictions, U.S. companies tend to disclose much more about individual executive and director compensation. In some ways it is ironic that this is the case, given the at times extreme levels of management remuneration involving not only base salaries, but also option grants, restricted stock, severance packages, and other perquisites enjoyed by executive management of U.S. companies.

U.S. companies are required to disclose the names and remuneration of directors and CEOs in their regulatory filings. The amount of shares held by the directors and CEO of the company as well as the identity and number of shares held by any beneficial owner of more than 5 percent of any class of the company's voting securities also must be disclosed in the regulatory filings.

NOTES

1. Marco Becht, "Beneficial Ownership in the United States," Fabrizio and Becht, 2002, p. 285.

2. New York Stock Exchange, March 2003.

3. The Business Round Table, May 2002.

4. World Bank, 2000–2001.

5. New York Stock Exchange Corporate Accountability and Listing Standards Committee, 2002.

6. NASDAQ, www.nasdaq.com, 2003.

7. Patel and Dallas, 2002.

REFERENCES

Allen & Overy. "Sarbanes-Oxley Act of 2002: The Most Significant Corporate Governance and Securities Law Reform Enacted in the US in Years," *Allen & Overy Bulletin* (August 2002).

Allen & Overy. "SEC Proposes Rules for Non-GAAP Financial Disclosures Required by the Sarbanes-Oxley Act of 2002," *Allen & Overy Bulletin* (December 2002).

American Society of Corporate Secretaries, www.ascs.org/

California Public Employees' Retirement System, www.calpers.ca.gov/

Council of Institutional Investors, www.cii.org/

Cowan, L. "Excessive Executive Pay Tops Shareholder Resolutions," *The Wall Street Journal Online*, www.WSJ.com (February 12, 2003).

Fabrizio, B. and M. Becht. "The Control of Corporate Europe," Oxford University Press (2002).

Financial Accounting Standards Board, www.fasb.org/

Georgeson Shareholder, www.georgeson.com/

Georgeson Shareholder, "Annual Corporate Governance Review: Shareholder Proposal and Proxy Contest" (2002).

International Accounting Standards Board, www.iasc.org.uk

Monks, R. A. G. and N. Minow. "Corporate Governance" 2d ed., Blackwell Publishers Ltd (2001).

Morrow & Co., Inc., www.morrowco.com/html/frameset_parent.htm

NASDAQ, www.nasdaq.com

NASDAQ, "Regulatory Requirement," www.nasdaq.com/about/RegRequire
ments.pdf

National Association of Corporate Governance, www.nacdonline.org

National Investor Relations Institute, www.niri.org

New York Stock Exchange, www.nyse.com

New York Stock Exchange, "New York Stock Exchange Corporate Accountability
and Listing Standards Committee," www.nyse.com (June 2002).

Nobes, C. W. (ed.), "GAAP 2001—A Survey of National Accounting Rules
Benchmarked against International Account Standards," (2001).

Patel, S. A. and G. Dallas. "Transparency and Disclosure: Overview of Methodology and Results: United States," Standard & Poor's (2002).

Shearman & Sterling. "SEC Adopts Final Auditors Independence Rules,"
www.shearman.com (February 7, 2003).

Shearman & Sterling. "SEC Adopts Final Rules Requiring Disclosure Relating to
Audit Committee Financial Experts and Code of Ethics," www.shearman.com
(January 30, 2003).

The American Institute of Certified Public Accountants, www.aicpa.org/

The Business Roundtable. "Principles of Corporate Governance," www.brtable.org
(May 2002).

The Conference Board, www.conference-board.org/

The Corporate Library, www.thecorporatelibrary.com/

The IIA Research Foundation, "Assessment Guide for U.S. Legislative, Regulatory,
and Listing Exchanges Requirements Affecting Internal Auditing,"
www.theiia.org (2003).

Teachers Insurance and Annuity Association—College Retirement Equities Fund
(TIAA-CREF), www.tiaa-cref.org/

U.S. Securities and Exchange Commission, www.sec.gov/

U.S. Securities and Exchange Commission, "Final Rule: Conditions for Use of
Non-GAAP Financial Measures," www.sec.gov/rules/final/33-8176.htm
(2003).

U.S. Securities and Exchange Commission, "Final Rule: Strengthening the
Commission's Requirements Regarding Auditors Independence,"
www.sec.gov/rules/final/33-8183.htm (2003).

"U.S. Securities and Exchange Commission Staff's Response to CORSA's
Questionnaire on Corporate Governance," www.sec.gov/ (2000).

World Bank, "Governance Research Indicator Country Snapshot 2000/01,"
www.info.worldbank.org/governance/kkz/sc_country.asp

CHAPTER 16-2

United Kingdom

Nick Bradley and Gurinder K. Badial

INTRODUCTION

The United Kingdom (U.K.) has demonstrated global leadership in both the codification and practice of good corporate governance. Following the governance scandals in the U.K. in the early 1990s involving well-known companies such as Maxwell Communications, BCCI, and Polly Peck, the U.K. government initiated the development of the Cadbury Committee's *Code of Best Practice,* which was published in December 1992. The Cadbury Code was the world's first corporate governance code and is the forerunner of several subsequent governance codes of practice.

The U.K. is the home of one of the world's largest, most international and most liquid stock exchanges. In common with the United States (U.S.) and a number of other "Anglo-American" markets such as Canada, Australia, and New Zealand, the U.K. exhibits widely dispersed ownership structures and liquid stock markets, which have shaped U.K. corporate practices over the years.

A long-established legal and regulatory framework for the protection of shareholder rights, robust accounting standards, and a strong auditing environment also reinforce the strength of the governance environment in the United Kingdom. U.K. company law, mainly the Companies Act of 1985, is a major part of the framework, which provides companies with the structure and guidance required to conduct business in an ethical manner with high standards of corporate governance. The government also recognizes the changing dynamics within the business environment and as a result, a significant revision of British company law is taking place. Following an independent three-year review the final report entitled *Modern Company Law* was published in 2001 by the

Company Law Review Steering Group. In response to this, the government published a white paper in 2002, *Modernizing Company Law*, which makes key proposals for company law reform. The report recommends many changes to promote improved corporate governance and a greater balance between the interests of various stakeholders including shareholders, employees, customers, and creditors. The aim is for company law to be flexible enough so that it is competitive and adaptable to market and technological changes.

The U.K. has established provisions in place that protect the interests of shareholders and ensure they are able to exercise certain basic rights including the maintenance of preemptive rights and the powers to call special meetings of shareholders, to appoint or remove directors, to vote on directors' remuneration, and to vote on transactions that would fundamentally affect the company, including takeovers and mergers. In turn, the boards of directors of U.K. companies have a fiduciary responsibility to manage with good judgment in the best interest of the company. There are legal penalties in place for directors that conduct business in an unethical manner and who disobey the law.

According to the World Bank, country governance indicators for the rule of law and rule of regulatory quality (2001) show that the U.K. scores highly and is among the highest in comparison to other western countries. In fact, the U.K. scores are higher than those of the U.S. in these two governance categories.[1]

Overall, the U.K. government's philosophy appears to support the notion that improved corporate governance can be gained through voluntary codes of best practice rather than legislation. Accordingly, many of the U.K.'s financial regulations are based on best practice rather than statutory requirements. A range of initiatives has been in place since the early 1990s based on a "comply or explain" basis, such as the introduction of the Cadbury Report (1992), Greenbury Report (1995), the Combined Code (2000), (2003), and the Myners Report (2001). More recently, the government-commissioned reports by Derek Higgs and Sir Robert Smith, whose committees examined the role and effectiveness of nonexecutive directors and ways of enhancing the role and effectiveness of audit committees, respectively. Higgs's proposals are based on enhancing board independence and include having a majority of independent directors on the board and separating the roles of the chairman and CEO. Sir Robert Smith's report also emphasizes the need to have independent and objective auditors, and suggests that the audit committee should include at least three independent directors.

In addition to voluntary codes, the U.K. also has a strong regulatory framework consisting of many regulatory bodies all with a specific role to play to ensure financial stability and to protect the interest of various stakeholders. The Financial Services and Markets Act 2000 (FSMA) provides the framework in which the financial regulatory bodies work. The three financial authorities, including HM Treasury, the Bank of England, and the Financial Services Authority (FSA), collectively work together to achieve U.K. financial stability. The FSA, as the main financial regulator, ensures that only those financial sector firms that meet the criteria for engaging in regulated activities and mainstream financial services are authorized. The U.K. also has procedures in place to maintain market confidence such as the Financial Ombudsman Service (FOS), which has a dispute resolution procedure.

There also exists the Office of Fair Trading (OFT), which protects the interest of U.K. consumers and ensures that companies conduct fair and competitive business. In addition, the Stock Exchange regulates the market and is itself regulated by the FSA. Investors are also protected through the well-established listing rules managed by the U.K. Listing Authority (UKLA), part of the FSA.

The U.K. is also recognized for its high standards of auditing and accounting practices and has effective processes and procedures in place to review the state of financial reporting and accounting standards and practices. Three key bodies promote good financial reporting: the Financial Reporting Council (FRC), the Accounting Standards Board (ASB), and the Financial Reporting Review Panel (FRRP). Recently, the FSA and the FRRP have been given joint responsibility to investigate the accounts of companies suspected of breaching accounting standards. In addition, the U.K. has a range of key accounting professional bodies, which have established guidelines to help auditors develop the capabilities and competence to work in a professional manner, such as the Institute of Chartered Accountants in England and Wales.

The U.K. government continues to promote the increased transparency and accountability of companies by extending the list of information that must be disclosed on an annual basis, such as a director remuneration report for quoted companies and an operating and financial review for those companies that are "economically significant." Following the recent report on accounting and auditing, the government has decided on many initiatives to enhance auditor independence and accounting

practices such as the rotation of key auditors every five years and the introduction of a more detailed breakdown of payments to auditors.

In contrast to U.S. Generally Accepted Accounting Principles (U.S.
GAAP), U.K. GAAP takes a principles-based approach to accounting,
namely that good accounting standards are underlined by reasoning
and guidance, as opposed to a strictly rules-based approach. Following
the European Commission (EC) announcement in 2000, all publicly
traded companies in the European Union (EU) will be required to use
International Accounting Standards (IAS) in their consolidated accounts
from January 1, 2005 (with some deferral until January 1, 2007).

Overall, the U.K.'s legal, regulatory, and information environment
supports and motivates good corporate governance practices by individuals and companies making the U.K. an attractive financial market for
domestic and foreign businesses and investors.

MARKET INFRASTRUCTURE

Types of Business Organization

There are approximately 1.5 million companies in Britain. Some of these
are large companies whose shares are traded internationally, but most are
small private companies. There are approximately 12,000 public companies, of which approximately 2000 are quoted on the London Stock
Exchange (LSE). Public companies have to conform to higher disclosure
requirements than private companies.

Financial Markets

The financial markets in the U.K. are well-regulated and are among the
most liquid markets in the world. The three financial authorities in the U.K.
are HM Treasury (the U.K.'s Ministry of Finance), the Bank of England, and
the FSA. While fulfilling their individual roles, they also work together to
achieve the common goal of financial stability and the efficient and effective
running of the U.K. economy. The LSE is the main market for the listing and
trading of U.K. equities and provides a means of raising capital for U.K. and
international companies through equity, debt, and depositary receipt
issues. Approximately 2000 U.K. companies, and more than 470 foreign
companies from over 60 countries, are listed. The LSE is one of Europe's
leading and most liquid stock exchanges. TechMARK is the exchange's

market for technology companies and lists approximately 200 companies from over 20 different subsectors. The Alternative Investment Market (AIM) is the market for small and expanding companies covering over 350 companies from the U.K. and overseas.

Investors

The attitude of U.K. investors has changed following the emergence of accounting irregularities and fraud investigations at a number of internationally known organizations.

Evidence shows that investors in U.K. companies are increasingly more active and vote more frequently in recent years. Research conducted by ProShare (an independent not-for-profit organization) shows that private investors are more active and that company directors and company accounting procedures and communication materials are heavily scrutinized. According to research by Pensions & Investment Research Consultants (PIRC) (an independent consulting firm), the average voting level at FTSE 350 companies (prominent U.K. index) was 55 percent in 2002, an increase from 51 percent in 2001.[2]

There are two main types of investors:

+ Institutional investors and asset managers who manage pooled funds on behalf of the ultimate investors such as pension funds and private investors and hold the majority of U.K.-quoted stocks.
+ Private investors who tend to invest their own money directly into the stock market. There are more than 12 million people in the U.K. that invest in both stocks and shares.[3]

The Institutional Shareholders' Committee (ISC) is an informal association of four investor bodies that represent institutional shareholders. These are: the National Association of Pension Funds (NAPF), the Association of British Insurers (ABI), the Investment Management Association (IMA), and the Association of Investment Trust Companies (AITC). The ISC has developed a series of best practices for U.K. institutional shareholders that require them to communicate with investee companies, intervene when necessary in companies in which they hold shares, and monitor the impact of their activism.

The NAPF represents the U.K. occupational pension schemes, which account for approximately £700 billion in pension fund assets and over 20 percent of the U.K. stock market.

The ABI is the trade association for authorized insurance companies operating in the U.K. and represents approximately 400 companies, which transact over 97 percent of the business of U.K. insurance companies and account for over 20 percent of investments in the London stock market.

The IMA represents the U.K. unit trust and investment management industry. IMA members manage approximately £2 trillion in assets. The IMA cooperates with the government on legislative and regulatory matters and with the FSA on regulatory matters affecting both investment fund and asset management.

Increasingly there is a growing interest in socially responsible investment (SRI) from U.K. investors. U.K. occupational pension funds are now required to disclose how they account for ethical, social, and environmental matters in their investment strategies. This requirement was included in a July 2000 amendment to the Pensions Act (1995). A recent survey of current practice of SRI (July 2002) conducted by *Just Pensions* highlights that despite the fact that an increasing number of pension funds are taking an active interest in SRI, the survey also pointed out that "Unless pension funds take urgent steps to improve their implementation of socially responsible investment strategies, the case for regulatory action by government will only increase."[4]

Some pension funds have their own social responsibility guidelines, which they follow when making investment decisions. For example, the NAPF has published guidelines on socially responsible investment for institutional investors and companies and is planning to increase its team on corporate governance matters. The ABI also has "disclosure guidelines on social responsibility" which outline the type of information companies should disclose in relation to social, environmental, and ethical issues.[5] ABI hopes that such guidelines will enable companies in which they invest to develop appropriate policies on corporate social responsibility.

LEGAL ENVIRONMENT

Legal Tradition

The U.K. consists of three distinct legal jurisdictions, England and Wales, Scotland, and Northern Ireland. Each has its own court system and legal profession based on the traditions of common law. In 1973, the U.K. became a member of the European Economic Community, now the EU. Since its transition to the EU, the U.K. has been required to include European legislation into U.K. law.

Principal Legal Provisions

U.K.-incorporated companies must register with Companies House, a government agency for public records, and also must fulfill certain legal requirements. These include the notification of any modifications to their memoranda or articles of association, any changes of registered office, the issuance of new shares, notification of special and extraordinary resolutions passed by the members, any charge or mortgage over the company's property, and any change, appointment, and/or resignation of directors or the secretary.

Company Law

Company law, principally the Companies Act of 1985, is a significant part of the framework in which companies operate. The present law describes three key purposes:[6]

- ◆ Companies are formed and managed for the benefit of shareholders.
- ◆ Accounting and disclosure requirements are for the benefit of actual and potential shareholders and creditors.
- ◆ Public disclosure of information is for the benefit of the wider community.

U.K. companies traditionally have had a unitary board of directors that has the responsibility of managing the company in accordance with the company's articles of association and the law, and are obliged by fiduciary duties to manage the business with good judgment in the best interest of the company. However, it is recognized that the current law needs to balance the interests of various stakeholders, including shareholders, employees, creditors, and customers, and that it needs to be flexible enough to be competitive and adapt to market and technology changes. In response to this, the government launched an initiative in 1998 to review British company law and in July 2002 the government published a white paper, *Modernizing Company Law*, which outlines proposals for company law reform and promotes improved corporate governance.[7] Some of the key recommendations within the white paper for reform of company law include the following:

- ◆ Private companies will no longer have to hold annual general meetings (AGM) or appoint a company secretary.
- ◆ Smaller companies will be able to produce simpler accounts.

♦ The time in which to file accounts with Companies House will be reduced to 7 months from 10 months for private companies and 6 months from 7 months for public companies.

♦ Listed companies will be required to publish their accounts on company websites within 4 months of their year-end.

♦ A new standards board is to be created based on the current ASB whose role will be to make detailed rules on areas including accounting, reporting, and other disclosure issues. The standards board will be responsible for the form and content of the annual financial statements and reports.

♦ Companies and their directors can be named in a central register if they are convicted of breaking company law.

♦ The law regulating companies that are incorporated overseas and operating in Britain will be simplified.

♦ Auditors will have a statutory right to ask employees, contractors, and directors for company information.

Shareholder Meetings and Voting Rights

Shares can be held in different ways including nominee accounts, personal membership of CREST (the real-time settlement system), and share certificates. Companies should provide specific information to shareholders who are listed on the register of shareholders, such as the annual report and details on any major company restructuring. These shareholders also are entitled to attend the shareholders' AGM and must be given at least 21 days notice regarding the time and venue of the meeting. Shareholders can vote at the AGM or by post by using proxy cards. With the recommended changes under company law, shareholders will be given the option to use e-communication to appoint proxies and for voting. Although it is rare, shareholders can demand an extraordinary general meeting (EGM) if they have the backing of 10 percent of the company's share capital.

Companies must ask shareholders to vote on matters that will have an impact on the company such as the appointment and removal of directors and auditors, the issuance of additional shares, approval of nonexecutive directors' and auditors' fees, amendments to the company's articles of association, approval of the final dividend, and the dissolution of pre-emption rights. Shortly, a new regulation is to come into effect that will require most companies to submit a report by the remuneration committee to shareholders for a nonbinding advisory vote.

Votes are generally taken at a general meeting or at a meeting for a specific class of shareholders. A simple majority passes ordinary resolutions either at a shareholders' meeting or by proxy. Extraordinary resolutions require at least 75 percent of the members' vote in order to be passed. Individuals or groups of shareholders can put resolutions to the shareholders' meeting for a vote if they gather 5 percent of the company's voting rights or if 100 shareholders each with at least £100 worth of shares agree.

REGULATORY ENVIRONMENT

Financial Services and Markets Act 2000

The FSMA was introduced in December 2001 and replaced the Financial Services Act (1986). The Act abolished self-regulating organizations which formerly had direct responsibility for governing investment businesses and introduced an integrated regulatory regime for investment resulting in a single regulator—the FSA.

Financial Services Authority

The FSA is the main financial regulator in the United Kingdom and regulates the key exchanges in the U.K. such as the LSE, LIFFE (the futures exchange), the London Metal Exchange, the International Petroleum Exchange, and Virt-x (the pan-European exchange for "blue chip" shares). The FSA also is responsible for the oversight and review of exempt professional firms (solicitors, accountants, and actuaries) and how designated professional bodies regulate them. In addition, the FSA regulates various organizations including banks, insurance companies, and building societies.

The government intends to take a more proactive approach into account investigations to prevent company account abuses. It has recently been agreed that this extended role and responsibility should be shared between the FSA and the FRRP, a small regulator reporting to the Department of Trade and Industry (DTI), which currently examines U.K. accounts following registered complaints and media attention.

Financial Ombudsman Service

When the FSMA (2001) came into effect, the FOS became the statutory ombudsman's scheme. All the previous dispute resolution schemes for investment business, insurance, and banking services were consolidated into this scheme.

Office of Fair Trading

The OFT is an independent competition and consumer protection authority that supports and protects the interests of U.K. consumers by ensuring businesses are both fair and competitive. To achieve its objectives, the OFT has three operational areas, competition enforcement, consumer regulation enforcement, and market policies and initiatives.

The Panel on Takeovers and Mergers

The Panel on Takeovers and Mergers is a regulatory body that administers the City Code on Takeovers and Mergers. The panel came into existence in 1968. Its objective is to ensure that all shareholders gain equal and fair treatment in takeover bids.

Department of Trade and Industry

The DTI works with a wide range of groups and organizations, to enhance U.K. productivity and competitiveness.

Companies House

Companies House is a government agency within the DTI, which holds the records of approximately 1.4 million live companies and 2.6 million dissolved companies. Its key functions include the registration of new companies, registration of documents that must be filed under insolvency, dissolution and striking-off companies from the register, and the provision of company information to the public that is in compliance with legal requirements.

London Stock Exchange

The LSE aims to provide issuers, intermediaries, and investors with well-regulated markets in which to raise capital. It has rules to ensure that markets work efficiently and monitors the operations of its markets to ensure that the rules are being followed. Stock exchange notices are issued throughout the year to inform member companies of changes to the stock exchange regulation and modifications to existing rules. Of particular importance are the disclosure requirements imposed by the LSE. Companies must disclose price-sensitive information on an immediate basis. Companies must transmit their information to the marketplace through a designated primary information provider (PIP). A set of special rules apply to any price-sensitive information that occurs after trading hours on Friday, whereby the company must send the information through two newspapers and two newswires during the weekend and through the designated PIP.

U.K. Listing Authority

The UKLA (formerly part of the LSE but now under the jurisdiction of the FSA) manages the listing rules, which govern the obligations of quoted companies. Its responsibilities include the admission of securities to listing and the enforcement of obligations outlined in the listing rules.

Companies must provide information such as listing particulars and prospectuses before their securities are eligible for admission to the official list. The U.K. listing rules require companies to disclose specific information on a continuous basis such as financial statements and directors' remunerations and dealings. As discussed above, price-sensitive information, which is information about the company that may have an impact on its share price, must be released "without delay" through a PIP to ensure that all investors have equal access to the information and that one group of investors is not disadvantaged by the selective release of information. Where listed companies or directors breach the rules, the UKLA will enforce the rules with financial penalties. If companies do not provide enough information to the market, their securities can be suspended from the official list. The UKLA aims to protect investors by ensuring they have access to accurate and timely company information.

A study conducted by PricewaterhouseCoopers concludes that the U.K. has well-developed capital markets and is generally regarded as a "high-quality market" which does not require significant change.[8] However, the European directives, which are incorporated into the U.K. listing rules, are currently undergoing some amendments, and these may affect the U.K. listing rules in the future. These changes are based on the standardization of capital market regulations across EU Member States. At present, the listing rules are mainly taken from the Consolidated Admission and Reporting Directive (CARD), which outline the "existing framework for listing."[9] However, it is likely that the Prospectus Directive and the Transparency Obligations Directive will replace a large degree of the CARD.

In addition to the EU directive requirements, the U.K. places additional obligations on listed companies, which are regarded as the "super-equivalent" requirements (these are listing rule requirements, which are above those provisions set out in the CARD). The FSA believes these requirements help to safeguard investor interests and maintain market confidence. However, with the proposed changes associated with the EU directives this could restrict the U.K. from imposing some of these super-equivalent requirements which would have an impact on the current listing rules in specific areas such as corporate governance, financial information, and shareholders' rights and obligations. The extent to which the U.K. listing rules will be affected will depend on the framework adopted for the EU directives, which is likely to be mid 2004.

Professional Accounting Bodies

The following key bodies are recognized as supervisory boards for registered auditors. The bodies ensure that auditors have the capabilities required to conduct their jobs in a professional manner.

+ The Institute of Chartered Accountants in England and Wales, which is the largest professional accountancy body in Europe
+ The Institute of Chartered Accountants of Scotland
+ The Institute of Chartered Accountants in Ireland
+ The Association of Chartered Certified Accountants
+ The Association of Authorized Public Accountants

Best Practice Corporate Governance Codes

Many reports emerged during the early 1990s after a series of company scandals and public outrage over large remuneration packages awarded to some CEOs. A series of regulatory responses emerged including the codes of best practice that are presented below.

Cadbury Code

In 1992 the Cadbury report was established to address concerns in corporate performance and financial reporting.[10] The key recommendations of the report focused on control and reporting functions of boards, taking a perspective on board performance and governance that focuses explicitly on financial stakeholders. The recommendations were incorporated into the LSE's listing rules on a "comply or explain" basis.

Greenbury report

In 1995, the Greenbury report on directors' remuneration was issued and addressed concerns about the large remuneration packages that had been awarded to some directors.[11] The code describes the information that should be made available by the company in its annual report. The report requires the linking of executive directors' remuneration to company performance and to the disclosure, in the annual report, of the directors' remuneration packages including pension entitlements.

Hampel and Turnbull Committees

In 1995 the Hampel Committee was established to review the work of the Cadbury and Greenbury codes and to create a consolidated and integrated set of principles and codes. The resulting "Combined Code of the Committee on Corporate Governance" was published in 2000 and incorporated the recommendations from both the Cadbury and Greenbury Committees as well as some amendments from the LSE.[12] The Code is appended to, but is not part of, the LSE listing rules. Companies that are listed on the LSE and are incorporated in the U.K. are required to comply with the Combined Code and if they have not, they must explain why.

A new Combined Code was published in July 2003, which replaces the existing Code. The new Code was created following a review of Higgs's Report on the role and effectiveness of nonexecutive directors (2003) and Sir Robert Smith's review of audit committees (2003) (both are referred to below in more detail).[13] The Code will take effect for companies whose reporting year commences on or after November 1, 2003.

The Combined Code requires a company to have an effective board of directors who are "collectively responsible for the success of the company." Two different individuals should hold the role of the chairman and CEO. Their lines of responsibilities should be transparent, where the chairman is responsible for the "running of the board" and the CEO is responsible for "running the company's business." The Combined Code also requires that the board should have "both executives and nonexecutives," which should include independent nonexecutive directors. The directors should be provided with quality information in a timely manner so that they can effectively fulfill their responsibilities.

There should be a "formal, rigorous and transparent" procedure in place to appoint new directors, who should all receive an induction when joining the board and continuously "update and refresh their skills and knowledge." The board is required to evaluate its performance on an annual basis and also the performance of its directors and committees. There should exist "regular intervals" for the re-election of directors depending on their performance. A "significant proportion" of the executive director's remuneration should be tied to corporate and individual performance. The levels of remuneration also should be "sufficient to attract, retain, and motivate directors" so that they effectively run the company. The directors should not be able to determine their own remuneration; instead there should be clear procedures in place to develop a "policy on executive remuneration and for fixing the remuneration packages" for all the directors.

In terms of financial reporting, the Code states that it is the board's responsibility to present a "balanced and understandable assessment of the company's position and prospects." An effective internal control system should be sustained to protect "shareholder investment and company assets." There should be clear provisions in place for "considering how the board should apply the financial reporting and internal control principles and for maintaining an appropriate relationship with the company's auditor."

In relation to shareholders, it's the board's responsibility to ensure that there exists "satisfactory communication" and that the communication which takes place is "based on the mutual understanding of objectives." Institutional shareholders also should communicate with companies "based on the mutual understanding of objectives" and make "considered use of their votes." Institutional shareholders are expected to consider all the facts when evaluating a company's governance and when companies deviate from the Code. And finally, companies should use their AGMs as a means of communicating with investors and engaging their participation.

Latest Proposals

Myners review

Paul Myners, former Chairman of Gartmore Investment Management Group, conducted a review of Institutional Investment, which was published on March 6, 2001.[14] This report was commissioned by the government to determine whether there were any factors distorting the investment decisionmaking of institutions. One of the outcomes of the review shows that fund managers do not actively engage with companies in which they invest, especially in the area of corporate underperformance, even though this could lead to a possible increase in the value of investment. The review highlights key principles of an effective approach to investment decisionmaking and suggests that funds should comply with these principles and that those that do not must explain why to its members and to the public at large.

Derek Higgs report

In 2002 the Secretary of State for Trade and Industry announced a review into the effectiveness of nonexecutive directors by Derek Higgs, a senior adviser to UBS Warburg and holder of a number of directorships including Prudential, British Land and Egg.[15] The report was published in January 2003 and builds on the work of the Myners review (2001) and the Company Law review. As with the Combined Code, Higgs's proposals also are subject to the "comply or explain" approach. The key recommendations include the following:

+ Companies should have a majority of independent nonexecutives on the board.
+ A separation of the chairman and CEO roles, where a former CEO should not become the chairman of the same company.
+ The formation of a new role—that of a senior independent director—who would be available to shareholders and act as an intermediary to management.
+ Nonexecutive directors should serve a maximum of 6 years on the board.

The business community has expressed concerns over Higgs's proposals and believes that some of the report's provisions could foster divisiveness and boardroom rivalries. Formal adoption of Higgs's recommendations into the revised Combined Code by the FRC and FSA was delayed due to this initial opposition.

Sir Robert Smith's report

Also published in January 2003 was the government-commissioned report by Sir Robert Smith (Chairman of Weir Group, a Member of the Board of Trustees of the British Council, and a past president of the Institute of Chartered Accountants of Scotland), inquiring into the role of company auditors in the U.K.[16] The report emphasized the need for audit committees to have a larger role to ensure good financial reporting. Although most listed companies do have audit committees, not all comply with the requirements of the Combined Code. The report will lead to modifications in the best practice code on corporate governance for listed companies. The key recommendations propose that the:

♦ Auditor must be independent and objective.
♦ Audit committee should include at least three independent nonexecutive directors.
♦ Audit committee should take an adversarial approach to management if it discovers misleading or poor financial reporting.

Overall the government, and the business community more generally, believes that better corporate governance can be gained through best practice codes rather than legislation.

INFORMATIONAL INFRASTRUCTURE

Financial Reporting

Three bodies work together to promote good financial reporting in the U.K.: the ASB, the FRC, and the FRRP.

The ASB's role entails issuing, amending, and withdrawing accounting standards and is recognized for its role in the Companies Act of 1985. Many of the accounting standards are set out in a series of Financial Reporting Standards (FRS) and some are in the Statements of Standard Accounting Practice.

The FRRP's role includes the tracking of annual reports of large companies where there is divergence from the requirements of the Companies Act of 1985. Where necessary it will involve the courts to ensure the required corrective action is taken. Each year the FRC publishes a review of the state of financial reporting and gives its views on accounting standards and practice. The FRC provides support and policy guidance to the ASB and FRRP.

Accounting Practices and Disclosure

At present, directors are required to report to shareholders once a year on the state of the business by presenting the company's balance sheet, profit and loss account, and a short directors' report about the business. It is also the directors' responsibility to ensure the deliverance of the annual report and other material, such as the consolidated accounts, to the Companies House within the statutory time frame. For U.K. companies, semi-annual reporting is the norm as opposed to quarterly reporting, which is conducted widely in the United States. The Companies House website states that, on average, more than 1000 directors are prosecuted each year for not delivering accounts and returns to the registrar on time.

Under the changes proposed in the company law reform, the government has agreed to abolish the narrative directors' report and instead replace it with a short supplementary statement and an operating and financial review for those companies that are "economically significant." In order to strengthen the transparency and accountability of directors, in the future companies will be required to prepare the following information on an annual basis: financial statements, a supplementary statement, an operating and financial review for economically significant companies, a directors' remuneration report for quoted companies, and an optional summary statement.

Accounting standards play a key role in determining how accounts are prepared. Public and large private companies are required to include a cash flow statement in the annual accounts. In addition, listed companies have other sources through which they can communicate financial and nonfinancial information to shareholders, such as interim reports, stock exchange announcements, press releases, analyst briefings, and the Internet. There also are an increasing number of companies that are reporting on environmental and social matters. In addition, companies have the ultimate responsibility to ensure price-sensitive information reaches the market place in a timely manner.

The new Standards Board will assume responsibility from the FRC for keeping the Combined Code under review and also will assume responsibility of enforcing certain rules from the UKLA. These rules include the requirement for listed companies to disclose their compliance with the Combined Code. At present, U.K. listed companies must show in their annual reports and accounts how they have applied certain principles and complied with the detailed provisions outlined in the Code. The auditors' report based on financial statements also must cover specific disclosures.

The new Standards Board also will consider whether this code requirement should be applied to companies that are not listed.

Government Changes and Initiatives

The government recently introduced its report on accounting and auditing, which it hopes will enhance confidence in audited accounts, improve corporate governance, and protect companies against Enron-style cases.

Professional accounting bodies are expected to insist that firms change audit partners every five years in order to ensure auditor independence. In addition, to ensure greater transparency, the DTI is expected to enact legislation to ensure that companies provide a detailed outline of payments to auditors for both audit and nonaudit services. Large accounting companies are to provide financial and nonfinancial information in their annual reports on a voluntary basis. U.K. government ministers have also expressed views in this debate, advocating audit committees to consist of nonexecutive directors and for the committee to make recommendations on the appointment and remuneration of company auditors.

The existing regulator of the accountancy profession, the Accountancy Foundation, will be dissolved, as will some of its operating bodies. Its other operating bodies will continue to function under the FRC. The functions of the review board will be taken over by a new Professional Oversight Board and it will also have additional functions concerned with the oversight of auditing and, in particular, for an audit inspection unit. The audit inspection unit will be responsible for inspecting the audit firms of listed companies and other public interest entities. Most of the planned changes are due to be in place by the beginning of 2004. The Auditing Practices Board will continue to be responsible for setting the auditing standards and it will also have a new function of setting the standards on auditor independence. As the FSA and FRRP take a joint proactive approach to investigating accounting abuses by companies, the Inland Revenue may also be given responsibility to act as a "whistleblower" on companies involved in accounting abuses. It would be involved in passing information on to the FRRP about companies that are not complying with the accounting standards.

There has been much discussion regarding the introduction of quarterly reporting in the U.K. However, many companies are opposed to this largely on the basis that it is costly and promotes a short-termist perspective. The introduction of quarterly reporting was one of the changes in the listing rules proposed by the FSA and originally put forward by the EU. The FSA will publish further consultation papers on the listing review later this year and take into account issues such as quarterly reporting.

U.K. GAAP–IAS

In 2002, a regulation was approved on the application of IAS across the EU. This followed the announcement by the EC in 2000 that all EU-listed companies would be required to use IAS in their consolidated accounts from January 1, 2005. However, in specific cases member states have the option of deferring the application of the regulation until January 1, 2007. The U.K. firmly supports this regulation and the move to use International Accounting Standards Board standards.

The U.K.'s approach to accounting standards is principles-based, with an emphasis on producing financial statements that are based on underlying reasoning and guidance. U.K. GAAP is closer to IAS than the accounting standards of other EU Member States. Although many U.K. companies already comply with IAS, those that do not will have to adapt their financial reporting. Following IAS gives U.K. companies greater flexibility in their financial reporting, as they do not have to comply with aspects of the FRS. By conforming to IAS there is greater international comparability for listed companies although this would reduce the comparability of listed and nonlisted companies within the United Kingdom.

NOTES

1. World Bank, 2000–2001.

2. International Governance Corporate, 2002.

3. The Association of Private Client Investment Managers and Stockbrokers, www.apcims.co.uk, 2003.

4. A discussion took place with 14 pension funds in the U.K.—all holding approximately 20 percent by value of the assets held by pension funds in the U.K. Coles and Green, 2000.

5. Association of British Insurers, 2001.

6. Company Law Review Steering Group, February 1999.

7. Department of Trade and Industry, 2002.

8. PricewaterhouseCoopers conducted a study of primary market regulations for the FSA. This included interviews with approximately 50 market participants and

entailed over 100 interviewees, which were conducted between August 2001 and January 2002. These participants were spread across various countries and included listed companies, investors, lawyers, investment bankers, stock exchanges, and representatives of regulators. PricewaterhouseCoopers, April 2002 and July 2002.

9. In July 2001, the Listing Particulars Directive, Admission to Listing Directive, Major Shareholding Directive, and Interim Reports Directive were consolidated into the Consolidated Admissions and Reporting Directive. Financial Services Authority, 2002.

10. Cadbury Committee, 1992.

11. Greenbury Committee, 1995.

12. Committee on Corporate Governance, The Combined Code, 2000.

13. Financial Reporting Council, The Combined Code on Corporate Governance, July 2003.

14. Myners, 2001.

15. Higgs, 2003.

16. Smith, 2003.

REFERENCES

Accounting Standards Board, www.asb.org.uk/
Association of British Insurers, www.abi.org.uk/
Association of British Insurers, "Investing in Social Responsibility: Risk and Opportunities," Association of British Insurers, www.abi.org.uk, 2001.
Bank of England, www.bankofengland.co.uk
Cadbury Committee, "The Financial Aspects of Corporate Governance," *Cadbury Report*, www.ecgi.org/codes/country_pages/codes_uk.htm, 1992.
Carpenter, R. "PR Newswire's Guide to European Disclosure," PR Newswire United Business Media, 2002.
Chartered Institute of England and Wales, www.icaew.co.uk
Chartered Institute of England and Wales, "Convergence with International Accounting Standards," www.icaew.co.uk, February 2003.
Coles, D., and D. Green. "Do U.K. Pension Funds Invest Responsibly?—A Survey of Current Practice on Socially Responsible Investment," *Just Pensions*, www.justpensions.org, July 2000.
Committee on Corporate Governance, "Hampel Report," (Final Report), www.ecgi.org/codes/country_pages/codes_uk.htm, 1998.
Committee on Corporate Governance, "The Combined Code—Principles of Good Governance and Code of Best Practice," www.ecgi.org/codes/country_pages/codes_uk.htm, 2000.
Companies House, www.companieshouse.gov.uk/
Companies House, "Administration and Management," www.companieshouse.gov.uk/, 2002/2003.

Companies House, "Formation and Registration," www.companieshouse.gov.uk/, 2002/2003.

Company Law Review Steering Group, "Modern Company Law for a Competitive Economy: The Strategic Framework," *Consultation Document*, February 1999.

Company-Solicitors.co.uk, www.company-solicitors.co.uk/

Croftm, J. "Companies Oppose Proposal for Quarterly Reports," *Financial Times*, 2003.

Dalla-Costa, J. "U.K. Pensions to Boost Private Equity Presence," Greenwich Associates, www.institutionalinvestor.com, November 13, 2002.

Department of Trade and Industry, "Modern Company Law for a Competitive Economy," www.dti.gov.uk/cld/, 2001.

Department of Trade and Industry, "Modernizing Company Law," White Paper, www.dti.gov.uk/companiesbill/whitepaper.htm, 2002.

Department of Trade and Industry, www.dti.gov.uk/, 2003.

Dickson, M. "Accounting Reform: Cosily, Oh So Cosily Does It," *Financial Times*, January 30, 2003.

Eaglesham, J. "Minister Set to Snub Pleas on Non-executives," *Financial Times*, February 26, 2003.

Financial Ombudsman Service, www.financial-ombudsman.org.uk/

Financial Reporting Council, www.frc.org.uk/

Financial Reporting Council, "The Combined Code on Corporate Governance, July 2003," www.frc.org.uk/publications/content/CombinedCodeFinal.pdf, July 2003.

Financial Review Reporting Panel, www.frrp.org.uk/

Financial Services Authority, "Financial Services Authority—Review of the Listing Rules," Discussion Paper, www.fsa.gov.uk/, July 2002.

Financial Services Authority, www.fsa.gov.uk/

Greenbury Committee, "Greenbury Report," www.ecgi.org/codes/country_pages/codes_uk.htm, 1995.

Gregory, H. J. " 'Comply or Explain' Governance Approach Could Work in U.S. as Well as U.K.," *DowJones Newsletter Corporate Governance*, 4, 7, January 23, 2003.

Guerrera, F. "Regulators Press on with Plan for Quarterly Reports," *Financial Times*, February 24, 2003.

HM Treasury, www.hm-treasury.gov.uk/

Higgs, D. "Review of the Role and Effectiveness of Non-executive Directors," www.dti.gov.uk/cld/non_exec_review, 2003.

Institutional Shareholders' Committee, "The Responsibilities of Institutional Shareholders and Agents—Statement of Principles," www.ecgi.org/codes/country_pages/codes_uk.htm, 2002.

International Accounting Standards Board, www.iasc.org.uk/cmt/0001.asp

International Governance Corporate, "Dissent Comes into Season: The 2002 Annual Meeting Season Is Over. The Results Are In," *International Governance Corporate*, no. 108, 2002.

Investment Management Association, www.investmentfunds.org.uk

KPMG, "Corporate Governance in Europe—KPMG Survey," www.kpmg.co.uk/kpmg/uk/, 2001/2002.

Law Firm Ltd, "U.K. Companies," www.lawfirmuk.net

London Stock Exchange, www.londonstockexchange.com

London Stock Exchange, "A Practical Guide to Investor Relations," www.londonstockexchange.com, 2000.

Myners, P. "Institutional Investment in the U.K.," *Myners Report*, www.hm-treasury.gov.uk/, 2001.

National Association of Pension Funds (NAPF), www.napf.co.uk/

Nobes, C. W. (ed.), "GAAP 2001—A Survey of National Accounting Rules Benchmarked against International Account Standards," 2001.

Office of Fair Trading, www.oft.gov.uk

Parker, A. "Audit Panels 'Must Challenge Management'," *Financial Times*, January 17, 2003.

Parker, A. "Call for In-house Clampdown on Cosy Auditor Relationships," *Financial Times*, January 21, 2003.

Parker, A. "Controversial Accounting Reforms Ruled Out by Hewitt," *Financial Times*, January 30, 2003.

Parker, A. "Deal Set to Resolve Dispute on Accounts Clampdown," *Financial Times*, January 22, 2003.

Parker, A. "Treasury Backs FSA Drive for More Power," *Financial Times*, January 17, 2003.

Parker, A., and C. Pretzlik. "FSA Seeks to Extend Powers," *Financial Times*, January 16, 2003.

Parker, A., and J. Eaglesham. "Inland Revenue May Get Whistleblowing Power," *Financial Times*, January 30, 2003.

Parker, A., and T. Tassell. "Boardroom Drama as Shake-up Plans Turn Radical," *Financial Times*, January 19, 2003.

PricewaterhouseCoopers, "Primary Market Comparative Regulation Study—Key Themes," (April 2002), *Financial Services Authority—Review of the Listing Rules*, Discussion Paper, www.fsa.gov.uk/, July 2002.

ProShare UK Ltd, www.proshare.org

Sharing Pensions, www.sharingpensions.co.uk

Smith, Sir Robert "Audit Committees—Combined Code Guidance," www.ecgi.org/codes/country_pages/codes_uk.htm, 2003.

Take Over Panel, www.thetakeoverpanel.org.uk/

Tassell, T., A. Bolger, and A. Parker. "Fear of Board Splits over Higgs Code," *Financial Times*, January 21, 2003.

Tassell, T. "Higgs' Package of Reforms Aims to 'Blow Away the Last Cobwebs'," *Financial Times*, January 21, 2003.

The Association of Private Client Investment Managers and Stockbrokers, www.apcims.co.uk

U.K. Financial Sector Continuity, www.financialsectorcontinuity.gov.uk/

U.K. Listing Authority, www.fsa.gov.uk/ukla/

Weil, Gotshal & Manges LLP, "Discussion of Individual Corporate Governance Codes Relevant to the European Union and Its Member States," *Annex IV*, 2002.

World Bank, "Governance Research Indicator Country Snapshot 2000/01," www.info.worldbank.org/governance/kkz/sc_country.asp

Similarities and Differences in the United States and United Kingdom

Dan Konigsburg

T he United Kingdom and the United States are often assumed to be similar in the matter of corporate governance; after all, the two countries share much of the same history, have similar legal foundations in common law, and are perceived to have open, transparent markets that actively encourage takeovers. The visible features of companies and their governance also look a lot alike; both British and American companies combine managers with outside directors into a unitary board, boards contain large numbers of outside, or nonexecutive directors, both markets tend to have companies with widely dispersed share ownership, high levels of public disclosure, relatively low levels of outside regulation, and clearly defined legal duties of care and loyalty to shareholders.

But despite the similarities, there are differences just beneath the surface—differences that are no less real for being subtle.

Boards of Directors

Company boards reflect some of the more significant differences. Both countries have boards that are relatively small in size, with between 7 and 12 directors, though British boards tend to be slightly larger than their American counterparts. Much of this has to do with different approaches to board balance. British boards tend to have more executives on their boards—at least half of most British boards are composed of company executives, and often they are a substantial majority. Compare this to the U.S. where, especially among larger companies, the CEO is often the only executive on the board. This fact itself reflects not just different approaches to board balance, but different approaches to the role of nonexecutives. Evidence from Standard & Poor's governance-related work in both countries shows that, in general, British boards tend to see their executives and nonexecutives working together as a collective body more than do American boards. A majority of nonexecutives on a British board might imply a distrust of management, or an "us versus them" mentality that is generally eschewed in the United Kingdom. The British like their nonexecutive directors to be comparatively more involved in running the day-to-day operations of the company, in partnership with the executives. Americans, on the other hand, have grown to see the role of the nonexecutive directors as a more circumscribed one—at many companies they are there to monitor management and not to get more involved in operational matters than absolutely necessary. If the American view can be described as "nose in, fingers out," then the British can be fairly said to have perhaps just a few more fingers in than the Americans.

This may be changing, however, as several recent British reports on governance have recommended increasing the numbers of nonexecutives on corporate boards. The Combined Code on Corporate Governance (1998) recommended at least three independent directors, regardless of board size. The more recent Higgs Report (2003) recommended raising this to at least half (though this recommendation has not been universally welcomed—many continue to be fearful of upsetting comity on boards and others question where the necessary nonexecutives will come from). The U.S., for its part, has found more consensus on the issue. Most, if not all, of the governance recommendations that came out of the Enron and WorldCom crises of the 2001–2002 period have suggested that boards be composed of a substantial majority of outside, independent directors. This recommendation has been perhaps less controversial in the U.S. than in Britain, despite the many smaller companies that will have to increase their board size or remove executive members to meet it. Today, the Americans may see the British minority-outsider board as a weakness in its governance system, but this is an area where the two markets may likely soon converge.

Board committees are another difference. Boards with audit, nomination, and compensation committees are almost universal in both countries (British compensation committees are called remuneration committees), but they are used in different ways. British nomination committees, for example, tend to include the CEO or another executive, reflecting the belief that bringing new members on to the board is a process that should involve management, since they will have to work together closely. Most American boards will insist on a nomination committee completely independent of management—some of the CEOs Standard & Poor's have interviewed have in fact boasted that they never even met some of their nonexecutives prior to the nonexecutive's first board meeting. Whether one considers this a good thing or not again depends on one's conception of the role of the outsider board. If it is to police the actions of management or to inspire outside confidence in a system discredited by scandal, then this may be helpful—if the role combines policing with the idea of partnership with management, then it may do more harm than good.

Another consequence of these different conceptions of outside directors is the prominence of the committees themselves. The work of many an American board is run through its various committees. It is not unusual for larger U.S. boards to set up any number of additional bodies, from strategy committees to corporate governance committees, to industry-specific committees like investment or liability committees. By contrast, it is still unusual to find separate board-level governance committees in the U.K., as boards there tend to prefer to raise these issues at plenary board meetings, together with managers. British board committees work separately from the board to the extent that they cover issues where conflicts of interest would otherwise arise (audit, compensation). By contrast, some agendas of U.S. board meetings are dominated by presentations of the work that the board committees have completed since the last meeting.

Of the various differences in boards of directors between the U.S. and the U.K., there are few as stark as that of whether the roles of board chairman and CEO should be combined. Today, 95 percent of FTSE 100 companies have separated the two positions, while the number of S&P 500 companies to have done so is a distinct minority (as of January, 2003, only 21 percent of these companies had done so[1]). The British have made the case that there are distinct dangers to combining the two roles—from the possibility of an imperial or overpowering CEO leading to abuse, to the idea that if the chairman's role is to evaluate and, if necessary, fire the CEO, a combined leader cannot impartially pass judgment on him- or herself. The Americans surely recognize the dangers as well as the British, but value the efficiencies and speed of decisionmaking gained by having one clear company leader. One U.S. CEO/chairman told Standard & Poor's that America had chosen a system of checks and balances for its government but not for its businesses, because of a

rational mistrust of the former and a desire not to slow down the competitiveness of the latter. There are also concerns about perception—historically, independent board chairmen have been acceptable at U.S.
boards only during periods of transition or where the CEO is weakened
or new. The preference also may reflect the prized American idea of
CEO as "Superman," which may indicate deeper cultural currents, and
to which we will return in our discussion of differences in executive pay.

But at the core, differences in this area may reflect differing conceptions of what an independent chairman actually does. U.S. companies
with combined chairman/CEO positions tend to fear a separate chairman
as a competitor for the CEO's job, or as someone that might put forward
a competing strategy. British boards often draw sharp boundaries: The
chairman leads the board; the CEO leads the company.

But in this area too, there is a trend toward convergence. In the
United States, the recommendations of the Conference Board[2] included
the only slightly qualified recommendation to split the two roles.[3] Many
others, including the Business Roundtable, are proposing alternatives
palatable to both sides of the debate like lead directors or presiding directors, who would provide leadership for nonexecutives without assuming
the role of chairman. In the United Kingdom, things are moving ever forward: The Higgs report recommended against former CEOs taking the
chairman's seat, and proposed the idea of a "senior independent director"
in addition to the chairman, whose role would be to bridge the board
and institutional directors. To some extent structural features offset one
another: The higher proportion of outside directors on U.S. boards may
lessen the need for an independent chairman in the United States, and the
split roles at the heads of most British companies may allow for strong
board independence even with fewer outside directors.

Regulation

Differences in corporate governance regulation between the U.K. and the
U.S. are quite stark. A major difference here is centralization. While the U.S.
preference for decentralized and checked power is reflected in the balanced
roles of the SEC, exchange listing rules, and state statute, the British have
consolidated almost all public company oversight in the Financial Services
Authority, a super regulatory body.

In terms of corporate law, the two markets are also distinctive. The
United Kingdom has the 1985 Companies Act, which regulates all aspects

of shareholder voting, meeting procedures, ownership rights, and directors' duties. The United States, on the other hand, has no federal body of corporate law; though there are SEC rules governing certain aspects of securities law and disclosure, basic corporate law is left to each of the 50 states, resulting in a multiplicity of approaches. U.S. companies can and do reincorporate in other states that offer greater flexibility in a number of areas, including takeover defenses. And while Delaware has been able to attract the majority of large U.S. companies thanks to its consistency in applying its law and the sophistication of its courts, there is no guarantee that this will continue. Large numbers of companies left New Jersey for the greater attractions of Delaware in the 1910s. Corporate law–shopping such as this is unknown in the United Kingdom.

Finally, the U.K. has been, since the innovation of the Cadbury Code in 1992, a proponent of self-regulation in corporate governance to a greater degree than the United States. The Cadbury Code and its descendants champion the idea of "comply or explain"—that is, a company should either comply with a recommendation or, if it does not, it should explain why. The U.S. has come late to this method (it has incorporated aspects of it into the recent NYSE and NASDAQ listing rule enhancements) preferring instead to introduce binding laws like Sarbanes-Oxley, which have been criticized as potentially developing into minimum requirements or safe harbors rather than incentives for improvement.

Ownership Rights

Shareholders in British companies enjoy more numerous and specific ownership rights[4] than their American counterparts. British companies routinely allow shareholders to vote on dividends, share buybacks, acceptance of financial statements, preemptive rights, and small acquisitions and spin-offs. American shareholder meetings, though they increasingly allow votes on more stock option plans, ask shareholders to vote for little more than director elections (typically in a block slate, rather than individually), approval of the auditors, and other business.[5] U.K. listing rules require companies to turn to shareholders for relatively small matters like related party transactions where, for example, a director of a property company intends to purchase a company-built apartment, or for acquisitions representing as little as 10 percent of assets. In the U.S., most of these decisions are reserved for the board, to which power has been delegated by shareholders and with whom fiduciary duties are entrusted.

The same is true of preemptive rights—current shareholders' right of first refusal over dilutive share issues—which is jealously guarded in the U.K. but which disappeared from U.S. by-laws by the 1980s[6] as companies required more speed and flexibility with their capital structures. Dual-class share structures—where one class of common shares has more voting rights than the other—are more common in the U.S., especially among family-managed companies and real estate investment trusts (REITs).[7] Rights to call a special meeting or to nominate a director to the board are also broader in the U.K. compared to the U.S., where alternatives like proxy contests are more unwieldy and costly to dissidents.

British holders' increased ability to call special meetings to replace directors explains why a common governance trait, classified boards (also known as staggered boards), is viewed so differently in the two countries. In the U.S., classified boards, where directors are divided into three groups, or "classes" of directors, each elected to staggered, three-year terms,[8] is viewed by many investors as an anti-takeover defense lengthening the time needed to change the board,[9] and viewed by boards as protection from opportunistic, nil-premium changes in control. In the U.K., classified boards with three-year terms are uncontroversial, as they are required by law, and because lower thresholds for calling special meetings allow holders to replace all directors at once. Despite a small trend in the U.S. to discard the structure, British classification is likely to continue, not least because English law is unclear as to who will run a company if all directors are removed at once and if there are no immediate replacements.

Two areas where British ownership rights compare less favorably to those in the U.S. are shareholder proposal mechanisms and the antiquated method of voting on a show of hands. U.S. SEC rules allow holders with minimal share ownership to put forward proposals, though companies have wide discretion, under the SEC's guidance, to exclude proposals. Moreover, most U.S. shareholder proposals are "precatory," meaning that management is not obliged to act, even if a proposal wins majority shareholder approval. U.K. holders need 3 percent of shares out or the support of 100 other shareholders to do the same. Voting by show of hands is also problematic in the United Kingdom. Though there are a few progressive British companies that have abandoned the practice, the vast majority still vote this way which, unless a poll is called to count the mailed-in proxies, skews voting power to the smaller number of shareholders present regardless of shareholding size. Voting by shareholders attending the company meeting may outweigh the much larger number of posted proxies, usually institutional investors. In the U.S., hand voting, if it exists, is accompanied by a count of the proxies, and voting by telephone and the Internet has facilitated the voting right to an extent not seen in the U.K.

Despite the stark differences in ownership rights, there is some reason to doubt their practical import. U.S. shareholders may have fewer individual control rights, but with few exceptions many doubt that American holders have substantially less control over companies than their British equivalents. Differences are likely to be a matter of emphasis—there is some thought that the U.K.'s emphasis on ownership and preemptive rights compensates for a weaker judiciary that, in its American incarnation, has been so active as to make numerous control rights less necessary.

Takeover Defenses

Closely related to ownership rights are takeover defenses and the market for corporate control, a broad area on which Britain and America have built very different approaches. In the U.S., defenses are common and are regulated by state statute (see Regulation, above) and run the gamut from classified boards to poison pills, greenmail, dual-class voting stock, or blank check preferred stock provisions.[10] Whatever one thinks of takeover defenses (and there is some academic research that shows that they may increase shareholder value by allowing incumbent directors more time to negotiate higher prices), their prevalence in the U.S. is owed to the fact that law and regulation have entrusted to directors immediate decisions on offers for the company. U.S. directors may adopt a poison pill defense, may pay greenmail, and may increase the size of the board without first seeking shareholder approval. U.S. directors may choose to send a recommended bid to shareholders or, if the offer is unwanted, they may simply choose not to. The latter option, known as the "just say no defense," has been tested and upheld many times in the Delaware Chancery Court. Moreover, directors using this defense are afforded the protection of the business judgment rule, which protects defensive boards against claims of liability if decisions are informed and made in good faith. Confirming the large role of the judicial system in U.S. governance, new defenses, as companies introduce them, are typically challenged in court.[11, 12]

In the U.K., directors are given little latitude to decide on business combinations on behalf of shareholders. Instead, they must follow the rules of the City Code on Takeovers and Mergers, administered by the quasi-governmental Takeover Panel, which ensures that shareholders decide on mergers rather than incumbent managements. The Code, set up in 1968 in response to concern about practices unfair to shareholders, sets out specific timetables for voting on bids, ensures equal treatment to shareholders and, in its preference for auctions, regulates statements both sides may make to the market after an approach. Structural defenses, like poison pills, freeze out provisions, and greenmail are not allowed under the Code and the self-regulating structure aims to keep takeovers out of court. Despite its benefits, the City Code is not without its limitations: It has few avenues of censure for rule-breakers beyond requesting a judicial review, and its effectiveness depends to a great degree on upholding an honor system.

The takeover debate is a good example of how the two markets at times do not speak the same language. In this area, the British governance system runs counter to the anything-goes, litigious system of the U.S. and its takeover defenses, under the belief that there is a conflict of interest when boards decide on mergers. However, most U.S. boards would claim it is in fact their responsibility to protect shareholders against opportunistic takeovers. The U.S. approach emphasizes directors' fiduciary duty to adopt maximum defenses, particularly in industries where volatile share prices and ready cash make them more attractive targets. These differing conceptions of the role of the board and the duties of directors are marked, particularly the extent to which shareholders delegate decisionmaking to the board.

Level and Tone of Debate

Highlighting many of the differences discussed so far is the tone of the debate about corporate governance in the two jurisdictions. Debate in the U.S. can be more strident and confrontational than in the United Kingdom, with a focus on rules and who may be breaking them at the moment. There is no one recognized American code of best practice; governance rules instead tend to be established in law, like the recent Sarbanes-Oxley Act.[13] In the U.K., there is a consensus around voluntary compliance, as exemplified by the pioneering 1992 Cadbury Code,[14] which asks companies to comply with its recommendations or, if companies do not comply, to explain why.

Consensus may be easier to achieve in a smaller market like the United Kingdom, where most of the major players are in one city, but it also may be a weakness. Contrarians point to a British business culture that likes to avoid rocking the boat, and to a consensus that may mask a deeper complacency. Those who remember the first governance consultations in the early 1990s point out that Cadbury was adopted by a business community threatened with regulation if they did not do something to curb perceived abuses. This itself may reflect weaker regulation, or perhaps a comparative reluctance for government to involve itself too closely in the affairs of business.

The U.K.'s response in the early 1990s is an instructive reminder of U.S./U.K. differences in governance culture. If today's British structures have grown out of scandal (Maxwell, Polly Peck, BCCI: all British governance failures in the late 1980s), Americans have looked not to business, but to Congress and the SEC for reform in the wake of the Enron and WorldCom collapses. Equally, this could reflect a stronger American belief in rule of law or simply increased mistrust of corporations. But perhaps the most overlooked difference in corporate governance is just how little consensus there is on the way forward in the U.S. as compared to the U.K., where there is more confidence that the present system is working.

Role of Institutional Investors and the Media

Of course, one of the factors behind the lack of consensus in the U.S. today is the role of institutional investors. Despite liquid markets and quite similar dispersed ownership structures (holders above 5 percent are unusual in both markets), the two markets have large investors like pension and mutual funds that behave quite differently, affecting governance debate in different ways. U.S. institutions, most notably public pension funds, tend to engage in a more adversarial relationship with companies than do British institutions, and are not shy about voting against management when it is in their interest to do so. U.K. institutions will do the same, but in a difference of degree, are generally more reluctant to take a public stance against a company. This again reflects the value of consensus in the U.K., but it is also fair to say that large investors have achieved more success through behind-the-scenes negotiations rather than through public bickering.[15] Another difference of degree is found in U.S. and U.K. institutions' focus on short-term profits over longer-term performance, a malaise blamed for everything from increased CEO turnover to fraudulent reporting; its more virulent form in the U.S. may perhaps correlate with a more competitive investment industry.

There are also differences among investors in the U.K. and the U.S. as to how actively they should look at corporate governance in their investments. Most U.S. investors outsource their voting responsibilities to a proxy adviser like Institutional Shareholder Services or the Investor Responsibility

Research Center; a large majority tend to be passive shareholders until a crisis erupts. U.S. institutions tend to keep proxy voting in-house, but separate from fund managers who, like their U.K. counterparts, tend to see corporate governance issues as not very relevant, both before and after the investment decision has been made. There are exceptions in both countries.

One not so obvious difference here is that the United Kingdom has had to get used to foreigners representing a large part of the shareholder base (especially among larger companies, where non-U.K. holders are near a majority). This sort of change is something U.S. companies and investors are less exposed to—U.S. companies generally remain focused on the interests of their domestic shareholder base. This is not the case in the U.K., where one driver of domestic engagement has been the emergence of more aggressive U.S. co-shareholders. If U.K. investors were to ignore this, they would see others changing their companies for them. If companies were to ignore this, they may find themselves targeted by unwanted activism, as oil giant BP discovered in a 2000 shareholder proposal conflict with its American investors.

Finally, the media plays a role here. U.S. companies are perhaps the most watched, scrutinized in the world, covered by numerous business dailies, specialist papers, online websites, and myriad cable channels. These aggressively track quarterly earnings reports, and are quick to dig up controversy or scandal. Business news in the U.K. is concentrated in one major business daily, *The Financial Times*, and the focus here and elsewhere tends to be on executive pay issues at the expense of other areas. There is an argument that heightened media scrutiny in the U.S. may make up for cases where there is an absence of direct short-term performance pressures from shareholders.

Disclosure

Among differences in disclosure, the U.K. does not require quarterly reporting (companies report twice yearly), the U.S. requires more consistent reporting on director backgrounds in AGM notices, the American SEC provides free access to an online database of public filings that simply does not exist in the U.K., the SEC's MD&A[16] requirements are much more comprehensive than the FSA requires, and there are small differences in continuous disclosure regulations. U.K. companies have one main avenue of disclosure to investors—the annual report and accounts—while U.S. companies produce an annual report in addition to a 10-K, proxy statement and other SEC filings.

From an accounting perspective, there are a number of small, yet material differences between U.S. and U.K. GAAP. Accounting for depreciation of intangible assets and goodwill is one difference (goodwill cannot be amortized in the U.K.), and there are small differences in purchase and disposal accounting methods as well as differing guidance for segment reporting. In general, however, U.S. GAAP is characterized much more by specific rules than by broad principles.

Reporting on governance has its areas of convergence, yet the U.K. still demands quite specific disclosures about the board and its functioning that are not standard in the U.S. In general, U.S. companies would likely argue that they disclose much more valuable information than companies in the U.K., while British corporates might respond that their disclosure is more targeted and thoughtful, and most importantly, does not overwhelm.

Activism

While investor activism is growing in both countries and is becoming more forceful everywhere, it is still the case that British activism tends to be much less grassroots in nature and is effected more behind the scenes than in the U.S. market. British institutions wield most power by threatening to vote against directors or items in the weeks before a meeting: means to an end that are rarely known publicly. Shareholder proposals and proxy contests are much less common in the U.K. than in the U.S., where smaller groups of investors, and increasingly labor union pension funds, are making their voices heard. However, more recently, U.K. shareholders have begun to assert themselves on executive compensation packages.

The emergence of socially responsible investment, or SRI, is another difference. SRI as an investment trend has been more pronounced in the United Kingdom than in the United States, and the 2001 Myners Report on Institutional Investment[17] recommended that pension and investment funds monitor their fund managers' approach to shareholder activism. Since the report's appearance, perceived lack of compliance with this recommendation has prompted the government to threaten legislation that would make shareholder activism by funds mandatory.

Executive Pay

There is perhaps no governance-related issue over which the United States and United Kingdom more thoroughly differ than that of executive pay. British investors may disagree with combined chairmen/CEOs in the U.S., but they can express defiance at the level of U.S.-style compensation, and in particular, multimillion dollar executive salaries, bonuses, and stock option awards, crossing the Atlantic to the boardrooms of their largest companies. For example, in 2003 the U.K. shareholders of Glaxo SmithKline reacted very negatively to the pay package of its CEO, notwithstanding the fact that this pay package was not inconsistent with that of CEOs of U.S. multinational pharmaceutical companies.

There are many possible reasons for the disagreement: Philosophically, there is a feeling in the U.K., reinforced by recent U.S. scandals, that excessively high pay can encourage abuse. There may be cultural reasons as well, including different attitudes toward the balance of CEO rewards compared with that of other employees in the United Kingdom. However, even in the U.K. it is the case that senior executive compensation is increasing at rates in excess of the growth rates of compensation of the average employee.

On the other hand, until recently, very high levels of executive pay have not been as controversial in the United States. Options were pointed to as the force driving the Internet revolution and making the economy more competitive. Markets swooned to star CEOs who could drive companies from rags to riches single-handedly. Much of this has not survived the bubble and the accounting scandals. But much of it remains. There is still an idea that someone who creates $100 billion in new value for shareholders should not be begrudged a mere $1 billion reward.[18] There is a dimension in size to this, too—even Americans can be awed by the size of a Microsoft or a General Electric, which had market capitalizations, until recently, equal to the size of a number of smaller European countries.

Other specific differences in executive pay include those of nonexecutive options, performance conditions on options, and golden parachutes. Most British investors do not support the granting of options to nonexecutives, which they view as confusing the roles of outside and inside directors. Performance requirements for option exercise, which U.S. companies have historically not required, are commonplace among U.K. companies' option plans. Finally, golden parachutes, or executive severance agreements, are prevalent among U.S. companies, while British investors have insisted on rolling employment contracts of no more than one year.

NOTES

1. This number falls to less than 5 percent if one asks whether the chairman is independent of the company (i.e., not an executive, the CEO, or a former CEO). (See Corporate Library.)

2. The Commission on Public Trust and Private Enterprise, The Conference Board, Findings and Recommendations, January 9, 2003. Taken from www.conference-board.org.

3. Or at least to introduce the role of presiding director when the two roles are combined.

4. Here defined more as control rights as opposed to cash flow rights, like the right to receive a dividend or payment upon liquidation.

5. Some U.S. companies do not even ask shareholders to approve the auditors, though the number is likely to fall in the wake of Andersen's collapse.

6. Though there are no preemptive rights among U.S. companies per se, exchange listing rules govern voting on share issues, and shareholders generally vote on corporate actions resulting in the issuance of 20 percent or more of current shares outstanding.

7. Though dual-class structures are, on the whole, uncommon under both systems.

8. Exchange listing rules do not allow staggered boards with more than three classes. NYSE Listed Company Manual, Section 304.00, www.nyse.com/content/publications/NT0006F742.

9. Under a classified board system, a dissident shareholder would require three years to effect a full change in board composition, as one-third of directors stand for re-election each year.

10. Many U.S. defenses were introduced as a reaction to the leveraged buyout and merger boom of the 1980s.

11. In practice, some have argued that the virulence of defenses like the poison pill have in fact been weakened by increasing numbers of independent directors and incentive pay, which may make value-increasing takeovers more likely. (See Kahan, Rock.)

12. The debate about U.S. takeover defenses often ignores the fact that, despite the level of protection available, M&A activity reached record levels in the late 1990s.

13. Sarbanes-Oxley Act of 2002, January 23, 2002, House Resolution 3763. news.findlaw.com/hdocs/docs/gwbush/sarbanesoxley072302.pdf.

14. Cadbury Report (The Financial Aspects of Corporate Governance), Committee set up by the Financial Reporting Council, the London Stock Exchange, and the accountancy profession, December 1, 1992.

15. The case for behind-the-scenes pressure in the United States has been made by Fidelity, Vanguard, and others in their unsuccessful lobbying against an SEC rule to require a proxy voting disclosure from private investment funds. The rule was approved by the SEC in January 2003.

16. Management Discussion & Analysis, a multipage discussion of strategy, risk, and performance review that must form a part of each company's 10-K, or annual report.

17. The Myner's Report, 2001.18. This is related to the assumption, long held in the United States, that people who are successful should and deserve to get rich, an idea that has few counterparts in the United Kingdom. See Monks & Minnow, 2001.

REFERENCES

Buckingham, L. "Greens Take on BP Amoco," *The Guardian* (January 27, 2000).

Burke, K. S. "Regulating Corporate Governance Through the Market: Comparing the Approaches of the United States, Canada and the United Kingdom," *Journal of Corporation Law*, vol. 27, no. 3, Spring 2002, pp. 341–380.

Grone, J. "The Skeptic: Softly, Softly Suits the City Just Fine," *Dow Jones Newswires* (January 20, 2003).

Higgs, D. "Review of the Role and Effectiveness of Non-executive Directors," www.dti.gov.uk (January 2003).

Hyde, D. "Nine in 10 UK PensionFund Managers Embrace Guidance on Shareholder Activism," *AFX European Focus*, www.afxnews.com (February 26, 2003).

Kahan, M., E. B. Rock, and S. A. Fox. "How I Learned to Stop Worrying and Love the Pill: Adaptive Responses to Takeover Law," *The University of Chicago Law Review*, vol. 69, no. 3, Summer 2002, pp. 871–915.

Keegan, V. "Master of the High-Wire Risk," *Guardian* (January 9, 1997).

Monks and Minow, "Corporate Governance," (2d ed), Blackwell Publishers Ltd., Oxford, 2001, p. 224.

Myners, P. "Institutional Investment in the United Kingdom: A Review," www.hm-treasury.gov.uk (March 2001).

Nobes, C. W. (ed), "GAAP 2001, A Survey of National Accounting Rules Benchmarked Against International Account Standards," *Pricewaterhouse-Coopers Publication* (2001).

The Combined Code: Principles of Good Governance and Code of Best Practice, Derived by the Committee on Corporate Governance from the Committee's Final Report and from the Cadbury and Greenbury Reports, www.fsa.gov.uk (May 2000).

The Corporate Library, "2003 Report on CEO/Chairman splits in the S&P 500: How Many and How Independent?," www.thecorporatelibrary.com (2003).

CHAPTER 17

Continental Europe and Japan: The "Insider" System

European Union

Gerben de Noord and Nick Bradley

The European Union (EU) was originally founded to bring peace and stability to the region following World War II. Led by the French-German axis, the Union expanded over the period, reaching 15 member states[1] by 1995. An additional 10 new member states[2] (predominantly from Central and Eastern Europe) also are expected to join by 2004 and a number of other countries[3] are waiting in the wings. Consequently, the EU is a powerful economic block with converging legislation, predominantly covering single-market issues.

The EU's member states are in different stages of economic and financial market development. The predominant concept is that of a social market economy; in which employees' interests are more explicitly taken into consideration than in the Anglo-Saxon market model. In some countries, e.g., France, Belgium, and Greece, the state plays an important role in the economy through shareholdings (including golden shares after privatization) and boardroom influence. In Germany, there is a strong sense of codetermination and consensus between the social partners (employees and employers) and the other key players in the economy—the state and the banking sector. Banks play a leading role as suppliers of capital to businesses in Germany and often designate representatives to sit on the boards of companies to whom they supply this capital. Workers have boardroom influence as well, as is the case in Germany and the Netherlands. In both the United Kingdom and in the Netherlands, institutional investors, particularly pension funds, play a large role in the economy whereas in Italy, families traditionally play a key role in the economy. In some of the smaller countries, a number of large companies dominate the financial landscape.

EU LEGAL AND REGULATORY ENVIRONMENT

The European Commission is the executive arm of the EU and has sole responsibility for initiating proposals for new legislative acts. The European

Parliament and the Council (consisting of representatives of member states) examine, amend, and approve these legislative proposals. Although EU law takes precedence over domestic law, not all EU law is directly applicable at member state level. The predominant instruments are regulations, directives, and recommendations.[4]

EU Enlargement

In May 2004, the European Union is scheduled to welcome 10 new member states—subject to approval by referenda in most countries concerned—and this will have a big impact on decisionmaking in the EU. A new European Parliament will be elected shortly after enlargement and a new European Commission will be installed after the summer of 2004. This change of power, combined with the inexperience of delegates from new member states, will likely slow down the legislative process, and there is severe pressure on the EU institutions to complete a number of key legislative proposals before enlargement—especially in the field of financial services and other policy areas sensitive to member states.

CORPORATE GOVERNANCE BACKGROUND

Corporate governance has become more relevant in the European Union in the wake of the single currency, the integration of capital markets, increased merger and acquisition activity (including consolidation of securities exchanges), and the appearance or development of an equity culture in most member states. Corporate governance codes of individual member states are remarkably similar, and most of the differences in corporate governance practices are embedded in the legal and cultural environment. Therefore to date, the EU has adopted the view that it is more sensible to establish common corporate governance reporting methods than to impose common rules. Some of the main differences among EU member states are the following:[5]

1. *Employee representation:* In roughly half of the EU member states, employees have boardroom influence. Employees have the right to elect board members in Austria, Denmark, Germany, Luxembourg, and Sweden; articles of association may provide employees with electoral rights in France and Finland, while the Works Council has an advisory role in France and the Netherlands.

2. *Shareholder-stakeholder:* The shareholder is not necessarily recognized as the prime constituency in every country. For example, in France, Germany, Italy, and the Netherlands there is a broader perspective, where the company as a whole takes the central role.

3. *Board structure:* Companies in most countries have single boards while in Austria, Denmark, Germany, and the Netherlands dual boards are predominant and in Belgium, Finland, and Greece both forms can be found. In Portugal and Italy, a separate board of auditors is required.

4. *Board committees and independence:* A recent study (KPMG, 2002) found that the number of board subcommittees is growing, encouraged by codes. Board subcommittees are least common in Germany and the Netherlands (countries with a dual board system), while, on average, only a minority of surveyed firms had nomination committees in place. In addition, the definitions of "independence," when describing directors, vary widely from country to country.

5. *Disclosure practices:* Transparency and disclosure standards vary significantly between countries[6] and information varies widely, e.g., information about board members.

6. *Voting rights:* Dual class shares can be found in Sweden, Denmark, Finland, France, Spain, and Italy, but not in the United Kingdom and Germany—where they have been prohibited recently. A recent survey found that ceilings on voting rights and ownership are not uncommon among the largest European companies.[7] Golden shares may be found in privatized companies throughout the EU.[8] The issue of disproportional voting rights may be addressed through pending EU takeover regulation (see below).

McCahery and colleagues (2003) summarize key characteristics of ownership structure in Continental Europe as the following:

+ High shareholding concentration;
+ Pyramidal and complex ownership structures to retain control;
+ The corporate sector owns a large stake in itself;
+ Bank holdings are generally small unless banks are part of a financial group; and
+ Institutions and directors do not hold much voting power in Continental Europe.

Until recently, corporate governance was not regarded as an issue for action at the Community level—predominantly because of the subsidiarity[9] of company law. Deeper capital market integration did, however, inspire the Commission to mandate a study comparing EU corporate governance codes[10] in the Financial Services Action Plan—an ambitious program to remove obstacles to the EU Single-Capital Market. The process was taken forward through the High-Level Group of Company Law Experts, chaired by Dutch professor Jaap Winter, set up in September 2001 by the Commission.

The first report of the High-Level Group dealt with specific issues regarding EU takeover regulation and a second report concerned best practice in a number of areas of company law, including shareholders' rights and general aspects of corporate governance.

Corporate scandals from the United States, particularly Enron, caused concern over corporate governance in Europe, and at a subsequent informal ECOFIN Council[11] at Oviedo, Spain, in April 2002, the Commission prepared a briefing paper that proposed EU policy responses, including the widening of the mandate of the High-Level Group by adding corporate governance issues (including the role of nonexecutive and supervisory directors, management remuneration, and the responsibility of management for the preparation of financial information) to its mandate.

The High-Level Group presented its second and final report, "A Modern Regulatory Framework for Company Law in Europe" ("Winter Report") in November 2002, having widely consulted industry representatives and others.

The key recommendation in the Winter Report was for the Commission to launch an Action Plan on Company Law, including corporate governance. This approach, and indeed the report as a whole, has been well received by EU institutions and most stakeholders. The Commission, Parliament, and the Council responded favorably to the recommendations of the High-Level Group and launched an informal debate, between and within EU institutions, on the way forward for corporate governance in the EU, at Community as well as member state level.

The Commission presented a communication detailing its proposal for an action plan on modernizing company law and enhancing corporate governance in the European Union (Company Law Action Plan) in May, 2003.[12]

The EU Action Plan on Company Law and Corporate Governance

The Company Law Action Plan will aim to facilitate harmonization of a framework of corporate governance structures for EU listed companies—

appreciating the variety of corporate governance practices and different legal systems and cultures by avoiding a "one-size-fits-all" single EU corporate governance code—while breaking down those barriers that inhibit a single EU capital market. The ambitious aims of the project include shareholder and third-party protection as well as improvement of the competitiveness and efficiency of EU businesses.

The Commission makes several recommendations for policy actions on corporate governance and company law for the short term (2003–2005), medium term (2006–2008), and long term (2009 and later).

These policy actions are based on the recommendations from the Winter Report, which were affirmed by the Council. The Commission approach is market-based and contains core elements of disclosure and transparency in addition to a number of rules and regulations. As mentioned, there will be no single EU corporate governance code, but each country should designate one code—containing minimum standards addressed in the action plan.

The proposed short-term policy actions contain the following elements:

1. A directive is proposed, requiring listed companies to publish an annual corporate governance statement, including a "comply-or-explain" reference to a national corporate governance code and several disclosure requirements related to the composition of the board and shareholders' rights. The board also will have collective responsibility for this report as well as for key nonfinancial information.

2. Collective responsibility of the board for the disclosure of key financial and nonfinancial information will be pursued through amending existing legislation.

3. The European Commission will coordinate corporate governance practices at Community level by the coordination, monitoring, enforcement, and facilitation of the convergence of corporate governance codes through the establishment of a European corporate governance forum.

4. The role of nonemployed (or nonexecutive) and supervisory directors, and board committees will be addressed in a recommendation, suggested to be taken forward by a comply-or-explain provision.

5. An appropriate regime for the approval of remuneration programs of executive directors will be set out in a recommendation.

6. There will be a directive to overcome obstacles to cross-border shareholdings and the use of voting rights across borders— hence facilitating shareholder participation.

On a medium-term basis, the Commission will request, in a directive, that institutional investors disclose their investment and voting policies, and that beneficial holders be able to obtain specific voting records. A further directive will allow companies to choose between a single-tier or dual-tier board. Another directive will target sensitive issues, enhancing boardmembers' responsibility by setting out procedures for directors' disqualification, wrongful trading, and a special investigation right for investors.

If those issues addressed in its recommendations are not adequately applied, it is likely that the Commission will push for a directive to achieve its targets.

While the action plan has laudable aims, there are some concerns regarding the implementation and the mix of policy instruments. There appears to be an overreliance on legislative proposals, which may undermine the current convergence of corporate governance practices in the EU. The proposed directive on the annual corporate governance statement, for example, and some of the requirements on board composition and members may, through the backdoor, lead to a pan-European corporate governance code, by setting minimum legal standards.

There is a clear concern when more detailed descriptive language would be used, which is not unlikely to be amended with technical details throughout the legislative process. This would further restrict the choice of corporate governance practices and codes. The Commission argued that certain disclosure elements need legislative enforcement, portraying, perhaps, a lack of trust in market discipline in adhering to Commission recommendations and, ultimately, codes.

In a union of 25 members, it may be hard to agree on any technical issue, but the legislative Action Plan may be delayed further, since the accession countries have not been consulted. While some of these countries may welcome the action plan, there are likely to be serious concerns over the applicability of some of the measures. While directives could perhaps provide Accession Countries with more time for implementation, recommendations would have provided appropriate incentives.

There is also a concern over the coordination mechanism. The Commission requests every EU country to nominate one code, and will enforce minimum standards if the European Corporate Governance Forum, or perhaps the Commission, deems the code to be unambitious. It could be more effective if the coordination mechanism for codes is used to address ineffectiveness of aspects of certain codes, or entire codes—e.g., when "explain" would dominate "comply."

Apart from the corporate governance elements, the Action Plan also addresses capital maintenance, more disclosure on groups of companies and pyramids, restructuring, and other new legal forms for companies. Progress on some of those issues may prove to be very difficult, considering the relevance of legal structures, like pyramids, in EU member states. Where progress in securities law has been painful and slower than expected, company law will prove to be even more difficult—especially since it is much more sophisticated and rooted more deeply than securities law has been in most countries.

Related EU Initiatives

The Company Law Action Plan is strongly linked to the Financial Services Action Plan (FSAP), launched by the European Commission in 1999. The aim of the FSAP is to remove the remaining barriers to a single EU for financial services. The European Commission has recently launched a number of related initiatives:

International Accounting Standards

Despite the existence of accounting directives, there are still major differences in accounting and measurement rules and also in the quantity and quality of disclosure throughout the EU. This severely impedes cross-border investment and in an attempt to address this issue, the Regulation on International Accounting Standards will require EU listed companies to prepare their accounts in accordance with IAS from 2005 (N.B. States will be allowed to defer the application of certain provisions until 2007 for those companies publicly traded both in the EU and on a regulated third-country market which are already applying another set of internationally accepted standards as the primary basis for their consolidated accounts as well as for companies which have only publicly traded debt securities.) The adoption of IAS' principles-based accounting rules is consistent with the EU's move away from prescriptive rules toward principles-based regulation.

The European Union takes a coordinated "hands-off" approach to the drafting of IAS/IFRS (International Financial Reporting Standards)[13] by the International Accounting Standards Board (IASB), the independent international standards setter, based in London. The European Commission coordinates the approach of the EU member states through a complex framework of advisory committees of regulators and an advisory committee of market participants, European Financial Reporting Advisory Group (EFRAG), an independent high-level group providing technical advice to the European Commission on the applicability of existing and proposed IAS in the EU. EFRAG also coordinates the views of interested parties on IAS and provides a proactive contribution to the work of the IASB. Accordingly, the EU expects to have considerable influence over the IASB, but the complex structure is expected to provide enough support for the independence of the IASB.

Several European companies—especially banks—strongly oppose the current Exposure Drafts of IAS 32 and IAS 39. These standards concern financial instruments; IAS 32 defines recognition and measurement and IAS 39 sets out the treatment for disclosure and presentation. These two standards are based on U.S. GAAP—one of the few accounting systems to contain recognition and measurement standards for financial instruments. IAS 32 and 39 are prescriptive—some argue too detailed— and not principles based, and while the IASB recognizes that these standards are imperfect, it does not want to change the fundamentals. The main points of criticism are the lack of involvement from private sector entities, the tight timetable for implementation (2005) as well as the contents of the standards. The European Parliament and member states also are concerned over the impact of the proposed standards on the banking sector and the lack of accountability of the IASB. There is also some concern over the application of IAS to nonquoted companies, as IAS have been developed for the capital market, but may be applied to unlisted companies through EU domestic regulation or through other regulation such as the Basel II Capital Adequacy regime for banks.

Nonendorsement of the standards on financial instruments may create an à la carte EU version of IAS, incompatible with other versions of IAS, fundamentally different from "pure" IAS. Moreover, it would probably signal the end of IAS as a global standard and remove incentives for the United States to accept accounts prepared under IAS or to replace U.S. GAAP with IAS.

The entire exercise of integration of EU capital markets would be severely hindered by incomplete adoption of IAS, especially since EU companies with a dual listing in a third country, e.g., the United States, would have to comply with two standards. Another criticism of the IASB is that some standards are complicated and are unsuitable for nonlisted companies and may therefore widen the gap between IAS and national accounting standards for small and medium-sized entities (SMEs).[14]

IAS versus U.S. GAAP

In September 2002, the FASB and the IASB signed "The Norwalk Agreement"—a memorandum of understanding that pledged to coordinate future work programs and to make the existing standards compatible. The key target date in this agreement is January 1, 2005, when the IAS regulation comes into force in the European Union.[15]

While both IAS and U.S. GAAP have an underlying principle of prudence and a strong information function, there are some key differences. Generally, IAS is principles based in contrast to U.S. GAAP, which is rule based. U.S. GAAP therefore has a higher density of regulations and offers less scope for interpretation, but, consequently, may provide more legal certainty.

Institutionally, the SEC enforces U.S. GAAP but there is no universal enforcer for IAS. Enforcement in the EU is coordinated by CESR,[16] but without a single EU enforcement agency there may be differences in local implementation of the standards. Links between the enforcement agencies and the IASB, and particularly with the International Financial Reporting Interpretations Committee (IFRIC), must be strong to ensure consistency and comparability.

Disclosure and Transparency Agenda

In March 2003, after extensive consultation, the European Commission proposed to amend the periodic and ongoing transparency obligations for listed companies. The important "transparency directive" requires quarterly reporting for EU listed companies, although not as extensive as in the United States. For example, issuers are only requested to publish certain, unaudited key financial data. Eight member states already require quarterly reporting for some regulated markets, but a number of issuers have voiced their concerns; shareholders are broadly in favor. The Commission also proposed more prompt publication of annual and interim reports, and requires increased transparency of significant shareholdings and voting rights. Information regarding participation in general meetings and proxy voting must be provided so as to facilitate shareholder participation, while the use of corporate websites was suggested for dissemination of key information.

Other disclosure and transparency initiatives are the market abuse directive and the prospectuses directive. The former requires immediate ad-hoc disclosure of inside information, while the latter addresses initial disclosure requirements. The market abuse directive was adopted in December 2002, while the prospectuses directive is scheduled for adoption by 2003 year-end. The transparency directive is expected to be adopted by 2005, although technical details may cause setbacks.

The EU directive on disclosure requirements for listed companies has been reviewed to allow for the use of modern technologies in shareholder communication, filing, and to accommodate cross-border access to company information. Moreover, as a mere formality, the accounting directives have been updated to allow for application of IAS.[17]

Auditing

The European Union has come forward with a number of initiatives to enhance best practice. In May 2003, the Commission presented a "10 Point Action Plan on Statutory Audit."[18] Similar to the Company Law Action Plan, the plan consists of short-term (2003–2004) and medium-term priorities (2004–2006).

Some of the short-term priorities address reinforcement of the EU regulatory infrastructure and strengthening of EU public oversight on the audit profession. Also, it will be proposed to require the use of International Standards on Auditing from 2005. The directive regulating statutory audits also will be updated in the near term. Some of the medium-term issues will address sanctions, auditor liability, and the lack of competition. Disclosure requirements for audit firms and relations with their clients will enhance transparency, while not prohibiting the provision of nonaudit services.

A key medium-term priority are audit committees and internal control systems. The Commission may make proposals regarding the role and functioning of audit committees, but initially relies on self-regulation and corporate governance codes to reinforce this area.

In May 2002, the Commission presented a *Recommendation on Auditor Independence*. In 2005, the Commission will review implementation at member state level, and may come forward with a legislative proposal or, if it is not satisfied with the implementation process, may propose legislation at an earlier stage.

Auditors will be required to ensure their independence—ultimately this may prohibit a firm from performing certain nonaudit services. They will not be allowed to have any direct or significant indirect relationship and partner rotation is required after seven years. Auditors will be required to provide their clients with full disclosure, at least annually, of fees for audit and nonaudit services and must provide written declarations of independence to nonexecutive directors or to the supervisory board.

The "soft" EU approach in this area clearly contrasts with the more prescriptive U.S. approach in the Sarbanes-Oxley Act. While encouraging good auditing practices in some countries, the approach may not lead to improvements in countries where existing standards are already high. Moreover, this approach may pose problems for EU companies that are dual-listed in the United States, as the U.S. SEC may be reluctant to accept accounts prepared by auditors that are subject to a less strict regulatory regime. As part of the 10-point-plan, the EU has affirmed that it will continue negotiations with the SEC regarding auditor independence.

Takeover Directive

One of the most sensitive issues in EU policymaking has been the takeover directive. Since 1989, the EU has tried to reach agreement over a common framework for cross-border takeover bids. Member states have been very hesitant, and a recent proposal fell at the last hurdle in a historic vote in the European Parliament in July 2001. A carefully redrafted proposal is currently being considered.

The common takeover code aims to provide a fair framework for all parties concerned, including protection for minority shareholders and legal certainty for companies. The latest proposal contains the following principles:

♦ Equal treatment for shareholders in identical situations;
♦ Full information about the offer;
♦ Institution of a mandatory bid;
♦ Control by supervisory authorities and distribution of competencies between them;
♦ The definition of the applicable law;
♦ Board neutrality;[19]
♦ The definition of equitable price for the mandatory bid;
♦ Squeeze-out and sell-out rights;[20] and
♦ A procedure for the bidding process, which aims at improving the transparency of capital and control structures of all listed companies.[21]

A controversial element from the Report of the High Level Group of Company Law Experts—the Break-Through Rule,[22] which overturns multiple voting rights has not been included in the proposal but may be considered by the European Parliament.

There is a broad difference of opinion between the Nordic states and the rest of the Union. Nordic countries oppose the abolition of multiple voting rights, as the system is said to encourage entrepreneurship and to protect highly innovative companies from being taken over. In France, some companies may reward loyal shareholders with double voting rights after holding shares for two years, while companies in the Netherlands and Belgium may issue nonvoting shares. Germany abolished multiple voting rights and is pressing for the same to happen throughout the EU. Some commentators argue that the abolition of multiple voting rights is against shareholder democracy and is counter to the spirit of freedom of contract—that a voluntary acceptance of inferior voting rights, often in return for a discounted share price, does not contravene good governance principles. The European Commission has proposed to undertake a study into the consequences of a one-share-one-vote regime, as a medium-term priority in the Company Law Action Plan, to be published before 2008.

Bolkestein-Winter versus Sarbanes-Oxley

The EU regulatory response to corporate governance concerns differs significantly from the approach taken in the United States. Europeans would argue that Winter's response has been more measured. Some EU countries are proposing financial market legislation, but the bulk of the work has been coordinated by Commissioner Bolkestein, which demonstrated the Commission's intent to converge and enhance corporate governance practices in the European Union.

The U.S. Sarbanes-Oxley Act of July 2002 proposed a system of rigid regulations—some of which have extraterritorial effects. The EU proposed, and will hopefully deliver, a consistent, principles-based framework—without extraterritorial spillovers.

NOTES

1. Austria, Belgium, Denmark, Finland, France, Germany, Greece, Ireland, Italy, Luxembourg, Netherlands, Portugal, Spain, Sweden, and the United Kingdom.

2. Cyprus, Czech Republic, Estonia, Hungary, Latvia, Lithuania, Malta, Poland, Slovakia, and Slovenia.

3. Currently, Bulgaria and Romania are scheduled to enter the EU in 2007 while Turkey does not have a firm target date for EU accession. A number of Balkan countries also may join at a later stage.

4. A *regulation* is directly applicable and binding in all EU member states without the need for any national implementing legislation. A *directive* binds member states as to the objectives to be achieved within a certain time limit while leaving the national authorities the choice of form and means to be used. Directives have to be implemented in national legislation in accordance with the procedures of the individual member states. A *recommendation* is not binding.

5. Weil, Gotshal & Manges, 2002.

6. Standard & Poor's Transparency and Disclosure Study, 2003.

7. DWS (2001, p. 30, as quoted by Weil, Gotshal & Manges (2002)) found that among Euro Stoxx 50 companies:

> A ceiling (or limitation) on voting rights is used by twenty-three percent (23%);
>> An ownership ceiling is used by ten percent (10%) of the sample.

8. A number of cases brought before the Court of Justice of the European Communities by the Commission against member states addressed the use of Golden Shares. Golden Shares were only accepted for "strategic" sectors, such as defense and energy, www.curia.eu.int/en/.

9. The subsidiarity principle is intended to ensure that decisions are taken as closely as possible to the citizen and that constant checks are made as to whether action at community level is justified in light of the possibilities available at national, regional, or local level. Specifically, it is the principle whereby the Union does not take action (except in the areas that fall within its exclusive competence) unless it is more effective than action taken at national, regional, or local level. It is closely bound up with the principles of proportionality and necessity, which require that any action by the Union should not go beyond what is necessary to achieve the objectives of the Treaty. Source: EU website, www.europa.eu.int/scadplus/leg/en/cig/g4000s.htm.

10. Weil, Gotshal & Manges, 2002.

11. The ECOFIN Council consists of economics and finance ministers of EU member states.

12. www.europa.eu.int/comm/internal_market/en/company/company/news/index.htm.

13. In May 2002, the IASB decided that IAS would be known as International Financial Reporting Standards (IFRS). Since not all standards have been approved to become IFRS, we use IAS when referring to IAS, IFRS, or IAS/IFRS.

14. BDO et al., p. 4.

15. Other countries, including Australia and New Zealand, also have agreed to endorse IAS.

16. Committee of European Securities Regulators.

17. The full text of these directives can be found at www.europa.eu.int/comm/internal_market/en/finances/mobil/index.htm.

18. www.europa.eu.int/comm/internal_market/en/company/audit/index.htm.

19. Obligation for the board of the target company to obtain the authorization of the shareholders before adopting any defensive measure after a bid has been launched. Source: Speech of Commissioner Bolkestein, European Commission, www.europa.eu.int/comm/internal_market/en/speeches/index.htm.

20. The squeeze-out right basically refers to the right of a majority shareholder in a company to compel the minority shareholders to sell their shares to that majority shareholder at an appropriate price. Conversely, the sell-out right refers to the right of a minority shareholder to compel the majority shareholder to purchase their shares at an appropriate price. Source: High Level Group of Company Law Experts (2002a), p. 54.

21. European Commission, October 2002.

22. This is "a rule, [...] which allows the bidder to break-through mechanisms and structures which may frustrate a bid, as defined in the articles of association and related constitutional documents, after completion of a takeover bid for all the risk- bearing shares of the company, which achieves such a measure of success as clearly to justify this." Source: High Level Group of Company Law Experts, 2002a, p. 4.

REFERENCES

BDO, Deloitte Touche Tohmatsu, Ernst & Young, Grant Thornton, KPMG, and PricewaterhouseCoopers, "GAAP Convergence 2002, A Survey of National Efforts to Promote and Achieve Convergence with International Financial Reporting Standards," 2002.

Deutsche Bank Research, "IAS: New Financial Reporting Rules in the European Union," *Frankfurt Voice*, EU Financial Market Special, January 2003.

Die Wertpapier Spezialisten ("DWS") Investment GmbH, 2002, DWS Corporate Governance Survey 2001: European Corporate Governance Ranking Report—Euro Stoxx 50, July 2001.

Economic and Financial Committee, "Corporate Governance Issues Linked to Financial Markets," Letter to the ECOFIN Council, www.ue.eu.int/en/summ.htm, November 27, 2002.

European Commission, "A First EU Response to Enron-Related Policy Issues," Note for the Informal ECOFIN Council Oviedo, April 12 and 13, European Commission, DG Internal Market, April 2002.

European Commission, DG Internal Market, www.europa.eu.int/comm/internal_market/en/index.htm.

European Commission, "Proposal for a Directive of the European Parliament and of the Council on Takeover Bids," European Commission, DG Internal Market, October 2002.

European Parliament, "Corporate Governance," Draft Briefing, Directorate General for Research, June 2002.

High Level Group of Company Law Experts, 2000a, "Issues Related to Takeover Bids," European Commission, DG Internal Market, January 2002.

High Level Group of Company Law Experts, 2000b, "A Modern Regulatory Framework for Company Law in Europe," European Commission, DG Internal Market, September 2002.

International Accounting Standards Board, www.iasb.org.uk.

KPMG, "Corporate Governance in Europe," *KPMG Survey 2001/2002* (2002).

McCahery, J., L. Renneboog, P. Ritter, and S. Haller. "The Economics of the Proposed European Takeover Directive," *CEPS Research Report, Preliminary Draft*, Brussels, 2003.

Weil, Gotshal & Manges LLP, "Comparative Study of Corporate Governance Codes Relevant to the European Union and Its Member States," European Commission, DG Internal Market, March 2002.

France

Liliane Kankindi Bwakira

INTRODUCTION

Corporate governance has become increasingly important in France in recent years and acceptable principles of corporate governance covered in domestic corporate governance codes have been translated into new corporate laws. Substantial reforms in French corporate law were first prompted by two reports prepared by a commission led by Marc Vienot. Today, there is renewed interest in reviewing the French governance code and limiting abuses of misappropriation of corporate assets and fraudulent financial statements. In 2002, Daniel Bouton, President of *Société Générale Bank,* led the latest review of the French governance code, together with chief executives of other prominent French companies.

French corporate law has traditionally been unique compared to other European countries due to the diversity in its legal structures. For several years, corporate governance in France has been structured in a way that allows a *société anonyme* (SA) to be governed under either a unitary or a two-tier board structure. Currently, French companies have even more flexibility than their European counterparts in choosing between various models of management and governing structures. Under French law, each SA can determine its own board structure in its "statuts." Dual auditorship is another specific feature of the French corporate governance system; in principle it allows for greater auditor independence.

From the end of World War I, the state has played a key role in the French economy. In the middle 1980s and the early 1990s, the government decided to accelerate privatizations while highly publicized corporate scandals, including Pechiney (1988), and Société Générale (1988), prompted the review of corporate laws. Most of these scandals, including the highly publicized Elf Acquitaine corruption scandal (2000) involving key senior officials of the French Republic during the Mitterand era, have exposed the complex interconnection between business and politics in

France. Nevertheless, the French privatization process has generated a cross-shareholding system in which the state still has an influence.

The corporate governance revolution in France was a result of various internal and external factors: privatization, the increasing presence of foreign shareholders, the emergence of the pension fund concept, increased activism by institutional and individual shareholders, and the publication of the two Viénot reports in 1995 and 1999. France implemented a wide set of corporate governance rules leading to changes in the voluntary disclosure practices of listed companies and a clearer allocation of duties among the board, the CEO, and the chairman. The latest reforms to date, referred to as *la Loi NRE*, or law on New Economic Regulation, were implemented in May 2001. This new economic regulation law introduced the option for companies with a board of directors to separate the functions of chairman and CEO or to keep them joined. Another new law, enacted in February 2002, mandates listed French corporations to report on the sustainability of their social and environmental performance. A new financial security bill, *la Loi de Sécurité Financière*, will soon be voted by the French parliament. This new bill is intended to help rebuild confidence in the financial sector by strengthening the role and efficiency of existing supervisory authorities and by creating new advisory bodies and institutions (such as the *Haut Conseil du Commissariat aux Comptes*) to protect financial transactions. With stronger supervisory bodies, this reform is expected to enhance corporate disclosure and protect shareholders. Among the reforms introduced by the draft legislation, corporate executives of listed companies are required to comply with financial transparency rules, to disclose internal audit procedures, and to report all their securities and stock option–related transactions to authorities.

Previously, French corporate governance had long been characterized by the vague definition and allocation of duties between a company's board and its CEO and the common practice of staggered boards, where several directors come up for renewal or replacement each year. Another common phenomenon and a key feature of French governance until recent reforms had long been known as the *cumul de mandats* which consisted of the accumulation of numerous posts which has allowed executives to hold various CEO positions or directorships. Linked to this is the concept of the *noyaux dur*, or "hard core" of French corporates that maintain a bond of loyalty often reinforced by cross-shareholdings and cross-board representation.

The working group, chaired by Daniel Bouton, was set up in 2002 to evaluate the corporate governance practices of listed companies and to provide "best practice" recommendations. More reforms are expected with the implementation of the Bouton report recommendations to all French listed companies proposed for the end of 2003. The Bouton report identifies areas of improvement needed to upgrade corporate governance practices of French listed companies. Findings suggest few boards have implemented the formal evaluations of their own operations and that to date there are no formal legal requirements for board members to be independent. Corporate governance remains a concern and has been in the headlines with news of allegations and investigation made against Vivendi over the firm's financial disclosures and financial irregularities.

MARKET INFRASTRUCTURE

Types of Business Organization

The main business entities under French law are the *société anonyme* (SA), which represents mostly large publicly limited companies, and the *société à responsabilité limitée* (SARL), which is a private limited liability company, a partnership used mostly by closely held limited liability companies with 50 or fewer shareholders. A few of the largest companies, such as Michelin and Casino, are organized under another type of company structure, the *société en commandite par action* (Sca), a partnership limited by shares that is mostly applicable to large family-controlled companies with access to equity market while maintaining control. There are various other forms of business partnership arrangements under French law including the *société en nom collectif* (SNC), a general partnership; the *entreprise unipersonnelle à responsabilité limitée* (EURL), representing a sole proprietorship with limited liability; the *société en commandite simple* (Scs), a limited partnership company; the *société en participation* (sp), a silent partnership; a *groupement d' intérêt economique* (GIE); European economic interest groupings (EEIG); or the *entreprise individuelle*, a sole proprietorship.

Traditionally, an SA's typical management structure consists of a board of directors whose chairman is the CEO, commonly called the *Président Directeur Général*, or *PDG*. Another common form has been the complex mixture of a management board (*Directoire*) charged with management functions and a supervisory board (*Conseil de Surveillance*) charged with oversight. A minority of publicly traded companies has mostly used this governance structure.

Corporate Ownership Structure

There is tremendous ownership and voting power concentration in France, although the degree of concentration is lower in CAC 40 companies. For CAC 40 companies, banks and insurance companies are the main category of voting block holders, followed by nonfinancial firms and individuals. Single majority shareholders have traditionally dominated France's shareholder ownership structure and families play a major role in ownership and voting power. Large publicly quoted companies have a single shareholder that owns up to 52 percent of capital. The largest identified shareholder of CAC 40 firms holds up to a 27 percent stake, however, with control of the company.[1] As a result, conflicts of interest between large controlling shareholders and the weak minority shareholders are important and a frequent phenomenon in France. The recent privatization process also has brought unexpected challenges in shaping relations between ownership and control in France.

Securities Markets

In France, company shares are listed either on the *Premier Marché, the Second Marché,* or *Le Nouveau Marché*. Requirements vary on each of these regulated markets concerning the percentage of total share capital floated. The Nouveau Marché, set up in February 1996 to allow small companies seeking development capital to raise equity, offers companies more flexible listing requirements but with stricter disclosure rules. Following the merger of exchanges in Amsterdam, Brussels, and Paris in 2000, Euronext has allowed companies to choose their preferred home market and home jurisdiction. For registration, Euroclear France acts as the central depositary but the record of ownership of securities is kept in the company register, which is maintained by the companies themselves. Custodians are responsible for registering shares in the name of the account holder by sending an electronic message to Euroclear France, which in turn, sends it to companies.

Role of Institutional Investors

A specific investor association, *L'Association Française de la Gestion Financière* (AFG-ASFFI) has played a visible role in terms of corporate governance. This organization has been actively involved in the review of key corporate governance issues and has been an advocate of wider discussions of corporate governance issues by extending and holding them at the European level. In 1998, the Commission on Corporate Governance of the AFG-ASFFI, chaired by Jean-Pierre Hellebuyck, drafted one of France's corporate codes. These recommendations on corporate governance were updated in October 2001. The organization's monitoring program also is aimed at extending the exercise of voting rights by fund managers and oversees draft general meeting resolutions of CAC 40 companies.

Institutional and Cultural Factors

A key feature of French corporate practice is the importance given to the social role and performance of the company, relative to the company's focus on shareholders and maximization of shareholder value. The company is defined in France as a separate economic agent, with its own objectives, which are distinct from those of shareholders, employees, creditors, suppliers, and customers. Relative to Anglo-American jurisdictions, France places a somewhat greater focus on the interests of nonfinancial stakeholders relative to financial stakeholders.

Role of the State

Although the current center-right government is undertaking economic reforms to maintain France's competitiveness within the EU, the French government continues to play an important role in the national economy and the government has controlling shares in strategic sectors in the economy. France also maintains a "golden share law" that requires government authorization before investing over a certain percentage of a firm's capital for the protection of French national interests.[2] The state holds controlling shares in approximately 1500 companies in France, including majority shares in major companies such as France Telecom and Air France.[3]

Corporate Control

Unlike in the United States and the United Kingdom, the market for corporate control is almost nonexistent in Continental Europe, and in France in particular, due to concentrated ownership of shares and anti-takeover regulation. Based on French law, every acquisition of more than 33 percent of the equity of the firm has to be followed by a tender offer to all voting shares at the same price. This law has implications: The law reduces the probability of takeovers taking place while preventing unequal treatment of shareholders in takeovers. As a result, there are very few hostile takeovers in France. Large shareholders and/or banks must generally be courted to support the bid to succeed. However, direct shareholder monitoring, dual board structure, creditor monitoring, and the main bank system could be perceived as alternative control devices and a substitute for hostile takeovers.

LEGAL ENVIRONMENT

Background on Legal System and Legal Tradition

French law allows for diversity in the legal structures that is rare in other European countries. French companies (SA) have a choice between three models of management and governing structures. A unique feature in France is the possibility for worker councils' representatives to attend board meetings, with an advisory voice on certain issues addressed by the supervisory body.

Principal Legal Provisions

French law provides French companies (both public and private) three main ways to organize a corporation (*société anonyme*): (1) with a board of directors, whose chairman is also the CEO; (2) with a management and a supervisory board, or (3) with a board of directors but with separate roles for the *président* (chairman) and the *directeur général* (CEO). Under French law, each SA can determine its own board structure in its "statuts."

The NRE Act of May 2001 introduced a distinction between supervisory and executive powers in the unitary governance structure. Currently, each individual may hold only up to five chairman positions in French SAs. A CEO is now limited to a maximum of one CEO position in France, but may be named a CEO in a second, affiliated SA (if not publicly traded). Currently, directors cannot serve on more than five boards with the exception of affiliated and nonpublic companies. At least two-thirds of the board must be nonexecutives (excluding executives of subsidiaries and affiliated companies who are not considered executives). Shares can be blocked in France. French law requires that shares be suspended from trading prior to the General Meeting for a period of five days in order to be voted in General Meetings.

Laws/Rulings on Corporate
Governance Practice

Compensation, stock options,
and director independence

Under new regulation, listed companies are now required to disclose specific information on remuneration of two to four of a company's top executives.

Since the NRE, French law requires the disclosure of officer and director compensation and allows the possibility of board of directors' meetings by videoconference. Since the laws introduced in 2001, it is now a requirement for listed companies to disclose the total compensation (salary, bonus, stock options, insurance policies, etc.) in their annual reports. Any shareholder is entitled by law to obtain details of the total amount of compensation given to the most highly compensated officers in the company. In 2000, MEDEF, the French employer association, had issued a strong recommendation to companies to voluntarily publish information on individual executive and director remuneration. Following recent amendments of the *Loi NRE*, nonlisted companies are no longer required to comply with requirements related to disclosure of officer and director compensation.

To limit misappropriation of corporate assets, companies are strictly prohibited from making loans to their executive managers or directors, including for the purpose of exercising options. Only general meetings of shareholders have the legal authority to grant stock options, to set their maximum number, and to determine the main conditions for granting them. In major French companies, stock options tend to be granted in the form of stock purchase options. Directors not considered corporate officers or employees are barred from receiving stock options.[4] French corporate law was recently amended to oblige listed companies to disclose in their annual reports how they take into account the social and environmental consequences of their activities, including how they conform to principles set by the International Labor Organization.

At present, there still is no law requiring the independence of one or more board members in French companies. To hold a director position, each director must be a shareholder with the minimum number of shares required as written by the by-laws.

Shareholder Rights

French shareholders generally are not active participants in the corporate governance process. Based on French law, each shareholder with one share in a company can submit written questions to the board and request the chief justice of the commercial court to call a shareholders' meeting, provided he or she states an urgent reason to do so.

One or more shareholders representing 5 percent or more of the capital of the company are accorded more right. They can submit, twice a year, questions to the chairman of the board of directors regarding threats to the continuity of the company's activities and request a court-appointed expert to investigate specific management actions within their company and within subsidiaries, without having to justify any urgency. Other rights enjoyed by shareholders include the right to request the removal of the company's auditors, to submit resolutions to be voted, and to request court intervention. French law allows both for individual lawsuits and "derivative" lawsuits in cases where harm is suffered by the company itself. French-style class action lawsuits are unique in that a group of shareholders may file a suit against executives on behalf of the company but only the company is considered the victim. Consequently, any compensation paid for damages caused benefits the company instead of the individual shareholders. For individual lawsuits however, compensation that is awarded for damages caused goes directly to the specific shareholder.

Shares of French companies come in two forms: registered or bearer form. Generally, shares carry proportional voting rights but the law allows that company articles or by-laws grant more voting rights to registered shares that are held for a two-year period (double voting rights after holding shares for two consecutive years). The Hellebuyck Commission Recommendations view double voting rights as "a way to reward the loyalty of certain shareholders," but is in favor of the "one share, one vote" principle. However, the commission takes the view that this practice can be abused. The recommendation put emphasis on equal and fair treatment of all shareholders and on the protection from controlling shareholders. Electronic signature is now legally recognized for all companies allowing this voting method in their by-laws.

In general, foreign investors have the same rights as local investors. However, occasionally foreign interests are restricted from participating or exercising their voting rights in certain corporate actions (corporate action announcement message).

Board Structure

Under French law, the board must be composed of at least 3 and no more than 18 directors.[5] On the subject of board independence, French law only imposes limits on the number of insiders who can serve on the unitary board. Only one-third may hold a contract of employment.

In France, the word *directeur* is exclusively restricted to members of management, and generally refers to the "manager" or the "executive." A member of a unitary board is titled *administrateur* which is the equivalent of "director" in English. When assigned managerial or executive functions, he or she holds the titles of *administrateur-directeur* or *administrateur-délégué* if he or she is appointed to replace an administrateur-directeur on leave or who is deceased.

REGULATORY ENVIRONMENT

General Protocol

Employee representation is allowed in France and in some cases company articles provide employees with a role in corporate governance by granting them the right to elect some members of the supervisory board. Employee representatives may have the right to attend board meetings, but not vote. When employee shareholdings reach 3 percent, employees are allowed to nominate one or more directors, subject to some exceptions.

The Annual General Meeting peak season is between May and June. Typical items reserved for shareholder action or approval in France include share issues, election or dismissing of supervisory board, articles of association, annual accounts, auditors, mergers, and dividends.

The rules regulating the publication of general meetings are the Commercial Company Acts dated July 24, 1966. French *sociétés par actions* (SA, SCA, SAS) and S.A.R.L are required to file their accounts with the *Greffe du Tribunal de Commerce* in their jurisdiction area within a month of the general meeting after financial statements are approved. Issuers are also legally obliged to publish meeting information in the *Bulletin des Annonces Légales Obligatoires* (BALO) within a month of the general meeting.

Investors in France can hold ordinary shares with voting rights and shares without voting rights that include certificates, preferred shares, and shares with priority dividends (*actions à dividendes prioritaires*, or ADP). Up to 25 percent of shares may be transformed into shares having no voting rights.

In wide contrast with recognized principles of corporate governance, French corporate governance does not follow the principle of "one share equals one vote." Voting rights of shares are increased in proportion to the share of capital represented and French law also allows for shares with voting rights to be eliminated or restricted, to protect minority shareholders. Double voting rights can be removed by the extraordinary shareholders' meeting or by shareholders with double voting rights in a separate meeting.

Regulatory Bodies and Prominent Market Institutions

There are an estimated 943 listed public companies in France with a total country market capitalization reaching EUR 3,817 billion ($3,435 billion).[6] The *Conseil des Marchés Financiers* (CMF) and *Commission des Opérations de Bourse* (COB) are the two main market authorities. The merger of the two institutions, announced in 2001, will be renamed *Autorité des Marchés Financiers* (AMF) later in 2003. Established in 1996, the CMF is the supervisory authority for all financial markets and determines the general rules under which regulated markets operate in France. The COB regulates the securities market by monitoring financial markets, verifying reports published by listed companies, and certifying portfolio management companies.

Since 1977, all firms with more than 300 employees have been required to submit a *bilan social* (social balance sheet) to the *Comité d' Entreprise* (works council). The bilan social considers employment, wage-related costs, health and safety protection, employee training, industrial relations, and other issues including transportation and housing.

Listing Rules and Compliances Practices

On March 15, 2000, the Council of Ministers adopted a draft legislation which subsequently was voted as the *loi NRE*, that would allow both listed and unlisted companies to separate the roles of chairman and CEO and require listed companies to publish the remuneration of the 10 most highly paid corporate officers.

Securities holdings exceeding 5, 10, 33.33, 50, or 66.66 percent of total company shares and/or of the voting rights must be reported to the CMF within 5 days and to the company within 15 days by the owner of securities. The investor is required to present the total number of shares as well as the total number of voting rights as soon as the limits are exceeded and when total holdings fall below limits.

BOARD STRUCTURE

Role of the Board and Outside Director

In accordance with French law, a director's term may not exceed three years if he or she is newly appointed when a company is started. In general, the term of all other directors does not exceed 6 years, and the number of directors who are over 65 years may not exceed one-third of the board membership. On average, listed company boards meet three or four times per year.

The Bouton code recommends that the number and structure of committees be matters for each board of directors to decide upon. The role of the board in France is to promote the interest of the company as a separate economic agent (Viénot I).

For several years the law applying to unitary boards has required that the leadership positions be combined. The *Association Francaise des Entreprises Privées* (AFEP) and *Mouvement des Entreprises de France* (MEDEF) released recommendations of the committee on corporate governance chaired by Marc Viénot in July 1999 on:

♦ The separation of the offices of chairman and CEO;

♦ Disclosure of the compensation granted to corporate officers of listed companies (executive remuneration policy and total amount of directors' remuneration);

♦ Disclosure of stock option and stock-purchase plans in listed corporations;

♦ Single-tier structure for boards of directors of public companies; and

♦ The French Financial Investment Management Association (AFG-ASFFI) created a Commission on Corporate Governance (the Hellebuyck Commission). The commission's task was to draft recommendations regarding publicly traded companies belonging to AFG-ASFFI.

The Viénot II Report recommends that independent directors account for at least one-third of the audit and nomination committees and make up a majority of the compensation committee. These recommendations were adopted by the AFG-ASFFI board in June 1998, and are used as the basis for discussion of corporate governance issues for listed companies throughout the Eurozone.

In director nominations, French codes recommend a nominating committee to reduce the CEO's influence on the body that is charged with monitoring his or her performance.

The board should evaluate its ability to meet shareholder expectations by reviewing periodically its membership, its organization, and its operation, and publish results of this review in corporate annual reports.

Role of Corporate Auditors

Dual auditorship is a specific feature of the French corporate governance system with the benefit of allowing for greater auditor independence. All major French companies appoint two independent statutory auditors for a six-year term, but the term can be renewable. Among key suggestions made in the Bouton report in this area of corporate governance were the increased need to inform the audit committee of fees paid by the company and the selection or reappointment of auditors through a tender process overseen by the audit committee.

Share Registration and Voting Procedures

Traditionally, shareholders could vote either by post or via physical representation and third-party representation is only possible by another shareholder. Since NRE reforms, voting by videoconference or electronic means are now allowed in France. There are no voting restrictions penalizing foreign investors. However, share blocking is mandatory as per the Commercial Company Acts of 1966 five days prior to the meeting. A blocking certificate is needed both for physical representation and for posting. Unblocking takes place a day after the vote. Vote counting methods consist of one vote per share, but split and partial voting also are allowed.

INFORMATIONAL INFRASTRUCTURE

Accounting Practices and Standards

French accounting requirements were formulated based on the *code de commerce* (commercial code), company law and decrees, and rules set by the main accounting body, the *Comité de la Réglementation Comptable*—including the *Plan Comptable Général* (PCG)—and interpretations of the *Comité d'Urgence*.

The latest code of best practice, the Bouton report, recommends the implementation of accounting procedures that allow better presentation of off-balance-sheet items in the financial statement. France has recently opted to upgrade reporting requirements by applying International Financial Reporting Standards (IFRS) and will convert to IAS/IFRS international accounting standards by 2005.

Financial Reporting

French companies are required to register with the local registrar of companies (*Greffe du Tribunal de Commerce*). Under French law, the public is entitled to access the company's constitution from the registration office or the local registrar. Registration documents are published in the *Bulletin Officiel des Annonces Civiles et Commerciales* (the official financial newspaper).[7]

Filing requirements include the annual report and accounts, and unaudited interim reports for SAs. The SA and SARL also provide the name and location of their parent company and their main affiliate companies, and percentage of ownership. SNC, Scs, and Sca have no obligatory filings. The information is published in the BALO.

All *sociétés par actions* and SARL companies must publish audited annual financial statements and a management report with the clerk of the court registry (Greffe) within a month after the annual general shareholder meeting to be held six months after the end of the fiscal year at the latest.

Financial statements must reflect the "true and fair" view (principle of *image fidèle*) of a company's financial position and include the balance sheet, income statements, and notes. The statement of changes in financial position is also mandatory and semiannual income statement summaries are published within four months after the end of the fiscal half-year.

Listed companies also are required to disclose their turnover at the end of each quarter and are required to appoint two statutory auditors for a six-year term.

All publicly traded companies have been required since 1986 to publish consolidated financial statements. No distinction is made between current and noncurrent assets and liabilities in the balance sheet (provided in the notes) and nonoperating balances are disclosed separately.

Most corporations publish an abbreviated consolidated statement (including an income statement, balance sheet, and notes) within four months after the end of the fiscal year and 15 days before AGM, in the *Bulletin des Annonces Légales Obligatoires* (BALO), the French legal-notices publication.

Disclosure

Annual financial statements are required within 45 days of the annual shareholders' meeting (no more than 6 months after the end of the fiscal year). Publicly owned companies must publish their turnover at the end of each quarter. French corporate law was amended in May 2001 to require listed companies to disclose in their annual reports how they take into account the social and environmental consequences of their activities. All firms with more than 300 employees now submit a *bilan social* (social balance sheet) to the *Comité d' Entreprise* with information such as employment, wage-related costs, health and safety protection, employee training, and industrial relations.

In the past 3 years, listing rules or legislation relating to increased remuneration disclosure have passed or have been proposed to require greater transparency in France. French codes of best practice call for enhanced disclosure of information to enable shareholders to judge the qualifications and independence of directors.

Disclosure of management remuneration is required for listed companies, and auditor rotation is mandatory every 6 years. The compensation of directors also must be disclosed and the overall amount of compensation to be set by the general meeting is determined by the board. All SA are required to disclose the overall remuneration of the 5 or 10 highest paid corporate officers *(mandataires sociaux)*. Only listed companies have to disclose individual pay for each of the corporate officers.

Standard & Poor's study of transparency and disclosure practices of French companies included in the S&P 350 index suggests that France's disclosure levels are among the highest in Europe and in the world, based on the 98 information items examined.

Although *documents de référence* filings are only legally required for companies listed on the Nouveau Marché, in practice, these regulatory reports have become very common in France and important corporate disclosure documents for French companies. These filings, which are registered with and certified by COB, are seldom available on corporate websites however, even if they are considered a key basis of company information disclosure in France. Few of the 45 French companies analyzed in this sample presented annual reports both in the form of a comprehensive document de référence and a discretionary annual report. Less than half of companies examined posted their latest documents de référence on their French corporate website although their certified and more detailed annual reports could be easily accessed and downloaded from COB's SOPHIE website in French. Only a handful of these companies (22 percent) translated and posted the documents de référence in English on their investor relations' website. Instead, most French companies generally prefer to present abbreviated discretionary annual reports to the public that are available both in French and in English versions on their corporate websites.

Stock Options and Areas of Improvement

Most major French companies tend to grant stock purchase options (of existing shares) rather than subscription options (subscribing for new shares). Only the general meeting of shareholders can authorize the granting of options.

Weak corporate governance areas identified by international investors and legal experts in France today include staggered boards of directors, shares with unequal voting rights, the need for a legal definition of independent director, the lack of law to have independent directors on boards, and weak committees.

NOTES

1. Bloch and Kremp, 1999.

2. Index of Economic Freedom, "France," Heritage.org, 2003.

3. *The Economist*, vol. 365, no. 8299, November 16, 2002.

4. "Promoting Better Corporate Governance in Listed Companies, Report of Working Group Chaired by Daniel Bouton," Working Paper, p. 16.

5. AFG-ASFFI Commission on Corporate Governance, "Recommendations on Corporate Governance," p. 8, adopted on June 9, 1998, amended in 2001.

6. Citibank Market Profiles, "France," Securities Services, www.Citibank.com, 2002.

7. Guide to International Filings, "France," Thomson Research, www.Primark.com, (2002).

REFERENCES

AFG-ASFFI (Association Française de la Gestion Financiere), *Hellebuyck Commission Recommendations sur le Gouvernement d'Enterprise*, June 29, 1998.

AFG-ASFFI Commission on Corporate Governance, "Recommendations on Corporate Governance," adopted on June 9, 1998, 2001 Amendments.

"A New Kind of Solidarity," *The Economist*, vol. 365, no. 8299, special section, p. 10, 4p, November 16, 2002.

Bloch, L., and E. Kremp. "Ownership and Voting Power in France," FEEM Working Paper No. 62-99, July 1999.

Bouton, D. "Pour Un Meilleur Gouvernement d'Entreprises Cotées: Rapport du Groupe de Travail Présidé par Daniel Bouton, Président de la Société Générale," MEDEF and FAFEP-AGREF, September 23, 2002.

Conseil National du Patronat Français (CNPF) [now retitled Mouvement des Entreprises de France] and Association Française des Enterprises Privees (AFEP), The Boards of Directors of Listed Companies in France (*Viénot Report I*), July 1995.

"Credit Where It's Due," The Economist, vol. 365, no. 8301, p. 64, 2p, 1c, November 30, 2002.

Gugler, K. et al., "Corporate Governance and Economic Performance," Oxford University Press, July 19, 2001.

Gregory, H. J., Weil, Gotshal & Manges LLP, "Comparative Matrix of Corporate Governance Codes Relevant to the European Union and its Member States," *Annex V*, 2002.

Gregory, H. J., Weil, Gotshal & Manges LLP, "International Comparison of Board 'Best Practices'"—Investor Viewpoints (2001 ed).

Maclean, M. "Corporate Governance in France and the UK: Long-Term Perspectives on Contemporary Institutional Arrangements," *Business History*, vol. 41, no. 1, 88p, 29p, January 1999.

Mesnooh, C. J. "Corporate Governance in France," *Corporate Finance*, supp. 2, no. 214, p. 8, 4p, September 2002.

Ministry of the Economy, Finance and Industry, Restoring Confidence, The Financial Security Bill, *Press Release*, France, February 5, 2003.

Mouvement des Entreprises de France (MEDEF) and Association Française des Enterprises Privees (AFEP), "Recommendations of the Committee on Corporate Governance," (*Viénot Report II*), July 1999.

Recommendation on Corporate Governance, AFG-ASFFI Commission on Corporate Governance, adopted on June 9, 1998, amended in 2001.

Stock Exchange Operations Commission, Regulation No. 98-01–98-10, English Translation, March 1999.

Weil, Gotshal & Manges LLP, Comparative Study of Corporate Governance Codes Relevant to the European Union and Its Member States, On Behalf of the European Commission, Internal Market Directorate General, *Final Report & Annexes I-III*, January 2002.

"Where's the Michelin Woman?," *The Economist*, vol. 358, no. 8209, p. 64, 2p, 1bw, February 17, 2001.

Germany

Merlin Underwood

INTRODUCTION

For much of the post-war era, the evolution of Germany's corporate governance showed a marked divergence from that which developed in more "market"-oriented economies such as the United States and the United Kingdom. This divergence was reflected in the marginal role of the stock market in the German economy, the concentration of share ownership and voting control, the limited size and role of the country's institutional investors, the statutory separation of the "supervisory board" from the "management board," the introduction of co-determination, and the level and components of executive compensation.

The system's opponents emphasized its weaknesses: the lower rates of return enjoyed by German shareholders relative to their British and American counterparts; the relative illiquidity of shareholder capital; the obstacles to management entrepreneurship; and the unequal treatment of (minority) shareholders. The system's defenders pointed to its strengths: the closer level of shareholder monitoring and the longer shareholder time horizon[1]—as evidenced by high levels of investment in the skills of the workforce, the fruits of which could be seen in the country's productivity gains.

This debate—between the proponents and opponents of the "German system"—intensified during the second half of the 1990s when the German productivity miracle began to lose its luster, with the average annual growth in real GDP per employed person falling below that of the United States for the first time in 30 years (see Fig. 17-3-1). With unemployment rates running at more than 8 percent and with a growing population of retirees, the increase in GDP per head was lagging far behind the rates achieved during the 1960s and 1970s and well below that of the United States (see Fig. 17-3-2). Faced with these ailments, the champions of market-oriented corporate governance prescribed a strong dose of "shareholder value"—to be administered via a (partial) privatization

F I G U R E   17-3-1

Average annual growth in real GDP per employed person (1960–1998)

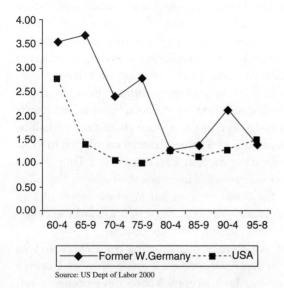

Source: US Dept of Labor 2000

F I G U R E   17-3-2

Average annual growth in real GDP per capita (1960–1998)

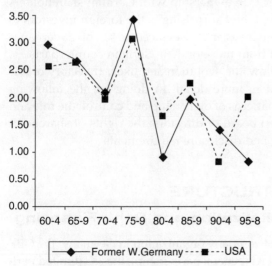

Source: US Dept of Labor 2000

of state-owned enterprises and a reform of the company's legal and regulatory infrastructures.

In accordance with this prescription, the German government took the first move toward a more Anglo-American system of corporate governance when it made a clear commitment to widening share ownership among German nationals and to making the German equity market more attractive to foreign investors. The strength of this commitment was demonstrated in 1996 with the Deutsche Telekom initial public offering—the largest ever in Europe—which raised some $13 billion in share capital.[2] Retail investors were offered the shares at a discount and were encouraged to hold their shares through bank accounts. In an effort to reduce share price volatility, dividend payments were guaranteed and bonus shares were offered to those who retained their holdings for a period of at least three years. Though critics argued that these practices deprived shareholders of one of the more powerful governance tools (the threat of share sales), most commentators saw the Deutsche Telekom privatization as a major step toward the development of a "shareholder culture" among German citizens.

The "governance shift"which took place during the 1990s also was promoted by the growth in foreign (portfolio) ownership of German shares and the rise in cross-border mergers. These developments left many German companies in the hands of Anglo-American shareholders who were unfamiliar with (and unsupportive of) the country's corporate governance practices. This cultural *cum* industrial convergence was well illustrated in the 1998 DaimlerChrysler merger which left 44 percent of the merged company under U.S. ownership with German shareholders accounting for just 37 percent. Not surprisingly, the foreign investors in companies such as DaimlerChrysler AG evinced a set of governance expectations quite different from those of their German counterparts.

In the sections that follow, the evolution and likely trajectory of this governance shift are traced in more detail. In doing so, the following changes are examined: the patterns of ownership and control; the role and composition of the (two-tier) board of directors; the rights of shareholders; and the key accounting and disclosure requirements.

MARKET INFRASTRUCTURE

Stock Market Capitalization and Bank Financing

There are five major forms of company organization in Germany: the GBR (civil law association), the OHG (general partnership), the KG (limited partnership), the GmbH (private limited company), and the AG (public limited company). The only form that can be listed on the stock market is the AG.

The stock market itself is composed of four segments: the Amtlicher Handel (the official market), the Geregelter Mark (regulated market), the Freiverkehr (over-the-counter market), and the Neuer Markt (intended, like the United Kingdom's Alternative Investment Market, for young growth firms). In the late 1990s, the Amtlicher Handel accounted for approximately 90 percent of the capitalization of the entire German stock market with shares traded on the Frankfurt stock exchange and the seven regional exchanges in Berlin, Bremen, Dusseldorf, Hamburg, Hanover, Munich, and Stuttgart (although Frankfurt accounted for 80 percent of the trading volume).[3]

In Germany, the number of listed companies—and the value of their equity in relation to the size of the company—is much smaller than in the United Kingdom or the United States. Although the number of German listed firms grew by 90 percent during the 1990s (in comparison to 18 percent in the U.K. and 26 percent in the U.S.), by the end of the decade, the number of listed German companies amounted to just 1043 in comparison to the 2292 companies listed in the U.K. and the 8110 listed in the U.S.[4] In relation to the country's GDP, the market capitalization of German listed companies stood at 68 percent in 1999 compared to 198 percent in the U.K. and 181 percent in the U.S.[5] Moreover, research by Wenger and Kaserer suggests that when market capitalization is adjusted for crossholdings, the relative capitalization of the German economy falls below 30 percent of GDP.[6] The marginal role of the stock market in the Germany economy is even more apparent when one considers the percentage of total turnover attributed to the country's stock corporations: just 21 percent in 1999.[7]

The relatively small size of the stock market is a reflection of German companies' traditional reliance on retained earnings, internal funds, and bank finance. In 1999, for example, nonfinancial German companies obtained 44 percent of their financing needs from internal funds, 16 percent from classical loan financing from banks, 22 percent from trade and financial loans from nonbanking institutions, and just 10 percent from equity investment.[8]

Corporate Ownership Structures and Voting Control

In comparison to corporate ownership in the United States and the United Kingdom, the ownership of German listed companies is remarkably concentrated. In a study of 171 listed industrial and commercial companies (including the largest German quoted firms), Franks and Mayer revealed that in 1990, 85 percent of these firms had at least one shareholder with a share stake in excess of 25 percent, and 57 percent of these companies had a single shareholder holding in excess of 50 percent.[9] This is in comparison to the U.K., where the corresponding figure was 16 percent.[10] Nevertheless, since the mid-1990s, there has been a slow de-concentration of the German stock market with one study reporting a 10 percent decline in the mean size of direct holdings between 1997 and 2001.[11]

In many cases, the concentration of "direct" ownership rights is accompanied by complex webs of "indirect" pyramidal and cross shareholdings, the effect of which ensures an even greater concentration of corporate control.[12] By way of comparison, La Porta and colleaques show that, in 1995, of the 20 largest and 10 medium-sized firms, 63 percent of German firms had a single shareholder with direct and indirect voting rights in excess of 20 percent. The equivalent figures for the U.K. and the U.S. were 13 and 17 percent, respectively.[13]

Moreover, statistics which measure the concentration of *ownership*, whether in direct or indirect form, are only a partial reflection of the concentration of *voting control rights*. This can be seen in the study by Baums and Fraune which analyzed AGM participation for the 24 firms—out of the top 100 German listed firms—that had more than 50 percent of their shares widely held.[14] In 1992, about 58 percent of outstanding voting rights within these "widely held" firms were present at the AGM, of which banks controlled 13 percent by virtue of their own shareholdings, 10 percent through dependent investment funds, and 61 percent by virtue of the proxy votes they exercised (and over which they were ceded the decision control right).[15] The status of banks as dominant "proxy shareholders" explains why bank representatives can be found on the supervisory boards of most of Germany's listed companies.[16]

The Market for Corporate Control

The (relatively small) number of listed firms and the concentration of ownership restricts the liquidity of the German stock. In 1999, trading in the shares of the top ten companies accounted for 50 percent of the total market turnover.[17] The relative illiquidity of the other companies on the German stock market makes it much harder for investors to apply the "Wall Street Rule"—the instrument of corporate discipline most favored by their Anglo-American cousins.

Hostile takeovers are also a rarity in Germany. Between 1945 and 1994, Germany experienced only four contested takeovers in comparison to the United Kingdom, which had an average of 40 a year.[18] A dramatic exception to this trend was the bid for Mannesmann made by Vodafone Airtouch in November 1999 but this event has yet to be repeated. The influence of the banks serves as a powerful deterrent against hostile takeovers, since (as noted above) they are often able to control the majority of shares voted at shareholders' meetings. An additional deterrent is provided by the German system of co-determination since the employee representatives on a company's supervisory board are likely to support the defensive actions of its management in the event of takeover battles. Takeover deterrents also can be found in German company law which provides, for example, that shareholder representatives on supervisory boards can only be removed before their term expires if the action is supported by a supermajority of 75 percent of the votes cast.

The force of these deterrents is particularly striking when one considers that it was not until 2002, with the introduction of the German Takeover Act, that Germany established a statutory framework for the regulation of takeover bids. This Act defines the role of a company's management and supervisory board in the event of a takeover bid. Acting in the best interests of the company, the board is required to issue statements of its position toward the offer in order to assist shareholders in making an informed decision. The Act also provides that, in order to initiate defensive measures, a 75 percent majority in a shareholder meeting and the approval of the supervisory board must be secured.

Nevertheless, despite the absence of hostile tender offers, there is an active market in large share stakes which often involve a transfer of control. Research by Franks and Meyer indicates that, during the 1990s, the overall turnover of large shareholders was more than 8 percent per year and was commensurate with the combined level of takeover activity and share block sales reported for the United Kingdom. However, although this market in share stakes bears a superficial resemblance to the Anglo-American tender offer market, the bid premia paid to selling shareholders is small compared with that observed in the U.S. and the U.K.[19]

The Role of Institutional Investors

The 1990s saw a sharp rise in the proportion of the German population who were investors in shares and investment funds; and by 1999 these investments accounted for 9.4 percent of total household financial assets (up from 3.8 percent in 1980).[20] Although Germany still has a long way to go before becoming "a nation of shareholders," this trend reflects a number of significant changes in the role of the state in German enterprise and pension provision. The first of these changes relates to the partial privatization of state-owned enterprises such as Deutsche Telekom and Deutsche Post, a major objective of which was to promote a "shareholding culture" among German citizens.[21]

The second change relates to the development of open-ended investment funds[22] (whose share of the stock market rose from 5.5 to 13.6 percent between 1991 and 1999) and, more recently, the growth of private pension funds.[23] The latter are relatively new because they were not formally recognized until the passage of the Third Financial Markets Promotion Act in 1998. Thus, in 1999, the total assets of private pensions in Germany stood at just 3 percent of GDP in comparison to the U.S. and the U.K. where the figures stood at 75 and 85 percent, respectively.[24] However, most commentators expect the value of private pension funds to increase rapidly over the coming years, helped along by the passage (in March 2001) of legislation to promote capital-funded provision for old age.[25] Under the terms of this legislation, the German ratio of wages to net benefits is set to fall from 67 percent in 2015 to 64 percent by 2020. Tax breaks were introduced to encourage employees to make up the difference by investing a percentage of their pay in equities (0.5 percent in 2002 rising to 4 percent of pay in 2008).[26] The significance of this development was nicely captured by *The Wall Street Journal* when it reported that:

> Fund managers are salivating over estimates that more than E260 billion will flow into the new pension funds annually once they are fully implemented. "You really only find good equity cultures when you have pension plans based on equities," said Klaus Martini, chief investment officer for global retail equities with DWS Investment, the mutual-fund arm of Deutsche Bank AG.[27]

Executive Compensation

The differences between the German system of corporate governance and that of the United States and the United Kingdom also are illustrated in the level of executive compensation. In 2000, for example, the average total pay for a chief executive in a large German company was 11 times the wages of an average worker, in contrast to the U.K. and the U.S. where the equivalent multiples were 25 and 531, respectively.[28] Differences in the structure of executive compensation also are noticeable, particularly in respect to the award of share options, a practice which is still a relatively new phenomenon among German corporations. In 1998, however, a change in German stock company law made it easier for German corporations to introduce share option schemes and by the end of 2001, 43 of the DAX 100 companies had introduced such schemes. Interestingly, the coverage of these schemes appears to be considerably wider than those operating in the U.K. In 2002, for example, the Deutsche Telekom share option plan included 350 executives in comparison to the 25 executives included in the BT stock option plan.[29]

LEGAL ENVIRONMENT

The German law on corporate governance has its origins in the nineteenth century. Drawing upon Roman and Teutonic tribal law, the founders of the German state developed a single, unified system of laws. This type of civil legal system has the benefit of certainty when compared to common law countries but is often criticized for being somewhat mechanistic and inflexible. This is particularly true of German company law—which is mandatory and prescriptive in nature. A corporation's article of association (*Satzung*) may only deviate from the provisions of the Stock Corporation Act to the extent that the Act itself permits.

Within this legal framework, German corporate governance is regulated through a combination of company laws, such as the Stock Corporation Act (Aktiengesetz) and the Commercial Code (Handelsgesetzbuch), securities laws, such as the Exchange Act (Börsengesetz) and Securities Trading Act (Wertpapierhandelsgesetz), and stock exchange listing rules, notably those of the Frankfurt Stock Exchange. The salient features of this system are described below.

Two-Tier Boards

Many private limited companies (GmbH) and all public limited companies (AG) are governed by a two-tier board system, with the supervisory board (*Aufsichtsrat*) presiding over the management board (*Vorstand*).[30] The supervisory board consists entirely of nonexecutive directors with the management board composed entirely of executive directors. Legally, the supervisory board and the management board have the same basic duty—to manage the business with the care of a diligent and prudent manager. There is no duty to maximize the value of shares—in fact, §76 AktG entitles the management board to take into account the interests of other "stakeholders." It is also standard practice for some of these "stakeholders" (e.g., employees and creditors) to be represented on the supervisory board.

The management board is responsible for the day-to-day running of the company and the supervisory board is responsible for monitoring the management board. Members of the management board are appointed and have their remuneration fixed by the supervisory board. There is a strict (and expanding) number of issues on which the management board must report to the supervisory board and—under the articles of the company, or by decision of the supervisory board—certain categories of transaction may be subject to the supervisory board's prior approval. However, if the supervisory board withholds consent, the management board may nevertheless act if it can obtain a three-fourths majority of votes at the annual shareholders' meeting.

While the two-tier governance structure benefits from having a clear division of authority between the boards, its critics argue that it suffers from poor information flows; that it is too large to make effective decisions (sometimes having up to 21 members); and that its members lack sufficient independence from shareholders, management, and employees. Despite this, the recent corporate failures in the United States have led some commentators to question whether the two-tier structure might not serve as a model elsewhere.

The issue is finely balanced and the recent Report of the High Level Group of Company Law Experts concludes that "no particular form of board structure (one-tier/two-tier) is intrinsically superior: each may be the most efficient in particular circumstances." The Group recommends that companies should have the right to elect whichever system (one-tier or two-tier) best suits their particular governance needs.

Co-Determination

One of the more controversial aspects of the German governance model does not relate to the two-tier system per se, but rather to the rules on co-determination. The system ensures the representation of employee interests at the supervisory board level, contributing to the unique nature of the German system of corporate governance[31] (see Fig 17-3-3). Under the 1952 Business Organization Act (Betriebsverfassungsgesetz 1952), corporations

F I G U R E   17-3-3

The German System of Co-Determination

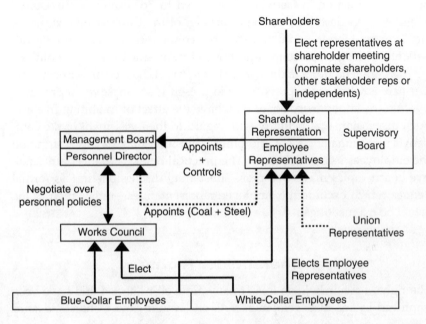

and private limited companies with more than 500 employees are required to establish a two-tier system and to let elected employees participate in the supervisory board. One-third of the members of the supervisory board of these companies consists of employees' representatives. Under the 1976 Co-Determination Statute, corporations and limited liability companies with more than 2000 employees have half of their supervisory board members elected by the shareholders and the other half elected by the employees and the trade unions. Despite their being equal representation in terms of numbers, the chairman, who is elected by the shareholders, has the casting vote in the event of a stalemate. The model is referred to as "quasi-parity co-determination" to reflect the slight superiority that shareholders enjoy.

The economic effects of co-determination on corporate performance have been well detailed in the literature but the empirical research has not generated consistent and convincing evidence about the impact of co-determination on corporate performance. The system is best characterized as being consensual in nature—with the potential for improving the relations between employers and employees. Supporters of the system of co-determination state that it is at least partly responsible for the low rate of industrial action in Germany (compared to, for example, the United Kingdom). As described by the Chairman of the Corporate Governance Government Commission: "practice has come to terms with co-determination, and it is not presently questioned by any side in German politics."

As a behavioral side effect, however, it has been observed by German governance experts that the presence of employee representatives on the supervisory board may have the effect of inhibiting free and open discussion—particularly with regard to the assessment of the company's senior management and other issues that may have a bearing on the employees as a stakeholder. The practical result is that certain sensitive board topics may have more substantial discussions in less formal venues which exclude the employee representatives—rather than in the actual board meetings.

Shareholder Rights

The rights of shareholders in Germany are well protected and have been improved by recent developments. As one would expect, shareholders in German corporations have the right to convene the shareholders' meeting—the supreme body of the company charged with making its fundamental decisions. A meeting can be convened by the supervisory board, the management board, or shareholders, provided their shares together amount to at least 5 percent of the company's issued share capital. In the meeting, most decisions are taken by simple majority vote, but the law or the articles of association can specify supramajority requirements. The principle of "one share, one vote" has recently been established and voting caps have been abolished—votes are determined by the nominal capital of the shares represented. The decision rights of the shareholder meeting are prescribed in detail by domestic law (as supplemented by the articles of the company) and have been expanded by recent reforms.

Nevertheless, a frequent criticism of the German system of corporate governance is that banks have control of the votes in German corporations far in excess of their direct holdings (for the reasons outlined earlier). In response to this criticism, it should be noted that were a beneficial shareholder to feel prejudiced by the strategy pursued by his or her bank, one could always revoke the proxy and vote independently (or move one's shares to another bank).[32]

The German Act on Corporate Control and Transparency (KonTraG), introduced in 1998, has also introduced the possibility of initiating a shareholders' suit against board members for breach of their statutory duties and responsibilities. The threshold for initiating a shareholder action was 5 percent or Euro 500,000 of the common share capital of the company. Despite this recent development, there is still no right of action by a governmental agency or regulatory body (unlike the United States where the SEC has wide-ranging powers of investigation); and shareholder class action suits are not possible in Germany.

Shareholder rights were further strengthened in 2003 when the Federal Minister of Justice and the Federal Minister of Finance jointly announced a catalog of measures which focus on improving investor protection and corporate integrity. The measures are designed to reinforce a culture of personal responsibility among management and supervisory board members. Under the proposals, which are to take effect from January 2005, small shareholders will be able to launch joint-action civil cases against individual executives and supervisory board members, in cases where the latter are suspected of spreading misleading information. In addition, the share ownership threshold above which shareholders can file for damages is to be lowered from 10 percent of the company's share capital to 1 percent. [33]

One of the more important (and distinctive) rights enjoyed by shareholders in a German corporation is the legal action to rescind resolutions passed in a shareholders' general assembly. Shareholders can file a court suit if a resolution is passed at a shareholders' meeting that is in violation of law or passed by majority shareholders who intend to harm the minority shareholder, thereby violating their fiduciary duties or the principle of equal treatment of all shareholders. An example would be a majority shareholder seeking to grant themselves an advantage that contradicts the interests of the company. Between 1980 and 1998, there were 408 legal actions brought to rescind such resolutions; half of which were instituted by shareholder groups of not more that 15 persons. Practioners acknowledge, however, that these recission rights are increasingly (ab)used by shareholder-raiders (*räuberische Aktionäre*) who use them to threaten companies with potentially long-lasting court procedures which can effectively halt important board decisions.

REGULATORY ENVIRONMENT

The German corporate governance framework is primarily provided through mandatory law. Unlike the United States, where the SEC both sets and actively enforces certain governance-related standards, in Germany the main regulatory body is the Landgericht, which arbitrates disputes but does not engage in proactive supervision of the capital market. Other regulatory bodies include the Federal Financial Supervisory Authority (BAFin), which is responsible for the supervision of securities, and the Supervisory Authorities of each of the stock exchanges, which are responsible for the enforcement of their respective listing rules.

Nevertheless, although much of the regulation of Germany's corporate governance is to be found in the rules-based provisions of the country's civil and commercial codes, recent developments have seen a shift toward a more principles-based approach.

German Act on Corporate Control and Transparency[34]

The shift toward a principles-based approach to regulation was already in evidence by the late 1990s with the introduction of the KonTraG, the provisions of which reflected the government's belief that the adoption of further mandatory provisions in company law should "be avoided as far as possible" and that "instead of strict legal directives, it is preferable to leave companies to organize themselves and for control to be provided by the existing supervisory bodies and the markets."[35]

This principles-based approach to governance regulation is reflected in each of the governance organs to which the Act applies. With respect to the supervisory board, for example, the KonTraG respects the organizational autonomy of the supervisory board, while encouraging the members to take responsibility for their own actions. The Act empowers the supervisory board to form committees, to meet more frequently and to take greater responsibility for the audit process.[36]

The provisions of the KonTraG which relate to the management board display the same concern with broad principles rather than narrow directions and the obligations they impose relate primarily to the systems of risk management and the reporting obligations (of the management board to the supervisory board). Under the KonTraG, the board is obliged to ensure the maintenance of adequate systems of risk management and internal monitoring. The KonTraG also explicitly provides that the management board must report to the supervisory board on matters of finance, investment, and personnel planning.

Outside of the main organs of the company, KonTraG also strengthens the rights of the company's external monitors, the shareholders, and the auditor. Banks are required to nominate a member of management who will ensure that the exercise of the banks' proxy voting rights will be more strongly oriented to the interests of the shareholder. Banks also must advise shareholders of alternative ways in which they can cast their vote. Two historic problems—the use of plural voting rights and voting caps— are no longer permitted. Additionally, the right of shareholders to bring an action for breach of duty against directors is made easier.

Corporate Governance Code [37]

By the end of the 1990s, the German government had made clear its intention that the regulation of corporate governance should "keep pace with the expectations of international financial markets."[38] But the problem it continued to face, despite the introduction of the KonTraG, was that many investors were not fully aware of the strength and advantages of this regulation because the key provisions were scattered throughout the stock corporation law, the securities trading law, the commercial code, and the co-determination law.

In 2000, the German Chancellor responded to this problem with the establishment of the Corporate Governance Government Commission under the guidance of Prof. Theodor Baums. A year later, the Commission presented its report, containing over 150 recommendations, on the modernization of German company law.[39] The principal aims of the recommendations were to enhance transparency and improve supervision of companies, enhance the efficiency of the company's main organs, both internal and external, de-regulate corporate law to make tapping of the equity markets more obtainable, and reconcile corporate accounting standards to international standards.

Acting on the recommendations of the Commission, the Federal Minister of Justice then appointed a government commission, chaired by Dr. Cromme, charged with developing a German Corporate Governance Code (DCGK) which was published in 2002. As described by its authors, the Code is intended to:

> ...Summarize major statutory corporate governance rules and to supplement them with standards of good corporate governance that businesses can fulfill in practice. The code brings together both types of provision in a concise, concrete and understandable way.[40]

Acceptance of the committee's recommendations was enhanced by the fact that a wide range of governance interests were represented, due to its diverse membership. In part a "communication document," the Code was designed to explain the key features of the German system of corporate governance in a way that makes it understandable to the international community. It also was designed to replace the proliferation of private initiatives in the area of corporate governance.

The DCGK establishes three categories of corporate governance principles. It reiterates the existing mandatory rules of German law, to which all companies must adhere. The Code then sets down a number of desirable practices that are divided into the form of recommendations (denoted by the word *shall*) and suggestions (denoted by the words *should* or *may*). In the words of Dr. Cromme, "the code provides capital market participants with a catalogue for evaluating good corporate governance which will allow especially foreign investors to obtain a clear picture of the corporate governance practiced by German corporations."

The Code deals with the key governance aspects of the corporation, laying down detailed requirements for shareholder meetings, the relationship between the management and supervisory board, the composition, tasks, and remuneration of both boards, transparency and accountability, and audit. Although detailed, the Code represents a departure from the heavily formalized, prescriptive means of regulation in Germany, preferring to rely on voluntary compliance. Each year the company must make a statement about its compliance with the recommendations of the Code. The auditors are required to verify the company's statement of compliance. It had been envisaged that the Code would adopt a "comply or explain" mechanism but the Transparency and Publicity Act[41] (TransPuG) only requires each listed AG to disclose whether it has complied with the Code during the previous year and whether it intends to comply with the Code in the current year. The company is not obliged to disclose its reasons for noncompliance.

INFORMATIONAL INFRASTRUCTURE

Audit Requirements

As a response to early corporate failures, the profession of "auditor" (*Wirtschaftsprüfer*) was given a statutory basis in 1931. Historically, the role of German auditors was to report to the supervisory board rather than shareholders.[42] The management board would forward the auditors' report to the supervisory board together with its drafts of the annual financial statements and annual report. The supervisory board was then responsible for reviewing these materials and submitting a written report on its examination to the annual shareholder meeting. The resolutions of the management board and supervisory board, in respect of the approval of the annual financial statements, also would be contained in the report of the supervisory board. Nevertheless, although the auditors did not report directly to the shareholder body, formal responsibility for the auditors' appointment rested with the shareholders in general meeting.

These procedures still characterize the relationship between the auditors, the supervisory board, and the shareholders but recent reforms have sought to secure the "independence" of the auditors, not just from the management board but also from the supervisory board. For example, the 1998 KonTraG empowers companies to form an audit committee,[43] requires the auditor to attend the supervisory board's closing meeting, and introduces new guidelines on the impact of nonaudit services and lengthy tenure on the independence of external auditors.[44] The TransPuG also has enhanced the role of auditors by expanding the content of the audit report and requiring that an independent auditor certify the company's statement of compliance with the DCGK.

Accounting and Reporting Standards

German companies are required to produce consolidated financial statements (*Konzernabschlüsse*) when the shareholders of the parent company or one of its subsidiaries are listed on a securities exchange.[45] Companies have the choice of preparing their financial statements in accordance with German accounting principles[46] or internationally recognized accounting principles (IAS or U.S. GAAP). All listed companies with a registered office in the European Union will have to prepare their consolidated financial statements in accordance with IAS from 2005.[47]

The pressure to introduce international accounting standards also was driven by the experiences of the late 1980s and early 1990s—when Germany witnessed the collapse of several large companies owing to severe mismanagement, speculation in the derivatives markets, manipulations of financial accounts, and other forms of criminal misbehavior. These cases led to serious concerns about the adequacy of the governance system of German firms in early 1998. The German legislator passed a bill which amended both the Corporation Act (*Aktiengesetz*) and the Commercial Act (*Handelsgesetzbuch*, HGB). The bill also established the German Accounting Standards Committee which aims at "introducing and financing standardization in accordance with the Anglo-American and international model."

The regularity with which German companies has been required to report to their investors also has increased as a result of recent reforms. For example, under the Exchange Act (*Börsengesetz*), listed companies are required to prepare at least one interim report each fiscal year[48] and companies that wish to be included in a market index of the Frankfurt Stock Exchange are required to report quarterly.[49] This has lead to some controversy, not least on the part of Porsche, who was excluded from Deutsche Borse's midcap MDAX index for refusing to report quarterly for fear that such regular reporting would promote short-termist investor behavior.[50]

Disclosure Standards

The 1990s saw a marked improvement in the disclosure practices of German corporations. These practices had previously been viewed as below the standards adopted by companies in the United Kingdom and the United States; but changes to both mandatory standards and voluntary norms have helped to improve the level of German disclosure on a global basis of comparison.

The reforms which have encouraged greater transparency among German companies include the 1998 KonTraG which provided for the use of electronic means of communication from both the company to shareholders (e.g., webcasting of the AGM) and from shareholders to the company (e.g., electronic proxy voting). The Act also provided that the *Bundesanzeiger* (the Official Gazette) be accessible online, making it more accessible to foreign shareholders.

German corporate transparency also reflects the impact of the Fourth Financial Markets Promotion Act 2002, much of which concerns the standard of company disclosures. Among its other provisions, the Act provides shareholders with the right to bring compensation claims in the case of unsatisfactory disclosures that influence the share price; and it also introduces strict disclosure obligations with regard to dealings by directors in the shares of the company.

NOTES

1. McCahery et al., 2002: 26-29.
2. Gordon, 1999.

3. Wojcik, 2001: 9.

4. Van der Elst, 2000: 6.

5. Jurgens & Rupp, 2002: 10. Note that, from the mid-1980s to the mid-1990s, the smaller German companies actually reduced their equity capitalization.

6. Wenger and Kaserer, 1997, cited in Boehmer, 1999:2.

7. As reported in Jurgens and Rupp (2002), sole proprietorships, general commercial partnerships, limited commercial partnerships, and limited liability companies, respectively accounted for 13, 6, 23, and 33 percent of total German turnover.

8. Jurgens and Rupp, 2002: 8.

9. Franks and Mayer, 2000.

10. Edwards, 1999: 4.

11. In a study of all domestic companies listed on the Amtlicher Handel (official market), Wojick (2001) reports a decline in the mean size of direct holdings of approximately from 32 percent in 1997 to 29 percent in 2001.

12. Franks and Meyer (2000) cite an example from the late 1990s when Robert Bosch held a 25 percent "blocking" minority stake in Stern Automobil, a company which itself held a 25 percent blocking stake in Mercedes which, in turn, held a 25 percent stake in Daimler Benz. As a consequence, Bosch had only a 1.56 percent cash flow right in Daimler Benz, the structure of this pyramid granted it effective voting control rights over 25 percent of the latter's equity.

13. La Porta et al. (1999) cited in Van der Elst, 2000: 14.

14. Baums and Fraune (1995) cited in Boehmer (1999: 5). The study by Baums and Fraune also suggests that the resulting voting power exercised by the banks was typically used to support management with legally mandated items on the AGM agenda approved with an average of 99.8 percent of attending votes.

15. Under the German system of proxy voting (Depotstimmrecht), private shareholders authorize the banks that hold their shares in custody to represent their interests at company AGMs. Banks are responsible for distributing the company's materials to the holders of bearer shares and are able to request the permission of the client to vote his or her shares for a period of 15 months.

16. Jurgens and Rupp, 2002: 6.

17. Wojcik 2002: 4.

18. Hutton, 1995: 156.

19. The evidence compiled by Franks and Meyer (2000) indicates that, even in the largest transactions, bid premia paid to selling shareholders are around half those in the United States and United Kingdom, while other shareholders incur significant discrimination and "obtain virtually a zero abnormal return." The authors ascribe the lower bid premia enjoyed by German shareholders to the (historical) absence of an equal price rule; in contrast to the United Kingdom, where takeover rules require that, once 30 percent of the shares in a target firm have been acquired, other shareholders receive at least an equal if not higher price for their shares.

20. Jurgens and Rupp, 2002: 30.

21. Gordon, 1998.

22. Gunter Deutsch and Stichnoth (2002: 12) suggest that, in addition to the absolute growth in the assets managed by German institutional investors, there also has been a major shift in the structure of their portfolios with equity investments accounting for 28 percent of total assets under management compared to just 10 percent in 1992.

23. Notwithstanding the direct appeal to retail investors of the Deutsche Telekom and Deutsche Post share offers, the percentage of German shares held directly by private households fell from 22.4 percent in 1991 to 17.5 percent in 1999. In other words, much of the growth in the share of household assets invested in the stock market is the result of investments in unit and pension funds rather than direct ownership of shares.

24. OECD, www.oecd.org/pdf/M00035000/M00035887.pdf, 2001.

25. During the 1990s, the arguments in favor of private pension funding made frequent reference to the future growth in the country's dependency ratio. A good example of this argument can be found in the work of Borsch-Supan and Winter (1999: 7), which suggests that the proportion of German pensioners will increase from 21 percent in 1995 to 36 percent in 2035, "the highest share among the industrialised countries." Borsch-Supan and Winter also predict that the German old-age dependency ratio will more than double from 21.7 percent in 1990 to 49.2 percent in 2030. But as Cohen (2002: 343) points out, this argument blithely assumes that the burden of dependency is not alleviated by increasing the proportion of those aged between 20 and 65 actually in work and/or by increasing the age of retirement.

26. Cohen, 2002: 261.

27. Rhoads, 2001.

28. Bogler, 2002.

29. Bogler, 2002 and Conyon and Schwalbach, 2000.

30. Hopt, 1997.

31. du Plessis, 1998.

32. Although, under law, investors must inform the company when they acquire at least 5 percent of share capital, this can be easily evaded through private holding companies in which no party owns a majority of stock. Indeed, the fact that share ownership among households is low, would suggest that there are relatively large blockholders who are unidentifiable to both the public and the corporation. This suggests that a significant proportion of the votes cast by the banks are ultimately controlled by large investors who ought to be more than capable of taking the steps required to exercise a responsible vote.

33. Williamson, 2003.

34. Gesetz zur Kontrolle und Transparenz im Unternehmensbereich (KonTraG) v. 30.4.1998, BGBl. I S. 786.

35. As described by Ministerial Counsellor Dr. Ulrich Seibert, Federal Ministry of Justice, Bonn.

36. There was concern voiced about the widening of the supervisory board role as there were fears that it might not be appropriate for the employee representative on the board to view sensitive company materials. However, the system of co-determination is so entrenched in German corporate practices that such fears have been allayed through past experience.

37. English version available at www.corporate-governance-code.de.

38. Seibert, ibid.

39. German Government Panel on Corporate Governance: Summary of Recommendations (English Translation, November 2001), available at http://papers.ssrn.com/paper.taf? abstract_id=290583 (SSRN).

40. Remarks by Dr. Gerhard Cromme, Chairman of the Government Commission German Corporate Governance Code on the publication of the draft German Corporate Governance Code, December 18, 2001 in Düsseldorf.

41. "Gesetz zur weiteren Reform des Aktien- und Bilanzrechts, zu Transparenz und Publizität (TransPuG) v. 19.7.2002, BGB1. I S. 2681.

42. Gietzmann & Quick, 1998.

43. A recommendation in the DCGK.

44. In addition to the reforms which aimed at securing the independence of the company's auditors, the KonTraG also sought to improve the flow of information that the supervisory board enjoys. It provides, for example, that the management board must deliver reports in an accurate and timely manner (the use of electronic communication is permitted), that each supervisory board member has the right to request additional reports, and that reports must reflect any changes in business policy and strategy—the "follow-up" requirement. In order to promote the free flow of information to all members of the supervisory board there are also increased penalties for a board member's breach of confidentiality.

45. Pursuant to the Seventh EC Company Law Directive of June 13, 1983 (83/349/EEC), p. 1, O.J. July 18, 1983 (L 193).

46. See §§ 290-315 Handelsgesetzbuch.

47. European Council Regulation (2002/1606/EC), p. 1, O.J. September 11, 2002 (L 243).

48. § 39 Exchange Act, as amended by the Fourth Financial Market Promotion Act.

49. The Fourth Financial Markets Promotion Act will also allow the securities exchanges to require a mandatory review of interim reports by independent auditors.

50. Wassener, 2001.

REFERENCES

Baums, T., and C. Fraune. "Institutionelle Anleger und Publikumsgesellschaft: Eine Empirische Untersuchung" *Die Aktiengesellschaft* 40, 1995.

Boehmer, E. "Corporate Governance in Germany: Institutional Background and Empirical Results," Humboldt University, March 24, 1999.

Bogler, D. "Greed as a Motivator: Share Option Schemes Are Helping to Expose German Executives to Closer Scrutiny," *Financial Times*, June 27, 2002.

Borsch-Supan, A., and J. Winter. "Pension Reform, Savings Behavior and Corporate Governance," Sonderforschungsbereich 504, Universitat Mannheim, April 1999.

Bratton, W. W., and J A. McCahery. "Comparative Corporate Governance and Barriers to Global Cross Reference," 2002, in *Corporate Governance Regimes and Diversity*, edited by Joseph A. McCahery, Piet Moerland, Theo Raaijmakers, and Luc Renneboog, Oxford University Press.

Cohen, R. "Banking on Death or Investing in Life: The History and Future of Pensions," Verso, 2002.

Conyon, M. J., and J. Schwalbach. "Executive Compensation: Evidence from the United Kingdom and Germany," *Long Range Planning—International Journal of Strategic Management* 33(4), 2000.

du Plessis, J., "Some Thoughts on the German System of Supervisory Codetermination by Employees," in *Festschrift für Bernard Großfeld*, edited by Ulrich Hubner, and Werner F. Ebke. Verlag und Wirtschaft, GmbH, 1998.

Edwards, J. S.S. "Ownership Concentration and Share Valuation: Evidence from Germany," University of Cambridge, July 15, 1999.

Franks, J., and C. Mayer. "Ownership and Control of German Corporations," London Business School, March 13, 2000.

Gietzmann, M.B., and R. Quick. "Capping Auditor Liability: The German Experience," *Accounting, Organizations and Society*, 1998.

Gordon, J. N. "Deutsche Telekom, German Corporate Governance, and the Transition Costs of Capitalism," *Columbia Business Law Review* 185, 1998.

Gordon, J. N. "Pathways to Corporate Convergence? Two Steps on the Road to Shareholder Capitalism in Germany: Deutsche Telekom and Daimler Chrysler," *Columbia Journal of European Law* 219 (5), 1999.

Gunter Deutsch, K., and H. Stichnoth, "Corporate Governance in Germany— Perspectives from Economics and Finance," *Deutsche Bank Research Notes in Economics & Statistics* 02-3, 2002.

Hopt, K., "The German Two-Tier Boar (Aufsichtsrat), a German View on Corporate Governance," (1997), in *Comparative Corporate Governance: Essays and Materials*, edited by K. Hopt, and E. Wymeersch de Gruyter.

Hutton, W. "The State We're In," Jonathan Cape, 1995.

Jurgens, U., and J. Rupp. "The German System of Corporate Governance: Characteristics and Changes," Wissenschaftszentrum Berlin fur Sozialforschung gGmbH (WZB), May 2002.

La Porta, R., F. Lopez-de-Silanes, and A. Schleifer. "Corporate Ownership Around the World," *Journal of Finance*, 1999.

McCahery, J. A., and L. Renneboog. "Introduction," *Corporate Governance Regimes and Diversity*, edited by Joseph A. McCahery, Piet Moerland, Theo Raaijmakers, and Lou Renneboog, Oxford University Press, 2002.

Rhoads, C. "Germany Is Set to Reform Pension System to Include Privately Funded Component," *Wall Street Journal*, May 10, 2001.

U.S. Department of Labor, "Comparative Real Gross Domestic Product Per Capita and Per Employed Person: Fourteen Countries 1960-1998," Bureau of Labor Statistics, Office of Productivity and Technology, www.stats. bls.gov/flshome.htm, March 30, 2000.

Van der Elst, C. "The Equity Markets, Ownership Structures and Control: Towards an International Harmonization?," Financial Law Institute, September 2000.

Wassener, B. "Porsche Faces Ejection by Deutsche Borse," *Financial Times*, August 7, 2001.

Wenger, E., and C. Kaserer, "German Banks and Corporate Governance: A Critical View," University of Wurzburg, 1997.

Williamson, H. "German Plan to Tighten Company Law," *Financial Times*, February 26, 2003.

Wojcik, D. "Change in the German Model of Corporate Governance: Evidence from Blockholdings 1997–2001," School of Geography and the Environment, University of Oxford, December 2001.

Japan

Hiroko Kiguchi

INTRODUCTION

The mandate for improving corporate governance practices has assumed new urgency in Japan in light of the country's ongoing economic problems over the last decade. Japan's deep-seated structural problems and inability to engineer a sustainable recovery in the 1990s—the so-called "lost decade"—have prompted a thorough inspection of the country's business practices and regulatory environment. The potential implications of this reexamination have significant consequences for transparency, disclosure, and corporate governance.

Japan's economic model was once widely admired as a central pillar of the nation's remarkable rebuilding during the postwar period. Under this model, corporate structures were consensual in nature and placed a strong emphasis on stability, the autonomy of management, and long-term relationships with suppliers, customers, and employees. Indeed, the needs of employees were typically regarded as having priority over those of a company's external shareholders. Most corporate groups were supported by a "main bank," which served as the primary source of capital for the family of businesses in which they engaged.

The heyday of this "convoy capitalism" ended abruptly with the collapse of the bubble economy between 1989 and 1990, which set into motion powerful forces that have the potential to remodel Japan's corporate landscape. Financial deregulation has been initiated and the presence of foreign companies—though still small by western standards—in what was traditionally a closed system has increased visibly in recent years. This shift in economic fortune, changing ownership structures, and the growing role of foreign investors have combined to place traditional Japanese governance practices under greater scrutiny, particularly in comparison with very different approaches to corporate governance found in other developed financial markets.

MARKET INFRASTRUCTURE

Types of Business Organization

The most common form of business organization in Japan is the *kabushiki kaisha*, which is equivalent to a public limited company in the United Kingdom. In this organization, the shareholders are liable only up to a certain amount of prescribed nominal capital. In this report, the word *company* refers to kabushiki kaisha.

Corporate Ownership Structure

Corporates in Japan have traditionally clustered into industrial group-ings, or *keiretsu*, developing long-standing and stable closed relationships among member companies. In each group, not only the core company or its main bank, but also member companies own equity in the other firms belonging to the keiretsu. This cross-shareholding relationship has shaped the development of corporate governance in Japan.

In recent years, companies have been unwinding their cross-share-holdings, a process accelerated by the adoption of market-to-market accounting, combined with the effects of a depressed stock market. Cumulative shareholdings of banks fell to 8.7 percent of the total market capitalization of Japan's five exchanges as of March 31, 2002, compared with a level of roughly 15 percent until the mid-1990s. In contrast, individ-ual investors' shareholdings have grown to 19.7 percent, thereby becoming a more important aggregate shareholder than the banking sector. Foreign ownership was 18.3 percent of total market capitalization as of March 31, 2002, and has shown growth in recent years. While the domestic corporate sector remains the leading source of share ownership, showing the contin-uing importance of cross-shareholdings in Japan, the growth of individual and foreign ownership has resulted in the proportion of domestic corporate ownership dropping to 21.8 percent at March 2002 from over 25 percent prior to fiscal 1999. These changes have had an important influence on the corporate governance debate in Japan.

Relationships with Banks

Banks have served as the main intermediaries for issuing debt, which is the major source of financing for corporations, and the keiretsu organizational structure has resulted in close and somewhat secretive relationships between the two. Main banks typically have had access to detailed financial information and knowledge about cross-shareholding patterns, even when such information was not in the public domain. The main bank has played an important supporting role, particularly when a group company has encountered financial difficulties.

While companies have benefited from the support of their main banks, the close relationships between the two have resulted in less rigorous investment scrutiny. Main banks have been less prone to question risky projects and are more likely to accept problems associated with moral hazard.

Corporate Control

In Japan, a common feature of companies' articles of incorporation is the absence of specific takeover provisions that could thwart an otherwise legitimate and shareholder value-enhancing bid. Nevertheless, the market for corporate control in Japan remains largely untested and this, coupled with the fact that the total number of outstanding shares is small relative to the total number of authorized shares, could theoretically be used as a means to delay or defer a legitimate bid, particularly as the board has the right to issue new shares without shareholder approval.

Macroeconomic Conditions

During the growth years of the 1980s, corporate governance was not an issue, as the strong economy and rising stock prices led to increasing profits for companies and shareholders alike. However, Japan's corporate governance system has come under renewed scrutiny following the prolonged downturn in the 1990s. Traditional organizational structures have been criticized for having created a bias toward overinvestment with little focus on returns on equity. Critics charge that the financial and ownership interrelationships between the main banks and member companies have failed to provide appropriate oversight, and have led to the approval of projects with very low chances of success.

Over the past 10 years, as corporates have begun to rely increasingly on capital markets to meet their funding needs and their dependence on bank financing has declined, the banks' corporate governance role has shrunk in prominence. More importantly, banks themselves have become very reluctant to extend credit to client companies in response to a mushrooming of bad assets in their portfolios. Banks have been dumping non-performing shares in an attempt to rebuild their eroded capital bases. The prolonged decline in equity and land prices also has applied similar pressure to companies, causing a dilution of the cross-shareholding arrangements between companies.

To survive in the difficult business environment, Japanese companies are increasingly resorting to practices that were once anathema in the old corporate culture. For example, executive salaries are being linked to company performance through the use of stock options, and new guidelines for greater disclosure are being established.

Institutional Investors

In terms of corporate governance, domestic institutional investors have not played a visible role traditionally, although this trend has shown some signs of reversal recently. For example, Nippon Life Insurance Co. (Nissay), Japan's largest life insurance company, with total assets of over ¥45 trillion (U.S. $375 billion), has reportedly been focusing more on corporate governance among large companies in which it is a major shareholder, aiming at higher returns on its investments.

There also has been a change in the attitude of public pension funds. The Association of Japanese Corporate Pension Funds (*Kosei Nenkin Kikin Rengokai*; KNKR) published guidelines designed to improve transparency and long-term shareholder value at trust banks and investment advisory companies, and is actively advising its dealing institutions to take actions to achieve maximum value from shareholdings. Other pension funds, however, remain less actively engaged in promoting higher governance standards.

One of the most noteworthy trends is that foreign institutional shareholders are increasingly establishing themselves as important players in the Japanese marketplace. They have been involved at companies' shareholder meetings and their actions have been visible in the marketplace, representing a more critical shareholding base than the typically quiet Japanese shareholder.

LEGAL ENVIRONMENT
Principal Legal Provisions

The accounting system has been influenced by three separate, and somewhat disparate, codes of law: the Commercial Code, the Securities and

Exchange Law (SEL), and the Corporation Tax Law. The roots of the Japanese legal system can be traced back to German origins.

The Commercial Code, administered by the Ministry of Justice (MOJ), governs matters related to corporate governance, information disclosure, and capital procurement. It is largely charged with ensuring that all parties in a contract are protected. The Code requires that all companies issue a balance sheet, income statement, business report, statement explaining how profits are distributed, supplementary information pertaining to reserve accounts, and transactions with directors and shareholders. However, requirements under the Code are not always stringent. Companies are allowed latitude in choosing from a number of acceptable methods. In addition, the Code requires an independent professional audit only for companies that exceed a defined threshold of liabilities or market capitalization.

A revision of the Commercial Code was completed in May 2002 and will take effect from April 2003, following several years of review aimed at separating everyday operating functions from management supervision. The major revisions included giving firms options to diminish the role of the corporate auditor on condition that:

♦ A company has more than two nonemployed directors;

♦ Over half the members of committees for board nomination, audit, and remuneration are nonemployed directors; and

♦ There exists a clear separation of directors and business operating managers.

The MOJ also administers the SEL, which stipulates the body of regulation to be followed by listed companies. The SEL provides more specific guidelines than the Commercial Code, and many of its requirements are patterned after the U.S. securities law. Every listed company is also required to produce audited registration documents and to submit accounting reports—a balance sheet, income statement, cash flow statement, profit distribution statement, and other supplementary information—to the Ministry of Finance (MOF) and the relevant stock-exchange authorities twice per year. Documents produced to comply with the SEL need to be audited by a registered independent CPA. The SEL also requires companies within its jurisdiction to abide by the rules articulated in the Financial Accounting Standards for Business Enterprises issued by the Business Accounting Deliberation Council (BADC), an advisory body to the Minister of Finance.

Unlike the situation in western countries, a third body of statutes, the Corporation Tax Law, also has a critical impact on corporate procedures in Japan, leading to accounting behavior that prioritizes tax minimization.

Shareholder Rights

The Commercial Code provides shareholders with the right to appoint and dismiss board members at annual general meetings (AGMs), to seek reports from management and auditors, and to vote on changes in corporate structure. Each shareholder has a single vote per share. Still relatively concentrated ownership structures in Japan have not made it possible for small shareholders as a group to have a large impact on management.

The Commercial Code does not guarantee the preemptive rights of shareholders. A board of directors has the authority to decide whether the company gives such rights to shareholders.

REGULATORY ENVIRONMENT

The approach to regulation in Japan differs from that in the United States and United Kingdom, but finds parallels in other code-based European countries (such as France and Germany). The Commercial Code, which applies to all companies, was formulated by the Civil Affairs Bureau of the MOJ, which continues to bear responsibility for any revisions.

General Protocol

A company can issue several types of shares, with varying benefit structures (associated with profits, interest, surplus assets, and retirement options). Every class of shares, however, holds the bearer liable up to the amount of the share value only. Most traded shares are ordinary shares, with each share entitling its bearer to a single vote.

Each company is required to hold an AGM at least once a year. All resolutions tabled at the meeting must be approved by a simple majority of the attending audience, representing more than 50 percent of the total voting rights. Certain critical decisions, such as the floating of new shares and merger and acquisition plans, must be approved by at least a two-thirds majority.

Under the Commercial Code, corporate governance in Japan has developed under a two-tier structure consisting of the board of directors and the board of auditors. The function and authority of corporate auditors have not been strictly defined, leaving room for operational discretion at each company.

Board Structure

Unlike its U.S. counterpart, a board of directors in Japan is typically responsible for making important strategic and management decisions that are implemented by the senior executives of the company.

On average, a board has 15 members (as of June 2002), down 25 percent from three years ago, the majority of whom are company employees. As a result, board members are intimately aware of the inner workings of the company. The board officially elects the company president, but this election process is largely symbolic. In most cases, the board simply accepts the nomination presented by the outgoing president. In each company, the president, as well as three or four senior-level directors, represent the company.

Board membership is frequently offered as a reward to long-serving, loyal employees. This system has two noteworthy implications: Board size can tend to expand, and the balance of power can be tilted in favor of senior management as opposed to board directors. Boards have traditionally been quiescent and have surrendered most of their authority to company presidents on a range of matters, including hiring and firing top executives, executive pay and severance packages, as well as other management decisions. Even though the board of directors theoretically has the ultimate authority to oversee the activities of a company on behalf of shareholders, in practice, boards in Japan have conventionally not been equipped with adequate governance power or capabilities to carry out this role satisfactorily.

Increasingly, the board's supervisory functions are being separated from the day-to-day operating functions of the company, aimed at ensuring the board takes charge of the former and that executive management is responsible for the latter. This separation of roles would ensure that a single person does not hold the chairmanship of both the board of directors and the executive board, other than in exceptional circumstances.

Role of Corporate Auditors

The corporate auditor is a statutory office required by Japan's Commercial Code. Corporate auditors are elected by shareholders at the shareholders' meeting and are charged with auditing the business operations of directors. However, as with directors, a corporate auditor is usually internally nominated by the president or top management and is often a long-time employee of the company. Large companies with equity of over ¥500 million are required to have at least one outside auditor for every three corporate auditors.

The range of auditors' authority is not clearly defined in the Commercial Code. As a result, each company has the discretion to conduct a corporate audit for purposes of compliance or the appropriateness of the business operations of its directors. In cases where a director acts outside the scope of the purpose of the company's business, or violates laws or the articles of incorporation, an auditor can request the director to cease these activities. However, an auditor does not have the authority to dismiss directors.

In some companies, the board of auditors performs functions similar to the audit committees of the board of directors in western companies. However, auditors cannot be defined as being independent considering the practice of nomination. Outside auditors are considered as being independent only if such a person has not held a management position in the company in the past five years.

Role of Outside Directors

There is currently no mandatory legislation requiring outside directors to be represented on company boards. However, under the revised Commercial Code (taking from April 2003), companies are required to have at least one outside director. Moreover, a company can replace its corporate auditor with three committees (nomination, audit, and remuneration) of which over half of the members are required to be independent directors under the revised Code. However, so far, only a few Japanese companies have signaled their intention to adopt these practices. As a result, the role of independent directors is likely to remain limited at most Japanese companies.

Shareholder Meetings

Shareholder meetings are largely clustered around peak periods, although some flexibility has been introduced in recent years, driven by companies' efforts to improve attendance. Leading companies are also making greater efforts to circulate AGM agendas in advance of meetings to generate increased awareness of company strategies among shareholders and encourage informed voting.

Share Registration and Voting Procedures

A person possessing share certificates is presumed to be the legitimate bearer and share registration is processed through a transfer agent, who enters the shareholder's details in a register. The shareholders' register is kept at the headquarters of the company or the transfer agent's office, and should be disclosed at the request of shareholders. A company addresses any peremptory and other notices to shareholders at the permanent residence entered in the register. Proxy voting and voting by mail are commonly followed procedures, with no material differentiation between domestic and foreign shareholders. It is noteworthy that around 50 companies accepted shareholders' votes via the Internet at their AGMs in June 2002.

Although there has been very little development of independent shareholder research and proxy voting associations, a change was observed at Sony Corp.'s shareholders' meeting in 2002, at which 27 percent of votes were in favor of disclosing the remuneration of each director.

Regulatory Bodies and Prominent Market Institutions

The regulatory function is fragmented and there is some tendency toward territoriality among diverse state agencies. The most notable overlap is between the MOF and the Ministry of Economy, Trade and Industry (METI), which often clash over priorities. At the same time, there are domains where regulatory responsibility is not well defined.

Prior to the eruption of a huge stock market scandal in 1992, the authority to monitor markets resided with the Securities Bureau of the MOF. Following the scandal, the Securities Exchange Surveillance Committee (SESC) was established to monitor compliance with securities law. The SESC's officers are appointed by the MOF and approved by parliament (the Diet). Since 1998, the role of supervising financial-market activity has been delegated to the newly created Financial Services Agency.

The Federation of Economic Organizations (*Keidanren*) also exercises influence with regard to the development of corporate governance, but is generally resistant to the so-called Anglo-American style of management characterized by a board consisting of external directors.

In recent years, the Tokyo Stock Exchange also has taken a more vocal role, particularly in corporate governance–related matters. Even though the exchange's listing rules do not yet explicitly require companies to comply with a specific set of corporate governance standards, certain information guidelines already have been implemented.

Accountability

The concept of board accountability has conventionally had a different focus in Japan. The emphasis on creating shareholder value is a relatively recent development. Boards are accountable for corporate performance, and it is not uncommon for directors to resign if their area of responsibility fails to meet expectations.

INFORMATIONAL INFRASTRUCTURE
Audit Requirements

Firms regulated by the SESC, as well as large firms covered by the Commercial Code, are required to undergo a financial audit by the company's statutory auditors. Large companies are required to undertake a financial audit by a nonemployed CPA. Financial auditing should be done independently from management, but, because auditors are appointed by the company, they have historically favored management's viewpoints. Companies have several options when adapting accounting rules so it is possible for a company to make up its financial statements in the range of Japanese-GAAP. Auditors tend to stay at the same company for long periods and are rarely changed.

In considering revisions to the Certified Public Accountants Law, the FSA originally had suggested that companies' auditors were to be replaced every five years, in line with the U.S. Sarbanes-Oxley Act of 2002. Lobbying by CPAs resulted in a recent decision to extend the period to seven years. In addition, the FSA had intended that revisions to the law would strengthen the independence of auditors and protect investors and creditors. However, apparent pressure from the ruling Liberal Democratic Party, insisting that accountants should promote the operations of their clients because they are paid auditing fees, may result in a watering down of the provisions.

Having experienced many scandals where fraudulent accounting has caused large bankruptcies, there has been a change in attitude among auditors. Auditors are now encouraged to announce a qualified opinion. Nevertheless, while there have been a greater number of qualified opinions provided for listed companies in recent years, this has not been viewed by the market as a serious enforcement mechanism.

Accounting Practices and Standards

The bulk of Japan's accounting procedures are developed and monitored by the government and the accounting profession itself has not contributed in setting standards. The MOF and MOJ both oversee accounting rules in Japan to varying degrees. The accounting system is somewhat unique insofar as it reflects the influence of three disparate codes: the Commercial Code, the SEL, and tax laws. Recently, efforts have been made to adopt a more unified, homogenized approach.

Government agencies, therefore, play an important role in setting accounting standards and administering CPA examinations. There is no autonomous accounting body charged with developing independent globally accepted best practices. Instead, accountants and the business community form a loose committee-based network. All members of the accounting profession are required to be members of the Japanese Institute of Certified Public Accountants (JICPA). JICPA, however, is not an independent, standard-setting body. It functions mostly as an advisory service to clarify accounting regulations set by the government. JICPA is represented on the Business Accounting Deliberation Council (BADC), an advisory body linked with the MOF that issues interpretations of accounting procedures. This organizational structure ensures that JICPA has a lesser impact on accounting procedures than the official BADC.

There has been a significant development in Japanese accounting rules in the past few years to match International Accounting Standards, including a shift to consolidated statements as a core of reporting, and market-to-market accounting. This shift has had an enormous impact on company valuations and has accelerated the dilution of cross-shareholdings. While catching up to global standards, there is no plan currently to apply market-to-market accounting to operating assets, or to recognize stock options as expenses. Thus, there is still room for Japanese accounting rules to become less conservative compared with those of other developed countries.

Financial Reporting

Currently, consolidated balance sheets, profit and loss statements, and cash flow statements are required to be submitted to the MOF. Segment-level information (both by lines of business and geography) is provided if the segment makes up at least 10 percent of a company's operations. Companies are also required to produce detailed projections of output, capital investment, and associated financing plans. Transactions with related third parties are also disclosed.

Disclosure

An emphasis on disclosure has developed in recent years alongside the collapse of several companies associated with poor disclosure. Because of the closed keiretsu business network, it has not been common business practice to make information publicly available in a timely manner. Instead, companies have offered information to a closed inner circle of major shareholders, which typically includes the company's main bank, and regulators. A rapid erosion of the cross-shareholding system and the recent influx of many foreign institutional investors have fueled pressure for more public disclosure of information by Japanese corporations.

The Commercial Code requires large Japanese corporations to report a balance sheet and profit and loss statement prior to the AGM. The SEL requires companies to submit copies of financial documentation to the local regulator, the stock exchange authorities, and the company's principal office twice a year.

The role of the government in corporate disclosure is important. Bureaus at the MOF (in particular, the tax policy subdivision) typically monitor disclosure practices of companies. Currently, consolidated balance sheets, profit and loss statements, as well as cash flow statements, with auditors' opinions, are required to be submitted to the MOF. This report (*yukashoken houkokusho*—literally "a securities report") is publicly available and easy to obtain. In addition, listed companies publish summaries of financial results (unaudited) at the end of the fiscal year, which is required by the listing exchange. The average number of days elapsed after March 31, 2002, for companies listed on the Tokyo stock exchange to publish their financial results was 49. According to the Tokyo stock exchange, this was the first time the average dropped below 50 days. Beginning in 2003, the Tokyo Stock Exchange announced its decision to require companies to publish quarterly statements, in addition to the currently required interim statements. This was based on a request from the FSA along with a plan by the Japanese government to boost reporting.

The FSA plans to require disclosure of total compensation paid to employed and nonemployed directors in the *yukashoken hokokusho* (financial reports) of listed companies after the fiscal year ending March 2004. In addition, the Ministry of Legal Affairs will require the disclosure of payments to companies' auditors, both for auditing and nonauditing fees, in the fiscal year ending March 2004.

Regardless of whether they are listed on overseas stock markets, most companies also prepare annual reports in English. However, this is not mandatory and the level of disclosure differs significantly. No Japanese companies disclose directors' remuneration individually. Along with the revision of the Commercial Code, some companies disclosed the total salaries and retirement packages of their management at AGMs held in 2002. In the revised Commercial Code, a company that changes its articles of incorporation to allow a board of directors to reduce the limit on liabilities from possible losses on derivatives should disclose total management remuneration in its financial report in fiscal 2003. As well as the revisions to the Commercial Code, pressure on disclosure is increasing in line with the increase of foreign investors and Japanese individual investors. More companies are expected to disclose the total amount of remuneration, but it is not yet known if and when companies will start to disclose the salaries of each individual director.

REFERENCES

Aoki, M., and G. Saxonhouse. "Finance, Governance and Competitiveness in Japan," Oxford University Press, New York, 2000.

Aoki, M. "Information, Corporate Governance, and Institutional Diversity: Competitiveness in Japan, the USA and the Transnational Economies," Oxford University Press, New York, 2000.

Chew, D. "Studies in International Corporate Finance and Governance Systems: A Comparison of the U.S., Japan, and Europe," Oxford University Press, New York, 1997.

Kanda, H. "The Role of the Board in Overseeing Financial Reporting and Disclosure," OECD, August 2000.

Nobes, C., and R. Parker. "Comparative International Accounting," Prentice Hall Europe, 5th ed., 1998.

Roberts, C., P. Weetman, and P. Gordon. "International Financial Reporting—A Comparative Approach," *Financial Times*, Pitman Publishing, Financial Times Professional Limited, 1998.

The Corporate Governance Committee of the Corporate Governance Forum of Japan, "Corporate Governance Principles, a Japanese View," October 1997.

Tokyo Stock Exchange, "The Role of Disclosure in Strengthening Corporate Governance and Accountability," Asia Corporate Governance Roundtable, May–June 2000.

Yasui, T. "Corporate Governance in Asia: A Comparative Perspective," OECD, March 1999.

Emerging Markets and Transition Economies

Brazil

Daniela Mesquita

INTRODUCTION

The last few years have seen significant reforms in Brazilian corporate governance. These reforms range from the introduction of the Novo Mercado to changes in company and securities law stemming from a conviction that capital markets ought to play a much larger role in the country's economic development than historically. Capital markets proponents in Brazil believe that one of the keys to achieving a healthy and successful capital market is through the introduction and support of strong corporate governance measures.

Historically, capital markets played only a minor role in providing for companies' financing needs as these were met from companies' retained earnings and government funding sources. However, the country's enormous social demands and scarce financial resources have limited the state's ability to maintain its role as a capital provider. This decline in funding was further compounded by the economic opening of the Brazilian markets in the 1990s. Companies now face intense international competition requiring more capital to upgrade and meet competitive threats. These capital demands can only be met by the growth and development of local capital markets. To aid this, local capital market development legislation was passed addressing governance problems, focusing primarily on greater transparency and disclosure requirements as well as protection of minority shareholder rights.

Current Corporate Governance Issues

Unlike the United Kingdom or the United States, where ownership is widely dispersed and conflicts are usually associated with the classic agency problem between professional managers and large and diffuse shareholder bases, Brazil's main source of governance conflict comes from the relationship between controlling and minority shareholders. Brazil's highly concentrated ownership structure and the lack of protection of minority shareholders rights are behind the most relevant governance problems. Current, as well as future, legislation is expected to continue to focus on improving these issues. Block ownership generates different governance concerns in contrast to developed markets. For example, in Brazil, prior to the introduction of new legislation, majority owners faced a perverse incentive to overemphasize bad news in an aim to depress a stock price, especially during a change in control event, to induce minority shareholders to accept lower bid prices. This asymmetric information deprives the minority shareholder of the knowledge and therefore the right to receive fair value for their stock holding. Brazil's efforts to eliminate such distortions include changes to the Company and Securities Laws and the introduction of the Novo Mercado—where listed companies must have higher governance standards than required by law. The establishment of the Novo Mercado and other securities law changes emphasize the promotion of ownership dispersion, better disclosure and transparency, and the protection of minority shareholder rights. This is complemented by greater regulation of audits and the professionals responsible to perform them.

Regulation of the Audit Profession

The regulation of the audit profession has been a priority for the Brazilian securities commission long before the recent accounting scandals brought the matter to the forefront of the global governance debate. In 1999, the Securities and Exchange Commission (CVM) issued a resolution prohibiting auditors from simultaneously providing auditing and consulting work to the same client and determined that auditors must be rotated at least once every five years, following a similar Central Bank rule in effect since 2000 for banks.

Not surprisingly, the resolution came under severe pressure from audit professionals, who have managed to suspend the resolution and keep on providing consulting work to audit clients. Companies must, however, disclose the extent of the consulting work as well as the fees paid for each service. Current lobbying efforts also could result in partner rotation, rather than the more extreme rotation of the audit firm itself, which will otherwise become effective from 2004.

MARKET INFRASTRUCTURE

General Stage of Economic Development

Brazil's per capita income classes it in the upper income levels of developing economies. However, there is great social inequality with almost 20 percent of the population living below the poverty line due to the income dispersion. Approximately 50 percent of the national income is concentrated among 10 percent of the population.

Having experienced more than two decades of military rule (1964 to 1985), Brazil returned to a democratic civilian government in 1985. On October 2002, Luiz Inácio Lula da Silva, a former metallurgical worker and founder of the left-wing PT party, was elected president with the support of over 61 percent of Brazilian voters. Among the many challenges facing the president and the country are the implementation of structural reforms in social security and taxation believed to be crucial steps to put the country back on a sustainable development path to enable the improvement of social standards.

Although market conditions have subsequently returned to "normality," the 2002 election process was surrounded by a market crisis that clearly exposed the country's vulnerability to wide fluctuations in capital flows. Uncertainty about the election's outcome, coupled with greater risk aversion in international capital markets, led to an increase in the risk premium on Brazil's bonds (EMBI spread) from approximately 800 points at the beginning of 2002 to over 2000 points some nine months later, by election time. As a result, international credit all but dried up to Brazilian companies, as investors worried about the country's ability (and willingness) to meet debt obligations. At approximately 55 percent of the country's GDP, and very high real interest rates to finance it, the dynamics of Brazil's public debt could indeed be a dangerous one. For some, the sustainability of Brazil's debt burden called for a measure of fiscal restraint that some viewed as incompatible with the political tradition of the front-running PT party.

Having survived the elections and avoided a meltdown, Brazil has seen the risk premium on its bonds return to the 700s range approximately one year after the elections. The elected government has initiated efforts to implement much needed structural reforms in social security and taxation, and there seems to be a general consensus that sustainable economic growth can only be achieved through responsible noninflationary policy-making. Such reforms, if successfully implemented, should help to reduce the country's vulnerability and avoid future confidence crises.

Ownership Structure and Market for Corporate Control

The ownership structure of Brazilian companies, in particular the concentration of control in the hands of a few shareholders, has been associated with many of the country's governance problems. These problems range from the poor functioning of boards to the disregard for minority share-holders' rights and the low liquidity of stock markets. In fact, more than 60 percent of publicly held companies have one single shareholder controlling over 50 percent of the voting shares and who on average controls over 70 percent of the total voting stock. With corporate control concentrated in the hands of few shareholders, if not a single shareholder, there is very limited scope for hostile takeovers. Thus, the managerial discipline imposed by such mechanisms is not a relevant feature of the market for corporate control in Brazil.

Financial Markets

Capital markets have traditionally played a small role in Brazil. It is estimated that less than 10 percent of public companies' investments were financed through capital markets in the last few years.[1] This, in part, is attributed to the legacy of decades of interventionist economic policy and the closed nature of the economy that limited the investment needs of companies and made the government a major source of capital.

With the economic opening and liberalization in the 1990s, financial markets have come to represent a much larger share of the country's GDP. The market capitalization of listed companies has increased from less than 8 percent in 1991 to more than 30 percent of GDP a decade later. Despite that impressive growth, the relative role of financial markets is still low compared to other emerging economies like South Africa, Taiwan, or Chile, where market capitalization exceeds 80 percent of GDP. The market expansion also has not altered the market structure that is characterized by high market concentration, low liquidity, and high volatility. On average, the 20 largest listed companies still account for 70 percent of the market's capitalization and only 4 percent of listed companies have daily liquidity.[2] As a result, financial markets are vulnerable to wide price and volume movements upon changes in capital flows, as well as to manipulation by large players, generating a precarious environment for the financial markets as a trusted long-term investment alternative for individual and institutional investors.

It should be noted that Brazil's macroeconomic conditions also have played a large part in the determination of the current structure and development of local markets, in particular the extremely high real interest rates practiced in the country. At approximately 15 percent in real terms,[3] interest rates impose extremely high financing costs to both government and business, making stock markets unappealing to corporations, who are unable to compete for capital at those rates, and to investors, who are better off lending their money to the government.

Privatization of Government Enterprises

Brazil's privatization program (1990–2002) did very little to remedy the capital market's structural problems. The main priority of the program was to maximize government revenues and this was accomplished by selling the government's ownership blocks to large, private controlling groups, rather than promoting dispersed ownership. In fact, in order to facilitate the privatization process, Company Law was amended for these sales so as to eliminate "tagalong rights" and maximize the potential control premium. Although this strategy must be understood in light of the government's precarious financial situation, it was nevertheless a missed opportunity to contribute to the development of the country's capital markets and governance environment.

LEGAL ENVIRONMENT
Primary Legislation

Based on Roman codes, Brazil's legal system is classified as a Civil Law Code, where three main laws guide the structure and functioning of the securities markets and address governance issues: the Securities Law, the Company Law, and the Bankruptcy Law. These laws are often complemented by resolutions or instructions issued by the regulatory agencies, the CVM, and the Central Bank, as well as by the stock exchanges.

The Securities Law sets forth the rules governing the securities market and its main regulatory body, the Securities and Exchange Commission. It is under the directive of this law that the markets are regulated. The Company Law provides the basic rules that determine the operation and governance of companies, both public and private. On October 2001, Company Law was expanded with the passage of Law 10.303 bringing with it significant governance changes.

Overview of key corporate law governance practices

Board structure and processes   Brazilian boards are composed of at least three members who must be approved by shareholders. Terms cannot be longer than three years and for companies listed on Bovespa's Level 2 or Novo Mercado, the term is one year.

Boards are responsible for the general strategy of the company and overseeing its implementation by senior executives as well as approving company finances and appointing and dismissing the independent auditors.

In general, boards are composed of company insiders and board processes are mostly informal. Frequently, the roles of chairman and CEO are combined and generally represent the company's controlling shareholder. As a result, majority ownership and executive control can be one and the same, with board structures maintained many times to meet legal requirements as opposed to providing a legitimate check and balance system. However, the evolving and expanding capital markets are resulting in more formalized board procedures and directors' duties in order to attract investors.[4] Brazilian best practice recommendations advocate that the board should be comprised of a majority of independent directors but there is no mandatory legislation requiring this and few companies go beyond what is required by law. Thus the role of independent directors is still fairly limited and there is little evidence that this will change in the near future.

Appointment of a board member   Shareholders representing at least 15 percent of the voting shares and preference shareholders with at least 10 percent of the total capital have the right to appoint and dismiss one member to the board of directors. That board member has the prerogative of vetoing the hiring of the independent auditor but not the firing of the auditor. However, this provision will have limited practical effect until

2006 when minority shareholders will not be limited to choosing the director from a list of three names determined by the controlling shareholders. It is a positive sign that some Brazilian companies have voluntarily eliminated the controlling shareholder's right to prepare the list of board appointees, leaving minority shareholders free to appoint whomever they want to be their representative.

Minority shareholders rights

Tagalong rights   Prior to the introduction of the new Company Law, upon a change of control Brazilian controlling shareholders received premiums for their shares that could reach 1000 percent at the expense of minority holders. With the passage of the new Company Law, the sale or transfer of shares representing a company's control obliges the buyer to make a tender offer for all common shares not in the controlling group for at least 80 percent of the price paid for each control share (tagalong rights), thereby limiting that premium to 20 percent. Such rights are, however, not extended to preference nonvoting shares, except for companies listed on Bovespa's Level 2, for which the exchange's listing rules determine tagalong rights for nonvoting preference shares of 70 percent. In the case of companies listed on the Bovespa's Novo Mercado, which requires all listed companies to issue ordinary shares only, tagalong rights are set at 100 percent, assuring equal treatment to all shareholders upon a change in control. This new Company Law significantly helps align the interests of controlling and minority shareholders and eliminates economic distortions that arise from the attempt by controlling shareholders to maximize the control premium through a depreciation of the remaining shares. Not surprisingly, the grant of tagalong rights to ordinary shares was reflected in ordinary share price appreciation relative to preference shares, with the price movement most evident for companies at a high change in control risk.[5]

Canceling the Registration of Publicly Held Companies

Brazilian Company Law has further enhanced minority shareholder rights by making it a requirement that acquiring companies repurchase all outstanding shares from minority holders at a "fair price." This is relevant when a bidder proposes to repurchase all remaining shares in the market in order to transform a publicly listed company to a privately held firm. Normally, in a large, diverse, liquid market the fair price is determined by the market's

last trade price. However, in Brazil concentrated ownership and market illiquidity make it difficult to determine a fair price especially when minority
shareholders fear that if the tender offer is not accepted there is no alternative to selling their shares. The law allows shareholders representing at least
10 percent of the outstanding shares to require a second opinion evaluation
of the fair price. Although this process may introduce subjectivity into the
pricing process, the right to formally challenge the tender offer price is a significant achievement for minority shareholder rights.

Conflict of Interests and Abuse of Voting Rights

In 1976, Company Law regulating conflicts of interest was introduced. The
law prevents shareholders from voting on resolutions that would lead to
their own benefit at the expense of the company. In a market like Brazil
where ownership and voting power are highly concentrated this law is crucial but still controversial, since identifying these cases is not straightforward. The Securities Commission analyzes such situations on a case-by-case
basis, but since the law's applicable criteria are not always clear, the
Commission is now having controlling shareholders disclose the characteristics and potential benefits of any transactions in which they are involved.
This is expected to lead to a better regulatory review of conflicts of interests.

Rights of Preference Shares

Preference shares are entitled to one of the following rights: (1) priority
dividends of at least 3 percent of the shares' book value; (2) dividends at
least 10 percent higher than that of ordinary shares; or (3) tagalong rights
and dividends equal to those of ordinary shares. Although most companies opt for offering higher dividends to preference shareholders, when
given the choice shareholders usually choose tagalong rights. This supports the view that eliminating potential conflicts of interest upon a change
in control is a priority for minority shareholders.

Voting Procedures and Proxy Rights

Each common share has the right to one vote in resolutions at shareholders
meetings. The one share/one vote right is waived for the board elections
where cumulative voting is usually applied.[6] Cumulative voting usually
ensures minority shareholders a greater chance of appointing at least one

member to the board. Preference shareholders are usually not entitled to vote at shareholders meetings, but the holders of these shares may attend and address the meetings.

Shareholder resolutions are decided on by a simple majority vote with certain exceptions that require a qualified quorum. Matters subject to a qualified quorum (approval requiring at least half of the voting shares) include changes to the privileges of preference shares, reduction of the compulsory dividend, mergers and consolidations, and other key corporate decisions. A shareholder is entitled to appoint a proxy to attend the meeting and vote in his or her place but telephone and electronic voting are not permitted. The proxy may be a shareholder, a corporation officer, lawyer, or a financial institution and the proxy document submitted cannot be older than one year.

Capital Structure—Ordinary Voting Shares and Nonvoting Preference Shares

The issuance of preference nonvoting shares is limited to one-half of a company's total capital, down from two-thirds prior to the introduction of the new Company Law. Although the two-thirds provision has been grandfathered in for companies with outstanding preference shares prior to the law change, these companies represent the majority of listed Brazilian companies.

The objective of the new limit was to reduce the discrepancy between economic interest and influence in Brazilian companies. Under the old limit, corporate control could be achieved through ownership of only 16.67 percent of a company's capital if only one-third of shares carry voting rights. Although the new limit reduces such distortions, the grandfather provision limits the practical effect of the law.

Dividend Policy

Brazilian Company Law determines the payment of a compulsory dividend of no less than 25 percent of net profits, and fiscal incentives provide further motivation for that form of distribution, as dividend payments are tax-exempt whereas capital gains are taxed at 20 percent.

As indicated in a related study,[7] the existence of such fiscal structure, coupled with the minimum dividend legal requirement, would lead one to reasonably expect higher dividend payouts in Brazil compared to countries where dividend payments receive less favorable tax treatment.

That is, however, not the case. The median payout for Brazilian companies was found to be 30 percent for the years 1994 to 2001, in line with the median payout found globally.[8] The fact that dividend payouts are not higher in Brazil, despite the strong fiscal incentive, has been cited as further evidence of the existence of private benefits of control in Brazilian companies, whereby controlling shareholders and managers can benefit from a preferential treatment at the expense of other investors.[9] Such preferential treatment can take the form of special terms for transactions with related companies, excessive salaries to family members, and other forms of expropriation of minority shareholders.

Bankruptcy Law

The Bankruptcy Law provides for two distinct legal proceedings to deal with companies in financial duress: *concordata* and *falência*. Concordata is a defensive mechanism under which troubled companies, under the supervision of a court-appointed commissioner, are granted partial debt forgiveness while maintaining control over the business. Falência is a conventional bankruptcy process analogous to a Chapter 7 proceeding under the U.S. Bankruptcy Code, which results in the public auctioning of the company's assets under court supervision and the liquidation of the business. Neither of these proceedings affords a troubled company the opportunity to reorganize its operations in a manner similar to that provided under Chapter 11 of the U.S. Bankruptcy Code.

Much needed changes to the Bankruptcy Law have been under negotiation by the National Congress for over 10 years, and are expected to be finally approved by the end of 2003. Among the proposed changes are measures to increase the ability of a company in financial duress to reorganize its activities. It also includes steps to increase the protection awarded to creditors, such as the creation of a creditors' assembly to regulate their participation in the process of judicial liquidation.

Law Enforcement

Court settlements of shareholders disputes have been almost nonexistent. Between 1986 and 1994 a total of 11 cases were judged, and some of these cases have not been concluded after 10 years.[10] The rigid legal system has led disputing participants to settle out of court. Most financially distressed companies also seek debt restructurings carried consensually in out-of-court negotiation.

In order to provide for a faster way to resolve disputes, the new Company Law has introduced a legal alternative to the traditional court approach—arbitration. That choice is voluntary and adoption has been very slow. In addition to the country's lack of arbitration tradition, and the natural suspicion toward any new system, there seems to be some concern that such an alternative would tilt the balance of power away from controlling shareholders in favor of minority shareholders. Although not openly admitted, both parties in a dispute do not always welcome a fast conclusion. Since minority shareholders often initiate legal proceedings, controlling shareholders hesitate to sacrifice the perceived benefit of a slow decision awarded by the traditional legal system. However, for companies listed under Bovespa's Level 2 and Novo Mercado arbitration is compulsory. Critics of arbitration cite this requirement as one of the main reasons for the small number of companies listed in those levels of the Exchange.

REGULATORY ENVIRONMENT
Key Regulatory Bodies

The key regulatory bodies overseeing corporate governance in Brazil are the Central Bank, the Securities and Exchange Commission (CVM), and the São Paulo Stock Exchange (Bovespa). In addition, independent and professional bodies, such as the *Instituto Brasileiro de Governança Corporativa (IBGC)*, which produced the country's first manual on best practice recommendations, and *IBRACON*, the Independent Auditors Council, actively contribute to the definition and enforcement of the country's regulations.

The Central Bank is responsible for the supervision of the country's financial system through its regulation of financial institutions. The CVM regulates all matters related to the securities markets, such as registration of publicly held companies, registration of public offerings, accreditation of independent auditors, and rules concerning the establishment and operation of stock exchanges and securities trading. The Bovespa, operating under CVM supervision, is empowered to establish rules and procedures as well as monitor compliance by brokerage firms, listed companies, and investors.

Both the CVM and the stock exchange have been very active in the promotion of better governance practices. The CVM published its Principles of Best Practice (Cartilha) and requires companies to comply with the principles or explain why they do not. Bovespa has segmented its listing requirements by levels of governance standards resulting in the Novo Mercado and Bovespa's Levels 1 and 2, in addition to regular listings. (See the following section for greater detail on the exchanges and their segmentation.)

Part of the changes in the new Securities Law grant the CVM independent administrative authority, fixed mandates, stable administrators, and financial and budgetary autonomy to better protect the Commission from political interference. These changes have significantly increased the Commission's punitive powers while ensuring the CVM's legal and financial autonomy. Despite such significant progress, the shortage of qualified professionals to implement the changes remains a considerable obstacle for more effective regulation.

New Market (Novo Mercado)

Inspired by Germany's now extinct Neuer Markt,[11] Brazil's Novo Mercado is a special listing segment that Bovespa introduced in 2001 as part of the Exchange's effort to promote better governance practices. In order to be listed in Bovespa's Novo Mercado companies must comply with a series of governance provisions not required by Brazilian law.

In addition to the Novo Mercado, two other listing segments—Level 1 (Nivel 1) and Level 2 (Nivel 2)—also were designated for companies with differentiated corporate governance practices. The extent of a company's commitment to the adoption of such practices classifies it as Level 1, Level 2, or Novo Mercado, where Level 1 has the least stringent requirements and the New Market the most comprehensive set of governance provisions. Level 1 listings require better information disclosure, including quarterly reports and ownership dispersion of at least 25 percent of total capital in circulation. For companies listed under Level 2, additional governance practices and minority shareholder rights are required, such as one-year term limits for board members, the adoption of internationally accepted accounting standards, and adherence to the arbitration chamber. For New Market companies, in addition to the requirements of Levels 1 and 2, all shares must be ordinary voting shares with tagalong rights.

Although adherence to the different levels of corporate governance has been slower than initially anticipated, with only 33 companies listed after more than two years in operation, recent studies suggest that listing on the Novo Mercado or Level 1 and 2 Exchange segments has had a positive impact on valuation, traded volume, and liquidity.[12]

The Fiscal Council

The Fiscal Council, a monitoring body that reports directly to shareholders, has no direct equivalent in other countries. Its main role is to supervise management and oversee company financial reporting. Although it bears some resemblance to audit committees in the United States or United Kingdom, the Fiscal Council is not a permanent body, but rather is assembled only upon shareholders' request for one-year terms.[13] These councils are normally requested by minority shareholders when they have a dispute with the controlling shareholders. As a result, the Fiscal Council has often come to be regarded as one element of shareholders conflicts rather than an independent and effective monitoring body.

INFORMATIONAL INFRASTRUCTURE

Key Accounting Practices and Standards

Two accounting frameworks are used in Brazil:

+ Company Law accounting and
+ Brazilian GAAP codified by the Federal Council of Accountants (CFC).

All Brazilian companies are required to prepare financial statements according to Company Law, with Brazilian GAAP statements provided supplementally by some companies. The Brazilian Institute of Accountants (IBRACON) publishes supplemental standards for both accounting frameworks and these standards are endorsed by the CVM and the CFC.

The main difference between the two accounting standards relates to their approach to inflation accounting. Brazil's historically high inflation rates required a methodology to account for or minimize the impact of inflationary distortions in financial statements. However, with the stabilization of the economy and dramatic reduction of inflation, Company Law principles no longer allow for monetary correction in financial statements after 1995. In contrast, Brazilian GAAP principles account for inflation using a constant currency approach and require inflation accounting for periods after 1995, if effects are material.[14]

Differences between Brazilian Accounting and Internationally Accepted Accounting Standards

Fundamental differences to principles-based International Accounting Standards (IAS) include:

+ Brazilian legislation does *not* require:
    + cash flow statements and segment information;
    + hedge accounting for financial derivatives; or

◆ specific rules requiring the disclosure of the fair value of investment properties, discontinuing operations, and diluted earnings
per share.[15]

A proposal to harmonize Brazilian accounting and IAS standards is
currently under consideration by National Congress, which if passed,
would minimize such differences.

Financial Reporting and Disclosure

Companies are required to prepare annual financial statements that include
a balance sheet, statement of retained earnings, income statement, statement of changes in financial statements, and notes to the financial statements. For comparative purposes, statements must show corresponding
amounts for the preceding fiscal year. Publicly held CVM registered corporations must meet the above filing requirements and also disclose their
management and auditor reports as well as a comprehensive set of quarterly and periodic information through the CVM's and Bovespa's websites
allowing online access to company regulatory disclosure for investors.

Despite the recent progress in the disclosure of information, notably
in the widespread use of the Internet, in most cases companies restrict the
disclosed information to regulatory requirements. Notwithstanding
Brazilian codes of best practice, annual reports are usually silent regarding practices and principles of corporate governance.

Audit Requirements

Independent auditors must audit the annual financial statements of publicly held corporations. Independent auditors must be both registered and
accredited by the CVM to do audited work in Brazil. The independent auditor's responsibilities include attending client's annual shareholders' meetings and providing shareholders' information regarding the company's
audit financial statements. Independent auditors are liable for any damages
incurred by third parties that rely on their audited statements.

NOTES

1. Kandir, 2001.
2. It is estimated that only 4.1 percent of listed companies have daily liquidity,
MB Associados, 2000.
3. ABN AMRO Bank estimate; Selic, September 2003.
4. McKinsey & Company and Korn/Ferry International.

5. That movement was particularly strong for telecom companies, since it was expected that the sector could undergo a strong consolidation.

6. The multiple voting process can be requested by shareholders representing at least 10 percent of the voting capital.

7. Cunha, M., 2002.

8. Shleifer, A. et al, 2000.

9. The existence of private benefits of control also is evident in the extremely high control premiums found in Brazil, previously mentioned.

10. Eizirik, N., 2002.

11. Similarities between the now defunct German Neuer Markt and Brazil's Novo Mercado refer to the governance practices required from listed companies. The listing of "new economy," companies that characterized German's Neuer Markt is not a feature of Brazil's Novo Mercado.

12. Carvalho, A. G., 2003.

13. The fiscal council can be a permanent body if so specified in the bylaws, but can otherwise be constituted upon the request of shareholders representing at least 10 percent of voting shares or 5 percent of nonvoting shares, for a 1-year term.

14. For further details see PricewaterhouseCoopers, 2003.

15. For further details see Nobes, 2001.

REFERENCES

Carvalho, A. G. "Efeito da Migração para os Níveis de Governança da Bovespa," *Bovespa Report*, 2003.

Carvalhosa, M., and N. Eizirik. "A Nova Lei das S/A," *Editora Saraiva*, 2002.

Cunha, Mauro, "O Mistério do Baixo Payout, " *Valor Econômico*, 23 set. 2002.

CVM, Gerência de Estudos Econômicos—GDE, "Panorama do Mercado Secundário International de Valores Mobiliários," www.cvm.gov.br (2003).

Dynanmo Administração de Recursos, "Prêmio de Controle no Brasil: por que, como e para quem?," *Cartas Dynam*, Dynamo.com.br, 2002.

Eizirik, N. "Sociedades Anônimas—Jurisprudência," *Editora Renovar*, 2001.

Kandir, A. "Lei das S/A, uma conquista a comemorar," *Folha de São Paulo*, Sept. 21, 2001, p. A3.

MB Associados. "Desafios e Oportunidades para o Mercado de Capitais Brasileiro," *Estudos para o Desenvolvimento do Mercado de Capitais*, 2001.

McKinsey and Company and Korn/Ferry International. "Panorama de Governança Corporativa no Brasil," 2001.

KPMG. "Accounting Practices Comparison," *DPP Brazil—Department of Professional Practices*, 2001.

Nobes, C. W. (ed). "GAAP 2001—A Survey of Accounting Rules Benchmarked against International Accounting Standards," 2001.

Pinheiro Neto—Advogados, "Corporate Governance Assessment—Brazil," www.pinheironeto.com.br (2000).

PricewaterhouseCoopers. "Brazil—An Overview of Accounting, Audit and Tax," www.pricewaterhousecoopers.com, 2003.

Shleifer, Andrei, R. La Porta, F. Lopez-de-Silanes, and R. Vishny, "Agency Problems and Dividend Policies Around the World," *Journal of Finance*, 2000.

China

Katrina Tai

INTRODUCTION

In August 2001, a local business publication, *Caijing Magazine*, unveiled the YingGuangXia RMB745 million fraud, the biggest economic scandal in Mainland China's history. This revelation not only drew attention from regulators and public investors to the importance of corporate governance but also exposed the weakness of the country's legal, regulatory, and accounting systems. Corporate governance since then has been placed at the very top of the government's agenda. This high-profile topic has been mentioned frequently in all of the recent keynote speeches by China's Premier, the Chairman of the Central Bank, the Chairman of the China Securities Regulatory Commission (CSRC), and numerous other government officials and scholars.

Within a mere two years, China has made some tremendous strides on the corporate governance front. The mandate to improve corporate governance is a top priority among all sectors, including government bodies, regulators, intermediaries, corporations, and investors. Legislators, regulators, and professional institutions have since issued various laws, rules, regulations, and standards with a view toward laying a foundation for good corporate governance. However, change will not happen overnight. The separation of ownership and management of a company is still a very new concept in China. Complete transparency of information disclosure, fairness to all shareholders, responsible and accountable board directors, and truly independent board oversight over executive appointments and compensation represent ideals that cannot be simultaneously legislated and implemented, particularly in the context of China's evolving market economy. While China's rules and regulations that dictate good corporate governance structures are important first steps, and may in some areas come close to reaching global standards, effective implementation and enforcement of such standards will prove elusive for years to come.

MARKET INFRASTRUCTURE

General Stages of Economic Development

Transforming from a planned economy to a market economy

Since its birth in 1949 until the late 1970s, modern-day China operated under a strict planned economy system. During the more than 30-year planned economy period, the Communist Party of China (CPC), under the leadership of Chairman Mao Zedong, was the sole ruler and creator of all policies and regulations. The country experienced remarkable economic development in the early stages but eventually witnessed a drastic downturn due to the political turmoil that culminated in the Cultural Revolution. As a result, in 1976 when the Cultural Revolution ended, the national economy faced a deep predicament.

When the new generation of government under the leadership of Deng Xiaoping assumed power, a market economy was introduced as a complement to the existing planned economy. During the 1980s, domestic economic reform officially took off nationwide. The entire 1980s represented an initial experimentation period for the market economy concept.

The first real and effective changes came in the early 1990s. In 1991, China established its very first stock exchange in Shanghai, and then in Shenzhen (1992). In 1992, Deng toured the major southeast coastal cities and re-emphasized the government's commitment to the development of a market economy and the establishment of market-based systems in China. Deng's "Communist market economy theory" was further carried forward by his predecessors Jiang Zemin and Zhu Rongji in the 1990s. By the end of the last century, the China market had become a market economy phenomenon.

Into the new century, the transformation continues. Although certain industries such as banking, telecommunications, media, and publication still remain highly regulated, China's accession to the WTO will help speed deregulation of these industries. As more international competitors enter the market, the PRC economy will need to break away from its heavy reliance on administrative and policy support from the government and adapt to the rules of a true market economy.

Role changes of government bodies

Under the leadership of the CPC, the Chinese government acted simultaneously as policymaker, implementer, enforcer, and evaluator. Unlike in other market economies, one of the Chinese government's roles was to approve or endorse any business activity. With government being the sole owner of most businesses, it also served as the strategic decisionmaker whose representatives managed and ran the state-owned enterprises (SOEs).

The late 1980s marked the beginning of a concerted effort to separate governmental functions from business functions within the SOEs based on the notion that government officials should not hold any executive position in any commercial entities. However, given the existing government structure, the top executives of the large strategic SOEs are all appointed by the Organization Department of the CPC Central Committee. These executives, inevitably, have strong ties to top government officials; thus, government is still the key influential force within these large SOEs. The management of the small- and medium-sized SOEs, theoretically, is appointed by their board, and thus should have operational autonomy and decision-making power. However, given the complex cross-shareholding situation that is common among the SOEs, government influence still plays a key role in impacting the SOEs' decision-making processes.

Furthermore, at the local government levels, a decentralization program was introduced in 1998 whereby the local governments were given more incentives and autonomy to introduce and implement local administrative and fiscal policies according to the local needs and economic condition. As a result, the bureaucratic entrepreneurialism at the local level generated dynamic growth rates at the beginning stages of the reform. However, this also created tensions between the local and central governments caused by sometimes-conflicting priorities.

Ownership Structure

State ownership

The largest owner of PRC businesses is the government. From the early 1950s to the late 1970s, the SOE constituted the sole corporate structure that was allowed to exist. Government owned every asset in the country, from farmland to large enterprises. The entire nation during this period was educated to work for the interests of the country and the Party only. Under this type of propaganda, different interests were not allowed to exist, and thus, no effective governance system was considered necessary.

Not until the 1980s when the market economy concept had been introduced did small, private workshops and entrepreneurs start to emerge, first in the rural areas and later in the cities. For example, in 1978, 100 percent of investment in China was from the provincial governments.

This figure reduced to 82 percent in 1980, and further reduced to 66 percent in 1985. However, most of the private businesses at the time were mainly owned and managed by the same group of people, and conflicts of interests had not been brought into the spotlight.

Privatization

The establishment of China's first stock exchanges in the early 1990s marked the beginning of a true ownership diversification process. Upon approval from the relevant ministries, SOEs can float a portion of their shares in the public markets. Listed companies' capital structure can consist of state-owned shares, legal person shares, A shares, B shares, H shares, and other foreign investment shares. Beginning in 2003, authorized foreign mutual funds with joint venture local partners (foreign stakes must stay below 33 percent in 2003, and below 49 percent in 2005) are allowed to invest in domestic securities. SOE ownership is thus further diversified by foreign shareholdings.

As of the end of 2002, the average state-ownership stake in Shenzhen and Shanghai listed companies stood at about 70 percent. This shareholding structure will not change significantly in the foreseeable future, given that the PRC Company Law stipulates that initial investors must maintain their investment for at least three years. Furthermore, the government, in general, may not yet want to sell down its controlling stakes in most key industries.

Financial Markets

Macroeconomic condition

China is one of the few markets that have maintained a strong growth trend during the recent global downturns. According to the National Bureau of Statistics, in 2002, China enjoyed an 8 percent GDP growth to reach RMB10.24 trillion (approximately U.S.$1.2 trillion), and became the world's second largest economy after the United States. Imports and exports remain strong. There is a U.S.$30.4 billion surplus in export figures. Foreign direct investment in 2002 reached U.S.$52.7 billion. At year-end 2002, national foreign reserve reached U.S.$286.4 billion, a 35 percent year-on-year growth from 2001. The national currency, RMB, is still not fully convertible. The official rate is fixed at U.S.$1 to 8.3 RMB range.

Despite the strong growth, there are some fundamental weaknesses in the fiscal and national economy. Shortage in effective demand, an imbalanced supply structure, the growing discrepancy in living standards between rural and urban areas, and an increasing unemployment rate are some of the primary issues yet to be addressed by the fiscal policymakers.

Banking industry

China has a savings rate equivalent to about 40 percent of total GDP, one of the highest in the world. In 2002, total savings reached U.S.$1 trillion. Most of the savings are in bank deposits, with a small percentage in equity investments. Bank financing is the primary funding source for companies in China. Corporations, especially SOEs, rely largely on bank loans and policy lending for their Cap-ex needs.

The "big four" state-owned commercial banks[1] and two state policy banks[2] dominated both lending and bank deposit markets. From the 1970s to the 1990s, while the PRC strived to transition from a planned economy to a market economy, most of the banks' lending was still policy lending. Coupled with the fact that all these banks had poor internal risk control mechanisms and the SOEs faced financial difficulties, and mounting nonperforming loan (NPL) problems became very serious. Official statistics estimated that NPL is about 24 percent of total lending. However, Standard & Poor's Ratings Services estimates that this figure could be as high as 50 percent.

The second group of banks forms the newer joint-stock banks.[3] Since these banks are owned jointly by government and by private entities, they have more operational autonomy compared to the state-owned banks. In addition, since these banks had less policy lending responsibilities and a shorter history, their NPL problems are far less serious than the state-owned banks. On the other hand, because of their smaller scale and less government linkages, their market shares and relative influence are also significantly smaller than that of the state-owned banks.

China's accession to the WTO will bring both opportunities and challenges to China's banking industry. In the initial stages, opening up the markets to international competition will put considerable pressure on the domestic banks. However, in the course of longer term, the foreign banks are expected to bring in positive influence to the domestic banks in terms of management skills, customer service awareness, product diversification, new technology, and additional funding sources. We expect to see a more open and competitive banking market by the end of this decade.

Development of the equity markets

Aside from bank financing, the equity market represents the other main funding source for corporations in China. The PRC equity market has developed into a size with market capitalization of RMB4,253.05 billion (over U.S.$500 billion), total of 1229 domestic listed companies, and total of 592.55 billion outstanding shares (as of the end of January 2003). Thirty-two and a half percent of the total capital is floating and tradable. There are two stock exchanges located in Shanghai and in Shenzhen, trading four types of equity stocks—Shanghai A shares, Shenzhen A shares, Shanghai B shares, and Shenzhen B shares. All stock issuance is subject to the approval of the China Securities Regulatory Commission (CSRC).

Individual investors dominate the PRC equity market. Of about 39.1 million investors, over 99.6 percent are individual investors. Only less than 0.4 percent of total investments are under the name of institutional investors.[4] However, since these institutional investors may be representing a group of individual investors, the actual percentage of institutional investors should be less than this official figure. Going forward, the percentage of institutional investors should increase as international funds are gradually allowed to enter the market.

Domestic bond market

The domestic bond market is small and underdeveloped. Issuance of corporate bonds is heavily controlled by the central and local governments. Though the central government has demonstrated a strong intention of encouraging the corporate bond market's development, the growth pace is much slower than that of the equity market. Similar to the equity market situation, retail investors make up a majority percentage of the investor base. Although there are over a dozen local credit rating agencies with the number constantly increasing, none of them has been able to establish a recognized domestic benchmarking standard.

Other Institutional/Cultural Factors

Role of state and nongovernmental organizations

Social and industrial associations in China also play important roles in providing guidelines, policies, and most important, business connections. These associations are categorized into three classes. The first-class institutions are directly under leadership of the State Council and/or the Ministries. The district and provincial associations normally are also members of these first-class associations. These associations normally act as quasi-government bodies in regulating and monitoring their members. They also may act as a positive enforcer in improving the corporate governance standards of their members. However, in certain situations, when the enforcement adversely affects the associations' own interests, they also may act as obstacles to achieving good governance.

The research institutes are the other type of nongovernmental organization (NGO) that exerts considerable influence. Such research institutes, including the one under the Chinese Academy of Social Sciences and the research center under the People's Bank of China, act as think tanks for the central government.

Lack of shareholder activism

As in most other emerging markets, shareholder activism is almost an unheard of term in the PRC market, although this is attributable mainly to this market's short history and lack of institutional investors. As of the end of March 2003, about 10 percent of the Shanghai and Shenzhen A-share companies are also listed at markets open for foreign investors,[5] and less than 1 percent of the A-share companies have cross-border capital programs. These companies are likely to be the first ones to make the most progressive strides toward better government standards. Looking forward, as China's capital markets open up more to international investors and the general public's awareness of corporate governance increases, shareholders should eventually become more actively focused on protecting their own interest and ownership rights.

Importance of relationships/connections

To transform from the traditional "rule of person" to the more systematic "rule of law" will require not only a good system but also a major learning and cultural transformation. Although China has already adopted the system to separate government from business over the past 20 years, strong personal ties and interlocked relationship networks still make the two inseparable. Relationships are still one of the most important factors in China influencing the conduct of business. In some situations, relationships can actually take precedence over legitimate decisions based on laws or regulations.

LEGAL ENVIRONMENT

Background on Legal System and Legal Tradition

Legal Development

This current Mainland China legal system has a history of only about half a century. Compared to the developed European continental and the U.S. legal systems, the Chinese system is only at a stage of infancy. PRC Constitutions were drawn out in 1949. The National People's Congress (NPC) has the highest authorization to legislate and to amend the constitutions and laws. The standing Committee of the NPC has the power to interpret laws and draw up decrees. Only the chairman of the PRC has the power to issue these laws and decrees.

Legal development was given the highest priority from 1949 to 1956. Many laws, rules, and codes were preliminarily drawn up during this period. Unfortunately, due to historical reasons and political turmoil, the system not only had not advanced, but rather, had retracted during the following 20 years. Not until 1978 was the importance of a sound legal system recognized and brought back to the top of the party's agenda.

Legal System and Tradition

The existing PRC legal system basically follows the Continental legal system, which in turn is based on fiduciary duty, governmental regulations, and legislation. However, the system is still heavily impacted by China's over 2000-year feudalistic history. Therefore, the true "system" consists of not only laws and rules, but also a large element of the Chinese culture, which in turn, allows the implementation and enforcement processes to be more discretionary. Under some circumstances, relationships can totally undermine a legal decision. Selective enforcement is often seen as a result of either the law enforcer's personal interests, or (better, but equally dangerous) the special interests of certain market groups.

Criminal laws were traditionally given more emphasis than commercial laws. The existing PRC legislation also inherited some of these traditions. Therefore, Criminal Law, Civil Procedures Law, Administration Law, People's Court Administration Law, among other areas of law, were some of the earliest ones to be issued (in 1978). The promulgation in July 1, 1979 of the Law on Joint Ventures Using Chinese and Foreign Investment marked a new era in China's legislation on foreign investment and corporate laws. It was not until the late 1980s and early 1990s that the bulk of rules and regulations dealing with civil and commercial law issues were promulgated.

Besides these issues, there are also some major conflicts or inconsistencies in China's existing legal system. Many of these issues were untouchable and were never publicly discussed during the first 30 years of PRC history. Most of these issues are still being debated among the legal scholars and practitioners. Legal versus human rights, the independence of the legal system, whether the CPC can overrule the laws, and whether the CPC can interfere with legal decisions, are some of these issues.

Principal Legal Provisions

Company Law

The PRC Company Law was first passed at the 8th National People's Congress in December 1993 (effective July 1, 1994) and amended in December 1999. The Company Law is intended to regulate corporate structures and activities, and to protect commercial interests of the companies, their shareholders, and creditors. Two types of companies are stipulated under the Company Law: limited liability companies and joint stock companies. The Law also articulates the responsibilities, rights, and liabilities of shareholders, the board of directors, managers, and the board of supervisors. Among the unique aspects of PRC Company Law are the requirements for minimum registered capital, fixed office space, and certain legal representatives.

All limited liability companies should set up a board of directors . For "large" companies, there should be a separate board of supervisors (BoS) consisting of at least three independent supervisors. Under the PRC Company Law, directors and managers are "insiders." Their responsibilities are articulated under the same section. However, the BoS is the independent "outsider" that should exercise supervision authority to monitor the company's activities. The Law also gives shareholders the right to appoint and to remove directors and supervisors and decide their remuneration.

A series of listing rules and regulations have been enacted to supplement the Company Law in terms of regulating capital market activities. This will be further discussed under the section on "Regulatory Environment."

Securities Law

The PRC Securities Law, passed and effective on December 29, 1998, is the law that regulates capital market issuance, trading activities, and related matters. The Law articulates that the regulatory organization under the State Council is the central regulator for the PRC's capital markets. The Law states that "a public stock issuance shall follow the conditions as stipulated in the Company Law and be submitted to the securities regulatory agency under the State Council for verification." It also stipulates that all stock exchanges, securities houses, securities clearinghouses, and securities regulators must file regular reports to the State Statistic Bureau for auditing purposes. The Law states that insider trading and market manipulation are strictly prohibited. It also provides specific guidelines for each of the areas relating to securities market activities.

Other commercial laws

The other major commercial laws that guide the PRC commercial world include

 - Contract Law (1999) which assigns rights and securities to all parties of the contracts;
 - Bankruptcy Law (1988) which addresses only bankruptcies of state-owned entities;
 - PRC Trust Law (2001) which deals with issues relating to the establishment and operation of trustees; PRC Security Law (1995) which stipulates the creation of security interests such as guarantees, mortgages, pledges, liens, and deposits; and
 - The Law of Commercial Instruments which deals with issues such as types of commercial instruments, and issue, transfer, endorsement, acceptance, recourse, etc., of commercial instruments.

REGULATORY ENVIRONMENT

SDPC and the Ministries

The State Council has final and overriding authority over all regulatory bodies. Under its supervision, there are 28 Ministries and the National Development and Reform Commission (NDRC), which is involved in overall strategic planning. With input from the Ministries, especially the Ministry of Finance (MOF) and the Ministry of Commerce (MOC), the NDRC researches and oversees implementation of nationwide strategic planning. One of the NDRC's core responsibilities is to balance out the overall economy in terms of demand and, the pace of growth, urban and rural resource allocation, and industrial adjustment. Companies that raise funds from the capital markets, either domestic or cross-border, need to get formal approval from the NDRC.

Banking Regulatory Committee

The People's Bank of China (PBOC) has been the regulator for PRC's financial industry since 1983. Besides regulating financial markets, the Bank also acts as an administrator in formulating and implementing monetary policy, issuing and administering the circulation of the currency, licensing and supervising financial institutions, managing official foreign exchange and gold reserves, acting as fiscal agent, maintaining payment and settlement systems, collecting and analyzing financial statistical data, and participating in international financial activities in the capacity of a central bank. To streamline the regulatory process while providing additional checks and balances to the existing PBOC functions, the State Council set up a new China Banking Regulatory Commission (CBRC) in the 10th National People's Congress in March 2003. This new CBRC is taking over the regulatory responsibilities from the PBOC to oversee banks, asset management companies, and trust investment companies. The CBRC also is responsible for drafting and enforcing banking-related laws, rules, and regulations.

Foreign Exchange

The PRC's national currency, RMB, is still not fully opened and convertible on the international exchange markets. Currency control therefore is one of the key functional areas under the central bank. The State Administration of Foreign Exchange (SAFE), under the supervision of the PBOC, is the regulator for the Chinese foreign currency market. SAFE, on a daily basis, looks after foreign currency trading, borrowing/lending, transferring, international clearing, and exchange rate setting. It also monitors foreign exchange market activities. Therefore, for cross-border debt or equity issuance, the issuer also needs to get SAFE's approval in addition to the NDRC's mandate.

Capital Markets

The PRC's capital market is highly and centrally regulated. The State Council Securities Commission (SCSC) is the highest authority for the capital markets. The China Securities Regulatory Commission (CSRC) is the executive arm of the SCSC responsible for conducting supervision and regulation duties.

With its centralized supervisory system, the CSRC establishes its supervisory authority over all securities and futures business, including stock and futures exchanges, the listed companies, fund management companies, investment consulting firms, and other intermediaries involved in the securities and futures business.

Key Listing Rules

Securities codes and regulations

There are four types of shares that list and trade in the domestic equity market. Shanghai A and Shenzhen A shares are for domestic investors, while Shanghai B and Shenzhen B shares are for foreign investors. All listings must comply with PRC Company Law, the Memorandum by the State Council Regarding Conversion of SOE to Joint-stock Company (1997), and the Circular by the State Economic and Trading Commission Regarding Standardizing Limited Company and Joint-stock Company According to Company Law (1995).

In January 2002, the CSRC released its Code of Corporate Governance for Listed Companies in China. The Code emphasizes the importance of credibility and integrity and identifies the relationship between shareholders and directors, executives, and management as that between the trustors and the trustees. The Code requires that all AGM details comply with PRC Company Law. Requirements for directors, supervisors, and stakeholders' rights and related items are articulated. The Code also sets additional disclosure requirements of corporate governance for listed companies.

Board structure

The Company Law requires listed companies to adopt a two-tier board structure. The board of directors consists of two-thirds top executives and one-third independent directors. The board of directors is accountable directly to shareholders. The second board, the board of supervisors, consists of independent shareholders and employees (employees cannot be less than one-third). According to the listing rules, directors and top management cannot be appointed as supervisors.

Under this two-tier structure, the board of directors, as the core board that works closely with the management (in most cases, board members and top management are held by same group of person), operates the company on a day-to-day basis. The BoS is the independent board that provides independent views and monitors the executive management and the board of directors. Given that, in most cases, BoS members are connected to major shareholder(s), they may only represent a single interest group but not all stakeholders. Furthermore, since the employee-members on the BoS must have a reporting line to the top management who make annual evaluation, promotion, and remuneration decisions, it is difficult for the employee-members to play a totally independent role without considering their personal career interests.

Shareholders' rights

Under the existing share registration system, all listed shares are secured and fully transferable. Shareholders should have equal rights in terms of profit sharing, participation in shareholder meetings in person or via proxy, voting, and monitoring/questioning/making recommendations to the management. However, given that the most common shareholding structures have one major shareholder, it is difficult for the minority shareholders to form a large enough pool to reach the minimum thresholds needed to enjoy some of their rights, such as nominating directors, calling special meetings, and raising a resolution to the board and/or at the shareholder meetings.

From a legal standpoint, a company's Articles of Association have binding force on all shareholders, directors, supervisors, and managers. The Articles should be approved at shareholder meetings. The Law also allows shareholders to amend the content of the Articles.

The PRC laws give shareholders preemptive rights. Such rights can effectively prevent the issuance of shares to new shareholders and thus mitigate the potential for dilution of existing shareholders' ownership stakes and voting rights.

Disclosure requirements

In addition to the Company Law, the Code of Corporate Governance requires listed companies to disclose corporate governance–related information such as composition of the board of directors and BoS, evaluation of the board of directors and BoS members, attendance records of independent directors and their independent opinion on connected party transactions and executive appointment/removal, establishment of functional subcommittees and their operating details, discrepancy between the actual situation and the requirements stipulated in the Code, and the improvement plan for corporate governance.

Other Recent Developments

Enforcement

Overregulation and underenforcement is a common theme that charac-
terizes most Asian governance systems. China is no exception in this
regard. Selective enforcement is commonly seen in all sectors across
China, including the capital markets. As a result, corporate risk-takers are
frequently willing to challenge the system, hoping that the laws or rules
would not be applied to them even if they were caught. Such practices are
highly detrimental to the integrity and development of China's legal and
regulatory system.

Incentive systems

The Code of Corporate Governance requires listed companies to set up
incentive and control systems. Listed companies are now required to establish a review system for directors, supervisors, and management, and set
up a performance-linked remuneration mechanism. Although nomination
and remuneration committees are not compulsory under the listing rules,
the relevant persons in most cases are not involved directly in the decisionmaking process in determining their own compensation packages.

However, recent statistics are not very encouraging. Of the 1124
listed companies, only about 6 percent currently have such incentive systems. Of the 6 percent that have incorporated incentive systems, only a
few companies have adopted corporate control systems.

Independent directors

It was required that all domestic listed companies have at least two independent directors on or before June 30, 2002, and one-third of the board
members had to be independent directors on or before June 30, 2003.
Though independent directors only comprise a minority percentage of the
board, it is important to have some independent voices heard. For major
transactions and connected party transactions, the guidelines require
independent directors' approval before the proposal can be submitted to
the entire board of directors. Independent directors also can provide independent views on issues such as important investment opportunities,
directors' appointments and removals, and directors' and executives'
remunerations. However, the true effectiveness of the independent directors remains to be seen in practical terms. In particular, it needs to be
demonstrated that independent directors are provided a meaningful role

on company boards—and are not just window dressing for compliance requirements. Active participation of the independent directors is more crucial than simple compliance with the regulatory requirements.

The CSRC regularly conducts training programs for directors and independent directors. However, these short two- to three-day training programs can merely provide general guidance. A lack of qualified persons to take up the over 3000 independent director positions is one of the major issues. Along with opening up the capital markets to foreign investors, more foreign directors will need to fill this gap.

INFORMATIONAL INFRASTRUCTURE

Accounting Practices and Standards

Accounting system

Except for some overseas listed companies, most companies in the PRC are only required to report their financial accounts under the local accounting standards. The local standards are based on PRC Accounting Law and individual company standards. Since 1993, under the supervision of the MoF, the China Accounting Standards Committee (CASC) started developing a range of accounting standards. This initiative was carried a step further in 1999 when a U.S.$27.4 million loan from the World Bank and a U.S.$5.6 million equivalent credit from the International Development Association (IDA) were provided to the Committee to fund the U.S.$85 million "Accounting Reform and Development Project." This project, in turn, completed the local standards by either introducing new standards or amending the old standards. In 2002 alone, 11 accounting standards were either introduced or amended by the CASC. As of the end of 2002, a total of 16 standards were issued.

Differences between local standards and IAS

Differences between the existing PRC standards and IAS have narrowed considerably. However, there are still some major differences in key areas such as consolidation basis, provisions, and off-balance sheet treatment. Table 18-2-1 contains a detailed list of discrepancies between the PRC accounting standards and IAS as noted by the major global accounting firms. On the other hand, the new national accounting standards became effective over the past 2 years. Key areas where PRC standards and IAS have started to converge include business combinations, lease accounting, impairment of

T A B L E   18-2-1

Differences between PRC Accounting Standards and IAS

Chinese accounting may differ from that required by IAS due to the absence of specific Chinese rules on recognition and measurement in the following areas:

Combining of interests	IAS 22.8
Provisions in the context of acquisitions	IAS 22.31
Employee benefit obligations	IAS 19
Discounting of liabilities	IAS 37.45
The treatment of an issuer's financial instruments	IAS 32.18/23
The de-recognition of financial assets	IAS 39.69
Hedge accounting for derivatives	IAS 39.142
The treatment of the cumulative amount of deferred exchange difference on disposal of a foreign entity	IAS 21.37

There are no specific rules requiring disclosures of:

A primary statement of changes in equity, exceptions for joint stock limited enterprises	IAS 1.7
The fair value of financial instruments (except for listed investments)	IAS 32.77
The fair value of investment properties	IAS 40.69
Discontinuing operations	IAS 35
Diluted earnings per share	IAS 33.47
The current or FIFO cost of inventory when LIFO is used	IAS 2.36

There are also inconsistencies between the PRC standards and IAS. Under the PRC standards:

Certain subsidiaries with dissimilar activities can be excluded from consolidation	IAS 27.14
Subsidiaries are excluded from consolidation if intended for sale, even if previously consolidated	IAS 27.13
For most business combinations accounted for using purchase accounting, the identifiable assets and liabilities of subsidiaries acquired are consolidated based on their book values	IAS 22.40
Either provisions for major overhaul costs or deferral of incurred major overhaul costs are allowed	SIC 23
Trading and derivative financial assets and liabilities generally are not held at fair value	IAS 39.69/93
Proposed dividends are accrued	IAS 10.11

T A B L E   18-2-1 (Continued)

Differences between PRC Accounting Standards
and IAS

There are also inconsistencies between the PRC standards and IAS. Under the PRC standards:	
Deferred tax accounting is uncommon and, when done, is calculated on the basis of timing differences, with the deferral method or the liability method allowed	IAS 12
Definition of extraordinary items is wider	IAS 8.6/12
Certain disclosures relating to primary segments (for example, acquisitions and depreciation of assets) are not required	IAS 14.57/58
There are no rules addressing the consolidation of special purpose entities	SIC 12
In certain enterprises, other issues could lead to differences from IAS:	
Finance leases can be recognized at the undiscounted amount of minimum lease payments	IAS 17.12
There is no specific requirement for segment reporting	IAS 14.44

Source: Andersen, BDO, Deloitte Touche Tohmatsu, Ernst & Young, Grant Thornton, KPMG, PricewaterhouseCoopers, GAAP 2001—A Survey of National Accounting Rules Section 3—Country Summaries.

assets, preoperating expenses, foreign currency translation, rules concerning the calculations of earnings per share, and segment reporting.

Implementation of the system

Aside from the accounting standards, the overall Chinese accounting system is still evolving. Implementation is the key governance challenge relating to the PRC accounting system. In December 2001, China's National Audit Office randomly checked the auditing work of 16 CPA firms. A total of 32 audit reports were examined, of which 21 were from local listed companies. Out of the 32 audit reports checked, 23 reports issued by 14 CPA firms were found to contain seriously inconsistent facts. The total fabricated amounts or discrepancies contained in these 23 financial reports reached as high as RMB7.1 billion (approximately U.S.$860 million). In this investigation, 72 percent of financial reports, 86 percent of the CPA firms' audit engagements, and 41 accountants were involved in fabrication of financial statements. These figures directly point to the urgency for improving governance standards among the corporate and professional firms. It also sent a strong message to the regulators for a more strict compliance requirement.

Transparency and Disclosure

Quality of disclosure

In 2001 and 2002, the CSRC released a series of disclosure standards and requirements. To ensure quality of disclosure, the new Ordinance on Disclosure requires the heads of the company, the accounting department, and the external accounting firm to make a public announcement ensuring true and complete disclosure of the reports. It also requires disclosure of any cross-shareholdings among the top 10 largest shareholders.

Timing of financial reporting

All publicly listed companies have to file and disclose financial results on a quarterly basis. Continuous disclosure is not required. However, any significant events that may impact stock prices have to be publicly announced immediately.

Remuneration and nomination

Matters involving executive nominations and remuneration are normally decided behind closed doors. Detailed disclosure on remuneration in the public domain is generally nonexistent. This is largely due to the fact that key directors and executive members are appointed by the major shareholder, i.e., the government. There is still a large gap between the salary levels of government official and private sector market rates. It remains culturally awkward and sensitive to publicly compare pay levels of government officials, directors, or top management appointed by the government in the listed companies, and the market rates. Disclosure of detailed remuneration information at the individual level is such a sensitive issue that even the new Corporate Governance Code did not address it.

Auditor independence

The national accounting professional organization, Chinese Institute of Certified Public Accountants, operated through the MoF, has administered and issued the professional designation "Certified Public Accountant" to qualified candidates since 1988. The national examination for Chinese CPAs was introduced in 1994. The CPA firms also are licensed and required to comply with the rules and standards.

The listing rules require the external auditor of a listed company to have CPA licenses. Most of these appointments are awarded without a public tendering process. Information on how and why a CPA firm is selected remains confidential within the "insider" circle of the top management. Furthermore, there is no requirement for disclosure of auditor fees versus nonaudit fees in the annual reports, and there is no specific rule or requirement on auditor rotations.

NOTES

1. Bank of China, China Construction Bank, Industrial and Commercial Bank of China, and Agricultural Bank of China.

2. Import and Export Bank of China and Development Bank of China.

3. China Everbright Bank, Huaxia Bank, Guangdong Development Bank, Shanghai Pudong Development Bank, China Merchants Bank, Shenzhen Development Bank, and Fujian Industrial Bank.

4. Figures are as of year-end 1998.

5. Chinese companies open for foreign investors (including Hong Kong investors) include: B-shares (listed and traded at the Shanghai and Shenzhen exchanges, and open for foreign investors); H-shares (listed and traded at the Hong Kong exchanges); N-shares (listed and traded at the New York exchange); L-shares (listed and traded at the London exchange); and Red-chips (domiciled in Hong Kong, as well as listed and traded at the Hong Kong exchange).

REFERENCES

Andersen, BDO, Deloitte Touche Tohmatsu, Ernst & Young, Grant Thornton, KPMG, PricewaterhouseCoopers, "GAAP 2001, A Survey of National Accounting Rules Benchmarked against International Account Standards," 2001.

China Economic Information Network, www.cei.gov.cn.

Caijing Magazine, www.caijing.com.cn.

Chen, R. H. "China Administrative Law," Joint Publishing (HK) Co. Ltd., Hong Kong, January 1998.

China Insurance Regulatory Commission, www.circ.gov.cn.

China Securities Regulatory Commission, www.csrc.gov.cn.

China Statistical Bureau, "China Statistical Digest 2001," China Statistical Publishing Ltd., 2001.

"China Statistical Yearbook 1993," China Statistical Information and Consultancy Service Center, International Center for the Advancement of Science and Technology Ltd., 1993.

Dong, S. Z., and R. Z. Li, *Finance Law*, Joint Publishing (HK) Co. Ltd., Hong Kong, December 1998.

Leung, H. X., Y. F. Long, and H. C. Chen. "China Property Law," Joint Publishing (HK) Co. Ltd., Hong Kong, July 1997.

Ling, B., and S. W. Shang. "China Contract Law," Joint Publishing (HK) Co. Ltd., Hong Kong, March 1999.

Liu, R. F. "China Company Law," Joint Publishing (HK) Co. Ltd., Hong Kong, June 2001.

Shanghai Stock Exchange, www.sse.com.cn.

Shenzhen Stock Exchange, www.sse.org.cn.

State Administration of Foreign Exchange, www.safe.gov.cn.

State Development Planning Commission P.R.China, www.sdpc.gov.cn.

The People's Bank of China, www.pbc.gov.cn.

Wang, G., W. S. Zhou, and M. F. Leung. "China Legal System," Joint Publishing (HK) Co. Ltd., Hong Kong, January 2000.

India

G. V. Mani

INTRODUCTION

India is an emerging market, transforming itself from an inward-looking, controlled economy to a liberalized and outward-looking country participating in the political and economic structures of the West. India is the second-largest country in the world by population, with a democratically elected government, a predominantly English-speaking populace, and extremely low penetration levels for most key consumer goods. In addition, large-scale investment is required in almost all areas of infrastructure such as roads, energy, and ports. India has a burgeoning software export industry and is increasingly becoming a global hub for outsourcing IT-enabled services such as data centers and transaction processing. The increasing interest among international investors in the Indian markets (total foreign direct investment in India over the five-year period 1997 to May 2002 is of the order of U.S.$12 billion compared to around U.S.$ 0.50 billion achieved in the prior five years[1]), coupled with the globalization of Indian industry, Indian industry's new presence in international capital markets, and also the large number of foreign mutual funds who manage India funds have all brought about an increasing awareness for corporate governance and its importance to the development of the Indian economy going forward.

The framework for improving corporate governance in India continues to take shape, building from its common law foundation. Improvements in recent years in Indian law, regulation, and accounting reflect positive steps forward. In particular the Birla Code and the report of the Naresh Chandra committee embody reforms that are similar in structure with reforms taking place in other countries around the world. However, in the case of India, improvements in written codes and laws are only a starting point to an improved governance environment. These must be better meshed with more effective legal and regulatory enforcement. In particular, the Indian legal system can be slow and bureaucratic. The Finance Ministry is seeking to bolster the practical enforcement power of its chief securities market regulator, the Securities and Exchange Board of India (SEBI). While these reforms show promise, the impact in practical terms remains to be seen. Moreover, these reforms must be appreciated in the context of a market environment where institutional and retail investors are relatively passive with regard to governance issues.

MARKET INFRASTRUCTURE

India's market infrastructure continues to grow and become more market oriented. However, the large role of the state and the legacy of the historically closed economy can still be felt. Corporate ownership is generally concentrated in the hands of "promoters," or family-owned conglomerates, which yield a great deal of power. Domestic investors are not generally active in pressing for greater shareholder rights, and there is relatively limited ownership from foreign institutional investors.

General Stage of Economic Development

During the last decade, the Indian economy has been in the midst of a transition from a closed, controlled economy to an open, liberalized economy. The first phase of reforms, begun in earnest in 1992 and which is largely seen to be over, involved the dismantling of government controls over the production, pricing, and distribution of almost all goods and services in the country except in some strategic and social sectors of the economy. The second phase of reforms has involved the further dismantling of trade restrictions, bringing the country in line with norms of the World Trade Organization (WTO), as well as the continued sale of the state's interest in government controlled units. After the current phase is completed, many consider capital account convertibility to be the only key area left to tackle, which is expected to be achieved once the already enacted reforms are seen to be working without affecting economic and market stability.

The Indian economy has experienced higher growth trajectories since the onset of reforms in the early 1990s. Growth in real GDP, which had averaged around 3.8 percent an annual basis between 1980 and 1990, increased to an average of 6.7 percent during 1992 to 1996 and to 5.9 percent during 1997 to 2000. The growth rate declined somewhat to 4.8 percent from then onward until 2002 to 2003.[2] These growth rates are impressive and India has demonstrated remarkable resiliency by being one of the few countries to actually record an increase in economic growth in the face of stabilization and adjustment measures that were implemented in 1991.

In recent years, however, economic growth has been constrained by the inability to achieve fiscal targets, infrastructure bottlenecks, and delays in implementing structural reforms. The government has recently taken a number of initiatives that suggest a strengthened commitment to structural reform, including liberalization of the insurance sector, automatic clearance for foreign direct investment in many sectors, reforms to the tax system (including a reduction in the number of tax bands, or brackets), convergence toward dual VAT, the phased elimination of the exemption of export income from taxation, and a landmark agreement on state sales tax rationalization.

A decade of economic reforms has altered the structure of the Indian economy by making it more resilient to external shocks than before. However, the reform process is far from complete, and there is general agreement that it needs further deepening to consolidate economic growth. Support for continued reforms is still strong, and there is a favorable environment for businesses and government to address corporate governance issues.

Ownership Structure

Corporate ownership in India is highly concentrated. Around 50 to 60 percent of the share capital of listed corporates is held by promoter families/parent companies (that is, other corporations; these parent companies are called "promoters" in India), around 15 to 20 percent is in the hands of financial institutions and mutual funds, around 5 to 10 percent with foreign institutional investors, while the balance of 15 to 20 percent is in the hands of the general public. Of these major players, the institutional investors are generally passive and the overall participation by public shareholders (at least as judged by their participation at general meetings) is relatively low. Concentration of ownership and influence of the promoters—or family members—in the management of companies remains a governance challenge for India.

Financial markets. The Indian capital markets are quite well developed with 2 major stock exchanges, 22 regional/other exchanges, and over 5000 listed entities. Trading is automated at both the major stock exchanges (The Bombay Stock Exchange [BSE] and National Stock Exchange [NSE]) and in some of the regional exchanges. A guaranteed settlement program has minimized the counterparty risk to a reasonable extent. Trading is largely in dematerialized form and settlement is handled through the depositaries and the clearing bank on a T+3 basis. The central clearinghouses associated with the stock exchanges settle trades of nondematerialized shares.

The lack of depth and breadth is a key challenge facing the Indian stock markets. Of the over 5000 companies listed, active trading takes place in around 1 percent of the scrips; top 20 to 30 stocks account for over 80 percent of market turnover; top 30 traded stocks account for over 65 percent of market capitalization[3]). Until recently, the Indian markets also showed a large volume of non-delivery-based trading. The Securities and Exchange Board of India (SEBI) has actively taken steps to reduce this activity by banning short sales and clamping down on carryforward trades. The introduction of derivative trading is a positive step in enhancing the depth and stability of the capital markets.

The ownership and management of the stock exchanges is the other challenge facing the markets. Only NSE, Over the Counter Exchange of India, and the Inter-Connected Stock Exchange of India are corporatized stock exchanges in India, managed by professionals who are not broker-members; broker-members manage all the other exchanges, including the BSE. However, SEBI has issued directions to most exchanges to review their ownership structure and to initiate processes to de-mutualize and eventually, corporatize.

The Indian debt market trades principally in government securities, corporate bonds, short-term certificates of deposit, and commercial paper. The government securities market is by far the largest of these and has expanded considerably since 1991, both in terms of range of available maturities and in terms of secondary market activity. The last few years also have witnessed increased regulatory activity with respect to the development of the debt markets. Among the recent developments are the adoption of a delivery-only against payment system (DVP), approval for foreign institutional investors to invest in debt securities, and the establishment of primary and satellite dealers to trade in government securities. Still the debt markets have a long way to go in terms of their development.

Other Institutional/Cultural Factors

Privatization. Privatization remains a crucial component of economic reforms and market development. The privatization process in India was initiated in 1991–1992 when the government divested its stakes (representing between 10 and 20 percent of such companies) in a clutch of selected state-owned companies. Since then, progress on the privatization front has been slow and while the government has been able to progressively reduce its stake in 48 state enterprises, it has been able to affect a majority sale only in 11 instances. The privatization process has had its political overtures and speedier pace of privatization would definitely contribute to speedier development of the financial markets.

LEGAL ENVIRONMENT

India's legal framework includes detailed and comprehensive company law, which has been augmented in recent years to address improvements in corporate governance practices. However, effectiveness of the legal system, particularly in terms of timely enforcement, remains a challenge and a priority.

Background on the Legal Systems and Legal Tradition

India's legal system has evolved over the years yet is based largely on the British common law system. Following U.K. practice, company law classifies most companies as either public companies limited by shares or private companies limited by shares. There are also a large number of government organizations that operate in the infrastructure sector (railways, postal systems, electric utilities, public work departments, ports, etc.). These entities are economically significant, but are run as quasi-government departments.

India's legal infrastructure is quite detailed and comprehensive. While the legislative process can at times be exceptionally slow, regulatory bodies such as SEBI (the market regulator) and the Reserve Bank of India (RBI)– the Central Bank, as well as professional bodies such as the Institute of Chartered Accountants of India (ICAI), the Institute of Company Secretaries of India (ICSI), and their professional members, have taken concrete steps to mitigate this impediment. The recent enactment of the Securitization and Reconstruction of Financial Assets and Enforcement of Security Interest Act (New Foreclosure Laws) are big steps in a positive direction. Despite this, enforcement of India's laws ranks among the largest roadblocks to further governance reform.

PRINCIPAL LEGAL PROVISION— THE COMPANIES ACT

The most important legislation governing corporate India is the Companies Act,[4] (amended in 2000). The Act regulates most aspects of a public company's life, including incorporation, formation of the board of directors, and a company's share capital. The Act was first introduced to Parliament in 1956 and was substantially updated in 1997 and again in 2000 through a series of amendments. The amended Act includes several improvements to India's corporate law and governance regime such as:

- Requiring mandatory appointment of audit committees in publicly listed companies.
- Requiring a Directors' Responsibility Statement to be included in the directors' report.
- Permitting small shareholders to appoint one director to the board.
- Instituting disqualification of boards of directors for default on public debt and nonpayment of dividends.

Some of the salient provisions of the 1956 Companies Act are outlined below.

Shares and Share Capital

- Shares can be issued only with specific shareholder approval; share issues only in dematerialized form.
- Shares can be issued with preferential rights; these preferences are to the right of a fixed dividend and to receive a preferential repayment over ordinary shareholders in the event of liquidation.
- Shares can be issued with different rights with respect to both dividends and voting.

Board of Directors

- Unitary board structure, executives, and nonexecutives sit together on the same board; minimum 3 directors, no maximum size (most companies have between 7 and 12).
- Alternate directors permitted; board can appoint additional directors without first seeking approval by shareholders. They may serve only until the next annual general meeting (AGM).
- Nominee directors from financial institutions (FIs) permitted.

- Maximum 15 board membership for a director excluding alternate directorships.
- Nonexecutive directors' required to retire by rotation; one-third of the current membership to retire every year; all directors serve three-year terms.
- Executive directors appointed for a period of five years, retirement by rotation rules are often not applicable to them.
- Directors usually elected by a simple majority of those shareholders present and voting. Cumulative voting rights not recognized.
- Shareholders can remove a sitting nonexecutive director before the expiry of his three-year term through an ordinary resolution (a simple voting majority).

Governing Documents of Companies

- *Memorandum of Association*: The Memorandum of Association (MoA) is a brief founding document that sets a company's self-allowed activities and scope of business.
- *Articles of Association:* These represent the fundamental working document of the company—how it organizes its board of directors, calls shareholder meetings, structures its share capital, etc. Articles are allowed wide latitude to operate within the framework of the Act. Articles typically include provisions relating to shares and share capital (classes of shares, variations of rights of shares, transferability, etc.), shareholders and shareholder meetings (which items require a majority, which a supermajority vote, etc.), the board and its meetings (size of board, the presence of alternate directors, filling casual vacancies, remuneration, voting procedures, quorum requirements, etc.).

Shareholder Meetings

- Companies to convene an annual general meeting of shareholders at least once every 15 months in addition to any special meeting that may have convened within the last year.
- AGMs, to be held only during business hours, cannot be called on a public holiday and must take place in the town or city where the company has its registered office.

+ Companies can convene special general meetings called extraordinary general meetings (EGMs).
+ Notice of every AGM/EGM to be sent to all shareholders
  approximately 25 days in advance. Companies must include in
  the notice annual financial statements, directors' and auditors'
  report, and a detailed explanation of all items requiring special
  resolution (three-quarters voting in favor) for approval.
+ Proxies permitted to attend and vote; to be intimated 48 hours
  before the meeting.
+ Voting by post permitted for certain matters.
+ Shareholders holding at least 10 percent of paid up capital or
  100 in number can requisition a general meeting; company has
  to treat this similar to EGM and send notices, and convene and
  conduct the meeting.

Minority Shareholder Rights

+ Shareholder-prompted investigations. India's Company Law
  Board may instruct the government to investigate a company for
  violating the rights of its shareholders on an application made
  by a shareholder or group of shareholders holding at least one-
  tenth of the company's total voting power or by at least 100
  shareholders. Applications to the Company Law Board can be
  brought on the basis of oppression (management of the company that is prejudicial to certain members and/or oppressive to
  others) or on the basis of mismanagement. If an investigation by
  the Law Board bears out any complaints, the Board may take
  action to correct the matter.

Duties and Liabilities of Directors

+ A director is considered to have a fiduciary relationship to
  shareholders, as he or she has been appointed to work in their
  interest. A director who has violated statutes or regulations or
  who is otherwise found deficient in the fulfilment of his or her
  duties is considered to be an "officer in default." These directors can be sued, fined, and imprisoned for offenses under
  the Act.

Disqualification of the Board of Directors

♦ The Act has imposed stringent conditions for the disqualification of company directors. The provisions disqualify every director of a company that has not filed its annual returns for any continuous period of three financial years (on or after April 1999) or who has defaulted on timely payment of interest and principal on deposits and debentures or failed to pay dividends. Such a director may not be appointed as a director of a public company for a period of 5 years.

Appointment and Powers of Audit Committee

♦ The Companies Act makes it compulsory for every company with a paid up capital of Rs. 50 million (approximately U.S.$1.06 million) to appoint an audit committee. The Act also prescribes wide-ranging powers to the audit committee, including the authority to ask management for information, seek clarifications, begin investigations as required, and make recommendations to the board on matters relating to financial management and the audit report, all of which are binding on the board. If the board does not accept the recommendations of the audit committee, then the committee can appeal directly to shareholders.

Takeover Laws

Takeover regulations in India are governed by SEBI under the SEBI Regulations 1997 (Substantial Acquisition and Takeovers). The regulation provides that anyone acquiring 5 percent of the equity capital of a company shall notify the company who in turn shall notify the stock exchanges. Following this procedure, the potential acquirer can then continue to acquire shares up to 15 percent. As soon as the holding reaches 15 percent, however, the acquirer must make a public announcement and offer to acquire a minimum of 20 percent of the voting rights in the company. There are provisions where the acquirer can make an offer for a lower number of shares than 20 percent, though this must be disclosed in the company's prospectus. These takeover laws have been tested in the last 12 to 18 months and appear to have resulted in increased protection of the interest of minority shareholders by obtaining better valuations for minority holdings.

Takeover rules in India are complicated by the ability of a family to control management with relatively low ownership stakes (sometimes as low as 12 to 15 percent) as well as by the new ability to issue shares with different voting rights, which may be used to defend against a takeover. Additionally, parent companies cannot acquire more than 5 percent of the shares of their daughter companies in any financial year under creeping acquisition rules. If an owner wants to acquire more than 5 percent in any year, the takeover code provisions will be triggered and they will have to make a public offer. This leaves daughter companies open to hostile takeovers, evidenced by the numerous takeover attempts of these kinds of companies in recent years. Nonetheless, India is still waiting for its first successful hostile takeover.

Insider Trading Laws

Insider trading rules are set out in the SEBI Insider Trading Regulations 1992. These rules prohibit insiders from dealing in securities on the basis of unpublished price-sensitive information. The law also prohibits insiders from communicating or passing on this information to other people who might benefit. If insider trading is proved against any person, he or she may be barred from securities trading in general, or prohibited from disposing of the acquired shares.

Price Manipulation and Fraud

SEBI also has set out the SEBI Regulations 1995 (Prohibition of Fraudulent and Unfair Trade Practices relating to Securities Market). These regulations seek to prevent practices such as price manipulation and fraudulent transactions. If SEBI proves such an act pursuant to an investigation, it can cancel broking cards (in the case of intermediaries) or may ban companies from accessing the capital markets if the guilty entity is a company.

Laws Related to Corporate Governance Practice

Clause 49—Birla Code. Clause 49, recently introduced to listing agreements at SEBI's insistence, requires every company to comply with certain standards of corporate governance. These standards are based on the report and recommendations of the Kumaramangalam Birla Committee set up by

SEBI to look into this issue. Clause 49 requirements include best practice instructions on the composition of boards of directors, disclosure of all related party transactions, requirements for audit committees (including their composition), remuneration and disclosure of director remuneration, frequency of board meetings, attendance requirements and disclosure of board meetings, segment analysis disclosure, business outlook disclosure, disclosure of shareholding patterns and major shareholders.

Clause 49 also requires disclosure of a report on corporate governance along with a compliance report from the statutory auditors of the company. Clause 49 is to be mandatorily complied with by all listed companies.

Naresh Chandra Committee Report. In light of the development in the U.S. markets, following the Enron debacle in 2001, the Department of Company Affairs constituted a high-level committee under the chairmanship of Mr. Naresh Chandra. The Committee's recommendation is similar to the Sarbanes-Oxley Bill and includes:

♦ Disqualification criteria for auditors in case they have any direct financial interest, business relationship, or personal relationship with the audit client. Audit fees from one client/group not to exceed 25 percent of total fees of the audit firm.

♦ Two-year cooling period for employment of audit partner by audit client or for key officer of audit firm by audit client.

♦ Prohibition on provision of nonaudit services.

♦ Compulsory audit partner rotation.

♦ Disclosure and auditors view on contingent liabilities.

♦ Auditors to highlight disclosure of qualifications.

♦ Management's explanation on auditor replacement; replacement only by special resolution of shareholders.

♦ Auditor appointment only upon recommendation of audit committee.

♦ CEO and CFO certification of annual audited accounts.

♦ Setting up of an independent quality review board to review the quality of audit, secretarial, and accounting firm.

♦ Proposal for specific disciplinary mechanism for auditors.

♦ Clear and exhaustive definition of independent directors.

♦ Minimum 50 percent independent directors; minimum seven directors on company boards of which minimum four shall be independent.

◆ Disclosure of duration of board/committee meetings; participation by teleconference and video conference permitted.
◆ Audit committee to be comprised of only independent directors.
◆ Regular training of independent directors.

REGULATORY ENVIRONMENT

India has a number of official and unofficial regulatory institutions, with the Securities and Exchange Board of India playing a key role with regard to corporate governance issues. Steps are being taken to bolster SEBI's regulatory clout. As with the general legal environment, the ultimate effectiveness of written regulation depends on practical enforcement powers.

The key players in the Indian regulatory structure, key regulations, and their relative level of influence on promoting good corporate governance are listed below.

Securities and Exchange Board of India

In 1992, following the onset of the liberalization process, India's government set up a formal regulatory body for the capital markets: the Securities and Exchange Board of India (SEBI). The establishment of SEBI has been among the most significant corporate governance–related developments in India. SEBI is the primary agency responsible for regulation of the capital markets and is India's SEC equivalent. It shares part of its responsibilities with the RBI India, which regulates Banks, Nonbanking Finance Companies (NBFC) as well as the foreign exchange and money markets. SEBI's remittance includes protecting the interests of investors in securities, promoting the development of the securities market, and regulating the capital markets.

SEBI has positively influenced the governance standards in India by calling for timely disclosure of price-sensitive information, publication of quarterly results and cash flow statements, requiring companies to have compliance officers and to adhere to corporate governance standards (in particular, the Birla Committee report—see above). SEBI also has provided clear guidelines and regulations with respect to insider trading, takeovers, and levels of disclosure in offer documents. SEBI also has set out guidelines and norms for the operation and functioning of stock markets, trading, and carryforward systems, and listing requirements.

SEBI has been vested with the powers of a civil court, although its decisions may be appealed at the local high court level as well as to the Supreme Court (India's two highest courts). The fines that SEBI is authorized to assign range from cash fines of Rs. 5000 per day to a maximum of Rs. 2.5 million (U.S.$50,000) or up to five years imprisonment.

SEBI has introduced a large number of regulations to effectively regulate the capital markets. Most of these regulations tackle key corporate governance issues such as insider trading, takeovers, mergers and acquisitions, and disclosure of information. Most recently, SEBI has introduced a formal requirement to disclose compliance with a corporate governance code of best practice. (See Legal Infrastructure—laws relating to governance practice.) The 2002 SEBI Bill, introduced by the Finance Ministry, is intended to bolster SEBI's enforcement powers.

Ministry of Finance (MoF). The MoF bears direct responsibility for the functioning of the financial markets and reports directly to the Parliament. The MoF prepares and presents the annual budget, which contains direct and indirect tax proposals and provides indicators of the direction of reforms, which are then followed up by the respective ministries. The MoF does not directly interfere in the functioning of the business and financial markets and is increasingly distancing itself from even indirectly influencing the policies of the various bodies operating in the country.

Department of Company Affairs (DCA). The Department of Company Affairs is responsible for administering the Companies Act, 1956, and other business legislations. The DCA drafts new legislation and amendments to existing legislation, circulates and obtains opinions of key constituents, and tables the results in Parliament for approval. It also is responsible for providing various clarifications with respect to the interpretation of legislation. The DCA operates under the administrative control of the Ministry of Law, Justice and Company Affairs.

Registrar of Companies (RoC). The Registrar of Companies is an independent body formed by the government to collect and disseminate information with respect to Joint Stock Companies in India. It is responsible for registering companies and calling for, collecting, and making available information on these companies including annual accounts, annual reports, and interim reports. The RoC has 31 offices across all the Indian states. In recent years, the RoC has begun computerizing the information/records so that access to information is available online.

Company Law Board (CLB). The CLB is the executive arm of the government for the exercise of its power under the Companies Act. While administratively, the CLB is under the DCA, it is an independent quasi-judicial body with the powers of a civil court. It provides approvals (required from the government under the Companies Act) as well as appeals under the various provisions of the Act. Its decisions can be appealed to the High Court and the Supreme Court.

Reserve Bank of India (RBI). The Reserve Bank of India is the country's central bank and plays a larger role in the Indian economy as compared to most central banks. It is responsible for monetary policy, setting benchmark interest rates, managing the treasury operations (both borrowings and redemption) for the government of India and as custodian and controller of the foreign exchange reserves. It is also responsible for regulating debt, money markets as well as banks and nonbanking financial services industries. The RBI also advises the government on key economic issues.

Stock Exchange Listing Agreement. The listing agreement forms the basis on which shares of a company are listed on any public stock exchange. The listing agreement contains a number of provisions requiring the company to keep the stock exchange informed about all material events at the company, both positive and negative. The listing agreement requires companies to publish quarterly results, half yearly results with a limited review by auditors, and audited results for the full financial year together with detailed cash flow statements. Explanations for any large variances (greater than 20 percent) between any two successive results, be they quarterly, half-yearly, or annual, also are required to be provided. Listing agreements also require companies to appoint a compliance officer (normally the company secretary), who is responsible for ensuring that the company follows all the various rules and regulations to which it is subject. The compliance officer also is responsible for addressing investor complaints.

Self-Regulating Organizations. India also has a host of self-regulating organizations who complement the efforts of the entities mentioned above. These comprise the Institute of Chartered Accountants of India (ICAI)—the principal body of accountants and audit professionals in India; the Institute of Company Secretaries of India (ISCI)—the principal body of Company secretaries in India; the Fixed Income Money Market and Derivatives Association of India (FIMMDA)—which focuses on encouraging the orderly development of the debt and derivative markets; and the Association of Mutual Funds in India (AMFI)—which is dedicated to developing the Indian Mutual Fund Industry.

From a regulatory standpoint, there is currently a strong focus on addressing structural and operational issues in India's capital market.

While these initiatives will very likely contribute positively to India's corporate governance practices, in the near term there remain concerns about the effectiveness of many of the country's regulations since the legal process can involve long timeframes in pronouncement of final decisions.

INFORMATIONAL INFRASTRUCTURE

Indian accounting principles are evolving toward international standards, and disclosure is improving. However, minor gaps still exist.

Accounting Standards

Accounting standards in India are influenced by the requirements of The Companies Act and to some extent the listing agreements. Accounting standards are driven by the Accounting Standards Board of the Institute of Chartered Accountants of India (ICAI). Actual accounting practices are influenced by a combination of statutory requirements as well as tax considerations (in India the marginal tax rate is relatively high at 35 percent).

India has 28 mandatory accounting standards. These standards must be adopted by all corporate entities. If there is any deviation from these standards, the professional accountant, who is the statutory auditor of the entity, shall disclose the nature and impact of the deviation in his or her report to the shareholders/stakeholders. All Indian companies are expected to prepare accounts and present them in accordance with Schedule VI of the Companies Act and in line with Indian Accounting Standards. The accounts of the companies are independently audited, and the auditors produce reports on whether the accounts present a "true and fair" view of the financial performance and financial position of the company for the accounting year under consideration.

Indian accounting standards were lagging behind IAS in many areas until around 2000. Since then the ICAI has issued 12 new accounting standards, which take these standards closer to International Accounting Standards (IAS). India today has standards on revenue recognition, valuation of inventories, accounting for depreciation, provision of cash flow statements and segmental reporting, reporting related party transactions, consolidation of accounts, reporting of interest in joint ventures, and accounting for retirement benefits. But gaps still exist. For example, consolidated statements are not required for quarterly reporting.

With regard to access to disclosure, the introduction in 2002 of the Electronic Data Information Filing and Retrieval system (EDIFAR) provides electronic access to financial and other company information filed with Indian stock exchanges. This currently covers the largest Indian companies, but is not in effect for the universe of listed companies in India.

Governance and Value Creation Rating

SEBI, along with credit rating agencies, also has been instrumental in the evolution of a model to rate companies on their governance practices, value creation record, and sustainability of value creation. The value creation being measured is for all stakeholders such as customers, suppliers, employees and the like, and not only shareholders. Titled the Governance and Value Creation (GVC) ratings, these ratings are globally unique since for the first time they set out to measure not only governance practices but also balanced value creation for all stakeholders. These ratings enable companies to be differentiated on the basis of their governance practices and sustainability of value creation, thus enabling SEBI to better focus its efforts.

The Indian accounting standards and the timing and periodicity of information dissemination (see Stock Exchange Listing Agreement above) are clearly in line with the best international standards. Measures such as GVC ratings would further add to the robustness of the information system. The key challenge, however, is access, which is being addressed by the regulators, stock exchanges, as well as companies by using technology effectively. In addition, the implementation of the recommendation of the Naresh Chandra Committee (see Laws Relating to Governance Practice) would strengthen the information infrastructure by further enhancing the purity of the auditor-client relationship.

CONCLUSION

India has made great strides in recent years to bring its corporate governance regime in line with international expectations and best practice. It has overcome the twin obstacles of bureaucracy and internal resistance to change to create a more rational regulatory environment, to increase the general level of disclosure and, via a series of well-publicized codes of best practice, to create an atmosphere of increased awareness and commitment to good corporate governance. However, challenges continue to exist in the area of speedy enforcement and decisionmaking, improving the depth and width of the capital markets, privatization, greater dispersion of shareholding, and distancing ownership and management.

NOTES

1. Government of India website, www.iic.nic.in/iic2_c04.htm.
2. Central Statistical Organization (CSO), Government of India.
3. Market data; CRISIL estimates.
4. Companies Act, 1956.

REFERENCES

"Annual Capital Market Review," The Stock Exchange, Mumbai, 2002.
Central Statistical Organization (CSO), Government of India, 2002.
Companies Act of 1956.
CRISIL Rating Methodology—Governance and Value Creation Ratings, 2003.
Department of Company Affairs, www.dca.nic.in.
India Investment Center, www.iic.nic.in/default.htm, 2003.
Institute of Chartered Accountants of India, www.icai.org.
Market data, CRISIL estimates, 2002.
Ministry of Finance, www.finmin.nic.in.
Ministry of Law and Justice, www.lawmin.nic.in.
National Stock Exchange of India Limited, www.nseindia.com.
Securities and Exchange Board of India, www.sebi.gov.in.
The Stock Exchange, Mumbai, www.bseindia.com.

Korea

Hyung Suk Kim, Nam Soo Kim, and Calvin Wong

INTRODUCTION

Korea has made rapid and significant progress in corporate governance since its economic crisis in the late 1990s. While this progress is set to be maintained, however, further improvements are still needed. The Korean government has placed strong emphasis on raising standards of corporate governance. This is complemented by recent improvements in the legal and institutional framework in Korea, active discussion by (and pressure from) civic groups, and significant efforts by leading companies to improve their governance systems. Furthermore, the inauguration of the highly reform-oriented Roh Moo-hyun administration is expected to add momentum for continuing improvements.

Nevertheless, corporate governance in Korea remains based on the combined "owner-manager" principle, and the functioning of governance systems and regulation is still not effective. Disagreement over the appropriateness of specific governance reform proposals among the corporate sector, led by the chaebols, on one side, and civic groups along with government on the other side, also has slowed the pace of change. Even individual companies that have independently streamlined their governance systems and policies still need to make significant improvement in specific practical areas.

On the positive side, access by enterprises to capital markets is good, as the restructuring of the banking industry has been implemented successfully even during Korea's fast economic recovery since its foreign exchange crisis. At the same time, the opacity of corporate ownership structures and the attitudes of controlling shareholders are key areas that need attention. Efforts by the government, based on recommendations made by international organizations including the International Monetary Fund (IMF), have enabled regulations and systems related to corporate governance to be brought close to international standards. Although regulatory agencies are undergoing integration, overlapping jurisdictions and resulting inefficiencies remain. The information infrastructure in Korea is reasonably developed, with accounting and auditing standards close to international standards, backed by relatively wide disclosure and satisfactory access.

The financial crisis that hit Asia in the late 1990s uncovered serious deficiencies in the Korean economy. These included: inappropriate supervision of the government-led financial system; indiscreet, "fleet"-type management by Korea's chaebol; and improper management decisions made by controlling shareholders. While progress has been made, Korea has failed to fully implement principles of market competition during the process of economic liberalization, and has failed to create a fully transparent economic environment.

Continued efforts by market participants to seek legal and institutional reforms and improve efficiency following the economic crisis have helped Korea to record economic recovery at a rate faster than any other Asian country in the aftermath of the crisis. In corporate governance, significant improvement has been made during a relatively short period. However, the speed of fundamental change in corporate ownership structures remains slow and the lack of a strong governance culture points to weakness of governance standards at individual enterprises. The success in Korea's implementation of stronger corporate governance practices will depend on the degree to which structural reform of the corporate sector, including the chaebol, will succeed in the future.

Current Corporate Governance Issues

Following the 1997–1998 financial crisis, Korean corporate governance has improved systematically. Nevertheless, systematic changes are not enough to ensure fundamental changes in corporate culture, business ethics, and among interest groups involved in policymaking. Discussion on potential improvements in corporate governance practice is continuing while interest groups argue for their own agendas.

The issue of how to reform the chaebol is challenging the effort to improve corporate governance in Korea while the nation is struggling to resolve the following key issues.

+ Class action suits;
+ Ceilings on conglomerates' equity investments;

+ Corporate governance in public companies; and
+ Strengthening the rights of shareholders and directors or external directors.

Class action suits

With a draft bill pending in the Korean legislature, the debate between the government (as well as) civil bodies and the business sector is still under way. The former group claims the introduction of class action suits would boost the rights of minority shareholders and transparency in the management of companies. In turn, the business sector argues that the implementation of such a legal system is premature in Korea and could impede corporate restructuring.

Ceiling on large corporations' equity investments

Under the Monopoly Regulation and Fair Trade Act, large corporations are allowed to own up to 25 percent equity in their subsidiaries. However, the effect of the ceiling is questioned because of various exceptions allowing business groups to exceed the ceiling. One interest group is calling for an overhaul in the relevant laws and regulations while the business sector insists the ceiling is undermining the growth potential of large corporations.

Corporate governance in public companies

The government is reviewing the possibility of promoting privatized public companies to impose corporate governance as efficiently as in the private sector. The government is considering the use of stakes in companies owned by the government, banks or other institutional investors, including pension funds and other funds, to improve corporate governance in public companies.

Strengthening rights of shareholders and directors or external directors

Issues on expanding directors' authority, specifying directors' commitments required to fulfill their duty to shareholders, and defining external directors' limited responsibility are being discussed. Furthermore, the approval of shareholders for new share issues, transactions with related parties, and the ban on excluding application of the articles of incorporation for cumulative voting are being considered.

MARKET INFRASTRUCTURE

Korea's political environment is characterized by the high geopolitical threat from the North Korean regime, a rapidly developing system of democracy, a government that exerts a significant amount of influence over the country's economic activities, and a lack of autonomy in the private sector as a result of such government influence.

Tensions between South and North Korea remain high, despite the "Sunshine Policy" pursued by the former President Kim Dae-Jung. A series of actions taken by North Korea has heightened fears of a conflict on the Korean peninsula. Although the possibility of a war between South and North Korea is considered low, the North's closed political system makes its future response unpredictable.

Korean enterprises in general follow a typical ownership and control form where the founders and their successors and other interested parties manage businesses as majority shareholders. This type of structure has the benefit of enabling quick and unified decisionmaking. At the same time, the structure does not protect the interests of minority shareholders, and hinders appropriate monitoring and control of management. It also creates problems relating to management succession and the role of family members versus professional managers.

Macroeconomic Stability

Korea's foreign currency sovereign credit rating has returned to the level recorded prior to the economic crisis of 1997, an indication of the extent of its economic recovery. The Standard & Poor's foreign currency rating is A-, with a stable outlook. The upward trend in the credit rating reflects Korea's ability to effectively deal with external shocks, its more flexible labor market, stronger financial liquidity, and restructuring initiated by the Korean government. Nevertheless, there are several factors constraining further improvement in Korea's ratings, including the unfinished restructuring in the private sector and the military threat from North Korea.

Korea's remarkable growth has been quoted as a model case for developing countries. However, the 1997 economic crisis disclosed structural weaknesses, particularly the need for greater liberalization to support a growth-centered policy, and the importance of adopting principles of market competition and creating a transparent economic environment.

Ownership Structure

The level of corporate ownership, standing at more than 93 percent by the private sector as of 2001, indicates that Korean enterprises are privately owned in general.

Following the election of Roh Moo-Hyun, the basic policy on the privatization of major public enterprises is expected to be maintained. However, the new administration will reexamine these policies for sectors of major public interest, such as transport and power.

Ownership structures of Korean enterprises are based on the conglomerates known as "chaebol." As of January 2003, there were 43 business groups and 728 subsidiaries subject to restrictions on mutual contributions. The relative importance to, and influence of these enterprises on, the Korean economy are absolute.

Korean enterprises in general are governed by a controlling shareholder and manager system under which controlling shareholders and managers act as owner and representative based on a high internal equity ratio resulting from mutual investment. In other words, the controlling shareholders exclusively control enterprises as managers, with ownership and control not separated. Table 18-4-1 shows that ownership concentration of leading chaebol (controlling shareholders plus their affiliates) has diminished somewhat from 1999 to 2001. But ownership concentration remains substantial at 45 percent.

Institutional investors, including banks, play minimal roles as shareholders, investors, and creditors. This is attributable to the high insider equity ratios of the conglomerates, banks' investment in stocks as rela-

T A B L E   18-4-1

Ownership Concentration in Korea

	[Share Ownership (% of total outstanding shares)]		
Item	Controlling Shareholders(A) and Interested Parties(A)	Affiliates(B)	Total(A+B)
1999	5.4%	45.1%	50.5%
2000	4.5%	38.9%	43.4%
2001	5.6%	39.4%	45.0%

Source: Fair Trade Commission. 30 chaebol.

tionship investments, and loans influenced by political judgment. Generally, institutional investors have tended to avoid conflict with the chaebols given that many are actually chaebol affiliates. This reality will not change significantly in the near term. National pensions, being subject to strong government oversight and influence, also have avoided conflict with the chaebols, who in turn had historically enjoyed strong government support. In the latter case, however, investors may exert more influence going forward as the government's position vis-à-vis the chaebols has shifted.

The monitoring function of external corporate control bodies is limited. The market for corporate control does not currently constitute a great discipline for company managers, reflecting in part a nonactive mergers-and-acquisitions (M&A) market and undeveloped markets for managerial talent. Since the financial crisis, there have been some institutional improvements, including the introduction of a tender offer system, to revitalize M&A activity.

Ease of Access to Public Exchanges

The stock markets in Korea consist of the Korea Stock Exchange (KSE) and the Korea Securities Dealers Association Automated Quotation (KOS-DAQ) market. As of February 2003, there were 685 companies listed on the KSE and 862 enterprises registered with the KOSDAQ.

KSE listing requirements are prescribed by its securities listing rules. Securities must satisfy the standards prescribed by the operating regulation of the KOSDAQ market and the Korea Securities Dealers Association registration regulations.

To qualify for listing stocks on the KSE, an enterprise should have been in operation for three years or more, and have capital stock of W5 billion or more, equity capital of W10 billion or more, sales averaging W15 billion or more during the past three years, with the figure for the recent year being W20 billion or more, and it is required to satisfy stock split requirements and financial standards (see Appendix, Article 15, Listing Rules).

Requirements for registration with the KOSDAQ market are similar to the KSE listing rules. However, the KOSDAQ registration requirements are far more relaxed than those of KSE because the KOSDAQ market is intended to supply stabilized, long-term funds to knowledge-based enterprises carrying high growth potential and technological power.

Banking System

Banks in Korea have played important roles in supporting industrial development and increasing exports under the supervision of the government. While the government pursued powerful growth-oriented policies, chaebol have enjoyed benefits from large, low-interest loans from the banks controlled by the government. Both chaebol and the banks have posted remarkable growth.

In the 1990s, banks gradually began to disclose problems. These problems can largely be classified into three types: management practices that put more emphasis on the size of operating income than profitability, inefficient regulation and supervision by the government, and the failure to adapt to changes in the operating environment. These problems were contributing factors to the foreign exchange crisis in 1997. Following the crisis, the industry was reorganized through the restructuring of the banks.

After the 1990s, the government implemented a financial liberalization policy, allowing interest rate liberalization, relaxing restrictions on the development of the financial industry, and expanding the business areas of financial institutions. Banks' discretionary power has increased with respect to their management—however, government support also has reduced proportionately. The survival of banks in the future will be determined based on independent competitiveness and financial solvency rather than on governmental support.

After the banks' first round of restructuring, large enterprise groups including Daewoo and Saehan became insolvent. This triggered a second round of restructuring, with the government injecting additional public funds and introducing a financial group system. A series of bank restructurings have been completed through the establishment of financial groups by Woori and Shinhan Bank, the merger between Kookmin Bank and the Housing & Commercial Bank, and the takeover of Seoul Bank by Hana Bank. However, there remains considerable room for bank sector restructuring given that the government still owns a substantial portion of the equity in several banks.

LEGAL ENVIRONMENT

The legal system in the Republic of Korea is based on principles derived from Germany's civil laws, although it retains elements of Japanese laws applied during the occupation up to 1945. Korea's commercial code was handed down from Japan based on Germany's stock-related laws, although the German system contains elements of the U.S. system.

Primary Legislation

The basic laws governing corporate governance are as follows:

+ The Commercial Code;
+ Securities and Exchange Act;
+ Act on External Audit of Stock Companies; and
+ Listing rules

Korea's Commercial Code (CC) comprehensively prescribes general matters related to the establishment, organization, and the operation of companies. The Commercial Code and the Securities and Exchange Act (SEA), both of which were amended several times after the financial crisis, reflect major restructuring projects contained in the Memorandum of Understanding signed with IMF and IBRD. The Code and the SEA have shifted emphasis to promoting the efficiency of corporate management, acquiring transparency, and strengthening the rights of minority shareholders.

Laws and Rulings on Corporate Governance Practices

Directors and nonexecutive directors

Appointment of directors   Directors are appointed at a shareholders' general meeting, and should be at least three in number. However, in the case of a company of which the total capital is less than W500 million, the number of the directors may be one or two. Unless prescribed otherwise in the articles of incorporation, shareholders representing no less than 3 percent of total voting shares may request the company to elect directors by means of a cumulative voting. The terms of directors may not exceed three years.

Duties and liabilities of directors   The duties of directors related to business pursuant to the Commercial Code are mainly classified into the duties to be faithful and duties to keep secret. In cases where a director has caused harm to the company, shareholders representing 1 percent of total outstanding shares may request the company to file a suit against such director.

Composition and appointment of nonexecutive directors   Stock listed corporations or KOSDAQ registered corporations prescribed by Presidential Decree shall appoint nonexecutive directors not less than one-quarter of the total number of directors provided that certain stock listed corporations (with total assets greater than W2 trillion) or KOSDAQ registered corporations as prescribed by Presidential Decree shall have not less than three nonexecutive directors. But it shall make the number of nonexecutive directors not less than half the total number of directors. Regulations are also available for the nominating committee to review nonexecutive director candidates.

Regulations on qualification of nonexecutive directors   The Securities and Exchange Law does not prescribe detailed qualification requirements for nonexecutive directors, but prescribes only passive limitations creating criteria which prevents certain people from becoming nonexecutive directors.

The provisions related to the disqualifications of nonexecutive directors, as stipulated in the Securities and Exchange Act, are outlined in considerable detail. The Korea Listed Companies Association established "Service Standards for Nonexecutive Directors" in November 2000. This standard, established on the premise that improved corporate governance strengthens corporate competitiveness and maximizes corporate value, contains comprehensive guidelines regarding the function and legal status of nonexecutive directors, basic authorities and duties, and remuneration.

However, due to the fact that the will of the management is strongly reflected in the nomination and appointment of nonexecutive directors, there is a limit on the extent to which many nonexecutive directors are truly independent of company management.

Audit committee regulations   The Commercial Code contains relatively detailed provisions governing auditors and the audit committee. The composition of the audit committee shall consist of at least three directors. According to the provisions of the Code, the directors engaged in the company business shall not exceed one-third of the total members of the committee. To guarantee the independent operation of the audit committee, the Code also prescribes that the chairman of the audit committee of securities companies must be a nonexecutive director (Paragraph 2, Article 54-6, Securities and Exchange Law).

Shareholders' meeting

Notice of shareholders' meeting   Shareholders must be notified, in writing or by electronic documents, of any general meetings at least two weeks prior to such meeting.

Proxy rights   Shareholders may have proxies to exercise the voting rights on their behalf. In this case, the proxy shall submit a document proving power of representation at the general meeting.

Voting procedures   There are no specific provisions within the Commercial Code regarding voting procedures and third-party verification of voting results. In general, a system where motions are passed when no objections are heard is used to decide most agenda items at shareholder meetings.

Minority shareholder rights

Regulations on minority shareholder rights can be considered to have made significant progress during the past few years in that the minimum shareholding requirements for exercising important rights have been significantly lowered. The legally guaranteed major rights of minority shareholders are listed in Table 18-4-2.

Other related regulations

Rights of foreign creditors and shareholders   There are no separate regulations governing the status of foreign shareholders. However, the Commercial Code specifies the principle of shareholders' equality indicating that shareholders' rights are not discriminated against according to nationality.

Preemptive rights   Shareholders have preemptive rights, but some exceptions are allowed. The CC stipulates that, "Pursuant to its articles of incorporation, a company may allocate new shares to persons other than current shareholders. However, such act shall be limited to situations where it is necessary for the company to achieve operational objectives, i.e., the introduction of new technologies, the improvement of financial structures, etc."

T A B L E   18-4-2

Requirements for the Exercise of Rights by Minority Shareholders

Rights of Minority Shareholders	KSE Listed Corporations · KOSDAQ Registered Corporations	General Corporations
Derivative suit (promoters, directors, auditors, liquidators)	Holding at least 0.01% of shares for more than 6 months	At least 1%
Rights to demand dismissal of directors, auditors, and/ or liquidators	Holding at least 0.5% of shares for more than 6 months (Large corporation: at least 0.25%)*	At least 3%
Injunction against directors' illegal acts	Holding at least 0.5% of shares for more than 6 months (Large corporation: at least 0.25%)*	At least 1%
Rights to inspect books and related documents	Holding at least 0.1% of shares for more than 6 months (Large corporation: at least 0.05%)*	At least 3%
Rights to convene shareholders' general meeting	Holding at least 3% of voting stocks for more than 6 months (Large corporation: at least 1.5%)*	At least 3%
Rights to demand appointment of auditors to inspect company business and financial conditions	Holding at least 3% of voting stocks for more than 6 months (Large corporation: at least 1.5%)*	At least 3%
Rights to make proposals	Holding at least 1% of stocks (Large corporation: at least 0.5%)*	At least 3%

* *Large corporation:* corporations having capital stock of more than W100 billion as of the end of the last fiscal year.

Insider trading   Securities and Exchange Law prohibits officers, employees, proxies, major shareholders, or other insiders from providing information to third parties in case they learn undisclosed important information in relation to the business. The provision specifies the effective date of the insider to be one year.

The inside trader shall be liable to compensate persons for any damage caused by securities trading and transactions.

REGULATORY ENVIRONMENT

Regulatory Bodies

Government regulatory bodies

There are two main government regulatory bodies in Korea: the Ministry of Finance and Economy (MOFE) and the Financial Supervisory Commission (FSC). The FSC has the Securities and Futures Commission under its control and the Financial Supervisory Services (FSS) as its executive body. Monetary policy is the responsibility of the Monetary Board of the Bank of Korea.

MOFE has the authority to set the principles and the basic directions of economic policy. The main duties of the Financial Supervisory Commission include the generation of policies for financial industry supervision, oversight of the FSS, and the development of guidelines for financial sector restructurings. The main purpose of the Securities and Futures Commission is to perform duties mandated by the FSC such as investigation into unfair trade in the securities and futures markets, business related to corporate accounting standards and audits, and the management and supervision of the securities futures markets.

The FSS was established by the FSC and the Securities and Futures Commission to regulate financial institutions and their functions, inspect the institutions' financial status, and to order corrective measures as required.

The MOFE, the Bank of Korea, and the FSC carry rights to mutually request the submission of related materials. Business cooperation between the regulatory bodies seems to be smooth. However, because some business areas overlap, the efficiency of the overall regulatory bodies still needs to be improved.

Self-regulatory bodies

The self-regulatory bodies include the Korea Stock Exchange (KSE), the Korea Securities Dealers Association, which supervises the KOSDAQ market, and the Korea Listed Companies Association.

The Korea Securities Dealers Association established the KOSDAQ market. The purpose is to perform duties related to market operations, including listed company disclosure, the execution of transactions, and market actions such as the suspension of trading.

The KSE was established to form fair prices for securities and to protect investors. It discloses corporate information, monitors unfair transactions, and examines trading. In case the KSE discovers an unfair act through its own monitoring system, KSE is obliged to report to the Financial Supervisory Commission, which has the right to take punitive actions.

The Korea Listed Companies Association is a nonprofit corporation established under the Securities and Exchange Law to handle matters related to securities. Its main duties include recommending improvement to the system related to securities firms, listed companies, and training. In addition, for use as a reference by listed companies seeking to appoint nonexecutive directors, it distributes a list of persons registered in the manpower bank and recommends candidates for nonexecutive directors. The Korea Corporate Governance Service (KCGS) also has been established and supported by the KSE to provide analytical services to enhance corporate governance awareness among listed Korean companies.

Enforcement of the Law

The FSS's investigative function is limited, because direct investigative rights with respect to financial institutions are maintained by the Securities and Futures Commission operating under the control of the FSC. However, actual investigative rights may be exercised through business association with the Securities and Futures Commission.

The punitive measures that may be taken by the FSS include the cancellation of business licenses or registration for certain institutions, suspension of all or part of a business, closure of business, suspension of part or all of branch business, and the issuance of warnings. Judicial action may be taken by indicting related persons to face prosecution. During 2000 and 2001, there were only two cases of partial business suspension, four cases of reprimand and/or institutional warning, and nine cases of other punitive actions taken by the Financial Supervisory Services. This indicates the relatively minimal level of its practical enforcement activities.

In case a violation is discovered during the process of examining trading or of monitoring members, the KSE may directly punish, or otherwise take other appropriate measures against, relevant members or related persons, pursuant to the KSE's Articles of Incorporation and service regulations. However, the punishment shall be limited to suspension of trading for a specific period, imposing fines in an amount not exceeding W1 billion, or instructing violators to be more careful in the future. In general, KSE reports such cases to the Financial Supervisory Services instead of taking its own investigation and punitive actions.

INFORMATIONAL INFRASTRUCTURE

The Financial Supervisory Commission has the final authority in setting, amending, and interpreting the Korean Accounting Standards (KAS) and the Korean Standards on Auditing.

In 1998, the Financial Supervisory Commission introduced major amendments to the then Korean Financial Accounting Standards and an old version of the Korean Standards on Auditing, in an effort to make them compatible with international standards. At the time, those amendments were issued based on International Accounting Standards (IAS). Meanwhile, the Financial Supervisory Commission revised Korea SubStandards on Auditing, supplemental schedules of the Korean Standards on Auditing, in 1999 by adopting International Standards on Auditing.

Korean Accounting Standards

The KAS consist of 91 articles and is supported by supplementary rulings. The Korea Accounting Institute (KAI) has issued 10 statements of KAS based on IAS, and has prepared more than 20 draft standards and exposure drafts.

In the process of formulating Korean accounting standards, KAI, once it decides IAS inputs are not sufficient for use in Korea, refers to accounting standards generally accepted in the United States. When the business environment in Korea precludes the application of both standards, KAI comes up with exclusively independent standards.

Korean Standards on Auditing

The Korean Institute of Certified Public Accountants (KICPA) has set Korean Standards on Auditing, described through 35 articles and Korean Sub-Standards on Auditing, which it believes are consistent with the International Standards on Auditing.

Public Auditors and Requirements for Independent Audits

A total of 6439 CPAs were registered with KICPA as of December 2002. Among them, 4954 members were working as auditors.

Four international accounting firms and six other local firms, which are member firms of the world's largest accounting firms, make up the mainstream accounting firms in Korea. In total there are 57 accounting companies, nine of which have more than 100 CPAs, and 3375 CPAs are working at all accounting firms combined. Remaining members of KICPA are working in private practices.

The External Audit Act requires financial statements of resident companies to be audited if their total assets reached a minimum of W7 billion in the immediate preceding fiscal year. The financial audit is to be conducted by a qualified CPA or audit teams of accounting firms. Auditors in turn are responsible for submitting the audit report to their client company, the Securities and Futures Commission, and KICPA within the deadline.

Comparison with International Accounting Standards

Consolidated accounts

KAS are generally deemed to comply with IAS. For instance, both accounting rules specify the same kind of financial information for disclosure requirements. But the former demands individual financial statements for key financial data while the latter requires consolidated financial statements. KAS does not have a clause regarding joint venture accounting.

Operating data in addition to financial data

KAS does not specify that the disclosure of financial statements should be accompanied by operating information of the company. However, the disclosure of operating data is essential for a company to go public, although it is not required under KAS.

Segment data

Standards for the definition of operating segments and reporting requirements set out in Korean Accounting Standards Interpretation 50-87 are consistent with IAS. But the requirements for reportable segments differ, making a distinction that KAS does not impose the equity method of accounting for a reportable segment on which the company's investment is concentrated.

Method of asset valuation

Aside from the circumstances under which revaluation of assets is allowed, the way changes in depreciation methods are interpreted and the level of disclosure necessary for related party transactions, there is no significant difference in the way Korean accounting standards and international accounting standards treat revaluation of assets.

KAS complies with IAS in many other aspects: definition of income, expense, profit/loss, cash flow statement, and all real and contingent liabilities. As for the accounting for related party transactions, KAS is more detailed by providing examples and sets forth different disclosure requirements from IAS in terms of coverage.

Required Timing of Disclosure

All resident companies are required to file financial statements with the Securities and Futures Commission to comply with the Commercial Code and publish their balance sheets in a major newspaper under the External Audit Act. Financial statements include a balance sheet, income statement, cash flow statement, and statement of appropriations of retained earnings approved in the general meeting of shareholders.

All companies with stocks listed on either KSE or KOSDAQ under the Securities and Exchange Law are required to disclose audited financial reports on a quarterly basis.

Under the Securities and Exchange Law, listed companies shall meet the periodic disclosure requirements by filing their audit reports and financial reports. In addition, these companies also are subject to prompt reporting of any material events that may affect investors' decisions in making their investment.

A regulatory system for fair disclosure was implemented in November 2002.

Ease of Access to Financial Statements

All companies are required to keep their audited financial statements as well as the audit report and make them available for their shareholders and creditors, if any of them seek access to the financial information during normal business hours.

The Financial Supervisory Service offers financial statements and audit reports of companies subject to the External Audit Act through its website (dart.fss.or.kr). Other financial activities of these companies, such as buy-back or disposal of shares, M&A plans, and purchase of new businesses also are posted.

REFERENCES

An, Ye-Hong. "Current Corporate Governance and Directions for Its Improvement," *The Bank of Korea Financial System Review,* August 1999.

Cho, Jang-yeon, Byung-min Kang, and Kyung-soon Kim. Position Report on Korean Accounting Standards, September 6, 2002.

Jang, Ha-sung. "The Korea Discount and Corporate Governance," November 2001.

Kim, Kak-jung. "Evaluation of Recommendations for Corporate Governance Improvement," October 2000.

Kim, Yong. "A Study on Corporate Governance Since the 1997's Economic Crisis," February 2002.

Kim, Yong-youl. "Corporate Governance Features Necessary for Developing an Advanced Economy," July 2000.

Lee, Sun. "Present and Future Corporate Governance in Korea," March 2000.

Lee, Young-Kee. "Korean Corporate Governance in an Era of Global Competition," April 1999.

OECD. "OECD Corporate Governance Guidelines," 1999.

Park, Se-Hyun. "A Study on Corporate Governance in Korea: Problems and Improvements," August 2002.

Seo, Jung-hwan. "Chaebol Ownership and Corporate Governance: Structures, Changes and Implications," March 2002.

Russia

Julia Kochetygova

INTRODUCTION

Despite significant improvements over the past several years, the level of corporate governance in Russia remains low. The vast majority of Russian companies still lack transparent operational and ownership structures, and suffer from weak internal control procedures. Affiliate party dealings are common, and there are many opportunities for the abuse of minority shareholders.

Legacy is partly to blame. The consolidation of ownership in Russian corporations following the Russian mass privatizations of 1992–1995 was accompanied by corporate "wars," and the weapons were false bankruptcies, improper notification for shareholder meetings, arrests of shares via suits filed by individual shareholders to prevent some owners from attending shareholder meetings, and discriminatory treatment of various shareholders.

During the Russian economic crisis of 1998, following the government's default on its domestic debt, many of the largest banks collapsed, with their owners stripping them of their assets. Meanwhile, the majority of foreign investors pulled out of the Russian market. In recent years, however, foreign direct and portfolio investment has begun to return, though with increased caution and upon the condition of improving corporate governance.

The Russian government and international organizations have put forward a number of initiatives for improving the standards of corporate conduct and governance in Russia. The most significant has been the introduction of the Code of Corporate Conduct, developed under the supervision of the Federal Commission of Securities Markets (FCSM) and sponsored by the EBRD and the government of Japan. Earlier efforts included the OECD's series of roundtable discussions on corporate governance in the 2000–2002 period and its White Paper on Corporate Governance in Russia.

The IFC launched the Corporate Governance Project to assist companies to introduce good governance practices and focus on actions to improve investment attractiveness; the IFC is now developing a corporate governance manual.

The redistribution of ownership stakes, the introduction of strategic shareholders—often in conjunction with significant investments—and the desire to attract outside capital are major driving forces in the improvement in governance standards in Russia.

Although the process of ownership consolidation continues with powerful interests competing for control of attractive assets, the positions of controlling shareholders and other strategic investors have become clearer and more stable in the case of many of Russia's major economic entities. Once the struggles for control are finally resolved, improving performance and attracting capital to fund growth will become top priorities. These objectives approach the paradigms by which international markets operate, and they improve Russia's acceptance within those markets.

MARKET INFRASTRUCTURE

Economic Situation

Russia's 1998 financial collapse closely followed the Asian financial crisis and a steep fall in international oil prices; the country's subsequent recovery, led by a sharp increase in oil prices and the economic benefits of a three-fold devaluation of the ruble, has been accompanied by increased political stability and significantly improved fiscal management.

Although Russia's recovery has been impressive (real GDP increased by an average of 6.5 percent in 1999 to 2001, by 4 percent in 2002,[1] and preliminary figures for January through April 2003 suggest GDP growth over 6 percent), and prudent economic management has supported fiscal and budgetary stability, analysts are still concerned by the country's dependence on oil and gas exports (over 50 percent of total exports). A $1 change in Russia's oil price per barrel has a corresponding $1 billion effect on Russia's budget. While Russia today would be much better able to withstand a sharp oil price drop than in 1998, a sustained low oil price would pose challenges for the country's budget.

Rising oil prices, a budget surplus, and the increasing reserves of the Bank of Russia have helped to resolve a $17 billion 2003 foreign debt–payment spike without IMF aid or new Eurobond issues this year. At the same time the continuing appreciation of the ruble—in particular against a weak

U.S. dollar—will have an adverse effect on Russia's international competitiveness. Although gradually reducing by a few percentage points a year in the past few years, inflation is still in the double digits (during 2001 and 2002, the consumer price index increased by 21.6 and 14.5 percent, respectively).[2]

In spite of the country's huge capital needs in order to repair and replace its aging industrial infrastructure, Russia has been unable to attract significant foreign direct investment in the post-Soviet period, with direct investment making up less than 1 percent of the country's gross domestic product. By contrast FDI accounts for 5 to 10 percent of GDP in central and eastern Europe. According to the Bank of Russia, the country received $3.3 billion in direct investment in 1999, $2.7 billion in 2000, $2.5 billion in 2001, and $1.8 billion in the first nine months of 2002.[3] Though it appears that investment has been stagnant, there are some recent positive signs of change. Most notably, in February 2003 British Petroleum announced a plan to invest $6.75 billion in a joint venture with the Russian oil major, TNK, and a number of consumer and auto sector investments also have been announced during 2003.

While Russia has made significant progress since 2000 in moving ahead with key structural reforms—including tax, land, pension, and judicial reforms—momentum has slowed and major issues of bank, administrative, natural monopoly, and other reforms remain to be tackled. A notable step forward, on the other hand, occurred when the individual income tax rate dropped to a flat 13 percent in 2001, and the profit tax was reduced to 24 percent in 2002. Nevertheless, tax collection, although improving, remains a concern.

The degree of government intrusion into the economy remains high. Tariff regulation in a number of industries (gas, electricity, transportation, and telecommunications) hampers growth and investment. Many industries rely heavily on government support, primarily in the form of cross-subsidies made at the expense of more lucrative and efficient businesses. Examples include fixed-line telecommunications services and local utilities, where certain subscriber categories are subsidized at the expense of others. The airline industry is fettered because some national air carriers are restricted in their ability to purchase more efficient foreign aircraft.

As Russia enters an election season, with Duma elections at the end of 2003 and presidential elections in the spring of 2004, substantial progress on reforms is unlikely until the electoral outcome is clear. At the subfederal level, strong regional governments continue to exert their influence over local companies, often interfering in commercial affairs in the attempt to strengthen hidden forms of cross-subsidization.

Another major concern is that, while Russia's credit and payment culture is gradually improving, corruption, excessive red tape, and a chronic lack of transparency in business practices persist as serious problems hampering the growth and expansion of Russia's private sector.

Prevailing Forms of Ownership and Ownership Structure

Since 1993, 130,000 Russian companies—66 percent of the total—have been privatized, and now account for 77 percent of Russia's GDP.[4] The government maintains controlling stakes in many key industries, including gas, oil pipeline, telecommunications, electricity, and transportation.

The mass privatizations of the 1993–1995 period largely determined the models for subsequent corporate ownership and governance in Russia. Seventy-five percent of Russia's enterprises scattered 51 percent of their shares among employees and managers. As a result, privatization gave the advantage to insiders, while it failed to bring money to the companies themselves. Intensive buy-out campaigns and questionable loans-for-shares deals made by the government led to the development of powerful financial-industrial groups (FIGs) and holding companies in the oil, metals, coal, chemical, food, automotive, and banking sectors.

T A B L E   18-5-1

The Concentration of Ownership of the 42 Largest Russian Companies[6]

	Number of Companies	Percentage*
Number of companies with large shareholders (more than 30%)	39	86
Of which, number of majority held companies (more than 50%)	31	60
Of which, number of companies with big stakes (30%) owned by holdings or part of FIGs	24	42
Of which, largely owned by the government (more than 30% directly)	9	32
Companies who are widely held (largest stakes less than 30%)	3	14

* Share of these companies' market capitalization (MC) in total MC of 42 companies ($104.14 billion as of August 13, 2002).

Today, eight business groups control 85 percent of the revenue from Russia's 64 biggest private companies.[5] Standard & Poor's research of the 42 largest publicly owned companies has shown that their ownership structures are highly concentrated and largely nontransparent (see Tables 18-5-1 through 18-5-3). Ownership is often obscured through shell companies registered in Russia or offshore, notwithstanding the legal requirement to disclose owners of stakes larger than 5 percent. Managers often indirectly own smaller companies.

T A B L E   18-5-2

The Transparency of Ownership of the 42 Largest Russian Companies[7]

	Number of Companies	Percentage[*]
Number of companies disclosing their beneficial majority and largest owners	32	74
Of which, disclosing the government and government-owned holdings	26	48
Of which, disclosing largest private owners	8	38
Of which, disclosing all beneficial owners having substantial stakes	4	34

[*] Share of these companies' market capitalization (MC) in total MC of 42 companies ($104.14 billion as of August 13, 2002).

T A B L E   18-5-3

Disclosed Ownership of the 42 Largest Russian Companies[8]

	Percentage[*]
Total disclosed share of ownership of 42 companies	40
Of which, total government and government-owned holdings' ownership	16
Of which, total private ownership disclosed	24
Share of disclosed private ownership in total private ownership	29

*Share of disclosed ownership in total MC of 42 companies ($104.14 billion as of August 13,2002).

Financial Markets and Their Infrastructure

Russian companies are undervalued because of sovereign and poor corporate governance risks. As a result, when compared to foreign markets, the Russian stock market is shallow. Despite a mostly upward trend in 2001 and 2002, the total capitalization of the Russian capital market in March 2003 was only $127 billion.[9] Daily traded volumes of equities on the major domestic exchanges (MICEX and RTS) and depositary receipts on foreign exchanges were approximately $300 million. Only three companies in Russia (Vimpelcom, MTS, and Wimm-Bill-Dann) have Level III ADRs listed on the NYSE; and only two companies (Rostelecom and Tatneft) have Level II ADRs. In February 2003, the weight of Russia in the S&P/IFCI Composite Index was 6.42 percent (increased from 3.56 percent in October 2001)[10]; weight in the MSCI Emerging Markets Index was 2.54 percent.

The domestic bond market, having emerged only in 2001, has rapidly grown. Accumulated domestic corporate debt issues doubled in 2002, and exceeded $3.5 billion by March 2003; 114 companies issued a total of 153 corporate bonds as of March 2003, including nonmarket issues.[11]

Domestic institutional investors are almost nonexistent, and capital is usually accumulated and invested through banks. Capital outflow, however, is generally declining due to Russia's improving investment climate.[12]

Both of the two leading Russian exchanges have introduced rigid disclosure requirements for their first-tier listed companies. Since 2002, they require listed companies to disclose their compliance with the provisions of the Russian Code of Corporate Conduct. Given the competition between the two exchanges, however, and the relatively weak domestic portfolio investment potential, most companies lack the necessary motivation for becoming listed or for upgrading their listing.

Nongovernmental public organizations have assisted in improving general governance standards. The National Broker-Dealer Association (NAUFOR) established a coordination center for investor protection in 1999 that later developed into the Investor Protection Association (IPA). The IPA has been defending investor interests through lawsuits and board nominations, while also consolidating investor votes. The IPA facilitated the placement of 49 independent directors on the boards of 55 companies in 2002.[13] The Association maintains an informative website that publicizes corporate actions and shareholder rights abuses. For its part, the decidedly influential Russian Union of Entrepreneurs and Industrialists has established a Supervisory Board on Corporate Governance, whose aim is to promote good governance standards among member companies; and it also has initiated the establishment of the National Council for Corporate Governance, whose first meeting was held on March 25, 2003.

The Association of Independent Directors (IDA) was established in February 2002, and has been actively assisting Russian companies to adopt best independent director practices. The Russian Institute of Directors is striving to improve the quality of directors through various training programs. Also, the Managers' Association has undertaken substantial research in the areas of management professional standards and corporate social responsibility.

LEGAL ENVIRONMENT

New laws are being adopted to guarantee greater accountability and corporate governance; these include The Civil and Arbitration Codes; the Joint Stock Company Law (JSC Law); the Law on Limited Liability Companies; the Law on the Securities Market; the Law on the Protection of the Rights and Legitimate Interests of Investors in the Securities Market; the Law on Banks and Banking Activities; and the Bankruptcy Law. A Franco-German model has been used for reforming the Russian legal system as a whole, but corporate law provisions also have Anglo-Saxon antecedents that were incorporated during the years of privatization. In some ways, Russian laws can be even more protective of the interests of minority shareholders than laws in other nations: for instance, Russia does not allow limitations on voting rights and anti-takeover defenses, and calls for a separation in the roles of the CEO and chairman.

The Major Legal Provisions with Regard to Shareholder Rights

Ownership rights

The law grants preemptive rights to shareholders for new share issues in cases of placement via closed subscription (for those who voted against it), and for all shareholders in case of open subscription. Also, the law prescribes that the share register should be kept by an outside, professional registrar in all companies having more than 50 shareholders. This does not suggest, however, that the registrar should be completely independent from an issuer.

Voting rights associated with different classes of shares

One share–one vote for common shares (except for cumulative voting); the law prescribes the voting rights of preferred shares in the most important cases (reorganization, liquidations, amendments to charter, etc.), and in the event that these shareholders do not receive dividends from the previous period.

The authority of a shareholder meeting and the board of directors

The range of issues exclusively reserved for the consideration of shareholders and directors is specified in the JSC Law.

Proper procedures for shareholder meetings

Companies must announce annual meetings at least 20 days in advance; 30 days in advance if reorganization will be discussed; and 50 days in advance if it will involve the election of a board of directors. Notification must be via registered mail or a mass-media publication. There are also detailed stipulations regarding who can attend, and about registration and voting procedures.

The placement of items on agendas

Shareholders owning (individually or in aggregate) at least 2 percent of the issued voting shares can introduce proposals for the agenda of the AGM and can nominate candidates for the board of directors.

Proper voting procedures

The law requires that large transactions, liquidations, amendments to charters, and changes in numbers of shares authorized for new issues are adopted by a supermajority of 75 percent. Companies having more than 1000 shareholders must apply cumulative voting for board elections.

Proxy rights

Shareholders may vote in person, in absentia, or by proxy. All votes are given equal rights. Companies with more than 100 shareholders must have voting by ballot. The charter of a company with more than 500,000 shareholders may stipulate the publication of ballots in a printed edition, available to all shareholders.

The composition of a board of directors (i.e., the number of outside and independent directors required)

The JSC Law makes stipulations in this area, but ones easy to circumvent. For example, it limits the percentage of members of a management board that can be on a board of directors (no more than 25 percent), but it does not say how many executives outside of the management board can be on the board.

The proper procedures for protesting corporate decisions

Shareholders who vote against a decision or have not taken part in a GSM can challenge a decision in court within six months.

The proper procedures for share buy-backs

A shareholder may demand a share buy-back in the event that he or she either refused or failed to take part in voting on reorganization or other major transactions, supplements, and amendments to the charter that violate his or her rights. In this case, the share valuation is to be made.

Regulations preventing insider trading

The Law on the Securities Market stipulates certain types of manager equity interest disclosure, as well as other reporting requirements; however, such regulations are easily skirted through the use of dummy companies.

Restrictions on the concentration of control

The Antimonopoly Law requires the Antimonopoly Committee's approval on acquisitions of 20 percent or more by an individual or single group, or if the face value of acquired securities exceeds 10 percent of the book value of fixed production assets and the intangible assets of the acquired company. Owners of 20 percent of a bank's equities must receive authorization from the Bank of Russia. In reality, this measure has little practical use because acquisitions are usually made in the name of different implicitly affiliated companies. The JSC Law stipulates a share buyout offer once a shareholder exceeds a threshold of 30 percent of ownership interest; however, the specific procedures for this are unclear.

Disclosure of affiliations and related party transactions, and the specific voting procedures for the approval thereof

A board of directors is to hold a vote, with the interested parties abstaining, once an affiliation between parties of the transaction is identified. For companies with more than 1000 shareholders, noninterested, "independent" directors, as defined by the JSC Law, take the vote. For large transactions, or in the event that the number of disinterested parties is less than a quorum, matters must be determined via a shareholder meeting.

Legal Loopholes and Improvements in the Legal Infrastructure

Company law in Russia has been evolving rapidly during the past several years with further changes anticipated. With both the letter and application of the law in a state of flux, reformers are targeting loopholes, though their success remains to be seen in most cases. This section surveys issues that are being, or need to be, tackled.

There is room for improvement regarding shareholder voting rights and shareholder meetings. Preventing shareholders from participating in meetings is still a popular tool in the corporate war for control. Shareholders can be prevented from participating in meetings through insufficient notification, or excessive registration requirements (the law allows for a disproportionately wide interpretation regarding registration requirements), or even physical hindrances; but the most frequent tactic is the arrest of shares under a court's mandate. Suits have been filed to prevent certain shareholders from participating in shareholder meetings, effectively barring them from participating in decisions on share dilution and other major transactions. In most cases, decisions have been handed down by courts that lack familiarity with equity market issues; and such cases have usually been taken up in the region where the plaintiff resides, sometimes so far away from the company's location that the company can hardly track them. Moreover, the independence and accountability of the courts have been questionable. There is little, if any, legal recourse for offended parties regarding discriminatory actions by those who did attend the general shareholders meeting. The new set of procedural (civil and arbitration) codes adopted in the second half of 2002 has, at least on paper, partly resolved this issue. Now, disputes between shareholders (individual and legal entities) and companies are to be resolved in arbitration courts. Claims are to be filed at the location of the company.

Bankruptcy procedures have been another way to abuse shareholders while remaining in full compliance with the law. Easily activated and sometimes false, bankruptcies have been widely used by creditors for purposes of acquiring companies. Through affiliate parties, a potentially solvent company could be stripped of its assets and then brought to bankruptcy—a scheme widely used in corporate wars in aluminum, oil, ferrous metals, and other industries for many years. An attempt to tighten bankruptcy procedures was made in the new version of the Bankruptcy Law approved by the State Duma and the Federation Council in July 2002. It sets hurdles for initiating bankruptcy: bankruptcy can now only be initiated if the debt of the company is in excess of a certain material threshold, and 30 days have passed since the company was obliged by a court to fulfill its obligations. It is too early to say, however, whether this law will provide better protection to shareholders.

With no concept of beneficial owners within Russian law, the provision on disclosure of block ownership beyond 5 percent of voting shares does not work adequately, and there are problems with the proper identification of affiliate parties in transactions. Transactions with possible affiliate parties are entered into without proper disclosure, without truly independent appraisal, without tender, and without proper approval procedures. Assets are sometimes stripped as a result. Also, there is no legal mechanism to disenfranchise shareholders who fail to provide personal information, as there is under U.K. law. This makes laws on affiliate party dealing ineffective.

There is a lack of definition of net income in the Russian law, although the term is mentioned in the context of dividends. As a result, companies can manipulate their financial results under Russian accounting standards to minimize dividend payments, particularly those that have an obligation to maintain a certain payout ratio on preferred shares. The State Duma, however, is expected to adopt amendments to the JSC Law that introduce a definition of net income on the basis of accounting information.

Corporate reorganization is still inadequately covered by the law, which allows for different accounting and value-setting procedures that may be detrimental to shareholders. The vagueness of existing "fair price" provisions provide inadequate protection. Also, the restructuring of banks in the form of consolidation is hampered by existing requirements on providing options for early debt redemption in the case of restructuring. This pushes banks into confusing ownership structures.

The law allows for discretionary dividend payment periods. As a result, late dividend payments have been commonplace—a particularly frustrating situation for shareholders during periods of double-digit inflation.

A serious issue is that ADR-holders cannot vote directly or through depositary banks on issues other than the election of the board of directors (where the cumulative vote is applied). This is because ADR depositary banks and custodians are regarded as owners, not nominees, and vote splits are only permitted in the case of registered nominee holders. Therefore, ADR blocks must be voted wholly for or against resolutions and not in accordance with their exact vote split; this can obscure the actual voting results. The FCSM has been saying that it will resolve this issue for some time now.

Changing the procedures for share consolidation has been a major step forward. Before recent improvements, the fact that fractional shares were not allowed left minority shareholders in a vulnerable position: holding companies would use swap coefficients to create fractional shares as a tool for forcing minority shareholders of consolidated subsidiaries (whose shares were being swapped for the holding company's shares) to sell at a loosely defined "fair price." In 2002, amendments to the JSC Law made allowances for fractional shares that destroyed these grounds for the forced sale of shares.

REGULATORY ENVIRONMENT
Enforcement and Accountability

The poor corporate governance record of Russian companies can be attributed in part to the generally weak rule of law, the sluggishness of reforms, and such specific cultural features as a lack of trust in government. As a result, enforcement remains ineffective, encumbering greater progress. The problems, typically, are poor transparency, insufficient experience, and widespread corruption. Despite increased activity on the part of the court system in this area, courts usually still fail in preventing or redressing the mistreatment of shareholders.

Current problems of accountability have historical roots. Many managers, for example, remain unclear as to what is even meant by "shareholder," because there was no historical precedent. The employee-oriented privatizations of the early 1990s gave rise to thousands of individual shareholders who did not bring capital investment to their companies. As a result, some managers have not been able to appreciate the connection between shareholders and investors. During the Soviet period, company managers typically reported to a single supervisory entity within the rigid hierarchy that dominated the country's industrial infrastructure. In this kind of framework, company information was confidential.

Today, secrecy has more contemporary foundations. Many managers, for example, now view disclosure requirements, such as the publication of CEO and director salaries, as dangerous to personal welfare. In other cases, with entities that work in areas connected to national security or national strategic reserves (such as Aeroflot and Norilsk Nickel), specific regulations actually *require* confidentiality and preclude better disclosure. Companies in corresponding sectors in many other countries are not similarly subject to secrecy laws.

Securities Regulations

The FCSM is a regulatory, coordination, and controlling body. Its main functions are to set rules for brokers, certify specialists in the securities markets, and register securities issues. It penalizes companies for noncompliance by imposing fines for inappropriate disclosures and late filings, by suspending trade in their securities, or by rejecting the registration of new issues. In 2000, it initiated the mandatory registration of the issuance of ADRs by Russian companies; and in 2001, it prohibited company management from automatically counting in its favor votes of ADR holders who had not forwarded proxy voting instructions. There are now stiff penalties for companies that fail to comply with disclosure requirements on time.

The Federal Law on the Securities Market, enforced by the FCSM, regulates registration and depositary procedures, and the Professional Association of Registrars, Transfer Agents, and Depositories (PARTAD) monitors licensed professional registrars and depositors. Most large companies now employ independent registrars, and the problems regarding the misuse of share registration procedures have mainly been resolved.

Other governmental bodies also play important roles in enforcement and accountability. For its part, the Bank of Russia regulates the issue of bank securities and provides prudential supervision; it imposes regulations on financial disclosure and the risk management of banks as well. The Ministry of Finance specifies rules for auditing and certifies auditors.

Russian regulators, however, lack the power to investigate ownership structures beyond what is disclosed in regulatory filings (quarterly
reports to the regulators mostly contain unhelpful information about nominee owners). This state of affairs, as we have discussed above, results in
the continued inadequacy of information disclosure, permitting the stripping of assets and other modes for fleecing shareholders.

Rules and Codes

A Code of Corporate Conduct (the Code) was developed in 2002 at the initiative of the Russian government and the FCSM, and sponsored by the
EBRD and the Japanese government. The initiative was first presented to
a public forum in late 2000; after more than a year of public deliberation
and revision, the Code was approved by the Russian government in April
2002 and recommended for voluntary implementation.

The goal of the Code was to fill the gaps in existing corporate laws
and to familiarize Russian companies with the best practices of corporate governance and conduct. The Code recommends the wider disclosure of owners beyond nominee holders and the disclosure of affiliate
relations and relevant information about directors; it advocates having
at least three-quarters of the board filled by nonexecutive directors and
one-quarter by independent directors (minimum three); it gives a definition of independent directors and explains why they are needed; and
it prescribes that directors have free access to all necessary information
and recommends the appointment of a corporate secretary to be
responsible for providing such information. The Code also stipulates
that a number of committees (strategic planning, personnel, remunerations, and settlement of corporate conflicts) are to be established by
the boards.

Implementation of the Code has been slow, however. At the
prompting of the FCSM, Russia's two major exchanges started promoting corporate governance standards by modifying their listing standards.
Companies included in the top-listing category, first-tier companies,
must comply with each provision of the Code, and second-tier companies must provide statements of their degree of compliance. Under the
RTS listing rules, first-tier companies are required to present IAS or U.S.
GAAP financial statements. The relative lack of interest in domestic listings, however, limits the impact by these measures on governance standards. It is not yet clear how compliance with the Code of Corporate
Conduct will be implemented.

INFORMATIONAL INFRASTRUCTURE

Financial Disclosure Standards and Requirements

Accounting practices in Russia are considerably behind the best international practices. In accordance with reporting requirements, companies must present the FCSM and tax authorities with quarterly financial statements, including balance sheets, profit and loss statements, cash flow statements, capital statements, an accounting of the use of funds, and notes on the balance sheets. Russian accounting standards differ greatly from IAS and U.S. GAAP standards, and, while they serve the purposes of tax authorities and other official bodies, they have little value for investors. One problem is that consolidated statements are not prepared in the Russian system, since tax authorities require only single-company tax returns. Other key differences include accounting for fixed assets, recognition of liabilities, policies on reserves, and use of estimates.

In 2001, the Ministry of Finance adopted a long-term plan for the development of a more compatible accounting system. This three-stage plan will culminate in 2010, and sets out steps to be taken for adopting and implementing an "IAS-compatible accounting system." It stipulates that as early as January 2004, Russian banks and public companies will have IAS-based reporting. This seems optimistic: In the middle of 2002, approximately 25 of Russia's 40 largest companies produced IAS and GAAP statements and reports[14] audited by one of the Big Four firms. Smaller companies are much slower to adapt to the newer practices because of the costs involved.

Progress also is being made in regard to the quality of training of the accountants themselves. The Institute of Professional Accountants has been issuing certificates to professional accountants since 1998. In 2000, the International Federation of Accountants (IFAC) awarded the Russian Auditors Collegium, a professional association of about 800 individual auditors, an associate membership.

There are approximately 75 Russian audit companies, though only a small number are considered reputable and meeting acceptable professional standards. As a rule, Russian auditors carry out statutory audits, though these are primarily viewed as tax returns. Tax and consulting services also are offered by these firms. The federal Auditing Committee regulates and certifies local audit companies, but the committee does not publicly disclose information about the number and quality of auditors.

Sources of Information and Disclosure Practices

Adequate and timely disclosure will only become a common corporate practice in Russia through the establishment of guidelines, greater market education, and consistent enforcement. Quarterly reports on securities to be filed with the FCSM must conform to specific guidelines in terms of structure and content, including the naming of the largest shareholders; they also must report on a company's governance structure, board composition, board remuneration, equity positions of 5 percent and more, affiliates, branches, number of employees, key business lines, authorized capital, outstanding shares, the names of the auditors, registrar, depositary, and major corporate actions. A company must present the report within 45 days of the closing of the reporting period. Also, public companies are required to inform the FCSM of any major developments and changes within the company's structure, and to disclose information about essential facts in the form of ad-hoc reporting to the FCSM within five days of the change or development.

Information provided to the FCSM, however, is rarely made fully or promptly public. The main informational resource regarding disclosure can be found at http://disclosure.fcsm.ru/. Corporate actions are published in the FCSM's special edition, *Vestnik FKTsB*. The FCSM website lists the quarterly reports of around 24,000 open joint stock companies [including quarterly financials under Russian Accounting Standards (RAS), corporate actions reports, and governance structures]. The information on the site is updated poorly, however, with lags that can exceed a year. The site for the Bank of Russia contains information about banks, included financial statements, though it too is not updated in accordance with the stipulated standards.

One of the weakest areas is ownership disclosure. Public companies must disclose information on shareholders who own more than 5 percent of share capital, including their names and addresses, and also the names and addresses of the owners of more than 25 percent in their parent companies. Other corporate issuers must disclose their total number of shareholders and provide more detailed information about those holding more than 20 percent of the shares. The Bank of Russia requires the same level of disclosure for banks. Nevertheless, as mentioned above, without a concept of beneficiary owners, reports on ownership structures are of little use when trying to understand real control structures. More optimistically, under the Registration Law, which went into effect in June 2002, LLPs must report all changes in their ownership structure and charters to the Tax Ministry. This information can then be made available to any person or company upon request.

The JSC Law requires companies to provide a list of those entitled to attend general shareholder meetings at the request of shareholders having at least 1 percent of the vote.

Annual reports have not yet become a normal source of disclosure for Russian companies. Only large companies produce annual reports, while the quality of information is uneven. Corporate Internet sites have increasingly become a major source of disclosure. In mid-2002, the amount of disclosed information on websites of the 42 largest companies was 41 percent of the maximum level of disclosure needed for investors, while statutory filings were responsible for 32 percent, and annual reports only contained 29 percent of the needed information.[15]

Media reporting on business is not always independent in Russia: financial groups own a significant portion of the Russian-language electronic and print media, and financial groups and the government own the major television networks.

NOTES

1. See H. Hessel, January 2003.

2. Ibid.

3. "Balance of Payments of the Russian Federation (analytical layout)." Central Bank of the Russian Federation. www.cbr.ru/statistics/credit_statistics/.

4. *Kommersant Vlast* #45 (447), November 13, 2001.

5. See P. Boone and D. Rodionov Denis, 2002.

6. Standard & Poor's Transparency & Disclosure Survey of 42 Russian Companies, 2002.

7. Ibid.

8. Ibid.

9. News of the Russian Economy. *RIA Novosti*, March 19, 2003.

10. "Emerging Stock Markets Review: Performance, Valuations and Constituents," Standard & Poor's, February 2003.

11. www.cbonds.ru.

12. www.cbonds.ru.

13. IPA reports, www.corp-gov.ru.

14. See Note 6.

15. Ibid.

REFERENCES

Boone, P., and D. Rodionov. "Rent Seeking in Russia and the CIS," *Brunswick UBS Warburg paper*, 2002.

Code of Corporate Conduct, *FCSM*, Moscow, 2002.

Corporate Consolidation—The Latest Lurch Towards Capitalism. *Renaissance Capital Russia Research*, March 2001.

"Corporate Governance. Foundation for Capital Flows," *Law in Transition, European Bank for Reconstruction and Development*, Autumn 1999.

Hessel H. "Russian Federation (The) Credit Rating Report," Standard & Poor's, *RatingsDirect*, January 2, 2003.

"Internal Audit Survey 2002—Russia and the CIS," Ernst & Young Business Risk Services, 2002.

Kostikov, I. "Board of Directors in the System of Corporate Governance," Russian Institute of Directors, 2002.

Krasnitskaya, E. "Corporate Governance Profiles. Long Crawl West," *Troika Dialog Research*, October 2002.

Miltner, S. "The Report on Corporate Governance in Russia: An Investor Perspective," Institute of International Finance, Inc., December 4, 2002.

"OECD White Paper on Corporate Governance in Russia," OECD Publications, 2002.

Radygin, A. "About Some Problems of Corporate Governance in Russia," *Institute of the Economy in Transition*, 2001.

"Russia Outlook," *Ernst & Young Monthly Review*, February 2002 and February, 2003.

The European Business Club in the Russian Federation, white paper, 2002.

CHAPTER 18-6

Turkey[1]

Melsa Ararat

INTRODUCTION

Located at the crossroads of Eurasia, Turkey is a rapidly growing emerging market and the largest economy lined up to join the European Union. Despite all the controversies about the prospects of Turkey's integration with Europe, considerable parts of the Turkish economy are already competing in the EU market. Turkey differs from many of the other candidate countries as it has a longer history of being both a market-based economy and an established capital market. However, in common with the transition economies, Turkey faces similar challenges associated with reducing the role of the state in the economy.

Since the foundation of the Turkish Republic in 1923, the state has been the major player in the economy and has subsidized the development of the private sector. The state's role has been gradually reduced especially after the liberalization reforms of 1980s that marked the beginning of a strong commitment to develop a market economy. The Capital Markets Law (CML) was enacted in 1981 and was followed by the foundation of the Istanbul Stock Exchange (ISE) in 1986. Turkey enjoyed high growth for two decades during which speculative investors enjoyed superior returns. This growth, however, was accompanied by high and persistent inflation due to successive governments' reluctance to attain fiscal discipline. Large public sector borrowing requirements, chronic high inflation, state insurance for deposit accounts, and undercapitalized state banks have all contributed to the fiscal deterioration in Turkey.

Turkey was plunged into a series of economic crises in 1994, 1999, and early 2001. Since 1999, Turkey has been following a structural reform program under an IMF Stand-by Agreement, which involved public sector reforms, the restructuring and strengthening of financial industry, a further reduction in the role of the state in the economy, and the implementation of measures to improve transparency and prevent corruption and expropriation. This restructuring program, in essence, constitutes the final phase of the establishment of a market economy in Turkey with all its institutions.

The implementation program was considered to be successful with the first signs of recovery and growth occurring during the second half of 2002. However, tight fiscal policies had caused the economy to shrink, leaving millions unemployed. Parliamentary elections, which took place in late 2002, brought a new political party to power with a substantial majority. Although some of the government's immediate practices (such as the recent appointments of insiders to the boards of state-owned public companies set for privatization, and rejection of the public procurement law) caused scepticism about its sincerity or capability to implement sound governance principles, the new government declared its strong commitment to continue the reforms.

Turkey's remarkably low share of global foreign direct investment, in comparison to its economic fundamentals, is a big concern for the government which needs to deal with the high levels of foreign and domestic debt and also for the Turkish private sector which needs foreign capital to finance delayed investment programs. These underpin the recent corporate governance debates and reform initiatives in Turkey. The Capital Markets Board's (CMB) efforts to deepen and strengthen the capital market via the improvement of the regulatory framework and the introduction of incentives to improve firm level corporate governance quality support the institutional foundations strengthened by the structural reforms.

Most of the corporate governance issues today are directly or indirectly related to the strong, but decreasing, role of the Turkish state in the economy and to the persistence of oligopolistic structures. Although Turkey's capital markets are much more developed than the neighbor economies in transition, Turkey is a typical emerging market with high ownership concentration, an underfinanced and inefficient legal system, and a highly volatile stock market. Corporate governance issues revolve around weak minority shareholders' and creditors' rights, a weak disclosure infrastructure, inconsistencies in the legal and regulatory framework, and a lack of enforcement. Together, these have produced an environment that is often conducive to market manipulation, asset stripping, share dilution, tunnelling, and transfer pricing.

MARKET INFRASTRUCTURE

Business Organization and Ownership Structure

The most common form of business organization in Turkey is *Anonim Sirket,* which is equivalent to a joint stock company with limited liability up to the amount of its prescribed nominal capital. There are roughly 85,000 joint stock companies in Turkey, out of which about 2500 are considered to be public and subject to the Capital Market Law (i.e., those companies with 250 or more shareholders). Ownership is highly concentrated in Turkey. Half of the 300 listed companies are controlled by one shareholder controlling more than 50 percent of the voting rights. Ultimate owners of listed companies are individual family members who exercise control through pyramidal structures and/or intercompany shareholdings. Families, directly or indirectly, own 75 percent of all companies and maintain majority control. In 2000, families ultimately controlled 198 of the 257 companies with an average 53.8 percent holding of the equity, although the pyramidal structures meant that average direct ownership was only 27.1 percent.

Business in Turkey is organized into group structures; corporations are affiliated with each other around a holding company whose purpose is to hold stock of other companies and manage them. Holding companies are the most significant majority shareholders of Turkish listed companies. All major groups also have a bank member that is ultimately owned and controlled by the same family. Although this structure may be advantageous in terms of the effective monitoring of management, efficient resource allocation and reallocation via an internal market mechanism and also may support pursuit of long-term growth strategies, the ultimate beneficiaries of these advantages are the majority owners that are able to maximize the returns from the total portfolio, often at the expense of individual companies and minority shareholders. Supporting this view, Yurtoglu's (2000) research on corporate structures in Turkey provides significant evidence that the holding company structure has a negative effect on many measures of the economic performance of Turkish firms— including profitability, return on assets, dividend payments, and investment decisions. Similarly, concentrated ownership and pyramidal structures also have resulted in lower returns on assets, lower market value to book value ratios, and lower dividends. Profit rates of Turkish companies tend to diverge from industry averages for longer time periods when these companies are part of a holding company structure. Anecdotal evidence supports the concerns of many investors that free cash flow might routinely be allocated to majority owners by means other than dividend payments. Therefore, companies within a group comprised of both listed and unlisted companies may be exposed to risks associated with reduced transparency, which may be higher if the holding company itself is not listed.

The original incentive for the formation of holding companies was the tax incentive associated with such structures, as taxes on revenues from holding companies' participations are payable only in the following fiscal year. The opportunity for "income shuffling" to reduce the overall tax burden of groups was another motive for their formation. Persistent and high inflation (without inflation accounting) and high corporate income tax rates have provided ongoing incentives for the continued formation of holding structures.

Although Turkey may be classified as an insider system, it deviates from typical examples in two areas; ownership disclosure and control leverage. Ownership structures are relatively transparent and ownership disclosure requirements are high. The voting rights deviate from cash flow rights but at a comparatively lower rate of 1.32 for all listed companies and even lower for ISE 100 at a rate of 1.26 in the year 2000, in relation to Asian and Latin American examples.

There is neither a tradition nor any requirement for independent board members at Turkish companies. Family members usually dominate both statutory and executive boards and their membership overlaps. Family members typically assume responsibility for the management of individual subgroups of the business and the board members of the holding perform the role of the chairman of the board for the individual companies. Genuinely independent board members are usually only found in joint ventures with foreign companies. However, anecdotal evidence suggests that companies are seriously considering the inclusion of independent members on their boards under pressure from investors and creditors.

Foreign investors ultimately own 15 listed companies and have stakes in a total of 40 companies. Their control leverage is minimal. Joint ventures between family holdings and multinational foreign companies based on equal ownership are common.

State-owned companies show a higher concentration of ownership with an average ownership stake of 80 percent in 6 listed companies within the ISE 100 and an average of 70 percent in a total of 13 state-owned listed companies. The expected acceleration of the privatization of state-owned enterprises is likely to play an important role in embracing better corporate governance standards.

According to McKinsey's investor opinions survey in June 2002 on corporate governance in emerging markets, the weight of key factors for investment decisions in Turkey shows a similar pattern to the average of all countries surveyed: accounting disclosure, shareholder equality, and property rights are the most important criteria that apply to all countries. Global institutional investors surveyed by McKinsey listed the top seven factors for their investment decisions in Turkey as follows:

+ Accounting disclosure (73 percent of the investors voted it as the most important factor)
+ Shareholder equality (64 percent as opposed to 47 percent for all countries surveyed)
+ Market regulation and infrastructure (55 versus 43 percent)
+ Takeover markets (45 versus 23 percent)
+ Property rights (45 percent)
+ Credit information (36 versus 29 percent)
+ Board independence (27 percent)

Turkey deviates from the sample group substantially with respect to the importance investors give to the presence of a market for corporate control. CMB has comprehensive regulations regarding takeovers and the respective protection of minority rights. However, due to the high concentration of ownership, hostile takeovers are simply not feasible. Hence the prevention of anti-takeover devices is not a significant matter in Turkey although some provisions exist to prevent poison pills. The deviations from the average with respect to the importance of credit information might be an indication of concerns about related lending. Although Turkish banking law has strict rules that forbid banks from lending to companies in which the bank owners have an ownership stake, difficulties associated with cascaded relations and the lack of mandatory consolidated accounts make enforcement difficult.

Financial Markets

The distinct feature of the Turkish case is the financing system that is structured around group-owned banks. The average free float of quoted Turkish banks is low (24 percent, mostly common shares). Market capitalization fluctuates around 20 to 25 percent of the GDP down from 35 percent in 2000 before the crises (this compares to an average of 135 percent for OECD countries). There have been no significant initial public offerings

(IPOs) since 2000, when a record of U.S.$2.8 billion was raised through the listing of 35 firms. Market commentators believe that a backlog of 10 to 15 IPOs is waiting for a more favorable environment. Market transactions are concentrated around financial institutions with the 25 most actively traded companies representing around 75 percent of the ISE's trading volume.

High volatility and low valuations discourage Turkish firms from pursuing a financing strategy through domestic equity markets. On the other hand, systemic risks associated with regional economic and political instability reduce corporations' enthusiasm for substantial investments and hence the need for high levels of new capital.

The banking system, although currently in recovery, has suffered from a lack of prudential regulation and supervision for a number of decades. The establishment of the watchdog Banking Regulatory and Supervisory Agency (BRSA) in 2001, and the subsequent restructuring and consolidation of the financial sector, which included risk management legislation, consolidated and inflation accounting legislation, the recapitalization of banking system, and debt restructuring for the corporate sector, were major steps in reforming the financial industry. Reforms aimed at the improvement of surveillance and the implementations of prudential standards have combined to reduce the losses of state banks, and have minimized the political influence on the state-controlled banks. However, despite these substantial reforms, the banking sector has low penetration rates due to the "crowding out" effect of public sector borrowing similar to the situation in Brazil. In 2002 more than 20 percent of deposit accounts were used to buy government bonds. Extremely high intermediation spreads (the difference between credit and deposit rates) limit the funds available to the real sector and encourage offshore banking.

Financing therefore is a main problem for Turkish firms, particularly for those small and medium-size enterprises without access to group bank finance. In 2001 credit volumes were reduced by 50 percent and investments fell by 35.1 percent. Similarly, there is a lack of venture capital and institutional investors (the army's pension fund is the only significant institutional investor). New legislation paving the way for private pension funds and allowing accumulated pension capital to be invested in stock markets is likely to change the situation in the medium term. Meanwhile the CMB needs to review the existing regulations forbidding institutional investors from pursuing the control of the companies they invest in. Currently, institutional investors or investment companies cannot be represented on company boards and they cannot own more that 9 percent of the voting rights in a company.

General Stage of Economic Development

Turkey ranks twentieth in terms of the size of world economies and has a young and well-educated population of 67 million and a GDP of €216 billion (in purchasing Power Parity €494.7 billion in 2001). Population growth is compatible with developed countries and is expected to fall to near zero in 2050. Thirty-five percent of the labor force of 22 million is employed in agriculture, a figure in rapid decline. GNP is expected to grow by 5.2 percent per annum on average in the 2003–2005 period and inflation is expected to fall to single-digit figures by 2005.

The Turkish economy has the potential and need to grow to finance the repayment of the public debt and to support Turkey's strategic role in regional political and economic stability. This growth can only be financed by substantial investments in the real sector. However, remarkably low foreign direct investments and high levels of foreign currency deposit accounts held by Turkish citizens (equal to 80 percent of GNP) indicate a problem of investor confidence. All these factors combined with the ongoing international focus on corporate governance bring the whole debate to the fore in Turkey.

On one hand, Turkish business, via the business leaders' organization Turkish Industrialists and Businessmen Association (TUSIAD), started focusing on corporate governance issues by forming an internal taskforce to draft a corporate governance code for its members and setting up an institute with Sabanci University to educate corporate boards and to create a pool of nonexecutive directors. On the other hand, the CMB established a committee to develop a recommended corporate governance code for companies listed on the ISE. The CMB's efforts to involve the business community in drafting the code, and the reciprocal enthusiasm of business to be involved indicate that a broad consensus has been reached on the vital importance to improve the investment climate in Turkey. As a result, 2003 has seen many conferences, panels, workshops, general assemblies, training programs, and seminars that focused on governance issues.

LEGAL ENVIRONMENT

Turkey is a civil law country in the French tradition. One of the building blocks of the corporate governance legislative framework, the Commercial Code (CC) was originally taken from France in 1850. The CC underwent various revisions subsequently with provisions taken from German, Swiss, and Italian law. The 1956 version, with its evidently eclectic nature, forms the basis of equity contracts and provides the general legal framework for incorporation, general assemblies, ownership rights, and the definition of shares and bonds and their issuance. It is important to note that the fundamental document governing the rights of shareholders is the company's articles of association, which should provide for a number of fundamental rights including the right of shareholders to participate in the general assembly, to vote and acquire information, to have the company audited, to file a complaint, and to take civil or legal action. The Commercial Code provides for privileged shares and does not impose limits to the extent privileges that may be granted. As a consequence, out of ISE 30 companies, 11 have different classes of shares with multiple voting rights and variations for dividend entitlement.

Capital Market Law (CML) borrows from the Anglo-Saxon legal system but still has its roots in civil law. It provides the legislative framework for the securities market activities and establishes the CMB. Separate laws legislate the banking and insurance sectors. A major issue associated with the existing legal system is the inconsistency between the Commercial Code, the Capital Market Law, and the Banking Law. The differences are more apparent in public disclosure, dividend payments, and shareholder rights. Therefore, the regulatory framework for nonlisted joint stock companies differs substantially from those listed in the ISE. The Commercial Code is currently undergoing a major revision in relation to Turkey's integration efforts in anticipation of joining the European Union and the consequent need for harmonization of certain laws, particularly those relating to competition, bankruptcy, and insurance.

There are severe operational problems with the legal process and the enforcement of law, as the legal system is complicated, slow, and costly. Since 2000, the CMB has filed complaints to the office of public prosecutors for around 100 violations of the CML each year, but only one case each year has reached a decree absolute, with the rest resulting in dismissals and adjournments. The average time between the CMB's appeal and the first verdict is 12 months and, to date; most cases have been related to market manipulation.

REGULATORY ENVIRONMENT

Turkey has a liberal foreign exchange regime and a fully convertible currency. There are no restrictions on foreign portfolio investors trading in the Turkish securities market or on the repatriation of capital and profits.

The CMB, the ISE, and Takasbank (Turkey's Settlement and Custody bank) are the major institutions involved in the capital market. The CMB regulates the operations of the ISE and its members are appointed by the Council of Ministers for six years. Although the CMB is equipped with ample regulatory powers and is capable of imposing penalties, including the suspension and cancellation of licenses, it cannot take cases directly to court as this right is granted to public prosecutors only.

The ISE's board is appointed by the government from among the nominees submitted by the CMB and is governed by a general assembly attended by its trading members which are licensed by the CMB. Takasbank, set up in 1996, is Turkey's central securities custody and national numbering agency and is compliant with ISSA G30 guidelines and U.S. SEC rules. It is owned by the ISE, 27 banks, and 77 brokerage houses and is regulated by the CMB and BRSA. It should be noted here that there are some restrictions for the transfer of shares of capital market institutions and banks. These transfers are subject to the approval of CMB and BRSA, respectively, due to the alleged need to consider the public interests.

Shareholders can vote in person or by notarized proxy, by appointing a representative through a power of attorney; however, the procedure is complicated and costly. Insider trading or trading on nonpublic information is a crime with penal liability and 2 to 5 years of imprisonment in addition to heavy fines. Dissemination of false or misleading information also is covered under the same provision. Similar penalties apply to the transfer of assets. The CMB can take any violations to the public prosecution; however, the provisions are not clear and are subject to interpretation. As in the case of all other countries where civil law traditions prevail, proof may be very difficult where judgment has to be based on a test of whether the directors have failed to exercise their duties of loyalty and care.

Recently, the CMB made substantial improvements to the regulatory framework. However, in most cases companies will have to amend their articles of association to incorporate the new provisions. Although the changes in articles of association is an important matter as this particular document is the basis for the governance of the company, there are no provisions mandating the public disclosure of changes in the articles of association.

In February 2003, the CMB promulgated new provisions for the sales of capital markets instruments during public offerings. These new provisions introduced new definitions covering various classes of investors:

* Institutional investors,
* Large-scale investors,
* Small-scale investors, and
* Foreign investors and require that at least 50 percent of the offered shares shall be allocated to small-scale investors.

Recent regulatory improvements also include regulations for investors including the requirement for accreditation of stock market professionals and the regulation of portfolio management companies. As of January 2003, portfolio management companies have to be joint stock companies and they have to establish internal audit and inspection units. They will only be able to charge fees based on performance and they have to disclose the last five years' performance to the public.

In summary, neither the listing requirements nor the structural fundamentals of capital market institutions should be viewed as imposing any problems for the performance of capital markets; however, their effectiveness is substantially reduced due to the weaknesses of enforcement mechanisms.

Corporate governance codes usually fill the gap between the legal and regulatory framework, and the desired practices. There are two corporate governance codes in Turkey; the first code was developed by TUSIAD and launched in December 2002 for consultation and discussion among its members. TUSIAD's code only focuses on the workings of the board and is expected to become TUSIAD's recommended code for board practices. The second code was developed by the CMB and addresses four main areas of corporate governance:

* Shareholders' rights and responsibilities,
* Disclosure obligations and transparency,
* The role and responsibilities of the board, and
* Stakeholders.

The CMB's code released for public consultation in February 2003 is very comprehensive and has used the Sarbane-Oxley Act's provisions as a benchmark. Initial reactions during the consultation period demonstrate support from professional organizations and companies; however, there is a strong emphasis on the need to achieve consistency of law and supporting legislation as well as on the need to develop capacity for nonexecutive board members. It is expected that the CMB's recommendations for corporate governance will be incorporated into the listing requirements on a "comply or explain" basis starting from 2004. The ISE has announced its intentions to float itself and to establish a separate segment within the main market consisting of those companies that comply with the recommended principles.

The launch of the recommendations for corporate governance and recent announcements from the Istanbul Stock Exchange are two major signals that the governance environment may become more investor-friendly especially after January 2004 when inflation-adjusted accounting and consolidated reporting will become mandatory.

INFORMATIONAL INFRASTRUCTURE

The Turkish CC has vague provisions related to the right of shareholders to obtain information. Shareholders have the right to receive financial statements, an audit report, and proposed dividend policy statements before the general assembly; however, their right to audit the company's records and request information on the company's business is subject to the consent of the company's board or the approval of the general assembly. The vaguely defined concept of "trade secret" is frequently cited in both CC and CML without any specific explanation. Company boards misuse the concept as an excuse for opacity. CML has comprehensive provisions on public disclosure but does not offer any remedies for the deficiencies in recognition of the rights of the individual shareholders to obtain information.

The lack of accounting standards that apply to all companies is a major concern. Existing rules are generalist; they only govern the aspects of accounting in the Tax Procedures Code, which prescribe a chart of accounts and a format for presentation of financial statements. Turkish accounting standards divert from IAS and GAAP in two major areas: inflation-adjusted reporting and mandatory consolidation for parent companies. Hence, financial statements do not correctly and consistently reflect economic realities.

Corporations often are motivated to conceal economic profits since high inflation can bring about an unfair tax burden. These deficiencies will be eliminated with the implementation of inflation-adjusted accounting and consolidated reporting after December 31, 2003, after which all listed companies will have to provide financial statements compatible with GAAP or IAS on a quarterly basis which should be audited by external certified audits semi-annually. Although major listed companies already produce quarterly IAS-compatible financial statements, they are rarely disclosed publicly. Another development worth noting is the new regulation of CMB requiring CEO and CFO certification on quarterly reports, which also will become effective in January 2004.

Some examples of how high inflation and inadequate accounting standards distort financial results are as follows:

+ Given that an important part of nominal interest income/ expense accounts for inflation (the rest being "real interest"), interest income and expense are both exaggerated, so that the net profit of a cash-rich firm is overstated whereas that of a leveraged firm is understated.

+ Due to inflation, industrial companies, which generally have high net working capital, tend to overstate their gross margins.

+ Accounting standards allow financial expenses to be capitalized in fixed assets or in inventory. This leads to the distortion of operating margins, value of fixed assets, and level of inventories.

+ Since interest expense and foreign exchange losses can be treated separately in different cases, financial expense cannot be accurately determined.

+ Since financial consolidation is not mandatory, the value of unlisted participations is distorted or understated, as they are not adjusted for inflation (unless a nominal capital increase is made).

+ Expense items that should take place in cost of goods sold are often put in operating expenses (and vice versa) thus distorting gross margins.

In addition to the above, there are many ways in which controlling shareholders can reduce or conceal profits. The most obvious mechanisms are:

+ Transactions with and/or participations in other unlisted firms controlled by the major shareholder,

+ Unregistered operating activities, and

+ Financing operations of the firm through debt capital (which is actually the majority shareholders' own equity) and the consequent escalation of financial expenses.

Deficiencies in the standards of transparency and accountability allow corporate managers to avoid disclosure and manipulate markets by misinformation. These weaknesses often also encourage asset transfers and asset stripping. Some of the most common and confidence-eroding cases taken to the public prosecutors by the Istanbul Stock Exchange involve the following violations:

1. Failure to disclose merger intentions to investors to allow time for insider trading.

2. Tunneling of free cash flow to owners while defaulting on payments to creditors.

3. Manipulating share prices by blocking the sales by the board.

4. Tunneling through excessive compensation for owner/managers.

5. Market manipulations to increase the share price to qualify for high levels of bank credit and to facilitate insider trading.

6. Substantial insider trading enabled by avoiding disclosure requirements in case of acquisition of more than 1 percent of the shares.

7. Dividend payments based on false financial statements.

8. Sales of shares to manipulators below market prices.

9. Tunneling via applying higher than market interest rates to credits received from group bank and lower than market rates for interests applied to deposit.

Current regulations require the notification of insider trading in excess of 1 percent of share capital; however, disclosure is rarely timely and the use of offshore funds dilutes the accuracy of information. One other important aspect to note is that the banks that are listed on the Istanbul Stock Exchange are subject to banking law with respect to disclosure requirements, a situation that prevents the effective monitoring of banks by the CMB.

External audits are mandatory for listed companies whose auditors have to be certified by the CMB. The professional associations do not have statutory positions to self-regulate. The CMB itself defines the professional standards of the auditors as well as the certification requirements for the audit companies. The internal audit framework is defined in the Commercial Code, but the provisions are vague. A new regulation put out by the CMB in November 2002 requires that a minimum of two board members of listed companies who do not hold executive positions will act as the audit committee and supervise the accounting system of the company, a change most welcome by market commentators. In case of complaints, regulatory audits are conducted by the CMB or by external auditors appointed by the CMB.

Companies usually hesitate to implement better disclosure policies voluntarily, fearing that this may provide competitive information to their rivals. The concept of "trade secret" finds its use again as an excuse for opacity. The lack of investor activism does not help the situation. Regular analyst meetings are very rare, although there are signs of change.

CONCLUSION

Turkey's corporate governance framework and company practices are set to go through a major improvement and the picture presented here may appear outdated soon, should Turkey manage to unleash its potential once the systemic risks are removed and macroeconomic stability is achieved. Meanwhile, it is of vital importance to analyze nontraditional firm-level factors more closely when evaluating the governance quality of Turkish firms.

Articles of association and groupwide business controls need to be examined closely to understand the basic rights of the shareholders and constraints on good governance. The identity of the owners and individual board members, the nature of their relationship, an analysis of intergroup dynamics and the exposure of the owners to reputational risks, and finally the identity of the auditor and the duration of their engagement would give indications about the business culture. Further analysis may include the history of violations (not only of the companies but also of individual board members); the level of unlisted exposure; the history of dividend payments; typical agendas of board meetings; existence and quality of shareholder relations management; the history and frequency of issuing IAS-compatible reports; cross listings; and the use of ADRs, GDRs, or Eurobonds.

It is probably safe to assume that the picture presented here will change in the medium term due to accelerated privatization and the implementation of pension reforms together with new legislation governing private pension funds, the close monitoring of banks by BRSA, the CMB's commitment to the improvement of the regulatory framework, the provision of incentives for better governed companies, and NGO-induced activism. The recent Corporate Governance Code developed by the CMB has very high requirements compatible to the regulations and codes adapted or promoted by the most developed capital markets in the areas of disclosure, minority rights, board structure, and management oversight. Meanwhile Turkey's progress in achieving full membership of the European Union will provide a critical stimulus in establishing the "rule of law" if not better corporate governance practices.

NOTE

1. This article is extracted from the original paper by Ararat and Ugur (2003) with some update based on the actual developments in Turkey after the article was written.

REFERENCES

Ararat, M., and M. Ugur. "Corporate Governance in Turkey: An Overview and Some Policy Recommendations," *Corporate Governance: The International Journal of Business in Society*, vol. 3, no. 1, 2003.

Capital Markets Board (CMB), www.spk.org, 2003.

Interviews and discussions with R. Tanör (June 2002), S. Taha (January 2003), D. Meen (December 2002) C. Ba_aran (January 2003), B. Elmaa_açlı (March 2003).

Istanbul Stock Exchange (ISE), www.imkb.gov.tr, 2003.

McKinsey & Company. "Global Investor Opinion Survey on Corporate Governance," www.mckinsey.com, July 2002.

Turkish Industrialists and Businessmen Association (TUSIAD), www.tusiad.org, 2003.

Ugur, M., "The European Union and Turkey: An Anchor/Credibility Dilemma," Aldershot: Ashgate Publishers, 1999.

Yurtoglu, B., "Ownership, Control and Performance of Turkish Listed Firms," *Empirica*, No. 27, Kluwer Academic Publishers, Netherlands, 2000, pp. 193–222.

Case Studies

$\mathbf{T}$his Appendix contains case studies of two very different corporate governance situations, presented in the form of a Standard & Poor's corporate governance scoring evaluation.[*] The companies covered include Fannie Mae in the United States, and Central Telecommunications Company (CTC) in Russia. Each study represents a holistic application of the governance scoring criteria developed in this book, and in each case Standard & Poor's analysts conducted extensive interviews with company managers, directors, and professional advisers.

Fannie Mae, one of the leading providers of mortgage finance in the United States, has a special corporate status given its public mission. In terms of Fannie Mae's governance, this status as a "government-sponsored enterprise" affects its board structure and disclosure requirements. Its overall governance assessment is "very strong." Russia's CTC's governance score was assessed as "moderate," but in a generally improving overall environment for governance in Russia. In CTC we see governance issues related to the influence of blockholders in the ownership structure and in terms of how this translates into specifics of board procedures.

The corporate governance score that is represented is on a scale from 1 to 10, with 10 being highest. The scoring process entails a review of each analytical subcomponent, and the assigning of an overall score from 1 to 10 to each of the four analytical components that were discussed in

---

[*]A Standard & Poor's Corporate Governance Score (CGS) is defined as reflecting Standard & Poor's assessment of a company's corporate governance policies and practices, and the extent to which these serve the interests of the company's financial stakeholders, with an emphasis on shareholders' interests. It is based on information provided to Standard & Poor's by the company, its officers, and any other sources that Standard & Poor's considers reliable. A CGS is neither an audit, nor a forensic investigation of a company's governance practices. Standard & Poor's may rely on audited information and other information provided by the company for the purpose of the governance analysis. It is neither a credit rating, nor is it a recommendation to buy, sell, or hold any interest in a company, as it does not comment on market price or suitability for a particular investor. The studies are dated as of the point of time referenced in each text, and have not been adjusted for any changes in the companies since the date of publication.

Chapters 3 through 6. The final, or composite, score is drawn from the four composite scores. In the cases of Fannie Mae and CTC, each of the four main analytical components was equally weighted. While these factors would have been considered by the analyst, the text represents the analyst's emphasis on the specific factors driving the governance analysis in the given company.

These scores do not address specific legal, regulatory, and market environment issues at the country level and the extent to which these may help or hinder governance at the company level. There is scope for further country analysis—along the lines discussed in Chapters 7, 16, 17, and 18—to fully appreciate any additional risks that may come from ineffective market, legal, regulatory, and informational infrastructures.

Case Study/Corporate Governance Score: Fannie Mae

January 30, 2003[*]

ANALYSTS

Dan Konigsburg, Standard & Poor's, London

Andrea Esposito, Standard & Poor's, New York

UNITED STATES

Overall Company Score (CGS)	CGS—9.0 (Maximum CGS—10)
Component Scores	
Ownership structure and external influences	9.0
Shareholder rights and stakeholder relations	8.7
Transparency, disclosure, and audit	9.0
Board structure and effectiveness	9.3

EXECUTIVE SUMMARY

Standard & Poor's has assigned Fannie Mae a corporate governance score of 9.0 on a 10-point scale, reflecting governance practices that are consistently strong or very strong across each of our areas of analysis.

Fannie Mae's unique corporate status, its size and influence in the housing market, its connection with the government, its public interest

---

[*] This analysis reflects the company's corporate governance practices as of this date of publication. To the extent that there have been changes in the company's governance structures or practices since this publication date, these are not reflected in this report.

mission, and the scope of its activity in the fixed income capital markets are all distinctive features of its operating environment. These factors increase its public visibility and invite scrutiny from the private and public sectors and the media. In addition, they allow more scope for external stakeholder influence at Fannie Mae than would be the case for companies with lower public profiles.

Particular governance anomalies that come with Fannie Mae's special status include appointment by the President of the United States of 5 of its 17 board members (board size is set by statute at 18 members; the board size of 17 used throughout this report reflects a current vacancy); special corporate status as a government-sponsored enterprise (GSE); regulatory status under the U.S. Department of Housing and Urban Development (HUD); and an historical exemption from both state and local taxes and from registering its securities with the U.S. Securities and Exchange Commission (SEC). While in certain respects the company's governmental dimension and its corporate status may challenge traditional views of investor rights, it is our view that Fannie Mae manages its governance process capably, and that external influences do not materially distort or negatively influence Fannie Mae's governance vis-à-vis its financial stakeholders.

Our conclusions in the individual categories of our analysis can be summarized as follows:

Ownership structure and external influences are assessed as very strong, as Fannie Mae discloses significant detail about who owns its shares and there is little possibility for conflicts of interest or undue influence among its widely dispersed shareholdings. The role of the government in its current operations is not considered a material governance issue at the moment, though given Fannie Mae's special status and strong political influences this is a factor that requires ongoing monitoring—particularly with regard to potential conflicts between the interests of financial stakeholders and Fannie Mae's public mission.

Shareholder rights and stakeholder relations are assessed as strong, as the company has assured equal rights for all of its owners. Our assessment of ownership rights reflects the fact that Fannie Mae's shareholders do not have the right to elect a certain meaningful number (28 percent) of directors, given the five directors appointed by the President. Fannie Mae has no takeover defenses per se, but the market for corporate control for Fannie Mae is likely to be inhibited by its special status and market position.

Transparency, disclosure, and audit at Fannie Mae is assessed at a very strong standard. Fannie Mae's size, and the complexity of particular accounting practices, notably FAS 133, make its financial practices subject to high levels of external scrutiny. However, the company's website and annual report provide a very strong basis of disclosure that meets or in some cases exceeds SEC requirements. While historically the company has been exempt from registering its securities with the SEC, it will voluntarily do so with respect to its common stock, and will be in line with the Securities Exchange Act of 1934 in early 2003. This should improve access to Fannie Mae's disclosure through the SEC's online EDGAR system, and will bring Fannie Mae into conformity with other U.S.-listed companies. It should not however, materially change the level of disclosure that Fannie Mae currently provides. We assess positively Fannie Mae's audit process and how its independence is maintained, but note a high level of nonaudit fees paid to the company's auditor.

Board structure and effectiveness scores very high in our analysis. The company combines a good mix of new and longer-serving directors, directors of high caliber, and with a diversity of skills and a strong voice of independence and engagement. From our meetings with a number of Fannie Mae directors and from access to board notes and meeting minutes, board effectiveness appears strong, particularly in the strength of its committees. The presence of presidentially appointed directors (presidentials) on the board might on its face appear to be a negative factor, but we have seen no evidence to suggest that the presidentials act in any way inconsistent with their fiduciary duties to the company's shareholders and on balance find their presence to be mildly positive to the board's effectiveness. In January 2003, the Fannie Mae board chose to establish a formal presiding director structure that could provide a counterbalance to the combined chairman/CEO role. The structure has largely been in place in all but name for some time. We have seen evidence that this role is in practice similar to that of a lead director. Although the concentration of power in the combined chairman/CEO position brings some positives as well, it warrants monitoring. However, it is our view that this has not proven to be a practical concern at Fannie Mae given its strong and independent board as well as the constraints and regulatory oversight that come from Fannie Mae's special corporate status.

COMPANY OVERVIEW

Fannie Mae (formally The Federal National Mortgage Association) is the largest provider of low-cost financing for mortgages in the United States.

It is the second-largest company in the United States by assets and the largest nonbank financial services company in the world. Fannie Mae was established by Congress in 1938 as a federal agency to support home ownership and the economy at large and was fully privatized in 1968. The company received its listing on the New York Stock Exchange in 1970. Today, Fannie Mae is one of only a handful of companies in the United States (Freddie Mac, Farmer Mac, and Sallie Mae are others) that enjoy the status not of a typical corporation, but of a GSE, a type of federally chartered corporation. As such, Fannie Mae is not incorporated in any state, though it has chosen to follow the corporate governance laws of Delaware.

As a GSE, Fannie Mae has a congressional charter that gives it a public interest mission to increase the availability and affordability of housing to low-, moderate-, and middle-income households in the United States. In addition, as a GSE Fannie Mae is exempt from SEC registration and enforcement actions from potential violations of most federal securities laws, although it is subject to antifraud securities laws. However, Fannie Mae's imminent voluntary registration with the SEC will improve access to disclosure and assure regulatory oversight and its securities will remain exempt under the Securities Exchange Act (see below). Fannie Mae receives no financial backing from the U.S. government and its debt is not officially guaranteed by the government. However, there is an implied basis of financial support, in part based on the Secretary of the Treasury's "discretionary authority" to purchase up to $2.25 billion of Fannie Mae's securities at any one time (though this amount would cover far less than 1 percent of Fannie Mae's obligations) and the general belief that the government would step in if necessary to protect the stability of the secondary market. Implied governmental support also allows Fannie Mae to borrow at favorable interest rates. Fannie Mae is closely regulated by HUD and the Office of Federal Housing Enterprise Oversight (OFHEO), whose sole mission is to ensure the safety and soundness of both Fannie Mae and Freddie Mac.

In 2001 and 2002, criticism has been raised over Fannie Mae's corporate governance and regulatory environment from several quarters: In Congress, Richard Baker, Chairman of the Capital Markets, Insurance and Government Sponsored Enterprises Subcommittee of the House Financial Services Committee, and a long-time critic of Fannie Mae, has raised questions about the oversight role of OFHEO in regulating Fannie Mae and its sister company Freddie Mac. Such criticism has been seconded by a few media sources and by FM Watch, a micro-lobby backed by some of Fannie Mae's competitors, upset at what they view as unfair government support for the company and for Freddie Mac, another GSE, and critical of these companies' public interest role in directing additional money into the housing market (see "Influence of ownership and external stakeholders" below).

In response to some of these criticisms and the market's increased focus on issues of corporate disclosure, Fannie Mae has decided to voluntarily register its common stock with the SEC, but not its unsecured debt and mortgage backed securities (MBS) that it uses to facilitate its main business of creating a secondary mortgage market (see "Content of public disclosure" below). Fannie Mae's first SEC filings occurred in the first quarter of 2003. These filings will end the anomaly that gives Fannie Mae more discretion than other listed companies regarding its disclosure obligations.

SEC oversight aside, Fannie Mae is among the most tightly regulated financial companies in the world. OFHEO, for example, completed a risk-based stress test for capital adequacy in 2001 that ties capital requirements directly to the risk profile of its assets, hedging strategies, and off-balance sheet exposures, a measure that is not even contemplated by the New Basel Capital Accord. According to published statements, the stress test is said to require a level of capital to allow Fannie Mae to remain solvent throughout a 10-year span of "depression-level" economic conditions plus, "for good measure," an additional 30 percent to account for operations risk.

The company chairman and CEO is Franklin Raines, who has served in these roles since 1998. Standard & Poor's Rating Services has assigned a "AAA" (triple A) credit rating to Fannie Mae, reflecting both its own operating and financial strength as well as the implicit governmental support that comes from its unique corporate status.

OWNERSHIP STRUCTURE AND EXTERNAL INFLUENCES

Component Score—9.0

Transparency of ownership

Fannie Mae has a transparent ownership structure. The company discloses all major shareholders above 5 percent of shares outstanding.

Key Analytical Issues	Assessment
There is adequate disclosure of shareholdings in public reports, e.g., identification of major shareholders.	Positive
The company identifies indirect holdings to the extent possible given regulation.	Positive

Fannie Mae is a widely held company and its shareholding structure is broadly transparent. The company discloses in its annual proxy statement all beneficial owners of its common stock above 5 percent in line with, but not subject to, SEC regulation. With a holding of 10.4 percent, FMR Corporation, the parent of Fidelity Management & Research, is the only holder with more than 5 percent of shares outstanding. The company does not disclose smaller stakes. Fannie Mae also does not disclose breakdowns of its shareholders by type.

Shareholdings of directors and senior executives in the company are adequately disclosed, as are shares held under option by directors and executives.

Influence of ownership and external stakeholders

Fannie Mae shares are widely held. There is no evidence of large block shareholders with disproportionate influence on company management. Fannie Mae's public mission, enforced by its congressional charter, gives it both more responsibilities and restrictions than a typical corporation.

Key Analytical Issues	Assessment
The majority of shares are widely held.	Positive
There is no evidence of a tendency toward greater concentration of shareholdings.	Positive
No blockholder has veto power; there are no cross-shareholdings.	Positive
Managerial holdings are not large enough to confer actual control.	Positive
There is no evidence of disproportionate exercise of power by one shareholding group.	Positive
Managers have no external relationships with large shareholders.	Positive
The company's congressional charter bestows additional responsibilities and restrictions.	Mixed
The company's status, size, and public mission results in strong political and regulatory scrutiny.	Mixed

Fannie Mae's shares are widely held and the largest shareholder, Fidelity, is a nominee representing the interests of thousands of smaller shareholders. As such, there is little reason to suspect that any one shareholder or group of shareholders has a disproportionate influence on the management of the company and there is little potential for conflicts of interest between owners and managers. Directors and officers themselves hold far less than 1 percent of outstanding shares. Minority interests are protected by a strong combination of legislation, listing rules, and independent board oversight.

While not owners themselves, Congress and the federal government are major stakeholders in Fannie Mae. Their interest is clearly to use the financial flexibility of a private company to pursue societal goals of increased home ownership. The government, through congressional oversight, the congressional charter, and regulation by OFHEO and HUD, restricts the business of Fannie Mae to supporting the housing market, which it does by buying and securing mortgages. Fannie Mae may not expand into other, potentially more profitable areas of business, and may not pursue business outside the United States. Moreover, there are more direct interventions in the day-to-day business of Fannie Mae: all debt and MBS issued by the company must receive approval from the U.S. Secretary of the Treasury. Whether these can be considered negative influences is questionable; investors have long known that Fannie Mae is a product of the federal government and has a narrowly defined social mission.

The potential for conflict between the company's social mission and the interests of its shareholders is mitigated to the extent that directors' fiduciary duties—including the presidential directors—are to the shareholders, not to the furtherance of the company's social mission. Indeed, except for the role of the Treasury and the company's congressionally defined business, Fannie Mae's chartered restrictions might not be considered materially different from regulatory restrictions on banks and other financial institutions.

While the influence of its regulators and of Congress may not materially affect Fannie Mae's corporate governance at present, there is a possibility that this could change in the future. In 2001, for example, OFHEO proposed regulatory changes that would have, among other things, lowered the liability threshold for Fannie Mae's directors as well as introduced new legal duties of directors potentially in conflict with Delaware law and potentially making it more difficult for Fannie Mae to recruit new directors. Another example of political influence comes from Congress, where representative Richard Baker, Chairman of the Capital Markets, Insurance and Government Sponsored Enterprises Subcommittee of the House Financial Services Committee and a long-time critic of Fannie Mae, has been a proponent for a top-to-bottom, congressional-led review of Fannie Mae's corporate governance practices and for increased disclosure of its debt securities in addition to its common stock (criticism seconded by the editorial page of a prominent national newspaper and FM Watch). In both cases, Fannie Mae to this point has been able to use persuasion, its political connections, and supportive legal opinion to maintain the status quo that it clearly believes serves the interests of its shareholders. In our interview with one of Fannie Mae's directors, it was observed that dealing with external political, regulatory, and legislative risk is something that the company is quite good at; a skill that has helped the company and its shareholders over the long term. Political attempts to challenge Fannie Mae's current role will doubtless continue, and it will remain an ongoing requirement for the company's managers and directors to govern the company in the context of these strong external influences.

SHAREHOLDER RIGHTS AND STAKEHOLDER RELATIONS

Component Score—8.7

Shareholder voting and meeting procedures

Fannie Mae's commitment to shareholder democracy is strong. The company supplies comprehensive information to shareholders well in advance of company meetings. Voting procedures are fair and in line with typical procedures for a Delaware corporation.

Key Analytical Issues	Assessment
Fannie Mae informs shareholders of upcoming meetings sufficiently in advance (at least 30 days' notice, often 50 or more) to consider and execute their votes.	Positive
Notices of meetings are sent individually to shareholders and posted on the company's website. Notices are comprehensive and provide enough information to reasonably allow the making of voting decisions.	Positive
There is evidence of attempts to ensure that notice reaches beneficial shareholders before shareholder meetings.	Positive
Shareholders' meetings are rotated among major cities throughout the country, allowing the maximum number of shareholders to participate in meetings.	Positive
Shareholders may put forward shareholder proposals, nominate directors, pursue proxy contests, and may convene special meetings.	Positive
Shareholders unable to attend meetings may vote by proxy, and may send instructions by mail, telephone, or the Internet.	Positive
Brokers may not use a discretionary proxy for nonvotes received in relation to all voting items.	Positive
All votes, whether cast at the meeting or in absentia, are given equal weight.	Positive

Fannie Mae has well-established procedures for both conducting shareholder meetings and disseminating shareholder meeting information. Registered shareholders are mailed notices of meetings and proxy statements, together with the annual report, sufficiently in advance of meetings to make informed voting decisions, usually more than 30 days in advance. Proxy statements include detailed explanations of each voting item and good information on voting procedures, rules, instructions, and deadlines. All information is simultaneously posted on Fannie Mae's website, although it is not as yet posted to the SEC's online reporting system, EDGAR.

Voting at shareholders' meetings is by poll, and all votes, whether physically present at the meeting or represented by proxy, are counted equally. Beginning in 2002, shareholders wishing to vote by proxy may do so by mail, telephone, or email. Shareholders vote on all major company decisions including the annual election and removal of directors (with the exception of presidentially appointed directors), appointment of auditors, remuneration plans, substantive bylaw amendments, and major mergers and acquisitions that qualify under New York Stock Exchange listing rules.

Fannie Mae does not count so-called "broker nonvotes" in shareholder approval of voting items, even items classified as routine by the New York Stock Exchange. This makes Fannie Mae unusually progressive in its voting policies, especially in comparison with other U.S. companies we have reviewed. Broker nonvotes occur when shareholders holding shares through their brokerage accounts do not provide voting instructions and brokers themselves vote in the assumed interests of the beneficiaries.

Fannie Mae also has quite positively ensured that shareholders have voted to approve each of its equity-linked compensation plans, including its ESOP, something that until recently few companies have undertaken to do.

Shareholders also may put forward, with a very small amount of equity, shareholder proposals at shareholder meetings, in line with current SEC rules (again, that Fannie Mae is not required to follow as an exempt issuer). Fannie Mae reports that it has entered into discussion with every shareholder resolution proponent in its history and has allowed virtually every shareholder proposal it has received onto its agenda, a decision that U.S. companies have significant discretion over when proposals deal with "ordinary business" issues, as defined by the SEC. A proposal to restore cumulative voting to the company's bylaws has been on the agenda each year since 1988; it has never received majority approval from shareholders. Though cumulative voting for directors was once in Fannie Mae's articles, the company has argued that, as a widely held company, cumulative voting might result in the election of directors representing specific interests, rather than shareholders as a whole. Cumulative voting can be beneficial in cases, unlike at Fannie Mae, where the share structure includes a large blockholder. Shareholders also may nominate directors to the Fannie Mae board in line with clear procedures set out in the company's bylaws.

Ownership rights

Ownership rights are clearly stated and well protected. The bylaws include a number of provisions that increase shareholder oversight beyond what is typical for a U.S. corporation, although shareholders do not have the opportunity to vote on all directors.

Key Analytical Issues	Assessment
Ownership rights are secured via a strong combination of internal bylaws, Delaware Law, and regulation by the New York Stock Exchange (but not the SEC).	Positive
Share structure consists of one class of common shares and seven classes of preferred shares.	Positive
Bylaws clearly establish a one share, one vote principle.	Positive
The company has a stated dividend policy and declared dividend payments have been made.	Positive
Shareholders may request that directors convene special shareholder meetings.	Positive
Shareholders do not vote on a number of routine items common among non-U.S. companies.	Negative
Shareholders' right to elect directors is limited to 13 of the current 17 board members.	Negative

Rights attached to Fannie Mae shares are secure and fully transferable. All common shares have equal rights and there are no multiple classes of shares with variable rights. Owners of common shares have the right to vote, to receive dividend payments and, in the case of liquidation of the company, to receive proportional payment in turn.

Voting rights attached to Fannie Mae shares are laid out in the company's bylaws and the Delaware General Corporation Law (DGCL), the state corporate law that the company chose to follow in a number of respects in 2001 in response to an OFHEO requirement. Shareholders vote on all major company decisions including the annual election of 13 of the 17 directors (Fannie Mae has determined that an unclassified board is appropriate for its current circumstances), appointment of auditors, remuneration plans, substantive bylaw amendments, and major mergers and acquisitions that might qualify under New York Stock Exchange listing rules.

One-third of Fannie Mae shareholders also may petition the board to convene a special shareholder meeting, a shareholder right that a minority of U.S. corporations allow. Calling a special meeting allows shareholders to propose changes to a company's governance structure that would not be possible under the SEC's shareholder proposal guidelines, and would perhaps be less expensive and disruptive than a proxy contest. Fannie Mae holders do not enjoy preemptive rights over new share issuances, another right that most U.S. companies removed by the 1980s, and shareholder class action securities suits are unlikely to be allowed at Fannie Mae because, as a GSE, the company is exempt from most federal securities laws.

The company has a clearly articulated dividend policy, underpinned by an annual peer analysis against the dividend policies and payout ratios of the financial companies on the S&P 500 index and with an intention to remain at about the 65th percentile in payout. Recently, Fannie Mae has responded to its investors who wanted a more tax-friendly method of returning value to shareholders, and it has, until January 2003, been reducing its payout ratio and using the difference to repurchase stock.

Finally, we note that shareholders cannot vote for, or indeed, vote to remove if necessary, all directors on the Fannie Mae board, as 5 of the board's 17 members are appointed by the U.S. President (typically, this is 5 of 18; one director has recently left the board). The system is a fact of life at Fannie Mae, and there are broad positives as well as negatives that accrue to the board by having these members (see "Role and independence of outside directors" below), yet fundamentally, the owners of the company cannot pass judgment on all 17 board members each year. Fannie Mae shareholders also do not vote to approve dividends, to receive the financial statements, to approve technical bylaw changes, or to waive rights to new share issuances, as these rights of ownership are typically reserved for the board at U.S. companies.

Takeover defenses and corporate control issues

While Fannie Mae's bylaws contain no takeover defenses, its unique position in the markets and as a regulated, congressionally chartered company makes a potential change in control unlikely.

Key Analytical Issues	Assessment
Fannie Mae has no takeover defenses per se.	Positive
The company's special status, scale, and governmental links are likely to inhibit the possibility for external challenges for corporate control.	Mixed

Key Analytical Issues	Assessment
Whether a proxy contest could successfully remove the presidentially appointed directors is unclear and untested, as the company's congressional charter governs their appointment.	Negative

Fannie Mae's bylaws do not contain any takeover provisions as such. There is no classified board, no poison pill, no freeze-out provisions on large share purchases or other devices that are normally used to frustrate takeover bids. Yet Standard & Poor's also recognizes that, as a highly regulated and congressionally chartered company, Fannie Mae is unlikely to be the target of a takeover. And even if this were to occur, there is a question of whether Congress would allow a change in control.

To some extent this might provide Fannie Mae management with fewer short-term performance pressures that can keep the company focused on its long-term strategy. However, it also can have the effect of limiting the channels that shareholders have to exercise change in corporate control. Moreover, it is unclear and untested whether a proxy contest for large changes to the board could remove the five presidential appointees because their appointment is governed by the company's charter, which only can be amended by Congress.

TRANSPARENCY, DISCLOSURE, AND AUDIT
Component Score—9.0
Content of public disclosure

While Fannie Mae has not been obliged to report to the SEC as an exempt issuer, the company has adopted a program of voluntary disclosures and publication on its website that meets or exceeds SEC disclosure requirements. Less is disclosed about noncommon stock than about common shares, and the depth of Web-based disclosure has improved over the last year.

Key Analytical Issues	Assessment
Though Fannie Mae does not have to make periodic disclosure to the SEC, the company has a policy of voluntary disclosure for its common stock that meets or exceeds SEC disclosure requirements.	Positive
The company maintains a number of disclosures that are unmatched by similar or competing companies.	Positive
Although disclosure of Fannie Mae's MBS continues to evolve, we expect further improvements in disclosure of these securities. Disclosure relating to non-MBS debt is strong.	Mixed
Nonfinancial disclosure is strong and comprehensive.	Positive

As an SEC-exempt issuer until early 2003, Fannie Mae has had few disclosure requirements other than its frequent reporting to its regulator, OFHEO, and before that, to HUD. Despite this, Fannie Mae has consistently undertaken to provide disclosure to its shareholders and stakeholders at a level that meets or in some cases exceeds that required by the SEC. In recent years, a combination of voluntary initiatives and specifics of OFHEO's oversight have resulted in disclosure about Fannie Mae's financial health that is unavailable from other, similar financial institutions.

Fannie Mae's financial reporting includes not just the typical financial statements and notes, but also a review of its derivative and hedging activities, its off-balance sheet risk, and an overview of its outstanding mortgage portfolio. Audited financial statements are included in an annual report sent to shareholders each year. In addition to these disclosures, the company adopted a series of voluntary initiatives in October 2000, designed to increase financial transparency in light of increasing market expectations and investor scrutiny. The company launched six voluntary initiatives in total (the seventh is voluntary SEC registration) that seek to provide investors with more information about its financial condition and risk management. The initiatives are as follows:

1. Fannie Mae periodically issues small amounts of publicly tradable subordinated debt, with the assumption that such debt is a useful gauge of market confidence in the company;

2. A commitment to maintain at least three months' worth of liquidity, assuming there is no access to public debt markets;

3. Implementation of Fannie Mae's own version of a risk-based capital stress test (since superseded by OFHEO's stress test);

4. Monthly interest rate risk disclosure that provides the financial impact of interest rate fluctuations on its business, including its duration gap, or the extent to which the duration of its assets and liabilities are matched;

5. Quarterly disclosure of credit loss sensitivity (the sensitivity of its future credit losses to an immediate 5 percent decline in home prices); and

6. Obtaining an annual "risk to the government" or financial strength rating from a nationally recognized rating agency.

Taken together, the voluntary initiatives meet or exceed what is generally expected in terms of disclosure from other U.S. financial institutions, particularly the disclosure that is forward-looking. Fannie Mae intends to continue its monthly disclosures under its voluntary initiatives, even as these are not required by the Exchange or the SEC.

We also note the publication of an "operating EPS" figure, which strips out the effects of FAS 133, a measure that Fannie Mae undertook to provide increased clarity to investors in light of the new accounting rule that brought all of Fannie Mae's derivatives onto its balance sheet. The company quite positively provides substantial disclosure on its website that helps investors understand the new rule. Separately, but also positively, Fannie Mae was among the first 10 companies in the United States to announce that it would expense the full cost of stock options, it discloses insider trades of Fannie Mae stock on its website within the current regulatory timeframe (though not, as yet, to the SEC), and provides strong disclosure of special-purpose vehicles and risk management techniques that it employs, arguably among the most important disclosures the company makes given its business. It also is assessed positively that the company has defined and publicized a clear corporate mission, and has set clear and challenging financial goals that can be measured and tracked by investors (the 1999 goal to double the rate of operating EPS growth within five years, for example).

We note that Fannie Mae has come under some criticism during the past year for its disclosure relating to its debt and MBS. While Fannie Mae will voluntarily register its common stock with the SEC under the 1934 Act, its securities offerings, including offerings of debt securities, remain exempt, primarily because of the number of securities issued (Fannie Mae estimates that its issued securities represent between five and six times the total number of such securities of all other U.S. issuers combined). Were Fannie Mae forced to register each of these securities, a challenging administrative burden could arise for both Fannie Mae and the SEC, and the offsetting benefits might not match the cost. For example, more disclosure (like loan-to-value ratios of loans within particular MBS, or credit scores of the borrowers within MBS, as smaller, private-label issuers of MBS include) could have the impact of reducing the number of MBS that could be sold. This could contribute to increased disclosure at the expense of liquidity in the MBS market itself. Standard & Poor's believes that Fannie Mae, together with its regulators, the Treasury, and the SEC, has for the moment decided that the value of liquidity and efficient markets exceeds the benefits to be gained from increased disclosure.

This argument has not convinced everyone though, and Standard & Poor's believes it is possible that Fannie Mae will decide to disclose more about its MBS in the medium term. One argument, that more should be disclosed about Fannie Mae's derivative counterparties, is less convincing. While Fannie Mae discloses concentration of the total notional amount of derivative transactions outstanding among its counterparties, disclosing more details is unknown among commercial banks and has never been required by the SEC. Fannie Mae, for its part, has argued that all its derivative transactions are collateralized and that counterparties maintain strict controls and enjoy high credit ratings themselves.

Nonfinancial disclosure reaches a high standard and is assessed positively, reflecting substantial disclosed information about the board, compensation, and corporate governance policies, and information and research about the American housing market that the company makes available on its website. The company has recently improved disclosure about its own governance practices, and will post, as of January 31, 2003, committee and governance charters and its own definition of director independence on its website.

Finally, Fannie Mae ranked among the 8th decile in Standard & Poor's 2001/2002 Transparency & Disclosure study—a level that ranks favorably with its U.S. peers in the S&P 500 index and with other non-U.S. companies in a broader global context.

Timing of and access to public disclosure

Timing of and access to public disclosure are strong. Access has improved as a result of the company reporting to the SEC in 2003. Its annual report and quarterly filings are posted to EDGAR, the SEC's online searchable database.

Key Analytical Issues	Assessment
Access to disclosure is expected to improve when the company begins reporting electronically to the SEC.	Positive
The company has long complied with Regulation Fair Disclosure.	Positive
The company comes closer than most U.S. companies to continuous disclosure, reporting monthly in some areas.	Positive
In line with the SEC's recommendation, Fannie Mae has created a senior-level disclosure committee.	Positive
The company's website is used to communicate effectively with shareholders, creditors, and other stakeholders.	Positive

Though the company has never been subject to Regulation Fair Disclosure (Reg FD), Fannie Mae has voluntarily complied with the rule since its introduction in 2000. Following Fannie Mae's registration with the SEC, it will be formally subject to the rule, although nothing of substance is expected to change. In a similar way, Fannie Mae's continuous disclosure policies follow those required by the SEC; all material changes to Fannie Mae's financial position are posted to its website without delay. Moreover, its monthly financial reports come closer than any other U.S. company's, financially or otherwise, to continuous disclosure: monthly reports include operational EPS numbers, changes to its duration gap, and updates of many of the voluntary disclosure initiatives. Fannie Mae's website also assists in creating a continuous disclosure regime: It includes speeches, presentations, testimony before Congress, as well as downloadable copies of all its public disclosure, including some historical disclosure as well.

Finally, we note that Fannie Mae has followed the SEC recommendation to form a high-level disclosure committee. The committee is designed to keep the board and management apprised of changes in disclosure expectations as well as to ensure that material issues are disclosed to the market on a timely and ongoing basis. Fannie Mae's disclosure committee includes its controller, general counsel, treasurer, senior credit officer, head of investor relations, head of internal audit, and chief of communications.

Audit process

Fannie Mae's audit committee demonstrates a commitment to the independence of the audit process. Its members are actively engaged with both the internal audit team and the outside auditors.

Key Analytical Issues	Assessment
The outside auditors are reputable and experienced.	Positive
An audit committee, composed entirely of independent outside directors, owns the relationship with the outside auditors.	Positive
There is an explicit, transparent, and accountable process for selecting the auditor.	Positive
There is evidence of processes that ensure auditor independence.	Positive
Audit committee members are actively engaged in the audit process.	Positive
Nonaudit fees are high relative to audit fees, though the audit committee has instituted processes to separate the tender processes for audit and nonaudit work.	Negative/Neutral

Fees		2001 (in $ millions)
Audit	1.05	12.84%
Nonaudit	7.13	87.16%
Total	8.18	100%

Fannie Mae's auditors, KPMG, are appointed by shareholders on an annual basis, upon the recommendation of the independent audit committee and the board as a whole. The audit committee addresses the effectiveness of the auditor's service on an annual basis and is responsible for monitoring their independence. In line with the provisions of the New York Stock Exchange's recommendations concerning audit committees, and in line with the 2002 Sarbanes-Oxley Act, Fannie Mae's audit committee is composed entirely of independent, nonexecutive board members, at least one of whom meets the NYSE financial expertise requirements, and the auditor's reporting relationship with the company is through the audit committee of the board, rather than with the CFO's office or with management in general. In addition to its audit work for Fannie Mae, KPMG provides the company with other services and their fees for this work are shown below.

While the nonaudit fees are substantially higher than those for audit, 86.2 percent of all nonaudit services provided to Fannie Mae by KPMG represent tax advice and comfort letters on the company's REMIC securities (Real Estate Mortgage Investment Conduit, a type of security representing ownership in a trust of multiple securities pegged to cash flows from different mortgages). The audit committee took the extra step to put this significant amount of business out to tender, though it did not decide to exclude KPMG from the tender itself, deciding that to do so would be to give in to the appearance of a conflict of interest when at the same time the committee agreed that the REMIC services did not affect the auditor's independence in fact. A statement testifying to the committee's confidence in the auditor's independence, despite the extra fees, is included in Fannie Mae's latest annual report. While Standard & Poor's found no evidence that challenges the committee's assessment of auditor independence, outside confidence in the process may rely on both the perception of independence in appearance as well as in fact. KPMG has acted as Fannie Mae's auditors since the company was split off from the federal government in 1968.

Standard & Poor's met with members of Fannie Mae's audit committee, internal audit department, and the KPMG lead partner and saw evidence of a strong commitment to audit independence, to robust audit and internal control procedures, and to a strong policy to avoid conflicts of interest. The committee has put substantial time and effort into building a strong working relationship with the internal audit team and the outside auditors and meets frequently with both groups, often without management present.

Linked to this is the company's serious focus on risk management, given the nature of its operating activities. Fannie Mae actively monitors and discloses key aspects of its risk management exposures relating to credit and interest rate risks. The company's internal auditor reports on a direct basis to the chair of the audit committee and works together with the financial management to ensure audit committee understanding of Fannie Mae's operating complexities and to provide timely information with regard to Fannie Mae's key financial exposures.

BOARD STRUCTURE AND EFFECTIVENESS
Component Score–9.3
Board structure and composition

Fannie Mae's board is well structured, if somewhat large, as a result of the presidential appointees. It has a solid committee framework.

Key Analytical Issues	Assessment
A substantial majority of directors are nonemployee and are independent in appearance and in action.	Positive
The CEO and chairman positions are combined; a formal presiding director has been identified.	Mixed
The presidential directors add a distinctive feature to Fannie Mae's board, providing both a basis of broader diversity and a perspective that may in theory differ from the shareholder-elected directors.	Mixed
There are audit, compensation, nominating and corporate governance, assets and liabilities policy, and technology committees, all of which are highly independent.	Positive
Board size is slightly larger compared with other major U.S. companies.	Neutral/Negative

Fannie Mae's board structure meets or exceeds the latest rules on board composition proposed by the New York Stock Exchange, and has for some time. Fannie Mae's board has a clear and substantial majority of independent, nonexecutive directors, a combined chairman and CEO, (see "Role and effectiveness of the board"), a presiding director that provides leadership for the nonexecutives, and independent board committees. At 17 members, the Fannie Mae board is somewhat larger than most corporate boards in the United States. An overview of the current board's structure is shown below.

	Executives	Shareholder-elected non-executives	Presidentially appointed non-executives	Total
Full Board[*]	3	9	5	17
Audit Committee	0	3	2	5
Compensation Committee	0	3	0	3
Nominating and Corporate Governance Committee	0	4	0	4
Assets and Liability Policy Committee	0	4	4	8
Technology Committee	0	3	4	7
Executive Committee[**]	1	5	0	6

[*] We note that Stephen Friedman, a shareholder-elected nonexecutive, left the board in December 2002 upon his appointment to head the President's National Economic Council and that Jamie Gorelick, a Vice Chair and executive of the company, has announced that she will leave the board in July to focus on her work with a federal commission investigating the September 11 attacks and to pursue other interests. The company has announced that it intends to propose CFO Tim Howard as her replacement on the board. The board has begun a search for a replacement for Mr. Friedman.
[**] The executive committee is authorized to transact business for the corporation in between board meetings. The committee did not meet in 2001.

One feature of the board, the five presidential appointees, can be viewed both positively and negatively. These members bring to board discussions a diversity of viewpoints and opinions that may not normally make it onto the board of a company Fannie Mae's size. Though turnover of the presidentials has not been especially frequent, the constancy of change every several years has meant that the board has become very good at bringing new members on, familiarizing new members with its complex business, and integrating them into the larger group.

For all of its negatives in terms of shareholders' right to elect all directors, it is also true that, like the occasional rotation of audit firms, the presence of five directors over whose appointment management has no authority can be a check against behavior that might not be in the best interests of shareholders. On the other hand, the tenure of presidentially appointed directors is typically shorter than that of their shareholder-elected colleagues, and many Fannie Mae directors recognize that the presidentials make the size of the board quite a bit larger than it would be otherwise, with an inevitable effect on efficiency and formality. (Average board size among larger U.S. companies is not constant, but is generally between 8 and 12 members.) Its large size would appear to be another reason why so much of the board's decisionmaking is run through its committees. (For more about the role of the presidentials, see "Role and independence of outside directors" below.)

Role and effectiveness of the board

The board appears to be an effective monitor of management. Directors appear to be engaged and show a desire to demonstrate leadership in board effectiveness and governance.

Key Analytical Issues	Assessment
The board has articulated for itself a set of matters reserved for its decision.	Positive
Much of the board's work is accomplished in its committees.	Neutral
The board sees its role in part to monitor management, including the chairman/CEO.	Positive
Board members express a conscious focus on leadership in governance/best practice and to increase board effectiveness over time.	Positive
The board has an appropriate mix of skills experience and background for its industry.	Positive
The presence of the presidential appointees, as a group, does not appear to materially influence the overall board's performance either positively or negatively.	Neutral
There are regular board performance evaluations.	Positive

Fannie Mae's board met eight times in 2001 and slightly more frequently in 2002. Attendance rates are reported in aggregate, and no board director attended less than 75 percent of official meetings. In common with many U.S. boards, much of the work at Fannie Mae is accomplished through its various committees, which meet before board meetings and throughout the year. While there is always a chance that heavy committee work will create divisions among, or different classes of, directors, we note that every Fannie Mae director sits on at least one board committee and from our director interviews we detected little if any division of this kind. Committee chairmen are nominated by the Governance and Nominating Committee and approved by the board as a whole. Given the lead role of the committees, a potential concern worth monitoring is that several committee chairs serve on several other outside boards. There is no concern about conflicts of interest in this regard; the key area of focus is whether this could result in insufficient focus on Fannie Mae responsibilities. We have no evidence to suggest this is a practical problem to date. For most of Fannie Mae's directors, this is their primary board membership, or they have resources to help them with their duties that lessen risk of overload. Moreover, the company's corporate governance guidelines require nonexecutives to inform the Corporate Governance and Nominating Committee before accepting any new outside directorships. The committee will then form a judgment about how any new board seat may affect board service at Fannie Mae.

From our access to board minutes, committees themselves appear to be efficiently run and cover a large amount of ground in each meeting. For example, Standard & Poor's reviewed with audit committee members the process through which it decided to continue to use its auditor KPMG for important nonaudit work relating to its REMICs. The committee decision to employ KPMG was justified ultimately on the basis of cost and the assertion that the nature of this work would not compromise the integrity of the audit process. On this basis the company appears to have consciously chosen what it viewed as the most cost-effective provider of these services, in full awareness that this would not create positive optics with regard to the balance of audit versus nonaudit fees. While in our view the absence of nonaudit fees in this case would create fewer questions about the independence of the audit process, we assess positively from a procedural perspective the fact that this question was seriously and thoughtfully addressed by the audit committee.

The audit committee is chaired by Thomas Gerrity, a professor and former dean at The Wharton School of Business of the University of Pennsylvania, and is distinguished by the high amount of both formal and informal interaction among its members. Again it is notable that Fannie Mae's chief internal auditor reports to the head of the independent audit committee on the board on a straightline basis.

The Nominating and Corporate Governance Committee is chaired by Ann McLaughlin Korologos, a professional and experienced board member who sets high procedural standards for the board as a whole. For example, this committee has undertaken a comprehensive comparative review of the changing corporate governance landscape with a view to maintain Fannie Mae's leadership in this area. In this, the committee has been supported by a strong team out of the corporate secretary's office.

Like a majority of U.S. companies, Fannie Mae's board is led by a combined chairman and CEO. Standard & Poor's is agnostic as to the relative merits of a split chairman and CEO, believing that there are potential risks to board effectiveness and oversight under both systems (split CEO/chairmen can themselves lead to competing power centers on the board and also can damage board effectiveness). In Fannie Mae's case, the combination does represent a significant concentration of power, but the board has taken the position that this concern is outweighed by the benefits of clear leadership and quick decisionmaking, particularly given the politics and competitiveness of its industry. Concerns also are lessened by the way that the CEO is monitored by a strongly independent board with strong, formalized leadership by a presiding director. (See "Role and independence of outside directors" below.) In our analysis, we have no evidence to raise concerns about the concentration of power, but given this structure, the strong role played by the chairman/CEO warrants ongoing monitoring in this context.

There is a thoughtfulness to the board's activities that is designed to increase effectiveness and cohesion as a group: There are frequent meetings of the nonexecutives separate from management, including unstructured meetings and day retreats to discuss strategy or other issues, and other meetings are organized where the nonexecutives can dine casually with the CEO; trips have been organized to neighborhoods where the effects of Fannie Mae's work can be seen by the directors; there is a robust orientation program for new directors that is both deep and broad (developed for the presidentials but of benefit to everyone), and there are regular evaluations of both board and CEO effectiveness that are completed with more than a pro forma approach.

Finally, the strength of the board is seen in a variety of areas, but two can be singled out here: the speed and effectiveness of the board's response to OFHEO's proposed changes in 2001 to its corporate governance (including the introduction of specific director responsibilities that may have been in conflict with most states' business judgment rules and lowered thresholds for director liability), and the way that the board has led a strong branding effort over the last several years that focuses equally on Fannie Mae's social mission and its leadership in technology and electronic commerce. Standard & Poor's has seen evidence, both in board of director meeting minutes and in meetings with directors themselves, that the board met these very different challenges with a seriousness of purpose and in partnership between management and the outside directors.

Role and independence of outside directors

The quality of Fannie Mae's independent directors is very strong. Directors are highly independent and demonstrate a clear commitment to the strength and independence of the board as a body. The presence of the presidential appointees does not appear to impair the independence of the nonexecutives as a group.

Key Analytical Issues	Assessment
All of the nonexecutive directors are assessed as independent in their actions.	Positive
There is strong, formalized leadership for the nonexecutives in a presiding director role.	Positive
In addition to qualification and experience, the director selection process includes explicit consideration of independence. The process includes evaluation of monetary, financial, and commercial relationships that might lead to conflicts of interest.	Positive
There are frequent opportunities for nonexecutives to meet independently of executives and management, both formally and informally.	Positive
The board has established 10-year term limits for nonexecutive directors.	Positive
Existing external directorships held by board members do not appear to interfere with the quality of their involvement, although this could be a challenge in the future.	Positive
Relationships that external directors have with the company are limited.	Positive
The presence of the presidential appointees does not appear to affect board independence.	Neutral

In our interviews with nonexecutive directors, we have assessed them to be intellectually independent and independent in their actions and have no reason to believe this is not representative of the nonexecutive directors as a whole. Two potential conflicts have been disclosed in the company's public reports (one director has received consulting fees from the company and another is president of a local university whose neighborhood has received significant help from Fannie Mae and its foundation). While these reflect potential areas of outside concern, we have seen no evidence that these factors materially impair the independence in fact (as opposed to in appearance) of the individual directors in question. For its part, the company has disclosed a specific definition of independence for its board, and has identified the former director as not independent according to this criteria.

In all respects Fannie Mae's nonexecutive director selection criteria and processes are very strong, and Standard & Poor's saw evidence that great care is taken in selecting new members with appropriate skills, experience, and knowledge. Independence is a specific consideration in the selection process. Moreover, consideration of independence among the nonexecutives continues after appointment, and there are procedures in place to track material changes.

Leadership for the independent directors exists, and has recently been formalized in the position of the chairman of the Nominating and Corporate Governance Committee (the current presiding director is Ms. Korologos). The chairman of the Nominating and Corporate Governance Committee takes the lead when nonexecutives meet alone, an opportunity given at each board of directors meeting. Directors we spoke with report that they can equally approach Mr. Raines or Ms. Korologos with concerns. Fannie Mae's board committee chairmen tend to be more experienced and longer-serving directors, and we understand these directors play subtle leadership roles for other nonexecutives as well. We note that the company has decided to link its presiding director (as well as the chair of its audit committee) to shareholders by publishing an email and mailing address for these board members on its website and will include these addresses in its next proxy statement. While this was a recommendation of the Sarbanes-Oxley legislation, Standard & Poor's positively assesses attempts to strengthen communication between nonexecutives and the shareholders they represent.

Worries that several directors sit on a large number of other boards are mitigated in practice: although there is always concern about the impact on a director's time should a crisis occur on another board, for most of Fannie Mae's directors, this is clearly their primary board membership or they have resources to help them with their duties that lessen risk of overload. In this way, Standard & Poor's does not find a one-size-fits-all rule governing board seats particularly helpful.

As mentioned above, five members of Fannie Mae's board are appointed by the President of the United States and do not stand for election by holders of the company's common stock. Five new directors may technically be appointed each year, but in practice, appointees tend to stay through the majority of each administration. According to Fannie Mae's charter, one of the five appointees must come from the mortgage lending industry, one must come from the real estate industry, and according to the Federal Housing Enterprises Financial Safety and Soundness Act of 1992 (the 1992 Act that created OFHEO), one of the appointees must have represented community or consumer interests, or have committed themselves to provision of housing for low-income households. In practice, Fannie Mae has no influence or say in the presidential appointment process, and does not provide the White House with recommendations, though the White House will often share names of potential appointments to Fannie Mae before they are announced, but only to ensure they meet Fannie Mae's standards of independence and to preclude any conflict of interest. The appointments are acknowledged to be among the more sought-after at every change in administration, both because they offer directorships of one of America's largest companies and because they are considered to be well-paid.

Standard & Poor's meetings with Fannie Mae board members confirmed that, despite the appointment process, no instructions are given to appointees on how to vote or otherwise behave on the board and the five appointees do not meet together as a group. All directors, whether presidentially appointed or not, share the same fiduciary duties of care and loyalty to shareholders and there is little in appointees' appearance, voting patterns, level of board activity, or other behavior that distinguishes them from their stockholder elected colleagues. Moreover, Standard & Poor's has found no evidence that the presence of these directors has diluted the board's independence or that they have hurt the board's effectiveness in any way other than board size.

Director and senior executive compensation

Compensation policies at Fannie Mae are competitive and transparent. The company attempts to link a substantial majority of executive pay to the performance of the company, at levels that increase in seniority. Standard & Poor's has seen evidence that the Compensation Committee limits the influence that executives can have on their own pay.

Key Analytical Issues	Assessment
The company has made efforts to link executive pay with increases in broad measures of performance.	Positive
The process by which pay is set is independent from executive influence.	Positive
The company has a clearly articulated compensation philosophy, which is followed in practice.	Positive
Potential dilution and cost to shareholders from option exercises is modest.	Positive
Pay packages for executives is competitive but not overly aggressive.	Positive

Fannie Mae's congressional charter requires the company to pay its executives compensation that is comparable to other publicly traded financial institutions and also sets a broad rule that "a significant portion" of pay should be connected to Fannie Mae's own performance. Another overarching compensation principle is the independence of the process by which executive pay it set.

The company has applied these principles to its compensation structure for its senior executives, which is composed of four main components: a base salary in cash, annual benefits, annual incentives, and long-term incentives. Except for base salary, each of these components is linked to increases in annual and multi-year performance. Moreover, Standard & Poor's has seen evidence that the board has limited the influence of executives on their own pay levels.

Fannie Mae's compensation policies for its CEO and senior executives are benchmarked and reviewed each year against a peer group of financial and financial service companies under the supervision of the board's Compensation Committee, composed entirely of independent, outside directors. Moreover, the Committee uses an outside consultant to assist with the process and discloses its name in public reports. Fannie Mae aims to be at or slightly below the 65th percentile in each of the four main components of pay packages, except for cash compensation (salary and bonus), which it benchmarks to the 50th percentile.

Standard & Poor's assesses positively the Committee's efforts to connect pay with performance: Annual bonuses are paid out entirely on growth in EPS (although the company does not disclose required growth levels or whether it uses its operating or GAAP EPS figures for this); longer-term incentives like performance shares or restricted stock only pay out over three- and four-year performance cycles, respectively, again linked to EPS measures and underpinned by participants' achievement of preestablished goals related to Fannie Mae's business, as assessed by the Committee (performance shares have a three-year performance cycle and payout to 50 percent in the fourth and fifth year after grant; restricted stock pays out in tranches of 25 percent over a four-year period). Stock options, with the exception of an EPS-linked challenge grant in 2000, pay out simply upon increases in the company's share price and do not include performance-linked criteria for option exercise. In today's environment, investors increasingly expect earnings or other financial performance hurdles for all equity-linked awards.

Expected dilution to current shareholders' stakes when outstanding awards are exercised is, at less than 5 percent of outstanding shares, modest compared with Fannie Mae's U.S. peers (overhangs at financial service companies are often twice as large). Moreover, dilution fears are lessened by the company's current policy to cover restricted stock awards with repurchased shares and the company's lowered share price. CEO pay at

Fannie Mae, while not especially modest, is well-disclosed and not out of line with its peers (it also is benchmarked to the 65th percentile of its U.S. peers). In 2001, base salary was set at just under U.S.$1 million and annual bonuses and longer-term option and performance awards increase total pay to just over U.S.$7 million, with approximately an additional U.S.$3.2 million (current value) paid and deferred. In the most recent year, performance criteria attached to these longer-term awards were fully met and the full compensation awards were granted to the CEO.

We note that the board has established challenging stock-retention rules: The CEO must hold a minimum of five times his or her base salary in Fannie Mae stock, and is given three years to attain this level. For the vice chairman, the minimum is three times salary; for executive vice presidents, it is two times salary. Standard & Poor's believes that stock retention can better align the interests of executives with shareholders than stock options alone.

Executive severance arrangements are modest and fully disclosed. Parties to these agreements may receive payments if they are not reelected by shareholders, upon a change of control or a few other reasons, though payouts are comparatively modest and do not extend beyond one year. Moreover, there are no unusual retirement benefits to a leaving CEO or other executives and all termination benefits are submitted to OFHEO for approval.

Board evaluation and succession policies are assessed as very strong: Although the board has avoided individual director performance reviews because they are seen as too divisive, this does not detract from the serious CEO and board evaluations that are conducted each year. The process is managed through the company's strong corporate governance committee and the company secretary's office. Unlike many U.S. companies, executive succession at Fannie Mae is far from ad hoc. The board regularly reviews contingency plans and meets to agree on their approach to both expected and unexpected changes in leadership.

Each nonmanagement director of Fannie Mae receives an annual cash retainer of U.S.$35,000 in addition to payments of U.S.$1000 for each board or committee meeting they attend and U.S.$10,000 if they chair a board committee. In addition, they participate in a restricted stock program and separate stock option program for directors that awards set amounts of stock at set dates, limiting discretion. The terms of these plans appear to be well-structured and are intended to align outside directors' interests with those of shareholders. Nonetheless, it would be positive if shares received under these plans could not be sold, or if awards did not fully vest, until directors leave the board.

Case Study/Corporate Governance Score: Central Telecommunication Company

March 21, 2003[*]

ANALYSTS

Julia Kochetygova, Standard & Poor's, Moscow

Nickolai Popivshchy, Standard & Poor's, Moscow

Vera Vitalieva, Standard & Poor's, Moscow

RUSSIA

Overall Company Score (CGS)	CGS—5.3 (Maximum CGS—10)
Component Scores	
Ownership structure and external influences	5.5
Shareholder rights and stakeholder relations	6.7
Transparency, disclosure, and audit	4.7
Board structure and effectiveness	4.5

---

[*] This analysis reflects the company's corporate governance practices as of this date of publication. To the extent that there have been changes in the company's governance structures or practices since this publication date, these are not reflected in this report.

EXECUTIVE SUMMARY

Central Telecommunications Company (CTC) is a fixed-line telecommunications service provider based in Moscow and servicing the central part of Russia. It is one of the seven supraregional telecom operators formed as a result of the consolidation of regional telecom companies in Russia. The company merged with 16 other telecom operators. However, the new governance structure is yet to be implemented based on the decisions of the first joint shareholder meeting in February 2003. We found the governance system at CTC to be rapidly developing, although it still has a number of weaknesses, some of which arise from the influence of its majority shareholder, Svyazinvest, which dominates the decision-making process at CTC.

The *ownership structure and external influence* component of our analysis, and the company's score of 5.5 for this component, reflect the fact that beneficial owners of 60.3 percent of the shares are identified, but there is little detail about other holders. On a positive note, the stated aim of the government-controlled Svyazinvest (holding 50.69 percent of the voting capital of CTC) is to improve the liquidity and value of the equity of its subsidiaries, primarily by conducting a reorganization of the industry, which is beneficial for all shareholders. The component score also reflects a number of other factors: (1) the high degree of regulatory influence and the limited commercial freedom enjoyed by the company, and (2) the sometimes controversial influence that Svyazinvest has due to conflicts of interest within the Svyazinvest group. The strong leadership and decision-making process exercised by Svyazinvest often lacks transparency, including the absence of tender procedures or public justification for significant transactions entered into by CTC, either directly or via an intermediate entity established by a group of Svyazinvest subsidiaries.

We positively assess the *shareholder rights and stakeholder relations* component of our analysis, assigning an above-average score of 6.7. All major shareholder rights appear to be respected and shareholder-meeting procedures are well articulated and observed, apart from the nondisclosure of existing limitation on splitting the votes of ADR-holders—a common problem for Russian companies. The quality of information provided for shareholder meetings and published on the company's website is adequate, but could be improved by the incorporation of English-language materials, of details of the reorganization, and further information about candidates for election to the board. It is a negative governance feature that the company's new share registrar is appointed and indirectly controlled by Svyazinvest and cannot, therefore, be fairly regarded as completely independent. In terms of financial rights, some of the solutions proposed by Svyazinvest and company management cannot be viewed as necessarily optimal for the interests of all other shareholders. Positively, the company has a good dividend payment history, although there is no articulated dividend policy.

CTC's standards of financial transparency and disclosure, receiving a score of 4.7, are affected by the continued absence of published IAS financial reports, although the company has produced these since 2001 for Svyazinvest's own use. The information about the ongoing reorganization, provided by the company, cannot be considered sufficient for various investors' purposes. It is a negative governance feature that the company does not provide analytical forecasts and segment analyses in its annual report or on its website. We also note that some transactions, including those where potential or actual conflicts of interest cannot be ruled out, are not fully transparent. There is not enough information about their terms, counterparties' ownership structure, and potential benefits. There is also a lack of English-language disclosure and a lack of transparency with regard to the auditor's fees and fees and consulting mandates that the auditor receives from an intermediate entity affiliated with CTC and other Svyazinvest subsidiaries. We further note that there is no audit committee to oversee the auditor's independence.

We assigned a score of 4.5 for the board and management structure and process component. The board's composition includes minimal (2 out of 11) representation of outside shareholders' interests and does not include specialized control committees. Although the board is actively involved in control and planning, most board sessions are held via mail voting, which is a negative governance feature, particularly given the need for wider discussion as representatives of Svyazinvest dominate the board. Major governance weaknesses include the lack of justification for certain proposals made by Svyazinvest and the company's management. Positive governance features include the increasingly transparent executive remuneration policy, although we note that the director remuneration policy encourages the short-term focus of directors.

COMPANY OVERVIEW

OJSC Central Telecommunication Company (CTC) is the largest fixed-line telecom operator in Eastern Europe and Russia, servicing the area covering about 20 percent of the country's population with about 6 million access lines in service, and a staff exceeding 70,000. It has evolved from a monopoly fixed-line telecommunications service provider, OJSC Electrosvyaz of the Moscow Region (ESMR), servicing the Moscow Region (excluding the City of Moscow), to a supraregional provider in the central region of Russia. This occurred as a result of the reorganization (initiated by Svyazinvest, a 51 percent owner of CTC, and the Russian Ministry of Telecommunications) to consolidate the telecommunications industry in Russia and, as part of this process, to merge CTC with 16 other telecom operators of the regions. The merger was completed in November 2002, when shareholders of the 16 regional companies swapped their shares for shares of CTC. The general shareholder meeting of the new mega-regional company (MRC) took place on February 20, 2003.

CTC's ordinary and preference shares are traded on the RTS and MICEX exchanges but have moderate liquidity. Trading volumes totaled $1.3 million in 2002.

The company issued Level 1 ADRs in 2001, which are now traded over the counter in the United States and Europe.

OWNERSHIP STRUCTURE AND EXTERNAL INFLUENCES

Component Score—5.5

Transparency of ownership

Public disclosure of CTC's ownership structure both before and after the merger contains minimal detail (see Table CS-1). Only the ownership interests of the holding company and the government are publicly disclosed. The disclosure of changes in individual directors' and executives' interest in the company is a positive governance feature.

Key Analytical Issues	Assessment
CTC provides information about the beneficial owners of 60.3 percent of its voting shares—Svyazinvest and the government.	Positive
Beneficial owners of 39.7 percent of voting shares are not directly identified. However, the company believes that this ownership is highly dispersed.	Negative
The direct shareholdings of individual directors and executives and changes therein are disclosed.	Positive

T A B L E   C S - 1

Large Holders of Voting Shares (with More Than 1 Percent) as of Year End 2002

Owner	Status	Share in Common, %	Share in Capital, %
OJSC Svyazinvest*	Owner	50.69	38.02
Russian Federal Property Owner Fund (RFPF)*	8.81	7.19	
ZAO DKK*	Nominee	7.39	10.02
ZAO ING Bank (Eurasia)*	Nominee	6.93	10.77
ZAO AKB Promsvyazbank	Nominee	3.28	3.06
ZAO Brunswick UBS Nominee Warburg Nominees	2.32	2.70	
Lindsell Enterprises Limited	Owner	2.01	2.73
OAO Bank Rossiyski Kredit	Nominee	1.16	1.25
ZAO ABN AMRO Bank A.O.	Nominee	0.70	4.46
OAO Commercial Investment Bank Euroalliance	Nominee	0.00	1.68

* The name, share in capital, and share in common stock are disclosed by CTC.

The company's public reports disclose the personal interests of CTC's managers and directors, and changes in their ownership interests. The aggregate disclosed stake of managers is 0.019 percent of the capital (we also note that there is no disclosure of the share of votes). We assume that only direct stakes are disclosed, and we are unable to determine whether managers and directors have any indirect interests in CTC via nominee shareholders.

Influence of ownership and external stakeholders

The political and social sensitivity of the telecom sector, together with its high level of regulation, may hamper the commercial success of CTC. Although the influence of CTC's majority shareholder is to a large extent aimed at increasing the company's value, improved disclosure of the reasons for certain investment decisions and commercial transactions would be a positive governance step.

Key Analytical Issues	Assessment
The telecommunications industry in Russia is highly regulated, primarily through tariffs.	Negative
Svyazinvest, which owns 50.69 percent of voting shares, exerts significant control over the company's decisions.	Neutral
This control is mostly aimed at increased shareholder value and stock liquidity.	Positive
Certain transactions, proposed by Svyazinvest, have taken place in less-than-transparent circumstances. It is therefore difficult to assess whether these are to the disadvantage of other shareholders.	Negative
Svyazinvest's commercial arrangements with the company lack rationale and can be frustrating for other shareholders of CTC.	Negative

CTC has been majority-owned by Svyazinvest, both before and after the merger. As Svyazinvest is 75-percent-owned by the government, and also because fixed-line telecommunications is a highly regulated industry in Russia, CTC is subject to significant government influence. This influence takes several forms:

1. All of the core business lines are licensed and the licensees have the obligation to provide consistent and secure telecommunications linkage for residential and governmental subscribers in their regions. Even though commercial factors (e.g., the late payment or nonpayment of bills) would normally require it, licensees are not allowed to disconnect those subscribers who are part of the social or governmental infrastructure (hospitals, army, police, etc.). Regional companies also are restricted in their ability to provide the services of long-distance and international communications.

2. The Ministry for Antimonopoly Policy (MAP) regulates the tariffs of regional telecom operators for fixed-line communications. Subscriber fees for governmental and residential customers are subsidized by higher tariffs for business customers, and traffic-based fees for long-distance and international connections. The average difference between subscriber fees for business customers and for residents in the central region is approximately twofold. Also, the 17 CTC regional branches have different tariffs for similar kinds of services. The introduction of per-minute billing is hampered by social policies and was only introduced in Voronezh, Yaroslavl, and five towns of the Moscow Region. Such

a situation limits the commercial success of CTC and makes it less attractive to investors. At the same time, we positively view MAP's recent decision to consider MRCs' suggestions on tariff rebalancing and unifying the tariffs within MRC.

3. Although the government provides direct subsidies to certain categories of low-income subscribers (which are paid directly to the telecom companies), in many regions these payments are late, resulting in substantial bad debts. As of September 30, 2002, short-term debtors of CTC amounted to $28 million, or 15 percent of assets; in July 2002, the company introduced a provision for bad and doubtful debts in the amount of $3.5 million, three-quarters of which represented debts of the federal budget. Although the government cannot be defined or treated as an interested party under Russian law, we believe that disclosure of the terms of commercial relations with governmental subscribers and of the essence of negotiations with government representatives on timely debt repayments could be improved.

4. It is encouraging to note that, associated with its decision to sell a further stake in Svyazinvest the government has established targets for the improvement of the financial standing of its subsidiaries. This aligns the interests of the government with the interests of other shareholders.

Svyazinvest has significant responsibility for the strategic decisions of its subsidiaries, including CTC. Svyazinvest has departments that are specifically in charge of monitoring its subsidiaries' activities, and its representatives typically dominate every stage of discussion at board meetings. Svyazinvest also is entitled to give direct instructions to managers serving on the boards of subsidiaries about "issues involving security matters." In the case of CTC, their influence is further strengthened by the appointment of one of the managers of Svyazinvest to the management board of CTC.

We note that a number of decisions proposed by Svyazinvest often lack transparency and appropriate justification and are not always accompanied by open tender procedures. This in turn obscures an assessment of the efficiency gains of these transactions, such as in the following cases:

1. *Appointment of consultants and other service providers.* We saw no evidence to suggest that CTC used a tender process for the selection of a consultant to advise on the merger with regional telecom companies. In the case of CTC and all other companies of the central

region, the merger adviser was LV-Finance. There is no evidence to suggest that shareholders were dissatisfied with the merger terms, or that the use of one adviser could not lead to economies of scale. Although LV-Finance's effectiveness as an adviser is not questioned, we believe that governance practice would have been enhanced if a separate adviser, hired by each side of the merger, had been selected via tender. Also, the auditors (Andersen originally, followed by Ernst & Young in 2002) and the registrar (Registrator-Svyaz) were proposed to all major Svyazinvest subsidiaries and automatically received the approval of shareholders and boards. Despite the potential economic synergies of having a single auditor and a single registrar for all Svyazinvest-controlled companies, we do not assess this practice as positive in the absence of tenders and the full disclosure of terms and competitive advantages. In the case of auditor selection, the situation may be further aggravated by (1) the fact that Ernst & Young (previously Andersen) simultaneously serves as an adviser, and (2) the lack of disclosure of the terms of these arrangements.

2. *Financing of intragroup projects.* Svyazinvest uses the cash flows of its subsidiaries to finance certain projects via an intermediary, the Noncommercial Partnership—Center for Research of the Telecommunications Development Problems (NP CRTDP). These projects require Svyazinvest's subsidiaries to transfer 1 percent of their revenues on a regular basis following the approval of the transfers by their boards. In 2002, the existing MRC transferred about $5 million after a board decision justified with the briefest of rationales—"for the financing of intra-corporate needs." While we appreciate the need for large-scale consulting projects, the absence of a tender process for the selection of contractors by Svyazinvest, or a disclosure of these projects, and of a full discussion by the board of CTC, does not, in our opinion, represent a strong basis of transparency and accountability in these actions.

3. *Procurement policy.* Svyazinvest appears to have a high degree of influence over CTC's procurement policy, in particular, its purchases of telecom equipment. In early 2002, Svyazinvest completed a tender for certain classes of equipment and recommended nine producers and a leasing company, RTK-Leasing, for all leasing projects. According to industry analysts, there was no open tender procedure for suppliers. The public dis-

closure of RTK-Leasing's shareholding structure gives very limited information about its owners apart from the stake owned by Rostelecom, another subsidiary of Svyazinvest. As the terms of the transactions with RTK-Leasing (amounting to $18 million in 2002 for the companies merged to CTC, currently CTC branches) were not transparent and there was no evidence of tender procedures applied, it is hard to tell whether these projects were beneficial for the MRC.

4. *Business models for new value-added services.* Svyazinvest to a great extent determines CTC's policy with respect to the provision of value-added services (Internet access, IP-telephony, mobile telephone services), for which MAP does not regulate tariffs. Despite the cancellation of MAPs instruction to spin off all value-added services to separate entities, in January 2003, Svyazinvest supported CTC management's suggestion to spin off certain value-added services (such as IP-telephony and access to the Internet) to a 75-percent-owned ZAO CenterTelecom Service, where the other founding partner, ZAO Telecom-R, does not have a fully transparent ownership structure. There was also little disclosure of the size and form of contributions expected from ZAO Telecom-R. In our opinion, such poor transparency and a lack of justification of the benefits from the existence of the founding partner do not correspond to practices of leading international companies and may give rise to questions about potential conflicts of interest.

5. *Financial settlements with Svyazinvest itself.* We note that it is difficult to assess whether certain commercial arrangements between CTC and Svyazinvest are always in the best interests of all other shareholders. In 1997 for example, ESMR, the predecessor of CTC, entered into a loan agreement with Svyazinvest (the size of the loan was 10 million rubles) that included a provision for the repayment to be made in Russian rubles or in U.S. dollars. However, after the 1998 crisis and the abrupt depreciation of the ruble, ESMR renewed the loan contract and cancelled the option for the repayment in rubles. Under pressure from Svyazinvest, CTC recalculated the amount to be repaid in U.S. dollars according to a precrisis exchange rate (making the principal equal to approximately $1.5 million, which CTC is currently repaying with interest). In our opinion, poor transparency regarding the rationale for such a decision is a negative governance feature.

SHAREHOLDER RIGHTS AND STAKEHOLDER RELATIONS

Component Score—6.7

Voting and shareholder meeting procedures

Procedures and disclosures related to shareholder meetings are generally adequate. Improved disclosure through the website would bring the company further into line with the practices of leading international companies. The problem, common for all Russian companies, is the risk associated with vote-split limitation for the ADR depositary.

Key Analytical Issues	Assessment
The notification procedure is in line with legislation, which is generally protective of shareholders.	Positive
Information provided to shareholders is adequate, although disclosure of information about candidates for nomination to the board and the revision commission is not comprehensive. Disclosure of the details of the reorganization before the 2002 EGM was incomplete.	Neutral
English versions of the materials relevant to shareholders' meetings are not available on the company website.	Negative
The registration, discussion, voting and vote-counting procedures are shareholder-friendly.	Positive
The chief executive officer acts as the chairman of shareholder meetings and has several powers concerning the modification of meeting procedures when necessary.	Negative
Some resolutions concerning the reorganization were combined into one at the EGM in 2002.	Negative
There are cumulative voting rights for board elections, a positive feature given the presence of a 50.69 percent majority shareholder.	Positive
The depositary agreement contains a provision that votes, corresponding to ADRs, for which no voting instructions have been provided, cannot be considered in determining quorum in GSMs and transferred to other parties.	Positive
While it is not possible under Russian law for the depositary bank to split the votes of ADR holders (i.e., they either have to vote all "for" or all "against" a resolution), the company treats separately votes of different ADR owners provided that the depositary gives it a list of such owners.	Neutral

It is a positive governance feature that CTC provides detailed notification of upcoming meetings to shareholders. It does this by publishing a notice in a widely circulated newspaper, on the company website in two languages, and by sending individual announcements via registered mail with the voting ballots no less than 20 days in advance. The materials on the issues proposed for voting are made available at locations convenient for most shareholders. ADR holders get all the relevant information in English via the depositary bank at least 28 days prior to the meeting.

The information package, provided to shareholders during GSMs, is generally comprehensive and relevant to the agenda; presentations and speeches, provided in relation to and during GSMs, are adequate. In particular, this relates to an extraordinary general shareholder meeting that was held on February 22, 2002, that dealt with the issue of reorganization: LV-Finance, the adviser on the merger, provided shareholders with a presentation about the merger and drafts of the merger agreement. However, in our opinion, the presentation by LV-Finance lacked the important details of the reorganization that were provided, for instance, by the advisers of the North-West Telecom and South Telecom. At the same time, before the two latest shareholder meetings (the AGM of 2002 and the EGM of 2003), the company had only Russian-language versions of materials displayed on the website.

With regard to the reorganization, we also believe that the combination of resolutions for the approval of swap coefficients with the approval of the merger itself is a negative governance feature, even though the high level of approval of the merger terms during the EGM suggests that minority shareholders generally supported the merger.

Positive governance features are that the registration continues throughout the GSM; shareholders are entitled to appoint proxies to attend or to vote by mail; voting on all items of the agenda lasts during the whole meeting and 30 minutes afterward; voting is by ballot, not via a show of hands; and vote-counting is done by an outside registrar. Votes cast in person or in absentia are given equal weight and all voting shares have one vote. The existence of cumulative voting rights for board elections is viewed positively given the presence of a 50.69 percent majority shareholder.

It is a positive feature that, in contrast with the practice employed by many Russian companies until recently, the depositary bank does not have the right to transfer voting proxies to any person nominated by the company's management for those ADRs where the owners have not been advised of their voting instructions before the GSM. In our opinion, under such provisions, ADR-holders' voting rights are better protected.

The company's attempt to treat votes of different ADR-holders separately, in spite of the law to give only one vote to the stake registered with the depositary bank, can be viewed positively as it allows ADR-holders to exercise their voting rights and does not lead to distortions in voting results. However, in such situations, there is still a risk that GSM results will be reversed by a court, as the law does not allow vote splits. The company does not inform its shareholders of this risk.

Ownership rights

All major ownership rights are well articulated and observed. Affiliation of the company's registrar with the controlling shareholder is viewed by Standard & Poor's as a negative governance feature.

Key Analytical Issues	Assessment
Svyazinvest appointed ZAO Registrator Svyaz as a single registrar for all subsidiaries without an open tender. Svyazinvest has a direct and indirect ownership interest of 25 percent of the capital of ZAO Registrator Svyaz.	Negative
CTC's charter provides for full transferability of shares.	Positive
Shareholders, holding at least 5 percent of the company's shares can call a board meeting, and those holding 10 percent of shares can call a GSM.	Positive
During the company restructuring, the proposed buy-back prices were based on the valuation made by an independent appraiser, although these were below the market price for the preceding period.	Negative/ Neutral
Financial rights of shareholders can be affected by nontransparent deals with the NP CRTDP, and there is a potential for financial rights abuses coming from the establishment of a 75 percent subsidiary for value-added services with a low-profile 25 percent partner.	Negative
CTC does not have an articulated dividend policy.	Negative
The company has a long history of stable and timely dividend payments.	Positive

During the reorganization, shareholders had the right to require the company to purchase their shares if they voted against the reorganization or abstained from voting. The price of the company shares for the buy-back purposes, determined by the board of directors, was based on the valuation made by an independent appraiser, ZAO Unicon/MS Consulting Group. The buy-back price, however, was below the market price (by 10 percent for preference shares and by around 50 percent for ordinary shares) for the period preceding the valuation. Should the price have gone down as a result of the EGM's decision on reorganization, shareholders' rights to offer their shares to the company at a fair market price would have been violated. In fact, the price went up, and for this reason, the valuation had no negative implications.

While an articulated dividend policy is absent, the company has a history of paying annual dividends since 1994. The dividends for ordinary shares are paid within a one-year period; the payout ratio for the last three years remained relatively stable (ranging from 7 to 9 percent). For preference shares, the dividend payout ratio is fixed at 10 percent of the net income.

Takeover defenses and corporate control issues

It is a positive feature that there are no anti-takeover defenses in the company's by-laws. The government's strategic interests, however, through the majority owner Svyazinvest, negatively influence a free market for corporate control, despite the government's plans to reduce its stake in Svyazinvest.

Key Analytical Issues	Assessment
No structural anti-takeover provisions exist in the company's by-laws (there are no restrictions on takeovers, no provisions for the establishment of a classified board, and a modest severance package for the CEO).	Positive
Supermajority provisions exist, but they are positive because of the existence of a majority owner.	Positive
Change in control in CTC is a matter of uncertainty despite the government's declared intention to sell its stake in Svyazinvest. The government has stated its intentions to sell its stake in Svyazinvest. When or if this will happen is unclear, as are the control-issue implications for CTC, if it does.	Negative

There is little likelihood of a change in control due to the political and social interests of the government in the telecommunications industry. However, we understand that the government is planning to sell its stake in Svyazinvest but that there is uncertainty over the timing and exact outlook of the sale.

Nevertheless, we take a positive view of the lack of structural anti-takeover provisions. The CEO's contract for 2000 contained a very modest severance agreement of one-year's fixed salary in case of premature termination of his contract initiated by the company or following the liquidation of the company; a new draft contract that is to be signed soon does not stipulate any severance payments at all.

TRANSPARENCY, DISCLOSURE, AND AUDIT

Component Score—4.7

Content of Public Disclosure

The information disclosure of CTC is not as comprehensive as many international investors require. Financial statements in accordance with IAS have not been produced and the company does not provide adequate disclosure of information about the ongoing reorganization. At the same time, the charter and by-laws are presented on the website, and individual remuneration of managers and directors are disclosed.

Key Analytical Issues	Assessment
Accounting statements conforming to IAS have been prepared since 2001, although these are yet to be published.	Neutral/Negative
The company discloses management and directors' personal remuneration.	Positive
Reviews of the last GSMs are published with accompanying materials, but in the "News" section only.	Positive/Neutral
Revenue and earnings forecasts are not disclosed.	Negative
Management's equity interests in CTC and outside directorships are disclosed.	Positive
Comprehensive segment analyses are not provided since the third quarter of 2001.	Negative
Disclosure of the parameters of the ongoing reorganization is insufficient.	Negative
Auditor fees and a breakdown of work by the auditor are not disclosed.	Negative

Financial transparency of CTC is hampered by the absence of publicly available financial reports conforming to international accounting standards, although we understand that the company started to produce financial statements under IAS in 2001 for the internal use of Svyazinvest. These were not audited and are not disclosed. As a result, there is no disclosure about related party transactions—a significant weakness. The absence of IAS financials is not consistent with the practice of most Russian blue chip companies, and is assessed as a negative feature. In the telecommunications sector, Rostelecom and Uralsvyazinform produce IAS audited statements with notes and include substantial information about related party transactions. Sibirtelecom, which also did not have audited financials for 2001 until recently, provided unaudited financial statements in accordance with IAS on its website in 2002. CTC is expecting to have fully audited 2002 financials at the end of May 2003.

CTC's bilingual annual report for 2001 contains operational analysis, an audited balance sheet, and profit and loss statements for 2001 in accordance with RAS. We found neither details of major transactions nor information about director or management equity interests. At the same time, we understand that Svyazinvest has issued instructions regarding the contents of annual reports of all MRCs covering the last five years and require disclosure of key financial data, major transactions, board and executives' backgrounds and equity interests, etc.

The company also has made an attempt to improve its information disclosure by producing quarterly "profiles" containing comprehensive segment analyses, operational data, and details of investment plans and requirements, and placing them on the corporate website; yet it terminated this practice in the third quarter of 2001. From the presentations available to us, we also understand that disclosure of the details of the reorganization, before and after the 2001 EGM was insufficient.

A positive governance step is the public disclosure of details concerning director and senior managers' remuneration, including those of the CEO, although only in Russian. Before 2002, CTC had translated its quarterly reports, containing such information, into English. Unlike most U.K. and U.S. companies, however, CTC does not disclose information about the nonaudit work of its auditor or the fees paid to the auditor either directly or via the intermediate company, NP CRTDP.

Timing of, and access to, public disclosure

The company has two websites, one of which is bilingual and comprehensive, and the other containing only recent information in Russian. Links between the two sites are not provided. Filings with the Federal Commission for Securities Markets (FCSM) are timely and informative, and are published on the website along with by-laws and company news. Only a very limited part of the most relevant information, however, is available in English. The company places emphasis on the improvement of its investor-relations policy.

Key Analytical Issues	Assessment
The company is shifting from the older site to an updated version. At this point, the new version has limited information and is in Russian only. The older version is comprehensive and bilingual.	Neutral
The two websites do not have links to one another, making searches difficult.	Negative

Key Analytical Issues	Assessment
Although the 2000 report can be found on the website, there is no inclusion of the 2001 report.	Negative
By-laws are presented on both websites, but in Russian only.	Neutral
Statutory information is filed with the FCSM on time.	Positive
Quarterly reports are disclosed on the corporate website. Before late 2001, they were in two languages, but now they are in Russian only.	Positive/Neutral
IAS statements for 2001 were selectively disclosed to the majority owner only.	Negative
The company has adopted a proactive approach to investors that is stipulated in its Investor Relations Program for 2002.	Positive

In accordance with the new organizational structure of CTC, the Department of Securities and Capital Markets includes four functional departments with duties and responsibilities related to investor relations and general disclosure.

CTC has two websites: an older, but relatively informative site (www.esmr.ru), and an updated, but not yet completed version (www.centertelecom.ru). At this point, however, the co-existence of two different websites with different information and without proper links to each other creates confusion, and we assess such a situation negatively. For example, the www.esmr.ru site provides quarterly reports, company profiles before 2002, the 2000 annual report, and news in English. Yet the information concerning the 2003 EGM (notice, draft charter, by-laws, and the list of candidates for the board) can be found on the new site and in Russian only. Also, we assess as negative the absence of the 2001 annual report on the company's website. The company had informed us that it has established a special working group (including one of CTC's independent directors) to investigate ways to further develop the website and is expecting to fill its Russian and English versions in the near future.

Before the fourth quarter of 2001, quarterly reports were produced in two languages and published on the company's website; subsequently, the practice of translating the reports into English was abolished. We positively assess the company's efforts to improve information disclosure by contracting a public information resource, SKRIN (www.skrin.ru) to publish its brief profile, including condensed RAS financials. A list of affiliates, quarterly reports, by-laws, and information about dividend payments are not available, however. In comparison, Southern Telecom, Uralsvyazinform, and Dalsvyaz are included into the upper tier of companies, providing such information in the public domain.

A one-year investor-relations program, approved by the board of CTC in January 2002, is aimed at increasing share liquidity. It provides for a number of new channels of information-dissemination for the public, development of a new website, the publication of presentations to analysts, specialized conferences, road shows, and an expansion of information to be provided to the media. The company also has a disclosure policy and maintains a focused mailing list of investors and other interested parties who receive quarterly and annual reports and reports on substantial news and events. Some of them are selectively translated into English and published on the website.

Audit process

CTC has hired a reputable international auditor for its RAS and IAS financial statements, although there was no tender for the appointment. The IAS financials have not yet been published. The auditors do not have any limitations on liability for damages. Fees and the amount of nonaudit work performed by the auditor are not disclosed.

Key Analytical Issues	Assessment
CTC has employed an international audit firm since 2002.	Positive
To date, IAS financials have not been published.	Negative
Auditor selection did not involve a tender process.	Negative
The auditors do not have any limitations on liability for damages.	Positive
Audit fees are not disclosed.	Negative
The auditor (previously a Russian branch of Arthur Andersen, and, since 2002, part of Ernst & Young) is involved in a number of large-scale consulting projects with the company directly and via an intermediate entity. The scope of, and fees for, the consulting work are not publicly disclosed.	Negative
The board has no audit committee to oversee the auditor's independence.	Negative

In 2001 Arthur Andersen audited CTC's RAS financials and consulted CTC on preparation of IAS financials. Andersen was appointed on the instructions of Svyazinvest. In 2002, due to the merger of Andersen's Russian operations with Ernst & Young, CTC (in common with all other key subsidiaries of Svyazinvest) contracted Ernst & Young to audit both RAS and IAS financials. There is no evidence that a competitive tendering process was used.

In our opinion, the lack of information about audit and nonaudit fees is a negative governance feature. We note that Andersen (and Ernst

& Young subsequently), in addition to its audit function and the related training of CTC staff on IAS methodology and procedures, is involved in a number of large-scale consulting projects for Svyazinvest companies. It is a negative governance feature that the terms and the contents of these projects are not disclosed, which, combined with the absence of an independent audit committee, makes it difficult to assess the impact that this might have on the audit process and auditor independence. As far as we understand, Svyazinvest companies are charged proportionally to their annual sales revenue, and fees are paid through the payment agent (NP CRTDP). Although there is no indication of the size of these projects on the website of NP CRTDP, we understand that the most significant ones include the following: (1) the validation of consolidation scenarios and procedures proposed by the company's restructuring advisers in each region, (2) the development of budgeting and investment planning systems for Svyazinvest's subsidiaries, (3) tax planning, and (4) reform scenarios in the telecommunications sector.

The absence of an independent, board-level audit committee is a significant weakness in CTC's audit process.

BOARD STRUCTURE AND EFFECTIVENESS
Component Structure—4.5
Board structure and composition

Svyazinvest's representatives dominate the structure of the board. There are two representatives of the government—one of which was nominated by Svyazinvest. At the 2003 EGM, the number of directors that can be considered independent increased from one to two, but the size of the board has also increased. The board has no independent control committees (see Table CS-2).

Key Analytical Issues	Assessment
Most directors are representatives of the majority shareholder, Svyazinvest.	Neutral
Before the 2003 EGM, there was only one independent director on the board; now the number of independent directors has increased to two, but the size of the board has increased from nine to eleven.	Neutral/Positive
The board has no independent committees.	Negative
The chairman of the board is a key manager of Svyazinvest, the company's majority shareholder.	Negative

TABLE CS-2

The Composition of the Two Latest Boards of Directors of CTC as Elected by the Annual GSM on June 5, 2002, and EGM on February 20, 2003

Name	Member Since	Position of the Board	Nominated by	Votes Received, %*	Votes Received, %**
Valery N. Yashin	2000	Svyazinvest,CEO; Chairman of the board of CTC	Svyazinvest	11.11	11.90
Vadim E. Belov	1999	Svyazinvest, deputy CEO	Svyazinvest	10.02	5.93
Alexandr V. Lopatin	2000	Svyazinvest, First deputy CEO	Svyazinvest	10.01	6.44
Oxana V. Petrova	2000	Svyazinvest, Corporate Governance Department, Deputy head of the Division of Methodology and Information	Svyazinvest	10.01	6.40
Ruben A. Amarian	2000	OJSC CenterTelecom, CEO	Svyazinvest	11.43	6.68
Alexander P. Gribov	2002	RFPF, deputy head of Federal Property Management department	RFPF	9.13	9.62
Alexander V. Ikonnikov	2002	Investor Protection Association (IPA), CEO; Independent Directors Association (IDA), president	Lindsell Enterprises Limited	9.22	8.35
Viktor D. Savchenko	2003	Svyazinvest, director of legal department	Svyazinvest	—	6.37
Stanislav P. Adviyants	2003	Svyazinvest, executive director, director of the Department of Economic and Tariff Policy	Svyazinvest	—	6.45
Alexei B. Panteleev	2003	First deputy chairman of the Government of Moscow Region	Svyazinvest	—	6.37
Grigori M. Finger	2003	NCH Advisors, Inc., executive director of the Moscow representative office	Lindsell Enterprises Limited	—	8.72
Yuri A. Pavlenko	2001	OJSC Megafon, CEO	RFPF	9.17	—
Oleg I. Betin	2002	Head of the Tambov region administration	Svyazinvest	9.15	—

* Votes received in cumulative voting at the 2002 annual GSM as a percentage of votes represented by the total number of voting shares.
** Votes received in cumulative voting at the 2003 EGM as a percentage of votes represented by the total number of voting shares.

Effective February 20, 2003, the number of board members has increased from 9 to 11 persons; while the proportion of directors representing Svyazinvest has risen, we appreciate the fact that in addition to one independent director, a representative of a minority shareholder has been elected to the board. We consider this representative to be independent. At the same time, the proportion of independent elements on the board is still low in comparison to leading international companies.

The roles of the chairman and the CEO are separate in accordance with Russian law. In line with common practices applied by Svyazinvest to all its subsidiaries, the chairman is a representative of Svyazinvest, which further reinforces Svyazinvest dominance. More significantly, it is a major negative consideration that, in addition to Svyazinvest representatives, the company's CEO and the government representatives, nominated by Svyazinvest, have to vote in accordance with Svyazinvest instructions.

There are no board committees, although the company by-laws do not rule out their existence. In our opinion, it would be a positive governance feature if the number of independent directors was increased and independent control functions were given to independent board committees.

Role and effectiveness of the board

The board of directors has significant authority, including the power to approve strategic plans and evaluate the performance of the company. The balance of interests is in favor of Svyazinvest, which allows it to pursue a common policy toward its major subsidiaries. A number of board decisions have lacked background information and have not necessarily been consistent with the interests of minority shareholders.

Key Analytical Issues	Assessment
The board regularly discusses strategic planning, financial and operating performance evaluations, the realization of investor-relations programs, and approves annual budgets, major plans of action, and participation in other entities.	Positive
The board has to approve all the transactions exceeding 0.4 percent of the company's assets and is to be informed about all transactions exceeding 1 percent of the company's quarterly revenue.	Positive
The board approves the composition of the management board and the appointment of key executives of regional branches.	Positive
The board evaluates the performance of the CEO on a quarterly basis and approves his or her bonuses.	Positive
There is evidence that certain transactions were not put on the board agenda despite requirements to the contrary. Subsequently, actions have been taken to correct this problem.	Neutral

There have been a number of occasions when transactions approved by the board were accompanied by the limited disclosure of supporting information. It is difficult to assess to what extent these transactions might have been subject to potential conflicts of interest.	Negative
Decisions on some important issues are made in absentia, with limited interactive discussion.	Negative
Although external directorships of board members are disclosed, the board does not identify whether its members have equity interests other than in CTC or its subsidiaries.	Negative

The board appears to control the company and its management within the scope of its exclusive responsibility as prescribed by the law. Among particular issues considered by the board are: approval of strategic planning (including the company's restructuring program), material financing and investment decisions, and investor-relations plans. A positive feature is that the board considers business plans and financial management issues (including the terms of short-term borrowing exceeding the prescribed threshold) in great detail. At the same time, the minutes of board meetings do not reveal whether the board considered any risk management issues, except for those relating to the company reorganization. Also, the CEO undertook certain short-term borrowing transactions without the board's consideration (although according to company by-laws, they had to be put on the board agenda). In 2002, the board created a group that would be responsible for ensuring that all the appropriate questions are put on the agenda of board meetings.

The board approves the appointment of CEO deputies and heads of branch offices, and the list of executives to be included on the management board. Also, according to the latest version of the company's charter, the right to appoint and dismiss the CEO has been transferred from GSMs to the board of directors.

It is a very positive feature that the latest version of the company's charter has lowered the threshold from 1 to 0.4 percent of the company's assets for which large transactions are required to have board approval. Both thresholds are lower than required by law (25 percent). Also, the CEO has to inform the board about transactions for sums exceeding 1 percent of the company's quarterly revenue (2 percent according to the new CEO draft contract). Nevertheless, we note as a negative feature that service providers proposed by Svyazinvest and discussed by the board are usually not chosen as a result of open tenders. For example, we saw no evidence that tendering procedures were used in the selection of LV-Finance, and Ernst & Young (formerly the Andersen group).

We also could not find evidence that tender procedures were used for the selection of RTK Leasing by companies of the central region, currently branches of CTC.

A strong governance feature is that the board discusses participation in other entities (creation of subsidiaries and changes of ownership interests). At the same time, such decisions were sometimes made in absentia, with limited supporting information, as was the case with the creation of a subsidiary Center Telecom Service with an outside partner in January 2003 (see "Influence of ownership and external stakeholders"), and the decision on the purchase of a 51 percent stake in ZAO Moteko in December 2001.

Despite the fact that board meetings take place on average twice a month, negative features are that a substantial proportion is in absentia, and that face-to-face discussions of important questions often do not take place. Examples of issues that were decided without adequate discussion include: the approval of the payment of funds to NP CRTDP in June 2002 and in August 2001; the approval of CTC responsibility within the credit line (for the sum of $18 million) between the Sberbank of Russia and RTK-Leasing.

Role and independence of outside directors

The nonexecutive directors representing Svyazinvest are active in executing control over the company in the interests of the main shareholder, but there have been examples where their actions were not fully transparent and therefore difficult to assess whether they were in the interests of all shareholders. In 2002, there was only one independent director on the board, and in the number of cases, his influence persuaded the board against taking decisions that were potentially disadvantageous to outside shareholders.

Key Analytical Issues	Assessment
An independent director since 2002, Mr. Ikonnikov is fully involved in board functions, and there is evidence that in some cases he has prevented nontransparent transactions that could have been unprofitable for the company.	Positive
Mr. Finger, a representative of a minority shareholder elected in February 2003, can be considered independent, although it is too early to assess his effectiveness as a board member. We have seen examples of the involvement of directors representing his company on other company boards.	Positive/Neutral
The influence of directors who represent Svyazinvest is mostly aimed at improving CTC's performance, but some decisions might not be consistent with the interests of all shareholders.	Negative/Neutral

Directors representing the main shareholder have corporate rather than individual membership on the board, as they always vote in coordination and in accordance with Svyazinvest's recommendations.	Negative
One of the government representatives nominated by Svyazinvest is obliged to vote in accordance with Svyazinvest's directives.	Negative
Despite the fact that the outside directors can get virtually any information the company is able to provide, their ability to participate in face-to-face discussions on some important questions is limited due to frequent meetings in absentia.	Negative

All directors except the company CEO are nonexecutives and mostly nominated by Svyazinvest (6 out of 8 during the 2002 AGM, and 7 out of 10 during 2003 EGM). Svyazinvest's influence is further reinforced by the obligation of all Svyazinvest-nominated directors, including the CEO and one of the government representatives to sign a special agreement that requires them to vote in accordance with the instructions of Svyazinvest. Although we understand that Svyazinvest's ambitious plans to reorganize the fixed-line telecommunications industry require a high concentration of influence, we assess this as a negative feature, as these agreements may have the effect of requiring the directors nominated by Svyazinvest to act as corporate rather than individual members and in the interests of Svyazinvest rather than the interests of CTC. For example, certain board decisions proposed by Svyazinvest were not necessarily made in the best interests of all shareholders (see "Influence of ownership and external stakeholders" and "Role and effectiveness of the board").

In our opinion, Alexander Ikonnikov, the executive director of IPA (nominated by Lindsell Enterprises Limited, a nominee owner in CTC), can be considered fully independent. He is an active director and in most cases, he analyzes the fundamentals of proposed items that are brought for board approval. We understand that he opposed certain transactions as a consequence of insufficient disclosure and justification (such as the creation of Center Telecom Service; the approval of CTC quota within the credit line between the Sberbank of Russia and RTK-Leasing; and the approval of payment of funds to NP CRTDP in 2002—see above). We also appreciate the fact that, according to this independent director, he has blocked certain proposals via informal discussions with Svyazinvest representatives before they were brought to board meetings.

We also appreciate the role of one of the government's representatives, Alexander Gribov, in providing inquiries and critical remarks in the

course of board discussions. At the same time, as a government representative normally voting according to instructions provided by Russian
Federation Property Fund, he cannot be considered independent.

Although it is hard to assess the effectiveness of board members
elected during the 2003 EGM, we believe that the balance of power
between the representatives of Svyazinvest, the government, and minority shareholders on the board will be preserved. The election of Grigori
Finger is a positive development in the governance practices of CTC:
He is a representative of a minority shareholder, Lindsell Enterprises
Limited, a well-established long-term institutional investor in the Russian
telecommunications industry. We assume that the role of Mr. Finger will
be to protect the shareholder value of CTC, and thus will be in line with
the interest of all shareholders.

Director and senior executive compensation

There are no committees for remuneration and nomination, but director
and senior executive compensation is articulated in internal documents and
contains performance-related factors. Based on the decisions of the February 2003 EGM, remuneration of executives and the CEO will be discussed
by the board, which includes only one executive. There are no articulated
board evaluation and succession policies, although evaluation procedures
exist. Details of compensation paid to managers and directors are disclosed
as required by law.

Key Analytical Issues	Assessment
Individual remuneration of executives and directors is disclosed in quarterly FCSM filings.	Positive
Directors' remuneration is approved by AGMs.	Positive
Directors' compensation is tied with the short-term financial performance of the company. Furthermore, some bonus plan components are contingent upon achieving revenue, and not net income, targets.	Negative
Under recently adopted rules, the board approves CEO nominations and all issues relating to the CEO's compensation and bonuses, in addition to his or her contract terms.	Positive
The discussion of executive compensation, besides that of the CEO, has become the board's responsibility under the new rules.	Positive
Compensation for the CEO and other top executives is largely performance-driven with a substantial "at-risk" component.	Positive
There are no articulated evaluation procedures for board members.	Negative

Before the 2003 EGM, the board could receive remuneration once a year in an amount not exceeding 0.4 percent of net income. According to company by-laws adopted by the 2003 EGM, the board receives quarterly and annual remunerations. Quarterly remuneration is defined as a percentage of quarterly sales, and is allocated to individual directors in proportion to their attendance at board meetings. The annual directors' bonus is defined as a shareholder-approved percentage of net income of the reporting year, which is then to be distributed by the board of directors to its members according to individual performance of each director. As a result of this scheme, there is a risk that the board might focus on short-term results rather than pursuing long-term targets; this, we assess negatively from the point of view of optimal motivation of the director's contribution. It is a negative governance feature that the company does not have an articulated set of criteria for the evaluation of the board and individual director's performance, while according to new by-laws adopted in 2003, the board has to assess the personal impact of each director on the company's performance. Before 2003, personal compensation of the members of the managing board was fully regulated by their contracts and the payment of bonuses was at the CEO's discretion. According to new by-laws adopted in 2003, the bonuses are paid on a quarterly basis and are determined, according to the CEO's suggestions, by the board of directors as a percentage of net income prescribed in the budget.

Only the CEO has a contract that additionally describes his or her compensation plan. For the CEO, the quarterly and annual bonuses are conditional on meeting business plan objectives and special tasks assigned to him or her by the board. In the case of successfully realizing set targets, the performance-related part of this compensation can be as high as 50 percent of the total package offered. The board makes decisions on bonus payments. The CEO contract of 2000 contained a very modest severance agreement of one year's fixed salary in case of the premature termination of his contract, which is going to be eliminated in a new draft contract. We do not think it is a positive decision with regard to the CEO's incentives.

We notice that executives of the company buy the company's shares on their own behalf. We regard it as a positive sign, proving the long-term interests and optimistic expectations of the top management of the company, even in the absence of a stock option program.

APPENDIX B

The Evolving Role of Corporate Governance in Credit Rating Analysis*

Clifford M. Griep and Solomon Samson

The links between credit quality and corporate governance—or, more correctly, certain elements of corporate governance—can be extensive. Governance issues that are germane—such as ownership structure, management practices, and financial disclosure policies—are regularly examined as part of the credit ratings methodology, although they have not traditionally been labeled with corporate governance nomenclature.

Credit rating analysis has focused on many specific corporate governance elements but has not aggregated these into one category or attempted to arrive at an overall assessment of corporate governance.

Until recently, greater emphasis has been placed on corporate governance factors in the rating analysis in countries with less-developed capital markets. However, given the recent spate of management scandals in the United States and Europe, Standard & Poor's is subjecting these issues to greater scrutiny globally in its credit ratings analysis.

It is clear that weak corporate governance can undermine creditworthiness in several ways and should serve as a red flag or warning indicator to credit analysts. Alternatively, strong corporate governance, demonstrated in part by the presence of an active, independent board that participates in determining and monitoring the control environment, while not a guarantee of creditworthiness, can serve to support the credibility of financial disclosure and, more broadly, management.

---

*Cliff Griep is Executive Managing Director and Chief Credit Officer of Standard & Poor's Credit Market Services. Soloman Samson is Managing Director and Chief Quality Officer of Standard & Poor's corporate credit ratings group. This article was originally published in Standard & Poor's Ratings Direct, in October 2002.

Recent examples of poor corporate governance, which contributed to impaired creditworthiness, include:

◆ Uncontrolled dominant ownership influence that applied company resources to personal or unrelated use.
◆ Uncontrolled executive compensation programs.
◆ Management incentives that compromised long-term stability for short-term gain.
◆ Inadequate oversight of the integrity of financial disclosure, which resulted in heightened funding and liquidity risk.

Standard & Poor's Governance Services group, which operates separately from credit rating activities, offers full-scope corporate governance analysis and scores—services geared largely to the equity investor's perspective. It is not the current operating practice of the credit rating or governance groups at Standard & Poor's to collaborate in the analysis of specific companies, particularly in situations where confidential information has been exchanged. However, to ensure a methodological consistency of approach relating to broad corporate governance issues, collaboration at a technical level between credit and governance analysts does occur to review points of general analytical criteria.

The following elements of corporate governance have traditionally formed part of ratings analysis. The significance of each element as a rating factor can vary greatly.

OWNERSHIP

Identification of the owners is an obvious requirement. It is a fundamental rating criterion that entities are never rated on a standalone basis; links to parent companies or affiliates are important considerations. Ownership by stronger or weaker parents substantially affects the credit quality of the rated entity. The nature of the owner—government, family, holding company, or strategically linked business—also can hold significant implications for both business and financial aspects of the rated entity.

CONTROL

The existence of more than one owner introduces additional issues regarding potential conflicts over control. Joint owners might disagree on how to operate the business. Even minority owners can sometimes exercise effective control or at least frustrate the will of the majority owners. Whenever control is disproportionate to the underlying economic interest, the incentives for the stakeholders could diverge. This could result from existence of classes of shares with super voting rights or from owning 51 percent in each of multiple layers of holding companies. In either example, control might rest with a party that holds only a relatively small economic stake. Cross-shareholding of industrial groupings and family-controlled networks are commonplace in certain parts of the world. Such group affiliations can have positive or negative implications, depending on the specific situation.

Conventional, equity-oriented corporate governance analysis is very sensitive to share structure (for example, does each type of share provide representational voting?) out of concern that actions will be undertaken to the detriment of minority shareholders. Although this concern is not the direct focus of credit analysis, there is a penalty for companies that are considered abusive to minority holders. Perception of such conduct would, obviously, impair the company's access to investment capital. Furthermore, if a company mistreated one set of its stakeholders, there would be serious concern that the company could later try to short-change other stakeholders, including creditors.

MANAGEMENT AND ORGANIZATION

Assessment of management is an especially significant determinant of credit-rating assignments. Rating analysis considers many factors that pertain to management, including:

- ♦ Track record and competence.
- ♦ Management background and reputation.
- ♦ Management depth and turnover.
- ♦ Professional or entrepreneurial style of management.
- ♦ Any tensions among operating functions, the finance function, or shareholder interests.

POLICIES AND STRATEGIES

Financial policies are assessed for aggressiveness or conservatism, sophistication, and consistency with business objectives. Policies should optimize for the typically divergent interests of the firm's stakeholders—shareholders, creditors, customers, and employees, among others. Specifically, the firm's goals with respect to its credit rating need to be consistent with the balancing of those interests.

Business strategies are evaluated for realism, comprehension of competitive risks, and contingency planning. Comparisons of policies and projections with a company's track record form the basis for judging management credibility.

INFORMATION DISCLOSURE AND FINANCIAL TRANSPARENCY

Ratings are based on audited financial data plus supplemental data (including detailed financial projections) that might be provided confidentially. Ratings agencies enjoy unique access to data given their status under disclosure regulations in many jurisdictions and their impeccable track record regarding confidentiality.

In judging the reliability of data, Standard & Poor's considers the accounting standards used as the basis of the financial statements, the reputation of the auditor, and the degree of openness of the local business practice. Qualms about data quality (dubbed "information risk") would translate into a lower rating and preclude a rating in the upper part of the rating spectrum.

A review of accounting quality is a critical prerequisite of the financial analysis. Comparisons of financial measures need a common frame of reference. Consolidation standards, revenue recognition methods, and depreciation methods are all scrutinized, as is off-balance sheet financing, such as leasing, securitizations, trust vehicles, and contingent liabilities. Adjustments are regularly made to recast the financial statements—and the credit ratios based on them—to better reflect economic risks and to allow better benchmark comparisons.

However, Standard & Poor's does not conduct audits, and there are limitations to analytical methods. A company bent on deception might succeed in misleading both its auditors and the rating analysts.

Apart from disclosure to Standard & Poor's analysts, though, public disclosure and transparency can be important. If a firm maintains an aura of secrecy, investors will be suspicious and skittish. In addition, the firm is more prone to so-called headline risk, the consequences of which can be very damaging, especially in the current environment.

INTERCOMPANY AFFAIRS AND AFFILIATED PARTY TRANSACTIONS

These activities pose special challenges, since it is difficult to ascertain that they are done on a truly arms-length basis. A propensity to engage in deals with inside parties would give rise to skepticism about the company's conduct of its affairs, even if they were fully disclosed.

A component of corporate governance that has historically not figured prominently in the rating process is board structure and involvement. Of course, if it is evident that a company's board of directors is passive and does not exercise the normal oversight, that weakens the checks and balances of the organization and represents a negative credit factor. But considerations such as the proportion of independent members on the board of directors, presence of independent directors in board-level audit committee, and direct reporting of internal auditor to board or independent internal audit committee at board level have not been systematically examined.

Similarly, relatively little attention has been paid to the compensation of directors and senior management teams. These issues are focused on more extensively in Governance Services' corporate governance scores and will receive more scrutiny in the ratings process as well. This can be a qualitative area of analysis, and it can be difficult to determine objectively if a given level of compensation is excessive or will result in a company strategy that is overly aggressive or mainly focused on short-term performance. As board practices change in the wake of management and accounting abuses—and directors take on a more active role in the company direction and oversight—more weight to the role of the board of directors could be warranted from the perspective of credit rating.

Quite obviously, strong corporate governance does not, by itself, indicate strong credit-worthiness—just as a company being open and fair does not equate with the company being well managed. In addition, companies with high credit ratings could have governance standards that are problematic, particularly from the perspective of minority shareholders. In the end, weak corporate governance practices can undermine credit-worthiness, but it would depend on the specific aspects of governance that led to the poor assessment.

Going forward, the links between corporate governance and credit ratings stand to evolve as more research and case studies bring new issues to light.

INDEX